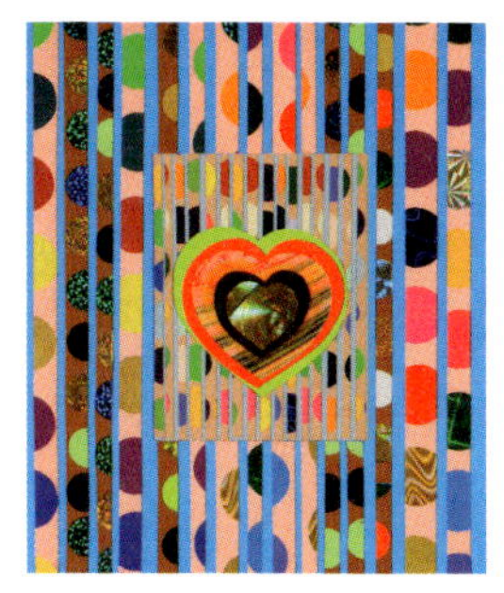
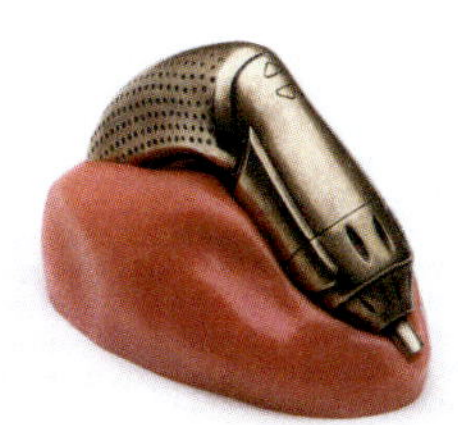

AF411645
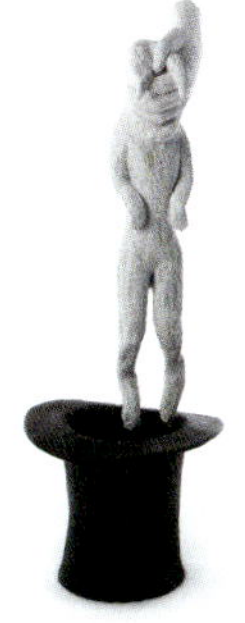
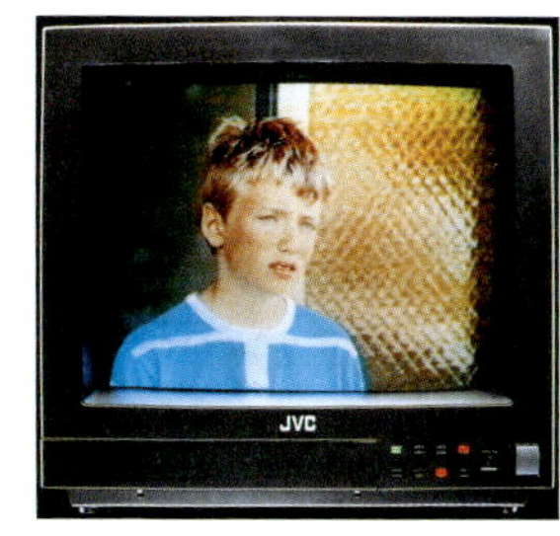
JVC
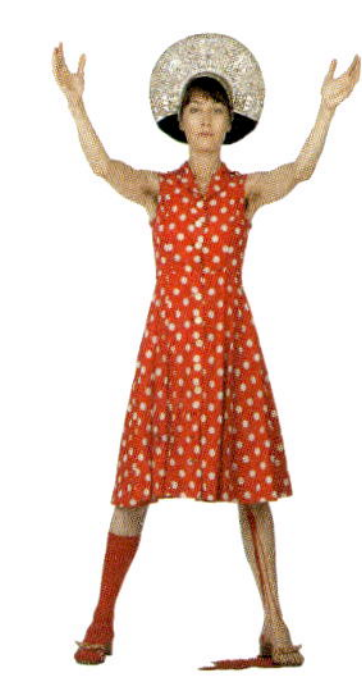
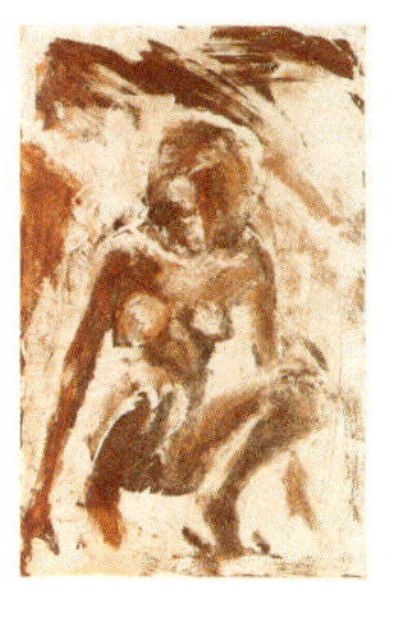
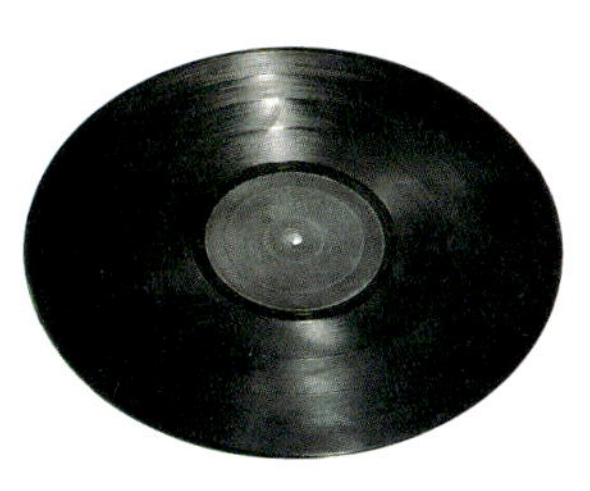
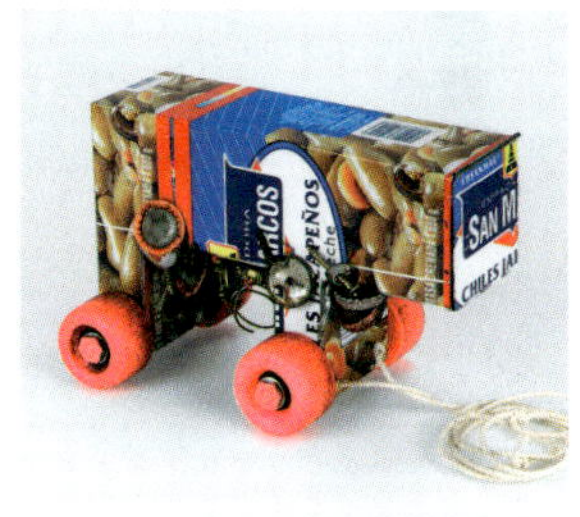
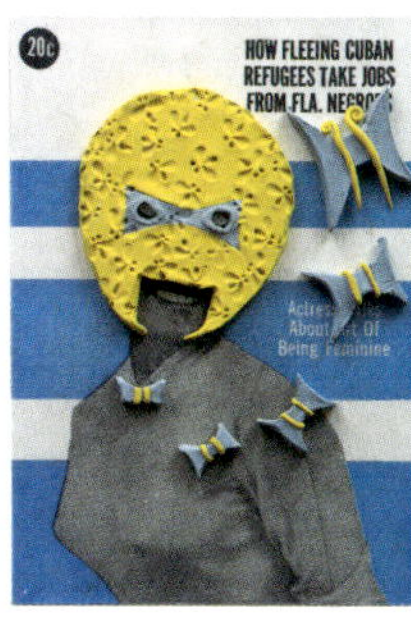
20c
HOW FLEEING CUBAN
REFUGEES TAKE JOBS
FROM FLA. NEGROES
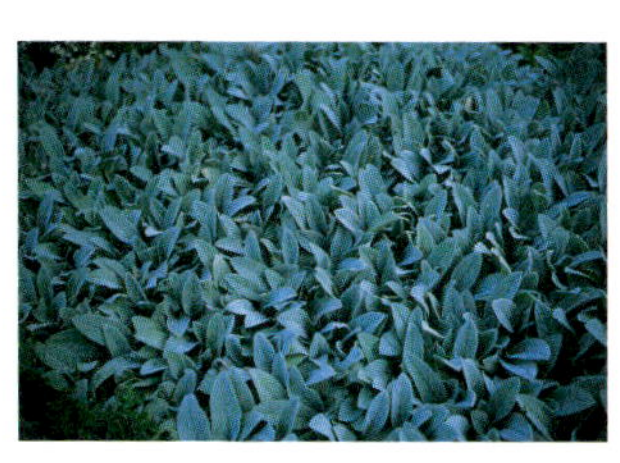
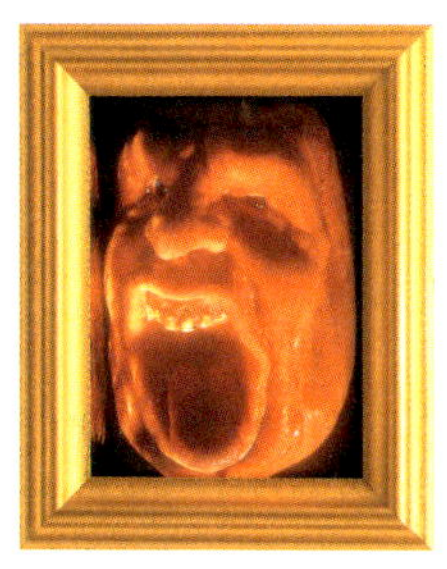

200 ARTWORKS 25 YEARS

PARKETT

パルケット・エディションズ

ARTISTS' EDITIONS FOR PARKETT

カタログ・レゾネ　執筆:スーザン・トールマン、デボラ・ワイ
付属資料:アーティストの自筆資料、パルケット誌インサート(ページ・アート)、
背表紙、バックナンバー表紙、執筆者一覧

発行:パルケット出版社(チューリヒ／ニューヨーク)

200 ARTWORKS 25 YEARS

ARTISTS' EDITIONS FOR PARKETT

Catalogue raisonné with essays by Susan Tallman and Deborah Wye
and additional chapters on Parkett's Inserts, Spines, Covers,
Artists' Documents, and a complete Authors' Index

Parkett Publishers, Zurich – New York

目　次

Table of Contents

PARKETT

200 ART WORKS - 25 YEARS
パルケット・エディションズ

執筆:スーザン・トールマン、デボラ・ワイ
編集:マーク・ヴェルツェル
翻訳:木下哲夫
デザイン:ハンナ・コラー(チューリヒ)
撮影:マンチャ/ボドマー(チューリヒ)、リック・ズィマーリ(チューリヒ)、レト・ロドルフォ・ベドリーニ(チューリヒ)
製版・印刷:チューリヒ湖印刷会社(シュテーファ/チューリヒ)

日本語版編集協力:
眞田一貫、イッカンアートインターナショナル(ニューヨーク)
株式会社アート・アドバイザリー・バンク(東京)
淡交社(東京)

賛助金提供:LUMA財団(スイス)

本図録は、2009年9月、金沢21世紀美術館市民ギャラリーAを皮切りに開催される、パルケット誌25周年記念展覧会
「200 ARTWORKS - 25 YEARS、パルケット・エディションズ」を機に出版された。

販売:パルケット/D.A.P.(アメリカ/カナダ)
　　　アート・アドバイザリー・バンク(日本)

発行:パルケット出版社(チューリヒ/ニューヨーク) 2009年7月

www.parkettart.com

Printed in Switzerland
ISBN 978-3-907582-25-1

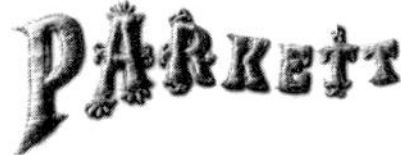

200 ARTWORKS – 25 YEARS
Artists' Editions for Parkett

Texts: Susan Tallman, Deborah Wye
Managing Editor: Mark Welzel
Japanese Translator: Tetsuo Kinoshita
Design: Hanna Williamson-Koller, Zurich
Photographers: Mancia/Bodmer, Zurich, Rikk Zimmerli, Zurich,
Reto Rodolfo Pedrini, Zurich
Color separations, typesetting and printing: Zuerichsee Druckereien, Staefa/Zurich

Special thanks:
Ikkan Sanada, Ikkan Art International, Inc., New York,
Art Advisory Bank, Inc., Tokyo
Tankosha Publishing Co., Ltd., Tokyo

With the generous support of the LUMA Foundation

Published on the occasion of Parkett's 25-Year Retrospective
"200 Artworks – 25 Years" first exhibited at the
21st Century Museum of Contemporary Art, Kanazawa, Japan (September 2009)

Distributed by Parkett, D.A.P. (USA & Canada), Art Advisory Bank (Japan),
Central Books (UK), GVA (Germany), Idea Books (Benelux), AVA (Switzerland)

Parkett Publishers, Zurich – New York, July 2009
Quellenstrasse 27, CH-8005 Zurich, Switzerland +41 44 271 8140
145 Ave. of the Americas, New York, NY 10013 +1 212 673 2660

www.parkettart.com

Printed in Switzerland
ISBN 978-3-907582-25-1

前書き

このカタログ・レゾネは、長年パルケットが目指してきた、素晴らしく魅力的なアーティストの仕事を、かれらとのコラボレーションを通じて探る作業の記録の集大成にあたります。ここにはアーティストが1984年以来パルケットのために制作したエディション、版画、写真、オブジェなどの作品200点が収められており、金沢21世紀美術館を皮切りに催されるパルケット創刊25周年記念展のカタログとして刊行されます。

スーザン・トールマンのエッセイ『美術館のままごと遊び』は、これらの作品の多様性と奥行きの深さを明らかにします。これらの作品群は、世界の最先端で活躍する影響力あふれるアーティストたちの、独特の個性の発露です。ニューヨーク近代美術館の版画・挿画本部門の主席学芸員を務めるデボラ・ワイは、エディション、インサート（ページ・アート）、背表紙、表紙、記事、さらには誌面デザインにおよぶ、パルケットとアーティストとの様々なコラボレーションのあり方を考察します。また本カタログは、パルケットに寄稿し、ひいては現代美術を巡る1400本以上の記事からなる厖大な資料集の創出に寄与した執筆者の方々への謝意を評するものでもあります。

他に類例を見ないパルケットの出版プロジェクトは、多くの方々の協力を得て初めて実現しました。創刊にも参加した編集長のビーチェ・クリガー、そしてジャクリーヌ・ブルクハルト、現在のチームはもとより過去の一時期、ともに働いてくれた同僚の面々、そして86巻の刊行にいたる今日まで、わたしたちを支えてくださったすべての方々にお礼を申し上げます。わけてもアーティストと執筆者のみなさんに、心から感謝いたします。この「小さな美術館、大きな図書館」が、かれらの献身的な協力があってはじめて現実のものとなったことは、言うまでもありません。

パルケット社長
ディーター・フォン・グラフェンリード

Foreword

This catalogue raisonné documents Parkett's longstanding goal to explore the work of compelling artists in direct collaboration with them. The book features 200 editions, prints, photographs, objects and works made by artists for Parkett since 1984; it is published on the occasion of Parkett's 25-year retrospective, which is first exhibited at the 21st Century Museum of Contemporary Art in Kanazawa, Japan.

Susan Tallman's essay "The museum plays house" traces the diversity and depth of these works, which represent distinct responses from many of the most influential artists worldwide. Deborah Wye, Chief Curator, Department Prints and Illustrated Books, at MoMA, looks at the various ways in which Parkett collaborates with artists, including the editions, inserts, spines, covers, texts, and the design of the publication. At the same time this catalogue pays tribute to all of the authors who have written for Parkett and created a formidable library of more than 1400 texts on the art of our time.

Parkett's singular publishing project has been made possible by the contributions of many people. Our thanks go to my co-founders, Bice Curiger, editor-in-chief, and Jacqueline Burckhardt, to our team past and present, and to all those who have enabled us to publish 86 volumes to date. Above all we wish to thank the artists and authors, whose dedicated support and commitment have made this small museum and large library come true.

Dieter von Graffenried
Publisher

Collaborations with Parkett:
1984 to Now

By Deborah Wye

Deborah Wye is Chief Curator,
Department of Prints and Illustrated Books,
at the Museum of Modern Art, New York.

"We are aiming to produce a vehicle of direct confrontation with art, providing not only coverage *about* artists, but original contributions *by* them."[1] Thus reads the stated goal in the first issue of *Parkett*, a journal of contemporary art and ideas, in 1984; it has remained the editorial challenge through volume 86, in 2009. This exhibition focuses on the original contributions by artists that have resulted from *Parkett*'s project of editions, inserts, and spine designs. Over the past twenty-five years the editors have collaborated with 200 artists, resulting in an extraordinary array of prints, page art projects, photographs, drawings, paintings, multiples, videos, DVDs, sound pieces, and other inventive formats, all available to subscribers in editions. While most are small in scale and imbued with the fascination that comes with miniaturization, others expand across the space of a billboard or require the walk-around room of a full-size sculpture. They are encompassed here within one gallery, where a concise survey of contemporary art unfolds. A full set of these works was acquired by The Museum of Modern Art in 1998, with new publications added to the collection as they appeared. This exhibition provides an opportunity not only to celebrate the remarkably diverse art of our own time, but also to highlight the creative forces at work in this innovative publishing venture.

The Parkett Project

In Zurich in the early 1980s, a group of friends, stimulated by the new level of communication between art communities in Europe and the United States, hoped to contribute to the burgeoning dialogue. Bice Curiger, Jacqueline Burckhardt, Peter Blum, Walter Keller, and soon thereafter, Dieter von Graffenried, decided to create a new periodical that would present articles in both English and German and be "an equal pleasure to read in both languages."[2] Their goal was a journal that would be not academic but artist-driven, necessitating active collaboration. Artists would be chosen to take part in shaping each issue by suggesting authors, conferring on layout, proposing cover ideas, and creating a separate artwork that could be editioned and offered for sale to subscribers. Eventually, additional artists were asked to contribute inserts to the magazine, most often in the form of page art bound into the volume, and also designs for the spines. With offices in Zurich and New York, cross-Atlantic communication and the efforts needed for translation made the process slow and thoughtful, something the editors valued.

When the journal appeared in New York, there was immediate talk about the meaning and pronunciation of its title. The editors responded with a piece in the second issue entitled "?Parkett?" that would become a hallmark of their thoroughness, poetic imagination, and humor. They explained that this German noun derives from the French word *parquet* and that it is "a term for a whole variety of inlaid wooden floors …" They alluded to the word's relationship to dance floors, as well as diplomatic statesmanship, and also invoked the theater by noting that it can refer to seats in the audience closest to the stage. Wittily, they even uncovered obscure connections to "the office of the public prosecutor" and "the stock exchange," and noted the similarity of the sound of the word *parkett* to the English word *parakeet,* and even to the combination of the words *parking lot* and *luncheonette.* In explaining their title, the editors hinted at the richness, complexity, and pleasure that would unfold in their dialogue with people who speak different languages but share a passion for art and ideas.

Twenty-five years later, *Parkett* has enlisted nearly 800 writers in addition to their artist-collaborators, and the magazine is printed in 11,000 copies. Such growth and longevity is a significant accomplishment when one looks back in the modern period on the relatively short runs for periodicals that base their activities around contributions from artists. Its erratic nature notwithstanding, the tradition is a rich one. In the 1890s—a time when many artists and literary figures shared close bonds with each other, and similar thematic concerns vis-à-vis Symbolism—journals such as *La Revue Blanche* commissioned prints to be bound into their pages, or offered portfolios to subscribers. In the twentieth century, such periodicals were generated from a variety of impulses. Some were political and/or satirical, such as *L'Assiette au Beurre*, *The Masses*, and *The New Masses*. In other instances, artists and like-minded editors joined forces, as they did during the German Expressionist period, and upon the arrival of the Dada, Surrealist, and Cobra movements. In the 1960s the adventurous publication *S.M.S.* appeared, with each issue in the form of a small portfolio containing ephemeral artworks by such artists as Christo, Roy Lichtenstein, On Kawara, and Joseph Kosuth.

Among the most illuminating precedents for the *Parkett* project, however, is the work of Marcel Duchamp, whose interest in reproduction found expression through designs and inserts for periodicals, and the publication of multiples. His *Box in a Valise* intersects tellingly with the *Parkett* project. In 1941 he issued his first edition of this carrying-case containing a carefully-constructed display box packed with color reproductions and miniature replicas of his past works. The artist characterized this piece as a "portable museum" and sold it over the years in various editions, for a total of about 300 copies. In homage to this concept, *Parkett*'s editors look back over the small-scale, editioned artworks created in conjunction with their journal, and characterize them as a kind of *Musée en Appartement*.

In addition to its collaborations with artists, *Parkett* provides a variety of thematic sections for ideas and opinions by critics, historians, curators, and other writers interested in contemporary art, but it does not contain exhibition reviews or art-world news items. Several conceptual rubrics under which authors are invited to participate are as follows: "Cumulus" brings together one art professional from the United States and one from a European country to write on any subject of current interest; "Balkon" offers "observations from a certain distance, as if from a balcony rather than the seats up front in the parquet area;" and "Les Infos du Paradis" is described as including "the delicate, the unexpected, the seldom-seen, the theoretical." These various components, along with articles devoted to collaborating artists and the commissioned artworks, create a kind of synergy that is unique to each issue and form a kind of event-between-covers. The periodical becomes a medium or, as the editors have called it, an "instrument."

The Editions: 1984–2009

Conceived during the period in which Neo-Expressionism held center stage in the art world, *Parkett* collaborated on its first issue with the Italian artist, Enzo Cucchi. For his edition, Cucchi created a rich black aquatint and drypoint that was bound into a separate copy of the journal. This version of the journal was published in an edition of 80 and was available for purchase to subscribers of the regular, trade version of *Parkett*. While many artists have decided on editions to be bound into special versions of the journal in this way, others created them as entirely free-standing works. As each issue of the trade version arrives, subscribers can see what the edition consists of through a reproduction, and then decide whether or not to purchase it.

Parkett's collaborating artists, and the editions they have created, represent a variety of artistic generations and directions. Artists such as Louise Bourgeois, born in 1911, and Vanessa Beecroft, born nearly sixty years later in 1969, for example, fit within these parameters. Artistic strategies representing Neo-Conceptualism and language-based ideas, social and political themes, Pop and consumer-based imagery, performance art, feminist issues, documentary and staged photography, and pure abstraction, are all to be found in these projects.

Popular culture merges with feminist issues, for instance, when artists Mariko Mori and Sylvie Fleury bring together elements of performance art, installation, and video in their startling "products." Mori created *Star Doll*, her version of the ubiquitous Barbie, and Fleury duplicated a stylish shoe from the fashion line of a hot designer with *Her Mistress' Toy*. Both objects provoke a certain delight: there is the possibility of playing with Mori's little self-portrait figure as a child would, posing and dressing her; and one can try on Fleury's rubberized stiletto platform mule, or throw it to the dog and hear it squeak. Social and political issues infuse the work of Kara Walker, whose black and white linoleum cut *Boo-Hoo*, falls within the long tradition of incisive prints that express social injustice. Her silhouetted figure takes on an abstract and decorative shape that provokes a kind of tension when joined to her narrative of racism and exploitation. With a uniquely Californian sensibility, Ed Ruscha gives his own slant to conceptual and language-based art. In the lithograph *Hell 1/2 Way Heaven*, Ruscha takes the format of the book into consideration—involving the reader not only in the act of opening his edition, which is bound into the volume, but also in unfolding it and deciding the orientation from which to view it.

The Book as Medium

Ruscha's edition draws attention to the book as a creative medium. Throughout the twentieth century and into the present, there has been a proliferation of deluxe books in a tradition developed particularly in France and known as the *livre de peintre*. Picasso, Matisse, and Miró, among many others, have linked their etchings, lithographs, woodcuts, and screenprints to accompanying literary texts, with masterful results. During the 1960s an alternative phenomenon called "artists' books" gained momentum; this format took advantage of the less costly technique of offset lithography for small, illustrated volumes in large editions. During this idealistic period, the affordable artists' books were meant to be available to a very broad audience, and the page became an alternative exhibition venue.

The structure of *Parkett* combines elements from both these book traditions, as well as from the exhibition catalogue, and becomes a variant genre. Artists provide many of its distinctive attributes. Their suggestions for covers include images for the front and back as well as the inside flaps. Charles Ray's cover of supermodel Tatjana Patitz is integral to the work he created for his separate edition. Executed as a standard fashion shoot, it includes credits for art direction, makeup, and hair. In contrast, Ray's edition consists of a series of nine snapshots of that same model taken at home, where she appears not with professionally designed makeup and hairdo, but in everyday outfits, sitting around the house, and doing everyday tasks.

Artists' interactions with the book-like quality of *Parkett* exist in many guises. Several have referenced the structure and proportions of the journal's pages. Alighiero e Boetti did this with his double twins portrait collotype, which simulates a double-page spread and incorporates a fold and a compositional element drawn down the center where the gutter of the magazine would be. Similarly, Günther Förg responded to the page proportions with his two sculptural editions, both of which include components to be installed side by side on the wall. Others who have incorporated the framework of the book include Georg Baselitz, who chose the traditional frontispiece as the location for a jewel-like drypoint, and Brice Marden and Robert Wilson, each of whom conceived foldout panels connected to prints bound into the magazine.

Some artists have devised separate books for their editions. Martin Kippenberger created eighty small, unique volumes, each with pages showing the same snapshot or found image from his personal archive. Raymond Pettibon fashioned an accordion construction that proposes a reading from left to right. Sigmar Polke subverted the act of reading with fifty unique books that look exactly like issues of *Parkett* but consist of pages rejected during the journal's printing process due to double-printing or other errors.

Parkett's insert series has given page art a regular platform. Over seventy artists have participated thus far. A few have chosen to reproduce works as posters to be folded and tucked into the journal, but most have put together sequences of up to twenty pages to be bound in. Cindy Sherman, whose photographs in series are shown together on gallery walls, generated a very different kind of anticipation, suspense, and drama, with her sequence of images for *Parkett*. Damien Hirst, who has produced ambitious pop-up books among his many other mediums, provided a chilling insert on the subject of cigarette smoking.

By *Parkett*'s fifteenth issue, the editors realized that the spines of a yearly set offered yet another opportunity for artistic collaboration. A composition now completes itself at the end of every year as issues arrive in the mail, are read, and then placed in sequence on the bookshelf. Christian Marclay took the opportunity to put an image of each of the four Beatles on separate spines, and Niele Toroni arranged diamond shapes to make a playing card. Ross Bleckner's abstract composition can be read as a reference to the bones of a human spine.

Art and Dissemination

Publishing in the art field is a risky and adventurous activity which has produced a wide array of works available in editions. Many examples by the most significant artists of the modern period are included in the Museum's collection. These works came into being through the instigation of such historic publishers as Ambroise Vollard, Daniel-Henry Kahnweiler, Aimé Maeght, Tatyana Grosman, and others. The editions commissioned by *Parkett* are now included alongside these examples. Sometimes referred to as "democratic" mediums, printmaking and book formats have provided artists with distinctive forms of expression while also enlarging the community of those who have the opportunity to experience these works up close by owning them. The inventive artworks published by *Parkett*, available to a relatively broad audience, carry on this rich tradition and demonstrate its potential for new and fertile developments.

1
Quotations are from editorial statements in various issues of *Parkett* and from conversations with the editors in Zurich, summer 2000.

2
Peter Blum eventually left to concentrate on activities in New York; Walter Keller left to found the Scalo publishing imprint. Karen Marta, Louise Neri, Cay Sophie Rabinowitz (assisted by Ali Subotnick), and now Bettina Funcke (assisted by Jeremy Sigler) have served as New York editors. Managing editor is Mark Welzel. Editions are handled by Beatrice Fässler in Zurich, and Andrea Urban in New York. Subscriptions are managed by Mathias Arnold and bookshop distribution by Nicole Stotzer.

3
Reprinted with permission from an essay by Deborah Wye in the brochure *Collaborations with Parkett: 1984 to Now*, © 2001 The Museum of Modern Art, New York. The dates, names and other facts have been updated for Parkett's 25th anniversary issue, 2009.

『パルケット』とのコラボレーション
1984年から現在へ

ニューヨーク近代美術館
版画・挿画本部門主席学芸員

デボラ・ワイ

　わたしたちはアーティストに「関する」情報ばかりでなく、アーティストが「自ら手がけた」オリジナル作品を提供して、アートとじかに触れ合う手段の創出をめざす[1]——現代美術と思想の専門誌『パルケット』は1984年の創刊号にこう記した。以来86号を数える2009年の今日まで、この目標は揺らぐことがない。本展は、『パルケット』の企画で制作された、エディション、インサート、背表紙デザインを契機に、アーティストが手がけた独創的な作品から構成される。過去25年の間に『パルケット』は200人のアーティストと手を携え、版画、ページ・アート（誌面を用いたアート作品）、写真、素描、絵画、マルティプル、ビデオ、DVD、サウンド・ピースを初めとする斬新な形式の作品を制作し、雑誌の定期購読者に頒布してきた。作品の大半はサイズが小さく、ミニチュア化の面白さに富む一方で、大きな看板に匹敵する空間を占めるものや、大型の彫刻のように、周囲を歩いてまわれる広さを必要とするものもある。そのすべてをひとつの展示室に収めた本展は、現代美術の全体像を簡潔に示すことになるだろう。ニューヨーク近代美術館は全作品を網羅するセットを1998年に収蔵し、新作はその都度コレクションに加えている。本展はわたしたちの生きるこの時代に生み出される美術のめざましい多様性を明らかにするばかりでなく、新たな試みに意欲的な出版事業にみなぎる創造力の豊かさにも光をあてるものになるだろう。

　1980年代初めのチューリヒで、気の合う数名が、ヨーロッパとアメリカの美術界の結びつきの飛躍的な高まりに刺戟をうけ、芽生え始めた対話をいっそう深めたいと考えた。ビーチェ・クリガー、ジャクリーヌ・ブルクハルト、ピーター・ブラム、ヴァルター・ケラー、そして間もなくディーター・ヴォン・グラフェンリードも参加し、英語／ドイツ語の二ヶ国語による「どちらの言葉でも、同じように読んで楽しい」[2]雑誌の刊行が始まる。かれらが目指したのはアカデミックではなく、アーティストを主体とするものであったから、アーティストの積極的な関わりが欠かせない。アーティストには寄稿者の選択、レイアウトの打ち合わせ、表紙のアイデア作りに関与して各号の制作に参加するのに加えて、定期購読者に頒布する雑誌とは独立したエディション作品の制作が求められる。その後、他のアーティストにも誌面をアート化し、雑誌の綴じ込み付録や背表紙のデザインの制作を依頼することになった。チューリヒとニューヨークのオフィスが大西洋を挟んで行う様々なやりとりに加え、翻訳にも手間暇がかかるため、制作作業は多大な時間と配慮を要するが、『パルケット』はそこにもかけがえのない価値をみいだした。

　雑誌がニューヨークで発売されると、たちまちタイトルの意味と発音をめぐって議論が起こる。制作者がこれに応えて第2号に「?パルケット?」と題して寄せた文章は、制作側の緻密な配慮、想像力の豊かさ、ユーモアを人々に強く印象づけた。制作者たちの説明によると、ドイツ語の単語「Parkett」の語源はフランス語の「parquet」にあり、この語は「多種多様な寄せ木細工の床の総称」である。またこの語は比喩的に舞踏場の床、外交面での政治手腕を表わし、さらに舞台に向かって最前列の客席をも意味するため、演劇との関わりも感じさせる。そして茶目っ気もみせて、「検察局」や「証券取引所の立会所」との曖昧な関係まで打ち明け、ドイツ語の「Parkett」の発音が英語の「parakeet（小型のインコ）」に似ていること、「parking lot（駐車場）」と「luncheonette（軽食堂）」を組合せた単語のようにも見えると記した。雑誌の題の説明を通じて、制作者はふだん用いる言語は異なっても、美術と思想に寄せる情熱をともにわかちあう人々との対話がもたらすはずの豊かな稔り、意味の深さ、そして歓びをさりげなく示したのだった。

　それから25年を経た今日までの間に、『パルケット』は共同制作者となったアーティストの他に約800名もの著述家の賛助を得て、発行部数も11,000部に達する。アーティストとの共同制作を基本にすえた雑誌が、近代ではどれも短命に終わっていることを考え合わせると、『パルケット』のこうした発展ぶり、息の長さにはとくに意味があるようにおもう。安定性を欠くのはその性質からやむをえないとしても、この分野には豊かな伝統が育まれてきた。1890年代にはアーティストと文学畑の作家たちが深い絆で結ばれ、ともに象徴主義に関心を抱く時代背景のなかで、『ルヴュ・ブランシュ』などが版画制作を委嘱してこれを雑誌に付録したり、何点かをまとめたポートフォリオを定期購読者に頒布した。20世紀にも、同様の雑誌が多様な意図のもとに世に送りだされた。『L'Assiette au Beurre』、『The Masses』、『The New Masses』などは政治や諷刺を目的とした。ドイツ表現主義の全盛期、さらにはダダイスム、シュルレアリスム、コブラの台頭期にはアーティストと志を同じくする版元が協力した例もみられる。1960年代に創刊された進取の気性に富む『S.M.S.』では各号がクリスト、リキテンスタイン、河原温、ジョゼフ・コスースらによる華奢な作品を収め、ささやかなポートフォリオの形態をとった。

　『パルケット』に先駆ける試みのなかで、とくに示唆に富むのは、雑誌とは異なるものの、マルセル・デュシャンの作品だろう。デュシャンは複製に関心が深く、雑誌のデザインや付録の制作、マルティプルの刊行にも手をそめた。デュシャンの《トランクの中の箱》と『パルケット』の試みには多くの関連性があり、様々な思考をうながす。デュシャンは1941年に過去の作品の色刷りの複製、あるいはミニチュア化したレプリカをぎっしりと収めて展示も可能な箱を丹念に組立て、それを持ち運びできるようにトランクにいれた最初のエディションを発表する。デュシャンはこの作品を「ポータブル美術館」と形容し、長年の間に幾度かエディションを重ねて、合計約300部を販売した。このアイデアに敬意を表して、『パルケット』の編集者たちは雑誌との関わりを契機に制作された小さなサイズのエディション作品群を顧みて、「アパルトマンのなかの美術館」と呼んだ。

　アーティストとの共同制作にくわえて、『パルケット』は評論家、歴史家、キュレーター、あるいは現代美術に関心のある作家たちが多様なテーマに関して考えや意見を表明できる誌面を用意はしても、展覧会の批評や美術界のニュースは掲載しない。毎号登場する項目はいくつかあり、「Cumulus（積雲）」はアメリカとヨーロッパから美術を職業とする専門家ひとりを選び、時の話題の中から好きなテーマについて執筆してもらう。「Balkon（バルコニー）」は「舞台に近い『Parkett（最前列）』ではなく、『balcony（2階正面席）』からのように、一定の距離を置いた観察」を提供し、「Les Infos du Paradis（天井桟敷の見聞）」は「微妙なもの、予期せぬもの、めったに目につかないもの、理論的なもの」をとりあげる。これらの多種多様な要素が、共同制作に携わるアーティストと委嘱作品に関する記事とあいまって、各号毎にユニークな相乗効果を生み、表裏の表紙に挟まれた「出来事」を創りだす。雑誌はメディア、あるいは編集者たちの呼び方にならえば、「道具・手段」となる。

エディション　1984年〜2009年

　新表現主義が美術界の主役を演じた時期に計画された『パルケット』は、創刊号でイタリアの画家エンツォ・クッキとの共同制作にとりくむ。クッキは表現力豊かな黒主体のエディション作品をアクアチントとドライポイントで制作し、これを特装版に付録として綴じ込んだ。特装版は部数を80に限定して刊行され、通常版『パルケット』の定期購読者向けに頒布された。このようにエディション作品を特装版に綴じ込むアーティストが多いなかで、雑誌とは別個に独立した作品を制作するアーティストもあった。通常版の雑誌が手もとに届く度に、定期購読者は複製によってエディション作品の内容を知り、これを購入するか否かを決めるのである。

　『パルケット』と共同制作を行ったアーティスト、そしてかれらが手がけたエディション作品は世代と方向性の両面でじつに多岐にわたる。たとえば1911年生まれのルイーズ・ブルジョワと、それからほぼ60年を経た1969年生まれのヴァネッサ・ビークロフトは年齢の幅を示す好例だろう。ネオ・コンセプチュアリズムから言語に基づく思想、社会・政治的テーマ、ポップや消費財のイメージ、パフォーマンス・アート、フェミニストのテーマ、ドキュメンタリー写真と芝居仕立ての写真、純粋な抽象作品まで、すべてをそこに見いだすことができる。

　森万里子とシルヴィ・フルーリがパフォーマンス・アート、インスタレーション、ビデオを一体化させて驚くべき「製品」を創りあげる過程では、大衆文化とフェミニズムの論点がひとつに溶けあう。森万里子が世界中いたるところで目につくバービー人形の向こうを張って自家製の《スター・ドール》を制作すれば、フルーリは《女主人の玩具》で人気絶頂のデザイナーによる靴の最新作の中から流行の尖端をゆくものを選び、瓜二つの作品をつくりあげた。どちらの作品も、見ていてある種の楽しさを感じさせる。自身をモデルとする森の小さな人形であれば、ポーズをとらせたり、服を着せたりして、子供のように遊ぶことができる。フルーリのゴムのようにやわらかいハイヒールのサンダルなら履いてみてもよいし、犬に向かって放り、キューキュー鳴るのを聞いてみてもよい。

　キャラ・ウォーカーのモノクロームのリノカット《ブー・フー》は、社会にはびこる不正を痛烈に抉る版画の長い伝統につらなり、社会、政治に関わる問題の浸透ぶりが目立つ。シルエットで描かれた人物は抽象化され、装飾性も帯び、それが人種差別と搾取を物語る作品の内容と結びつくとき、ある種の緊張を誘発する。カリフォルニア出身者ならではの感受性をいかし、エドワード・ルシェはことばを用いたコンセプチュアル・アートに独自の彩りをそえる。《Hell 1/2 Way Heaven（地獄・中途・天国）》と題するリトグラフで、ルシェは本の形態的な特徴を作品にとり入れた。雑誌に綴じ込んだエディション作品を読者に開いてもらうのにくわえ、開いたものをどの向きに見るかの決定を読者にゆだねたのである。

メディアとしての本

　ルシェのエディション作品をきっかけに、創造的なメディアとしての本に注目が集まった。20世紀全般を通じ、さらに今世紀に入ってからも、とくにフランスで発展し、「画家の本」とも呼ばれる伝統をなす豪華本の刊行は盛んに行われた。ピカソ、マティス、そしてミロを初めとする多くの画家たちが、文学作品にエッチング、リトグラフ、木版、シルクスクリーンを添えて、巨匠の名に恥じない成果を生んだ。1960年代にはこれに代わる「アーティスト・ブック」の制作に弾みがつく。これは費用のかからないオフセット・リトグラフを用いた挿画入りの小型本で、制作部数も多い。理想主義が通用したこの時期、比較的容易入手できるアーティスト・ブックは広範な愛好家層に提供され、誌面は従来と一味ちがう作品展示の場となった。

　『パルケット』の成立ちはこれらふたつの書籍の伝統にくわえ展覧会カタログの要素も加味して、従来からのジャンルの枠を乗り越える。『パルケット』ならではの性格の多くは、アーティストが授けてくれたものである。表紙に関するアーティストの提案は、表紙と裏表紙、さらに見返しの図柄にもおよぶ。スーパーモデルのタチアナ・パティッツをとりあげたチャールズ・レイの表紙デザインは、雑誌とは別個に制作したエディション作品と切っても切れない関係にある。通常のファッション写真として制作された表紙には、アート・ディレクター、メーキャップ、ヘアメークの担当者の名が入っている。それと対照的にレイのエディションは同じモデルを住まいで撮影した9枚のスナップ写真からなり、そこでは仕事中とは化粧も髪形も違い、普段着姿のパテッツが日常の家事をこなしている。

　書籍にも匹敵する『パルケット』の印刷物としての質の高さとアーティストの関わりは、様々な装いをとる。誌面の構成や形にちなむ作品を制作したアーティストも何人かいる。アリギエロ・ボエッティは見開きページを模してコロタイプで二組の双子のポートレートを制作し、のどあきに当たる中央部にできる折り目と構図の変化を作品にとりいれた。同じように、ギュンター・フェルクは判型に応じて2種の彫刻的なエディションを手がけた。そのどちらもが壁に並べて掛ける要素をとり入れている。本の枠組みをとり入れたアーティストにはこの他にゲオルク・バゼリッツがあり、宝石のようなドライポイントを口絵の定位置に配した。ブライス・マーデンとロバート・ウィルソンはいずれも、雑誌に付録した版画に合わせ折りたたみ式のパネルを作品化した。

　エディション作品用に、別冊を案出したアーティストもいる。マルティン・キッペンベルガーは一冊毎に内容の異なる小冊子を80冊制作した。自ら収集したスナップ写真や印刷物から一冊につき一つのイメージを選び、どのページにも同じイメージを配したのである。レイモンド・ペティボンはアコーディオン式の造りを工夫し、左から右に視線を誘う読み物を提示した。ジグマー・ポルケは『パルケット』と寸分ちがわない体裁をとりつつ、印刷過程で二重刷りなど乱丁ページばかりを集めて同じものがふたつとない冊子50部を制作し、読むという行為を破綻させた。

　『パルケット』の「インサート・シリーズ」は、ページ・アートに定期的に発表の場を提供することになった。これまでに参加したアーティストは70人を越える。作品の複製をポスターとし、折り畳んで雑誌に綴じ込んだアーティストも何人かいたが、大半は何ページ分かをひとまとめにしており、多いものではこれが20ページにおよぶ。シンディ・シャーマンの写真は画廊でもシリーズ化された作品が壁にまとめて展示されるが、『パルケット』のために制作した連作は予感、サスペンス、ドラマ性に富む異色作となった。多様なメディアを操るデミアン・ハーストは、野心的な飛び出す絵本も手がけているが、喫煙をテーマにぞっとするように恐ろしい付録を制作した。

　創刊から15号目を迎える頃、編集者は1年分の雑誌の背表紙を集めると、それもアーティストとのコラボレーションを行う場になりうることに気づく。郵送される雑誌を毎号読み、それを順番に本棚に並べると、年末にはひとつの作品が完成する。クリスチャン・マークレイはビートルズ4人の映像をひとりずつ4冊の背表紙に載せ、ニエーレ・トローニはダイアモンドの型をトランプのカードになるように配置した。抽象性の高いロス・ブレックナーの作品は、人間の脊椎を暗示するようにおもわれる。

アートと普及

　美術の分野で行う出版には先の見通しが立ちにくく、危険も伴うが、これによって多様な作品がエディション化され、手に入りやすくなった。近代を代表するアーティストたちが手がけ、出版された多くの作品が美術館によって収集されている。これらの作品は、アンブロワーズ・ヴォラール、ダニエル＝アンリ・カーンワイラー、エメ・マーグ、タチアナ・グロスマンら歴史に名を残す美術商や版画工房主が版元となり、彼らに誘われ、あるいは唆されて制作されたものである。『パルケット』が委嘱したエディションも、今ではこうした先例と肩を並べるまでになった。「大衆的な」メディアとも呼ばれる版画と書籍は、アーティストに他では得られない表現の形式を提供する一方で、作品を所有して間近に体験できる愛好家の層を拡大した。『パルケット』が出版する創意に富む作品群は、愛好家の間にひろくゆきわたり、豊かな伝統を受け継ぎながら、そこに新たな、そして実り多い発展の可能性のあることを実証している。

注

1. 引用の出典は既刊の『パルケット』に掲載された編集者の文章、および2000年夏にチューリヒで行われた編集者との会話。

2. ピーター・ブラムはニューヨークでの活動に専念するため、後に離脱した。ヴァルター・ケラーも独立してScalo Publishing Imprintを設立。ニューヨーク側の編集はカレン・マルタ、ルイーズ・ネリ、ケイ・ゾフィ・ラビノヴィッツ（アリ・スボトニクが補佐）を経て、現在はベッティーナ・フンケ（ジェレミー・ジグラーが補佐）が担当する。編集および制作統括はマーク・ヴェルツェル。エディション担当は、チューリヒがベアトリス・フェスラー、ニューヨークがアンドレア・アーバン、予約講読の受付はマシアス・アーノルド、書店配本はニコル・ストッツァーがそれぞれ行っている。

3. 本稿は、以下に所収のテキストを関係者の許可を得て再録した。再録にあたり、年や人名など事実関係を一部修正した。

Collaborations with Parkett: 1984 to Now. The Museum of Modern Art, New York, 2001.

The Museum Plays House

By Susan Tallman

Susan Tallman is an art historian
and author of several books.

Parkett describes itself as "a small museum and a large library on contemporary art." This is accurate enough—its 86 issues and 1400 texts offer a singular source of documentation and insight into the culture of our time, and its 200 artists' editions offer a global survey of contemporary art. But the ethos of these editions is more precisely captured by another phrase *Parkett* once employed—*"un musée en appartement."* The image of the *Musée en Appartement*, with its merger of the domestic and the grandiose, suits both the individual works and their collective presence. It is possible to imagine the history of *Parkett* publications as a real apartment, a suite of rooms in which art and life have ceased to occupy separable spheres.

In this imaginary *Musée*, even the foyer is a gallery: to the right, Malcolm Morley's Tang horses and Thomas Struth's Shanghai street, to the left, Anri Sala's mysterious runway and Gabriel Orozco's light-dappled Iris print. Near, far, nature, artifice, analysis and longing, presented in less space than you need to swing a cat.

A study would accommodate *Parkett*'s "large library"—86 volumes on a tidy rolling cart, one copy set out on a table with its own (slightly garish) tote bag. This is a museum, so a display case holds archival documents: photographs of Dan Graham and Vanessa Beecroft installations, a rock from the Valle Maggia with notes by Ugo Rondinone, a stack of notes by Trisha Donnelly, delivered individually over the course of the year. In keeping with the mood of studious intensity, the walls are lined with black and white prints: Julie Mehretu's masterful maelstrom of etching, Albert Oehlen's small etching-based cacophony, Richard Serra's arching ropes of black ink, Chuck Close's daguerrotype, Kara Walker's acerbic linocut. A small Ross Bleckner painting sits on a shelf. But this is also an apartment, and the large desk is scattered with bits and bobs bearing witness to life in progress: a postcard pinned down with a paperweight, an abandoned New York Times, a calendar for keeping track of appointments, a rubberstamp tipped on its side, a casually dropped pair of spectacles. The cushion on the chair has been nudged to the side.

Lingering traces of perfume waft from the bedroom where Elizabeth Peyton's *Oscar and Bosie*—the love that dare not speak its name—hangs above the bed, where a jacket, shirt and tie are laid out, waiting. Across the room, John Wesley's screenprint *Boyfriends* exerts its ambiguous narrative above the vanity, on which a pair of evening gloves and a silk scarf have been dropped beside the perfume bottle. An open jewelry box gleams silver and gold with rings.

The kitchen, as in any apartment, is a working space. The only recognizable art is Maria Lassnig's *Pair of Gloves* above the sink. The table is laid with a cutwork table cloth and covered with tools and utensils: a stack of Styrofoam cups, a striped rolling pin, a drill, a fire-proof glove, a small, stained bucket. Someone, playing with his food, has fitted out a lemon to look like a pig, with mushroom legs and strawberry eyes. The tinkle of a wind-chime floats in through the window and a weather vane turns out in the garden where the dog gazes longingly at a shoe-shaped chew-toy, and flies investigate a box left on the bench, oblivious to the fly-swatter beside them.

Down in the rec room (it is a small museum, but a large apartment), the walls are hung for entertainment: Franz Ackermann's glowing screenprint and Thomas Demand's airplane photograph announce travel; Sarah Morris' poster and Richard Phillip's Jane Fonda look-alike portrait advertise the attractions of cinema; Beat Streuli's *Oxford Street* reminds us of shopping; Dana Schutz's *Head of Timothy Leary* and Richard Prince's Woodstock snapshot offer drugs and rock and roll. Two new flat-screen TVs are lit up with swaying palms and busy bees, while two old tube televisions show a domestic dispute in progress and a crouching woman, ready to spring. By the turntable a black phonograph record has been forgotten on the shelf. Abandoned Poker hands, weighted down with card guards, litter the table.

But the busiest room may be the nursery. Animal pictures line the walls: Laura Owens' bats, Robert Frank's swans, Christopher Wool's black dog. Toys litter the floor: a colorful pull-toy, a cardboard suitcase of lead soldiers, a half-built tower of plexiglass panels, slightly too tall. Everything here is Brobdingnag or Lilliput: in one corner, an enormous balloon flower bumps against an enormous broken cardboard watch. In the other corner, a cow and a dinosaur small enough to fit on a plate stand by a plate-sized bear-skin rug, a pocket-sized pair of brown shoes. The dollhouse holds a blue-haired, Saturn-Moon-like figure, a dancing girl with a hoop, and a male figure dressed in an orange jumpsuit, masked and shackled, on its knees.

The orange figure is, of course, not a plaything—it is John Kessler's Guantanamo-era rumination on evil—and the nursery is not a nursery. This is not after all an apartment hung with art, it is an apartment *as* art, every object wreathed with meaning and allusion. Robert Frank's swans don't illustrate nature, they comment on social class, Christopher Wool's dog is a pun on the artist's *rundogrun* paintings. The colorful pull-toy is one of Francis Alys' magnetic *Ghetto Collectors*, pulled through city streets by the artist to accrue urban flotsam. The Saturn Moon-ish doll is by Mariko Mori, the apocalyptic ballerina by Mai-Thu Perret. The lead soldiers are neither lead nor soldiers, but cast tin figures from Pawel Althamer's autobiography. The balloon flower is by Jeff Koons, the watch by Thomas Hirschhorn, the bearskin rug by Susan Rothenberg. The wee shoes are replicas of those sold by Sherrie Levine in her first gallery show. The Plexiglas construction kit is by Liam Gillick (its too-large panels matched to the dimensions of *Parkett*); the paint-spattered cow and dinosaur by Isa Gentzken.

Back in the rec room, the domestic dispute is a video by Bruce Nauman, the swaying palms a DVD by Jennifer Allora and Guillermo Calzadilla, the buzz-less bees by Diana Thater. The crouching woman is a Pippiloti Rist 3D pin-up suction-cupped to the television screen. The card guards are not cheap and cheery tat, but hand-painted coins by Mark Grotjahn. The turntable is stacked with records by Katharina Fritsch. The record on the shelf, floppy and unplayable, is a Fischli / Weiss simulation, as is the paint-stained "bucket" in the kitchen.

The kitchen tablecloth is by Daniel Buren, the rolling pin by Cosima von Bonin, the glove is a reference to the fireworks of Roman Signer. The Styrofoam cups that shade so delicately from white to gray have been stacked and painted that way by Tom Friedman. The drill, by Monica Bonvicini, is set in a pinkly organic ooze, suggestive of both sex and dentistry. The lemon pretending to be a pig is actually Styrofoam pretending to be a lemon pretending to be a pig, by Olaf Breuning. The dog's fetish is by Sylvie Fleury, the weather vane is by Rodney Graham, the chime by Pierre Huyghe (its tones an aleatoric reordering of the Close Encounters theme). The fly-swatter by Ai Weiwei is gilded brass and beautifully inept at squashing bugs, but it doesn't matter because the flies are plastic, caught within an Ilya Kabakov pocket distopia.

Even the scent in the air is art, perfumed and bottled by Kai Althoff. The white shirt is alternatively stitched or silk-screened with a face by Luc Tuymans; the black jacket is by Eija-Liisa Ahtila; the tie by Sophie Calle. The gloves, white-skinned and red-veined are Surrealist traps by Meret Oppenheim; the scarf is a trompe l'oeil reproduction of the back of a painting by Michael Raedecker. The gold signet ring bears the initials RS for Rudolf Stingel, the silver ring bears a statement by Jenny Holzer.

The New York Times in the study is a fake: somewhere on the page there is a newsbrief to the effect that a boy named Robert Gober has drowned. The calendar has been designed by Dominique Gonzalez-Foerster to move in 13-month increments (January 2008 is followed by February 2009.) The postcard on the desk is by Tacita Dean, the paperweight by Keith Tyson, the rubber stamp by Lawrence Weiner. Open the issue of *Parkett* on the table and you will find it unreadable—the pages elaborately overprinted by Sigmar Polke. The purse is by Franz West, as is the rolling shelf. Even the cushion in the chair is allusive—Olaf Nicolai's replica of the one that graced George Lukacs' study in Budapest. And the spectacles on the desk clarify nothing: the lenses are etched with words by Rirkrit Tiravanija.

In the *Musée en Appartement* art may lurk anywhere: that light switch by the door isn't a light switch, it's Rachel Whiteread's cast inversion of one. The light bulb is turned up and down by Tony Oursler's recorded voice, part of a pre-fab installation work.

Parkett is now 25 years old—ample time in which to establish a signature style, but the editions remain as quixotic in temperament and as unpredictable in appearance as ever. If there is a house style at *Parkett*, it exists as an editorial fondness for ambigious situations, for crossovers, for artists and objects that confound the usual borders between art and life. Andreas Slominski, whose edition consists of a ready-made folding ruler, describes his work as "an experiment that explores what we can and cannot identify as art in this culture." Such experiments may be more effectively executed in an apartment than in a museum, where you know you've come to "see the art." In an apartment, you touch things, you smell things, you play with things.

Play, however, is serious stuff. It's how to investigate the world: inquiry and improvisation, disguise and discovery, rules devised and rules discarded. *Parkett* editions abound in games of deception and games of perception; solitary games and games for players; dress-up games and mind games. Sophie Calle's tie is printed with the story of her attempt to remake an attractive stranger through anonymous gifts of clothing; but since anyone wearing the tie has been "dressed by" Calle, it is difficult to tell the difference between owner, beneficiary, and victim. Like the best children's games, these works investigate the grown-up world of money, love, and power by inverting the roles, tweaking the rules, metaphorically putting clothing on the dog or, in the case of Gillian Wearing's mask, literally putting the artist's face on the collector.

In the *Musée en Appartement*, even the art on the walls seems to play at being art. The etchings of John Currin and Peter Doig are contemporary works in period costume; Glenn Brown's *Disorder* suggests an 18th century portrait dissolving into frenetic brushwork, but all of it is scrupulously concocted and false. Cindy Sherman's photograph bulges out from its gilded bijou frame, while Mike Kelly's intones a calligraphed quote from Goethe. Tomma Abts' photographed painting, Roni Horn's tumbling adjectives, Andreas Gursky's museum photograph, all come pre-framed, like IKEA *décor*. Rosemarie Trockel's photogravure comes mounted on wood, Alex Katz' *Sunny* is a tiny terrier head screenprinted on aluminum, Jean-Luc Mylayne's bird photographs are so massively framed they stand as sculptures. Other works, like Matthew Ritchie's adhesive wall drawing, are perversely unframable.

These works are designed not just as images, but as *products*. Jeff Koons' "collectible" plate and Rudolf Stingel's bling ring are play-acting as commodities—high art content in a low-brow box. They toy with our habits of categorization. But Richard Prince's pre-packaged gold record belies a wistful fascination with the power, authority, and distribution of real industry, as does Tacita Dean's postcard edition—100 were signed and numbered and posted for *Parkett*; the remainder were "distributed unsigned ... to be sold as normal tourist postcards," out in the real world.

The impulse to muck with the assigned role and location of art can be traced back to the original games master, Marcel Duchamp, whose rectified ready-mades—now nearly a century old—have proved an enduring inspiration to take what's on the ground and tweak it. Duchamp's game was chess, cerebral and sober, but the cross-dressing objects here are more Snakes & Ladders. Damien Hirst, Jason Rhoades, Karen Kilimnik, Anish Kapoor and Rebecca Horn all use pre-existing artifacts to wildly different effect: playful, analytical, mysterious, elegiac. As with Katharina Grosse's painted chunks of Carrara marble, equal weight is given to the presence of what is found and to the meaning of what has been done.

The wide range of eccentric supports employed by *Parkett* artists in place of paper or canvas is testament not only to an analytic engagement with the sociology of packaging, but also to lure the viewer into a more intimate, more physical relationship with art. Gary Hume and Louise Bourgeois chose to print on textiles, Yayoi Kusama on mirror, Fred Tomaselli on plexi, Rachel Harrison on polypropylene, Sue Williams on multiple layers of mylar. John Baldessari's grimacing faces are enameled on steel, "impervious to environmental influences." The quarter sheets of plywood that Wade Guyton ran through his printer, like

Günther Förg's mirror and copper diptych, insist on a specific, irreducible materiality. The substances of Matthew Barney's resin and sugar dumbbell carry as much content as the form. Cady Noland's spray-painted, perforated cardboard and Imi Knoebel's pigment brick have no image apart from their substance.

Some works simply beg to be touched: Sarah Lucas' *Lion Hearts* and Christian Marclay's *Bad Ear* are palm-sized and seductive; Ernesto Neto's quirky pillow-balloon-sculpture and Richard Artschwager's rubberized *Hair Box* lose half their meaning if they cannot be handled. Powerful indices of the artist's hand, the sculptures of Stephan Balkenhol and Rebecca Warren provoke tactile curiosity, as does Douglas Gordon's index of the artist's teeth.

The drypoints of Georg Baselitz, Francesco Clemente, Enzo Cucchi, and Martin Disler are, similarly, images that fingers long to know. Under most circumstances, the touching of such prints is taboo, but these are bound into the magazine. The only way to see them, or those of James Turrell, Eric Fischl, Jannis Kounellis or Mario Merz, is to hold open the magazine with (gasp!) your thumb on the art. To view Robert Wilson's lithograph or Brice Marden's etching, you have to seize the page and unfold it. The incipient naughtiness of this is captured in Ed Ruscha's bound-in lithograph, which unfolds to read, "hell"... "heaven"... "1/2 way."

From a marketing point of view, this is perverse: a loose print is a much more saleable commodity than one hidden in a book. That this is so suggests that art is more often purchased as a public statement than as a private pleasure, and one can see the decision to bind as an enforcement of intimacy. But this intimacy comes—literally—at a price. To be known, these works need to be owned: Laurie Anderson's *Hearring* can only be worn, and heard, by one ear at a time. Franz Gertsch, Raymond Pettibon, Gilbert & George, and Marlene Dumas all made works that need to be opened to be seen. Thomas Ruff's photo under vellum cannot be understood without taking it in one's hands. Christian Boltanski's disturbing book requires the owner to scratch through an opaque coating to reveal images of violent crime that no one should ever see.

Curiously, though many of the objects in the *Musée en Appartement* present themselves as pre-packaged products, almost none are mass-produced. The edition sizes are modest, and many are not editions at all in the customary sense of a set of identical things, distinguished only by a penciled number in the corner. Instead, they offer collections of unique objects joined together by that penciled number and some particular set of shared qualities. In the case of Jorge Pardo's hand-made sculptures, those qualities are little more than a material (paper) and an approximate size (10"x 4"x 4"). John Armleder's are individual manipulations of the same sized piece of Perspex. Paul McCarthy chose to produce 36 different billy clubs; Josh Smith, 38 double-sided collages; John Bock, 60 knitted undergarments. Ross Bleckner and Gerhard Richter simply painted a large number of small paintings. The fact that such things are so obviously hand-made seems to entitle them to a special kind of attention, the kind we take to the theater rather than leave in front of the television. The hand-stitched prints of Warhol and Bourgeois, the plasticine addenda on Ellen Gallagher's photogravure, and the improvisatory variation of Phillip Taaffe's monotypes, all add the immediacy of hand-facture to standard printing techniques. Wilhelm Sasnal's hand-engraved negative does the same for photography.

Of all the reproductive media photography is, seemingly, the most efficient, transparent, and ubiquitous—qualities exploited by Gregor Schneider's and Maurizio Cattelan's deadpan documentations of the absurd, and punned upon in Zoe Leonard's *One Hour Photo* photo and Angela Bulloch's photograph of furniture-sized "pixels". These same qualities are purposefully undermined, however, by Wolfgang Tillmans and Tracy Emin in their "editions" of unique photographs, which grant the medium an unexpected quality of preciousness. Christian Jankowski hired 50 different photographers to photograph him reading 50 different issues of *Parkett* to produce 50 unique photographs. Sigmar Polke took pictures of Goya's DISASTERS OF WAR but developed the film with his own barmy alchemy of Himbeergeist and Pril to produce 60 unique (and only occasionally pictorial) photographs. Here the seeds of transcendence don't lie outside the seemingly dehumanizing mechanisms of reproduction, but deep within it.

Making such irregular editions can be a way to emphasize the hazards of chance or the impulse to improvise, but they can also be a tool for demonstrating a priori: Keith Tyson's paperweights and Daniel Buren's tablecloths both work through a set number of variables within a specific formal problem. Each solution—each example—is unique, each equally valid. (Giving such conceptual tasks life as a utilitarian object for the bourgeois home is typical of the *Parkett* sensibility.) Martin Kippenberger's re-structuring of the edition was both methodical and perverse: instead of 80 books all reproducing the same photographs, he made 80 unique books each featuring a single photograph, repeated on all its pages.

All these interventions in the normal mechanism of the edition work to a purpose: they enjoin viewers to consider closely the thing before them: why *this* thing, rather than just any thing? Why this *thing*, rather than just an image?

The difficulty of seeing—really seeing—what lies before you is addressed repeatedly in *Parkett*, from Markus Raetz' vision of vision in *Parkett* 8, to Carsten Höller's anamorphic key. William Kentridge printed his anamorphic drawing atop an encyclopedia page: the text is interrupted by the drawing which can only be read in cylindrical reflection where the text becomes illegible—a lesson in not having your cake and eating it too. Olafur Eliasson offers a device that shows you only your own eye, looking at itself. There are objects that play at disappearing, like Doug Aitken's mirrored kite or the Ahtila jacket, printed with the words "veil of ignorance" on the back and the same phrase mirror-reversed on the front, as if you were seeing through the person in between. There are allusions to illusions, like Urs Fischer's sculpture of a rabbit being pulled from a hat.

Subterfuge, imitation, and re-presentation abound in the *Musée en Appartement*: the Fischli/Weiss and Robert Gober pieces that look like ready-mades but aren't; the defaced Lucy McKenzie silkscreen that might be an echo of Duchamp's LHOOQ, except the image vandalized is McKenzie's own age-progressed portrait of Hergé's imaginary Tintin. Alighiero e Boetti's twinned Time Magazine covers are hand-drawn. The piece that looks like a Marilyn Minter painting mimicking glamour photography, is actually a photograph mimicking a Marilyn Minter painting. Thomas Demand's photograph of too-perfect airplane stairs actually pictures a paper model. Like so many of the things in the *Musée en Appartement*, it is a trap, a lesson in not taking things at face value, an injunction to pay attention—to, in John Cage's phrase, "wake up to the very life we're living."

Life—the very life we're living—is ultimately lived on a human scale. The vastness of museums is a fantasy. In the *Musée en Appartement* the necessity of modest size (*Parkett* editions are delivered by post) has made for some profound rethinking of the customary scale of contemporary art. Sometimes this is a literal miniaturization (Sam Taylor-Wood's two inch high panorama,) sometimes a conceptual collapsing of distance. (Charles Ray's snapshots of Tatjana Patitz eliminated visual cues to her status as a "super-model"—professional lighting, hair, make-up, staging, mass-production offset-lithography on coated paper—giving the purchaser instead nine [unique] photographs of an unusually lovely girl sitting around the house.) Sometimes the problem is solved by offering a fragment: Tracey Moffatt's and Jeff Wall's photographs were once part of larger installations. James Rosenquist's lithograph looks like it could have been cut from one of the artist's immense works; Franz Gertsch's woodcut actually was. Nan Goldin's field of leaves and Thomas Schütte's dotty wallpaper are excerpts from larger fields. Vija Celmin's night sky and the boxed oceanscapes of Hiroshi Sugimoto are tiny and infinite—we understand that the edge of the picture is merely a convention, the reality extends beyond our perception.

This idea that the job of art is to convey a reality that extends beyond our perception forms the bricks and mortar of the *Musée en Appartement*. A century ago, this belief inspired artists to look beyond appearances, to ferret out principles from form, to make the concrete abstract. We, however, live in a world governed by abstractions—by money we never see, politicians we never meet, art that cannot be touched. In our time, the challenge is to make the abstract concrete.

This is precisely what Bernard Frize does—his double torus gives physical form to a topological conjecture (a three-dimensional variant of the four-color map problem) in something that looks like a chew-ring. It is what Richard Artschwager does in *1000 Cubic Inches,* offering five differently shaped packing cases of equivalent volume, a tangible illustration of Piagetian abstraction. And it is what artists as diverse as Wolfgang Laib, David Hammons, and Beatriz Milhazes do as well. It is a small museum, but it can hold a lot.

The largest work produced by *Parkett* is Felix Gonzalez-Torres' *Untitled*, a DIY billboard of footprints in the sand. One of the smallest is Juan Muñoz' *Augenblick* (Glance) a palm-sized rectangle of glass that is blank until you breathe on it, when a spare drawing briefly appears and then floats away. The picture is of a piggy-back ride. Brobdingnag and Lilliput. Eternal sands and fleeting joys. Presence and absence. Love and death. In the *Musée en Appartement* they might be placed as the two last things you see, just before going out the door.

Susan Tallman is an art historian specializing in issues of multiplicity and reproduction, and has been writing about *Parkett* editions since 1995. She is the author of *The Contemporary Print: Pre-Pop to Postmodern* (Thames and Hudson 1996) and, most recently, of *The Collections of Barbara Bloom* (Steidl 2008).

美術館のままごと遊び

美術評論家・美術史家

スーザン・トールマン

　『パルケット』は自分のことを「現代美術の小さな美術館、大きな図書館」と言い表す。これもたしかに正確にはちがいない。1400本のエッセイを掲載した86冊の本誌が記録として貴重なのと同時に、現代の文化に対する深い見方も提供してくれるのにくわえ、アーティストが制作した200点にのぼるエディション作品を見れば、世界中の現代美術のおおよその姿を知ることができる。もっともこれらのエディション作品の気風は、『パルケット』が以前にもちいたもうひとつの言い方、「アパート式美術館」のほうが、よりよく捉えている。身近な家庭と堂々とした美術館がひとつに溶けあうこのイメージは、個々の作品と全体が集まったときの存在感の大きさを、一言でうまく表わしている。『パルケット』の出版事業の歴史を、美術と人生が別々の世界に暮らすことをやめて、隣同士の部屋の住人となる、本来のアパートとみなしてもよいだろう。

　この「空想の美術館」では、玄関の広間がすでに作品を展示する場となる。右手にはマルコム・モーリーの描く唐時代の馬とトーマス・シュトゥルートの撮った上海の街頭風景があり、左にはアンリ・サラの神秘的な滑走路とガブリエル・オロスコの斑に光るアイリス・プリントが見える。近景、遠景、自然、人工、分析、そして憧憬が、猫の前肢をもってぐるっとひと回りするのに必要なスペースより狭いところに、ちゃんと並んでいる。

　書斎がひとつあれば、『パルケット』の「大きな図書館」を収めるのに不都合はないだろう。キャスターの付いたほどよい大きさの本棚に86冊が立ててあり、1冊はテーブルの上に（少々派手な）トート・バッグと一緒に置いてある。ここは美術館なので、展示ケースには保存用資料がしまってある。ダン・グレアムの写真、ヴァネッサ・ビークロフトのインスタレーション、ウーゴ・ロンディノーネがメモを添えたマッジア峡谷の石、1枚ずつ1年かけて配達されてきたトリシャ・ドネリーのメモの束。研究に取り組む真剣な姿勢にふさわしく、壁にはモノクロームの版画が列をなす。ジュリー・メーレトゥがエッチングで表現した見事な渦巻き、アルバート・オーレンの小さなエッチングの奏でる不協和音、リチャード・セラが黒のインクで描いたロープ、チャック・クロースのダゲレオ・タイプ、そしてキャラ・ウォーカーの辛辣なリノカット。ロス・ブレックナーの小さな絵が棚に載っている。とはいっても、ここはアパートなので、大きなデスクには日々の営みが今も続くことを示すあれこれが散らばっている。文鎮で抑えた絵はがき、読みさしの『ニューヨーク・タイムズ』、予定を記したカレンダー、横倒しのゴム印、何気なく置かれた眼鏡。ソファのクッションは隅に寄せてある。

　香水の残り香が漂う寝室の壁にはエリザベス・ペイトンの《オスカーとボウジー》（あえてその名を口にはしない愛）が掛かり、ベッドの上のジャケット、シャツ、ネクタイは主を待ちうける。部屋の奥には、ジョン・ウェスリーの曖昧な物語をつぶやくシルクスクリーン《男友だち》の下に鏡台があり、香水瓶の脇に夜会用の手袋とシルクのスカーフが脱ぎ捨ててある。蓋の開いたままの宝石箱は、指輪を収めて銀色、そして金色の光を放つ。

　台所はどこのアパートでもそうであるように、働くところ。美術作品と見分けがつくのは、流しの上にかかるマリア・ラスニックの《手袋》ただひとつ。模様を切り抜いたテーブルクロスで覆われたテーブルには、さまざまな器具や食器が並んでいる。いくつも重ねた発泡スチロールのカップ、縞模様の麺棒、ドリル、オーブン用手袋、汚れた小型のたらい。食べ物を玩具にして、レモンにキノコの脚と苺の目をつけ、ブタをこしらえたひとがいる。窓からウィンド・ベルのちりんと鳴る音が聞こえてくる。庭では風見鶏が向きを変え、犬は噛んで楽しむ靴の形をしたチュートイを物欲しそうにじっと見つめ、ハエはベンチに置いたままの箱の中身の詮索にいそがしく、すぐ脇にあるハエ叩きには気づかぬ様子。

　娯楽室（小さな美術館とはいえ、ここは大きなアパートです）の壁には、楽しい余暇に誘う品々が目につく。フランツ・アッカーマンの赤く燃えるシルクスクリーンとトマス・デマンドの飛行機の写真は、旅行を思わせる。サラ・モリスのポスターとリチャード・フィリップスのジェーン・フォンダ似の女のポートレートは、映画の楽しさを宣伝する。ベアト・ストロイリの《オックスフォード・ストリート》を見れば、買い物がしたくなる。デイナ・シュッツの《無題（ティモシー・リアリーの頭）》と、リチャード・プリンスがウッドストックで撮影したスナップ写真は、ドラッグとロックンロールへの誘い。2台の薄型テレビには揺れる椰子の木と忙しない蜂が映り、2台の旧式なブラウン管テレビの一方では夫婦喧嘩がまっさかり、もう一方には女がうずくまり、今にも飛びかかろうとしている。レコードプレーヤーの隣の棚には、置き忘れた黒いレコード。ゲームの途中で置き去りにされたポーカーの手札が、カード・ガードの下敷きになって、テーブルの上に散らばっている。

　とはいえ、どこより賑やかなのは育児室だろう。壁には動物の絵がずらりと並ぶ。ローラ・オーエンズの蝙蝠、ロバート・フランクの白鳥、クリストファー・ウールの黒犬。床にちらかした玩具の数々。色鮮やかな引き回し玩具、鉛の兵隊を入れるボール紙のケース、組立て途中のアクリルのタワーはすこし高すぎはしないだろうか。どれもこれも、ガリヴァーが巨人国か小人国から持ち帰ったお土産のよう。部屋の片隅で、風船でこしらえた巨大な花がやはり巨大な、壊れたボール紙の時計とこぜりあいを演じる。別の隅には一枚の皿に乗るほどの小さな牛と恐竜が、皿のサイズの熊皮の敷物の脇に立っている。茶色の靴はポケットに入りそう。

人形の家には青い髪のセーラームーンのようなフィギュアに、フープをもって踊る少女、オレンジ色のジャンプスーツを着て、枷をはめられ跪く男の人形が入っている。

　オレンジの人形はもちろん遊びの道具ではなく、グアンタナモ基地が捕虜収容所として使われていた時代に、ジョン・ケスラーが邪悪とは何か考えてこしらえたものであり、育児室は育児室ではなかった。ここは美術作品を展示したアパートではなく、アパートが作品そのものであり、どのオブジェにも意味するもの、ほのめかすものがある。ロバート・フランクの白鳥は自然の描写ではなく、社会に存在する階層に対する批評であり、クリストファー・ウールの犬は「RUN DOG RUN」の文字を並べた初期の絵との語呂合わせ。引いて回して遊ぶ色とりどりの玩具は、視線を引きつけてやまないフランシス・アリスの《ゲットー・コレクター》、これはアリスが都会の屑を集めに、街路を引いてまわったもの。セーラームーン風の人形は森万里子の作品、黙示録的なバレリーナはマイ＝チュー・ペレの作。鉛の兵隊は鉛でもなければ兵隊でもなく、パヴェウ・アルトハメルの自伝から抜け出した錫の人形たち。風船の花はジェフ・クーンズ、時計はトーマス・ヒルシュホーン、熊皮のラグはスーザン・ローゼンバーグの作ったもの。ちっぽけな靴はシェリー・レヴィーンが初めての個展で売った靴。アクリルの組立てキットはリアム・ギリックがこしらえた（もとのサイズは大きすぎるので、『パルケット』の判型に合わせてある）。絵具を塗りたくった牛と恐竜は、イザ・ゲンツケンの作品である。

　娯楽室に戻ろう。夫婦喧嘩はブルース・ナウマンのビデオ作品、揺れる椰子の木はジェニファー・アローラ＆ギリェルモ・カルサディーリャのDVD、ぶんぶん音の聞こえない蜂はダイアナ・セイターの作。しゃがむ女性はピピロッティ・リストが吸引カップを使い、テレビ画面に密着させた3D式のピンナップ。カード・ガードは手軽な安物ではなく、マーク・グロチヤーンがひとつひとつ手で描いたコイン。レコードプレーヤーにはカタリーナ・フリッチュのレコードがのっている。棚のレコード、ふにゃふにゃで音の出ないレコードはフィッシュリ/ヴァイスの模造品、台所にあった絵具の染みだらけの「たらい」も同様。

　テーブルクロスはダニエル・ビュレン、麺棒はコズィマ・フォン・ボニン、手袋はローマン・シグナーが花火にことよせてこしらえた。白からグレーに色調がわずかずつ変化する発泡スチロールのカップは、トム・フリードマンが彩り、積みかさねたもの。モニカ・ボンヴィチーニのドリルはピンクがかった艶かしい分泌物の上に置かれて、セックスと粘り気を感じさせる。ブタになりきったレモンは、じつは豚のふりをするレモンのふりをする発泡スチロールで、これを作ったのはオラフ・ブルーニング。犬の好物はシルヴィ・フルーリ、風見鶏はロドニー・グレアム、風鈴はピエール・ユイグ（ここで鳴る音は『未知との遭遇』のテーマ曲を無作為に並べ替えたもの）。アイ・ウェイウェイのハエ叩きは真鍮に金メッキしたもので、虫を潰すのには見事なくらい適さないが、ハエはといえばプラスチック製のうえに、イリヤ・カバコフのポケット・サイズのディストピアに捕まっているから、それでもちっともかまわない。

　空気の匂いもやはり作品で、こちらはカイ・アルトフが香りをつけ、瓶に詰めた。白いワイシャツに男の顔を縫いつけたのはリュック・タイマンス、黒いジャケットはエイヤ＝リーサ・アハティラの作、そしてネクタイの作者はソフィ・カル。白い肌に赤い血管の浮くシュルレアリスト好みの手袋はメレット・オッペンハイム、絵の裏側をだまし絵風に描いたスカーフはマイケル・レデッカー。印章付きの金の指輪はルドルフ・スティンゲルの作品、銀の指輪にはジェニー・ホルツァーの考えが記してある。

　書斎の『ニューヨーク・タイムズ』は模造の品、このページのどこかに、ロバート・ゴーバーという名の少年が溺れ死んだという短信が載っている。ドミニク・ゴンザレス＝フェルステルのカレンダーは１月毎に１３ヶ月前に進むようにデザインされた（2008年1月の翌月は2009年2月になる）。デスクの上の絵はがきはタシタ・ディーンの作、文鎮の作者はキース・タイソン、ゴム印はローレンス・ウェイナー。テーブルの上の『パルケット』を手にとって開いてみれば、とても読めたものではないとわかるはず。これはジグマー・ポルケが念入りに重ね刷りしたせいだ。ポーチはフランツ・ヴェストが作ったもの。キャスター付きの本棚も同様。椅子におかれたクッションがいわくあり気なのは、ジェルジ・ルカーチのブダペストの書斎にあったもののレプリカだから。デスクの上の眼鏡をかけても、何もよく見えるようになりはしない。これはリクリット・ティラヴァニャがレンズにことばを刻みつけたのが仇になった。

　アパート式美術館では、美術作品は神出鬼没。ドアの脇の明かりのスイッチは明かりのスイッチではない。これもスイッチを裏返しに成形したレイチェル・ホワイトリードの作品。電球はトニー・アウスラーの録音した声にしたがい、明るくなったり暗くなったり、そしてプレハブ式インスタレーションの一部をなす。

　『パルケット』も当年とって25歳、ということは、一目でそれとわかる独特のスタイルを確立するのに十分な時間が経過したことになるけれども、エディションの気質はいまもドン・キホーテに通じ、見かけもおそらく予測の範囲を超える。『パルケット』に独自のスタイルがあるとすれば、それは編集人たちが曖昧な状況、クロスオーバー、芸術と人生の間に引かれる通常の境界線を混乱させるアーティストやオブジェを愛好する点にあるのではないだろうか。アンドレアス・スロミンスキーはレディ・メイドの折りたたみ式定規をエディションにして、この作品を「現在の文化のなかでアートと見なせるものと見なせないものを探る試み」と説明する。そうした試みには、美術館よりアパートの方が適しているようにもおもえる。美術館にいるとき、ひとは自分が「アート」を見に来たことを意識しているけれども、アパートならそこにあるものに触れたり、匂いを嗅いだり、遊んでみたりするはずだ。

　遊びとは、じつは真面目なものである。世界を探り究める方法でもある。探りを入れ、機知を働かせ、偽り、見いだす。ルールを考え出し、ルールを棄てる。『パルケット』のエディション作品には、ひとを欺くゲームや感覚の鋭敏さを試すゲームがいくらでも見つかる。ひとり遊び、チーム・ゲーム、着せ替えゲーム、知恵比べ。ソフィ・カルのネクタイには、見知らぬひとに匿名で衣服と装身具を送り、魅力的な人物に変身させようとした経緯がプリントしてある。ところがだれでもこのネクタイを着ければ、カルに「衣裳をあてがわれた」ことになり、持ち主、受益者、犠牲者を区別するのはむずかしい。よくできた子供たちの遊びと同じように、これらの作品は役割を取り替えたり、ルールをねじ曲げたり、隠喩的に犬に服を着せたり、あるいはジリアン・ウェアリングのマスクなら、収集家にアーティストの顔を被せたりして、金と恋、権力が物を言う大人の世界の内情を明らかにする。

　アパート式美術館では、壁にかかった作品までもが美術作品ごっこを楽しんでいるように見える。ジョン・カリンとピーター・ドイグのエッチングは、古い時代の衣裳をまとった現代の作品。グレン・ブラウンの《混乱》は、18世紀の肖像画が荒れ狂う筆遣いによってかき消されようとする様子を描いているようではあっても、じつはそのすべてが周到に仕組まれており、偽りなのである。シンディ・シャーマンの写真が見事な金の額縁からはみ出そうとすれば、マイク・ケリーの肖像にはゲーテの引用が達筆で記されている。絵を撮ったトマ・アブツの作品、ロニ・ホーンの転げ回る形容詞、美術館で撮影したアンドレアス・グルスキーの写真、これらはすべてIKEAの「室内装飾」さながら、額入りで配達される。ローズマリー・トロッケルのフォト・エッチングは、板にマウントしてある。アレックス・カッツの《サニー》は、ちっぽけなテリアの顔をシルクスクリーンでアルミに刷ったもの。ジャン＝リュック・ミレーヌの鳥の写真は額がとても頑丈で、支えがなくても彫刻のように立てられそう。これとは反対に、マシュー・リッチーの壁に貼るドローイングのような天の邪鬼は、額に入れようがない。

　これらの作品はたんなるイメージとしてではなく、「製品」としてデザインされている。ジェフ・クーンズの「コレクションに適した」皿やルドルフ・スティンゲルのけばけばしい指輪は、商品のふりをしてみせる。高級な芸術にふさわしい内容が、低俗な包装箱に収まっている。ところがリチャード・プリンスの包装済ゴールド・レコードとなると、こちらは実際の業界の権力、権威、販売力を羨み、憧れる気持ちが見え隠れする。これはタシタ・ディーンの絵はがきについてもいえることで、100部に署名、番号を入れて、『パルケット』に代わり投函した。残部は通常の世の中で「通常の観光客向け絵はがきとして販売してもらえるように……無署名のまま小売店に卸す」ことになっていた。

　芸術にあたえられる役割と、定位置をめちゃくちゃにしたいという衝動は、初代ゲームの名人マルセル・デュシャンにまでさかのぼることができる。デュシャンが矯正に手を貸したレディ・メイド——これにも今では100年の歴史がある——は、地面に落ちているものを拾って、ひとひねりしてやろうという気を起こさせるきっかけとして、いつまでも色あせることのない魅力をもつことが明らかになった。デュシャンの得意なゲームは知能を使い、冷静さの欠かせないチェスだったが、オブジェを別物に仕立てるこちらの手法は「蛇とはしご」のすごろく遊びに近い。デミアン・ハースト、ジェイソン・ローズ、カレン・キリムニック、アニッシュ・カプーア、そしてレベッカ・ホルンは、いずれも人の手で作られ既に存在していたものを使い、遊び心たっぷりに、分析力するどく、謎めかし、哀調も添えて、思いも寄らない効果を挙げている。カッラーラ産の大理石に絵具を塗ったカタリーナ・グロッセの作品では、見つけたものの存在感とそれに対して加えられた手数の意味に、等しい重みがあたえられている。

　『パルケット』のアーティストが紙やカンヴァスの代わりに、相当風変わりな支持体まで用いているのは、包装の社会学に分析的視点から取り組んだ証拠であるばかりでなく、鑑賞者にこれまで以上に美術作品と親近感を持って接し、身体をつかってじかに触れるように仕向けるためである。ゲイリー・ヒュームとルイーズ・ブルジョワは布地にプリントし、草間彌生は鏡に、フレッド・トマセーリはアクリルに、レイチェル・ハリソンはポリプロピレン、スー・ウィリアムズは何枚も重ねたマイラーにプリントした。ジョン・バルデッサリのしかめ面は鋼板にエナメル加工してあり、「外部からの影響に左右されない」。ウェイド・ガイトンが刷り機にかけた合板の四半分は、ギュンター・フェルクの鏡と銅板の二部作と同じように、何物にも換えがたい、物としての個性を強く主張する。マシュー・バーニーが樹脂と砂糖で作ったダンベルでは、素材がフォルムに負けないほど内容と深く関わっている。ボール紙に孔を開け、スプレー絵具で色を塗ったケディ・ノーランドの作品にも、イミ・クネーベルの顔料を塗布したレンガにも、素材のほかにイメージと呼べるものはない。

　なかにはとにかく触ってごらんとしきりに誘いかけるものもある。サラ・ルーカスの《ライオン・ハート》とクリスチャン・マークレイの《ぼくの悪い耳》はちょうど掌に乗るサイズで、どうしても触ってみたくなる。エルネスト・ネトの風船とも枕ともつかず、得体のしれないかっこうをした彫刻も、リチャード・アーシュワーガーのゴム引きの《ヘア・ボックス》も、もし手に取ってみることができなかったら、意味の半分は失われてしまうだろう。アーティストの手仕事の跡が強烈な印象を刻むシュテファン・バルケンホールとレベッカ・ウォーレンの彫刻は、どんな手触りか知りたいという好奇心を刺激する（本人の歯形を残すダグラス・ゴードンの作品も同様）。

　ゲオルク・バゼリッツ、フランチェスコ・クレメンテ、エンツォ・クッキ、そしてマルティン・ディスラーのドライポイントもおなじく、触りたくて指がむずむずしてくる作品である。たいがいの場合、版画に手を触れるのは禁物だが、これらは雑誌に綴じこまれている。これもそうだし、そのほかにもジェームズ・タレル、エリック・フィッシュル、ヤニス・クネリス、マリオ・メルツの作品を見ようとすれば、雑誌を開いたままにしておかなければならず、そうなると、どうしても親指を作品の上に載せなくてはならない。ロバート・ウィルソンのリトグラフとブライス・マーデンのエッチングを見るには、折り畳まれたページを指でつまみ、開く必要がある。ちょっと悪戯をしているようなこの気分を捉えたのが、本紙に綴じこまれたエドワード・ルシェのリトグラフで、ページを開いてゆくと「地獄」、「天国」、「中途」が現れる。

　マーケティングの観点からすれば、これはまるで要領を得ない。本誌の中に隠しておくよりも、別刷のほうが商品としてはるかに売りやすい。ということは、とりもなおさず美術作品は個人的な悦びのためよりも、世間に対する意思表示として購入されることを意味し、『パルケット』がエディションを本誌に綴じこむことにしたのは、作品と所有者との親密さの度合いをよりいっそう深めたかったからだろうと推測できる。ただしこの親密さは、掛け値なしに、犠牲をともなう。ひとに知ってもらうには、これらの作品は持ち主の手に渡らなければならない。ローリー・アンダーソンの《聞き飾り》は、毎回、片方の耳に着けて、聞いてもらう必要がある。フランツ・ゲルチュ、レイモンド・ペティボン、ギルバート＆ジョージ、そしてマルレーネ・デュマスは揃って、畳んであるものを開かないと見ることのできない作品を制作した。羊皮紙の表紙の下にかくれたトーマス・ルフの写真は手に取ってみないかぎり、理解はむずかしい。クリスチャン・ボルタンスキーの不穏きわまりない冊子は、不透明なコーティングを持ち主が削りとって初めて、人目に触れるべきではない残虐な犯罪現場の画像が姿を現す。

　奇妙なことに、アパート式美術館の展示品の多くは包装済の製品であるのに、大量生産されたものは皆無に等しい。エディションのサイズは控えめで、同一のものがいくつもあり片隅に鉛筆で書きこまれた数字だけが判別の手がかりという、通常の意味でのエディションとは似ても似つかないものも少なくない。『パルケット』のその種のエディションは、どれひとつとしてまったく同じ物はなく、鉛筆で書かれた数字と、いくつかの共通点によって、ひとまとまりのものとみなされる。ホルヘ・パルドの手製の彫刻では、共通点は素材（粘土）とおおよその大きさ（25×10×10cm）に尽きそうだ。ジョン・アームレーダーの作品は、サイズの同じアクリル板をひとつひとつ成形したもの。ポール・マッカーシーは色も形もちがう棍棒を36個作ることにした。ジョシュ・スミスは両面コラージュを38個こしらえた。ヨン・ボックはニットの下着を60着制作した。ロス・ブレックナーとゲルハルト・リヒターは、単純に小さな絵をたくさん描くことにした。これらの作品は見るからにひとの手で作られているので、特に注目されて当然と思われるようである。これならテレビの前に放っておくより、劇場に持っていきたくなる。手で綴じられたアンディ・ウォーホルとルイーズ・ブルジョワの版画、エレン・ギャラガーがグラビア印刷にとりつけたプラスチック粘土、フィリップ・ターフのモノタイプが見せる即興ならではの微妙な変化、そうしたすべては標準的な版画作りの技法に手仕事の生々しい感覚を添えている。ネガに手で文字を彫りつけプリントしたヴィルヘルム・サスナルは、同じ手法を写真に採り入れた。

　複製可能のあらゆるメディアのなかでも、写真はどうやらもっとも効率が良く、透明性が高く、しかも広くゆきわたっているようで、この特質を活かしたのが滑稽な様子をさりげなく記録したグレゴール・シュナイダーとマウリツィオ・カテランの写真、語呂合わせを試みたゾーイ・レオナルドの《1時間写真＆ビデオ》の写真、そして家具並の「ピクセル」を撮影したアンジェラ・ブロックの写真である。これと同じ特質がヴォルフガング・ティルマンスとトレイシー・エミンの「エディション」とはいいながら、全く同じものはふたつとない作品で、そのために写真でありながら思わぬ希少性を得ることになった。クリスチャン・ヤンコフスキーは写真家を50人雇い、50冊別々のパルケットを読む自分の姿を撮影してもらい、1点ずつ異なる50種の写真を制作した。ジグマー・ポルケはゴヤの《戦争の惨禍》を撮影したうえで、フィルムを現像するのに、ラズベリー・ブランデーや洗剤のプリルを用いた正気の沙汰ともおもえない錬金術を駆使して、ひとつずつ異なる60種の（絵柄が見分けられるのはごくまれにすぎない）写真をつくりあげた。ここでは超越の種子は一見したところ人間性を排除した複製のメカニズムの外側にあるのではなく、その内部の奥深くに巣くっているようだ。

　このように不揃いなエディションを制作するのは、偶然の働きや即興を求める衝動を強く訴える手段にもなるだろうが、それはまた予め定めた論理を実地に表現する手段にもなりうる。キース・タイソンの文鎮とダニエル・ビュレンのテーブルクロスはどちらも、一定の法則内で組み合わせの変化を試みたもの。個々の方法、あるいは個々の実例は他にふたつとなく、またその価値に優劣はない（ブルジョア家庭のための有用なオブジェを作るというきわめて観念的な課題をあたえるのも、いかにも『パルケット』らしい感覚といえるだろう）。マルティン・キッペンベルガーのエディションの組み直しは、整然としているようで、ひねくれてもいる。キッペンベルガーは80種の同じ写真を載せた80冊の同じ冊子の代わりに、どのページにも1枚の同じ写真を載せた冊子を、冊子毎に写真を変えて80冊制作した。

　エディション作りの通常の仕組みにさまざまな手をくわえるこうした試みは、ある目的を果たすのに役立つ。鑑賞者に、目の前にあるものについて詳しく考えてみるように求めるのである。なんでもよさそうなのに、どうして「この」物でなければいけないのか？ただの映像ですみそうなのに、なぜこの「物」でなければいけないのか？

　自分の目の前にあるものを見ること、本当の意味で見ることの難しさは、『パルケット』が何度もとりあげているテーマであり、視覚の見え方を描いた『パルケット』42号のマーコス・レーツも、鍵を歪ませたカールステン・ヘラーも、この問題に取り組んでいる。ウィリアム・ケントリッジは百科事典のページの上に、歪んだドローイングをプリントした。テキストはドローイングに遮られて、円筒に映ったものを読むしかないけれども、その時にはすでに読み取り不能になっている。一石二鳥を狙うとこうなるという教訓だろうか。オラファー・エリアソンは自分の目だけ、目を見つめる目だけが見える仕掛けを作った。たとえばダグ・エイケンの鏡の凧やアハティラのジャケットのように、姿を消すのを楽しむ作品もある。アハティラのジャケットには「無知のヴェール」という文字が背中にプリントしてあり、正面には同じ文字の左右が逆転した鏡像をプリントして、間にはさまった人物を透かして文字を見ているような気にさせる。幻覚をほのめかすものもあり、ウルス・フィッシャーはウサギを帽子からとりだしたように見える彫刻を制作した。

　アパート式美術館にはごまかし、模倣、表現のしなおしが目白押し。フィッシュリ／ヴァイスとロバート・ゴーバーの作品はレディ・メイドのように見えて、じつはそうでない。あとからの書きこみで汚れたルーシー・マッケンジーのシルクスクリーンは、デュシャンの《L.H.O.O.Q.》を手本にしたのかもしれないが、いたずらされた絵はエルジェ作の童話の主人公タンタンが年をとった姿を、マッケンジー自身が想像して描いたところが、本家とちがう。アリギエロ・ボエッティが双子のように並べた『タイム』誌の表紙は、手描きである。人気女優の魅力的な写真を模して描いた絵のように見えるマリリン・ミンターの作品は、実際にはマリリン・ミンターの絵を模した写真なのである。どこにも非の打ち所のないトーマス・デマンドの飛行機のタラップの写真は、紙製の模型を描いたもの。アパート式美術館にあるじつに多くのものと同じように、これは罠であり、物事を額面通りに受け取らないようにする訓練であり、よく注意を払い、ジョン・ケージのことばをかりると、「自分たちの営むこの生活に目を見開く」ようにとの指令でもある。

　生活、わたしたちが今こうして営んでいる生活は、つきつめてみれば、人間の尺度のなかで営まれている。美術館の果てしない大きさは幻想にすぎない。アパート式美術館では、控えめなサイズにする必要性（『パルケット』のエディションは郵送されてくる）が、現代美術作品の通常のサイズについて、根底から考え直すきっかけとなった。これが文字通りのミニチュア化（サム・テイラー＝ウッドの5センチのパノラマ）を促す場合もあれば、距離を概念的に押しつぶす（チャールズ・レイが撮ったタチアナ・パティッツのスナップ写真からは、彼女が「スーパー・モデル」

であることを視覚的に伝える手がかり――プロによる照明、ヘアメイク、メーキャップ、演出、コート紙にオフセット・リトグラフで大量にプリントした写真――は取り除かれていて、購入者はとびきり魅力的な若い女性が自宅のあちこちでくつろぐ様子を撮った9枚の写真を手にする）ものもある。断片を作品にして、課題に応えた例もある。トレイシー・モファットとジェフ・ウォールの写真は、大規模なインスタレーションの一部をとりだしたもの。ジェームズ・ローゼンクィストのリトグラフは、いつもの巨大な作品の一部を切り取ったのだとしてもおかしくない。フランツ・ゲルチュの木版は実際、そのようにして作られた。ナン・ゴールディンの草の葉の群れとトーマス・シュッテの点々の壁紙は、もっと大きな拡がりの一部をとりだしたもの。ヴィヤ・セルミンスの夜空と杉本博司の箱に収められた海景はとても小さいが、果てしない。作品の縁は単に慣習的にそうなっているにすぎず、現実は知覚できる範囲をこえて、どこまでもひろがっていることをわたしたちは知っている。

　アートの役割は、わたしたちの知覚力を越えた先にもつづく現実を伝えることにあるとの考え方が、アパート式美術館の土台にある。1世紀前には、この信念からアーティストたちは外観を越えたその先を見つめ、フォルムから原理を探し出し、形あるものを抽象化しようと思い立った。ところがわたしたちは今、抽象の支配する世界に暮らしている。目にしたこともない金、会ったこともない政治家、決して手で触れることのできない美術作品の言いなりといってよい。今や、課題は抽象的なものに形をあたえることにある。

　これこそまさにベルナール・フリズの試みであり、二重円環体は位相予想（4色で地図を塗り分ける課題の3次元的変形）に物理的な形をあたえ、犬が噛んで楽しむ輪に似た作品となった。それはまたリチャード・アーシュワーガーが《無題（1000立法インチ）》でめざしたもので、体積は等しく形は違う5個のパッキング・ケースは、ピアジェの言う抽象思考を手に取ってみられる形に表現したものである。これはまたヴォルフガング・ライプ、デイヴィッド・ハモンズ、ベアトリス・ミリャーゼスなど、多様なアーティストたちが試みていることでもある。美術館は小さいとはいえ、収蔵できる作品の数は少なくない。

　『パルケット』が制作した最も大きな作品はフェリックス・ゴンザレス＝トレスの《無題》、砂地に印された足跡の看板を購入者が自分で組み立てる作品である。小さいほうには、掌サイズのなんの変哲もないガラスに、息を吹きかけるとドローイングがほんの一時おぼろな姿を現し、まもなく薄れ、消えてゆくフアン・ムニョスの《瞥見》がある。目に映るのはおんぶの図。巨人国と小人国。永遠の砂と束の間の歓び。存在と不在。愛と死。アパート式美術館では、このふたつが出口のそばに置かれ、去ってゆく鑑賞者を見送る役を務めることになる。

スーザン・トールマンは作品の複数性、複製を専門に考察する美術
史家。パルケット・エディションについては1995年より著述があ
る。著書に『現代版画。ポップ以前からポストモダンへ』（テームズ・
アンド・ハドソン社、1996年）があり、最近刊は『バーバラ・ブルーム
のコレクション』（シュタイデル社、2008年）。

エディションズ
200 Art Works – 25 Years

Editions:
200 Art Works – 25 Years

Artists alphabetically
アーティスト総リスト（アルファベット順）

Tomma Abts, 84
Franz Ackermann, 68
Eija-Liisa Ahtila, 68
Ai Weiwei, 81
Doug Aitken, 57
Jennifer Allora /
Guillermo Calzadilla, 80
Paweł Althamer, 82
Kai Althoff, 75
Francis Alÿs, 69
Laurie Anderson, 49
John Armleder, 50/51
Richard Artschwager, 23, 46
John Baldessari, 29, 86
Stephan Balkenhol, 36
Matthew Barney, 45
Georg Baselitz, 11
Vanessa Beecroft, 56
Ross Bleckner, 38
John Bock, 67
Alighiero e Boetti, 24
Christian Boltanski, 22
Monica Bonvicini, 72
Louise Bourgeois, 27, 82
Carol Bove, 86
Olaf Breuning, 71
Glenn Brown, 75
Angela Bulloch, 66
Daniel Buren, 66
Sophie Calle, 36
Maurizio Cattelan, 59
Vija Celmins, 44
Francesco Clemente, 9 & 40/41
Chuck Close, 60
Enzo Cucchi, 1
John Currin, 65
Tacita Dean, 62
Thomas Demand, 62
Martin Disler, 3
Peter Doig, 67
Trisha Donnelly, 77
Marlene Dumas, 38
Olafur Eliasson, 64
Tracey Emin, 63
Urs Fischer, 72
Eric Fischl, 5

Peter Fischli /
David Weiss, 17, 40/41
Sylvie Fleury, 58
Günther Förg, 26 & 40/41
Robert Frank, 83
Tom Friedman, 64
Katharina Fritsch, 25
Bernard Frize, 74
Ellen Gallagher, 73
Isa Genzken, 69
Franz Gertsch, 28
Gilbert & George, 14
Liam Gillick, 61
Robert Gober, 27
Nan Goldin, 57
Dominique Gonzalez-Foerster, 80
Felix Gonzalez-Torres, 39
Douglas Gordon, 49
Dan Graham, 68
Rodney Graham, 64
Katharina Grosse, 74
Mark Grotjahn, 80
Andreas Gursky, 44
Wade Guyton, 83
David Hammons, 31
Rachel Harrison, 82
Thomas Hirschhorn, 57
Damien Hirst, 40/41
Carsten Höller, 77
Jenny Holzer, 40/41
Rebecca Horn, 13 & 40/41
Roni Horn, 54
Gary Hume, 48
Pierre Huyghe, 66
Christian Jankowski, 81
Ilya Kabakov, 34
Anish Kapoor, 69
Alex Katz, 21, 72
Mike Kelley, 31
Ellsworth Kelly, 56
William Kentridge, 63
Jon Kessler, 79
Karen Kilimnik, 52
Martin Kippenberger, 19
Imi Knoebel, 32
Jeff Koons, 19, 50/51

Jannis Kounellis, 6
Yayoi Kusama, 59
Wolfgang Laib, 39
Maria Lassnig, 85
Zoe Leonard, 84
Sherrie Levine, 32
Sarah Lucas, 45
Christian Marclay, 70
Brice Marden, 7
Paul McCarthy, 73
Josiah McElheny, 86
Lucy McKenzie, 76
Julie Mehretu, 76
Mario Merz, 15
Beatriz Milhazes, 85
Marilyn Minter, 79
Tracey Moffatt, 53
Mariko Mori, 54
Malcolm Morley, 52
Sarah Morris, 61
Juan Muñoz, 43
Jean-Luc Mylayne, 50/51, 85
Bruce Nauman, 10
Ernesto Neto, 78
Olaf Nicolai, 78
Cady Noland, 46
Albert Oehlen, 79
Meret Oppenheim, 4
Gabriel Orozco, 48
Tony Oursler, 47
Laura Owens, 65
Jorge Pardo, 56
Philippe Parreno, 86
Mai-Thu Perret, 84
Raymond Pettibon, 47
Elizabeth Peyton, 53
Richard Phillips, 71
Sigmar Polke, 2, 30 & 40/41
Richard Prince, 34, 72
Michael Raedecker, 65
Markus Raetz, 8
Charles Ray, 37
Jason Rhoades, 58
Gerhard Richter, 35
Bridget Riley, 61
Pipilotti Rist, 48, 71

Matthew Ritchie, 61
Tim Rollins & K.O.S., 20
Ugo Rondinone, 52
James Rosenquist, 58
Susan Rothenberg, 43
Thomas Ruff, 28
Edward Ruscha, 18 & 55
Anri Sala, 73
Wilhelm Sasnal, 70
Gregor Schneider, 63
Thomas Schütte, 47
Dana Schutz, 75
Richard Serra, 74
Cindy Sherman, 29
Roman Signer, 45
Andreas Slominski, 55
Josh Smith, 85
Rudolf Stingel, 77
Beat Streuli, 54
Thomas Struth, 50/51
Hiroshi Sugimoto, 46
Philip Taaffe, 26
Sam Taylor-Wood, 55
Diana Thater, 60
Wolfgang Tillmans, 53
Rirkrit Tiravanija, 44
Fred Tomaselli, 67
Rosemarie Trockel, 33
James Turrell, 25
Luc Tuymans, 60
Keith Tyson, 71
Cosima von Bonin, 81
Kara Walker, 59
Jeff Wall, 22 & 49
Andy Warhol, 12
Rebecca Warren, 78
Gillian Wearing, 70
Lawrence Weiner, 42
John Wesley, 62
Franz West, 37, 70
Rachel Whiteread, 42
Sue Williams, 50/51
Robert Wilson, 16
Christopher Wool, 33, 83
Yang Fudong, 76

Artists chronologically
アーティスト総リスト（年代順）

86 John Baldessari	71 Keith Tyson	55 Sam Taylor-Wood	37 Franz West
Carol Bove	70 Christian Marclay	54 Roni Horn	36 Stephan Balkenhol
Josiah McElheny	Wilhelm Sasnal	Mariko Mori	Sophie Calle
Philippe Parreno	Gillian Wearing	Beat Streuli	35 Gerhard Richter
85 Maria Lassnig	69 Francis Alÿs	53 Tracey Moffatt	34 Ilya Kabakov
Beatriz Milhazes	Isa Genzken	Elizabeth Peyton	Richard Prince
Jean-Luc Mylayne	Anish Kapoor	Wolfgang Tillmans	33 Rosemarie Trockel
Josh Smith	68 Franz Ackermann	52 Karen Kilimnik	Christopher Wool
84 Tomma Abts	Eija-Liisa Ahtila	Malcolm Morley	32 Imi Knoebel
Zoe Leonard	Dan Graham	Ugo Rondinone	Sherrie Levine
Mai-Thun Perret	67 John Bock	50/51 John Armleder	31 David Hammons
83 Robert Frank	Peter Doig	Jeff Koons	Mike Kelley
Wade Guyton	Fred Tomaselli	Jean-Luc Mylayne	30 Sigmar Polke
Christopher Wool	66 Angela Bulloch	Thomas Struth	29 John Baldessari
82 Pavel Althamer	Daniel Buren	Sue Williams	Cindy Sherman
Louise Bourgeois	Pierre Huyghe	49 Laurie Anderson	28 Franz Gertsch
Rachel Harrison	65 John Currin	Douglas Gordon	Thomas Ruff
81 Ai Weiwei	Laura Owens	Jeff Wall	27 Louise Bourgeois
Cosima von Bonin	Michael Raedecker	48 Gary Hume	Robert Gober
Christian Jankowski	64 Olafur Eliasson	Gabriel Orozco	26 Günther Förg
80 Allora & Calzadilla	Tom Friedman	Pipilotti Rist	Philip Taaffe
D. Gonzalez-Foerster	Rodney Graham	47 Tony Oursler	25 Katharina Fritsch
Mark Grotjahn	63 Tracey Emin	Raymond Pettibon	James Turrell
79 Albert Oehlen	William Kentridge	Thomas Schütte	24 Alighiero e Boetti
Jon Kessler	Gregor Schneider	46 Richard Artschwager	23 Richard Artschwager
Marilyn Minter	62 Tacita Dean	Cady Noland	22 Christian Boltanski
78 Ernesto Neto	Thomas Demand	Hiroshi Sugimoto	Jeff Wall
Olaf Nicolai	John Wesley	45 Matthew Barney	21 Alex Katz
Rebecca Warren	61 Liam Gillick	Sarah Lucas	20 Tim Rollins + K.O.S.
77 Trisha Donnelly	Sarah Morris	Roman Signer	19 Martin Kippenberger
Carsten Höller	Bridget Riley	44 Vija Celmins	Jeff Koons
Rudolf Stingel	Matthew Ritchie	Andreas Gursky	18 Ed Ruscha
76 Lucy McKenzie	60 Chuck Close	Rirkrit Tiravanija	17 Fischli/Weiss
Julie Mehretu	Diana Thater	43 Juan Muñoz	16 Robert Wilson
Yang Fudong	Luc Tuymans	Susan Rothenberg	15 Mario Merz
75 Kai Althoff	59 Maurizio Cattelan	42 Lawrence Weiner	14 Gilbert & George
Glenn Brown	Yayoi Kusama	Rachel Whiteread	13 Rebecca Horn
Dana Schutz	Kara Walker	40/41 Francesco Clemente	12 Andy Warhol
74 Bernard Frize	58 Sylvie Fleury	Fischli/Weiss	11 Georg Baselitz
Katharina Grosse	Jason Rhoades	Günther Förg	10 Bruce Nauman
Richard Serra	James Rosenquist	Damien Hirst	9 Francesco Clemente
73 Ellen Gallagher	57 Doug Aitken	Jenny Holzer	8 Markus Raetz
Paul McCarthy	Nan Goldin	Rebecca Horn	7 Brice Marden
Anri Sala	Thomas Hirschhorn	Sigmar Polke	6 Jannis Kounellis
72 Monica Bonvicini	56 Vanessa Beecroft	39 Felix Gonzalez-Torres	5 Eric Fischl
Urs Fischer	Ellsworth Kelly	Wolfgang Laib	4 Meret Oppenheim
Richard Prince	Jorge Pardo	38 Ross Bleckner	3 Martin Disler
71 Olaf Breuning	55 Edward Ruscha	Marlene Dumas	2 Sigmar Polke
Richard Phillips	Andreas Slominski	37 Charles Ray	1 Enzo Cucchi

TOMMA ABTS

Untitled (Uto), 2008

Archival pigment print
on Angelica paper,
mounted on sintra, framed,
paper size: 15 $^7/_8$ x 19 $^3/_4$" (50,5 x 40,5 cm),
image size: 15 x 18 $^7/_8$" (48 x 38 cm),
printed by Laumont, New York,
Ed. 45/XXV, signed and numbered
certificate

EDITION FOR PARKETT 84

Unpremeditated lines, encompassed by layer upon layer, barely concealing a color spectrum about to erupt.

"Abt's compositions in fact emerge out of the give-and-take that comes with the application of numerous successive layers of paint and through choices being elaborated over many months. Interlocking linear elements might float across densely layered fields, objective aggregations of the thin strata."

Suzanne Hudson
Parkett No. 84, 2008

トマ・アブツ

無題 (Uto)   2008

アンジェリカ紙に耐久性の高い顔料系インク
でプリント、シントラにマウントし額装、
紙：50.4×40.5cm、
図柄：48×38cm、
刷り：ローモント (ニューヨーク) 、
Ed. 45/XXV、署名、番号入り証明書

パルケット・エディション 84

心の赴くままに描かれた線が、層を重ねる毎に包囲され、今にも噴き出しそうな色彩のスペクトルをかろうじて覆い隠している。

アブツの作品は実は絵具を何度も塗り重ね、数か月かけて構想を練るなかで生じたやりとりから姿を現したものである。互いに交錯する線が、幾重にも層を成す背景の上に浮遊し、薄層の集積として目に映る。

スザンヌ・ハドソン
 (パルケット84号、2008年)

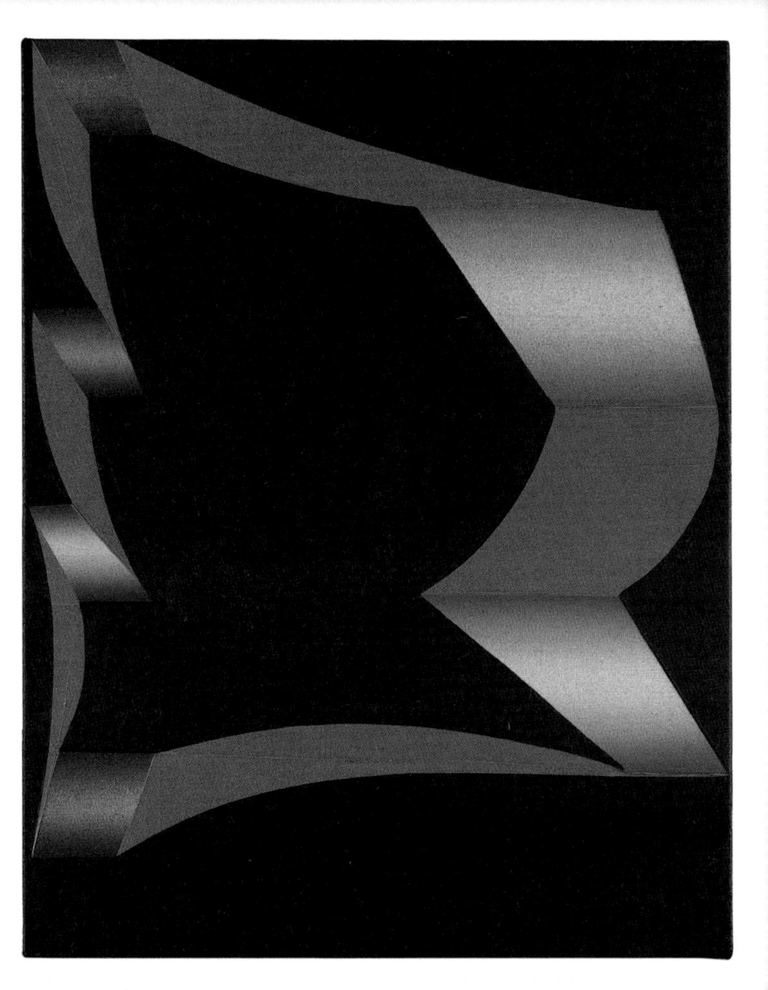

FRANZ ACKERMANN

Peak Season, 2003

10-color silkscreen print
on Somerset 300g/m^2,
paper size: 19 $^{11}/_{16}$ x 27 $^9/_{16}$" (48 x 68 cm),
image size: 18 $^7/_8$ x 26 $^3/_4$" (45,7 x 66 cm),
printed by Werkstatt
für Kunstsiebdruck Munich,
Ed. 70/XXX, signed and numbered

EDITION FOR PARKETT 68

Seasonal gravitation: individual traces and points of crystallization in the maelstrom of mass nesting from place to place.

"Ackermann is a painter for whom travel is a categorical necessity. However, when looking at his work it is clear that the road he travels is not that which we might associate with the classical grand tour. For Ackermann tourism is both a topic and a methodology. Since… he spent a year living in Hong Kong, Ackermann has evolved a set of Situationist-inspired visual practices that have actively investigated the 'psychogeographical' aspects of travel as embodied in the figure of the tourist."

Douglas Fogle
Parkett No. 68, 2003

フランツ・アッカーマン

ピーク・シーズン　2003

サマーセット紙300g/㎡にシルクスクリーン
10色刷り、
紙：48×68cm、
図柄：45.7×66cm、
刷り：ヴェルケシュタット美術印刷社（ミュンヘン）、
Ed. 70/XXX、署名、番号入り

パルケット・エディション 68

四季の引力。渦を巻きながら点在する塊のなかに結晶化の基点、痕跡がひとつひとつ描かれる。

旅を忘れて画家アッカーマンは存在しえない。ただし作品を見れば、彼の旅路が、わたしたちがかつてのグランド・ツアーから想起する旅程と異なるのは明らかだろう。アッカーマンにとって、観光は話題でもあれば、方法論でもある。香港に1年暮らして以降……アッカーマンは旅行者の姿が体現する「心理地理学」の側面を意欲的に検証するシチュエーショニストの思想に啓発され、数種の視覚表現を案出した。

ダグラス・フォグル
（パルケット 68号、2003年）

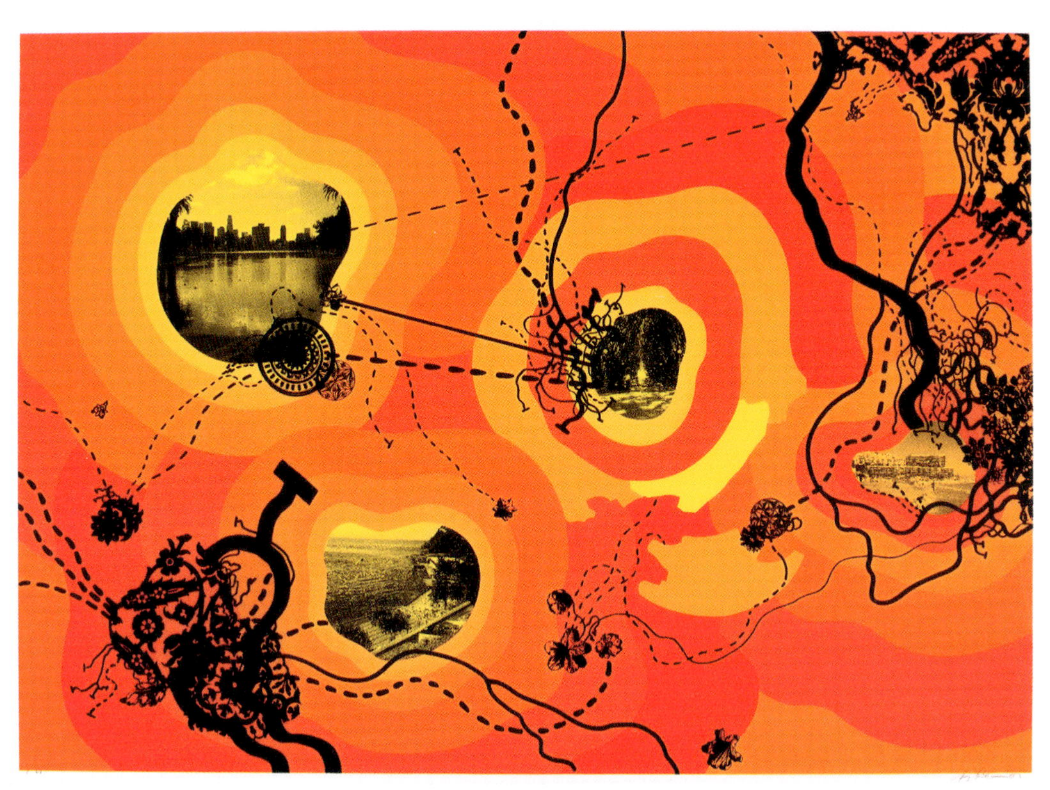

EIJA-LIISA AHTILA

Veil of Ignorance, 2003

Pure wool jacket
with text printed on front
(mirror-inverted) and back,
handprinted silkscreen lettering by
Atelier für Siebdruck Lorenz Boegli,
Zürich, available in 5 sizes,
Ed. 70/XXV, signed certificate

EDITION FOR PARKETT 68

Ignorance is the mirror of knowledge.

"Ahtila's moving pictures often revolve around the house: around the objects and people that enter it from the outside and close it off from the inside. Access roads, parking places, bridges along the way, doors that are opened into the house from outside by odd visitors, curtains that keep out the light, cars that traverse the walls of the rooms, beds under which one can hide, drafts that undo everything: the picture that Ahtila conjures of a house is a fragile affair, somewhere between dollhouse and house of cards, model and construction site."

Gertrud Koch,
Parkett No. 68, 2003

エイヤ＝リーサ・アハティラ

無知のヴェール　2003

テキストを純毛のジャケットの
胸（左右反転した鏡像）と背にプリント、
手刷りのシルクスクリーン、
刷り：ロレンツ・ボエリ（チューリヒ）、
サイズは5種類、
Ed. 70/XXV、署名入り証明書

パルケット・エディション 68

無知は知識を映す鏡

心に強く訴えるアハティラの絵画は、しばしば家をめぐって展開する。オブジェと外から中に入り、内側から扉を閉める人々。家につづく道、駐車スペース、道中に渡った橋、奇妙な訪問者が開いて中に入る扉、日差しを遮るカーテン、部屋の壁を通過する自動車、ひとが下に隠れることのできるベッド、すべてを緩めるすきま風。アハティラが家をもとに作り上げる絵は脆く、人形の家とトランプの家、模型と建築現場の狭間にある。

ゲルトルート・コッホ
（パルケット 68号、2003年）

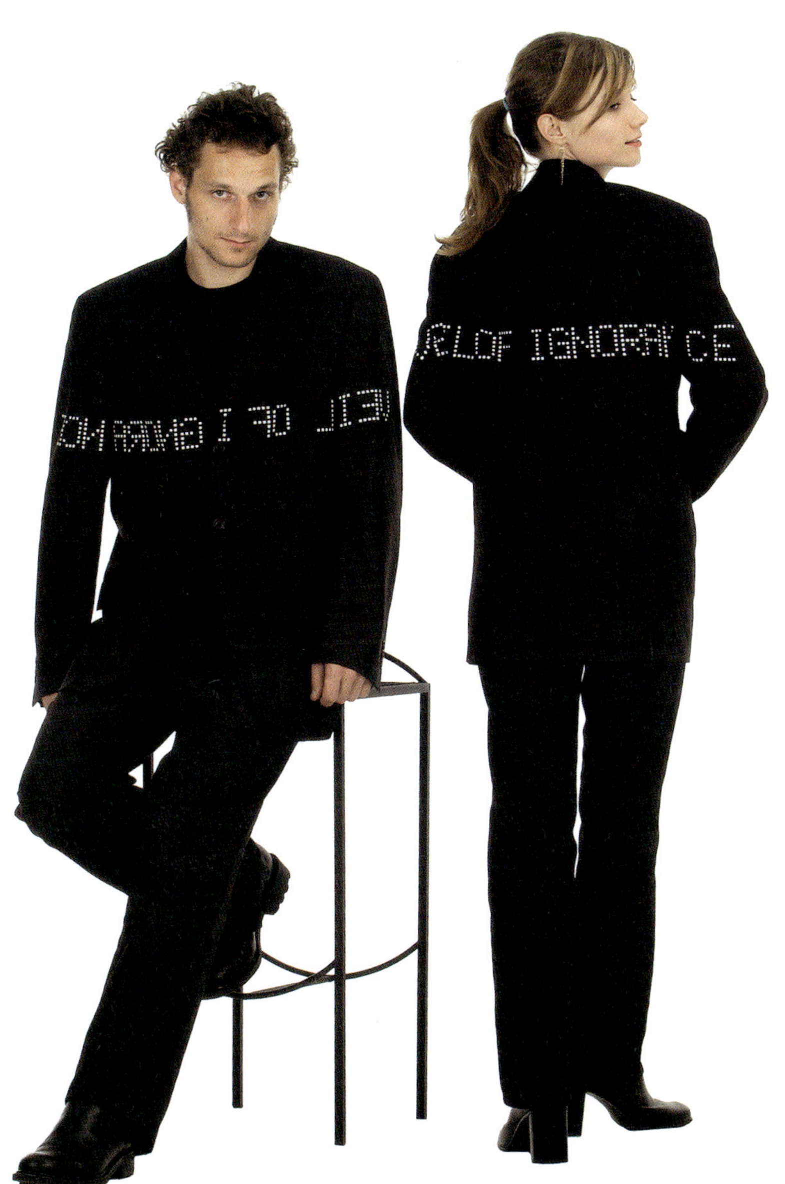
LEVEL OF IGNORANCE

AI WEIWEI

Swatter, 2007

Brass, gilded,
19 ³/₄ x 2 ³/₄ x ²/₈" (50 x 7 x 0,5 cm),
Ed. 55/XXV, signed and numbered
certificate

EDITION FOR PARKETT 81

How to kill two birds with one swatter:
exercise artistic license and create a
make-believe readymade.

"There was an ineffable sense, that grey afternoon,
that old hierarchies were on their way toward
obsolescence, that it wasn't quite as much of an honor
as it might once have been for a Chinese artist to be
visited by the New York Times."

Philip Tinari
Parkett No. 81, 2007

アイ・ウェイウェイ（艾未未）

蠅叩き　2007

真鍮、金メッキ、
50×7×0.5cm、
Ed. 55/XXV、署名、番号入り証明書

パルケット・エディション 81

ひとつの蠅叩きで2羽の鳥を落とす方法。芸術家に許された自由を行使し、架空のレディメイドを創る。

雲が灰色にたれこめたその日の午後、古い権力構造は消滅しつつあり、中国人アーティストにとっても、『ニューヨーク・タイムズ』の訪問を受けるのは、以前ほど誇らしいことではなくなったという、曰く言いがたい印象をもった。

フィリップ・ティナリ
（パルケット 81号、2007年）

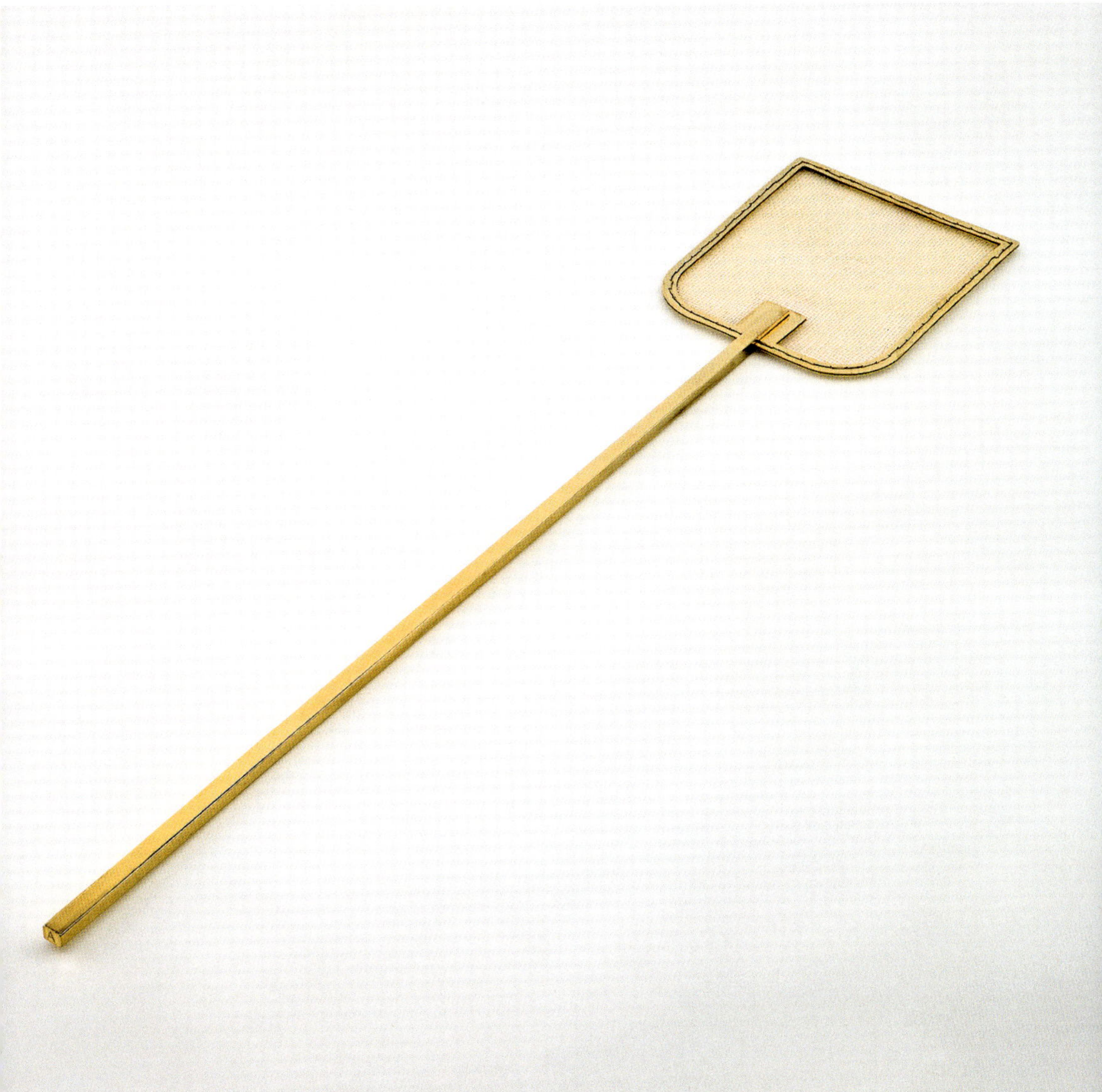

DOUG AITKEN

Decrease the Mass and
Run like Hell, 1999

Mirror kite, ca. 34 x 33 1/2" (86,5 x 85 cm),
tail 37 3/8" (95 cm), with poster of flying kite,
20 x 15 5/8" (50,8 x 38 cm),
Ed. 60/XX, stamped and numbered

EDITION FOR PARKETT 57

Feather the light and cast a spell:
This kite preys on reflection.

"Aitken's great technical mastery is obvious in the
framing of his shots, the precision with which he
captures the light, and the perfection of his editing,
which alternates shots of nature with the motion
of the machines. A sound mix of intelligent techno
music provides rhythm for the ensemble of screens
and images. A narrative subjectivity emerges out of
this unexpected encounter, one with an ideological
viewpoint on the world in all its contemporary
complexity."

Christine van Assche
Parkett No. 57, 1999

ダグ・エイケン

嵩を減らし、必死で走れ　1999

鏡状の凧：86.5×85cm、
尾：95cm、
空を飛ぶ凧のポスター：50.8×38cm、
Ed. 60/XX、スタンプ、番号入り

パルケット・エディション 57

翼で光をさえぎり、呪いをかけよ。この凧は光を捕
食する。

撮影した写真のフレーミング、光の精緻なとらえ方、自然を映
した映像と機械の動作を順次おりまぜる編集の完璧なしあげ
からも、エイケンの技量の高さはうかがえる。知的なテクノ・
ミュージックを用いた音響効果が、スクリーンと映像全体にリ
ズム感をあたえる。意外な出会いから、物語性をそなえた主観
性が浮上する。それはかぎりなく複雑な現代世界に向けるイデ
オロギー的視点と一致する。

クリスティーヌ・ファン・アッシュ
（パルケット 57号、1999年）

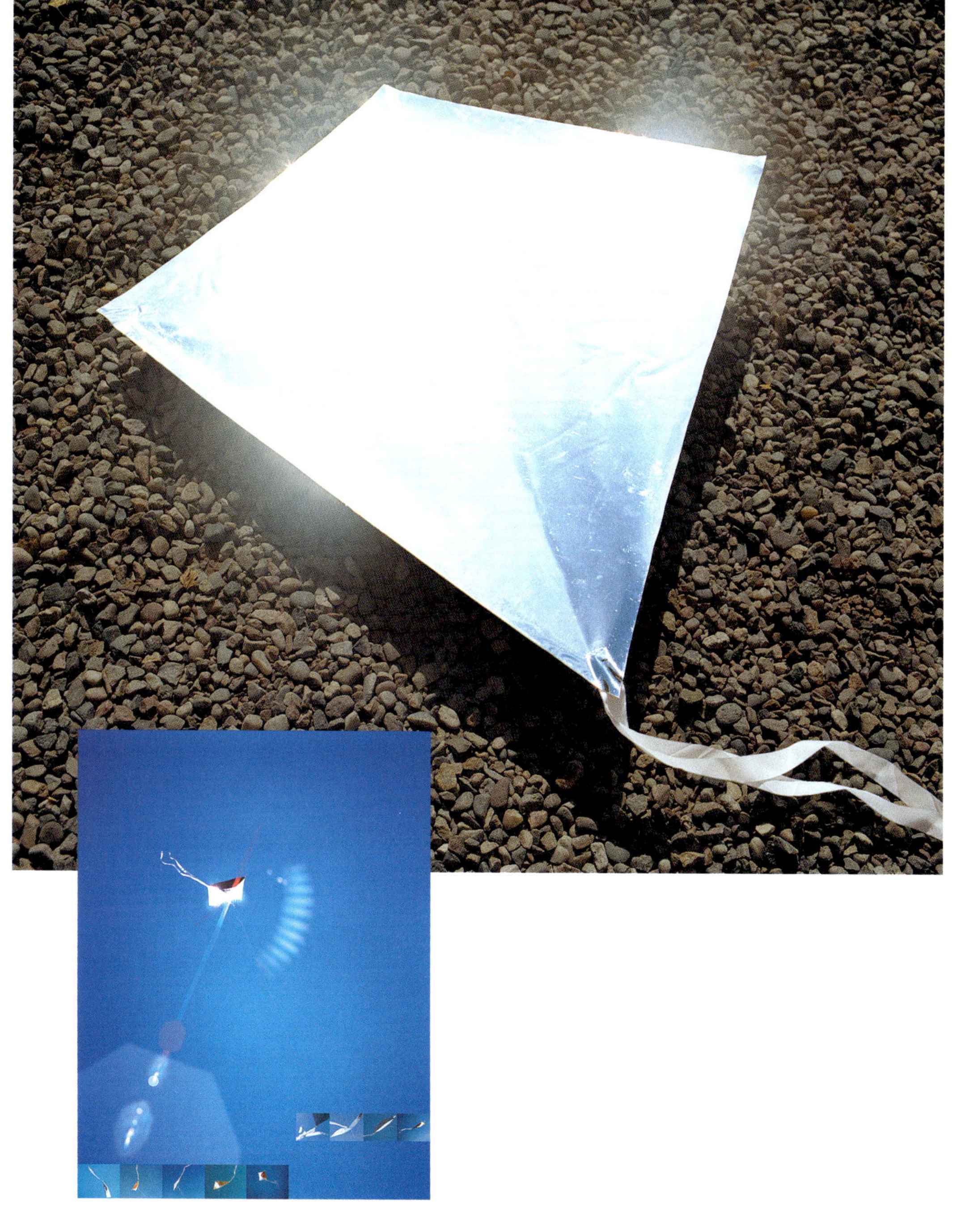

JENNIFER ALLORA &
GUILLERMO CALZADILLA

Deadline, 2007

DVD from 16 mm color film, 3 min.,
signed and numbered certificate,
Ed. 28/XVI

EDITION FOR PARKETT 80

Poetics and politics: mutually exclusive no
longer. For once the former holds the latter
in thrall.

"...materiality and metaphoricity constitute a couple.
In other words, a material is never simply self-evident
in its meaning; it is always marked with histories,
cultures, and politics that are at once irreducible
to and indissociable from the material in question.
Any material is going to have the weight of history
inscribed in it. The time of the world is there;
geologically, geopolitically, there is always an
allegorical dimension to materials. A tropical plant,
for instance, cannot be treated as a bare biological life
without effacing its colonial genealogy, even though
we are quite interested in the actual temporalities
and processes of the living organism as a sculptural
problematic."

Jennifer Allora / Guillermo Calzadilla
Interview in Parkett No. 80, 2007

ジェニファー・アローラ＆
ギリェルモ・カルサディーリャ

デッドライン　2007

16ミリ・フィルムに基づくDVD、3分、
署名、番号入り証明書、
Ed. 28/XVI

パルケット・エディション 80

詩と政治が互いに無関係だった時代は過去のもの。
この時ばかりは前者が後者を虜にした。

……物質性と隠喩性が対をなす。言い換えれば、物質の意味は決
して自明ではありえません。そこにはつねに歴史、文化、政治の
刻印があり、それらは物質に戻すことも、またそれと切り離すこ
ともできないのです。物にはすべて歴史の重みが銘記されていま
す。世界の時間がそこにあります。地質学的、地勢学的に見て、物
質はつねに寓話的な側面を伴います。熱帯植物であれば、植民地
時代の系譜を抹消しないかぎり、不確定な彫刻としての生命体の
時間性とプロセスには興味を惹かれても、単に生物学的に生き物
としてあつかうことはできません。

ジェニファー・アローラ＆ギリェルモ・カルサディーリャ
へのインタヴュー
（パルケット 80号、2007年）

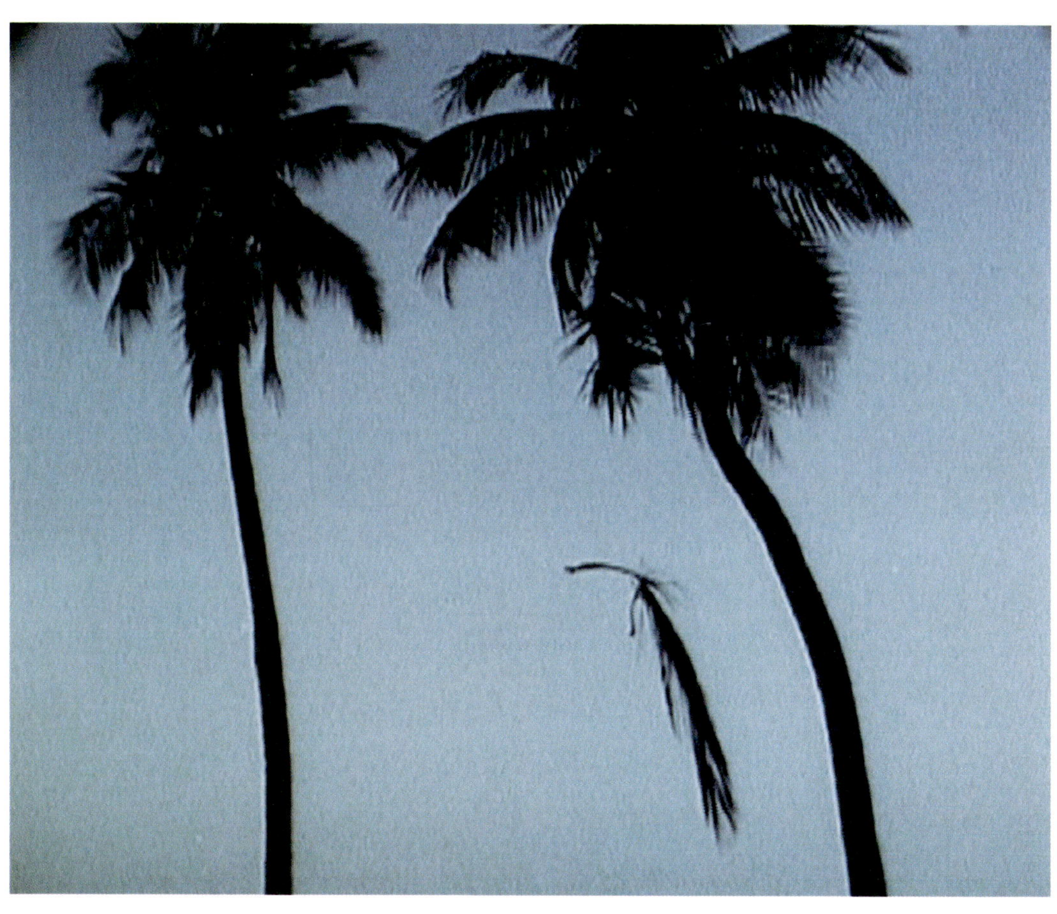

PAWEŁ ALTHAMER

Retrospective, 2008

12 tin figures,
each approx. 1 $^1/_8$ to 3 $^1/_2$" (3,5–9 cm) high,
cast by Michal Nowicki, Warsaw,
in custom-made cardboard suitcase,
6 $^5/_8$ x 9 $^1/_2$ x 3 $^1/_8$" (17,5 x 24 x 8 cm),
Ed. 38/XXV, signed and numbered
certificate

EDITION FOR PARKETT 82

The pilgrim's progress: twelve everymen
reenact the artist's journey into the origins
of the world.

"Althamer becomes a part of his medium, in both a
material and spiritual sense. It is as though he invites
us to share in a waking experience of lucid dreaming
where ordinary rules do not apply and where we may
begin to become newly absorbed by our surroundings
with an acute, hallucinatory perceptiveness."

Catherine Wood
Parkett 82, 2008

パヴェウ・アルトハメル

回顧　2008

錫の人形12体、各々高さ3.5-9cm、
ミカル・ノヴィッキー鋳造 (ワルシャワ) 、
ボール紙の特注スーツケース入り、
17.5×24×8cm、
Ed. 38/XXV、署名、番号入り証明書

パルケット・エディション 82

巡礼者の旅。12人の平凡な人物が世界の起源をもと
めるアーティストの旅を再現する。

アルトハメルは、素材と精神の両面から、自ら用いるメディアの一
部となる。鮮烈な夢から目覚める経験を、分かち合おうとするよう
にも見える。平凡な取り決めは通用せず、幻覚を呼ぶ研ぎ澄まされ
た感覚のうけとめる周囲の印象に、わたしたちはあらためてひきこ
まれる。

キャサリン・ウッド
（エディション 82号、2008年）

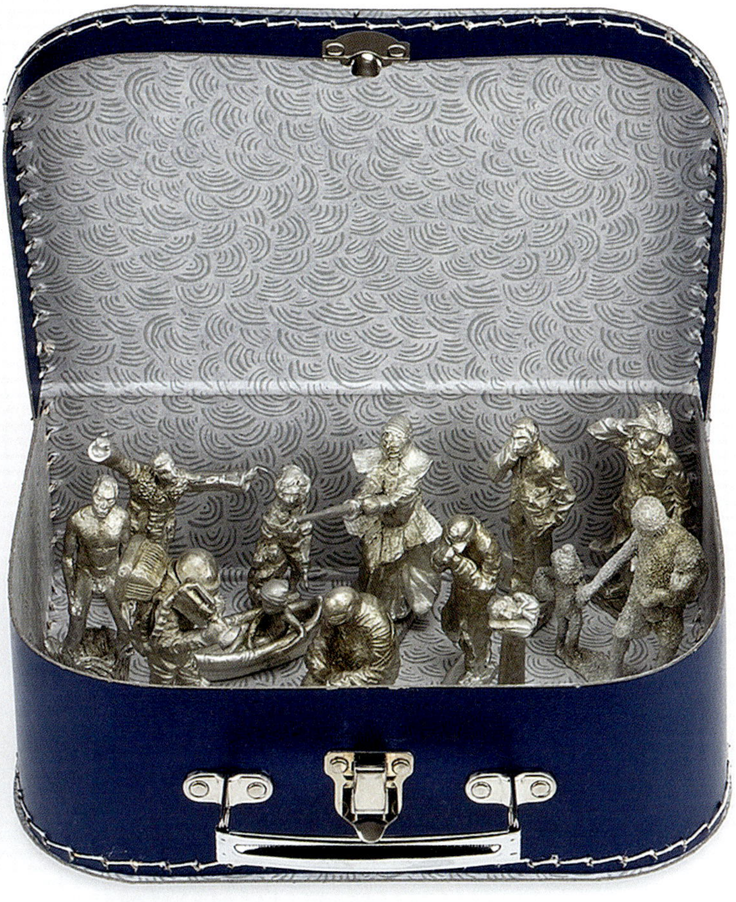

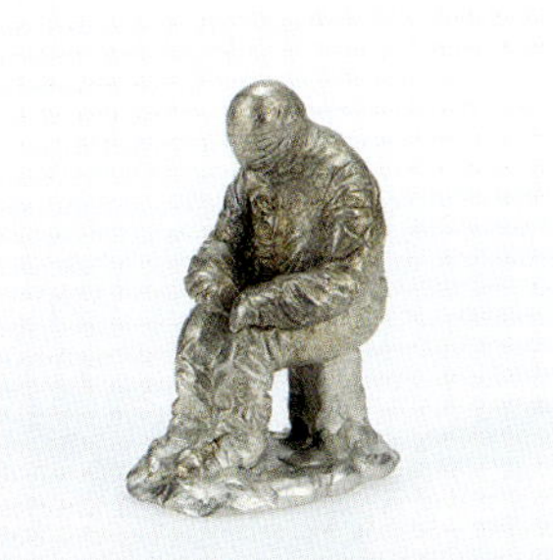

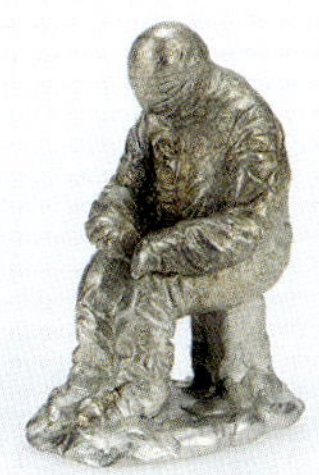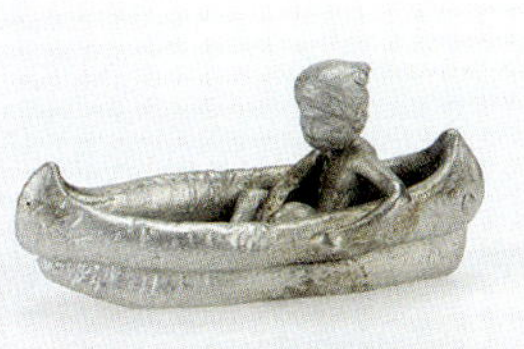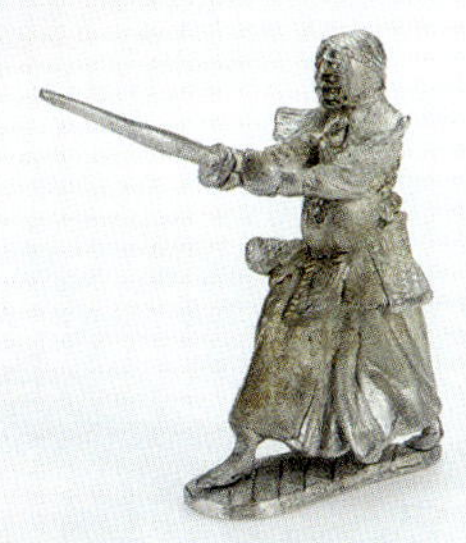

KAI ALTHOFF

Paden, 2005

Fragrance and bottle
conceived and designed by the artist,
mouth blown glass
with oxidation (each unique),
approx. 7 x 6 $^2/_8$ x 2" (18 x 16 x 5 cm),
production by Matteo Gonet,
Glassworks + Design, Zurich,
Ed. 55/XXV, signed and numbered

EDITION FOR PARKETT 75

Pandora's bottle: beware the sampling that
issues like whispers.

"Kai Althoff's installations are scenarios of initiation
that bring to life manifestations of extremely specific
worlds. They are populated by an arsenal of real or
invented characters, all of them absorbed by the artist
as alter egos. Detached from their original historical
and biographical contexts, they represent various
aggregate states of individual and collective being—
from compulsive brutality to ethereal spirituality."

Oliver Koerner von Gustorf
Parkett No. 75, 2005

カイ・アルトフ

パデン　2005

アーティストが考案、
デザインした香水とガラス瓶、酸化による着色、
吹きガラス（すべて一点物）、
18×16×5cm、
制作：マッテオ・ゴネ・グラスワークス
＋デザイン（チューリヒ）、
Ed. 55/XXV、署名、番号入り

パルケット・エディション 75

パンドラの瓶。囁きのようにしみでる見本にご用心。

カイ・アルトフのインスタレーション作品は、きわめて特殊な世界
の存在を生々しく蘇らせる秘儀のシナリオ。そこには実在の、ある
いは架空の人物たちが、いずれも作者に同化した分身として群れを
なしている。本来の歴史的背景、個人史から切り離されたかれらは、
衝動的な残忍さから霊妙な精神の気高さまで、個人と集団が集合
して示す多様な状態を体現する。

オリヴァー・カーナー・フォン・グストーフ
　（パルケット 75号、2005年）

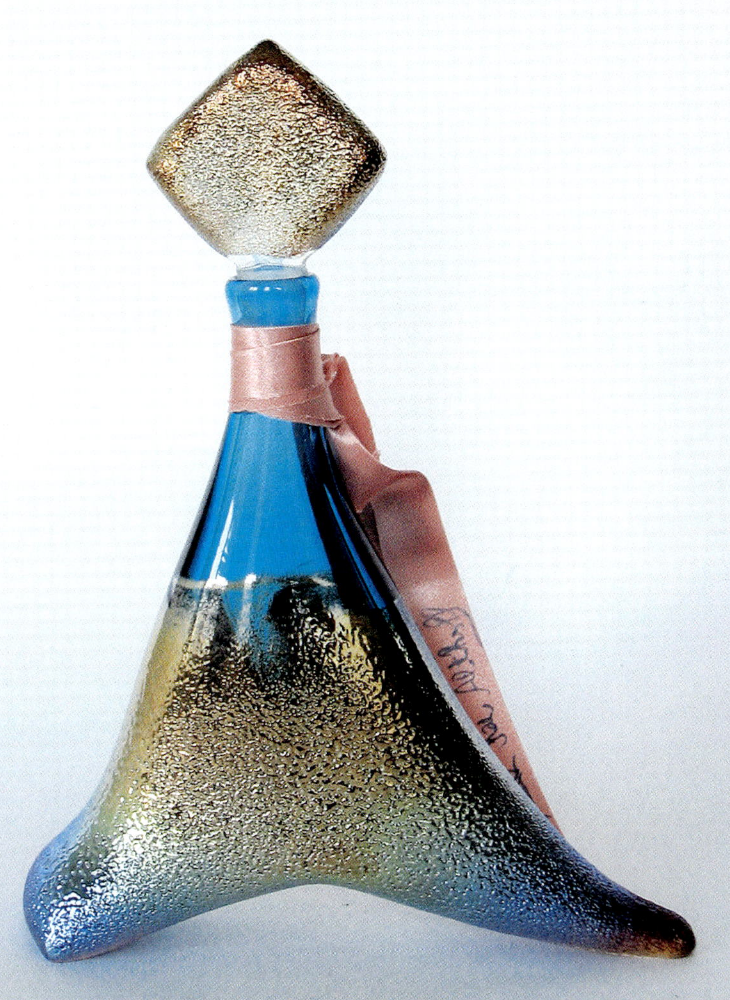

FRANCIS ALŸS

Ghetto Collector, 2003

Tin, magnets, plastic string,
rubber wheels, 25 design variations,
approx. 6 1/2 x 9 x 5" (15 x 24 x 13,8 cm),
Ed. 99/L, signed and numbered

EDITION FOR PARKETT 69

Collector of urban debris: the ultimate
accessory for every pooch-happy flaneur.

"Each of Alÿs's disturbances in the normal traffic
patterns of everyday life spans a portion of the city,
most involve a process of accumulation or depletion,
all are willful, deadpan, understated, and efficient
with regard to their apparent aimlessness.
And, whether documented in videos or photos,
all are visually memorable."

Robert Storr
Parkett No. 69, 2003

フランシス・アリス

ゲットー・コレクター　2003

錫、磁石、プラスティックの糸、
ゴム・タイヤ、25種のデザイン、
15×24×13.8cm、
Ed. 99/L、署名、番号入り

パルケット・エディション 69

都会のゴミ収拾車、愛犬家の散歩にうってつけの
アクセサリー

日々の暮らしの決まり事をかき乱すアリスの企みは、どれも都
会生活の一部として、物を溜め、あるいは失くす営みに関わる
ことが多く、いずれも頑固に、なに食わぬ様子で、でしゃばらず、
見かけどおりに役立たずであることを効果的に印象づける。ビ
デオ、写真を問わず、記録は長く視覚の記憶に残る。

ロバート・ストア
（パルケット 69号、2003年）

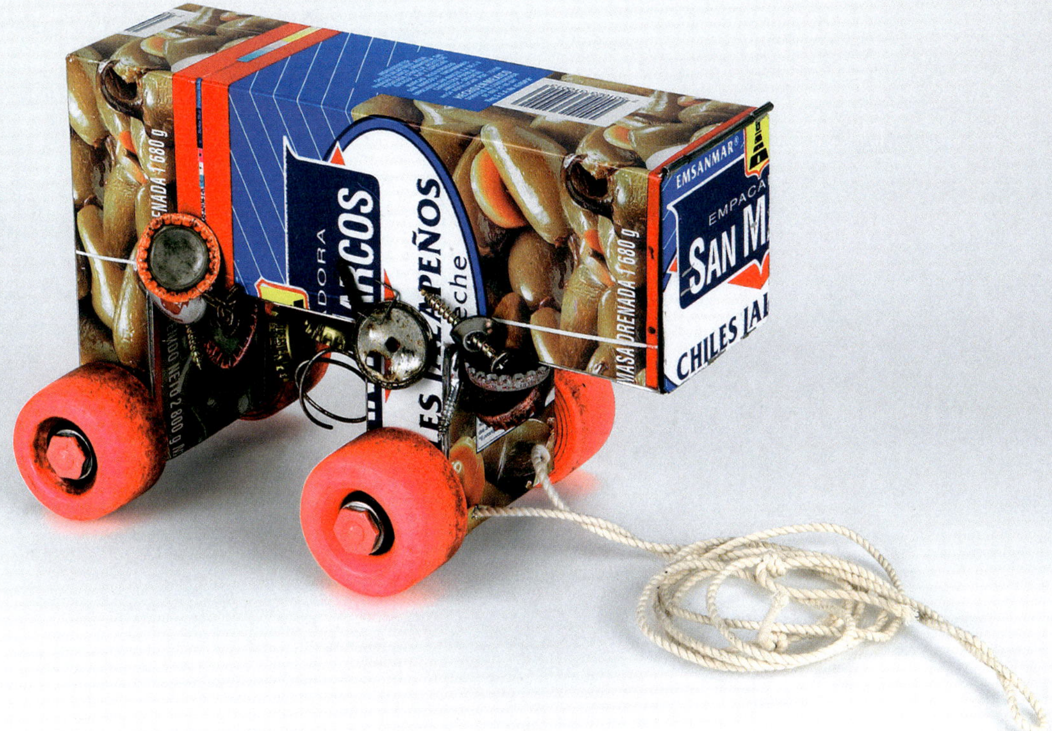

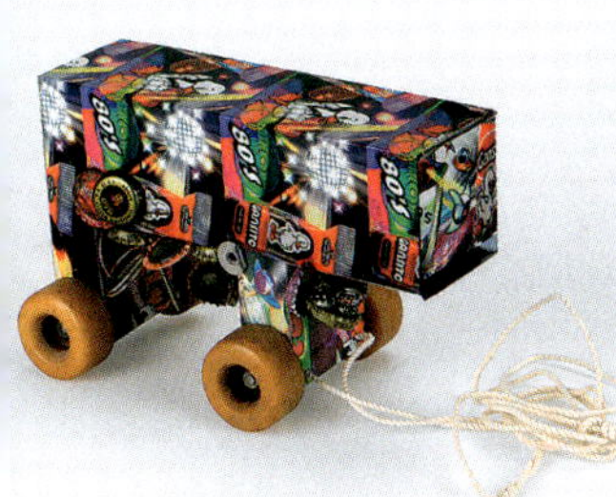

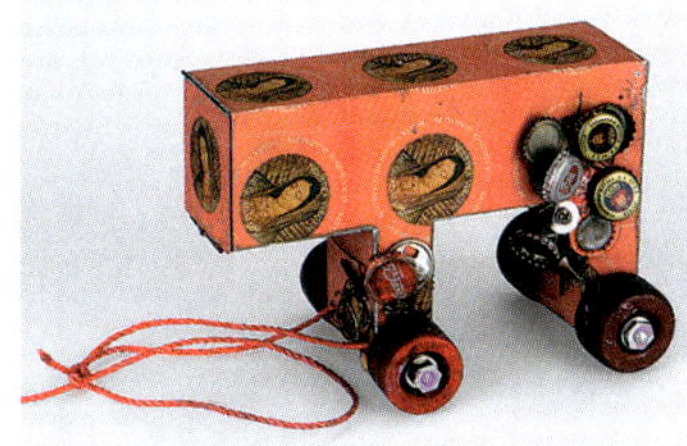

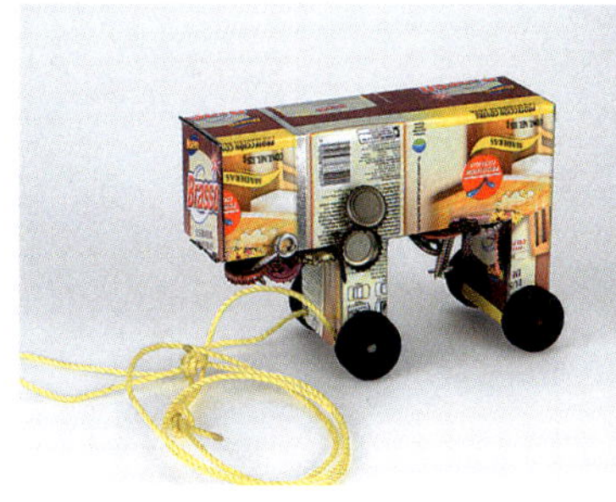

LAURIE ANDERSON

Hearring, 1997

Earring with playable sound message
(approx. 20 sec.), brass, copper,
circuit board, loudspeaker, lithium
battery, Plexiglas, wires, approx. size:
3 $^3/_8$ x 1 $^3/_4$ x 1" (10,2, x 4,5 x 2 cm),
jewelery by Josiah Dearborn,
engineering design Bob Bielecki
Ed. 150/XXX, with monogram and
numbered

EDITION FOR PARKETT 49

Tune in to the mysterious workings of a late
twentieth century baroque mind.

"Firmly rooted in time and in the world, her art explores
a territory between keen wakefulness and (day)-
dreams, where things of the real world and visions
together penetrate consciousness, where perception
stimulates dreams, and dreams sharpen perception.
...For almost three decades, ceaselessly circling
themes and motifs in text, image, and music have
been coupled in Laurie Anderson's performances and
installations with new material, forever evolving in a
cosmology-in-flux, in the endless flow of a great work
in progress."

Jacqueline Burckhardt
Parkett No. 49, 1997

ローリー・アンダーソン

聞き飾り　1997

再生可能な音声メッセージ（約20秒）を
収録したイヤリング、真鍮、銅、回路盤、
スピーカー、リチウム電池、アクリル、電線、
10.2×4.5×2cm、
ジュエリー・デザイン：ジョサイア・ディアボーン、
機械部分のデザイン：ボブ・ビーレッキ、
Ed. 150/XXX、イニシャル、番号入り

パルケット・エディション 49

20世紀後半を生きる奇怪な知性の神秘的な働きに
周波数を合わせましょう

時代と世界にしっかり根をはるアンダーソンの作品は、鋭敏な覚醒
と（白日）夢の狭間の、現実世界の事柄と幻覚が手を携えて意識
に浸透し、感覚が夢を誘い、夢が感覚にみがきをかける領域を探
究する……ほぼ30年に渡り、切目なく循環する文章、映像、音楽の
テーマとモティーフはローリー・アンダーソンのパフォーマンスと
インスタレーションを介して新たな素材と結びつき、流動状態の
宇宙論のなかで、制作途上の偉大な作品のはてしない流れのなか
で、永遠に発展をつづけている。

ジャクリーヌ・ブルクハルト（パルケット 49号、1997年）

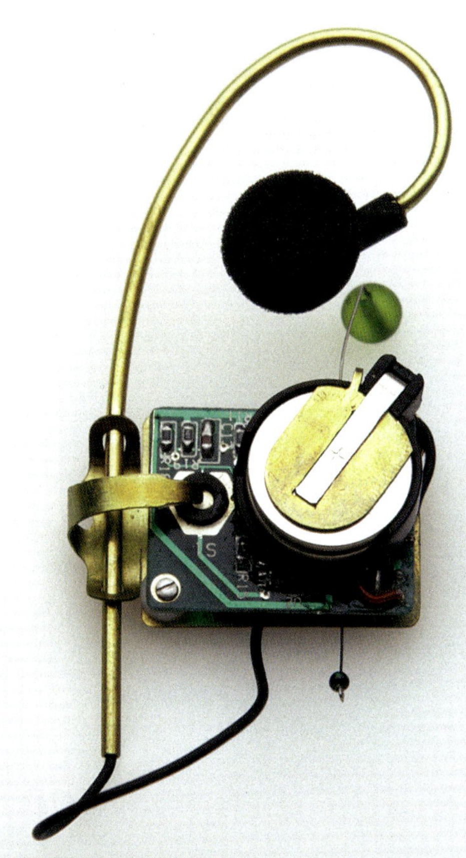

JOHN M ARMLEDER

Untitled, 1997

Unique Perspex sculptures in
fluorescent colors: yellow,
light blue, orange, or colorless,
approx. 16 x 16 x 8"
(40,6 x 40,6 x 20,3 cm),
Ed. 50/XX, signed and numbered,
yellow: 1–20, blue: 21–33,
orange: 34–42, colorless: 43–50

EDITION FOR PARKETT 50/51

Sculpted calligraphy. Translucent, ethereal
shapes in a state of suspended animation.

"The idea one gets when looking at the work of John
Armleder is the idea of the twentieth century itself,
the age of modernity. This is not only because he uses
an abstract pictorial vocabulary, but also because he
uses objects that have served to construct the new life
of this century."

Giacinto di Pietrantonio
Parkett No. 50/51, 1997

ジョン・M. アームレーダー

無題　1997

黄、明るい青、オレンジの蛍光色、
あるいは無色のアクリル製彫刻、
デザインは個々に異なる、
40.6×40.6×20.3cm、
Ed. 50/XX、署名、番号入り、
黄：1-20、青：21-33、
オレンジ：34-42、無色：43-50

パルケット・エディション 50/51

彫刻による書。半透明の華奢な姿が動きを中断して
そこにある。

ジョン・アームレーダーの作品を見てひとが何か考えるとすれば、
それは20世紀、すなわち近代性の時代そのものである。これは
アームレーダーが抽象的な絵画の表現法を用いるせいばかりで
なく、今世紀の新生活を築くのに役立った物を用いるからでもあ
る。

ジャカント・ディ・ピエトラントニオ
（パルケット 50/51号、1997年）

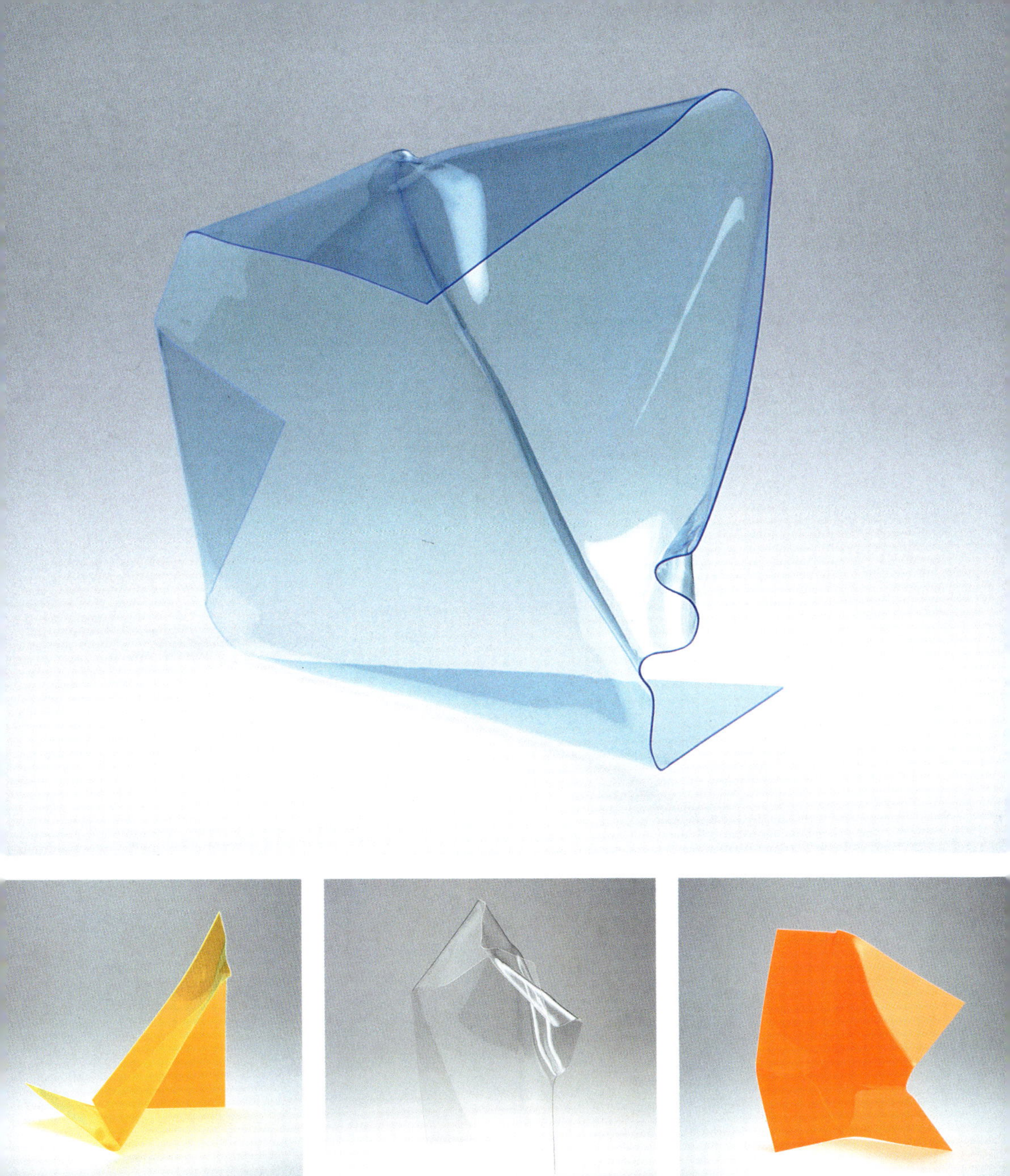

RICHARD ARTSCHWAGER

Hair Box, 1990

Paint on rubberized hair, wood backing,
10 x 15 x 5" (25,4 x 38 x 13 cm),
Ed. 100/XX, signed and numbered

EDITION FOR PARKETT 23

Industrial topiary. An enclosing wall, a
jutting ledge, a dark fibrous recess that
only the hand can enter: the impact of the
uncanny makes this box a surrealist object
for the modern age.

"An Artschwager chair is a chair distilled to its
platonic essence, all trace of ornamentation edited
and pruned away, abridged to the intellectual
state of chairhood, part of a kit through which we
teach the meanings of 'chair' and 'table.'"

Arthur C. Danto
Parkett No. 23, 1990

リチャード・アーシュワーガー

ヘア・ボックス　1990

ゴムを引いた髪を塗装、木で裏打ち、
25.4×38×13cm、
Ed. 100/XX、署名、番号入り

パルケット・エディション 23

植木の刈り込みの工業製品版。周囲をとりまく壁、
壁から突き出す棚、手のみが入れる暗い繊維質の窪
み。得体の知れない気配は、シュルレリアスムのオブ
ジェの現代版にふさわしい。

アーシュワーガーの作る椅子は観念の本質に純化された椅子で
あり、装飾の痕跡はことごとく取り除かれ、椅子という存在の知
的状況にまで簡約され、わたしたちが「椅子」や「テーブル」の意
味を教えるのに用いる道具一式の一部となる。

アーサー・C. ダントウ
（パルケット 23号、1990年）

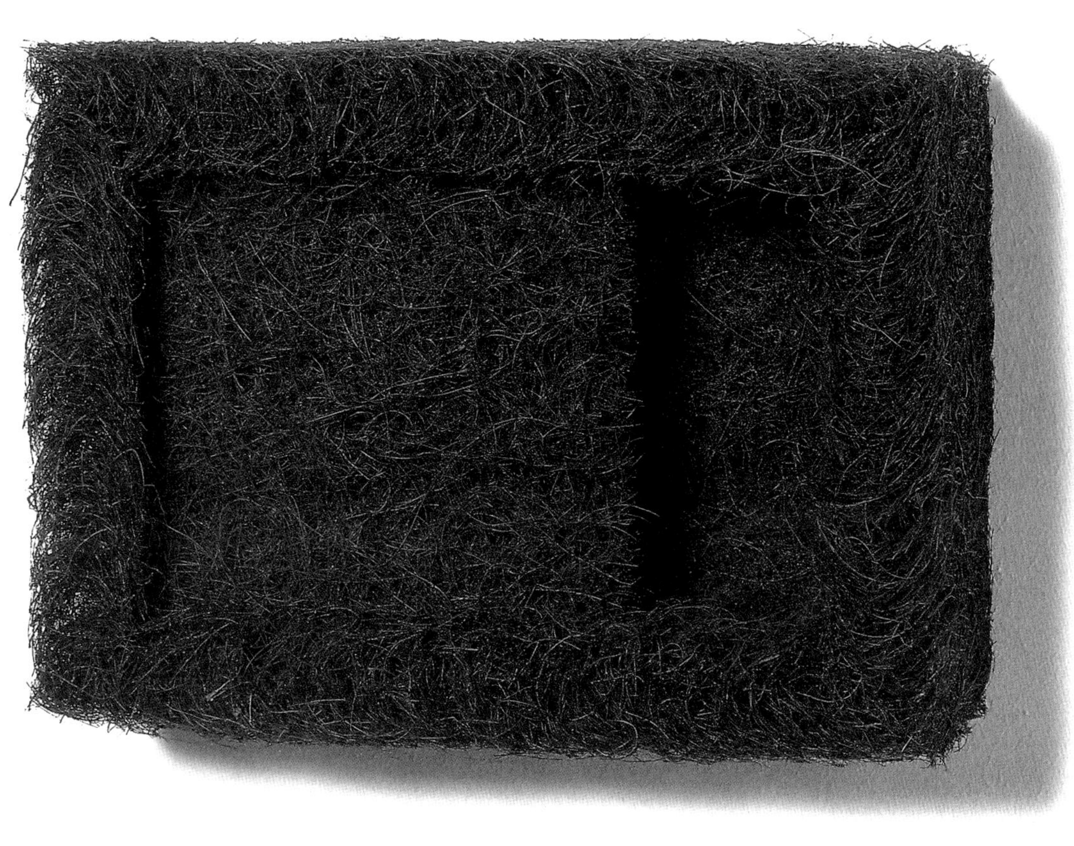

RICHARD ARTSCHWAGER

Untitled (1000 Cubic Inches), 1996

Plywood and pine with steel hardware,
Ed. 60/XL, signed and numbered
No. 1 ed. 1–12/60
No. 2 ed. 13–24/60
No. 3 ed. 25–36/60
No. 4 ed. 37–48/60
No. 5 ed. 49–60/60

EDITION FOR PARKETT 46

1000 cubic inches of space for your favorite ghosts—towering or flat, slanted or straight—they lie nestled and safe, inaccessible to unimaginative souls.

"What is American about Artschwager's objects goes beyond analogy—and there is more to it than the aggressive way they display their surface textures. Whether Formica or fiberboard, flowing grain or rigid pattern, their surfaces appear hermetic. Their sheer size further reinforces their presence as pure surface…They are like those organisms that have settled into extreme ecological niches, just below the boiling point of water, or in the anaerobic ocean depths. That is the kind of position that Artschwager's objects occupy in the realm of art objects: By scale and texture, they have one foot in the world of objects and one foot in the world of art."

Kurt W. Forster
Parkett No. 46, 1996

リチャード・アーシュワーガー

無題（1000立方インチ）　　1996

合板、松、ステンレス金具、
Ed. 60/XL、署名、番号入り
1号：Ed. 1/60−12/60
2号：Ed. 13/60−24/60
3号：Ed. 25/60−36/60
4号：Ed. 37/60−48/60
5号：Ed. 49/60−60/60

パルケット・エディション 46

あなたのお気に入りの幽霊のために、1000立方インチの空間をご用意しました。すっくと立ってもぺしゃんと寝ても、傾いてもまっすぐでも、散文的な連中に煩わされることなく、心地よく、安全にお休みいただけます。

アーシュワーガーの作品には他に類似するものが見当たらないアメリカ的な性格があり、それは表面の質感をむきだしにする荒々しさにとどまらない。材料が合成樹脂でも繊維板でも、粒子が流れても厳密な模様を描いても、表面の質感は秘密めいて、視線をはねかえす。サイズの桁外れの大きさも、純粋な表面としての存在感をひきたてる……沸騰寸前の水温や嫌気性の生き物のみを育む深海のような、ごく限られた環境条件の狭所に棲みついた生物体をおもわせる。美術作品の世界のなかで、アーシュワーガーのオブジェが占めるのは、そうした位置だろう。サイズと質感の点で、片足をたんなる物の世界に、もう一方の足を美術界においている。

カート・W. フォースター
（パルケット 46号、1996年）

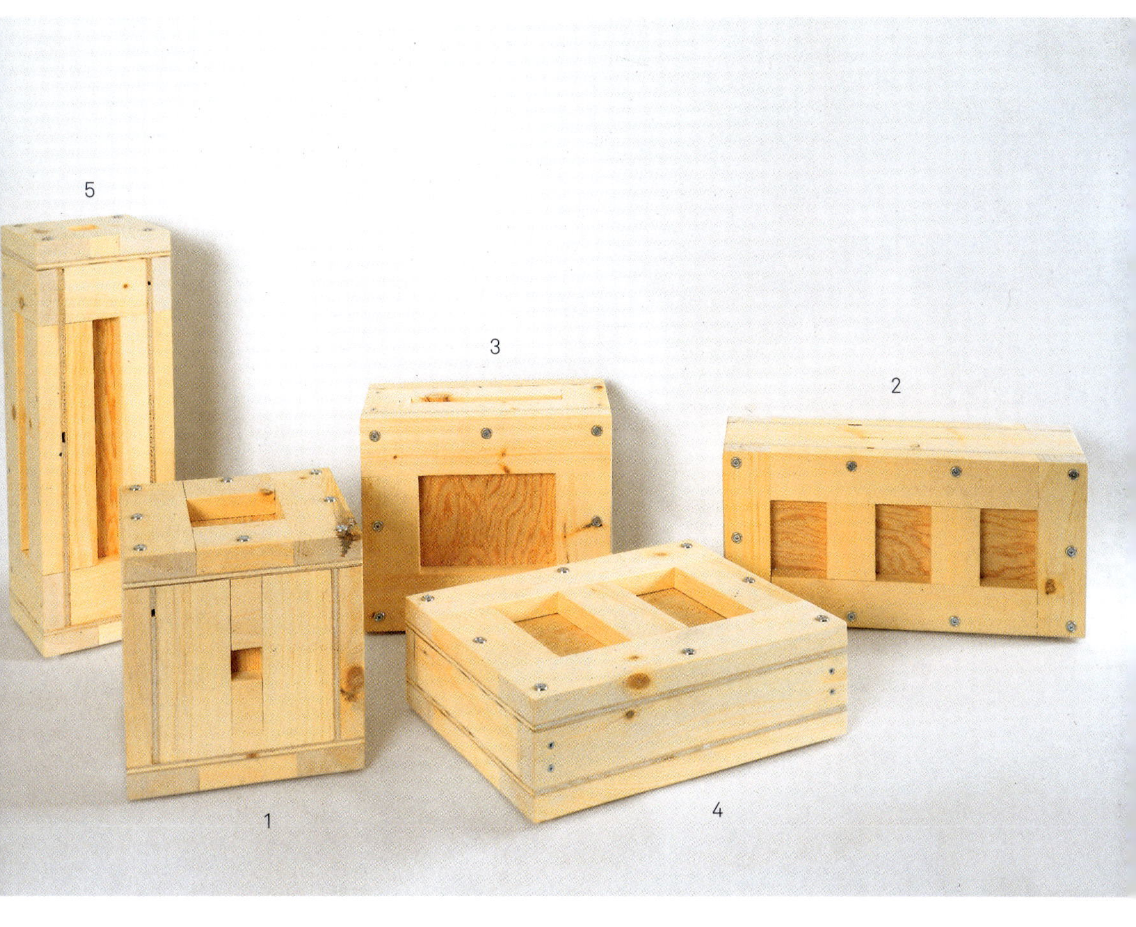

5
3
2
1
4

JOHN BALDESSARI

Six Colorful Expressions
(Frozen), 1991

Porcelain enamel steel plate, eight
color photographic screen process print,
imaged by a proprietary photographic
ceramic process, impervious to
environmental influences,
$10\,^{7}/_{16}$ x $4\,^{3}/_{4}$ x $^{1}/_{16}$" (26,5 x 12 x 0,2 cm),
Ed. 75/XX, signed and numbered

EDITION FOR PARKETT 29

Foul or fair weather friend. This technically
innovated object is guaranteed to be as
impervious to the ravages of everyday life as
the smile that defies misfortune.

"On the evidence of his images, Baldessari argues for
the metaphysical atmosphere of pictoriality and the
pictorial nature of abstraction… Thus, any image that
aspires to portray the historical moment must do so by
enclosing it—by stopping its pulse and suspending the
laws of its nature."

Dave Hickey
Parkett No. 29, 1991

ジョン・バルデッサリ

6つの彩り豊かな（凍てついた）表情 1991

スティール板をエナメル加工、
写真8点をスクリーン・プリント、
写真を陶磁器に転写する特殊製法により、
堅牢で外部からの影響に左右されない、
26.5×12×0.2cm、
Ed. 75/XX、署名、番号入り

パルケット・エディション 29

照っても友、降っても友。革新的な技術を駆使したこの
作品は、微笑みが不運を寄せつけないように、日々の惨
害をものともしないこと請け合いです。

自作のイメージに基づき、バルデッサリは絵画的な物は形而上学的
雰囲気を伴い、抽象に絵画性ありと主張する……したがって、歴史
的瞬間を描写しようと願うイメージはそれを包囲することにより、す
なわちその脈動を停止させ自然の法則を停止することにより、目的
を達するのでなければならない。

デイヴ・ヒッキー
（パルケット 29号、1991年）

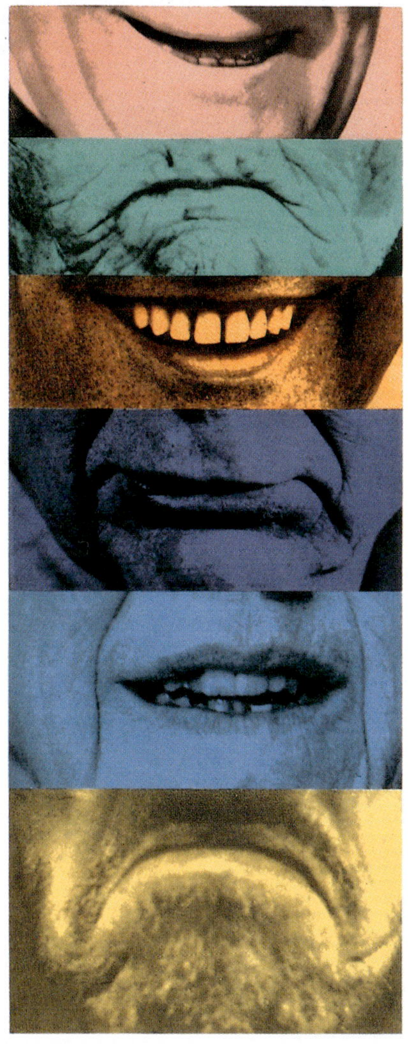

Six Colorful Expressions (Frozen)   Baldessari, 1991

JOHN BALDESSARI

Raised Eyebrows /
Furrowed Foreheads:
Crooked Made Straight, 2009

9-color silkscreen print on plexiglas,
5 x 12" (12,5 x 31cm)
Printed by Atelier für Siebdruck,
Lorenz Boegli, Zurich
Ed. 45/XX, signed and numbered

EDITION FOR PARKETT 86

Spots aside; it's the framing that counts.

"…when I was a painter I would work on a single image, because that's what you do. But when I got into photography I had the liberty of not using a single image. I'm not sure how I made that leap. I have a hard time with a single image because, in my mind, it's like one truth. And I'm always thinking, 'well, on the other hand there is this.'"

John Baldessari, interview with James Welling
Parkett No. 86, 2009

ジョン・バルデッサリ

眉を上げ／額に皺を寄せ
修正された歪み　2009

アクリル板（12.5×31cm）
にシルクスクリーン9色刷り
刷り：ロレンツ・ボエリ（チューリヒ）
Ed. 45/XX、署名、番号入り

パルケット・エディション 86

枝葉はさておき、肝心なのはフレーミング

絵描きだった頃は、ひとつのイメージに取り組むことにしていた。絵描きとはそうしたものだからね。写真を始めてからは、ひとつのイメージをつかわなくてもよくなった。その飛躍が、どのように起きたかは自分でもよくわからない。ひとつのイメージを相手にするのが難しいのは、わたしの考えるに、真実はひとつということになるからではないか。ところがわたしときたらいつだって、「とはいっても、それとは別に、こういうのもあるじゃないか」と考えているものだから。

ジョン・バルデッサリ
（パルケット 86号、2009年）

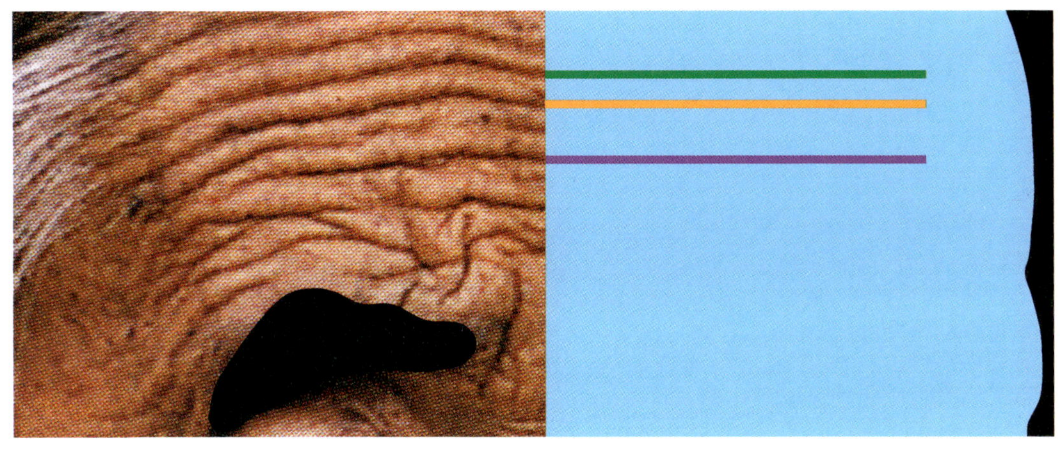

STEPHAN BALKENHOL

Two Lizards and a Man, 1993

Group of three cast lead figurines,
each figure approx. 11 $^7/_8$ x 5 $^1/_8$ x 1 $^1/_2$"
(30 x 13 x 4 cm), weighing approx. 4.5 lbs.,
cast by Bärtschi Foundry,
Aefligen, Switzerland,
Ed. 85/XXV, signed and numbered

EDITION FOR PARKETT 36

Graven image. A triumvirate of a man
and two lizards cast in lead—a substance at
once elemental and endearing—man
coexists with beast, devoid of fear or
hierarchy.

"Balkenhol's sculptures derive their qualitative
currency and significance from their origin in two
diametrically opposed fields. They draw on the
rational, sober, anorganic, and serial character of
Minimal Art; yet they also provide immediate sensual
access to the world."

Max Katz
Parkett No. 36, 1993

シュテファン・バルケンホール

2匹のトカゲとひとりの人間　1993

3個の小さな鉛の人形、
それぞれサイズは約30×13×4cm、重さ約2kg、
制作：ベルツキ鋳造所（エフリゲン市、スイス）、
Ed. 85/XXV、署名、番号入り

パルケット・エディション 36

彫像。元素のままの状態であり、しかも親しみを感
じさせる鉛を鋳造した人間ひとりとトカゲ2匹の3体
1組。人間が動物と恐怖心も上下関係も有さずに共存
している。

バルケンホールの彫刻は正反対の二つの世界を母体とするところ
から、広い通用範囲と意義を得る。合理的で飾り気がなく、有機
性から遠く、連続性を好むミニマル・アートをふまえながら、世界
との生々しい、感覚的なつながりも感じさせる。

マックス・カッツ
（パルケット 36号、1993年）

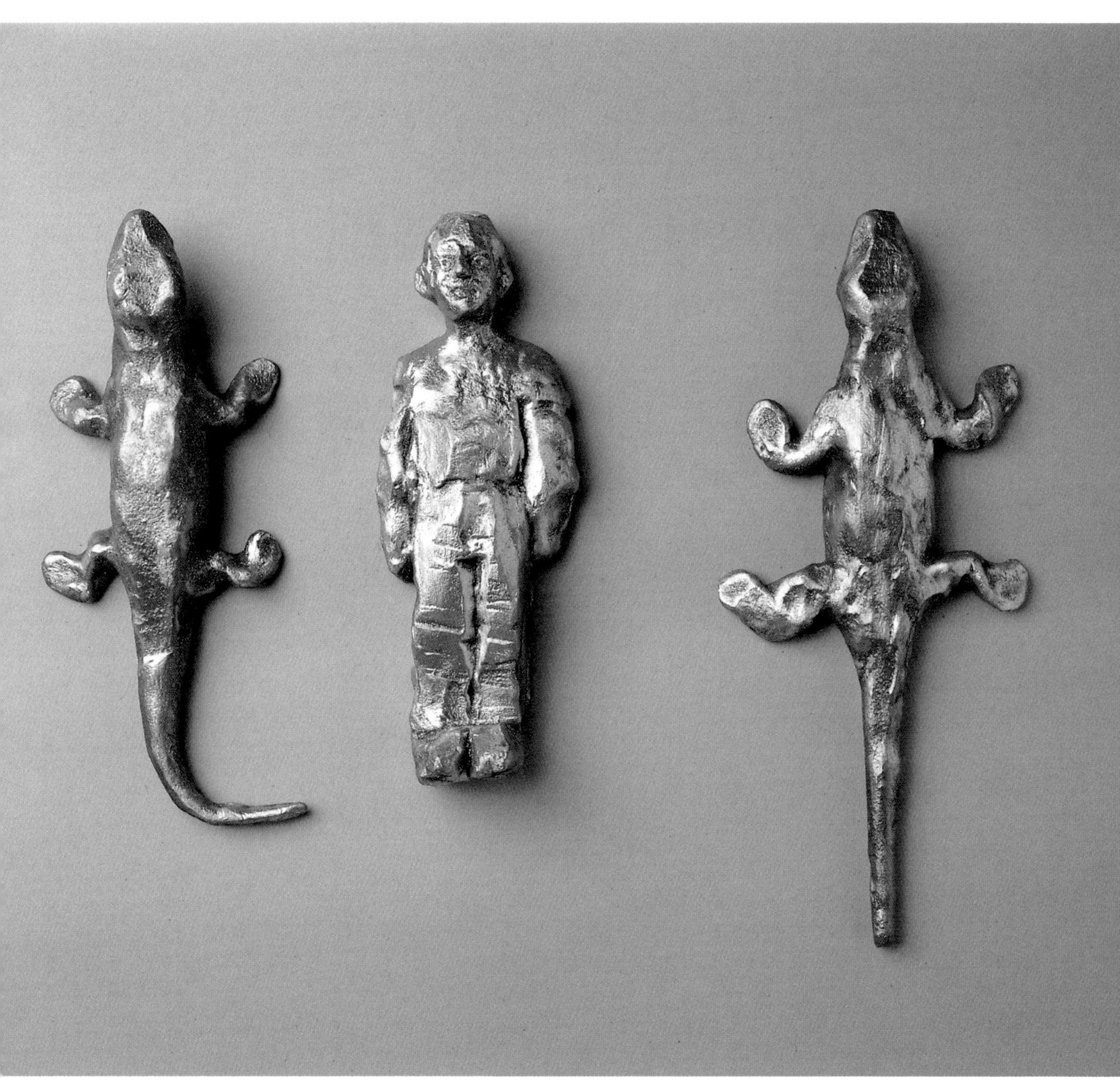

MATTHEW BARNEY

Sweet Bolus, 1995

Cast sugar and Viratex epoxy resin
on satin ribbon with single cultured
pearl, dumbbell: 3 $^7/_8$ x 4 x 11 $^1/_2$"
(8,5 x 9 x 30,7 cm), overall length
with satin ribbon 26 $^1/_2$" (67 cm),
Ed. 50/XXV, signed and numbered

EDITION FOR PARKETT 45

A crystallization of energies. A cast-sugar
dumbbell appears as a scepter waiting to be
wielded, cushioned on a white satin ribbon,
studded with a perfect pearl.

"Barney's work has always involved a carefully
balanced combination of exoteric and esoteric
elements, aspects that anyone can follow and enjoy
mixed in with cryptic signs and personal myths almost
impossible to decipher... Part of Barney's skill lies in
creating initial scenographies so compelling in visual
terms that it is almost impossible for the viewer not
to be drawn in by them."

Norman Bryson
Parkett No. 45, 1995

マシュー・バーニー

甘い丸薬　1995

砂糖とエポキシ樹脂を鋳型で固め、
サテンのリボンに養殖真珠1粒を添えたもの、
ダンベル：8.5×9×30.7cm、
リボンをふくめた全体の長さは67cm、
Ed. 50/XXV、署名、番号入り

パルケット・エディション 45

エネルギーの結晶。砂糖を固めたダンベルは、無垢な
真珠をあしらった白いサテンのリボンに護られ、振り回
される時を待っているようにみえる。

バーニーの作品にはだれにでもわかりやすい要素と、難解な要素が
常にほどよいバランスで入り混じり、だれでも理解し楽しめる側面
が、ほぼ解読不能な謎めいた記号、私的神話と混じり合う……バー
ニーの技量は、視覚的に惹きつける力がきわめて強く、見るものが
おもわず引き込まれてしまうような情景を創り出すところに発揮さ
れる。

ノーマン・ブライソン
（パルケット 45号、1995年）

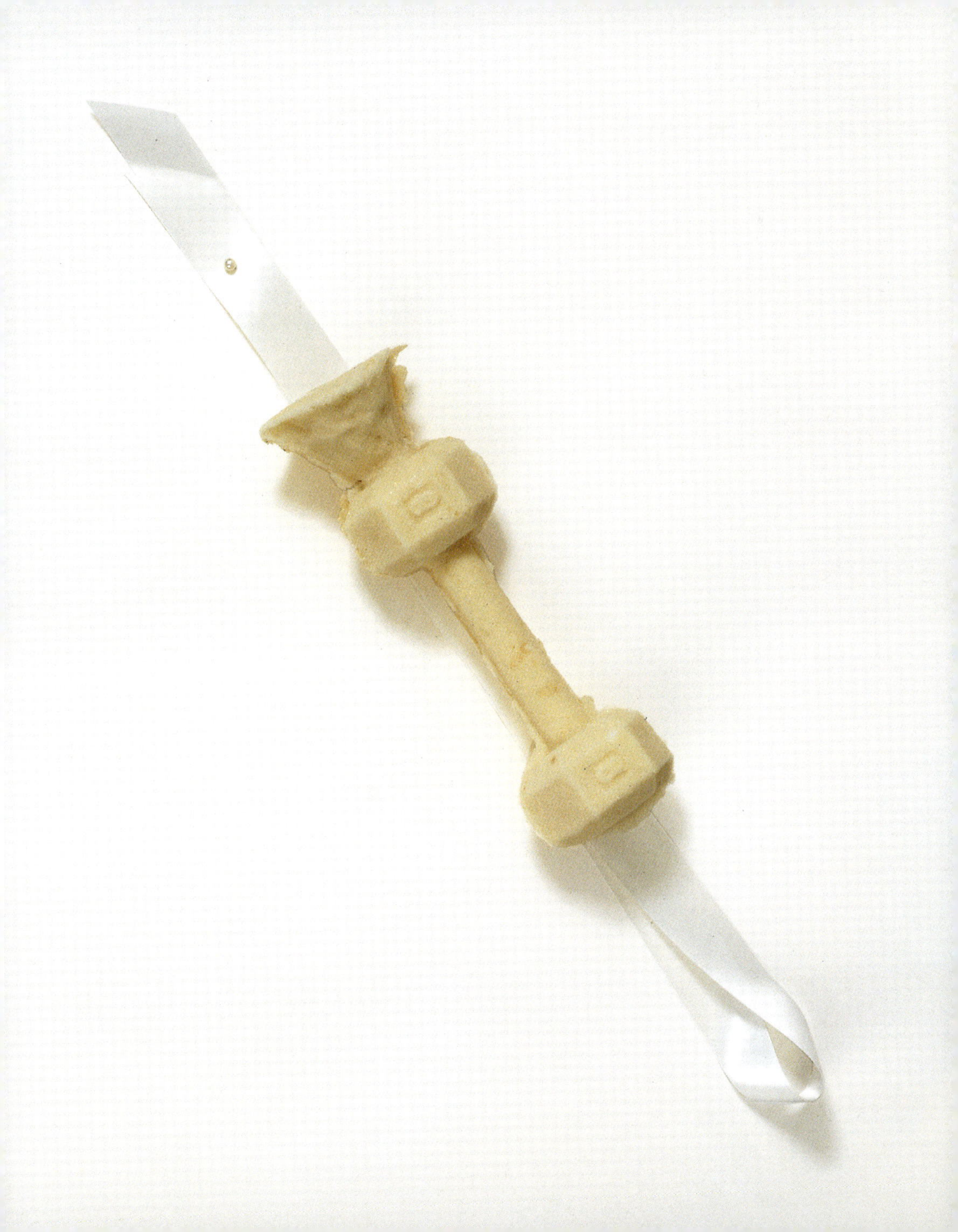

GEORG BASELITZ

Face and Teardrop, 1986

Drypoint etching
on stenciled english-red ground
of two plates on Zerkall
book paper 145g, bound in the magazine,
left plate: 5 x 3 1/8" (12,7 x 7,9 cm),
right plate: 4 13/16 x 2 13/16" (12,3 x 7,1 cm),
paper size: 10 x 8 1/4" (25,5 x 21 cm),
Ed. 60/XV, signed and numbered

EDITION FOR PARKETT 11

Frontispiece. Hair falling across the features or replacing them altogether covers the "face" of Parkett with a lushly enigmatic diptych.

"In Baselitz's work, sculpture and painting represent two forms of what might be called his 'opinione contraria,' to cite Vasari's Mannerist expression in referring to Rosso. It signifies the opposition and commitment involved in freeing expression and exposing the aggression of structure."

Eric Darragon
Parkett No. 11, 1986

ゲオルク・バゼリッツ

顔と涙粒　1986

2つの版を用いステンシルで染めた
イングリッシュ・レッドの地色にドライポイント、
ツェルカル社製書籍用紙145g、本誌に綴じこみ、
左の版：12.7×7.9cm、
右の版：12.3×7.1cm、
紙：25.5x21cm、
Ed. 60/XV、署名、番号入り

パルケット・エディション 11

口絵。垂れた髪が顔にかかり、あるいは完全にとってかわり、瑞々しく神秘的な2枚1組がパルケットの「顔」を覆う。

バゼリッツの作品、つまり彫刻と絵画は、ロッソについて語るヴァザーリのマニエリスム風表現を借りるなら「対立する意見」とも呼ぶべきふたつの形式に相当する。それは表現の解放、構造の攻撃性を露呈させるための異議申し立て、決意の表れである。

エリック・ダラゴン
（パルケット 11号、1986年）

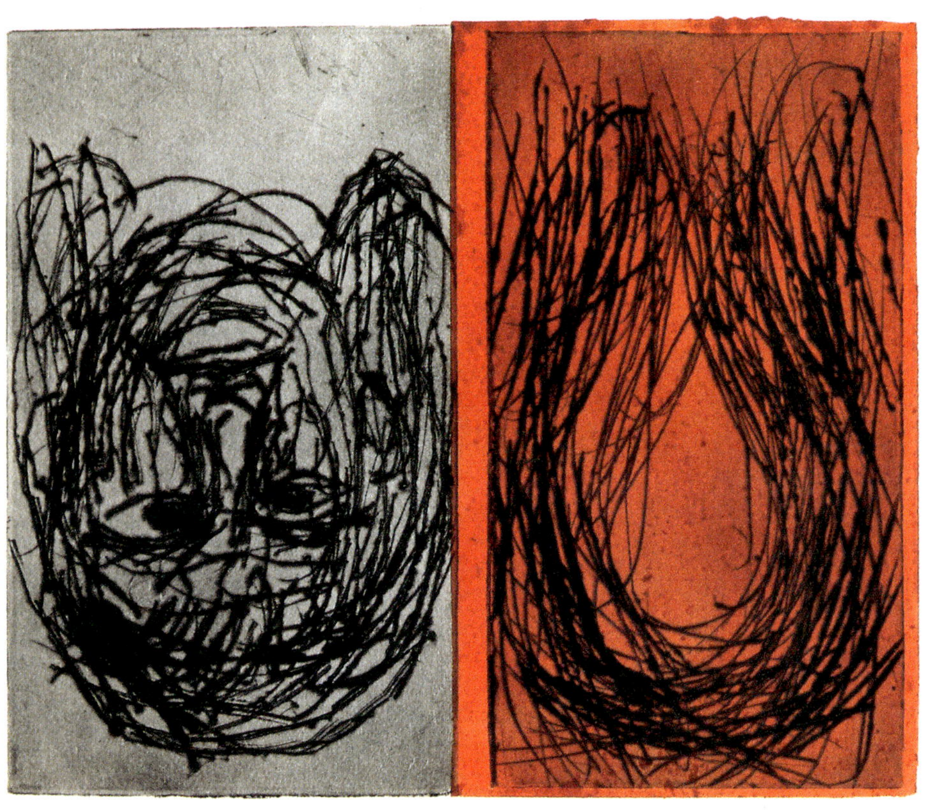

VANESSA BEECROFT

Untitled, 1999

Five silkscreen color prints
of photographs from the artist's archive
(VB08, VB35, VB16, VB39 & VB39),
19 $^7/_8$ x 27 $^7/_{16}$" (49,9 x 70 cm) each,
printed by Lorenz Boegli, Zurich,
Ed. of 50/LV, signed and numbered
certificate

EDITION FOR PARKETT 56

Dreams of corporeal identity.

"...Beecroft does something no one else does—she
does images live. And that changes everything. Even
though most viewers probably only know her work
through photographs and videos, it's the staging and
theatricality of the live event that make these images
of girls, whose vacancy and seductive appeal are
equally pronounced, so compelling."

Jan Avgikos
Parkett No. 56, 1999

ヴァネッサ・ビークロフト

無題　1999

作家所蔵の作品に基づく多色刷シルクスクリーン5点
　（VB08、VB35、VB16、VB39、VB39）、
49.9×70cm、
刷り：ロレンツ・ボエリ（チューリヒ）、
Ed. 50/LV、署名、番号入り証明書

パルケット・エディション 56

身体のアイデンティティを夢見る

ビークロフトはほかのだれもしないことをする。生のままのイメージをこしらえる。それがすべてを変化させる。鑑賞者の多くはビークロフトの作品を写真やビデオを通じてしか知らないだろうが、これらの娘たちのイメージの威力、空虚さと、男心をそそる魅力が等しく漲るイメージの威力がこれほど高いのは、写真の中のイベントが芝居がかった演出で実際に行われているせいである。

ヤン・アヴギコス
（パルケット 56号、1999年）

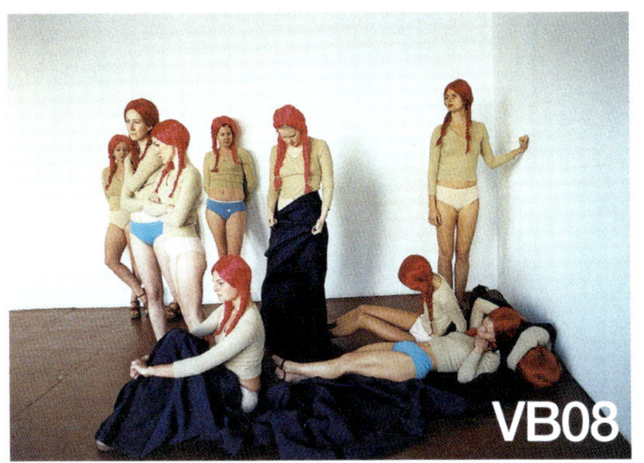

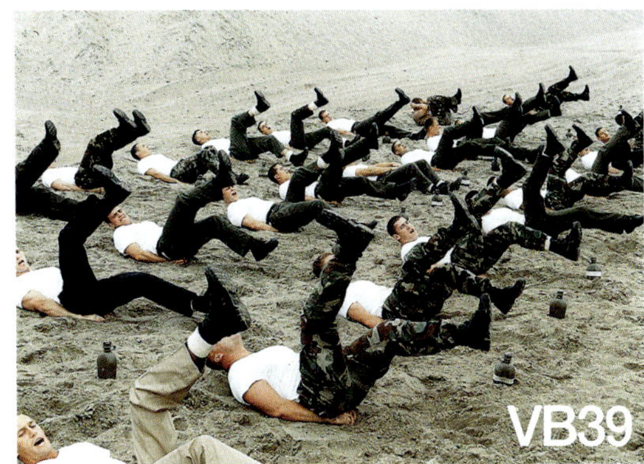

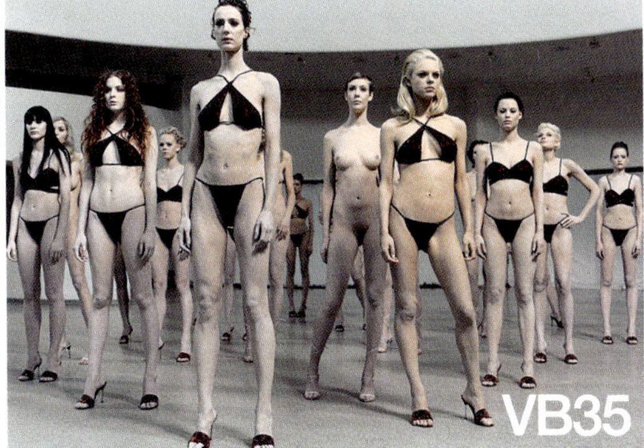

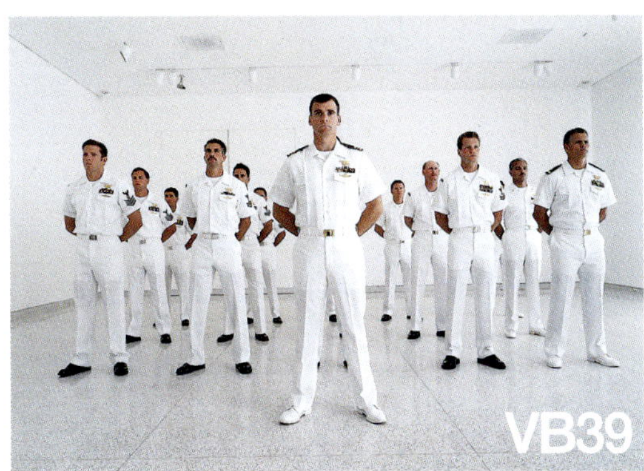

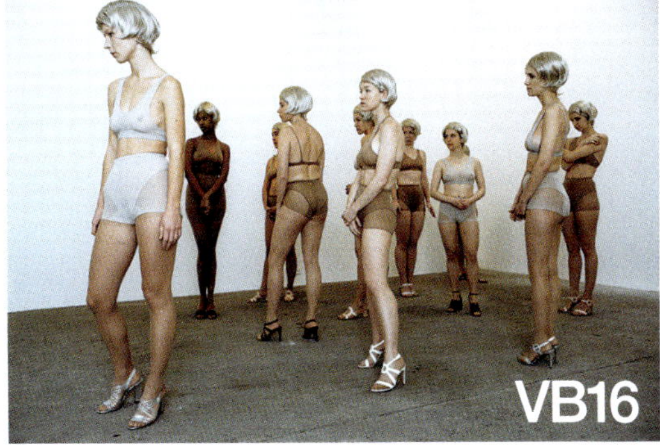

ROSS BLECKNER

Untitled, 1993

100 unique works, watercolor, inks,
and wax on watercolor paper in
handpainted and waxed wooden desktop
picture frame, 11 x 9" (27,8 x 22,8 cm),
Ed. 100, signed and numbered

EDITION FOR PARKETT 38

Forget me not. In handpainted portrait
frames, a simple-petalled flower goes
through a cycle of permutations, making each
a unique and distinctive watercolor.

"The question of whether Bleckner is an abstractionist
or an expressionist completely misses the point: that
he is avid to demonstrate the most intimate pulse
of consciousness lurking behind a veil of abstract
energy—'dematerialized life,' as he calls it. Or he can
call a painting 'a language to think thought…'"

Edmund White
Parkett No. 38, 1993

ロス・ブレックナー

無題　1993

100 点すべてに違いがある、
水彩画用紙に水彩絵具、インク、蜜蝋、
机上に置く額縁に手彩色、蜜蝋をかける、
27.8×22.8cm、
Ed. 100、署名、番号入り

パルケット・エディション 38

忘れな草。手で彩色したポートレート用の額縁のなか
で、ささやかな花びらをつけた植物がしだいに姿を変
える、ひとつひとつが他と異なる、唯一無二の水彩画と
なる。

ブレックナーは抽象画家か表現主義画家かを問うのはまったくの的
外れ。ブレックナーは抽象化をめざすエネルギーのヴェールの背後に
潜む意識の密やかな脈動、かれが「非物質化された生命」と呼ぶ物を
ぜひとも描きたいと強く願う。ブレックナーはまた絵画を「思考を思
考する言語」とも呼ぶ。

エドマンド・ホワイト
（パルケット 38号、1993年）

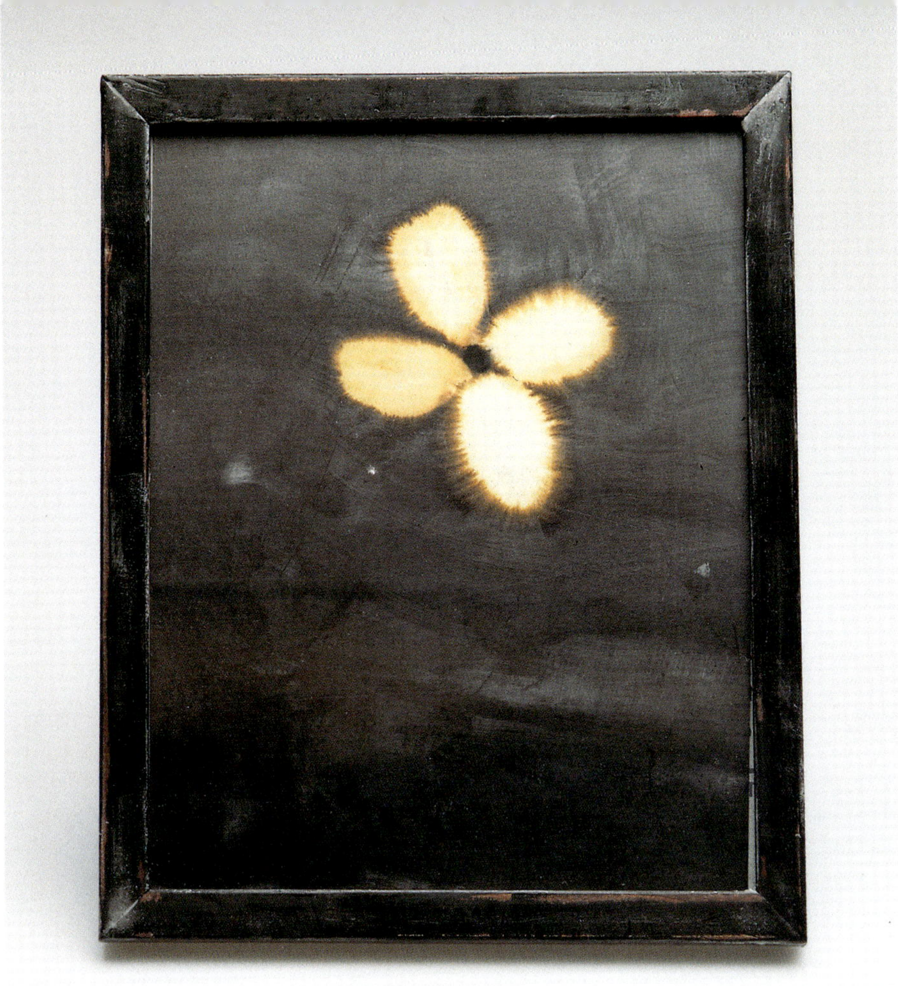

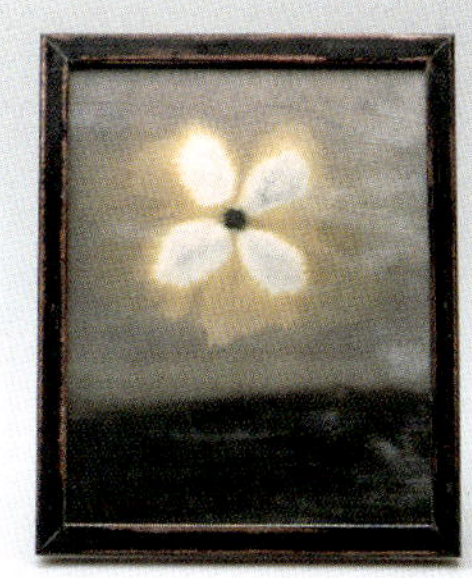
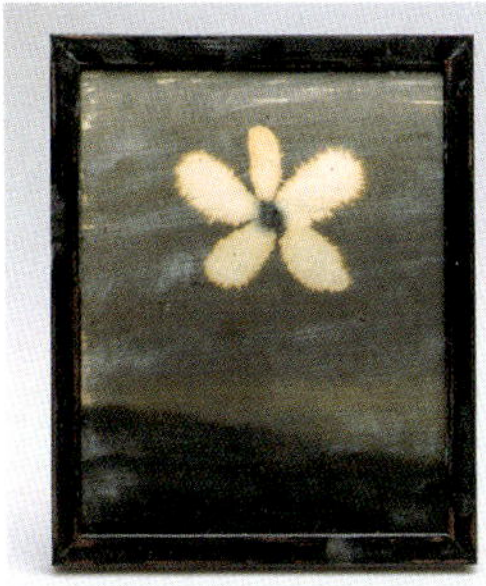
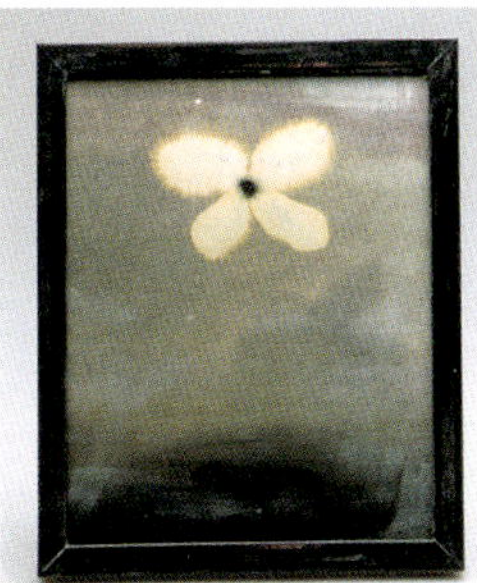

JOHN BOCK

Geometrischer Ort der 2 Mio. $
Knödelknickerbockermigräne-
hitshitbitssoufflévisage, drin
strohmulmige Isoquante touchiert
goldene Bilanzregel + Insolvenz-
snob, 2003

Unique underpants, knitted fabric,
gold sequins, straw, silicone,
bunny droppings, migraine pill,
Ed. 60/XX, signed and numbered
certificate

EDITION FOR PARKETT 67

Anti-Bunny Costume: the ideal get-up for
close combat, all-inclusive with headache
protection and the last straw.

"It is neither performance nor clearly installation,
neither sculpture nor solely slapstick happening,
neither film nor any known form of theater. Bock's work
is most likely a turbulent mixture of all of these—he
creates exuberant, extroverted, passionate, and often
forceful but always humorous and highly absurd pieces
of art. The range of Bock's artistic means is remarkably
diverse; in fact, it is impossible to pin him down at
all, since so much is ambiguous, cryptic, obscure,
enigmatic, and mysterious.—No matter how exhausted,
how worn out our world may appear, the artist confronts
us with an unstoppable avalanche of visual impressions
and artistic stunts, as if everything still remains to be
said, seen, or heard."

Jens Hoffmann
Parkett No. 67, 2003

ヨン・ボック

200万ドルの幾何学的空間。ジャガイモ団子
ニッカーボッカー頭痛とはスフレフェイス。麦
わら状等産出量曲線に内接する黄金会計規
定＋債務超過スノッブ　2003

一点もの下着、布地、金ラメ、麦わら、
シリコン、ウサギの糞、頭痛薬、
Ed. 60/XX、署名、番号入り証明書

パルケット・エディション 67

反バニーガール・コスチューム。接近戦に最適の身支度。
頭痛防止と辛抱の限界を超す藁一本までふくむ完全装
備。

パフォーマンスでもなければ、はっきりインスタレーションとも呼べず、
彫刻でもなければたんなるドタバタのハプニングでもなく、映画でもな
く、既存の演劇でもない。ボックの作品はこれらのすべてを混ぜ合わ
せて波瀾含み。威勢がよく、開けっ広げで、やる気満々、そしてしばしば
説得力にも富みながら、いつもユーモラスで、はなはだ不条理な作品を
手がける。ボックが創作に用いる手段は驚くほど多様で、実際のところ
あまりに曖昧、謎めいて、茫漠としており、不可解なうえ神秘的なので、
はっきりこうと言いきるのは不可能に近い。この世界がどれほど疲弊し、
くたびれ果てているように見えるとしても、いまでも言うべきこと、見
るべきもの、聞くべきものはいくらでもあると言わんばかりに、ボック
はしゃにむに視覚に強烈な刺激をあたえ、アーティストならではの離れ
業をやってのける。

イェンス・ホフマン
（パルケット 67号、2003年）

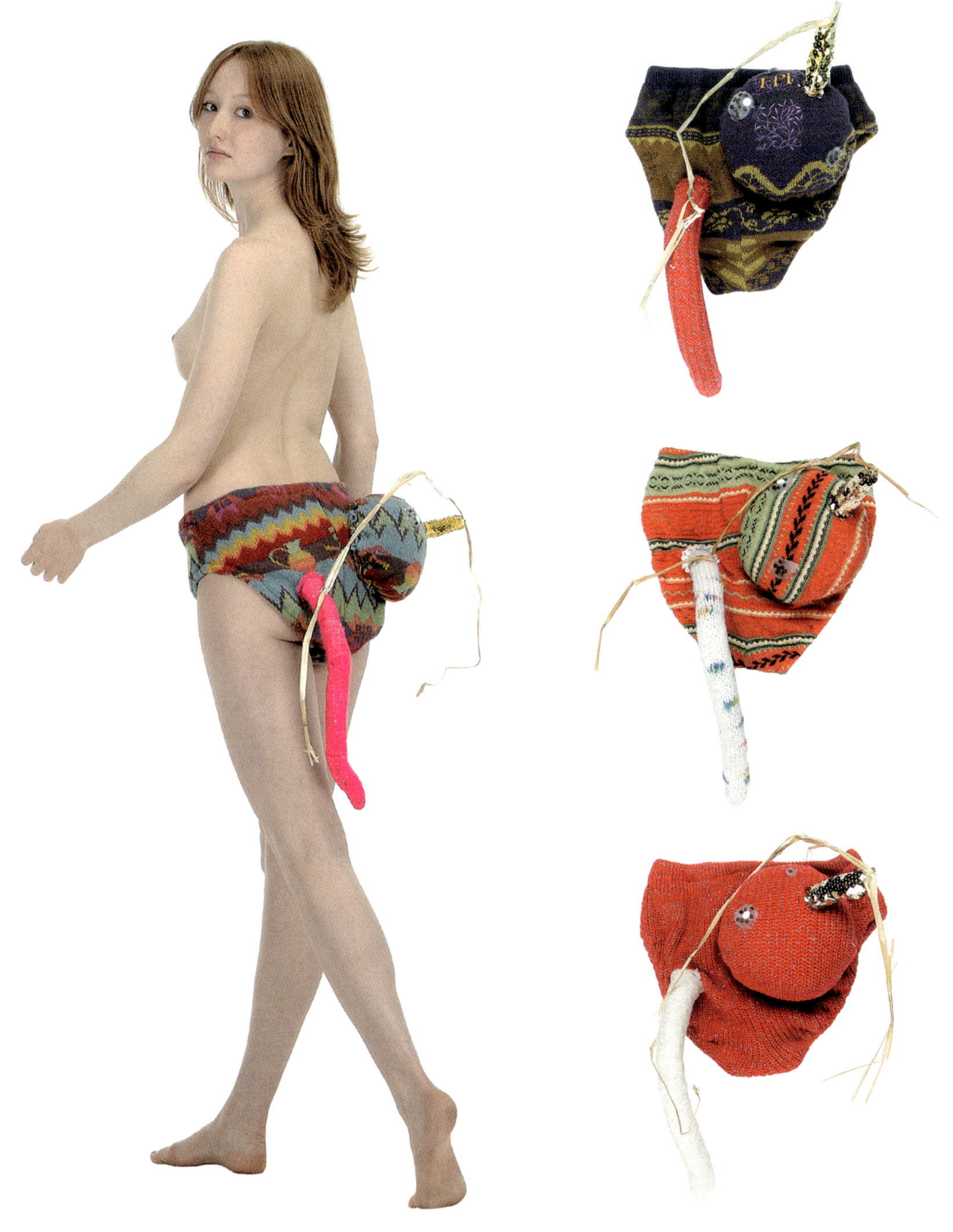

ALIGHIERO E BOETTI

Probing the Mysteries of a
Double Life, 1990

Collotype (Granolitho),
overpainted by hand in red,
19 ⁵/₈ x 27 ¹/₂" (49,8 x 69,8 cm),
printed by Lichtdruck AG,
Dielsdorf, Switzerland,
Ed. 100/XX, signed and numbered

EDITION FOR PARKETT 24

Double trouble. A perennial obsession with
dual identities and symmetry is manifested
in the systematic rendering of twin subjects
by two detectably different hands. A hand-
applied flash of vicious scarlet completes this
doubly complex Rorschach test.

"The works of Alighiero e Boetti open onto the world,
onto the fluid passage of forms; they capture chaos
without diminishing it, and one can always cross over
from one work into another, while maintaining the same
degree of precision, which demonstrates everything
with the facts. If there is a route, it is one that leads
where routes branch out, bifurcate and multiply. If there
is a key, it is a passe-partout that opens and at the
same time 'closes' every frame, every possible door."

Giovan Battista Salerno
Parkett No. 24, 1990

アリギエロ・ボエッティ

二重生活の秘密を探る　1990

コロタイプ（グラノリト）に手描きで赤を添える、
49.8×69.8cm、
制作：リヒトドリュック社（ディールスドルフ市、スイス）、
Ed. 100/XX、署名、番号入り

パルケット・エディション 24

非常に厄介。アイデンティティの二重性とシンメトリーに
対する長年の執着は、相違を見極められる2つの手によっ
て系統的に制作された一対の主題にも明らかに見て取れ
る。手で塗られた禍々しい緋色の線が、二重に複雑なロー
ルシャッハ・テストをしめくくる。

アリギエロ・ボエッティの作品は世界に向かい、流動的な形態の変転に
合流する。混沌を矮小化せずに捉え、ひとつの作品から別の作品へ乗
り移ることはつねに可能であり、しかもその間にも精度の高さは保た
れ、すべては事実の裏付けをともない提示される。通り道があるとすれ
ば、道が枝分かれして二叉になり、いくつにも分かれる地点へと導くだ
ろう。鍵があるとすれば、それはすべての枠組み、ありとあらゆる扉を
開けると同時に「閉ざす」親鍵にちがいない。

ジョーヴァン・バティースタ・サレルノ
（パルケット 24号、1990年）

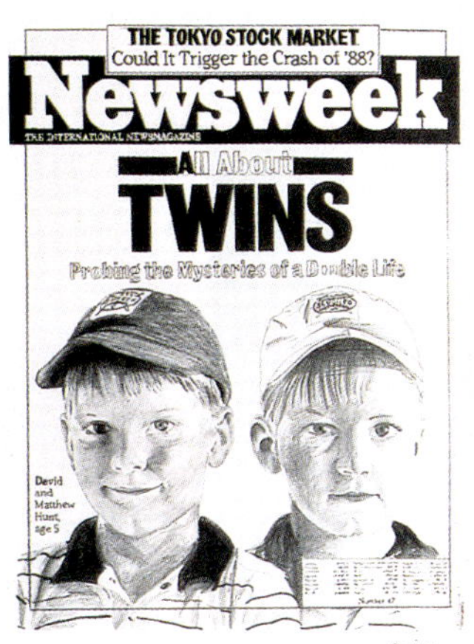

THE TOKYO STOCK MARKET
Could It Trigger the Crash of '88?
Newsweek
THE INTERNATIONAL NEWSMAGAZINE
All About
TWINS
Probing the Mysteries of a Double Life
David
and
Matthew
Hunt,
age 5

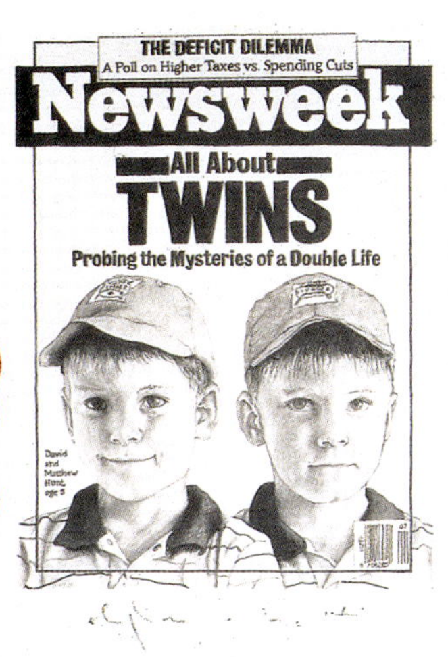

THE DEFICIT DILEMMA
A Poll on Higher Taxes vs. Spending Cuts
Newsweek
All About
TWINS
Probing the Mysteries of a Double Life
David
and
Matthew
Hunt,
age 5

CHRISTIAN BOLTANSKI

El Caso, 1989

Booklet with 17 photographs,
2 x 3 1/8" (5 x 8 x 0,6 cm),
Ed. 80/XX, signed and numbered

EDITION FOR PARKETT 22

Guilty not guilty. Themes central to Boltanski's
œuvre find devastating expression in this
tiny piece of pocket pornography containing
images of brutal murder rephotographed
by the artist from the Spanish detective
magazine El Caso.

"There is in the work of the artist something of the
high priest and something of the charlatan. Boltanski
transforms shards of nothing into art, bits of cardboard,
lumps of sugar, old photos, but plays the game of
showing us that his transformation is also mere
illusion, that this art is also the nothing or next to
nothing from which it has sprung."

Didier Semin
Parkett No. 22, 1989

クリスチャン・ボルタンスキー

『El Caso (事件)』　1989

17枚の写真入り小冊子、
5×8×0.6cm、
Ed. 80/XX、署名、番号入り

パルケット・エディション 22

有罪、無罪。ボルタンスキーが日頃から追求するテーマ
の核心が、このポケット版のポルノグラフィーにも、赤
裸々に表現される。写真はいずれもスペインの探偵小説
誌『El Caso』に掲載された残酷な殺人現場の様子を、
アーティスト自身が撮影しなおしたもの。

ボルタンスキーの作品は司祭長風でもあればほら吹き風でもある。
ボルタンスキーはボール紙の切れ端、砂糖のかたまり、古い写真など、
取るに足らないものの破片を芸術に変容させるが、その一方でこの
変容がじつは幻想にすぎず、アートは些細な起源と同じように些細か、
些細に近いことをわたしたちに判らせようと企む。

ディディエ・セミン
（パルケット 22号、1989年）

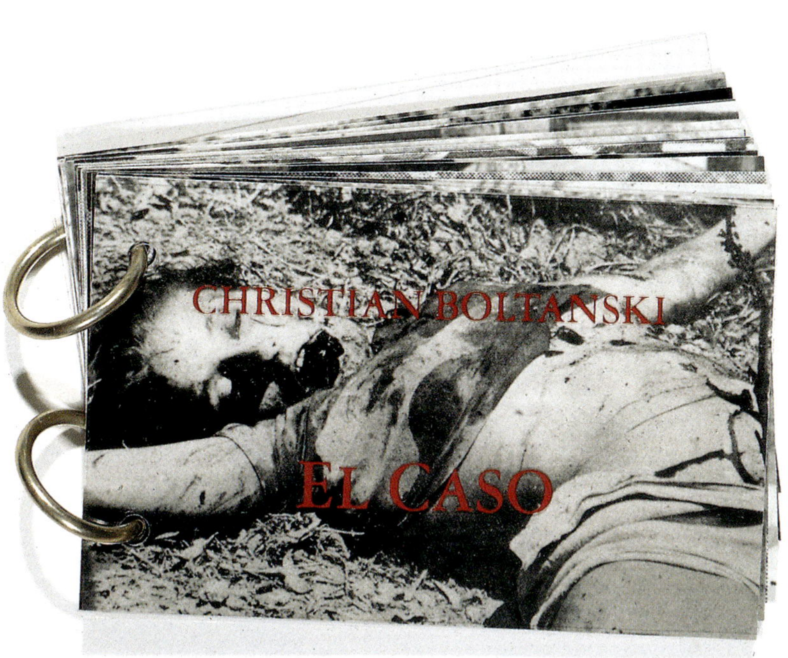

CHRISTIAN BOLTANSKI
EL CASO

MONICA BONVICINI

Drill 4 Chastity, 2004

2-part cast, bronze and resin,
4 1/8 x 5 7/8 x 3 1/2" (10,5 x 15 x 9 cm),
Ed. 35/XX, signed and numbered

EDITION FOR PARKETT 72

The eroticism of irreconcilable opposites united in the cool embrace of form and fetish.

"For Bonvicini titles are concrete, practical equivalents or absurd allegories. One way or another, language and built structures are positioned next to and on top of each other, abruptly engaging in blatant acts like the protagonists in a choreographed porn scenario. Fractured quotes and voiceless material mutually transform: it is as though words and sentences were materializing, developing a physical presence on the wall, in the dust, rigidified into fragmented letters; it is as though built structures were, in return, soaking up syntax and signification."

Jörg Heiser
Parkett No. 72, 2004

モニカ・ボンヴィチーニ

純潔をまもるための訓練　2004

ブロンズと合成樹脂を鋳造、
10.5×15×9cm、
Ed. 35/XX、署名、番号入り

パルケット・エディション 72

互いに相容れないエロティシズムが、フォルムとフェティッシュの冷めた抱擁により結ばれる。

ボンヴィチーニにとって作品のタイトルは具体的、有用で等しい価値を持つ物であるか、さもなければ不条理な寓話である。なにかしらのかたちで、言語と組み立てられた構築物は隣り合わせ、あるいは上下に重ねて置かれ、しっかり振り付けられたポルノ芝居の登場人物のように、いきなりあられもない演技にとりかかる。断片的な引用と声を奪われた素材が互いに変容する。それはあたかも単語と文が物質と化し、壁や埃のなかに物質としての存在感を形成するようにも、断片的な文字として硬直化するようでもあり、組み立てられた構築物はそれに応えて、語順と語義を吸収するようにも見える。

ヨルク・ハイザー
（パルケット 72号、2004年）

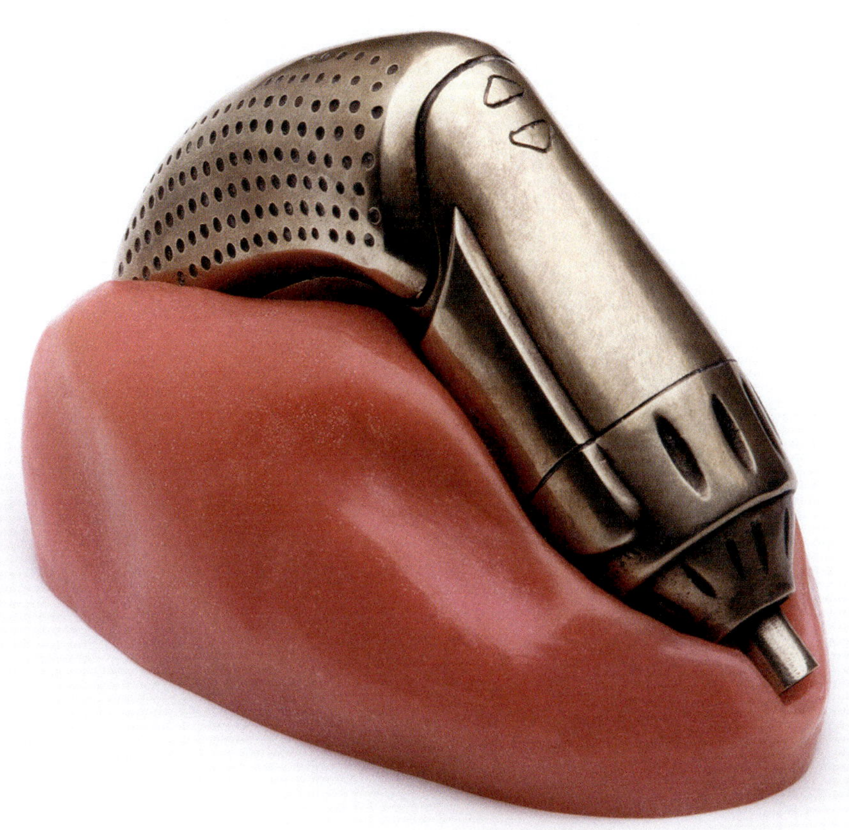

LOUISE BOURGEOIS

Reparation, 1991

Fabrication of printed and handcolored
paper, handtorn, pierced, and sewn
with thread, 10 x 8¼" (25,5 x 21 cm),
bound in the magazine,
Ed. 75/XX, signed and numbered

EDITION FOR PARKETT 27

A stitch in time. A patched and mended page
in a book fuses theory with biography—the
sculptor's approach to assemblage as a
reparative process and her origins as the
child of tapestry-restorers.

"[Under] the psychic conditions of production in which
Bourgeois works, the object is made for psychic use.
For Bourgeois, cathexis is often coupled with self-
representation, or more precisely, with a projection of
the self onto the object which becomes its substitute."

Mignon Nixon
Parkett No. 27, 1991

ルイーズ・ブルジョワ

修復　　1991

プリント、あるいは手彩色の紙を手でちぎり、
穴を開け、糸で縫い合わせて構成、
25.2×21cm、本誌に綴じこみ、
Ed. 75/XX、署名、番号入り

パルケット・エディション 27

遅れずに縫う。接ぎをあて、繕われ、本に綴じこまれた
ページに理論と生涯が溶け合う。アッサンブラージュを
修復の過程とみなすブルジョワの取り組みは、絨毯の修
復業を営む家庭に生まれた歴史をもうかがわせる。

創作にあたるブルジョワの心理状況をふまえ、オブジェは心理作用を
利用するために制作される。ブルジョワにとって、心的エネルギーが
特定の対象・人物・観念に結びつく作用は、しばしば自己表現、より正
確には、身代わりとなる対象への自己投影と一体化する。

ミニヨン・ニクソン
（パルケット 27号、1991年）

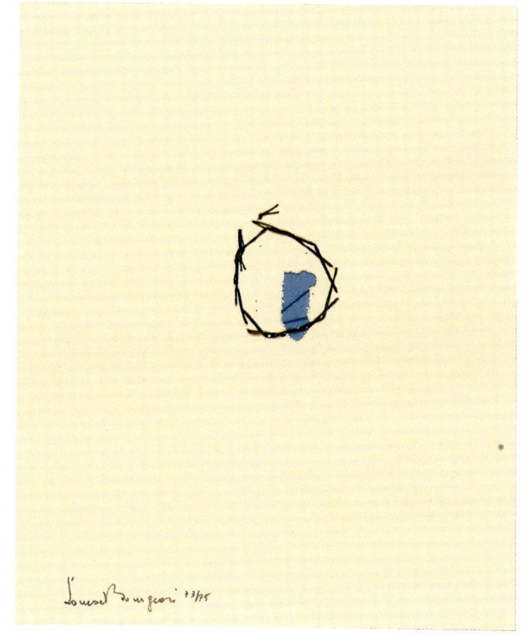

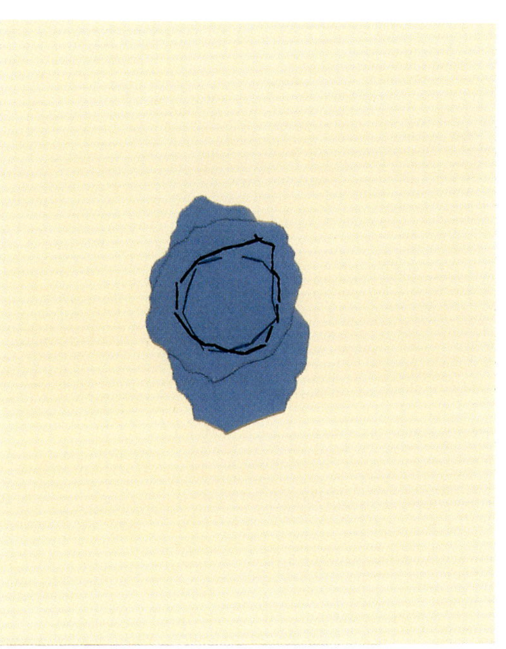

Front / 表

Back / 裏

LOUISE BOURGEOIS

The Maternal Man, 2008

Archival dyes printed on cloth,
10¹/₂ x 8" (26,6 x 20,3 cm),
LB stiched lower right, numbered lower left,
Ed. 33/XVII

EDITION FOR PARKETT 82

Mater-ializing the father.

"The artist follows its indirectly registered whims with a steadfast fidelity that is, perhaps, the source of the remarkable potency of Louise Bourgeois's always-surprising and even shocking visual inventiveness. She does not draw the world, but pictures the imagos of our psychic life."

Griselda Pollock
Parkett No. 82, 2008

ルイーズ・ブルジョワ

母方の男　2008

布に保存性の高い染料でプリント、
26.6×20.3cm、
右下にLB、左に番号を刺繍、
Ed. 33/XVII

パルケット・エディション 82

父親を（母／物）質化する

ブルジョワは遠回しに表された気まぐれに、ゆるぎない忠実さをもって追従するが、それこそがたえずひとの意表をつき、衝撃さえあたえるルイーズ・ブルジョワの独創的な視覚性の、めざましい効能の源泉なのかもしれない。ブルジョワは世界を描くのではなく、わたしたちの心理生活のイマーゴを絵画化する。

グリゼルダ・ポロック
（パルケット 82号、2008年）

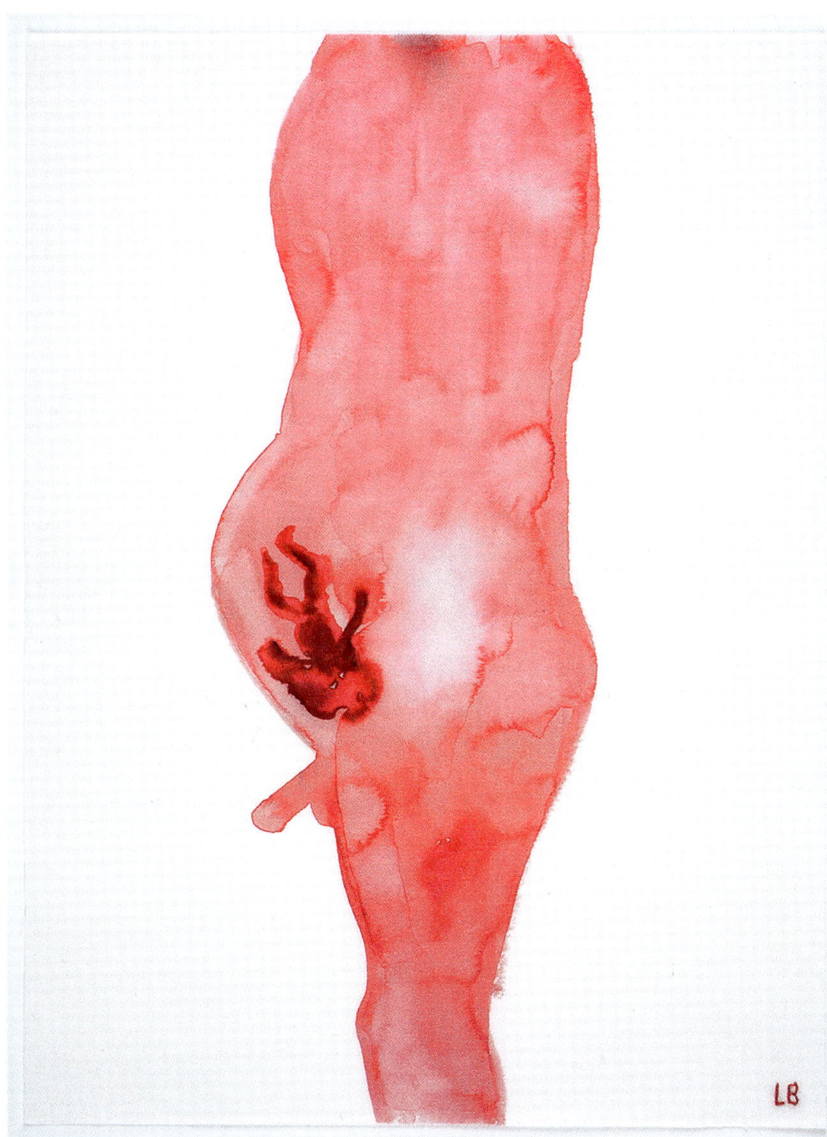

CAROLE BOVE

Untitled, 2009

Brass, mixed media, each work unique,
Brass frame: 8 $^5/_8$ x 3 $^1/_8$ x 3" (22 x 8 x 7,5 cm),
Object: approx. 2 $^3/_8$ x 1 $^1/_4$ x 11 $^7/_8$"
(6 x 3 x 30 cm),
Ed. 35/XX, signed and numbered
certificate

EDITION FOR PARKETT 86

Caught or liberated within the space of geometry?

"In the shelf-based arrangements of books and objects that became an early trademark of hers, and which she continues to produce, Bove combines a diversity of evidences that virtually release the perfumes of earlier eras—with the sixties at their center—and lets them commingle allusively."

Martin Herbert
Parkett 86, 2009

キャロル・ボウヴェ

無題　2009

真鍮、ミクスト・メディア、ふたつ同じものはない、
真鍮製枠組：22×8×7.5cm、
オブジェ：約6×3×30cm、
Ed. 35/XX、署名、番号入り証明書

パルケット・エディション 86

幾何学空間の中に、捕われたのか、解き放たれたのか？

初期のトレードマークとなり、現在も継続中の書棚に本と様々なオブジェを配置する作品に、ボウヴェは1960年代を中心に過去の芳香漂う多様な名残を組合せ、仄かな交わりを促す。

マーティン・ハーバート
（パルケット86号、2009年）

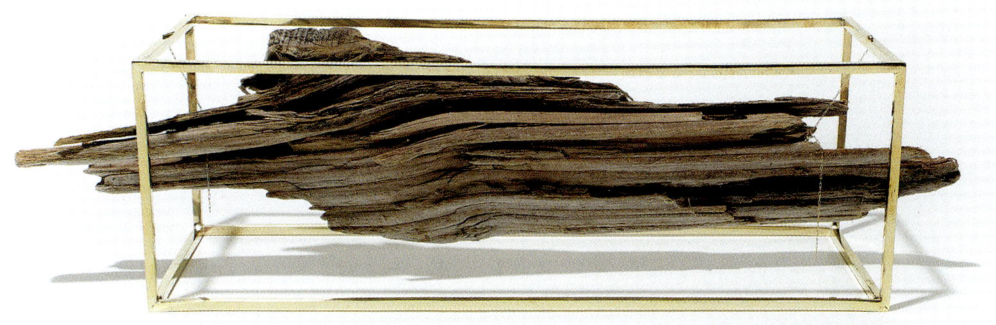

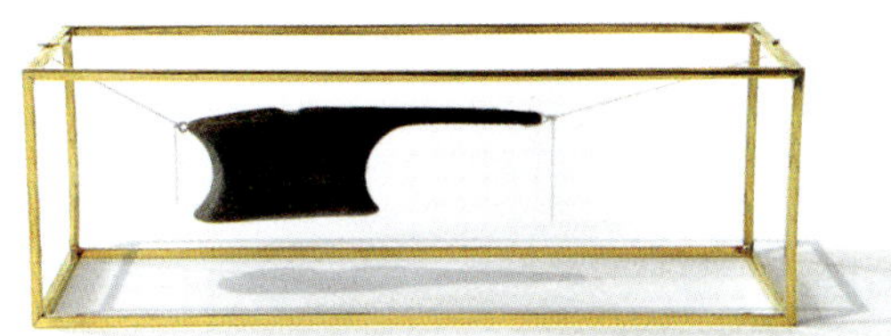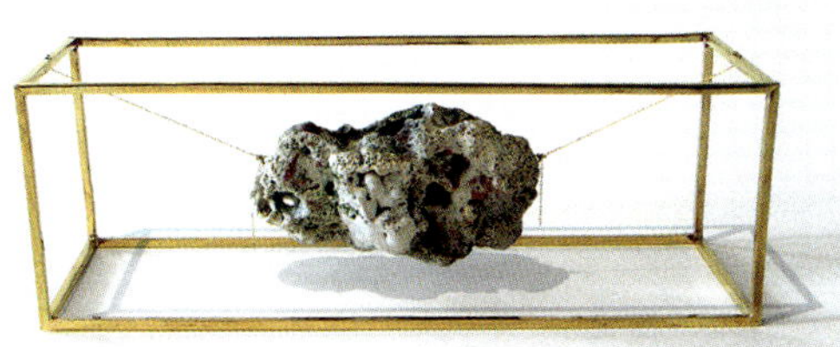

OLAF BREUNING

Lemon Pig, 2004

Styrofoam, ca. 9 $\frac{7}{8}$ x 9 x 12 $\frac{1}{8}$"
(25 x 23 x 31 cm),
Ed. 60/XX, signed and numbered

EDITION FOR PARKETT 71

A hiking viking in full armor boldly beats around the bush and braves the onslaught of the new millennium.

"The subject matter is of little importance, and ultimately, what is on view matters just a little. It is always the same story: all images are of equal value, all scenarios are possible. Breuning's motto encapsulates it: 'Whatever.' His works are extraordinary catalysts for interpretation, powerful scenario-machines, intriguing and visually fascinating tableaux, but at the end of the tunnel, the message is clear and unequivocal: 'Whatever.'"

Marc-Olivier Wahler
Parkett No. 71, 2004

オラフ・ブルーニング
レモンの豚　2004

発泡スチロール、
約25×23×31cm、
Ed. 60/XX、署名、番号入り

パルケット・エディション 71

防具も怠りなくハイキングに出かけたバイキングは大胆に藪を叩いて獲物を追い立て、新たな千年紀の到来に平然とたちむかう。

主題は結局のところほとんど重要ではなく、つきつめれば、目に見えるものにさほどの意義はない。何時も同じ話のくりかえし、イメージの価値はすべて等しく、あらゆるシナリオが成立しうる。ブルーニングのモットー「何でもござれ」はそれを要約したもの。作品は様々な解釈をひきだす素晴らしい触媒であり、強力なシナリオ製造機、視覚を魅了し、興味をそそるタブローでもあるけれども、最終的なメッセージは明快、そして誤解の余地がない。つまり、「何でもござれ」

マール＝オリヴィエ・ワーラー
（パルケット 71号、2004年）

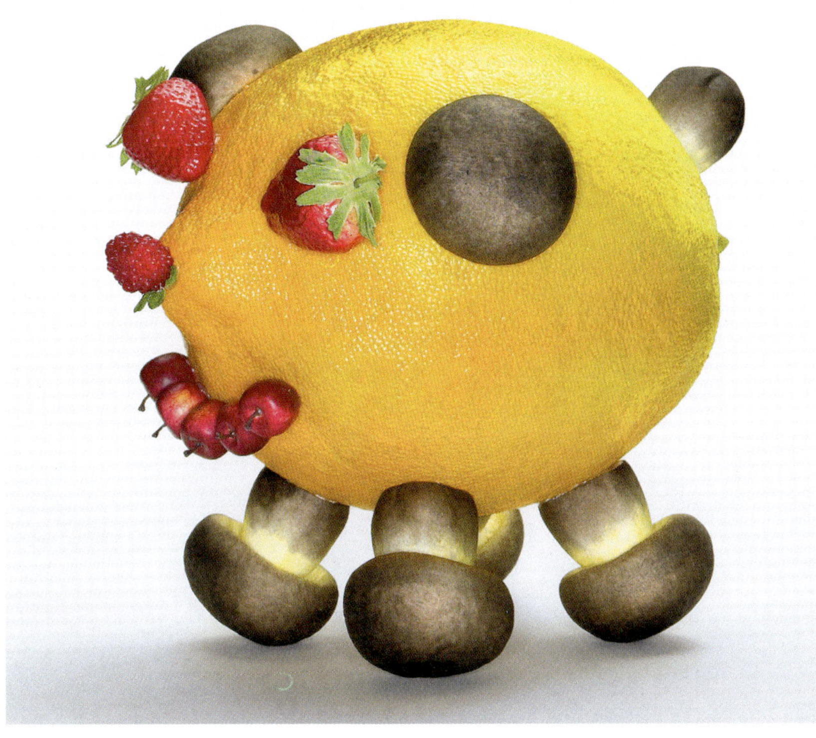

GLENN BROWN

Disorder, 2005

Digital print on archival paper,
surface mounted on Plexiglas,
paper size 32 $\frac{5}{8}$ x 25 $\frac{1}{2}$" (83 x 65 cm),
image 28 $\frac{3}{8}$ x 21 $\frac{5}{8}$" (72 x 55 cm),
Ed. 55/XXV, signed and numbered

EDITION FOR PARKETT 75

Thus is her cheek the map of days outworn when beauty lived and died as flowers do.

"A fresh and filthy flower, a flourish stilled; a streched torso, a face built from air. Details—a sickly eye, a boneless hand, a bloated toe—repel and attract with the confusion of a vicious joke turned tender. Every one of Brown's elegant arrangements of paint is an idea leavened with humor; greatness is simultaneously punctured and paid homage to. Such a mix of hyper-reality (the kind of reality that can only exist on canvas) and illusion can be disorienting; it is difficult to grasp that such complication is simply pigment painstakingly applied to a canvas with small brushes."

Jennifer Higgie
Parkett No. 75, 2005

グレン・ブラウン

混乱　2005

中性紙にデジタル・プリント、
アクリルにマウント、
紙：83×65cm、
図柄：72×55cm、
Ed. 55/XXV、署名、番号入り

パルケット・エディション 75

かくしてその女の頬は、美が花のように生きて死ぬとき、用済みの日々の地図となる。

清々しく薄汚れた花、開花は押し止められる。背筋を伸ばすトルソ、空気でこしらえた顔。病人のような目、骨のない手、腫れた爪先は、悪辣な冗談が穏健に変わる混乱に乗じ、反発を買いながら、興味をひきつける。ブラウンの優雅な絵具の配置はすべて、ユーモアを添えて変容させた思想にほかならない。偉大さは台無しにされると同時に、尊重もされる。ハイパーリアリティ（カンヴァス上にしか存在しえない現実）と幻覚のとりあわせは、分別を奪う。そうした混沌が、カンヴァスに小さな筆で塗られた顔料にすぎないと見抜くのは容易でない。

ジェニファー・ヒギー
（パルケット 75号、2005年）

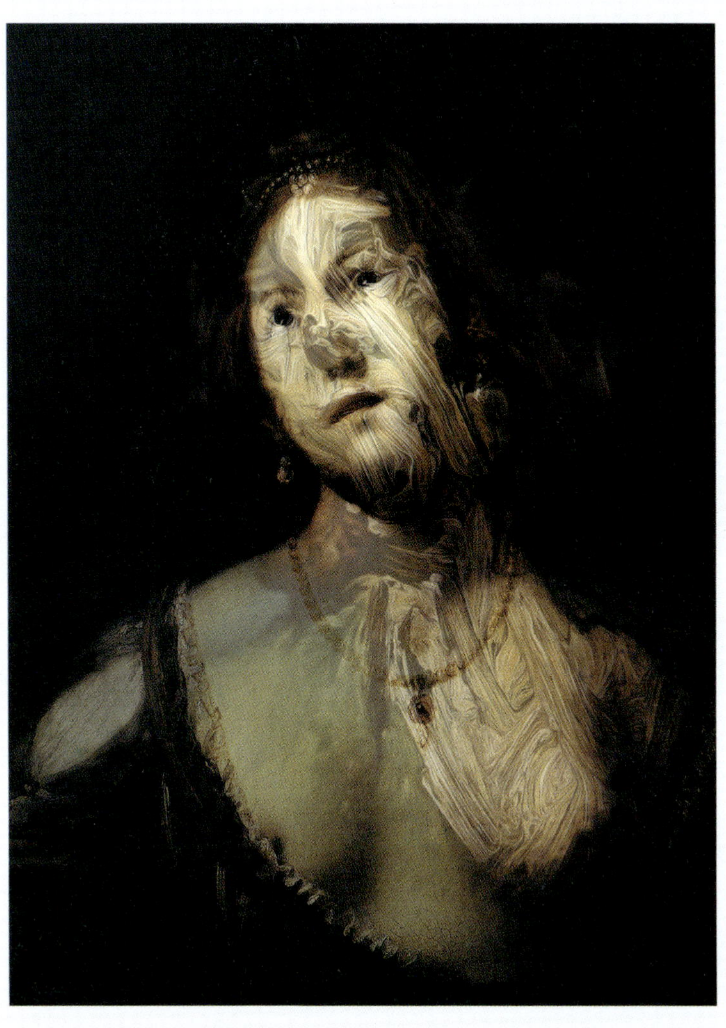

ANGELA BULLOCH

Horizontal Technicolour:
Stills with Negative Space, 2002

C-print,
sheet: 12 $^3/_{16}$ x 46" (30,9 x 116,6 cm),
image: 8 $^7/_{16}$ x 42 $^7/_{16}$" (21,5 x 107,8 cm),
printed by Philippe Laumont, Laumont
Editions, New York,
Ed. 80/XX, signed and numbered

EDITION FOR PARKETT 66

Mosaic of light: a composition culled
from the vast potential of untold shades
of color.

"Angela Bulloch's work is based on activating the
dynamics of [the] relationship between technical
possibility and cultural space of perception...
the presentation always takes the shape of a mix,
contains shifts in size and speed, and can therefore
never be reduced to one single interpretation."

Martin Prinzhorn
Parkett No. 66, 2002

アンジェラ・ブロック

水平のテクニカラー
負の空間のあるスチール写真　2002

カラー写真、
紙：30.9×116.6cm、
図柄：21.5×107.8cm、
プリント制作：
フィリップ・ローモン・エディションズ（ニューヨーク）、
Ed. 80/XX 、署名、番号入り

パルケット・エディション 66

光線のモザイク。色彩の未知、そして無尽蔵の潜在
力から選り抜いた作品

アンジェラ・ブロックの作品は、技術的な可能性と感覚に存す
る文化空間のダイナミックな関係性を活性化するところから始
まる．．．表現はつねに混合物であり、サイズと速度の変化を内
包するため、単一の解釈に還元されることは決してない。

マルティン・プリンツホーン
（パルケット 66号、2002年）

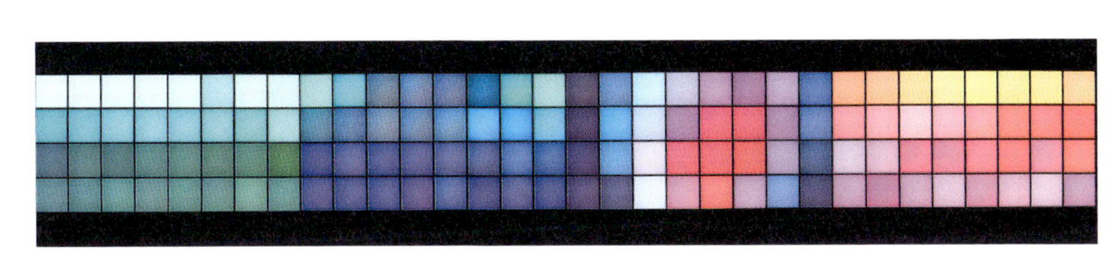

DANIEL BUREN

Unique Tablecloth with Laser-Cut Lace (Object to Be Situated on Table), 2002

Two-layered tablecloth:
off-white laser-cut design on monochrome underlayer, each tablecloth has a unique combination of design and color,
top layer: 70 $\frac{7}{8}$ x 70 $\frac{7}{8}$" (180 x 180 cm),
bottom layer: 67 x 67" (170 x 170 cm),
design: 30 $\frac{11}{16}$ x 30 $\frac{11}{16}$" (78 x 78 cm),
width of stripes: 3 $\frac{11}{16}$" (8,7 cm),
washable polyester, laser-cut and produced by Jakob Schläpfer AG, St. Gallen,
Ed. 78/XXIV, unique versions (design versions 1A–3A: 13 each on different colors, diagonal design versions 1B–3B: 13 each on different colors), numbered certificate

EDITION FOR PARKETT 66

Clarity of form and state-of-the-art technology conjure the baroque splendor of handmade lace.

"Buren's work is rooted in the artist's initial search for ways to strip painting of illusionistic and expressive reference as per his decision in 1965 to reduce the pictorial content of his canvases to the repetition of mechanically printed, alternating white and colored vertical bands 8.7 centimeters in width painted white on its outer stripes... Grounding his works in the real without espousing the grandiose or impositional, he has constantly sought to express the idea of the unfettered nature of aesthetic experience that (as he has demonstrated) may be proffered to spectators in relation to the temporal and spatial reality of architecture and its institutional affiliations."

Anne Rorimer
Parkett No. 66, 2002

ダニエル・ビュレン

レーザーカットによるレースの一点物テーブルクロス（テーブルに掛けること）　2002

2層のテーブルクロス。オフ・ホワイトのデザインをレーザーカットし無地の下層に重ねた、デザインと色彩の組み合わせにひとつとして同じものはない、
上層：180×180cm、下層：170×170cm、
柄：78×78cm、縞の幅：8.7cm、洗えるポリエステル、レーザーカットと制作：ヤーコブ・シュレップファー社（ザンクト・ガレン市、スイス）、
Ed. 78/XXIV、デザインは個々に異なる
（3種のデザイン：1A-3A、色違い13点、3種の対角線デザイン：1B-3B、色違い13点）、番号入り証明書

パルケット・エディション 66

フォルムの明瞭さと最先端技術が描き出す手作りレースのバロック的壮麗さ

ビュレンの作品は、カンヴァスに描く絵の内容を機械的にプリントした白ともう一色の幅8.7cm のストライプに限定するという1965年の決断にしたがい、絵画から目の錯覚、他者との関連の表現を排除する方法を探る当初の企図をふまえている。作品を現実に根づかせながら、大仰さやおしつけがましさに陥ることなく、つねに美的体験の自由を表現しようと試みるが、鑑賞者には（ビュレンがこれまでに見せてくれたように）、建築物の時間的、空間的現実、それが果たす機能と関連して提示されることもあるだろう。

アン・ロリマー
（パルケット 66号、2002年）

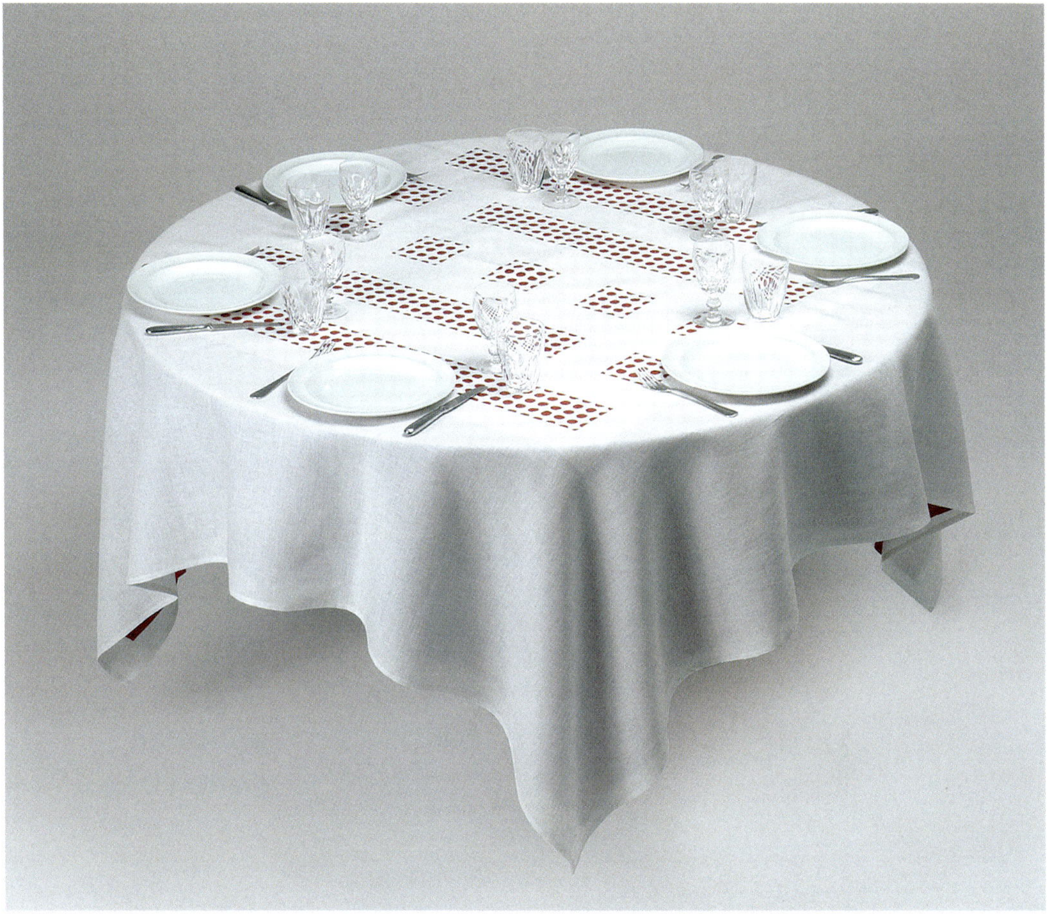

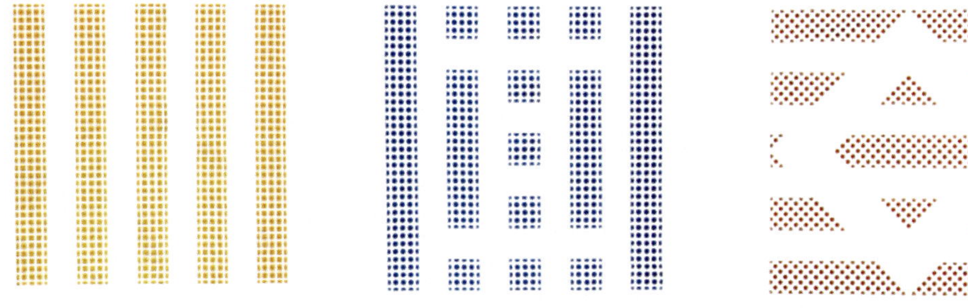

SOPHIE CALLE

The Tie, 1993

Pure silk crêpe-de-chine man's tie,
printed with an autobiographical story,
56 $^5/_8$ x 3 $^3/_8$" (70,7 x 21,2 cm),
produced by Fabric Frontline, Zurich,
Ed. 150/LX, signed and numbered

EDITION FOR PARKETT 36

Autobiographical story. A silken tie not only represents the first episode of a story in which a number of tasteful articles of clothing are sent to a badly dressed but attractive man; it also becomes the page on which the story itself is told.

"Like a sculptor of a past century, Sophie Calle in her art manipulates and reconfigures a commodity central to the economy of her time. This commodity does not happen to be bronze or marble, however, but information, the elusive stuff that circulates constantly between consciousness, document and cyberspace."

Luc Sante
Parkett No. 36, 1993

ソフィ・カル

ネクタイ　1993

絹100％クレープ・デシン、
男性用ネクタイ、
自身の体験にもとづく物語を印刷、
70.7×21.2cm、
制作：ファブリック・フロントライン社（チューリヒ）、
Ed. 150/LX、署名、番号入り

パルケット・エディション 36

自身の体験にもとづく物語。絹のネクタイは、男前なのに服の選び方が拙い男性に、趣味の良い衣服の数々を送り届ける物語の第1話を象徴するばかりでなく、物語そのものが綴られるページにもなる。

前世紀の彫刻家と同じく、ソフィ・カルの作品では彼女の生きる時代の経済を支える物資が操作され、再構成される。ただしこの物資はブロンズでもなければ大理石でもなく、情報、つまり意識、記録、電脳空間の狭間を滞ることなく巡回するとらえどころのないものである。

リュック・サント
（パルケット 36号、1993年）

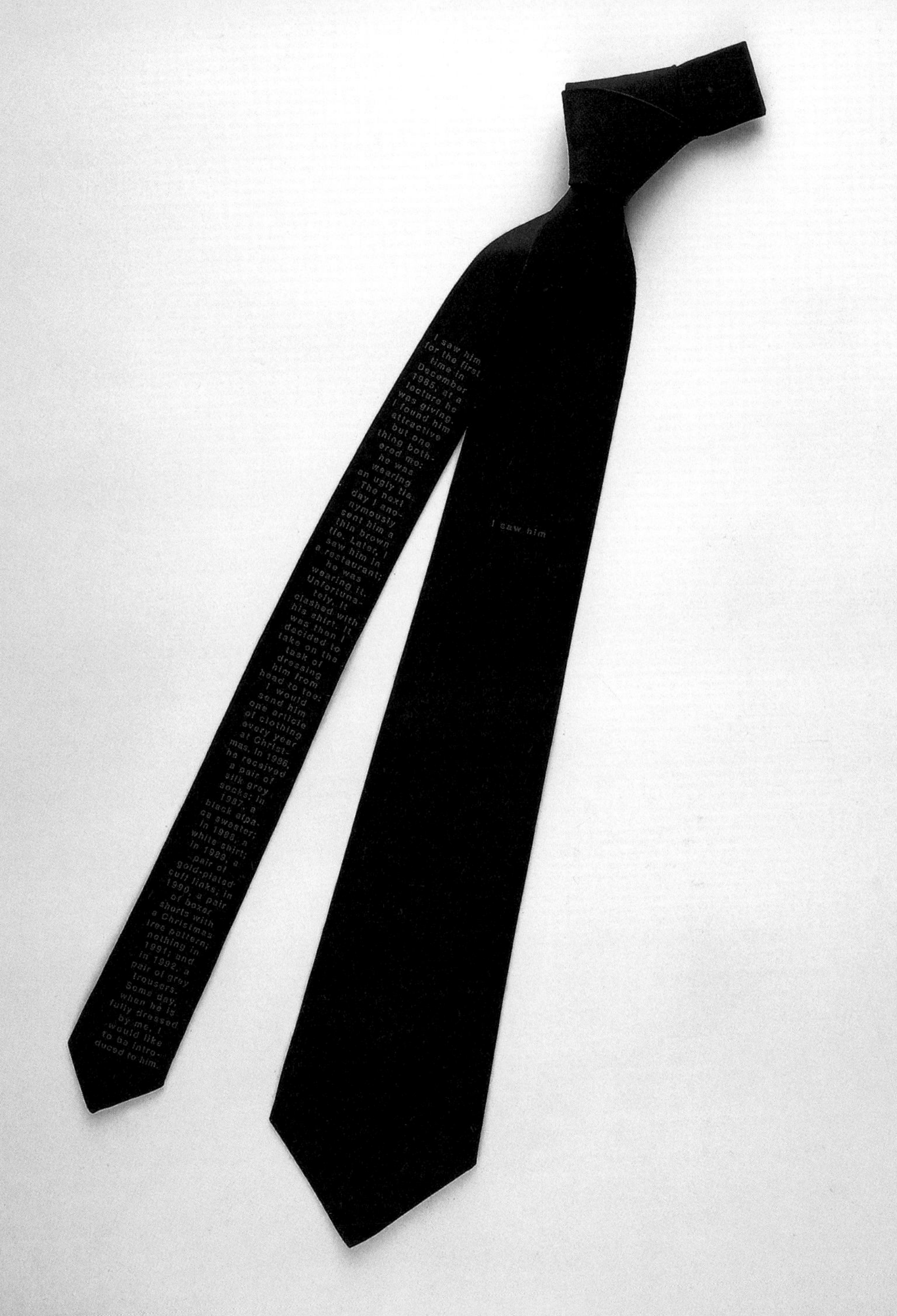

I saw him for the first time in December 1985, at a lecture he was giving. I found him attractive but one thing bothered me: he was wearing an ugly tie. The next day I anonymously sent him a thin brown tie. Later, I saw him in a restaurant; he was wearing it. Unfortunately, it clashed with his shirt. It was then I decided to take on the task of dressing him from head to toe: I would send him one article of clothing every year at Christmas. In 1986, he received a pair of silk grey socks; in 1987, a black alpaca sweater; in 1988, a white shirt; in 1989, a pair of gold-plated cuff links; in 1990, a pair of boxer shorts with a Christmas tree pattern; nothing in 1991; and in 1992, a pair of grey trousers. Some day, when he is fully dressed by me, I would like to be introduced to him.
I saw him

MAURIZIO CATTELAN

Untitled, 2000

Black-and-white photograph,
digital print on paper (Uso Mano)
16¼ x 13" (41,3 x 33 cm),
image size: 12 x 9½" (30,5 x 24 cm),
photo by Armin Linke,
Ed. 60/XXII, signed and numbered
certificate

EDITION FOR PARKETT 59

Gag or muzzle? Present-day sirens live dangerously.

"Cattelan, for his part, directs the forms he
manipulates towards conflict and comedy; through
works of the most embarrassing, constraining
and cumbersome sort he seeks conflicts with the
administrators of the art system. In a word, his conduct
as an artist consists of orienting the forms
he manipulates towards delinquency."

Nicolas Bourriaud
Parkett No. 59, 2000

マウリツィオ・カテラン
無題　2000

モノクロ写真、
紙にデジタル・プリント (Uso Mano)：
41.3×33cm、
図柄：30.5×24cm、
写真撮影：アーミン・リンケ、
Ed. 60/XXII、署名、番号入り証明書

パルケット・エディション 59

猿ぐつわか口輪か。現代のローレライの暮らしは危険と
背中合わせ。

カテランはフォルムを操作して諍いとユーモアをめざす。厄介で息苦
しく、始末に負えない質の作品を通じて、体制化した美術界の管理者
と揉め事を起こそうとする。一言でいえば、アーティストとしてのカテ
ランの振る舞いは、操作するフォルムを非行に追いやることから成り
立つ。

ニコラス・ブーリオ
（パルケット 59号、2000年）

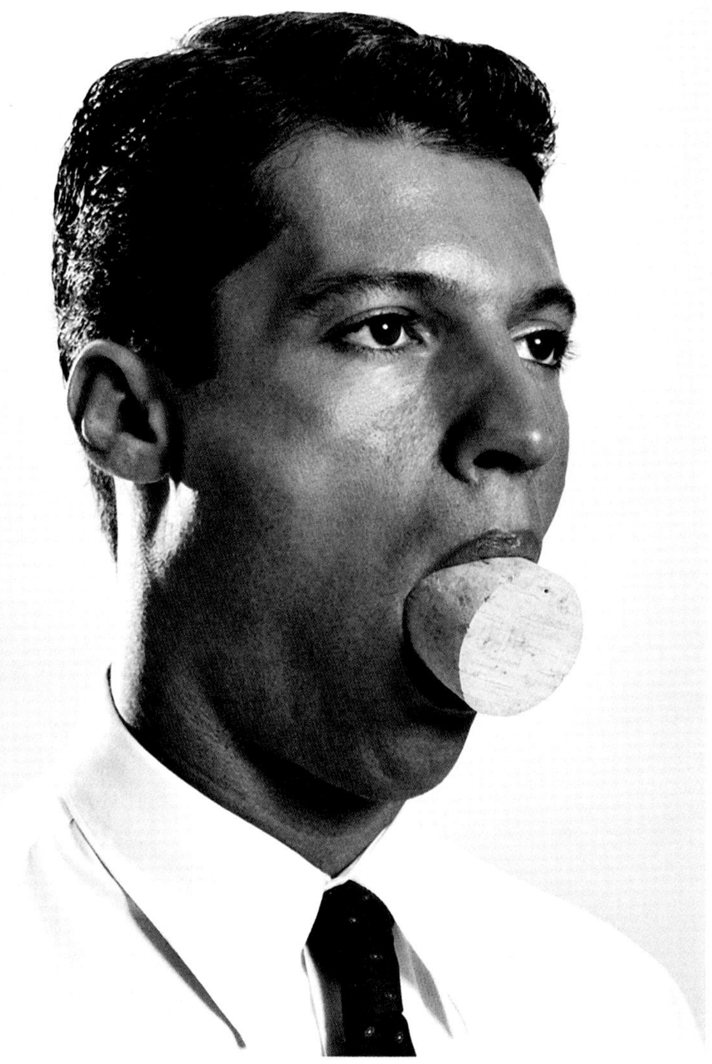

VIJA CELMINS

Untitled, 1995

Mezzotint (manière noire),
image size: 5 x 5 1/8" (12,6 x 13 cm),
on Rives, paper size: 16 7/8 x 14"
(40,6 x 35,5 cm), printed by Simmelink/
Sukimoto Editions, Los Angeles,
Ed. 60/XXV, signed and numbered

EDITION FOR PARKETT 44

The limits of infinity. The vast skyscape of an astronomical constellation plays host to an artist's acute discernment of surface and perspective.

"Vija Celmins's mature work is a repeated image of uninhabitability, without foothold or air. It depicts space liquefied or rarefied, and further carbonized in the rendering. It is a space of drowning or asphyxiation, and, though without fantasy's comforts, of dreams."

Nancy Princenthal
Parkett No. 44, 1995

ヴィヤ・セルミンス

無題　1995

メゾチント、図柄：12.6×13cm、
リヴ紙：40.5×35.5cm、
刷り：シマーリンク／
スキモト・エディションズ（ロサンゼルス）、
Ed. 60/XXV、署名、番号入り

パルケット・エディション 44

無限の限界。宇宙の星座またたく広大な空景を舞台に、表面と遠近に向かうセルミンスの鋭敏な感覚が羽ばたく。

円熟期を迎えたセルミンスの手がける作品は、足場もなく空気もない、人の住めない状況をくりかえし映像化する。そこには液状化、あるいは希薄化された空間が、制作過程でさらに炭化作用をうけ、描写される。空間は溺れ、窒息する場となりながら、幻想の癒しを保つ夢の場でもある。

ナンシー・プリンセンソール
（パルケット 44号、1995年）

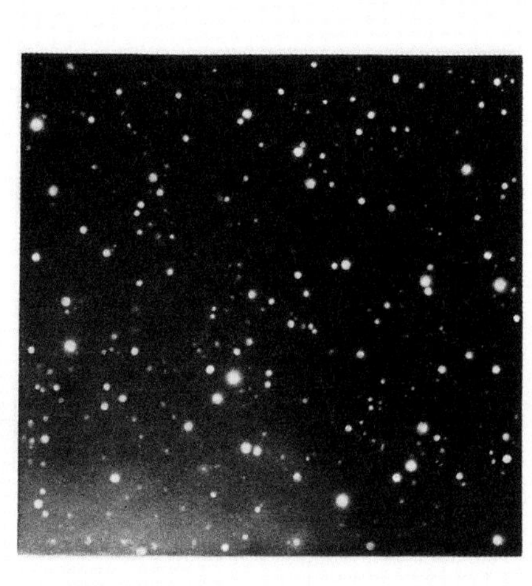

FRANCESCO CLEMENTE

Reconciliation, 1986

Drypoint etching
on Somerset Satin,
bound in the magazine,
10 x 16¹/₂" (25,5 x 42 cm),
printed by Jennifer Melby, New York,
Ed. 100/XV, signed and numbered

EDITION FOR PARKETT 9

Bestiary. Almost disarming in their linear simplicity, these figures function like a hermetic text in which the secrets of the universe can be contained in a few elemental forms.

"The intensity of Francesco Clemente's art is one that is never divorced from the flux of surfaces, from worldliness and its signs, from individuality and its ill-defined limits, and from the excess of action. Clemente participates not in the 'anxiety of influence,' but what may be justly called the joys of influence, a willingness to accept secondariness or 'belatedness' without pedantry or populism."

David Shapiro
Parkett No. 9, 1986

フランチェスコ・クレメンテ

和解　1986

ドライポイント、サマーセット・サテン、
本誌に綴じこみ、
25.5×42cm、
刷り：ジェニファー・メルビィ（ニューヨーク）、
Ed. 100/XV、署名、番号入り

パルケット・エディション 9

動物寓話集。線描の素朴さにおもわず肩の力が抜けそうになるが、ここに描かれたものたちは宇宙の神秘を一握りの単純な形状にこめ、秘教の経文として機能する。

フランチェスコ・クレメンテの芸術の強みは、絵画面の流麗さ、世俗性とその象徴、独特の個性と曖昧な境界、行き過ぎた行為と決して袂を分かたないところにあるのだろう。クレメンテは「影響を恐れる」のではなく、おそらく影響を受けることを歓び、衒学者ぶらず、大衆におもねることもなく、二度目であること、あるいは「おくればせ」を進んで受け入れる。

デイヴィッド・シャピロ
（パルケット 9号、1986年）

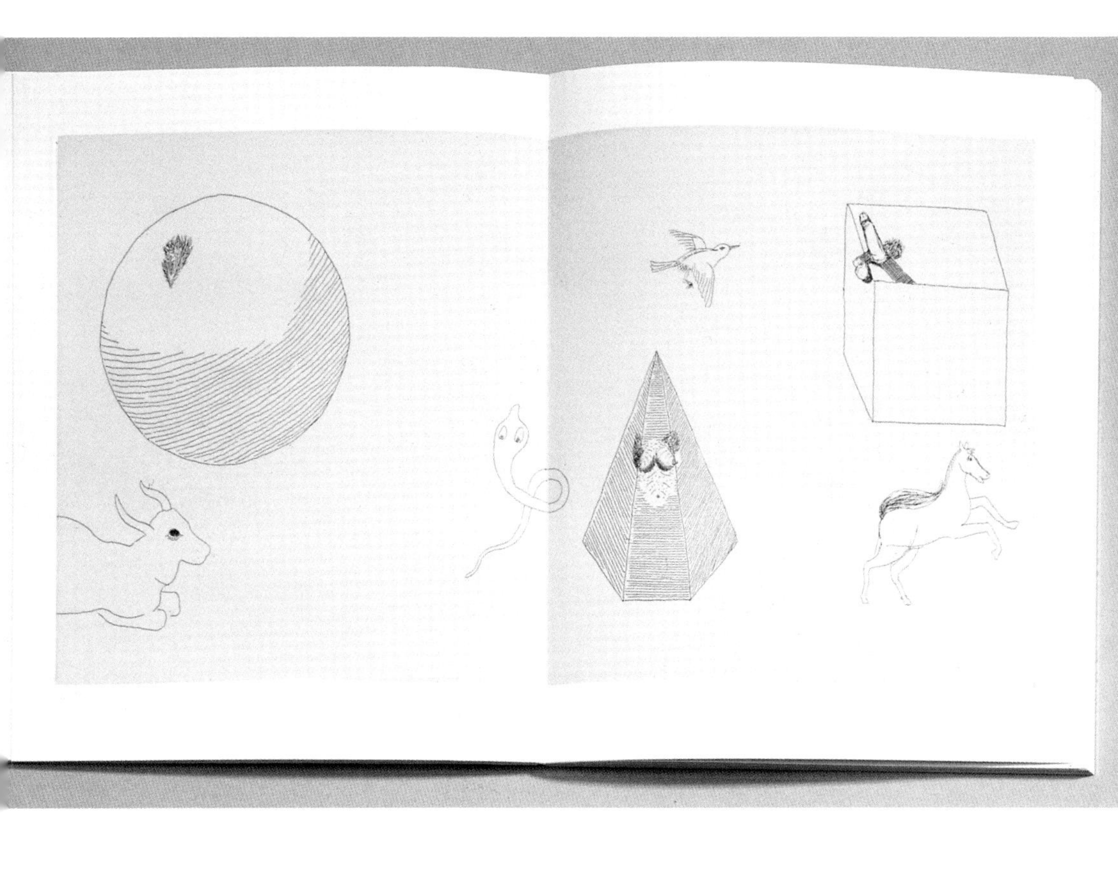

FRANCESCO CLEMENTE

Sorrow, 1994

Photo-etching,
printed by Peter Kneubühler, Zurich,
on handmade vellum paper,
11 $^4/_8$ x 8 $^1/_8$" (29,8 x 21 cm),
Ed. 60/XX, signed and numbered

EDITION FOR PARKETT 40/41

Balancing act. A whimsical lyricism
counterweighted by an aura of impossibility
haunts these simple figures.

"Is Clemente's art about the unsolid, about flux? An art
that doesn't want to linger, to revise, to build up, work
through? He seems to be moving from one picture to
the next without stopping; you are watching them the
same way, taking them in like a scent…"

Holland Cotter
Parkett No. 40/41, 1994

フランチェスコ・クレメンテ

かなしみ　1994

フォト・エッチング、手作りの模造皮紙、
29.8×21cm、
刷り：ペーター・クノイビューラー（チューリヒ）、
Ed. 60/XX、署名、番号入り

パルケット・エディション 40/41

バランスをとる。さりげない図柄に、気まぐれな叙情を
打ち消しそうな、ありそうもない気配がつきまとう。

クレメンテの芸術は形の定かでないもの、流動性に関わるのだろ
うか。立ちどまるのも、見返すのも、積み上げるのも、やり抜くの
も、気が進まないのだろうか。クレメンテはひとつの絵から次の
絵に、滞ることなく進んでゆくようにみえる。ひともまた同じように
絵をみつめ、まるで香りのように、それをうけとめる……

ホランド・コッター
　（パルケット 40/41号、1994年）

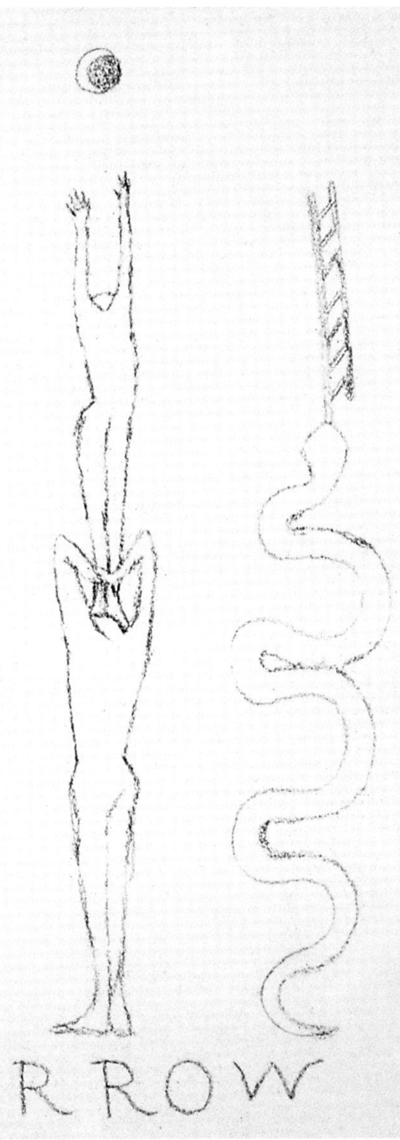
SORROW

CHUCK CLOSE

Self-Portrait, 2000

Digital ink-jet print of a daguerreotype
original on Crane Muséo paper,
printed by Adamson Editions,
Washington D.C., 22 x 17" (56 x 43 cm),
image size: 15$\frac{1}{2}$ x 12" (39,5 x 30, 4 cm),
Ed. 70/XXX, signed and numbered

EDITION FOR PARKETT 60

The artist's face afloat and yet immersed in the skin-deep confines of Daguerre's space.

"When I make someone flat I can remember that
image. I have an almost photographic memory for flat
things. Also, I'm really overwhelmed by the problem
of the whole: By breaking it down into these little
bite-size decisions, by not thinking about a face,
just a chunk, I'm not worried about what it's going to
end up as."

Chuck Close in conversation with Elizabeth Peyton
Parkett No. 60, 2000

チャック・クロース

自画像　2000

ダゲレオタイプの写真にもとづく
デジタル・インクジェット・プリント、
クレイン・ムゼオ紙、
刷り：アダムソン・エディションズ（ワシントンＤＣ）、
紙：56×43cm、　図柄：39.5×30.4cm、
Ed. 70/XXX、署名、番号入り

パルケット・エディション 60

クロースの顔が、肌の厚みほどのダゲレオタイプの写真の深みから浮き上がり、沈みこむ。

ひとの顔を平面にしてやると、そのイメージを覚えていられる。平面
のものなら、写真のようにはっきりと覚えていられる。それから、全
体を考えると、どうしてよいかわからなくなってしまう。こんなふう
に小さな部分に分割し、判断をその範囲に限って、顔のことは考え
ずに、その小さな部分のことだけを考えるようにすれば、最後にそ
れがどうなるか思い煩わずにすむ。

チャック・クロース、
エリザベス・ペイトンとの対話
（パルケット 60号、2000年）

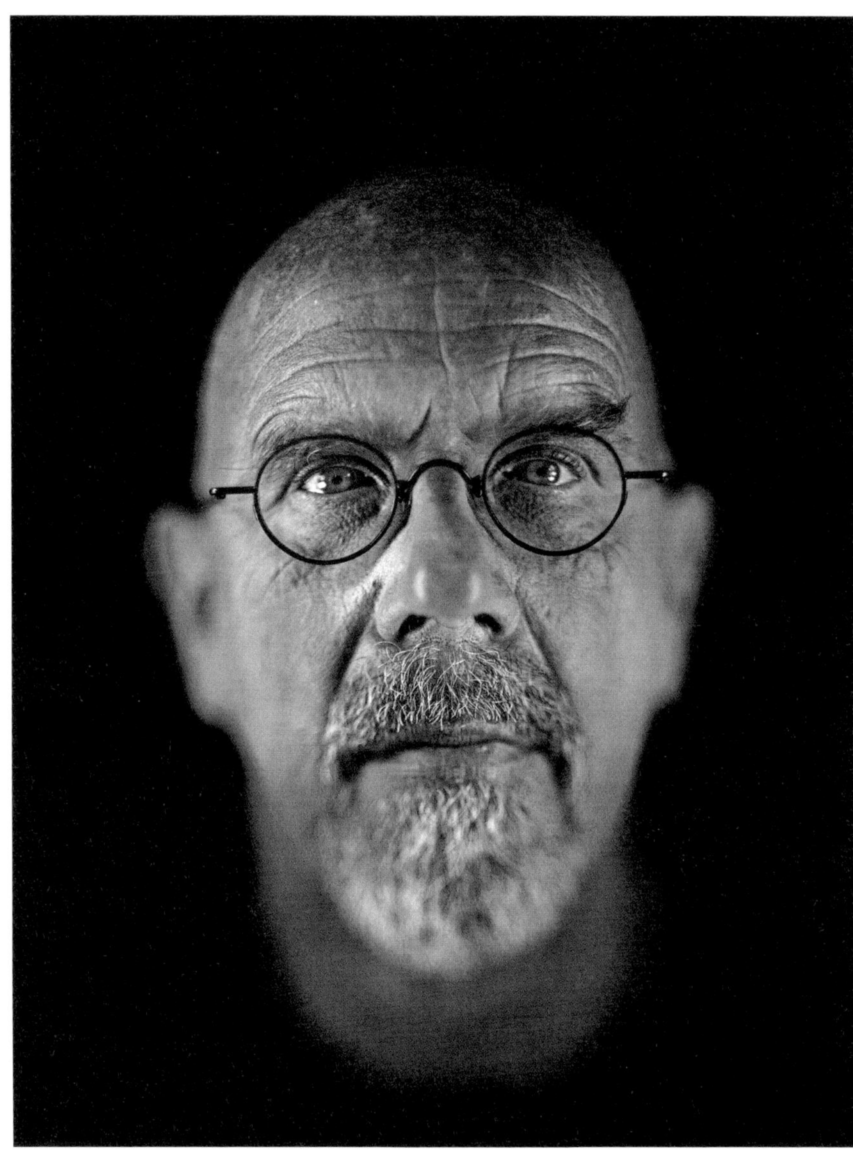

ENZO CUCCHI

Elegy and Etching, 1983

Aquatint and drypoint
on Vélin d'Arches,
bound in the magazine,
10 x 16½" (25,5 x 42 cm),
printed by Peter Kneubühler, Zurich,
Ed. 80/XVIII, signed and numbered

EDITION FOR PARKETT 1

Elegy for cities. A brooding and delicate etching imagining the transatlantic city that is partly Rome, partly New York, entirely dream.

"The present moment and far-reaching memories. Naked exposure and sheltered safety. Enzo Cucchi conjures up opposing forces from the depths of human emotions with such artistic power that his painting becomes itself the wave, the fire, the earth, the living objects it represents. 'Bisogna togliere I grandi dipinti dal paesaggio.'"

Bice Curiger
Parkett No. 1, 1984

エンツォ・クッキ

哀歌とエッチング　1983

アクアチントとドライポイント、
ヴェランダルシュ紙、
本誌に綴じこみ、
25.5×42cm、
刷り：ペーター・クノイビューラー（チューリヒ）、
Ed. 80/XVIII、署名、番号入り

パルケット・エディション　1

都会に寄せる哀歌。物静かで繊細なエッチングが、ローマでもあればニューヨークでもある、大西洋の向こう側の都会に想いを馳せる。すべては夢。

現在と遠い過去の記憶。剥き出しの露呈と保護された安全性。人間の感情の深い底から相反する要素を呼び起こすクッキの創造力はじつに逞しく、そのため絵画は波に、炎に、台地に、描写対象の生き物となる。風景画の大作は脇に退けておく必要あり。

ビーチェ・クリガー
（パルケット　1号、1984年）

Elegia

Il fumo di Roma
cammina sulle
gambe di una bestia antica.
I nostri scheletri
millenari si muovono
con rumore.
New York ci sentirà;
vedrà altri dinosauri
inoltrarsi sui tetti!!
Dentro le case di Roma
si respira. 7/8°
1983 Zurigo. Enzo Cucchi

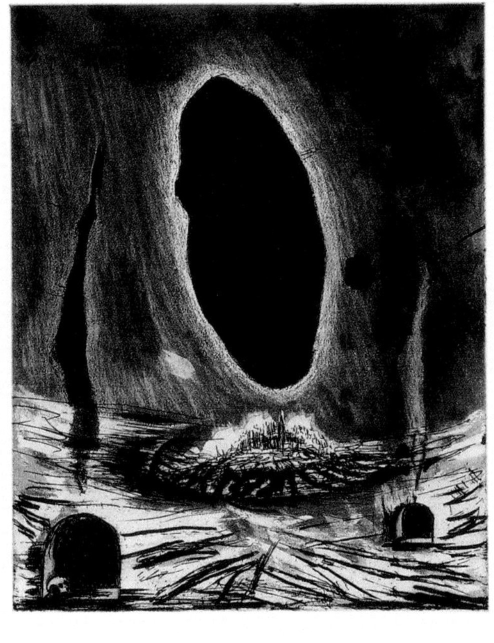

JOHN CURRIN

The Beggar's Alms, 2002

Etching with aquatint, sugarlift,
spitbite, and drypoint on Somerset
soft white textured, 250 g/m²,
paper size: 23 1/2 x 18 1/2" (59,6 x 47 cm),
image: 10 1/2 x 8 1/2" (25,4 x 20,3 cm),
printed by Greg Burnet,
Burnet Editions, New York,
Ed. 70/XXV, signed and numbered

EDITION FOR PARKETT 65

Past and present: sameness across centuries in radically different guise.

"He's not after anything as safe as a simple rehearsal of art history... what you're witnessing is an artist in the grip of a passion far stranger than any kind of kitsch love you could care to name: Currin has fallen for academic painting. He's found a fetish for technique, for style. And in a way, it's hard to imagine a less fashionable enthusiasm."

Mark van de Walle
Parkett No. 65, 2002

ジョン・カリン

貧者の施し　2002

アクアチント、シュガーリフト、スピットバイト、
ドライポイントによるエッチング、
ソフト・ホワイト・テクスチャード・
サマーセット紙 250g/㎡、
紙：59.6×47cm、
図柄：25.4×20.3cm、
刷り：グレッグ・バーネット、
バーネット・エディションズ社（ニューヨーク）、
Ed. 70/XXV、署名、番号入り

パルケット・エディション 65

過去と現在。まったく様相を異にする風を装いながら、数世紀を隔てても変わらない姿。

美術史を単純にくりかえすような安全策にはまったく興味がない……わたしたちが目の当たりにするのは、なにかしら名前を思いつけるようなキッチュ嗜好よりはるかに不可思議な、情熱の虜になったアーティスト。カリンは技法、様式を偏愛するにいたった。考えようによっては、それほど時代の流れとかけはなれた志向は想像しにくいのではないか。

マルク・ファン・デ・ワール
（パルケット 65号、2002年）

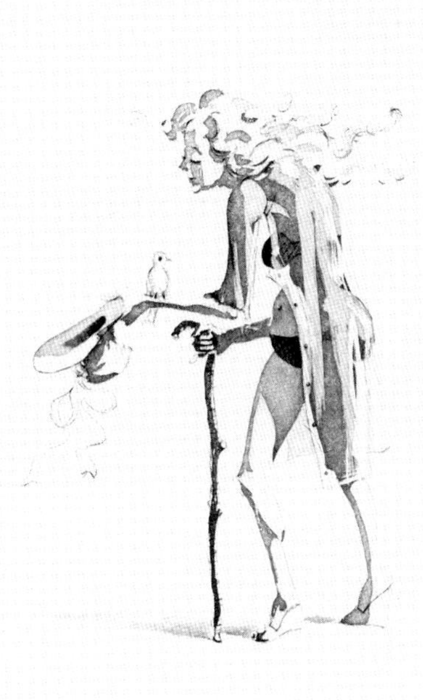

TACITA DEAN

The Green Ray, 2001

Color postcard,
4 1/8 x 5 4/5" (10,5 x 14,8 cm),
printed by Steidl Verlag, Göttingen,
Germany,
Ed. 100/XL, signed, numbered,
stamped and posted in Morombe,
Western Madagascar

EDITION FOR PARKETT 62

The enchantment of the green ray has captured the imagination of Jules Verne, Marcel Duchamp, and now Tacita Dean.

"When asked, 'What is the relation between sound and image in your work?' Dean answered, 'My interest resides in this gap between the sound and the image... I require sound to have its own autonomy.' Thus, in opposition to an approach to cinema in which the viewer experiences a sense of identification with the spectacle, Dean creates a mode of apprehension in which the observer feels at odds with what she sees. (...) The slightly disjointed relationship between the sound and image, compounded by the clearly physical presence of the projector creates caesurae, which force the beholder to return to real-time, lived bodily experience rather than that of the cinematic."

Paula Carabell
Parkett No. 62, 2001

タシタ・ディーン

緑の光線　2001

カラー写真のポストカード、
10.5×14.8cm、
制作：シュタイデル社（ゲッティンゲン市、ドイツ）、
Ed. 100/XL、署名、番号入り、
西マダガスカルのモロンベで切手を貼り投函

パルケット・エディション 62

緑の光線の美しさはジュール・ヴェルヌ、マルセル・デュシャンの想像力を刺激し、そしていま、タシタ・ディーンも魅了する。

あなたの作品のなかで、音と映像の間にはどのような関係がありますかと問われて、ディーンはこう答えた。「わたしは音と映像の間のギャップに興味があります……音には自立してほしいとおもいます」。したがって鑑賞者が目の前でくりひろげられる出来事と一体化する映画とは異なり、ディーンは鑑賞者が目にしているものに違和感を覚え、懸念を感じる方式を編み出す。音と映像のいささかぎこちない関係が、はっきり目に見えてそこにあるプロジェクターの存在とあいまって切れ目を形成し、鑑賞者を映画のなかの時間ではなく、生身の肉体が体験する現実の時間にひきもどす。

ポーラ・カラベル
（パルケット 62号、2001年）

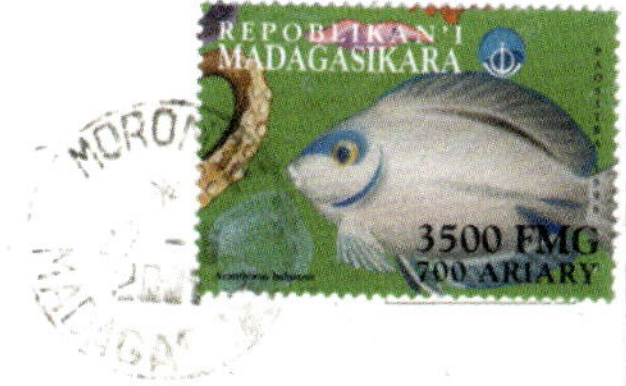

Editions for Parkett
No. 62
A/p I.
Tacita Dean
2001

Parkett — Verlag AG
Quellenstrasse 27
CH – 8031 ZURICH

SUISSE

THOMAS DEMAND

Gangway, 2001

Lambda print,
diasec on black acrylic glass
with attachable chromium-plate stand,
8 $^{1}/_{4}$ x 10 x $^{1}/_{5}$" (25 x 20,8 x 1,2 cm),
Ed. 75/XX, signed and numbered

EDITION FOR PARKETT 62

Where have all the travelers gone?
Long time passing.

"The last thing Demand wants to do is simulate reality.
His pictures have no intention of deceiving viewers;
rather, they give them the choice of taking part in the
illusion themselves. Illusion is not an act of deception;
it is play... In the case of Demand's pictures, it acquires
diversity by ceaselessly commuting between the
imitation and the construction of reality. You can never
quite tell what kind of reality prevails in these pictures:
that of the represented or the representation itself or
both at once?"

Andreas Ruby
Parkett No. 62, 2001

トーマス・デマンド

タラップ　2001

ラムダ・プリント、
黒のアクリルにディアセクでマウント、
クロームのスタンド付き、
25×20.8×1.2cm、
Ed. 75/XX、署名、番号入り

パルケット・エディション 62

乗客はどこへいったの？　あれから長い時間が経ちました。

デマンドは現実をなぞることにはまったく関心がない。デマンドの絵は、見るものを決して欺こうとしない。そのかわり、みずから幻影の仲間入りをするチャンスをあたえる。幻影は欺く行為とは異なる。それは戯れ……デマンドの絵であれば、現実の模倣と形成の間をたえず往復し、多様性を獲得する。これらの絵のなかでは、どのような現実が優勢になるか、まったく予断を許さない。描写されたものか、あるいは描写そのもの、はたまたその両方が同時に奏功するのか。

アンドレアス・ルビー
（パルケット 62号、2001年）

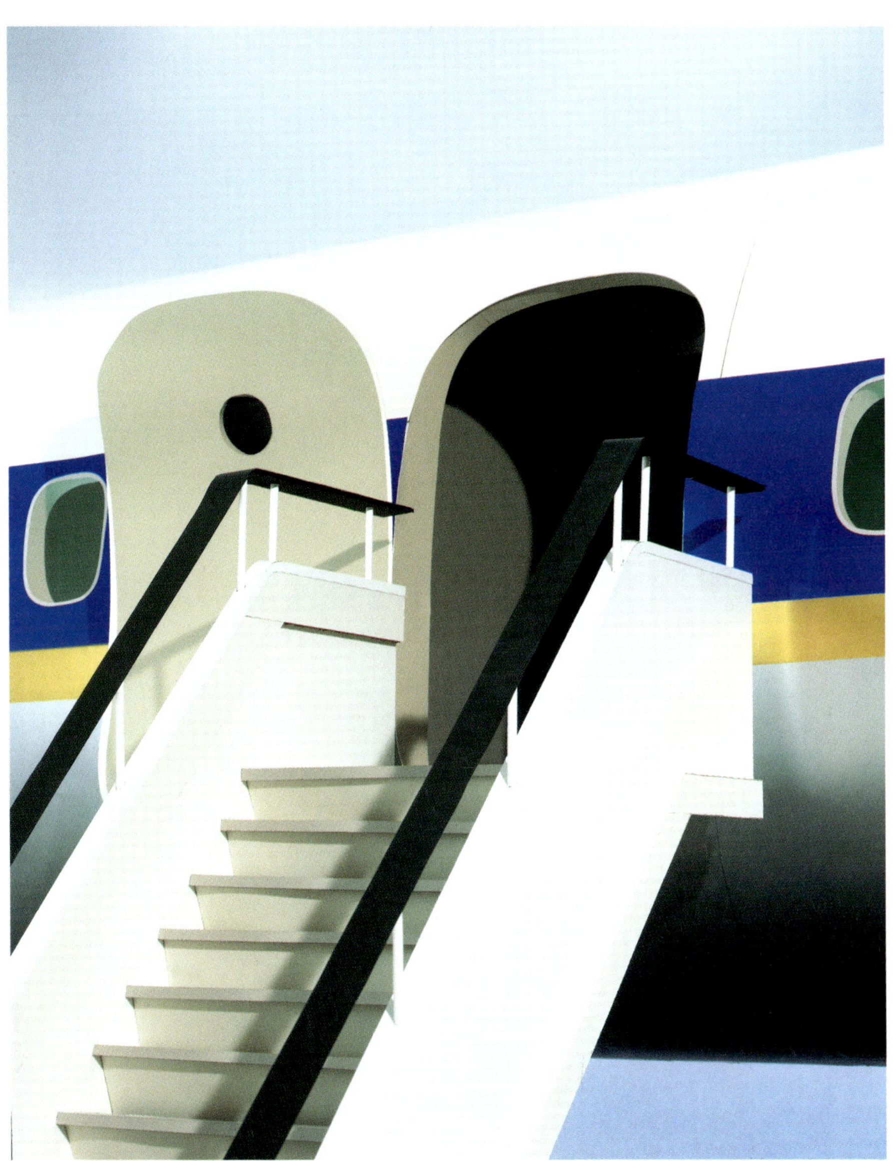

MARTIN DISLER

Little Red Pusher, 1984
In the Erotic Space of a Head, 1984

Leathercut and drypoint on Rives Wove,
bound in the magazine,
10 x 8¼" (25,5 x 21 cm),
printed by Aldo Crommelynck, Paris,
Ed. 50/X, signed and numbered.

Drypoint, aquatint, open bite and sugar lift
on Rives Wove, bound in the
magazine, 10 x 8¼" (25,5 x 21 cm),
printed by Aldo Crommelynck, Paris,
Ed. 50/VIII, signed and numbered

EDITION FOR PARKETT 3

The red and the black. With urgent,
emphatic scribbles and deep, palpitating
undertones, these etchings epitomize the
skill of a graphic master.

"It seems as if Disler were trying to recall (modern)
man's immense capacity to record and store images
in order to penetrate into the memory of mankind.
Unperturbed he surrenders to the excitement and with
invincible power paces off the boundaries of deeper
and deeper dimensions."

Bice Curiger
Parkett No. 3, 1984

マルティン・ディスラー

赤い小娘　1984／
頭のなかの官能空間にて　1984

レザーカットとドライポイント、
リヴ・ウォーブ紙、本誌に綴じこみ、
25.5×21cm、
刷り：アルド・クロムランク（パリ）、
Ed. 50/X、署名、番号入り

リヴ・ウォーヴ紙にドライポイント、
アクアティント、オープン・バイト、
シュガー・リフト、本紙に綴じこみ、
25.5×21cm、
刷り：アルド・クロムランク（パリ）、
Ed. 50/VIII、署名、番号入り

パルケット・エディション 3

赤と黒。切迫し、弾けるような筆勢と深部で震動す
る地色のあいまつエッチングは、画家の卓越した技
量を示す縮図となる。

ディスラーは（現代）人の物事を記録し、映像を保存する厖大
な能力を呼び起こし、人類の記憶に踏みこもうとするように思
われる。何事にも煩わされず、ディスラーは感興に身を委ね、何
者によっても挫かれることのない力をもって、深い、深い次元
の境界から立ち去ろうとする。

ビーチェ・クリガー
（パルケット 3号、1984年）

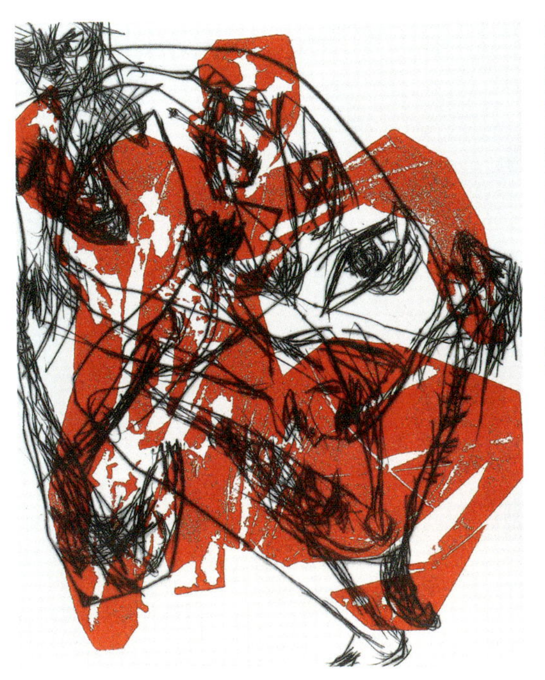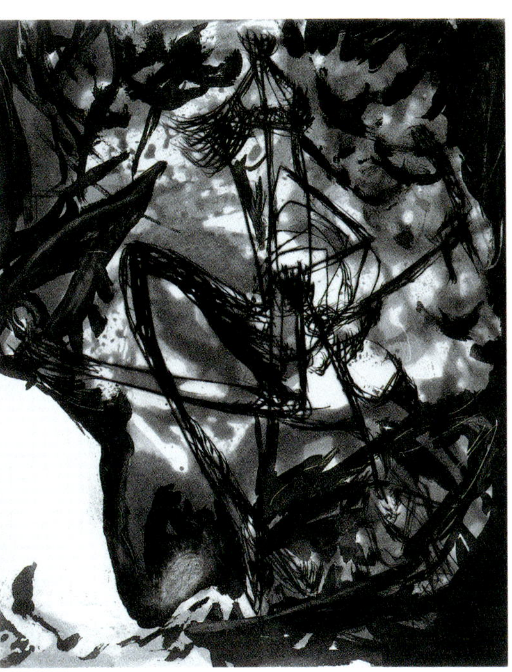

PETER DOIG

Gasthof, 2003

Etching with aquatint (7 colors),
26" x 22" (79 x 60,4 cm),
on Hahnemühle 300 g/m²,
printed by Hope Sufferance Press, London,
Ed. 70/XX, signed and numbered

EDITION FOR PARKETT 67

Law and order? Two characters no longer in search of a master.

"Peter Doig once said that one doesn't have to paint the present simply because it's there—his pictures depict the characteristics of painting itself and the spaces that can establish a relationship between pictures, reality and imagination for the artist and the viewer—just as he has presented it in practice, as multiple layers, as interlocking, shifting times and places, thereby re-actualizing our own connection to the places of our imagination and experience. 'I paint versions because I think that the best ones are never done—one desires to go back for more, like in lots of other areas of life... more. One wants to see more, hear more, experience more and also hope for the same sensations again in all of the above...'"

Beatrix Ruf
Parkett No. 67, 2003

ピーター・ドイグ

旅館　2003

アクアチントを用いたエッチング（7色）、
79×60.4cm、
ハーネミュール紙 300g/㎡、
刷り：ホープ・サフランス・プレス社（ロンドン）、
Ed. 70/XX、署名、番号入り

パルケット・エディション 67

法と秩序？　ふたりはもうご主人様を探そうとはしない。

かつてピーター・ドイグはただそこにあるからといって、目の前にあるものを描く必要はないと語ったことがある。ドイグの絵は絵の特質そのもの、さらに画家と鑑賞者のために絵画、現実、想像力の関係性を定めうる空間を描く。これまでドイグは実際に、それをいくつもの層をもつものとして、また相互に関連しながら転位してゆく時間と場所として提示し、そうすることによって、創造し、また体験する場とわたしたち自身の結びつきを再活性化させてきた。「わたしはひとつのモティーフをさまざまに形を変えて描きます。それは最高のものには決して到達できないと考えるからであり、ひとは何度でも、人生の他の多くの分野とも同じように、よりよいものを求めて後戻りしたいと願うものです。ひとはより多くを見たい、聞きたい、経験したいと欲し、またそれらのすべてについて、同じ感覚をもう一度得たいと望むのです……」

ベアトリクス・ルフ
（パルケット 67号、2003年）

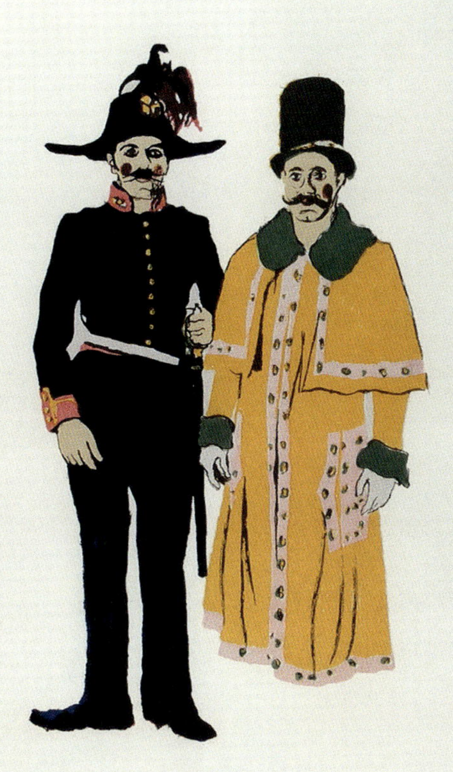

TRISHA DONNELLY

The Dashiell Delay –
an Edition Subscription, 2006

Edition in 10 installments made and
delivered every 1–2 months over a period
of one year, varied media, each approx.
8 x 10" (20 x 25 cm),
Ed. 45/XXV, signed and numbered
certificate

EDITION FOR PARKETT 77

Twelve months of mystery: ten unpredictable messages that will (or will not) be decoded in the record left behind.

"Trisha Donnelly, whose exhibitions suggest a
fundamentally iconoclastic approach, and who—
even in the sparsest showing of her pictures—will
punctuate their reception with unexpected bursts
of sound (in the same way that film scores influence
one's perception of the images on screen), seems to
be particularly interested in pictures, or rather in the
reconfiguration of our perception of pictures. She
has immense faith in the 'pictures' that she creates
through drawing, video, photography, sound, text, and
'demonstrations,' for her use of different media always
plumbs the depths of that realm, where, through force
of will, fantasy, and imagination, 'things' actually come
to exist and have meaning."

Beatrix Ruf
Parkett No. 77, 2006

トリシャ・ドネリー

ダシールの遅れ（予約出版）　　2006

月刊あるいは隔月刊で1年間、
送付される様々なメディアによるエディション作品、
サイズはそれぞれ約20×25cm、
Ed. 45/XXV、署名、番号入り証明書

パルケット・エディション 77

12ヵ月つづく謎。あとに残された記録に照らして解読
される（されない）であろう10通の予測不能なメッセー
ジ。

展覧会を見れば、絵を発表するのはごくまれではあっても、既存の価
値観を破壊しようとする意図は明確で、唐突な音響を添えて作品の受
けとめ方にアクセントをつける（これは映画音楽がスクリーン上の映
像の見方に影響をおよぼすのと同様）。トリシャ・ドネリーは、とりわ
け映画に興味がある、より正確にはわたしたちの絵の感知の仕方を
組み立て直すことに興味がある。ドネリーは素描、ビデオ、写真、音響、
テキスト、そして「実演」を駆使して創作する「絵画」に深い信頼をお
く。なぜならさまざまなメディアを用いてドネリーが探究を試みる世
界の深遠でこそ、意思、幻想、そして想像力の働きにより、「物事」は
実際に存在し、意味を持つからである。

ベアトリクス・ルフ
（パルケット 77号、2006年）

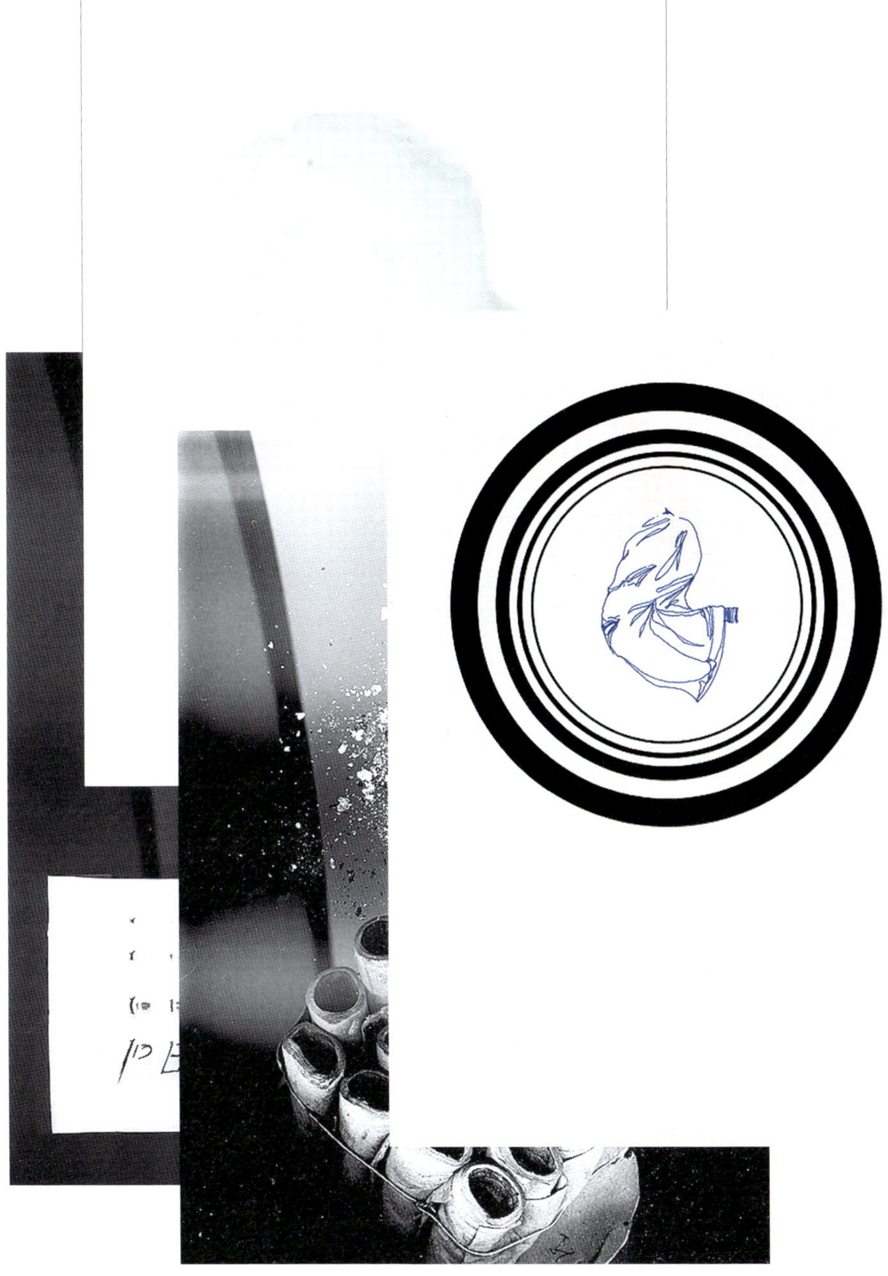

MARLENE DUMAS

The Black Man, the Jew,
and the Girl, 1993

Triptych printed by Marcel Kalksma,
Amsterdam, in three processes on
250g/m² Arches: blockprint in one color,
two transfer lithographs from one stone
rendered in two colors, inked and
inscribed by hand, with eyes and organs
scratched out, folded zigzag,
10 x 24¼" (25,5 x 63 cm),
Ed. 60/XX, signed and numbered

EDITION FOR PARKETT 38

Archetypical exorcism. The crude silhouettes
of street graffiti meet the painstaking
processes of the handmade print,
transforming familiar stereotypes into a
luxurious triptych.

"Ever-enquiring into what is reflection, what is real,
what is love, what is violence, what is pain, what is lust,
what is presence, what is absence, Marlene Dumas
constructs, like a piece of architecture, a feeling with
corridors, doors, rooms, and empty spaces, many
empty spaces, but without a single resting-place for
the banal which is perhaps the beginning of evil: the
banality of self-deception."

Anna Tilroe
Parkett No. 38, 1993

マルレーネ・デュマス

黒人、ユダヤ人、そして少女　1993

3点1組、
刷り：マルセル・カルクスマ（アムステルダム）、
3版、250g/㎡のアルシュ紙、
木版1色、石版1枚に2色、リトグラフによる転写2度、
アーティストの手でインクを塗り題名を記入、
目と器官の部分を掻きとりジグザグに折り畳んだ、
25.5×63cm、
Ed. 60/XX、署名、番号入り

パルケット・エディション 38

悪魔祓いの原型。街頭の落書きのように粗雑なシル
エットを、手刷りの版画の緻密な作業によって表現
し、目垢のついた陳腐なイメージを3点1組の豪華な
作品とした。

幻影とは何か、現実とは何か、愛とは何か、暴力とは何か、苦痛と
は何か、欲望とは何か、存在とは何か、不在とは何かをたえず問
いつづけながら、マルレーヌ・デュマスは、建築物のように、廊下、
扉、部屋、そして何もない空間、何もないいくつもの空間を用い
てひとの感覚を組み立てるものの、そこに邪悪の始まりにもなり
かねない凡庸さ、自らを欺く凡庸さの寛げる場はひとつとして存
在しない。

アナ・ティルロウ
（パルケット 38号、1993年）

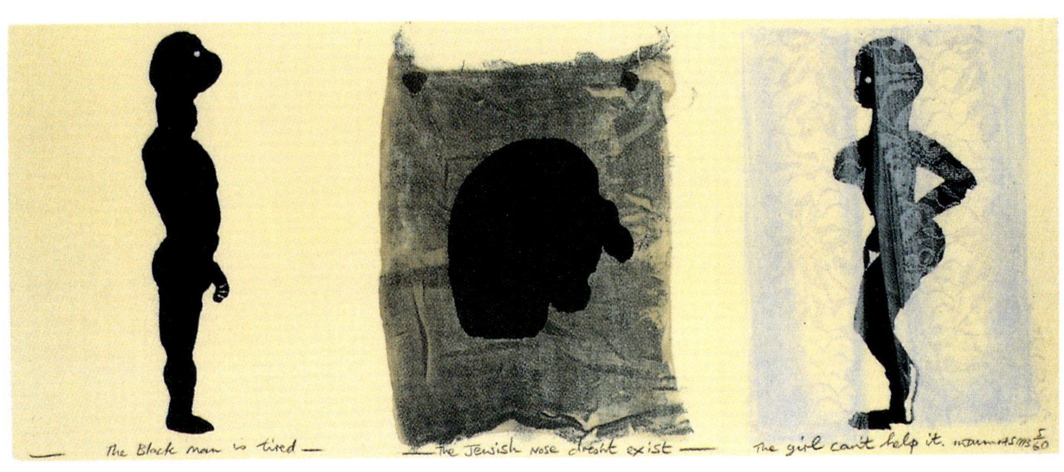
The Black man is tired
The Jewish nose dresn't exist
The girl can't help it.

OLAFUR ELIASSON

Eye Eye, 2002

Iris shutter, concave mirror,
wooden bracket, 8 11/16 x 8 11/16 x 10 1/4"
(27,1 x 22 x 25,5 cm),
shutter 4" (10,2 cm) diameter,
mirror 4 3/4" (12,1 cm) diameter,
Ed. 70/XX, signed and numbered

EDITION FOR PARKETT 64

Seeing ourselves seeing, we eye the ultimate in self-referentiality, where perception culminates in the blackness of invisibility.

"During the last decade the ambient has often been figured as a dwelling-place, a womb-like social idyll whose design-strategies approximately model the natural environment... By refusing this kind of unity, Eliasson's work recaptures an alternative, and more impatient type of production, which continually encircles and probes the sense of place itself — including some of the ideal places art occasionally manages to create for itself."

Ina Blom
Parkett No. 64, 2002

オラファー・エリアソン

目、目　2002

カメラの虹彩シャッター、
凹面鏡、木製ブラケット、
27.1×22×25.5cm、
シャッター：直径10.2cm、
鏡：直径12.1cm、
Ed. 70/XX、署名、番号入り

パルケット・エディション 64

見ているわたしたち自身を見るわたしたちは、究極の自己言及性を目の当たりにするが、そこでは知覚が不可視の闇に極まる。

過去10年、環境はしばしばひとの住まうところとして、自然環境を模すデザイン戦略にもとづき、子宮に似た社会的牧歌のように表現されてきた……こうした調和を拒むことにより、エリアソンの作品はそれにとって代わる、さらに切迫した作品づくりを捉えなおし、作品が折々みずからのために創りあげる理想的な場もふくめ、場そのものに伴う感覚を包囲し、探究を継続する。

イナ・ブロム
（パルケット 64号、2002年）

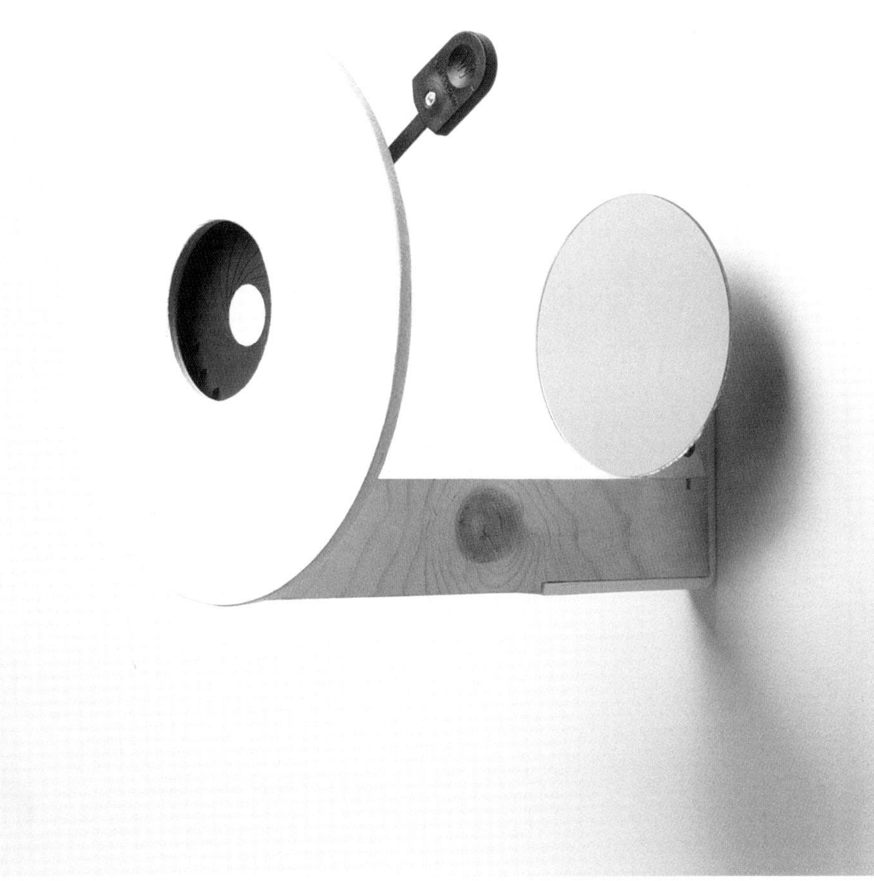

TRACEY EMIN

Self-Portrait, 12. 11. 01

Unique color print from original Polaroid,
all images taken on the same day,
image size: 8 x 7 $\frac{7}{8}$" (20,4 x 19,9 cm),
paper size: 15 $\frac{3}{4}$ x 15 $\frac{3}{4}$" (40 x 40 cm),
Ed. 80/XX, signed and numbered

EDITION FOR PARKETT 63

Tracey, eighty times: the faces and facettes of unqualified candor.

"Tracey Emin has no secrets, she exposes herself
utterly, you can see there are no skeletons in her closet
because the closet door is open and you are welcome
to look inside. Her art is not a record of emotion, but
the hot stew of emotion as it comes fresh from the
heart—anger, pain, confusion, desolation, occasionally
happiness—always with the implicit question 'What is
going on here?'"

Lynn Barber
Parkett No. 63, 2001

トレイシー・エミン

自画像　12.11.01

オリジナルのポラロイド写真にもとづくカラー写真、
映像は1点ずつ異なるがすべて同じ日に撮影された、
図柄：20.4×19.9cm、
紙：40×40cm、
Ed. 80/XX、署名、番号入り

パルケット・エディション 63

トレイシーを80回。率直きわまりない顔とその一面

トレイシー・エミンに隠し事はなく、なにもかも人目にさらす、タンスにはご覧のとおり骸骨は隠れていない、というのもタンスの扉は開いていて、中を見たいひとは見てもいっこうにさしつかえない。エミンの作品は感情の記録ではなく、心から湧きでる感情、とはつまり怒り、痛み、戸惑い、絶望、そしてときどき幸せなどの感情のごった煮で、そこにはつねに「いったいこれはどうなってるの」という問いが、密かについてまわる。

リン・バーバー
（パルケット 63号、2001年）

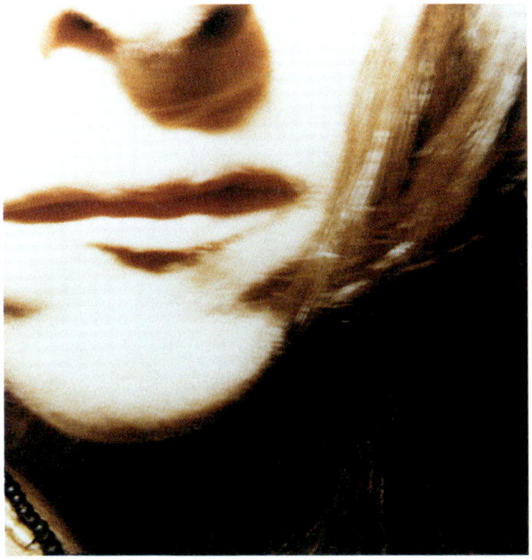

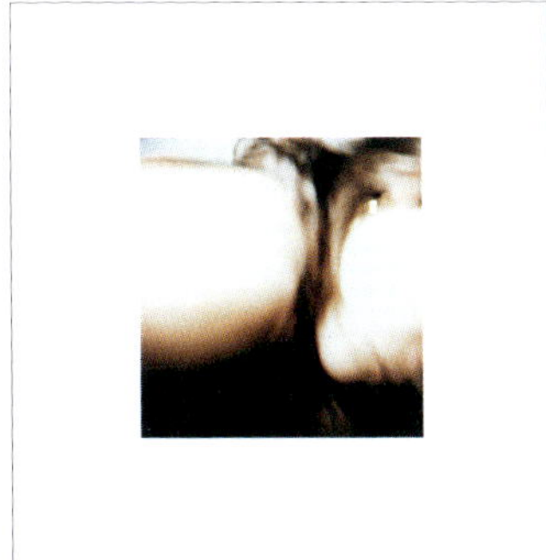

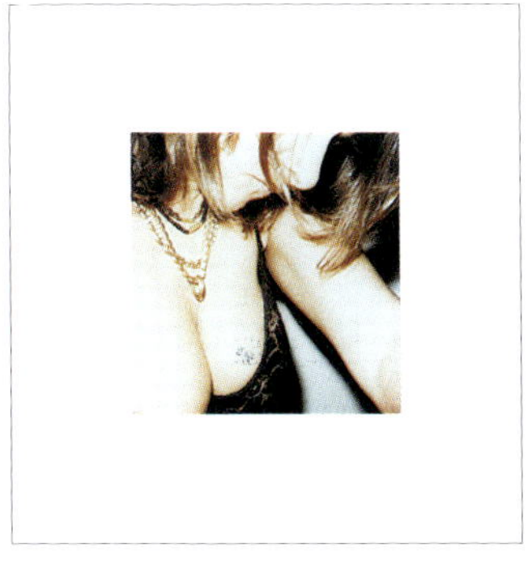

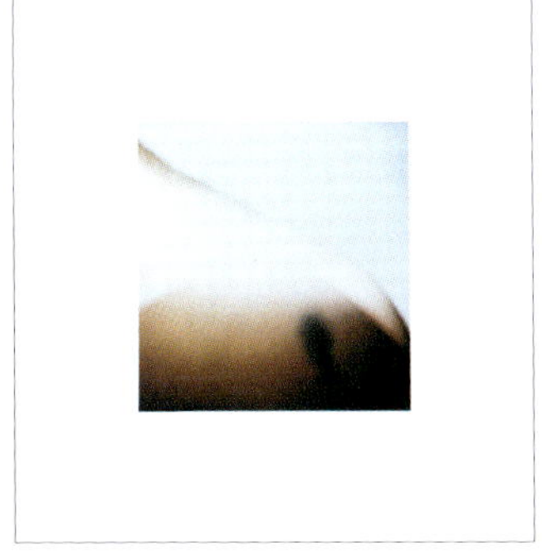

URS FISCHER

Sigh, Sigh, Sherlock!, 2004

Fiberglass reinforced plaster cast, partially painted, 36 1/4 x 12 5/8 x 12 5/8" (92 x 32 x 32 cm), cast by Kunstgiesserei Felix Lehner, St. Gall, Switzerland, Ed. 45/XXV, signed and numbered

EDITION FOR PARKETT 72

Sigh no more, ladies, sigh no more; men were deceivers ever...

"Wow! What a show! A real tour de force. I didn't want to leave. And when I did, finally, I left knowing that I had encountered an artist of mad ambition whose work – revelatory with inspired conjunctions and dazzling invention, the product of incredibly demanding labor carried out in a spirit of play – casts a spell of fairy-tale enchantment."

Brenda Richardson
Parkett No. 72, 2004

ウルス・フィッシャー

ため息、ため息、シャーロック！　2004

グラスファイバーで強化した石膏像、
一部彩色、92×32×32cm、
制作：フェッリクス・レーナー美術鋳造社
（ザンクト・ガレン市、スイス）、
Ed. 45/XXV、署名、番号入り

パルケット・エディション 72

もうこれ以上、ご婦人方、もうこれ以上ため息はつかないで、男はいつだって嘘つきなのだから……

うわっ！　これはたいへんな見物だわ！　すごい腕前、外に出たくなかった。けれどようやくその場を後にしたときには、桁外れの野心をもつアーティストに出会ったこと、そしてその作品は信じられないほど骨の折れる作業を、遊び心も忘れずなしとげた賜物であり、霊感にみちた連想と目ざましい発明の才に啓発され、おとぎ話のように楽しい魔法をかけてくれることがよくわかった。

ブレンダ・リチャードソン
（パルケット 72号、2004年）

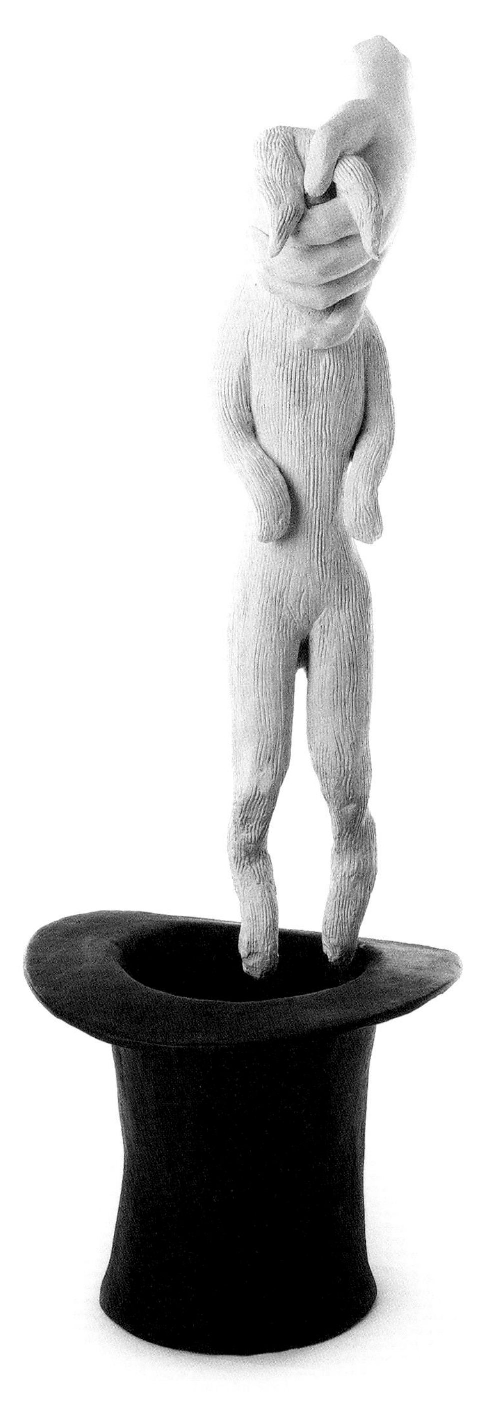

ERIC FISCHL

Squatter, 1985

Aquatint and sugar lift on Zerkall-
Vellum, bound in the magazine,
10 x 8¼" (25,5 x 21 cm),
printed by Peter Kneubühler, Zurich,
Ed. 80/XX, signed and numbered

EDITION FOR PARKETT 5

Pornography of gesture. The classical
archetype of the Squatting Venus is given
new and fleeting articulation in the vision
of an eminent voyeur.

"As for what has entered Fischl's work, it is simply
consciousness: a heightened, unhappy, ambivalent
consciousness that can no longer be confined to the
frame of primal scenes and suburban anecdotes.
Almost helplessly, it observes a constant ramification
of context and themes: context that links artist and
audience, audience and social class, social class and
the wider world..."

Peter Schjeldahl
Parkett No. 5, 1985

エリック・フィッシュル

しゃがむ女　1985

シュガーアクアチント、ツェルカル社製ヴェラム紙、
本誌に綴じこみ、25.5×21cm、
刷り：ペーター・クノイビューラー（チューリヒ）、
Ed. 80/XX、署名、番号入り

パルケット・エディション 5

姿勢の示す猥褻さ。古典的な、しゃがむヴィーナスを
原型に、覗き見で知られるアーティストの想像力が新
たに、つかのまの表現を生み出す。

フィッシュルの作品になにが入りこんだかといえば、それは意識
につきる。昂揚し、不幸せな、曖昧な意識は、もはや幼少期の情
景や都市近郊生活のエピソードの枠組みにはおさまりきらない。
ほとんど手も足もでない様子で、その意識は文脈やテーマがとめ
どなく分岐してゆく様を見つめる。アーティストと鑑賞者、鑑賞
者と社会階級、社会階級と幅広い世界を結びつけるのは、その文
脈であるにもかかわらず……

ピーター・シェルダール
（パルケット 5号、1985年）

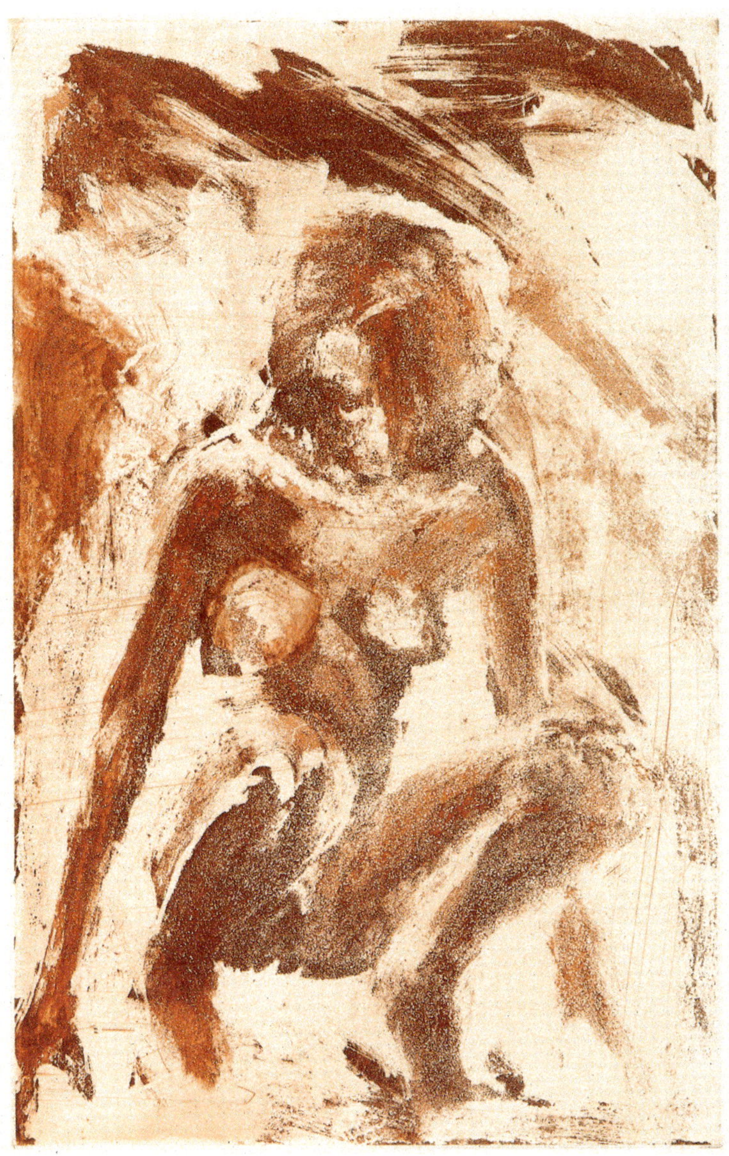

PETER FISCHLI / DAVID WEISS

Record, 1988

Record, beracryl, diameter 11 4/5" (30 cm),
Ed. 120XXVI, signed and numbered

EDITION FOR PARKETT 17

Extended play. A household object that is fast becoming a museum piece—a simulacrum of a record from the artisans of the ordinary. For those who don't mind ruining the needle of their phonograph, a cross-section of average disco will be audible on this acrylic "vinyl."

"In appearance, the work of Fischli/Weiss is ironic and humorous; oscillating between game and joke, it seems to mock the seriousness of art. The artists' combinations of things and objects, figures and actions, whether in balance or in movement, tend to restore the value of wit and playfulness to creative commitment, but their goal is to contest the claim to truth, to contest the absolutism of the art process, repudiating cleverness and replacing it with inept intentions... or removing its core... or even collapsing it."

Germano Celant
Parkett No. 17, 1988

ペーター・フィッシュリ／ダヴィッド・ヴァイス

レコード　1988

レコード、合成樹脂、直径 30cm、
Ed. 120/XXVI、署名、番号入り

パルケット・エディション 17

長時間演奏。瞬く間に博物館送りとなった家庭ではお馴染みの品。平凡のあつかいに長けた職人ふたりが送るレコードの模造品。レコードプレーヤーの針を傷めても構わないという方は、アクリル製「ビニール（レコードの意）」から平均的なディスコ・ミュージックの見本を聴くこともできます。

外見からすると、フィッシュリ／ヴァイスの作品は皮肉っぽく、ユーモアもある。ゲームとジョークの間をせわしなく往復しながら、芸術の真面目さを小馬鹿にするようにも思える。物とオブジェ、姿と動きをとりあわせるふたりの手さばきは、釣り合いがとれて静止しても、動いても、真摯な創作活動に頓智と戯れの価値を復権させるようでもあるが、かれらが目指すのは、真理は我にありとの主張や芸術の創作過程を絶対視する考え方に異議を唱え、器用さを退けて不器用な思いこみを活かし……あるいは核をとりのぞき……あるいは崩壊させることであるのかもしれない。

ジェルマノ・チェラント
（パルケット 17号、1988年）

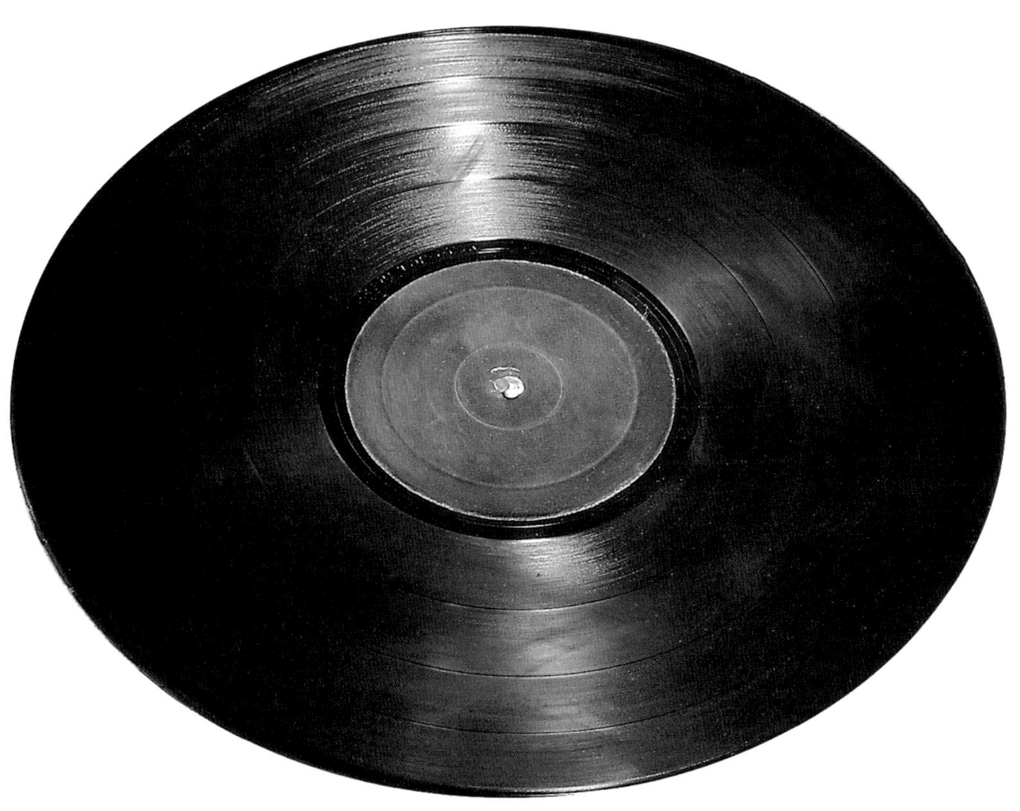

PETER FISCHLI / DAVID WEISS

Untitled (Small Bucket), 1994

Carved object, polyurethane,
acrylic, dispersion,
ø 7 $^5/_8$ x 3 $^2/_8$" (20 x 20 x 8,5 cm),
Ed. 32/X, signed and numbered

EDITION FOR PARKETT 40/41

The Real Thing. Confounding, delightful
decoys of everyday life reveal themselves
in the slow-release mechanism of human
perception.

"Peter Fischli/David Weiss's replicants refuse to give us
any insight into their inner nature and structure, which
we, as products of a scientific age, automatically want
to investigate. Instead, we are radically confronted
with a surface that cannot be penetrated because it
conceals nothing but a void."

Boris Groys
Parkett No. 40/41, 1994

ペーター・フィッシュリ／ダヴィッド・ヴァイス

無題（小さな盥）　　1994

ポリウレタン、アクリルを彫塑、
20×20×8.5cm、
Ed. 32/X、署名、番号入り

パルケット・エディション 40/41

本物。日常生活でお馴染みの品を模した楽しくもあり、
困惑もさせるオトリは、徐々に働きはじめる人の知覚作
用の覚醒をまって、本性を明らかにする。

フィッシュリ／ヴァイスの作るレプリカは、内部の構造、性質を明らか
にしようとしないが、科学の時代に生まれたわたしたちは、無意識の
うちに、それを探りたくなる。ところが、わたしたちの目の前には虚空
以外の何物も隠していないために、侵入することのできない表面が立
ちふさがる。

ボリス・グロイス
（パルケット 40/41号、1994年）

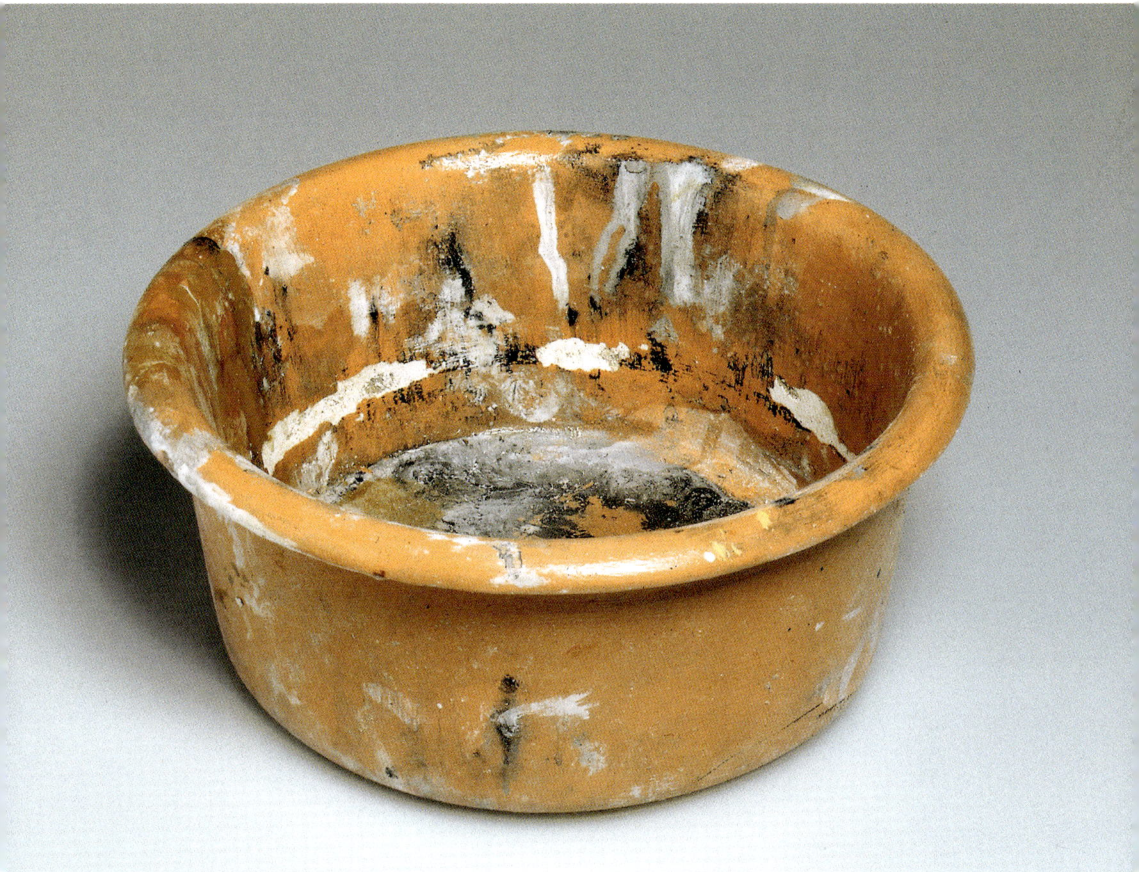

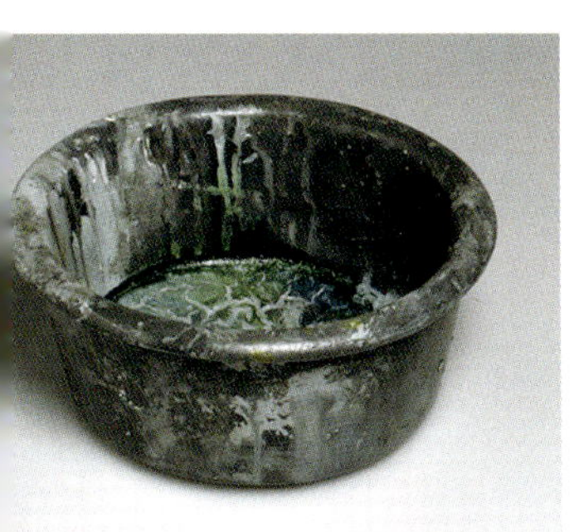
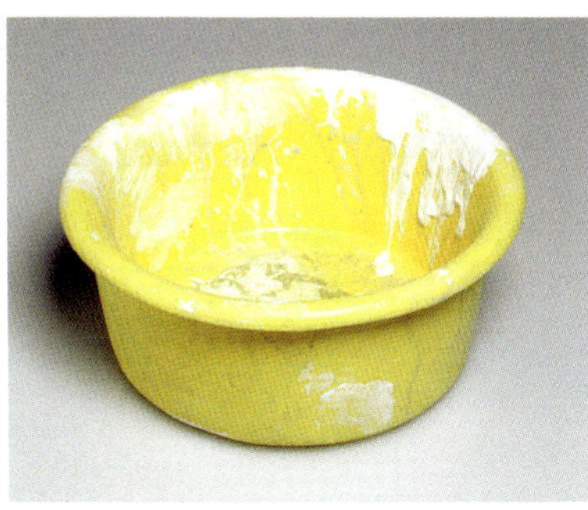
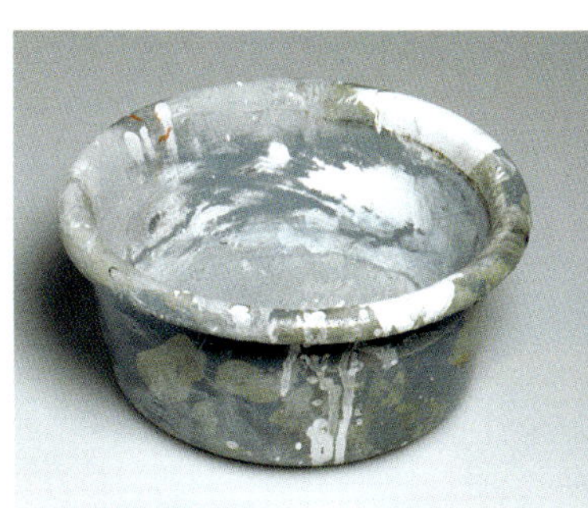

SYLVIE FLEURY

His Mistress' Toy, 2000

Size 37 women's mule cast in
polyurethane, with integrated noise
maker (squeak), produced at
T.E.S.T Kreashens, Saugus, CA, USA,
Ed. 99/XXX; no. 1–50 (left shoe),
no. 51–99 (right shoe),
engraved signature, numbered

EDITION FOR PARKETT 58

A shoe not made for walking. A graceful leap transforms frivolous footwear into squeaky plaything.

"Sylvie Fleury's 'studio work' thus takes place in all
the various realms of social added-value production
and fetishization, and she whirls together—codes
pertaining to fashion, art, high and low culture, models
of male and female self-configuration—appropriating
and playing with self-images, life-models, and forms
of existence in styling and manner that in effect
pulverizes every last hierarchy of sex, class, and genre."

Beatrix Ruf
Parkett No. 58, 2000

シルヴィ・フルーリ

女王様の玩具　2000

ポリウレタンを成形したサイズ37の婦人用ミュール、
（キーキーと）音をたてる仕掛けを組みこんである、
制作：T.E.S.T クリーシェンス社
（カリフォルニア州ソーガス市）、
Ed. 99/XXX、1-50（左）、51-99（右）、
署名を刻印、番号入り

パルケット・エディション 58

歩くためには作られていない靴。優雅な飛躍により、軽
薄な履物がキューキュー鳴く玩具に変身する。

シルヴィ・フルーリの「スタジオ・ワーク」はこうして社会的な付加価
値生産と物心崇拝化の多様な領域で展開され、フルーリはセルフ・イ
メージ、生きた手本、さらにセックス、階級、ジャンルに最後まで残る
力関係を実質的に粉砕する様式や流儀のあり方を拝借し、それと戯れ
つつ、ファッション、アート、高踏文化、低俗文化、男性、女性の自己形
成の手本に関わる決まり事を、ひとつにまとめてかきまぜてみせる。

ベアトリクス・ルフ
（パルケット 58号、2000年）

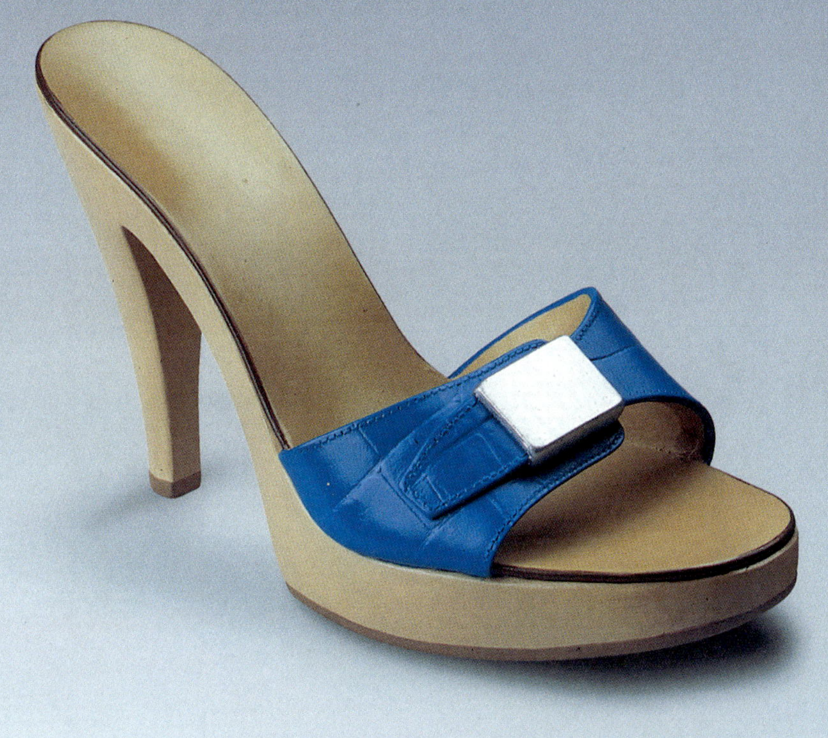

GÜNTHER FÖRG

Four Bronze Reliefs, 1990

10 x 8 1/4 x 1 3/8" (25,5 x 21,5 x 3,5 cm),
cast by Gogarte, Rancate,
Ed. 20/X each, signed and numbered

EDITION FOR PARKETT 26

Fingerpainting. Book-sized bronzes in four variations record the sensual and immediate pleasures of encounters with surfaces that yield to the finger's touch.

"Förg redirects painting by painting picture surfaces like a house painter, by composing rooms like a workman, by taking photographs à la Titian and painting photographs à la Godard... Förg opens a space and invites us to take a walk in it, with his eyes."

Wilfried Dickhoff
Parkett No. 26, 1990

ギュンター・フェルク

4つのブロンズ・レリーフ　1990

25.5×21.5×3.5cm、
鋳造：ゴガルテ、ランカテ、
Ed. 20/X、それぞれに署名、番号入り

パルケット・エディション 26

指で描いた絵。本のサイズのブロンズ4種に、指でさわれば凹む表面と触れ合う生々しく官能的な歓びが記録される。

フェルクは家を塗装するペンキ職人のように絵画の表面に絵具を塗り、大工のように部屋を構成し、ティツィアーノのように写真を撮り、写真をゴダールのように描くことによって、絵画の方向性を変化させる……フェルクは空間を開き、その中で散歩してみませんかと、わたしたちに目配せして招き入れる。

ヴィルフリート・ディックホフ
（パルケット 26号、1990年）

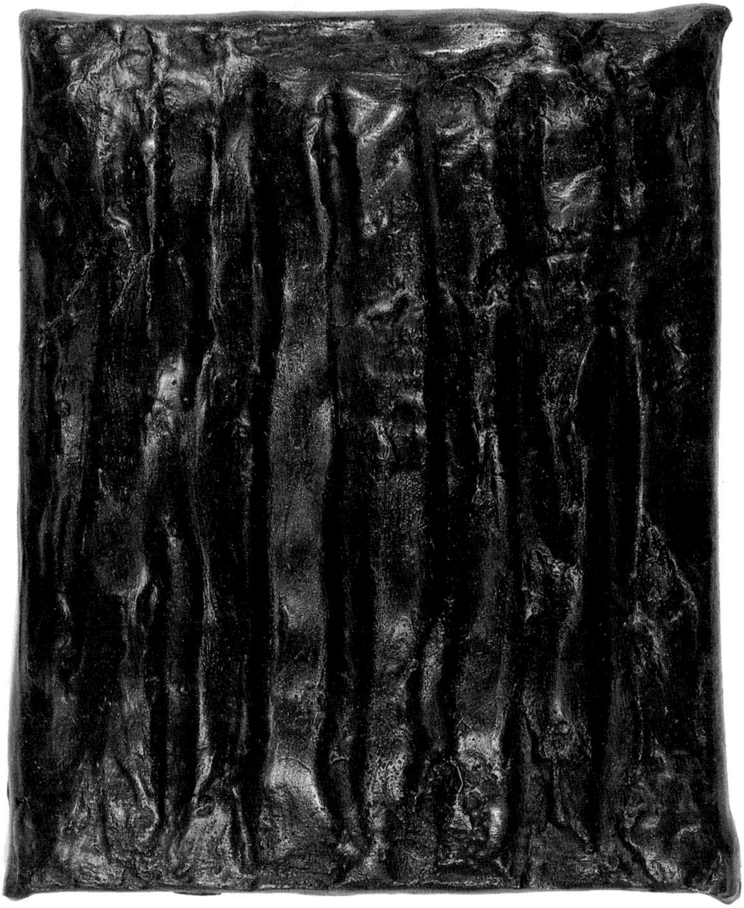

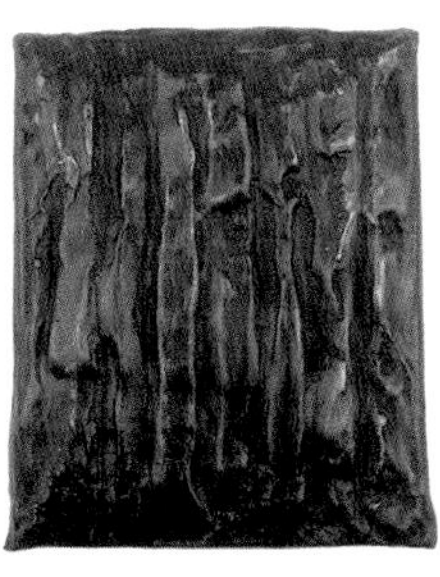
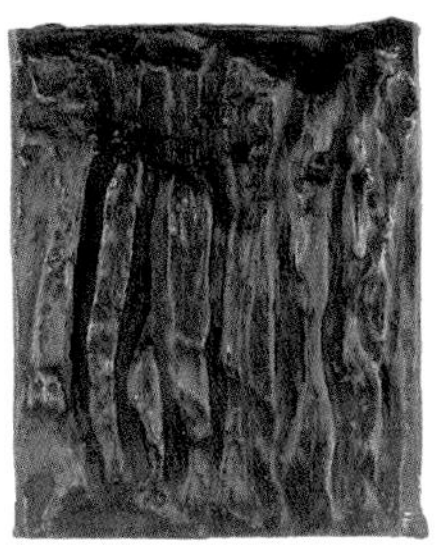
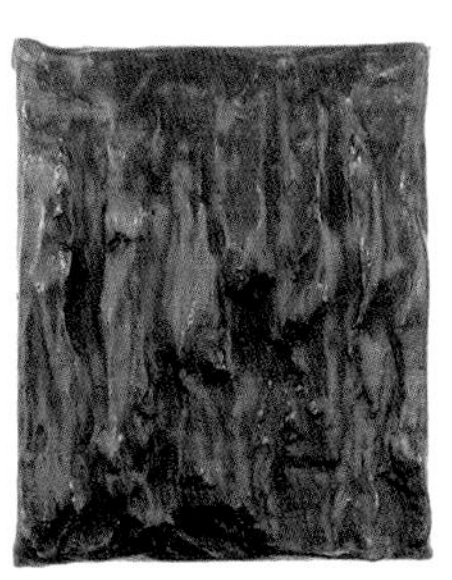

GÜNTHER FÖRG

Untitled, 1994

Two-part object, consisting of one
mirror and one copperplate each
mounted on wood in Parkett format,
each 10 x 8¼ x 1¼" (25,5 x 21 x 3,2 cm),
produced by Jürgen Zimmermann,
Karlsruhe,
Ed. 45/XV, signed and numbered

EDITION FOR PARKETT 40/41

Reality abstracted. Lightning strikes between mirrored reality and the abstract pattern of oxidation on a copperplate, both in Parkett format.

"Förg wants to access a past seemingly sealed off. He wants to reinsert himself within an apparently completed project, but a project the success or failure of which is still very much in question. It is inevitably a melancholy and nostalgic game, and regardless of the formal elegance and seduction that Förg's installations promise, he is always somewhat a loser. Maybe part of the point of his work is being just that, a graceful, good loser in a foreclosed historical gambit—and that way, surreptitiously, a success."

David Rimanelli
Parkett No. 40/41, 1994

ギュンター・フェルク

無題　1994

二部作、鏡と銅版をそれぞれ
パルケット誌のサイズの木にマウント、
各25.5×21×3.2cm、
制作：ユルゲン・ツィマーマン（カールスルーエ市）、
Ed. 45/XV、署名、番号入り

パルケット・エディション　40/41

抽象化された現実。鏡に映る現実と、銅版の酸化による抽象的な模様の間に、稲妻が走る。鏡と銅版はどちらもパルケット誌のサイズ。

フェルクは封印されたように見える過去と接触したいと願う。見かけは完了しているものの、その成否については大いに疑問の残るプロジェクトに、もう一度参入したいと考える。これはどうしても憂鬱で、郷愁を誘うくわだてにならざるをえない。インスタレーションの姿が優雅で、ひとの心を惹きつけるものであっても、フェルクはしたがって、つねにどこか敗者の趣から逃れられない。フェルクの作品の要点の一部は、そこにあるのかもしれない。すでに処理済の歴史的な先行作戦の、天晴れな敗者となること、それはつまり、人目を忍ぶ、成功でもあるだろう。

ダヴィッド・リマネリ
（パルケット 40/41号、1994年）

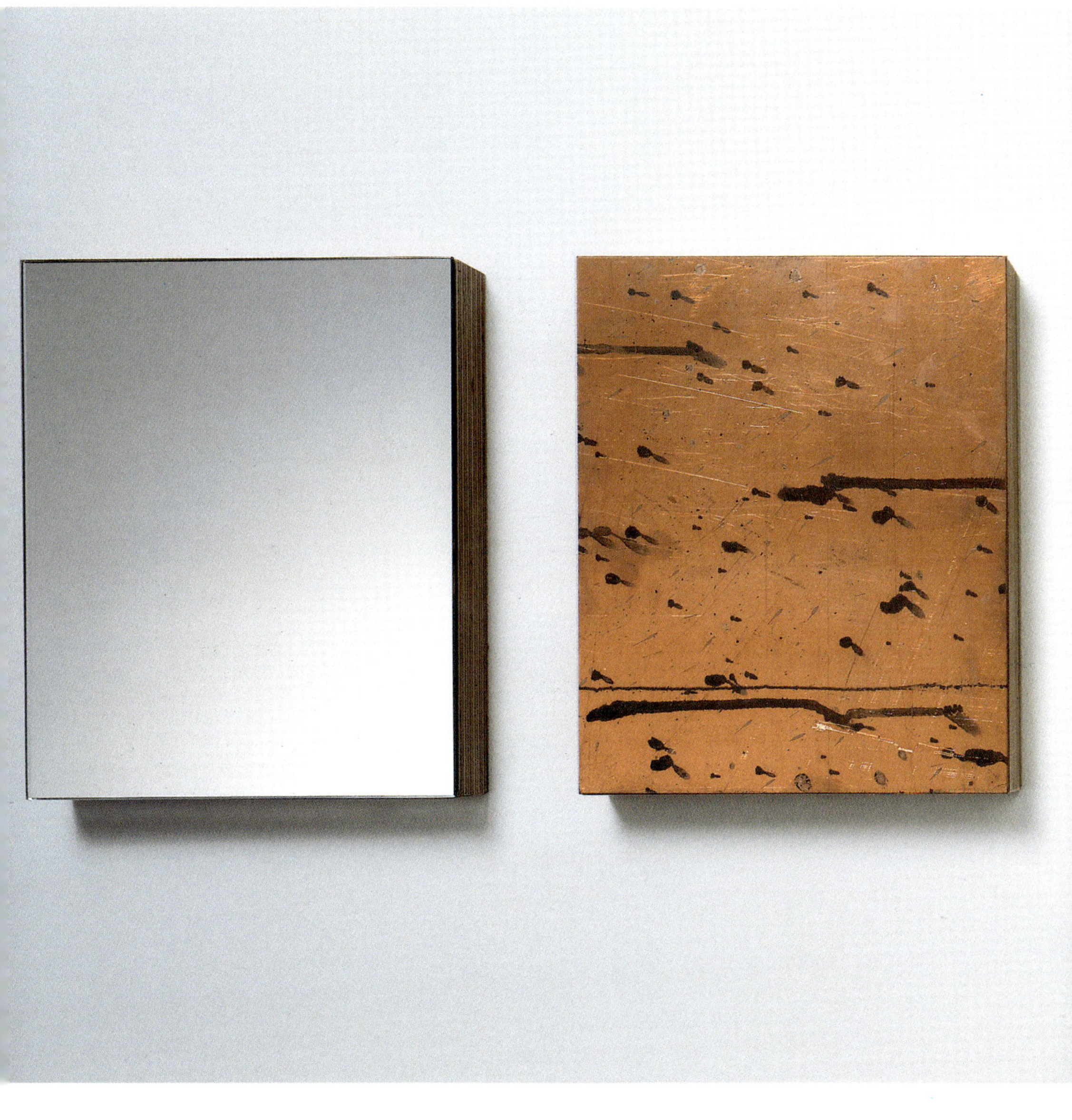

ROBERT FRANK

Untitled, 2008

Archival pigment print
on Hahnemühle paper,
11 x 8¹/₂" (28 x 21,6 cm),
Ed. 25/X, signed and numbered

EDITION FOR PARKETT 83

A droplet of colored deliberation in a stream of black-and-white consciousness.

"Frank understood that the essence of a subject was just as often found on the soft side of focus as in the sharp, and in the non-composition or the unbalanced, when people were off-guard or unaware… In this way, there is none of the hierarchy of quality so prevalent at that time, leaving Frank free to make his decisions elsewhere."

Tacita Dean
Parkett No. 83, 2008

ロバート・フランク

無題　2008

保存性の高い顔料系プリント、
ハーネミュール紙：28×21.6cm、
Ed. 25/X、署名、番号入り

パルケット・エディション 83

モノクロームの意識の流れに落ちる、彩色された思案のしずく。

物事の本質はピントの合っていないところにも、合っているところと同じ頻度で見つかるものであり、ひとが撮られると気づかず、身構えていないところを、構図を考えるでもなく、またバランスもとらぬままに撮った写真に見いだせるとフランクは理解していた……そのおかげで、当時あまりに広く世間に行き渡っていた写真の質の高さ低さにまどわされず、フランクはそれとは異なる方面で、自由な判断を下すことができた。

タシタ・ディーン
（パルケット 83号、2008年）

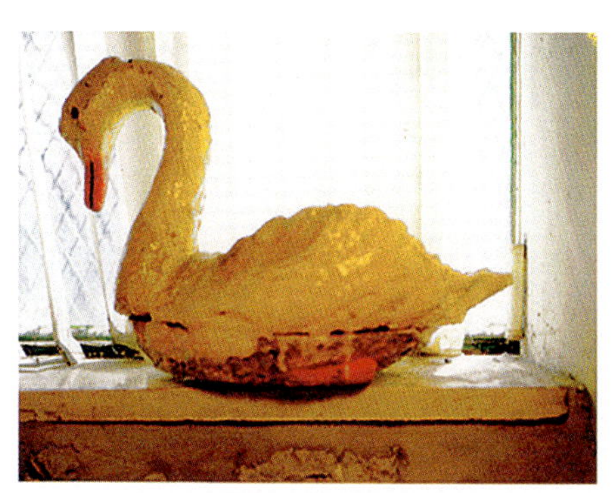

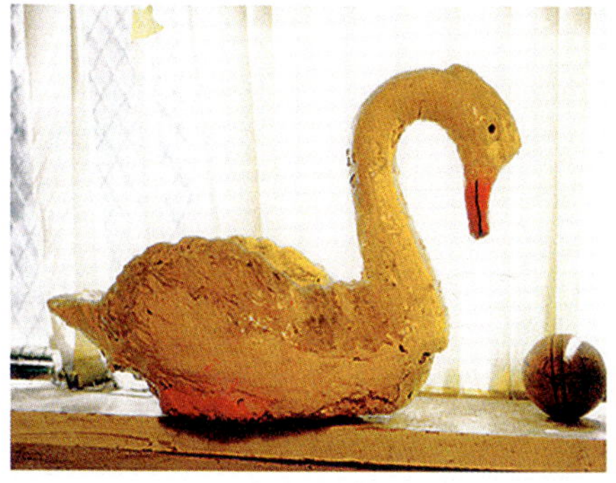

TOM FRIEDMAN

Untitled, 2002

75 Styrofoam cups painted by hand
with acrylic paint, glue,
40" (102,8 cm) high, 2" (7,1 cm) diameter,
Ed. 75/XX, signed and numbered

EDITION FOR PARKETT 64

Column or color chart. This fragile structure
begs belief, inviting scrutiny
and denying satisfaction.

"Tom Friedman's sculptural works radically modify
our view of things. Small and fragile, made of
mundane, frequently expendable materials, they evoke
meditation on the interconnectedness of natural and
industrial worlds, even suggesting that the human
mind, body, and inanimate things are all involved in the
same process of transmutation."

Midori Matsui
Parkett No. 64, 2002

トム・フリードマン

無題　2002

発泡スチロールのカップ75個、
アクリル絵具で手彩色、接着剤、
高さ102.8cm、直径7.1cm、
Ed. 75/XX、署名、番号入り

パルケット・エディション 64

柱またはカラー・チャート。華奢な造りは目を疑わせ、
しげしげと見るように誘うが、決して満足させることは
ない。

トム・フリードマンの彫刻作品は、わたしたちの物の見方を根底か
らくつがえす。小さくて壊れやすく、どこにでもありふれた、しばし
ば使い捨ての素材でつくられた作品は、自然と工業化された社会
がたがいに深く結びついていることへの思索をうながし、さらには
人間の知性、身体、そして生命のない物もすべて同じ変容の過程に
まきこまれていることまでも示唆する。

松井みどり
（パルケット 64号、2002年）

KATHARINA FRITSCH

Mill/Ambulance/Toads, 1990

Set of three single records,
ø 7 $\frac{7}{8}$" (17,5 cm),
Ed. 2000 sets, unsigned

EDITION FOR PARKETT 25

Music for the eyes. A set of three records, each pressed with a single ambient sound from the artist's aural memory—toads croaking, a watermill churning, a local ambulance siren wailing—and sealed with a corresponding emblematic color.

"All of Katharina Fritsch's works start with a clear and precisely visualized image of a thing: a situation that, by definition, incorporates both the individual view and the collective sign."

Julian Heynen
Parkett No. 25, 1990

カタリーナ・フリッチュ

水車／救急車／ヒキガエル　1990

シングル・レコードの3枚セット、
直径17.5cm、
Ed. 2000セット、署名なし

パルケット・エディション 25

目で見る音楽。レコード3枚1組のセット。それぞれにアーティストの記憶に残るヒキガエルの鳴き声、回転する水車、救急車のサイレンを録音し、それにふさわしい色のジャケットを用意した。

カタリーナ・フリッチュの作品はすべて、ある物を明瞭に、そして正確に視覚化したイメージから出発する。そうした状況であれば、必然的に、個人的な視点と集団的な象徴が内にふくまれる。

ジュリアン・ヘイネン
（パルケット 25号、1990年）

Unken

Krankenwagen

Mühle

BERNARD FRIZE

Percy John Heawood Conjecture,
2005

Double torus cast in Polyurethane, painted
in eight synthetic resin colors, the number
of colors sufficient for map coloring on
the surface of a double torus is given by
the Heawood conjecture, all eight colors
share a common border with each other,
10 $^5/_8$ x 6$^1/_4$ x 1 $^3/_4$" (24 x 8 x 4 cm),
2,75 lbs (1,25 kg),
production by Kunstgiesserei
Felix Lehner, St. Gall, Switzerland,
Ed. 45/XXV, signed and numbered
certificate

EDITION FOR PARKETT 74

The recipe: eight colors, seven borders, and
chance under control; for once, salvation is
immanent.

"Frize's paintings deploy colors in their multiplicity
of forces; far from any kind of composition, they are
machinations of forces—in all senses of the word: the
contrivance of a machine, a calculation, crafty plotting,
cunning, an event."

Patricia Falguières
Parkett No. 74, 2005

ベルナール・フリズ

ヒーウッドの公式　2005

ポリウレタンを成形した2重円環体、
8色の合成樹脂絵具で塗装、
2重円環体の表面の隣接面に同じ色が並ばない
ように塗り分けるのに最低限必要な色数は
ヒーウッドの公式によってあたえられる、
8色のすべてがたがいに境界を接する、
24×8×4cm、
制作：フェリックス・レーナー美術鋳造
　　（ザンクト・ガレン市、スイス）、
Ed. 45/XXV、署名、番号入り証明書

パルケット・エディション 74

レシピ／8つの色、7つの境界、偶然を意のままに
操る、救済は内在する。

フリズの絵画は色彩が多様な力を発揮するように配置する。いか
なる構図ともまったく性質の異なる、力を操る策謀、あらゆる語義
に照らしても、それはまさに策謀にほかならない。機械装置、計算
ずく、抜け目のない策略、狡猾、イベントである。

パトリシア・ファルギュイエール
（パルケット 74号、2005年）

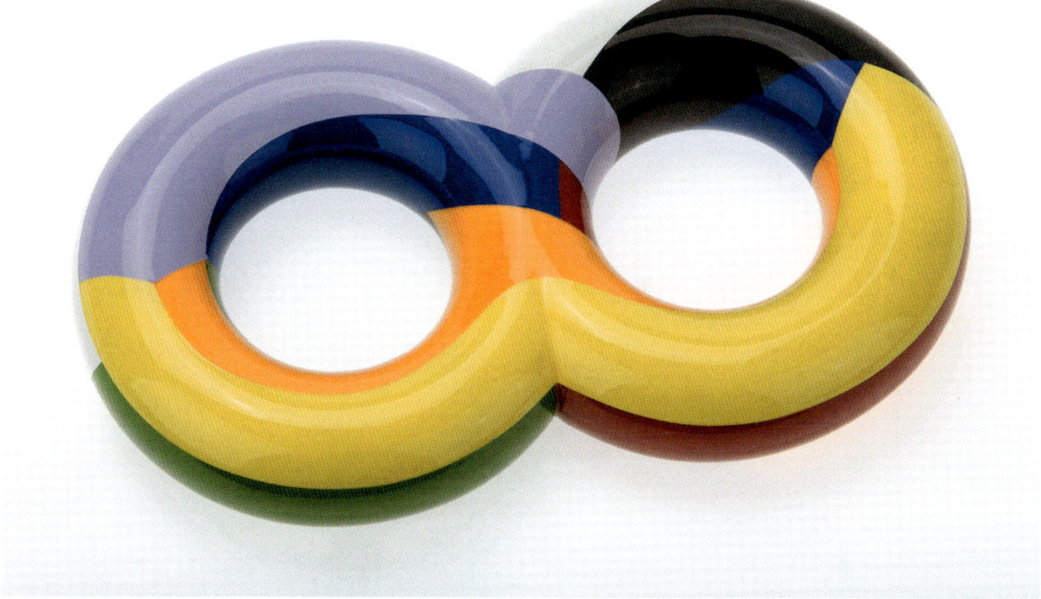

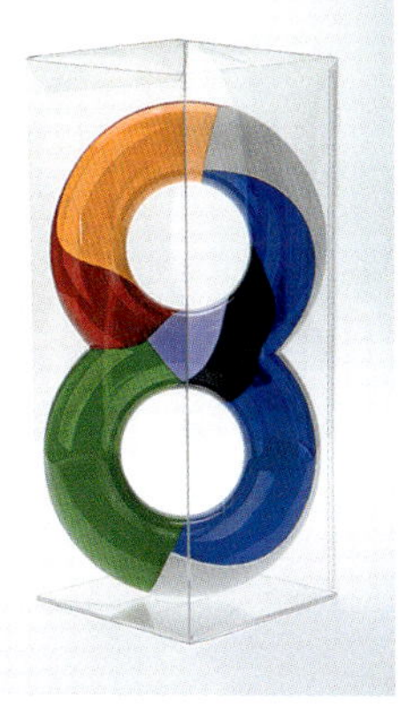
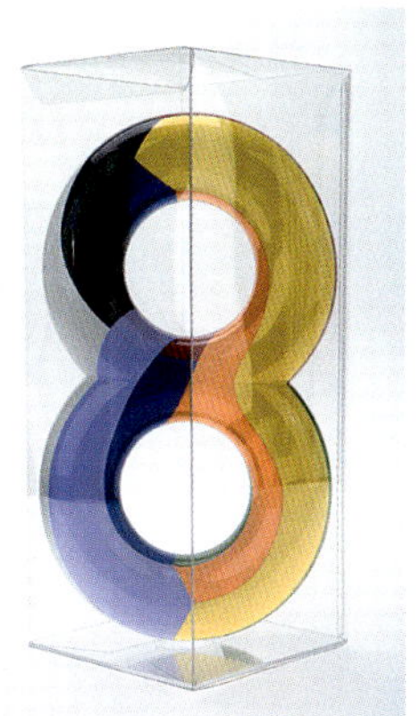

ELLEN GALLAGHER

Ruby Dee, 2005

Two-plate photogravure with aquatint
and unique hand-shaped plasticine
elements (in three colors) on multilayered
laminated paper, framed,
image size: 6 x 4 x $^1/_8$" (15,2 x 10,2 x 0,3 cm),
with frame: 9$^1/_4$ x 7$^1/_4$ x 1$^1/_4$"
(23,5 18,4 x 3,8 cm),
produced by Two Palms Press, New York,
Ed. 30/XV, signed and numbered

EDITION FOR PARKETT 73

A beehive of thoughts buzzing in the gulf
between womanhood and survival, past and
present, hunger and surfeit, work and play...

"Gallagher is a handworking, hand laborer (...). The
production of a simple, flat, engaging image is never her
sole purpose. This is why she works in print, as well as
in painting and in drawing. Process, layers, materials—
physicality is everything to her. Flesh is a texture as
much as a color. DeLuxe is collage (paper), photomontage
(digital), photogravure (the process of printing from an
intaglio plate, etched according to a photographic image);
it is mounted, built-up and –upon by: abrasion, aquatint,
burnishing, drypoint, embrossing, etching, laser cutting,
stenciling, tattoo-machine engraving (yes for skin)—
adding blue varnish, crystals, cut paper, toy eyeballs,
white spaces, glitter, gold leaf, pomade... and this is not
even the half of it."

Thyrza Nichols Goodeve
Parkett No. 73, 2005

エレン・ギャラガー

ルビー・ディ　2005

2版グラビア印刷にアクアチントと
プラスティック粘土による
手作りの個々に形の異なる要素を添え
積層紙に載せて額装、
図柄：15.2×10.2×0.3cm、
額入り：23.5×18.4×3.8cm、
制作：ツー・ポーム・プレス（ニューヨーク）、
Ed. 30/XV、署名、番号入り

パルケット・エディション 73

考え事でいっぱいの蜂の巣が、女であることと生き延び
るのがやっとの人生、過去と現在、飢餓と飽食、仕事と
遊びの間に横たわる深淵でブンブン音を立てている。

ギャラガーは手を使って働く、手仕事の働き手……素朴で、平面的、見
るものの興味をひきつけるイメージのみを目指したことはない。絵と
素描ばかりでなく、版画も手がけるのはそのせい。制作過程、重層性、
素材、物の手応えがギャラガーにとってはすべて。肉体は色彩と同じ
程度に質感が物を言う。《デラックス》はコラージュ（紙）、フォトモ
ンタージュ（デジタル）、グラビア印刷（写真の映像をエッチングした
凹版印刷）からなる。それをマウントし、組み上げ、組み上げられる。
磨耗、アクアチント、つや出し、ドライポイント、エンボス加工、エッ
チング、レーザー・カッティング、ステンシル、刺青機による彫版（そう、
皮膚用です）——青いニスをかけ、クリスタル、切り紙、玩具の目玉、
白い空間、きらめき、金箔、ポマード……これでもまだ半分以上残って
いる。

ティルザ・ニコルス・グッディーヴ
（パルケット 73号、2005年）

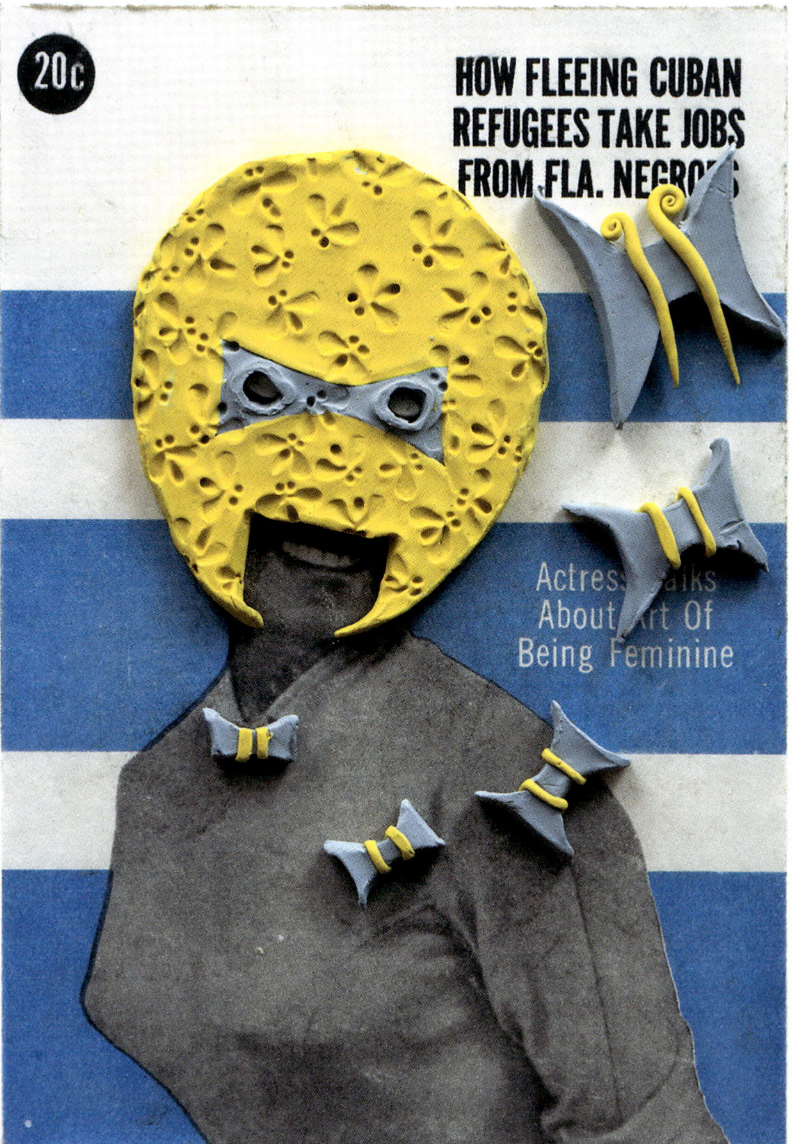

20c
HOW FLEEING CUBAN
REFUGEES TAKE JOBS
FROM FLA. NEGROES
Actress Talks
About Art Of
Being Feminine

ISA GENZKEN

Al Dente, 2003

Italian ceramic, lacquer, plastic,
plate with two toy figures (cow and
dinosaur), each unique and handmade
by the artist, approx. 11 $^{13}/_{16}$ x 7 $^{7}/_{8}$ x 10 $^{1}/_{4}$"
(29,7 x 20 x 26 cm),
Ed. 74/XX, signed and numbered
certificate

EDITION FOR PARKETT 69

Survival of the tastiest: evolution in a nutshell demonstrated by the odd couple.

"Models—I wanted the pieces to be like models—are usually more fragile than some monumental metal sculpture. And people often find it very pleasing when they can still see something old, intended as a sketch, because it's been preserved. Fragility can be a very beautiful thing, more beautiful then something that's obviously made to last forever. It's very important to me that the things I'm making are really by me, and not made by assistants or farmed out as commissions. Every piece is by me, made by my own hand."

Isa Genzken, interview with Michael Krajewski
Parkett No. 69, 2003

イザ・ゲンツケン

アル・デンテ　2003

イタリア陶器、ラッカー、プラスティック、
玩具の人形をふたつのせた皿、
すべてアーティストの手作りで個々に形がちがう、
約29.7×20×26cm、
Ed. 74/XX、署名、番号入り証明書

パルケット・エディション 69

もっとも美味なものが生き残る。おかしなカップルが、小さな貝のなかで実地に示す進化。

模型（作品には模型のようであってほしい）は通常、大がかりな金属の彫刻よりも壊れやすい。スケッチのつもりで描いた古い絵がまだ残っているのを見ると、それがとってあったことをとても喜ぶひとがいる。華奢なものは美しい、いつまでも残るように作られたものより、ずっと美しい。わたしにとっては、自分の作品がアシスタントに頼んだり、よそに注文したものではなく、自分の手で作られたものであることがとても重要です。作品はどれをとっても、わたしが作ったもの、わたしがこの手でこしらえたものです。

イザ・ゲンツケン、
ミカエル・クラジェウスキーのインタヴューに応えて
（パルケット 69号、2003年）

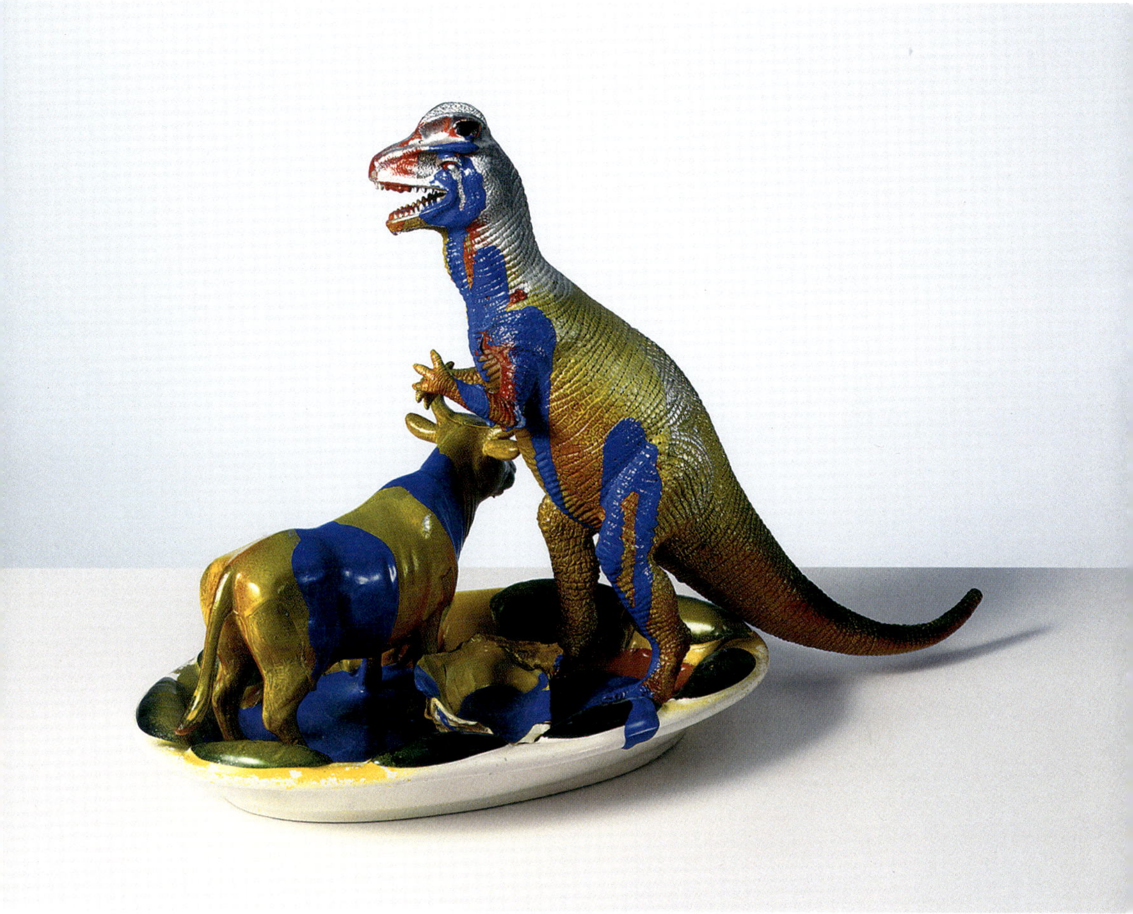

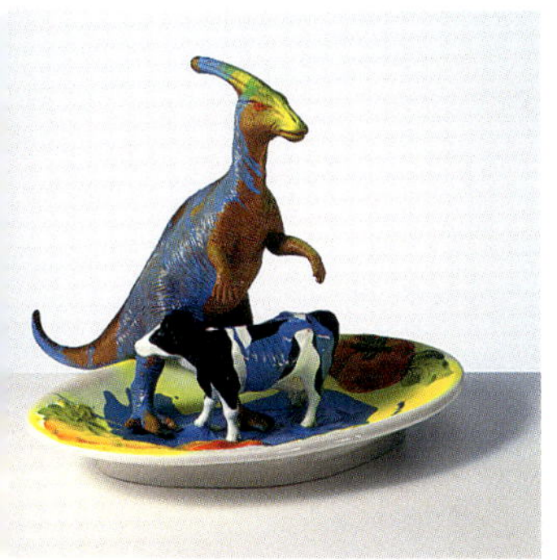

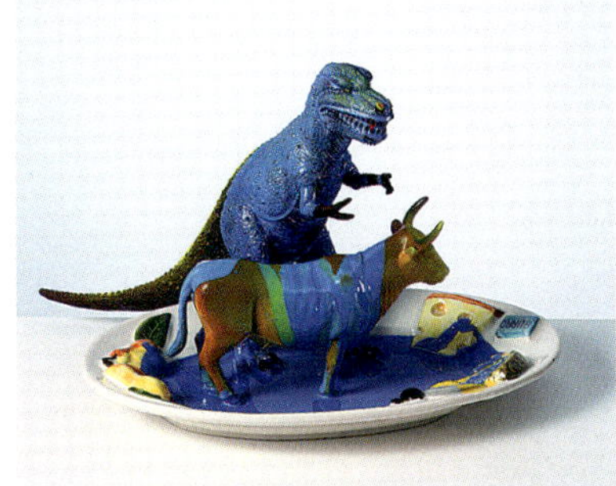

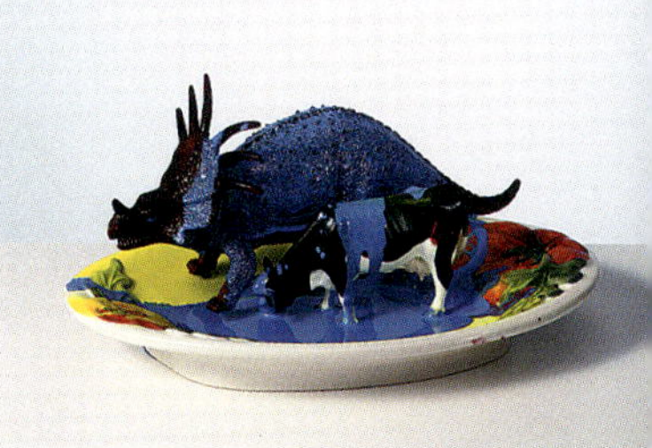

FRANZ GERTSCH

Cima del Mar (detail), 1990/91

Woodcut (cobalt turquoise and
ultramarine, half and half)
on Heizaburo Japan paper,
10 x 16 ³⁄₈" (25,4 x 41,6 cm),
folded, not bound in the magazine,
Ed. 80/XXX, signed and numbered

EDITION FOR PARKETT 28

Against the grain. Every point of light on this minutely described surface corresponds to the removal of a sliver of wood. This fragment was taken from a gigantic woodcut measuring more than 5 x 6 feet (170 x 152 cm).

"In Gertsch's woodcuts, everything makes it impossible to 'pocket' the image as a finite subject. One must go inside, adjust, let one's eyes wander, orient oneself. Beyond the dimensions of the block (and the print), there is no scale."

Rainer Michael Mason
Parkett No. 28, 1991

フランツ・ゲルチュ

外洋（部分）　　1990/91

木版（コバルト・ターコイズとウルトラマリンを半々）、
手漉き和紙（岩野平三郎）、
25.4×41.6cm、
本誌に綴じこまず折り畳み、
Ed. 80/XXX、署名、番号入り

パルケット・エディション 28

木目に逆らう。微細に描写された表面に光る点のひとつひとつが、木板から取り除いた裂片に対応する。この断片は170×152cmの巨大な木版画の一部。

ゲルチュの木版では、すべてが画像を完成品として「ポケットにいれる」ことを妨げる。わたしたちはその中に入り、適応し、目が彷徨うのにまかせ、方向を見定めなければならない。版木（そして版画）の大きさを越えれば、その先に尺度は存在しない。

レイナー・マイケル・メイソン
（パルケット 28号、1991年）

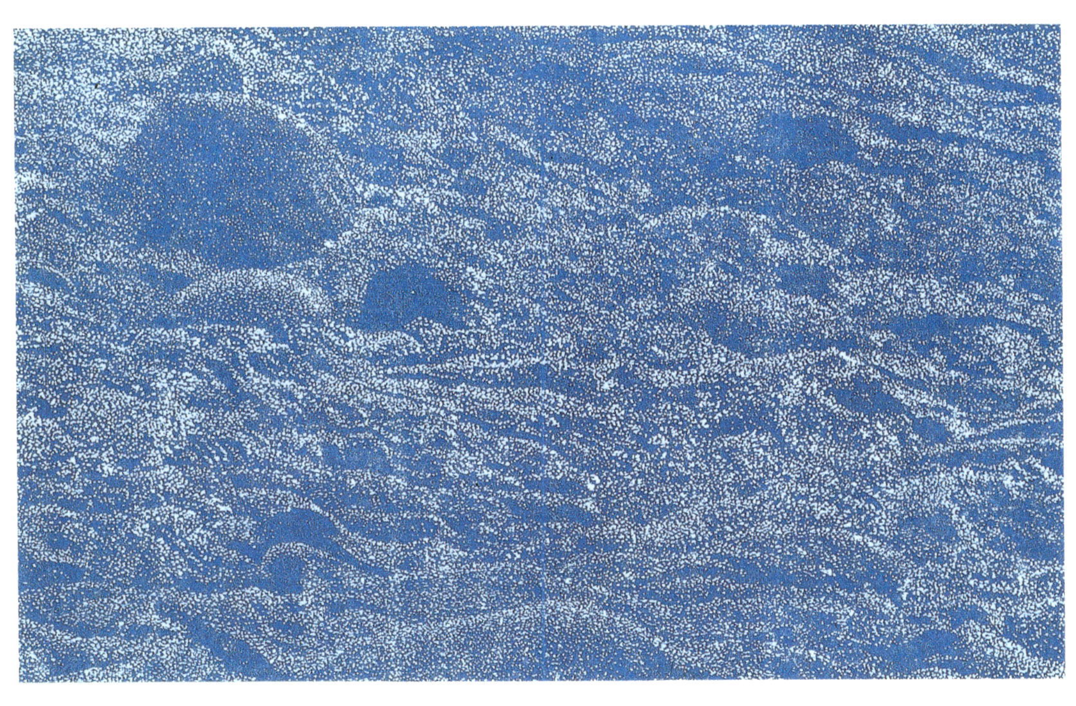

GILBERT & GEORGE

Gilbert & George, 1987

Photograph, mounted on cardboard
folded in the middle,
10 x 16¹/₂" (25,5 x 42 cm),
Ed. 200, signed and numbered

EDITION FOR PARKETT 14

Memorabilia from an art world Hall of Fame.
A provocative reshoot of the classic wedding
photo, the alumni portrait, the religious
diptych, Gilbert & George's stand-up self-
portrait will be an asset to the mantelpiece
of any self-respecting amateur.

"Gilbert & George consider themselves warriors
'fighting for a total expression.' They want to involve
all our experiences, intellectual and physical, even
the most dramatic, the most banal, the most shunned
by social custom. Their daily struggle for artistic
creative action becomes a metaphor of the unceasing
desperate activity of man."

Mario Codognato
Parkett No. 14, 1987

ギルバート＆ジョージ

ギルバート＆ジョージ　1987

写真、真ん中から二つ折りにしボール紙にマウント、
25.5×42cm、
Ed. 200、署名、番号入り

パルケット・エディション 14

美術界の栄誉殿堂のお土産。昔ながらの婚礼写真、
卒業記念写真、二連式宗教画を挑発的に焼き直した
ギルバート＆ジョージの立ち姿の自画像は、自尊心に
欠けるところのない美術愛好家すべてのマントルピー
スにいっそうの輝きを添えるでしょう。

ギルバート＆ジョージは自らを「完全な表現を目指して闘う」戦士
とみなしている。ふたりはわたしたちが経験するすべてを、知的な
ものから肉体的なもの、劇的の極み、凡庸の極みでさえ、そして
社会慣習がとりわけ避けようとするものまで、作品にとりあげよう
とする。かれらが不断に展開する芸術的な創作活動は、絶えること
なくくりひろげられる人間の絶望的な行為の隠喩となる。

マリオ・コドニャート
（パルケット 14号、1987年）

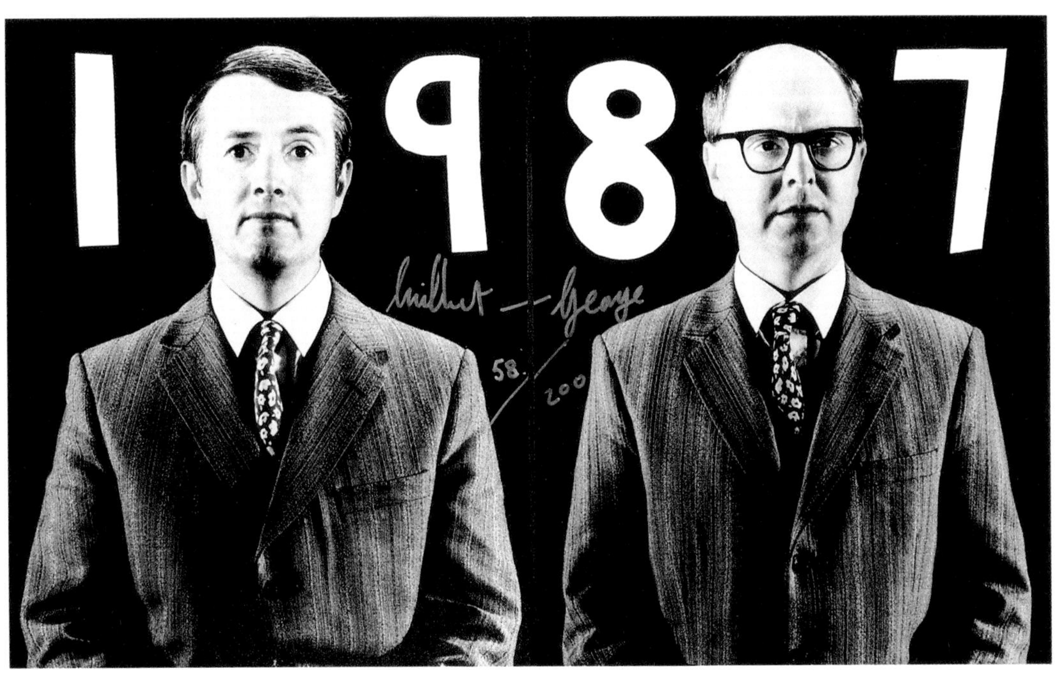

LIAM GILLICK

Literally No Place, 2001

5 plexiglas and 3 aluminum plates
in different colors,
8 x 10" (25 x 20,5 cm) each,
assembly ad libitum,
Ed. 70/XXV, signed and numbered

EDITION FOR PARKETT 61

The poetry of architecture: the house that Gillick built defies the conventions of presence and place.

"Gillick's platforms—Plexiglas panels in aluminum frames—do not obey gravity and lie on the floor like Andre's carpets of metal panels that viewers can step on. No, they are suspended from the ceiling, parallel to the floor so that viewers must tilt their heads to look up at the platforms and the way they are mounted. In his boxed and wall constructions, he uses materials like Plexiglas, plywood, pine, and aluminum as Donald Judd did before him, but without giving viewers the feeling of knowing where they stand. Instead they are awash with feelings of enigmatic and fluttering indeterminacy."

Gregor Stemmrich
Parkett No. 61, 2001

リアム・ギリック

文字通り場にあらず　2001

色違いのアクリル板 5枚、アルミ板 3枚、
25×20.5cm、
任意に組み立て、
Ed. 70/XXV、署名、番号入り

パルケット・エディション 61

建築の詩情。ギリックの建てる家は存在と場の慣例に従おうとしない。

アルミの枠組にアクリル板をはめたギリックの台座は引力にしたがわず、鑑賞者が上に乗れるカール・アンドレの金属製カーペットのように、床に置かれている。いや、天井から床と並行に吊るされているので、鑑賞者は台座を見るにせよ、それがどのように設置されているかを知ろうとするにせよ、首をかしげて見上げなければならない。箱や壁の形をした作品には、アクリル、合板、松材、そしてドナルド・ジャッドに倣ってアルミを使うけれども、鑑賞者は自分の居場所があやふやになる。いやそれどころか、得たいの知れない、心をかき乱すどっちつかずの感覚に襲われる。

グレゴール・ステムリヒ
（パルケット 61号、2001年）

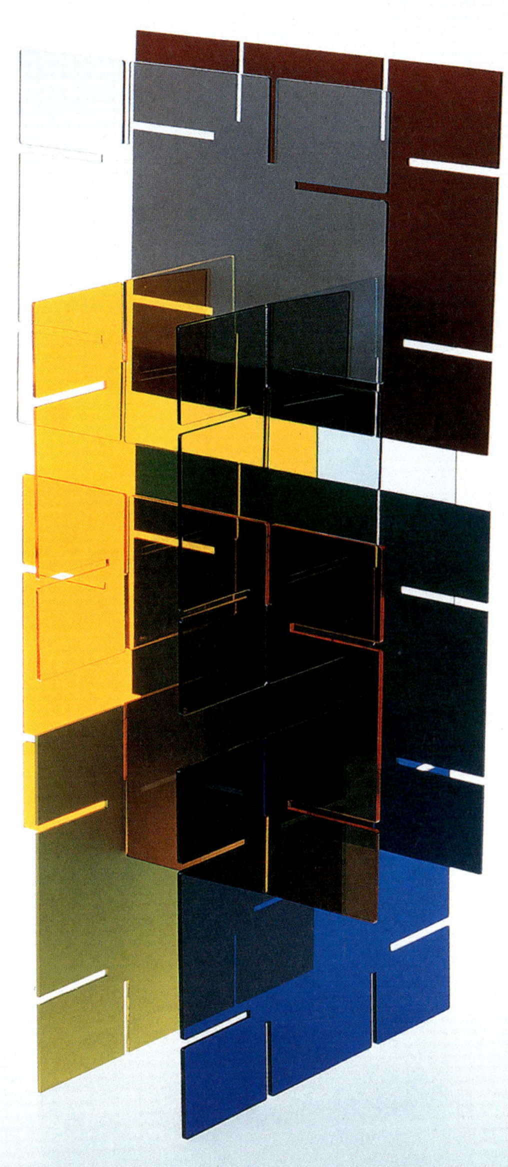

ROBERT GOBER

Untitled, 1991

Lithograph on newsprint
with handtorn edges,
printed on both sides and
folded three times,
22 1/8 x 13 7/8" (56,7 x 35,4 cm),
hand-colored with coffee
by the artist, printed by
Maurice Sanchez & Joe Petruzzelli,
Derrière L'Etoile Studio, New York,
Ed. 75/XXV unique pieces,
signed and numbered

EDITION FOR PARKETT 27

Day in the life. Amongst a scramble of
blushing brides and gruesome news on a
seemingly ordinary page of The New York
Times, dated October 4, 1960, we come
suddenly upon a brief notice of the artist's
own death as a boy of six.

"As assemblages of props, costumes, and sets, Gober's
installations of domestic dreamscapes pose as sites
for the unfolding of narrative sequences; each element
serves as a silent accoutrement to the human drama
awaiting to be enacted therein... in this potent mise-
en-scène we are implicated as participants. Gober's
fabricated, home-like spaces are uncanny in the truest
sense of the word."

Nancy Spector
Parkett No. 27, 1991

ロバート・ゴーバー

無題　　1991

手で縁を破いた新聞紙の両面にリトグラフでプリント、
3度折りたたむ、56.7×35.4cm、
ゴーバー自身がコーヒーで着色、
刷り：モーリス・サンチェス＆ジョー・ペトルッツェリ、
デリエール・レトワール・スタジオ（ニューヨーク）、
Ed. 75/XXV、同じものはふたつない、署名、番号入り

パルケット・エディション 27

人生のとある一日。頬を紅潮させる花嫁や身の毛のよだ
つニュースのひしめく一見ありきたりな、1960年10月4
日付けのニューヨーク・タイムズの紙面を見ていると、い
きなりアーティスト自身が6歳で亡くなったという短い記
事が目にとびこんでくる。

舞台装置、衣裳、小道具のアッサンブラージュと同じく、家庭内の情
景を夢見るゴーバーのインスタレーションは、物語が順次展開する場
としてそこにある。品物ひとつひとつが、演じられる時を待つ人間ドラ
マの無言の語らぬ備品の役割をはたす……見るものを強力に引きつ
けるこの演出では、わたしたちもいやおうなく芝居に参加させられる。
ゴーバーの手がける家庭まがいの空間は、薄気味悪いことおびただ
しい。

ナンシー・スペクター
（パルケット 27号、1991年）

Miss Rubinson, A Buyer, Marries

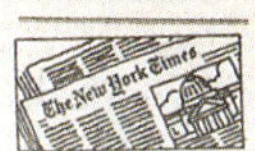

Heather Lina Rubinson, a daughter of Dr. Kalman Rubinson of New York and the late Irene Rowe Rubinson, was married yesterday to Michael Warren Schechter, the son of Ruth Canaan of Great Neck, L.I., and Marvin L. Schechter of Old Westbury, L.I. Rabbi Lawrence M. Colton performed the ceremony at the Tower Suite in New York.

Mrs. Schechter has a bachelor's degree in fine arts and an M.B.A. from New York University. She is an assistant buyer at Tiffany's in New York. Her father is an associate professor of physiology and biophysics at N.Y.U. Her grandfather, the late Dr. Irving Rowe, was a physicist and the chief scientist at the United States Office of Naval Research in New York.

The bridegroom, a magna cum laude graduate of N.Y.U., is an associate at Mentor Partners, an investment firm in New York. His mother is the vice president of corporate communications at N.S. Tele-Comm Inc., a private pay phone company in Great Neck. His father is the senior partner in the New York law firm of Tumstead, Schechter and Torre.

Girl Lived in a Closet, California Police Say

SAN BERNARDINO, Calif., Oct. 25 (AP) — A 12-year-old girl has been found locked in a filthy closet, where, the police say, her parents kept her confined for much of her life.

The girl was found Monday night in the reeking, cockroach-infested closet, which was kept closed by a bent nail, said Sgt. Jenifer Kauffman of the San Bernardino police.

Her parents, Joseph and Sandra Sauceda, were charged Wednesday with felony child endangerment, and the father also was charged with felony child abuse, Ms. Kauffman said.

The police were tipped by a relative. When they asked the Saucedas to show them the girl, they took officers to the closet, Ms. Kauffman said.

Officers said the girl was lying in her own feces and wore a urine-stained sweatsuit.

Investigators say the child rarely left the closet and had probably been kept locked up at other homes where the family lived during the past decade, Ms. Kauffman said.

"Obviously, it's a terrible, traumatic condition," said Sgt. Bob Evans. "It will probably take years to recover from."

The couple was held in this city 60 miles east of Los Angeles in lieu of $50,000 bail each.

The girl, whose name was not disclosed, and her six brothers and sisters, ages 2 months to 15 years, were turned over to the county Child Protective Services. There was no evidence that the other children were abused, Ms. Kauffman said.

Joseph Sauceda, 33, denied that he and his 31-year-old wife abused their daughter. He said the closet was not a cell and that his family was a loving one.

Randy A. Gilman, Gemologist, Weds

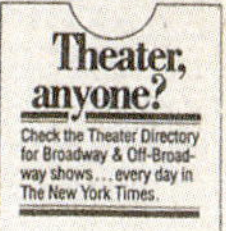

Randy Allyn Gilman, a daughter of Mrs. Herbert Gilman of West Hartford, Conn., and the late Mr. Gilman, was married yesterday at the Pierre in New York to Henri Zvi Bolimovsky, the son of Mr. and Mrs. Meisha Bolimovsky of Tel Aviv. Rabbi Sol Roth and Cantor Joseph Malovany performed the ceremony.

Mrs. Bolimovsky, a graduate of Union College, is a gemologist in New York for Best Products, a retail holding company in Richmond. Her father was the founder and chairman of Ames Department Stores in Rocky Hill, Conn. Her mother, Evelyn Gilman, is a retired teacher.

The bridegroom, a graduate of the University of Toronto, is an architect and commercial planner in New York. His father, who is retired, was a jeweler in Tel Aviv.

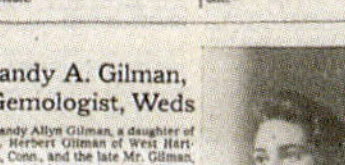

Theater, anyone?

Check the Theater Directory for Broadway & Off-Broadway shows... every day in The New York Times.

Lottery Numbers

Oct. 5, 1990

New York Numbers — 061
New York Win 4 — 3441
New Jersey Pick-It — 199
New Jersey Pick 4 — 6607
Connecticut Daily — 827
Connecticut Play 4 — 2622
Connecticut Lotto — 9, 10, 14, 17, 24, 43

Oct. 4, 1990

New York Pick 10 — 2, 3, 4, 6, 9, 11, 14, 17, 19, 21, 28, 43, 45, 49, 50, 58, 59, 62, 68, 71

Your Money: Saturday, In Business Day

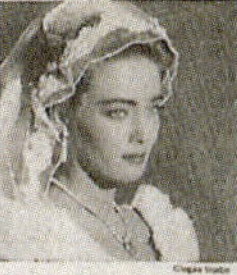

Susan and Robert Greenwood

Susan Fisher Weds R. A. Greenwood

Susan Grossman Fisher, the daughter of Mr. and Mrs. Bernard Grossman of Scarsdale, N.Y., was married yesterday at her home in New York to Robert Arthur Greenwood, a son of William Greenwood of Bradenton, Fla., and the late Mildred Greenwood. Rabbi Richard S. Chapin performed the ceremony.

Mrs. Greenwood and her husband, both 44 years old, are principals in the Berkshire Bank, a private commercial bank in New York. The bride graduated cum laude from the University of Wisconsin and has a master's degree in personnel administration and an M.B.A. from Columbia University. Her first marriage ended in divorce, as did her husband's. Her father, who is retired, was the president of Laurel Printing in New York.

Mr. Greenwood is the president of the New York Women's Forum and is a member of the National Advisory Council of the United States Small Business Administration.

The bridegroom is a graduate of the University of Oklahoma with an M.B.A. from Bucknell University. His father retired as a vice president of the Chase Manhattan Bank in New York.

Diane Dougherty Weds J. G. Chachas

Diane Young Dougherty, a television sales executive, and John Gregory Chachas, an associate at the First Boston Corporation, both of New York, were married in Washington yesterday afternoon at St. Sophia's Greek Orthodox Cathedral by the Rev. John Tavlarides. The ceremony was followed by another marriage service last evening at the Metropolitan Memorial United Methodist Church in Washington, conducted by the Rev. William Holmes.

Mrs. Chachas is a daughter of Mr. and Mrs. Thomas J. Dougherty of Bethesda, Md. The bridegroom is the son of Mr. and Mrs. Gregory Chachas of Salt Lake City.

The bride, 27 years old, is a national account sales executive with Capital Cities/ABC. She is a graduate of Barnard College. Her father is a senior vice president of the Metromedia Company. Her mother, Anne D. Dougherty, recently completed two terms as the president of Hospice Care of the District of Columbia.

The bridegroom, 25, is an associate in mergers and acquisitions at First Boston. He is a graduate of Columbia University and has an M.B.A. degree from Harvard University. His mother, Mary P. Chachas, is a community relations associate at the University of Utah Medical Center in Salt Lake City. His father is a lawyer and manages family mineral and other business interests in Salt Lake City.

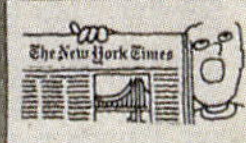

Diane Chachas

Teen Watches as Dog Is Killed With Wrong Injection by Vet

FORT WORTH, Sept. 29 (AP) — A teen-age boy who took his dog to a veterinarian for a rabies vaccination watched as his pet was mistakenly put to sleep.

"It was a real tragedy, very serious," said Dr. Keith Sultemeier, the veterinarian who operates the clinic in Azle, northwest of Fort Worth.

Tony McCarty, 15 years old, and his mother took their 2½-year-old dog, a pit bull and chow mix named Runt, to the clinic on Thursday, about the same time another similar dog, a female mix of pit bull and chow, was taken in for euthanasia, Dr. Sultemeier said.

The boy was with Runt when the dog got the lethal injection instead of the rabies shot. "The lady and her son came in with a dog for a fairly straightforward vaccination and walked out without the dog," Dr. Sultemeier said. "We are at fault."

The veterinarian bought the boy a full-blooded chow puppy. The mother, Pam Peyton, said she would not sue.

Ms. Froom Weds A Fellow Student

Mignon Froom and Brian Jeffrey Benjamin, both third-year medical students at the University of Rochester, were married yesterday at the Country House, a restaurant in Stony Brook, L.I. Rabbi Joseph Topek officiated. The bride, who is 29 years old, is the daughter of Dr. and Mrs. Jack Froom of Stony Brook. Her husband, who is 24, is a son of Mr. and Mrs. Harvey P. Benjamin of Voorhees, N.J.

Mrs. Benjamin, who is known as Mimi, is a magna cum laude graduate of Brandeis University.

Boy Drowns in Pool

WALLINGFORD, CT Oct. 3 (AP)— State officials are questioning a report by local authorities that the drowning of a small boy in a near-empty backyard pool was accidental. According to the initial police report the child's mother, Leah Gober, found her six-year-old son Robert late Monday evening face down in about three inches of water. State officials have refused to release details but are holding the child's mother for questioning. The family was draining the pool for winter.

Weather Report

Meteorology: Pennsylvania State University

Metropolitan Forecast

High pressure over the South will direct unseasonably warm air into the region this weekend. Aside from a few high clouds, skies will be clear and temperatures will average more than 15 degrees above normal. A cold front will reach northern New York state tomorrow and may cross the region early next week.

New York City: Today, sunny, breezy, warmer. High 83. Tonight, clear, quite mild. Low 64. Tomorrow, mostly sunny, very warm. High 85.

Long Island: Today, sunny, breezy, warmer. High 81. Tonight, clear, quite mild. Low 61. Tomorrow, mostly sunny, very warm. High 83.

Westchester and Rockland: Today, sunny, breezy, warmer. High 79. Tonight, clear, quite mild. Low 58. Tomorrow, mostly sunny, very warm. High 81.

New Jersey: Today, sunny, breezy, warmer. High 84. Tonight, clear, quite mild. Low 62. Tomorrow, mostly sunny, very warm. High 87.

Connecticut: Today, sunny, breezy, warmer. High 80. Tonight, clear, quite mild. Low 58. Tomorrow, mostly sunny, very warm. High 83.

Extended Forecast: Monday and Tuesday will continue to be unseasonably warm, though cloudier. Showers are possible later Tuesday as a cold front nears the region.

National Forecast

Powerful winds coursing through the northern Rockies (gusted to 87 miles an hour at Choteau, Mont. on Thursday, a precursor to a strong cold front coming ashore in the Pacific Northwest Today, the upper-level sections of the front, marked by a southwest sag in the jet shears from Montana to northern California, will start through tomorrow morning. In response, high-level winds will flow from the central Rockies to the Great Lakes, impeding the eastward advance of the cold front.

The delay of the front will allow an area of high pressure off the Middle Atlantic Seaboard to act like a heat pump, fostering sunny, unseasonably warm weather in the Northeast this weekend. Humidity will not significantly rise across the region before Monday, owing to the fact that moist air will have to take a circuitous route, slowly spreading north from the western Gulf Coast and then northeast from the lower Mississippi Valley.

The only snag in the weather pattern in the Northeast is the arrival of clouds and showers in northern New England. The cause of the showers there is the collision of cool air that is moving across eastern Canada and warm air from the heat pump high off the Middle Atlantic Coast.

In the wake of the sluggish front, cold air will continue to gather in the northern Rockies. Snow, caused by winds from the east being forced up the mountains, will fall in the Tetons of Wyoming, the Bitterrolls of Montana and in Yellowstone Valley, where two large forest fires, fanned by gale-force winds, were out of control on Friday.

Meanwhile, a disturbance from Mexico will spread showers into parts of Texas, Oklahoma and Kansas. In the Tropics, Hurricane Klaus will continue to drift northwestward in the Caribbean.

Today's High Temperatures and Precipitation

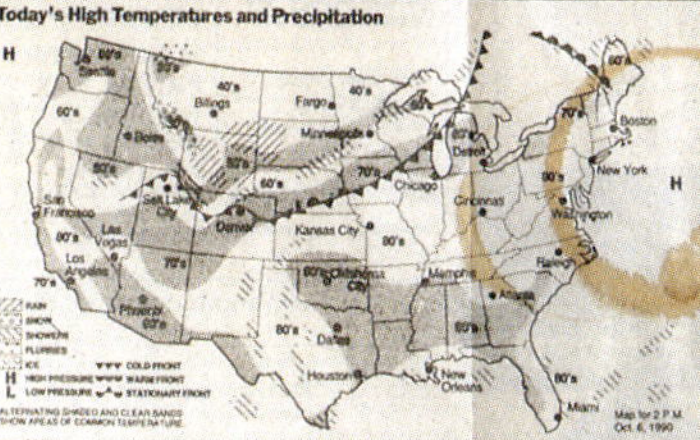

Today's Sunshine and Clouds

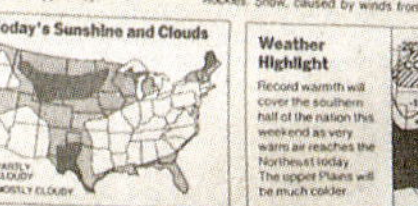

Weather Highlight

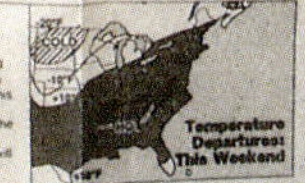

Metropolitan Almanac

Temperature · **Precipitation** · **Sun, Moon, Planets** · **Boating** · **Foliage Forecast** · **Reservoirs**

Regional Recreation

NAN GOLDIN

Lambs Ears, 1999

C-print, 15 ³/₄ x 23 ⁵/₈" (50,8 x 61 cm),
Ed. 60/XX, signed and numbered

EDITION FOR PARKETT 57

L'heure bleue: A moment of silence immerses us in the sensual fragrance of whispering sage.

"The states of subjectivity in Goldin's work are achieved by closing in on her subjects, sometimes almost to the point of addictive hallucination. Looking in the mirror. Lying in bed. Being alone. Being together. Dressing to go out. Hanging out in a bar. Talking. Sleeping. Crying. Kissing. The actions or feelings, the joys or sorrows, shown in the pictures relate neither to professional activity nor to public life: There's no school, shopping mall, or work, no doctors or teachers. Enemies have been removed. It is striking how the faces and their gazes, whether or not they are looking towards the lens, or the bodies, naked or dressed, evoke so little of our common cultural heritage."

Elisabeth Lebovici
Parkett No. 57, 1999

ナン・ゴールディン

子羊の耳　1999

Cプリント、50.8×61cm、
Ed. 60/XX、署名、番号入り

パルケット・エディション 57

L'heure bleue（蒼い時）。沈黙の時に囁くセージの官能的な香りがわたしたちを包む

ゴールディンの作品にみなぎる主観性は、ときには中毒性の幻覚を催しそうになるほど、主題にあくまで接近することよって達成される。鏡を覗きこむ。ベッドに身を横たえる。ひとりきり。だれかと一緒。服を着て外出する。バーにたむろする。話をする。眠る。泣く。キスをする。写真に映る行為あるいは感覚、歓びあるいは悲しみは、仕事や世間とのつきあいと関係しない。学校もショッピング・モールも映らず、仕事、医者、教師は登場しない。敵は追放されている。顔、そしてレンズを見ているいないにかかわらず眼差しが、裸か着衣かにかかわらず肉体が、わたしたちの共有する文化遺産をほとんど喚起させないことに、胸を打たれる。

エリザベス・レボヴィッチ
（パルケット 57号、1999年）

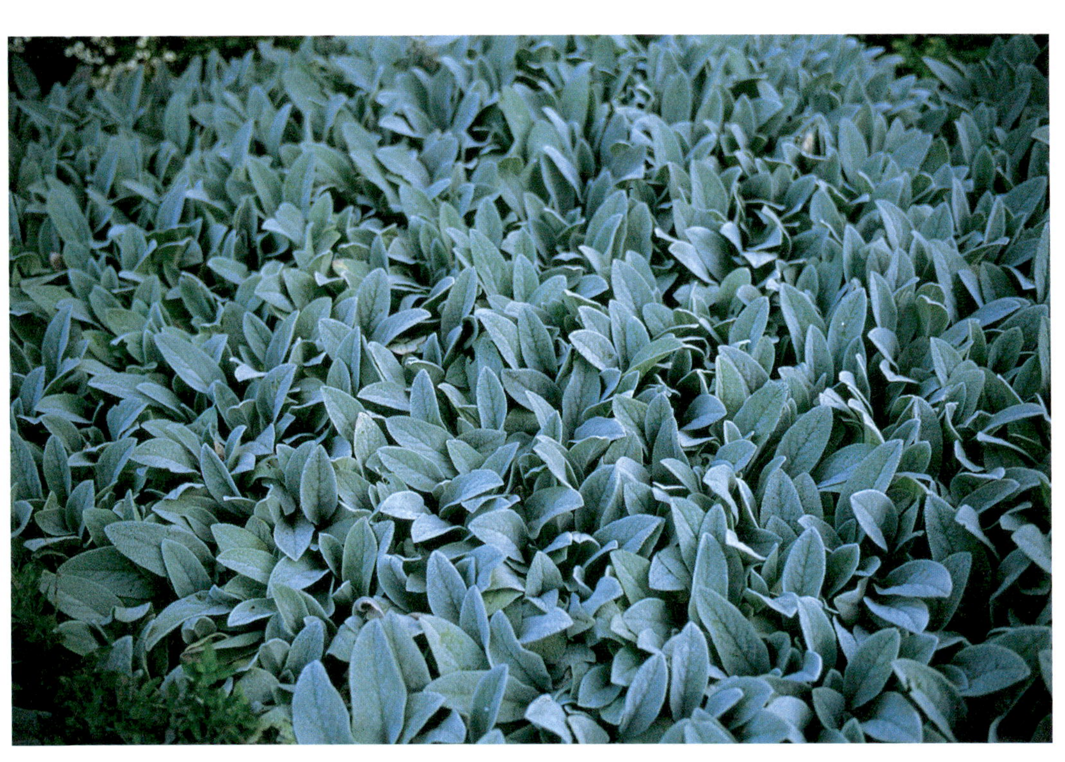

DOMINIQUE GONZALEZ-FOERSTER

Calendario 2020, 2007

Calendar for 12 months in 12 years
(January 2008–December 2019),
14 prints including 2 by Philippe Parreno,
color silkscreen on Munken 350g/m²,
paper size: 16¹⁄₂ x 19" (42 x 46,6 cm) each,
image size: 11¹⁄₂ x 16³⁄₄" (28,6 x 42,6 cm),
bound, printed by Atelier Lorenz Boegli,
Zurich,
Ed. 45/XX, numbered and signed

EDITION FOR PARKETT 80

A calendar in four dimensions, where the space of a year fills the time of one month.

"Gonzalez-Foerster has repeatedly used space as a central feature of her artistic practice. Her work hails from multiple places, sites, and milieus and is constructed from the storehouse of feelings that we all carry inside. It unapologetically alludes to emotional values while generating a sensible landscape within the spectator. From her vast body of work, it is specifically the environments that provoke the formation of these mental-affective landscapes, and with which we are here concerned."

Pamela Echeverria
Parkett No. 80, 2007

ドミニク・ゴンザレス=フェルステル

カレンダー 2020 2007

12年間の12か月のカレンダー
（2008年1月から2019年12月まで）、
フィリップ・パレノ作の2点を含むプリント 14点、
カラー・シルクスクリーン、ムンケン紙 350g/㎡、
紙：42×46.6cm、
図柄：28.6×42.6cm、
刷り：アトリエ・ロレンツ・ボエリ（チューリヒ）、製本、
Ed. 45/XX、署名、番号入り

パルケット・エディション 80

4次元のカレンダー。1年間の空間が1月の時間を埋める。

ゴンザレス=フェルステルは制作活動のなかで、何度となく空間を中心としてあつかってきた。作品は多様な場所、処、環境を起点とし、わたしたちが心のなかに抱く感情の宝庫から構築される。弁解がましさの素振りもみせず感情に訴える力に触れながら、鑑賞者の内部に感情の敏感に作用する風景を生じさせる。数多い作品のなかで、知性に働きかける風景の形成をうながすのは、なによりもまずこうした環境であり、わたしたちの関心もまたそこにある。

パメラ・エチェベリア
（パルケット 80号、2007年）

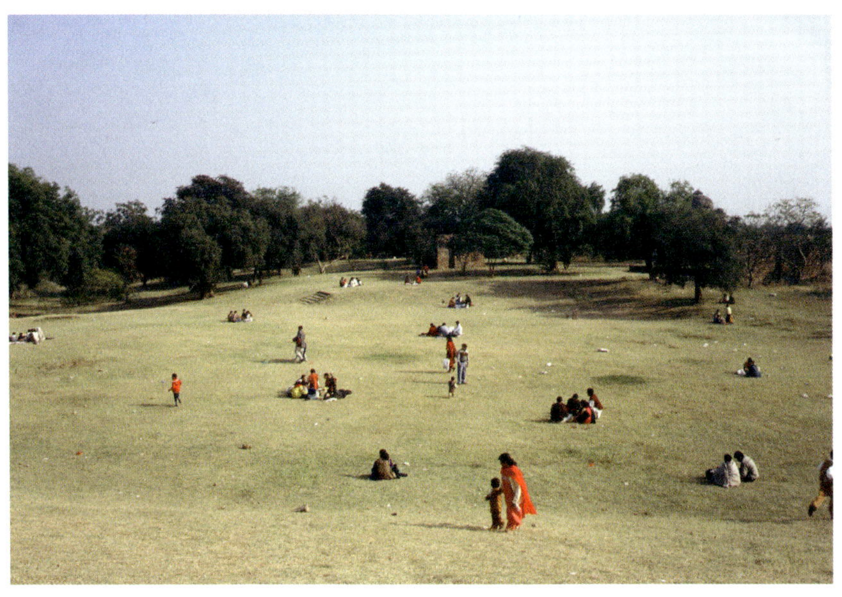

	1	2	3	4	5	6
7	8	9	10	11	12	13
14	15	16	17	18	19	20
21	22	23	24	25	26	27
28	29	30	31			

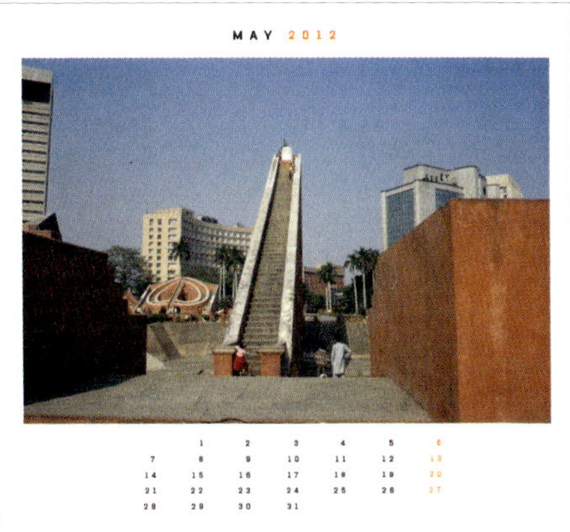

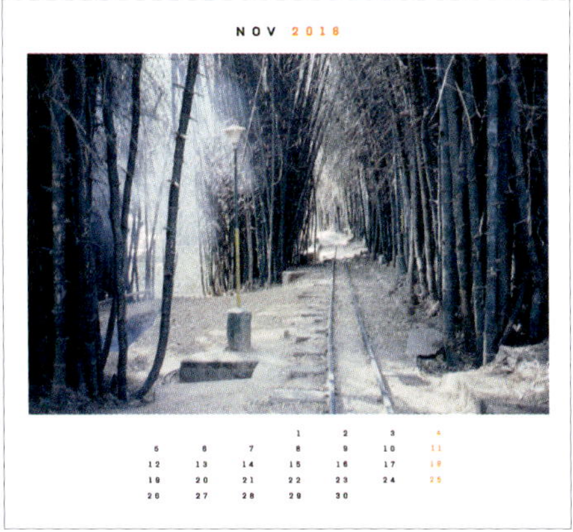

FELIX GONZALEZ-TORRES

Untitled, 1994

8-sheet billboard, silkscreen
on Appleton coated stock,
125 x 272" (317,5 x 690,9 cm),
printed by Triumph Productions, New York,
Ed. 84/XV, signed and numbered

EDITION FOR PARKETT 39

Emotional propaganda. Ephemeral footprints
in sand become an advertisement for the
ineffable in a gigantic billboard.

"Gonzalez-Torres finds and mobilizes materials
which may function as analogues for experience and
emotions which are not 'explained' in any extended
biographical supplementary exegesis. They are works
about love, desire, loss, death, and mourning, and
much of their extraordinary power derives from the
artist's refusal to retreat into didacticism."

Simon Watney
Parkett No. 39, 1994

フェリックス・ゴンザレス=トレス

無題　1994

シート8枚をつらねた広告掲示板、
アップルトンのコート紙にシルクスクリーン、
317.5×690.9cm、
刷り：トライアンフ・プロダクションズ（ニューヨーク）、
Ed. 84/XV、署名、番号入り

パルケット・エディション 39

感情に訴えるプロパガンダ。砂につかのま残る足跡が、
巨大な広告看板となってことばに尽くせないものを
宣伝する。

ゴンザレス=トレスは伝記を補足する詳細な評釈のどこにも「説
明」のない体験や感情の類似物として機能しうる素材を見いだし、
これを動員する。これらは愛、欲望、喪失、死、そして追悼をめぐる
作品であり、その比類ない威力の大きな部分は教訓主義に退去する
ことを拒むアーティストの姿勢に由来する。

サイモン・ワトニー
（パルケット 39号、1994年）

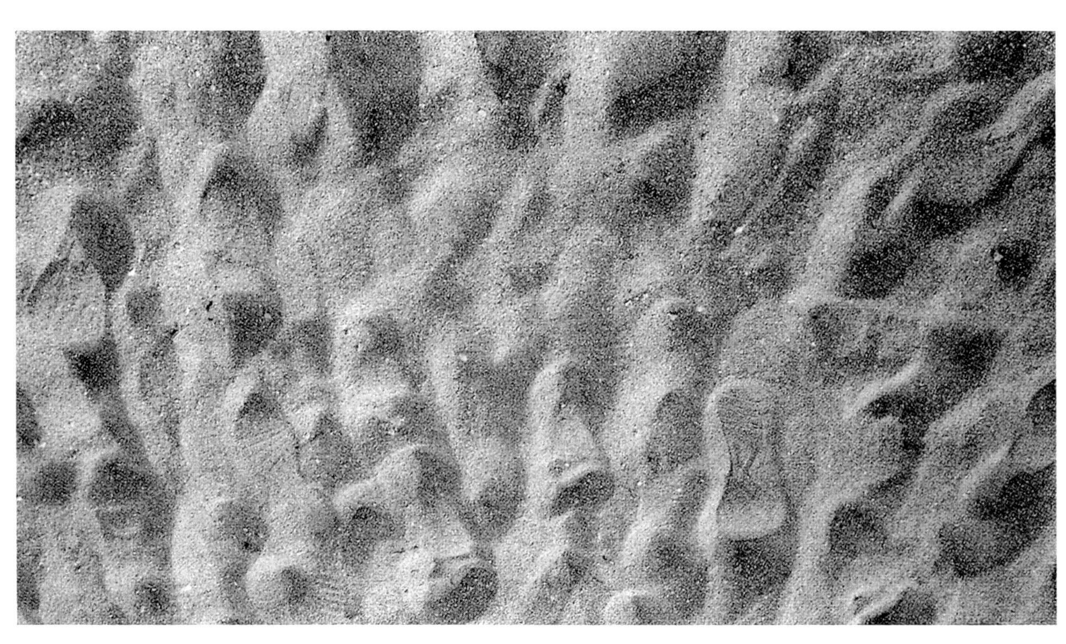

DOUGLAS GORDON

Signature, 1997

The artist's bite, 2 1/8 x 2" (5,5 x 5 cm),
on Fabriano paper 160g/m², 10 x 8 1/4"
(25,6 x 21,1 cm), bound in the magazine,
Ed. 50/XX, numbered

EDITION FOR PARKETT 49

The making of a sound bite: caught in the act and immortalized in silence.

"Douglas Gordon exposes certain time-based effects
that are at the root of our sense of psychological
security. This process is implemented by re-
emphasizing key elements from carefully researched
material, as well as using specially made video and
film footage to restructure the mass of connections
that influence an artist's activity. What could be
described as aestheticising the dynamic of trauma
and reassurance has been combined with an ongoing
desire to acknowledge his position as a self-conscious
artist working within the specific power structures of
the art world."

Douglas Gordon, interview with Liam Gillick
Parkett No. 49, 1997

ダグラス・ゴードン

署名　1997

アーティストの嚙み痕、5.5×5cm、
ファブリアーノ紙160g/㎡、25.6×21.1cm、
本誌に綴じこみ、
Ed. 50/XX、番号入り

パルケット・エディション 49

サウンドバイトのできるまで。行為のさなかを捉えられ、黙したまま後世に残される。

ダグラス・ゴードンはわたしたちの安心感の根底にある、時間を
ベースとする作用をあばきだす。この作業は、入念に検証した素材
の主要な要素を改めて強調することによって、またそのために用意
したビデオやフィルムを用い、アーティストの活動を左右する厖大
な関係性を改造することによって、履行される。トラウマと安堵の
ダイナミックな関係の美的表現とも形容しうるものが、美術界の具
体的な力関係のなかで自覚的に活動するアーティストとしての自ら
の立場を確認したいという、今もつづく欲求とむすびついた。

ダグラス・ゴードン、
リアム・ギリックのインタヴューに応えて
（パルケット 49号、1997年）

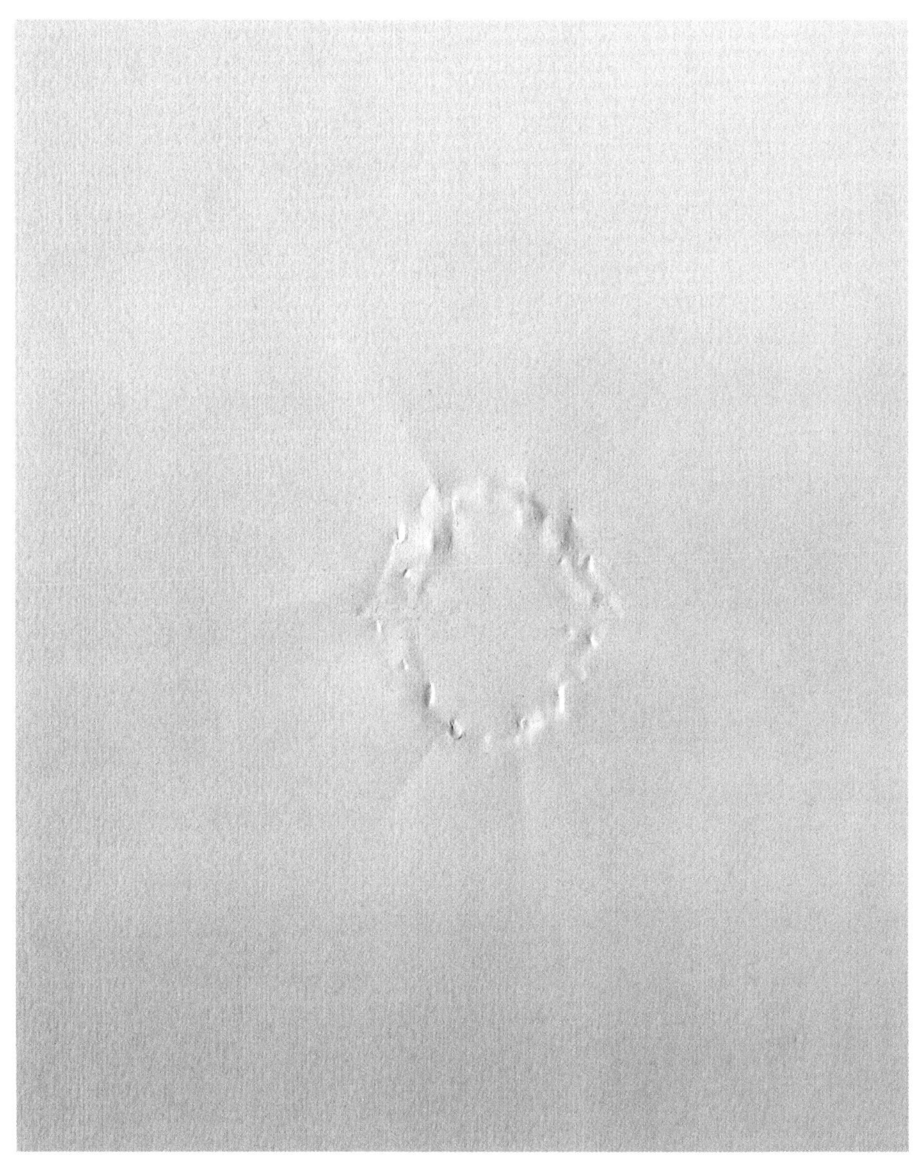

DAN GRAHAM

Fun for Kids at my Work in a Park
in Manhattan, 2003

Piezo Ultrachrome Pigment print
on Hahnemühle paper,
13 x 16½" (32,9 x 41,9 cm),
printed by Laumont Editions, New York,
photograph by Rosalind Cutforth,
Ed. 60/XX, signed and numbered
on the reverse

EDITION FOR PARKETT 68

Be your own architecture: reflect and be
reflected in walls and rooms that are none.

"I think I am experiencing my second childhood
through my two-way mirror work. I've never read Lacan,
but I feel my work involves the Lacanian 'mirror stage'
of childhood, when the young child first experiences
his/her sense or non-sense of an ego. I know that
through my art I make new friends, which I barely had
as a child. And through my 'hobbies' of rock music,
architectural tourism and travel, I stay young. I know
I am a child when I watch other Aries people (I am an
Aries) behaving childishly, like me."

Dan Graham, interview with Carmen Rosenberg Miller
Parkett No. 68, 2003

ダン・グレアム

マンハッタンの公園に置かれた
わたしの作品で楽しむ子供たち　2003

ピエゾ・ウルトラクローム顔料でプリント、
ハーネミュール紙、
32.9×41.9cm、
刷り：ローモント・エディションズ（ニューヨーク）、
写真撮影：ロザリンド・カットフォース、
Ed. 60/XX、裏面に署名と番号入り

パルケット・エディション 68

あなた自身の建築になってみませんか。不在の壁と部屋
に映ったり、映されたりしてみましょう。

マジックミラーを使った作品では、子供時代を追体験しているような
気がします。ラカンは読んだことがないけれど、子供時代に関するラ
カンの鏡像段階論、つまり幼い子供が初めて自我を感じたり自我のな
さを感じる時期の理論と、わたしの作品は関係があるように思います。
作品を通じて新しい友だちができるのですね。子供のころはほとんど
友だちがいなかったのに。それから「趣味」のロック音楽、建築観光
と旅のおかげで、若さを保っていられます。ほかの牡羊座のひとたち
（わたしも牡羊座です）が（わたしと同じように）子供っぽくふるまう
のを見ていると、わたしも子供だと気づくのですよ。

ダン・グレアム、
カーメン・ローゼンバーグ・ミラーとの対話
（パルケット 68号、2003年）

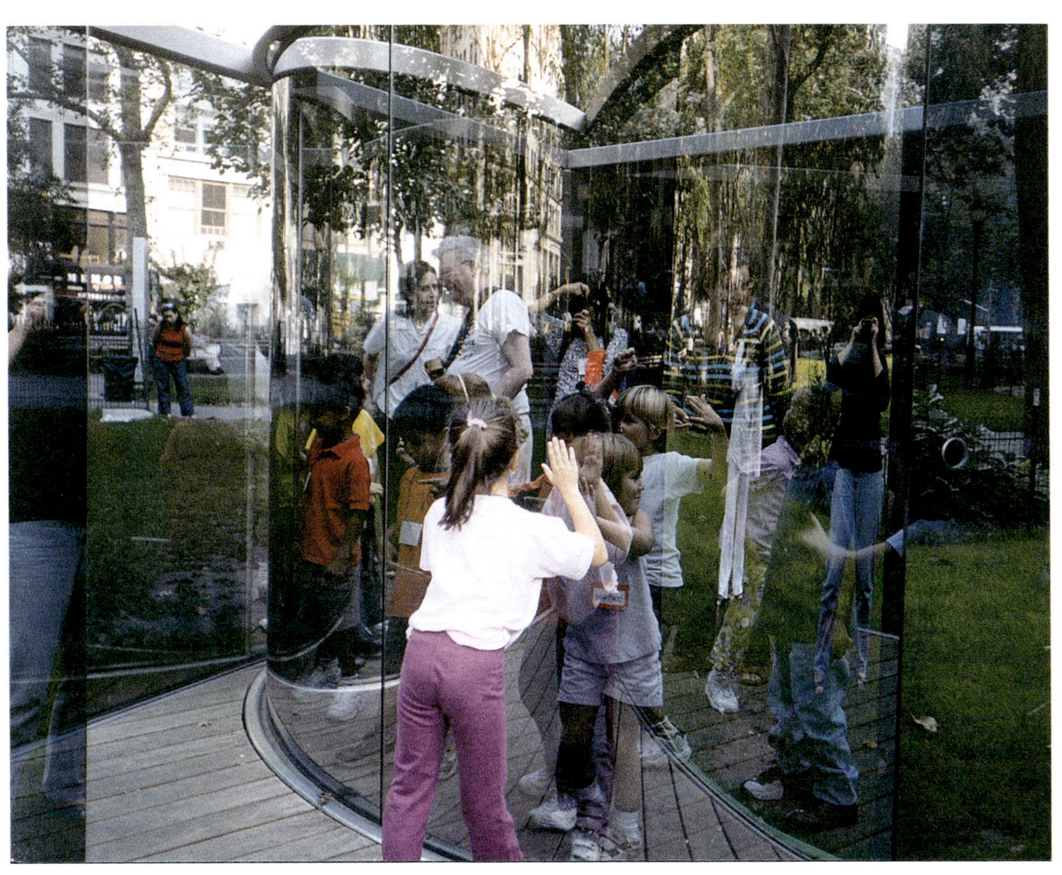

RODNEY GRAHAM

Weather Vane, 2002

Black enameled stainless steel,
approx. 26 $\frac{3}{4}$ x 24 $\frac{4}{5}$ x 21 $\frac{1}{2}$"
(40 x 53,7 x 53,7 cm) produced after
a drawing by Derek Root,
Ed. 70/XX, signed and numbered
certificate

EDITION FOR PARKETT 64

Effortless equilibrium. Waiting for a halcyon breeze to blow memory to the winds.

"...caught up in the loops of their own company, Graham's solitaries have a tendency to leave even themselves behind for periods, and journey inwards as we all do, at least in sleep... Graham keeps taking us back to the same impossible, giddy place; leading us right up to the border of someone else's thought; his thought; our own thought; the 'Edge of a Wood.'"

Mathew Hale
Parkett No. 64, 2002

ロドニー・グレアム

風見鶏　2002

黒のエナメル加工を施したステンレス・スティール、
約40×53.7×53.7cm、
デレク・ルートのスケッチをもとに制作、
Ed. 70/XX、署名、番号入り証明書

パルケット・エディション 64

軽々とバランスをとる。穏やかなそよ風が思い出を吹き流してくれるのを待つ。

仲間との煩わしいつきあいに厭いて、グレアムのとりあげる独り者はしばし自分自身からも逃げ出し、わたしたちのだれもがするように、自分自身の内面に、すくなくとも睡眠中は、旅立とうとしがちである……グレアムはわたしたちを、あいかわらずにっちもさっちもいかない、目まいのしそうな場所に連れ戻す。他人の考え、かれの考え、わたしたち自身の考えとの境にまで、わたしたちを連れてゆく。そこは「林の辺」。

マシュー・ヘイル
（パルケット 64号、2002年）

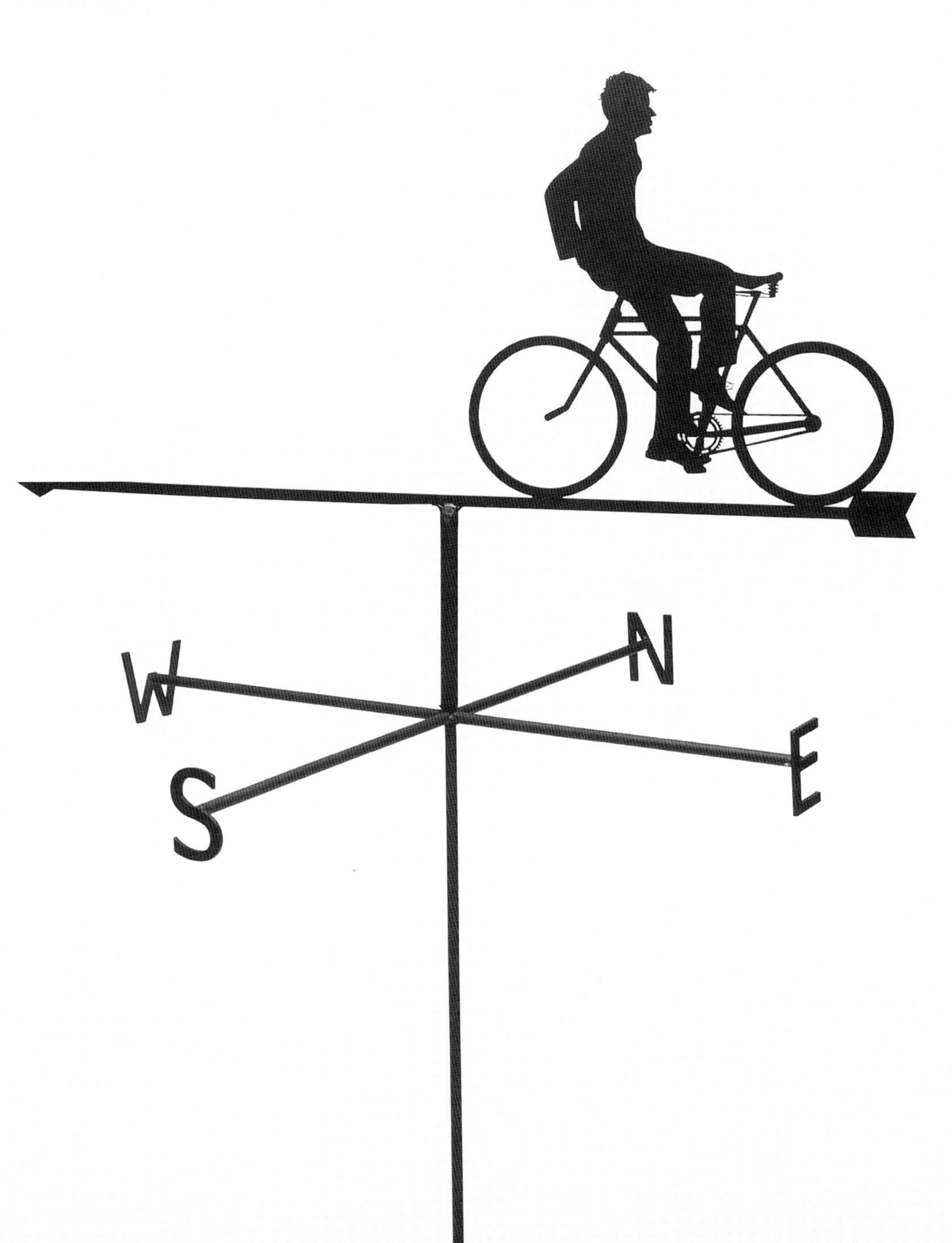

KATHARINA GROSSE

Rock, 2005

Carrara marble, acryl,
each unique, ca. 8 x 4 x 5¹/₂"
(20 x 10 x 14 cm),
15–20 lbs (7–10 kg),
Ed. 55/XXV, signed and numbered
certificate

EDITION FOR PARKETT 74

Perfectly packaged: color comes full circle,
embracing and concealing one of art's oldest
and most exquisite materials.

"Within my compositions, the colors have the function
of distinguishing between different movements.
I like working with a certain palette, one that is
usually very raw and very cold. It's extremely artificial,
like Pontormo's, for example. Then, within this
spectrum, there are some colors that develop certain
characteristics. A particular red, when it meets up
with blue, doesn't become purple but rather brown.
I like this ambivalence that makes colors surrender
their identity and yet still show signs of their origins."

Katharina Grosse, interview with Hans Ulrich Obrist
Parkett No. 74, 2005

カタリーナ・グロッセ

岩石　2005

カッラーラ産大理石、7-10kg、アクリル、
ふたつ同じものはない、
約20×10×14cm、
Ed. 55/XXV、署名、番号入り証明書

パルケット・エディション 74

完璧な包装。色は周囲を巡り、美術作品に用いられる
ものとしては最も歴史が長く、極上の素材のひとつを
抱擁し、人目から隠す。

わたしの作品では、色はことなる動きを判別する機能をもちます。わ
たしには好きな色使いがあって、たいがいは生々しい、寒色なのです。
非常に人工的で、たとえばポントルノに似ているかな。さてその範囲
のなかには、ある決まった性格をもつ色があります。ある種の赤は青
と混ざると紫にはならずに、茶色っぽくなってしまう。色に自分のアイ
デンティティを放棄させながら、それでもなお素性の名残りをみせる、
こうしたどっちつかずのところが気に入っています。

カタリーナ・グロッセ、
ハンス・ウルリヒ・オブリストのインタヴューに応えて
（パルケット 74号、2005年）

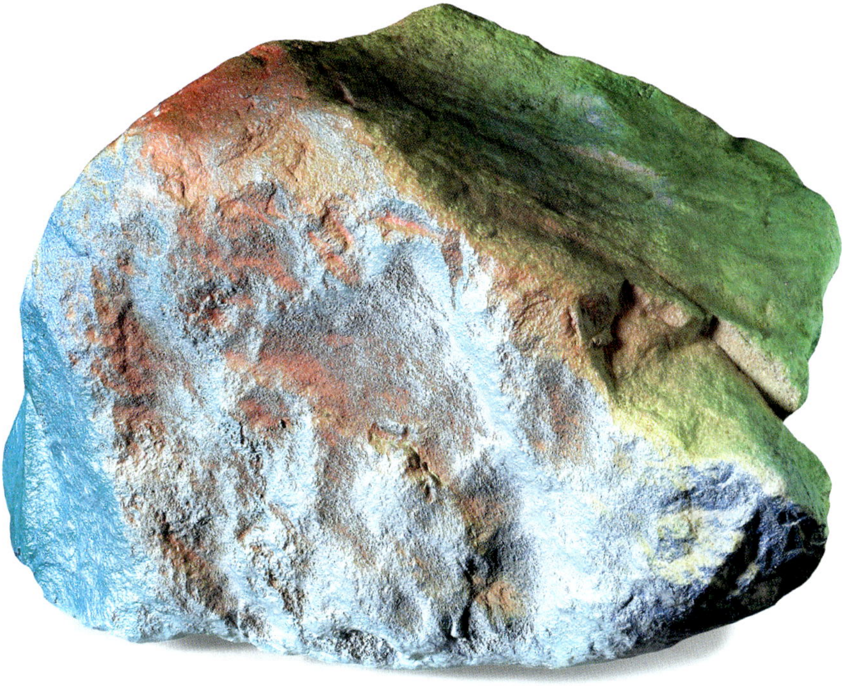

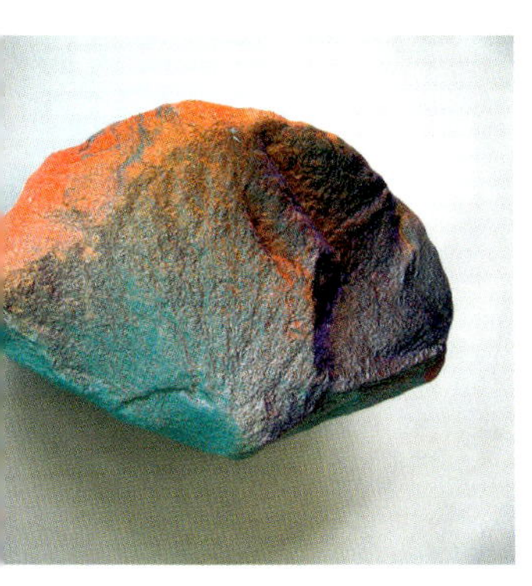
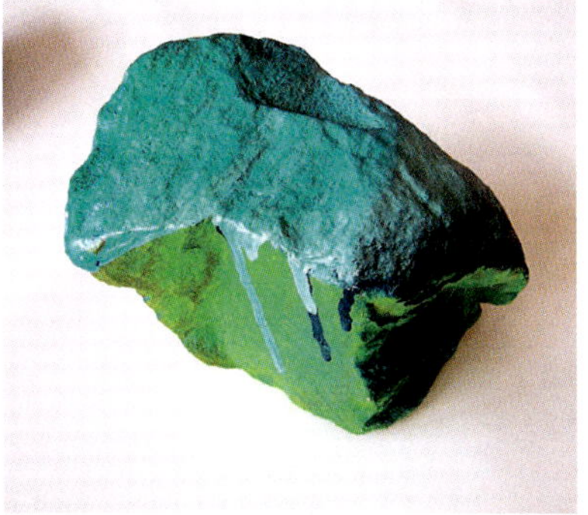
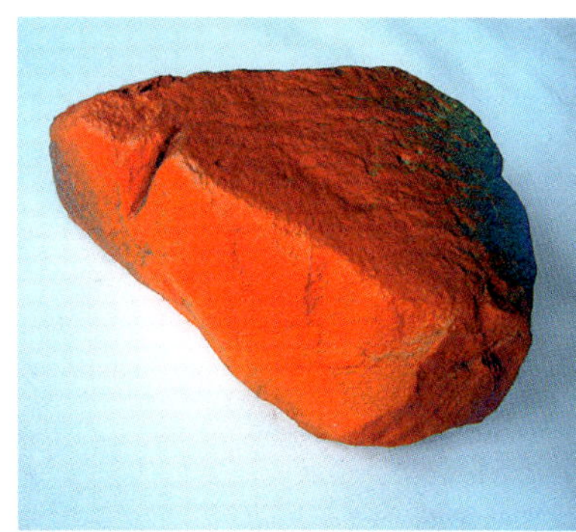

MARK GROTJAHN

Spinner Winner, 2007

Hand-painted coin in gold and silver,
1 1/2 x 1/8" (3,9 x 0,3 cm), each unique,
plexiglas case,
Ed. 13/VII in 18 carat gold,
engraved and numbered on reverse,
Ed. 30/X in sterling silver,
engraved and numbered on reverse

EDITION FOR PARKETT 80

Spin-spin: you do not get what you see; you will never see what you get.

"For me, the recent paintings of Mark Grotjahn retain and renew the tradition and potential of abstract painting. They have an intense physicality. The paint is thickly applied, luscious; the process of application, immediate, apparent; but the strokes are timelessly frozen. Their thousand edges bristle, catching light like a fractured prism, but with only white light. It is difficult for the eye to find a stopping point. With the slightest shift of the body, of the gaze, the glistening sheen of light instantaneously tips, slides, careens across the surface of the canvas, offset by deep, equally unstable, almost black, contrasts. Only near the center of the canvas, in the area where the two sets of points nearly meet, does the whitish gleam of light remain constant."

Garry Garrels
Parkett No. 80, 2007

マーク・グロチヤーン

スピナー・ウィナー　2007

金貨と銀貨に手描き、3.9×0.3cm、
すべて一点もの、アクリル・ケース、
Ed. 13/VII、18金、裏面に彫りこみ番号入り、
Ed. 30/X、純銀、裏面に彫りこみ番号入り

パルケット・エディション 80

回れ回れ。見えたものは手にはいらず、手にはいったものは決して見ることができないだろう。

わたしには、マーク・グロチヤーンの近作は抽象絵画の伝統と可能性を保持し、更新しているように思える。そこには物としての強烈な存在感がある。分厚く塗られた絵具は肉感を刺激する。絵具の塗り方は直接的で、明白だ。しかし筆痕は時間を越えて固定されている。無数にある縁は毛羽立ち、砕けたプリズムのように光を捉えるけれども、白い光のみを放つ。目にはどこでとまればよいのか、なかなかわからない。身体や視線をほんのすこしずらすだけで、きらきらした輝きはたちまち傾き、滑り、カンヴァスの表面を斜めに横切ると、深々とした、同じように不安定な、ほとんど黒に近いコントラストがそれを打ち消す。カンヴァスの中心のあたり、2組の先端が触れそうなところにだけ、白っぽい光が変わることなく輝いている。

ギャリー・ギャレルズ
（パルケット 80号、2007年）

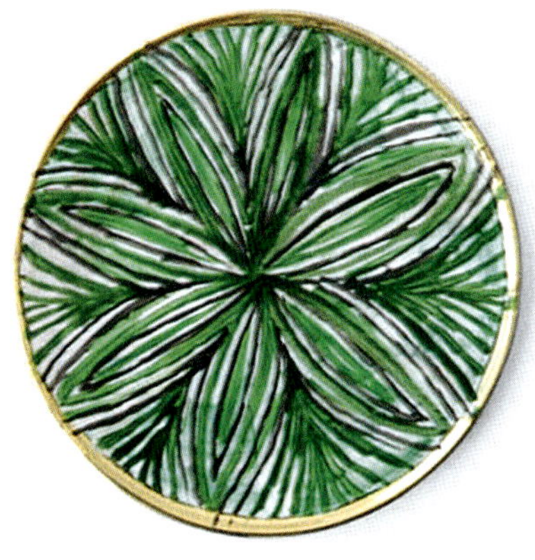
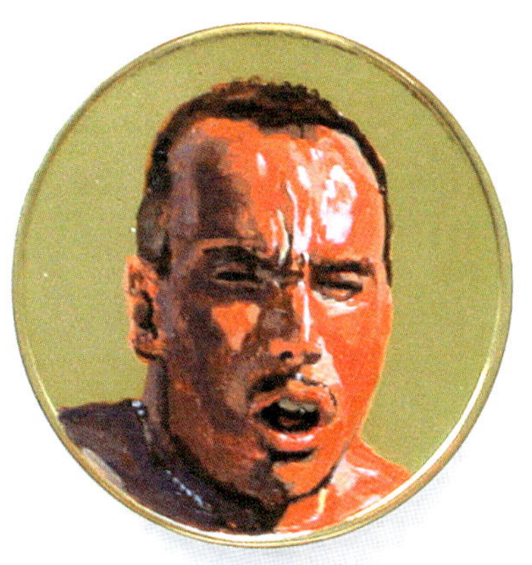
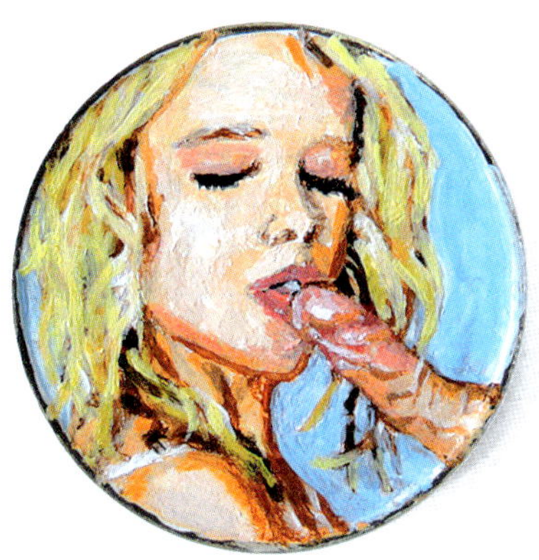
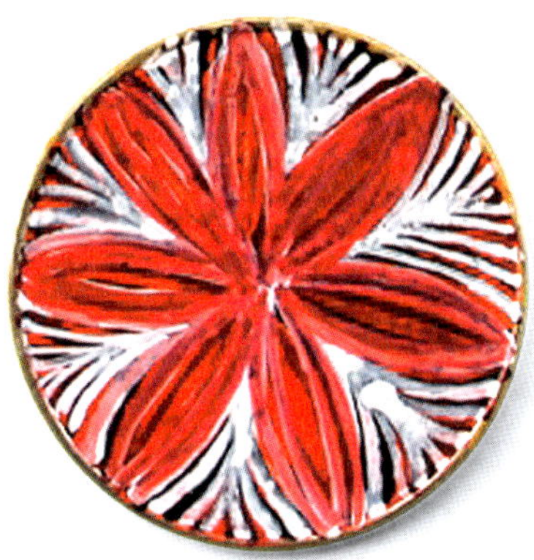

ANDREAS GURSKY

Centre Georges Pompidou, 1995

C-print
in wooden frame, Plexiglas,
21 1/4 x 27 1/2" (54 x 70 cm),
Ed. 60/XXV, signed and numbered

EDITION FOR PARKETT 44

Visualized attentiveness and concentration.
A drama of magnetic space and rhythmic
lines at the Herzog & de Meuron exhibition in
the Centre Pompidou, 1995.

"The rampant beauty of Gursky's photographs
culminates in his interiors of factories or stock
exchanges. That these places of labor, alienation and
of the most cynically disembodied business could
provide an opportunity for unparalleled visual delight,
even ahead of 'nature,' is a paradox that will perhaps
leave an ashen aftertaste."

Jean-Pierre Criqui
Parkett No. 44, 1995

アンドレアス・グルスキー

ポンピドゥー・センター　1995

Cプリント、木製額縁、アクリル、
54×70cm、
Ed. 60/XXV、署名、番号入り

パルケット・エディション 44

注意と集中の視覚化。1995年にポンピドゥー・セン
ターで開催されたヘルツォーク＆ド・ムーロン展に見る
磁場と躍動する動線のドラマ。

グルスキーの写真の奔放な美は、工場の内部や証券取引所を撮影
した作品で頂点をきわめる。このような労働、疎外、現実との皮肉
な乖離がとくに目立つ商取引の場が、視覚に比類のない悦楽をあた
える場となり、それがしかも「自然」にも優る事実は、砂を噛むよう
な後味を残すパラドックスにちがいない。

ジャン＝ピエール・クリキ
（パルケット 44号、1995年）

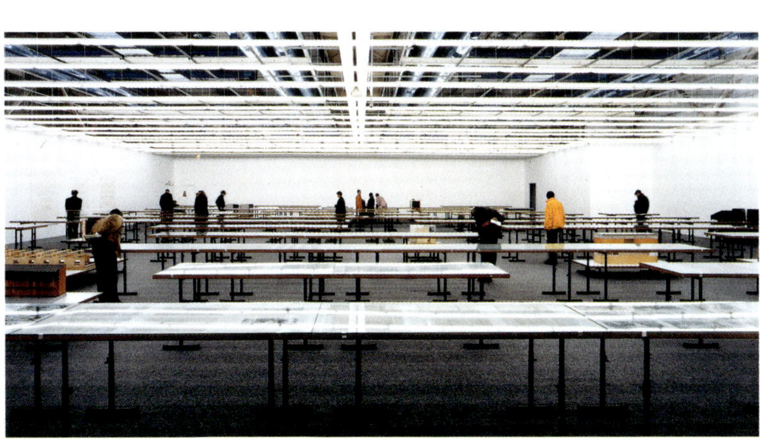

WADE GUYTON

Untitled, 2008

Pigment print on plywood,
48 x 24 x ¹/₂" (122 x 61 x 1,3 cm),
ca. 10 lbs.(4,5 kg),
Ed. 38/XXII, signed and numbered

EDITION FOR PARKETT 83

When signs have been all but obliterated,
what remains is an Xtraordinary vU.

"It is of significance that X is one of the most
rudimentary marks of acknowledgment or signature.
For Guyton, the notion of authorship is a pertinent
question, whether it be the distance he assumes with
regard to making the work or his varying artistic roles."

Suzanne Cotter
Parkett No. 83, 2008

ウェイド・ガイトン

無題　2008

合板に顔料でプリント、
122×61×1.3cm、
約4.5kg、
Ed. 38/XXII、署名、番号入り

パルケット・エディション 83

標識がほぼ塗りつぶされると、あとに残るは素晴らし
い景色

Xが確認の表示または署名代わりのもっとも基本的な記号なのは、
意義深い。ガイトンにとっては、作り手がだれであるかという問題
が、作品づくりとの間にとる距離であれ、アーティストとして果たす
多様な役割についてであれ、つねに関心の対象となる。

スザンヌ・コッター
（パルケット 83号、2008年）

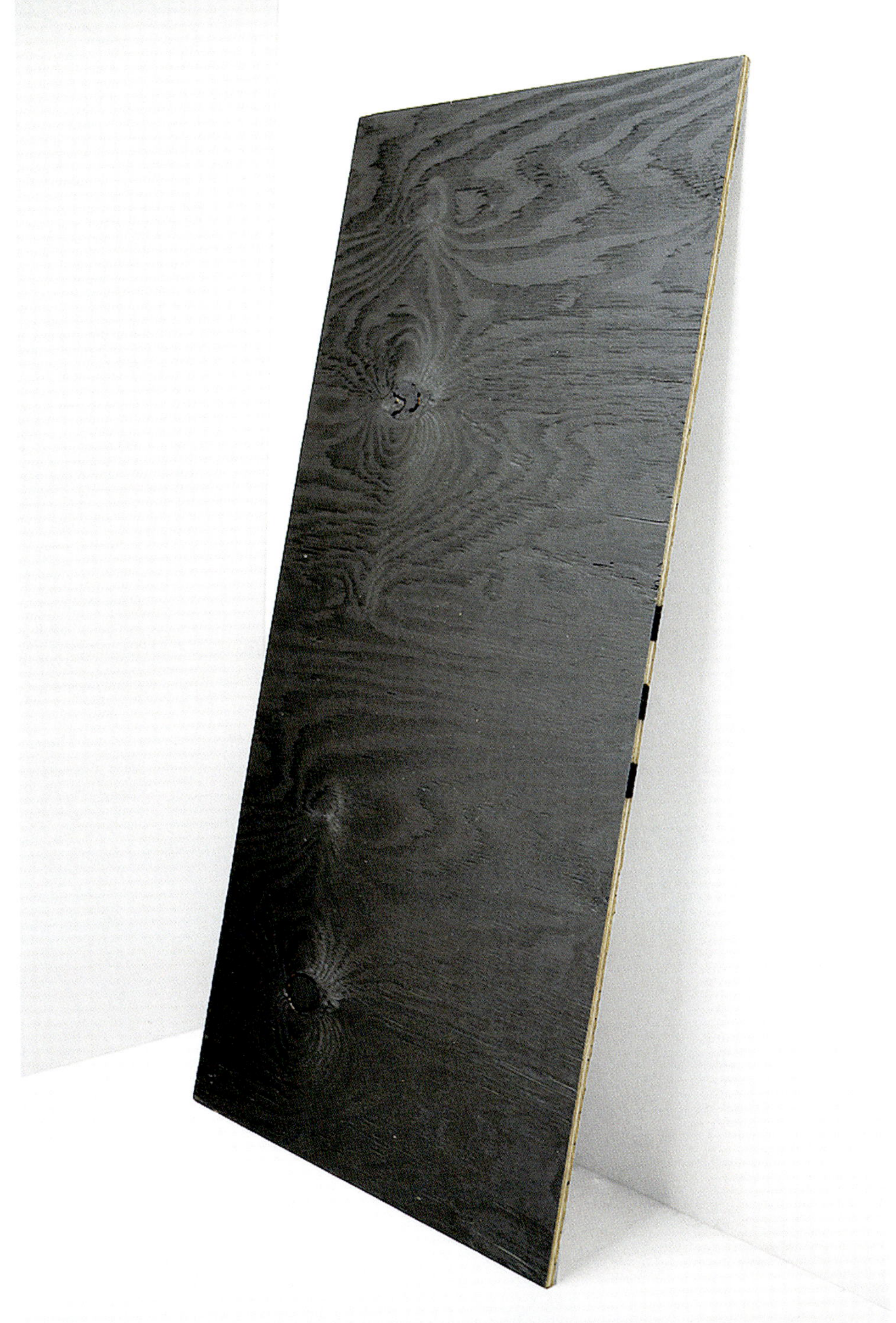

DAVID HAMMONS

Money Tree, 1992

Sepia-Print photograph,
16 1/2 x 11" (42 x 28 cm),
Ed. 70/XXV, signed and numbered

EDITION FOR PARKETT 31

Readymade magic. A basketball hoop fashioned from the rim of a bicycle tire, embedded in a living tree in a Charleston backyard, testifies to the ingenuity of its anonymous maker.

"Hammons has described his practice as 'tragic magic,' taking the discarded vestiges of black life and transforming them, restoring them to a lost potency reinvested with the power of the fetish."

Emma Dexter and Iwona Blazwick
Parkett No. 31, 1992

デイヴィッド・ハモンズ

金のなる木　1992

セピア色の写真、42×28cm、
Ed. 70/XXV、署名、番号入り

パルケット・エディション 31

レディメイドの魔術。自転車のタイヤのリムでこしらえ、チャールストンの裏庭に立つ木に埋めこんだバスケットのリングは、無名の作者の優れた発明の才を立証する。

ハモンズは自らの作家活動を、黒人の生活から廃棄された名残りをとりあげ、それを作り替え、一度は失われた効能をとりもどしてやり、物神崇拝の対象にまで祀り上げる行為と説明した。

エマ・デクスター、イウォナ・ブラズウィック
（パルケット 31号、1992年）

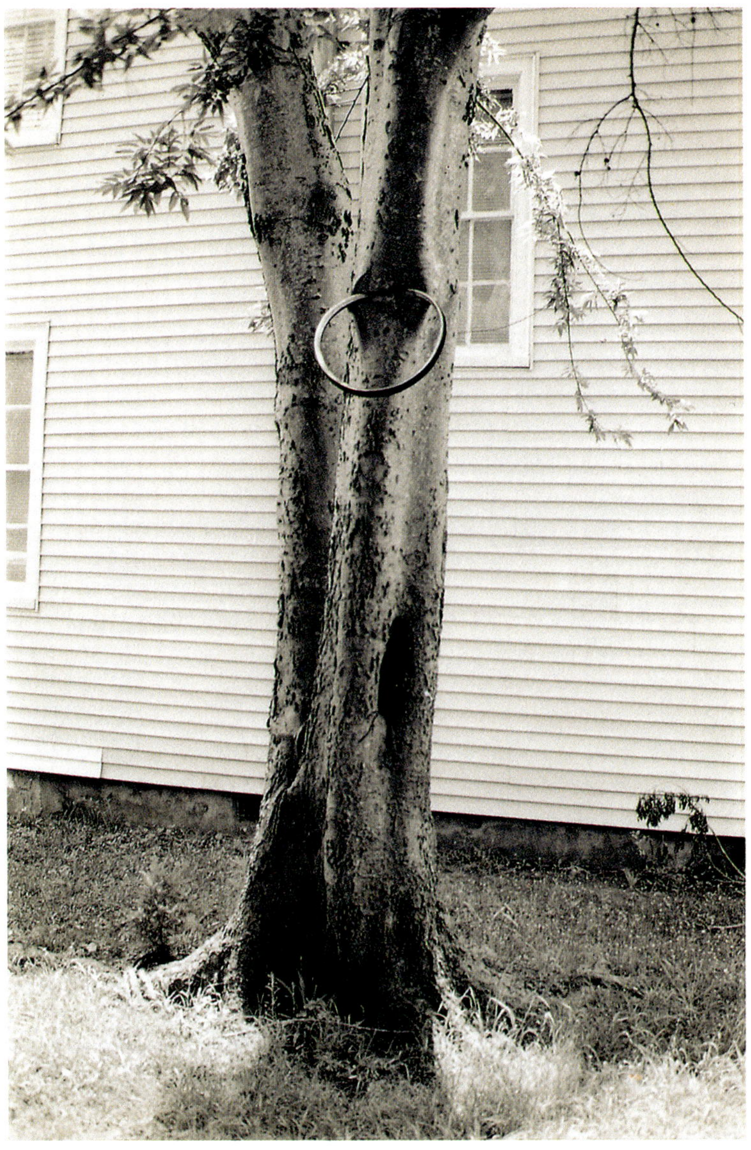

RACHEL HARRISON

Wardrobe Malfunction, 2008

10-color lithograph
on polypropylene,
26 ³/₈ x 18 ³/₈" (67 x 46,8 cm),
printed by Derrière L'Etoile Studio,
New York,
Ed. 48/XXII, signed and numbered

EDITION FOR PARKETT 82

Reverse portraiture: painterly sculptural inventions against the "generic of an iconic figure."

"To ask what these images want, then, is having to face the possibility that perhaps they want nothing at all, or nothing in particular. Except, of course, to stun and fascinate: to be allowed to 'matter,' to be taken into account, to be seen. And something in this scenario is of course reminiscent of the highly theatrical productions of rock, its quasi-ritualistic deployment of 'looks' and 'images' that revel in the crude, the incongruous, the over-sophisticated, and the plain stupid—in short, in the big whatever."

Ina Blom
Parkett No. 82, 2008

レイチェル・ハリソン

機能不全の舞台衣裳　2008

ポリプロピレンに10色刷リトグラフ、
67×46.8cm、
刷り：デリエール・レトワール・スタジオ（ニューヨーク）、
Ed. 48/XXII、署名、番号入り

パルケット・エディション 82

裏返しのポートレート。「偶像的存在の一般的イメージ」に逆らう絵画彫刻的捏造

これらの映像は何を求めているのかと問えば、ひょっとすると何も求めていない、とくに何も求めていないという可能性と向かい合わなければならなくなるかもしれない。もちろん、びっくりさせて、うっとりさせようとは思っているのだろうが。「かまう」ものでいさせてもらい、気にしてもらい、見てもらいたいのだろう。そしてこのシナリオのなかには、おそろしく芝居がかったロックのあり方、粗雑で辻褄が合わず凝りすぎそしてただの馬鹿、言ってみればビッグならなんでもありの風潮に大いに持て囃されるほぼ儀式化した「ルックス」と「イメージ」の利用のしかたを思い起こさせるものがある。

イナ・ブロム
（パルケット 82号、2008年）

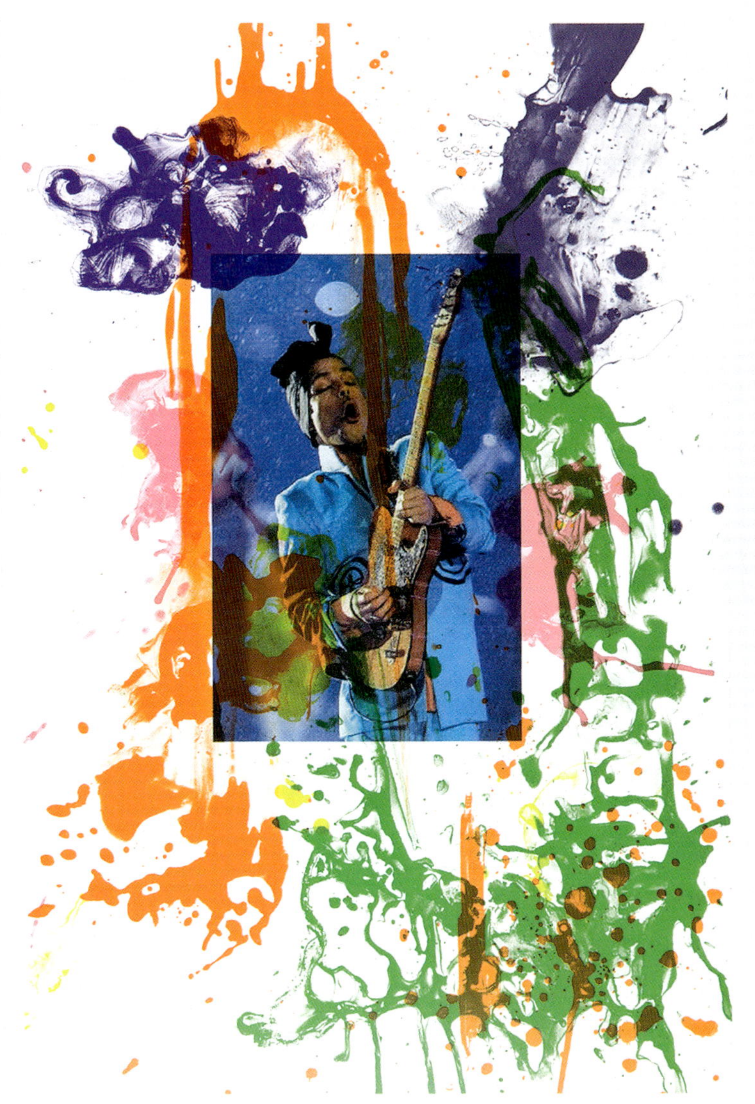

THOMAS HIRSCHHORN

Swiss Made, 1999

Cardboard, aluminum, foil, felt, wood,
plastic, transparent foil, in three pieces,
overall size approx. 86 $^5/_8$ x 19 $^{11}/_{16}$ x 3 $^1/_8$"
(230 x 52 x 6,5 cm),
Ed. 50/XX, signed and numbered

EDITION FOR PARKETT 57

The ultimate watch: a glittering lesson in mastering the millennium by exploding the fiction of time.

"Thomas Hirschhorn—an artist easily recognized for
his persistent use of low-grade materials such as
tinfoil, cardboard, plywood, plastic, and masking tape
in his sculptural assemblages—perfectly illustrates
cheapness in all of its senses. From the connotation
of poor quality or shoddy standing to appearing easily
made, despicable, or having little value, Hirschhorn
has cultivated more than aesthetic consistency in
his oeuvre. Underlying the objects that he fashions
out of these meager materials is a sophisticated
machine whose inner workings produce affects and
interpretations that extend beyond mere formal
statement. Cheap is no longer just an adjective;
Hirschhorn makes it a procedure."

Alison Gingeras
Parkett No. 57, 1999

トーマス・ヒルシュホーン

スイス製　1999

ボール紙、アルミニウム、ホイル、フェルト、木、
プラスティック、透明ラップ、3つの部分から構成、
約230×52×6.5cm、
Ed. 50/XX、署名、番号入り

パルケット・エディション 57

腕時計のきわめつけ。時間の虚構を粉砕しつつ千年紀を手懐ける眩い教え。

錫箔、ボール紙、ベニヤ板、プラスティック、マスキングテープな
ど安手の素材にこだわった彫刻風アッサンブラージュに特徴があ
り、作り手はだれとすぐに見分けのつくヒルシュホーンは、安っぽ
さをこれみよがしにひけらかす。品質の悪さやみすぼらしさから造
りが安易に見えたり、下らなくて、ほとんど価値がないように思え
るところまで、ヒルシュホールの手がける作品群には美術品として
の一貫性を越える内容が育まれてきた。こうした貧弱な素材から
ヒルシュホーンが作りだすオブジェの陰には、高度に洗練された機
械が潜んでおり、その内的作用が産みだす感動や解釈は通り一遍
の主張をはるかに乗り越える。安っぽさはもはや形容詞にとどま
らない。ヒルシュホーンはそれを過程とする。

アリソン・ジンゲラス
（パルケット 57号、1999年）

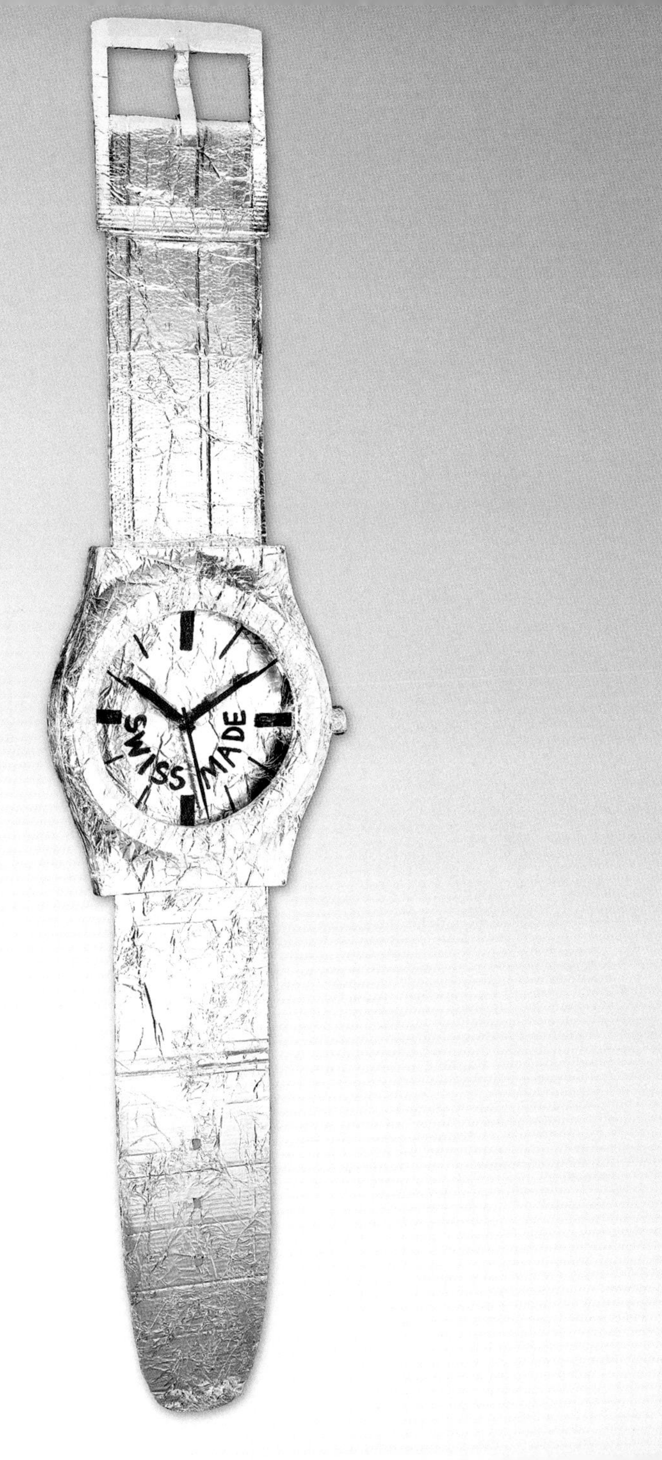

SWISS
MADE

DAMIEN HIRST

What Goes Up Must Come Down,
1994

Ping-pong ball, hairdryer,
Plexiglas container for laboratories,
approx. ø 12 x 12" (ø 30 x 30 cm),
Ed. 30/XV, signed and numbered

EDITION FOR PARKETT 40/41

Perfect control. An executive toy grown
to monstrous proportions, a laboratory
specimen jar houses a ping-pong ball held
in suspension on the up-draft of a domestic
hairdryer.

"The revolutionary geometrical ideal of the twentieth
century plays the same role for Damien Hirst that the
classical norm played for nineteenth century decadent
art. Hirst is primarily interested in the injuries inflicted
upon living reality by the canon of geometric form,
that is, the violence and terror that emanate from this
canon."

Boris Groys
Parkett No. 40/41, 1994

デミアン・ハースト

上ったものはいつかかならず下りる　1994

ピンポン球、ヘアドライヤー、
実験用アクリル容器、
径約30×30cm、
Ed. 30/XV、署名、番号入り

パルケット・エディション 40/41

完璧なコントロール。途方もない大きさに育った動く
おもちゃ。実験用の見本を入れる容器のなかで、ピン
ポン球が家庭用ヘアドライヤーの吹き上げる風に支え
られ、宙に浮いている。

20世紀が理想とした革命的な幾何学性がデミアン・ハーストに
とっては、古典のフォルムが19世紀の頹廃芸術に対して果たした
のと同じ役割を果たす。ハーストの主な関心は、幾何学的な形象を
礎とする規範、つまりこの規範を源とする暴力と恐怖が生きた現
実に負わせた損傷にある。

ボリス・グロイス
（パルケット 40/41号、1994年）

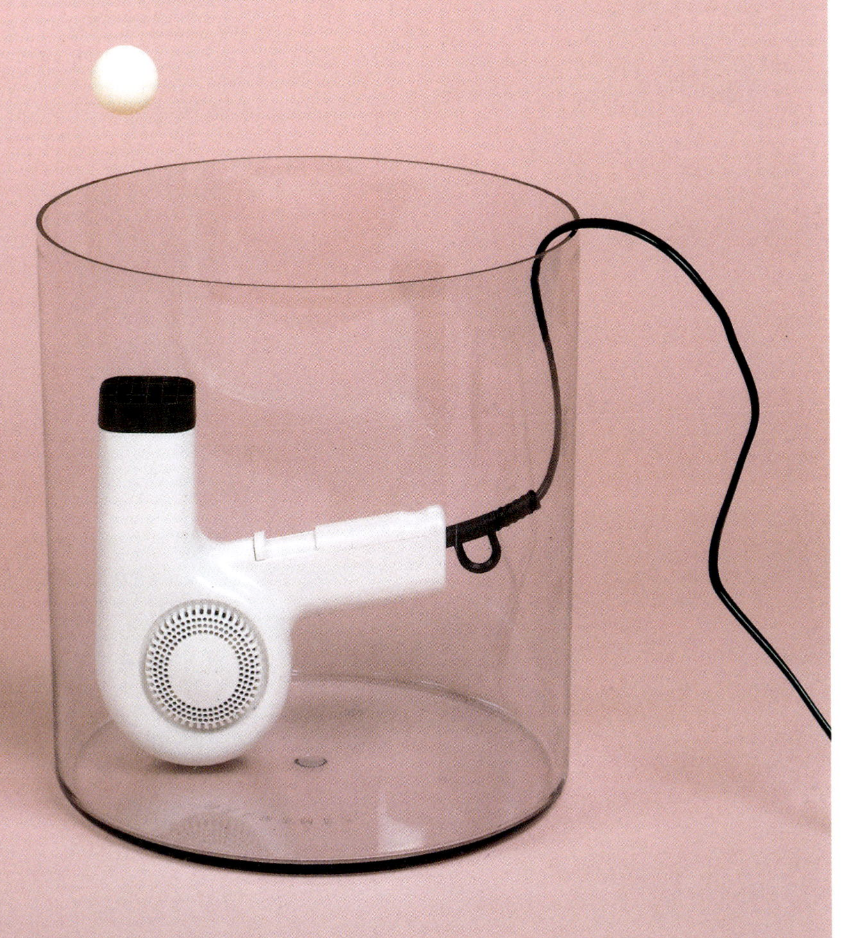

CARSTEN HÖLLER

Key to the Laboratory of Doubt,
2006

Anamorphic key, cast in sterling silver,
approx. 3 ¹/₈ x ³/₄ x ¹/₈" (8 x 2 x 0,5 cm),
silver cylinder, 1 ¹/₂ x ³/₄" (4 x 2 cm),
silver necklace approx. 27 ¹/₂" (70 cm),
black box with embossed print,
production by Factum Arte, Madrid,
Ed. 50/XXV, initials engraved and
numbered

EDITION FOR PARKETT 77

Begin with certainties and you shall end in
doubts. But beware: doubt is not the key to
certainty.

"Doubt and its semantic cousin, perplexity, which are both
equally important to me, are unsightly states of mind
we'd rather keep under lock and key because we associate them with uneasiness, with a failure of values. But
wouldn't it be more accurate to claim the opposite, that
certainty in the sense of brazen, untenable affirmation
is much more pathetic? It is simply its association with
notions of well-being that gives affirmation its current
status. What needs to be done is to sever the association
between affirmation and well-being."

Carsten Höller, interview with Hans Ulrich Obrist
Parkett No. 77, 2006

カールステン・ヘラー

疑惑の実験室の扉を開く鍵　2006

純銀で鋳造した歪んだ鍵：約8×2×0.5cm、
銀の円筒：4×2cm、
銀のネックレス：約70cm、
エンボス・プリントを施した黒箱、
制作：ファクトゥム・アルス社（マドリッド）、
Ed. 50/XXV、イニシャルを彫刻、番号入り

パルケット・エディション 77

確信から始めれば、しまいには疑問を抱くようになる。
とはいえ、気をつけなさい。疑問は確信に至る鍵にあら
ず。

意味論からすると疑念の従弟筋にあたる当惑は、わたしにとっては
おなじように大切なものですが、一般には見苦しい心理状態とされ
て、できれば鍵をかけてどこかにしまっておきたいものなのです。と
いうのもそれが不安や評価の低下に結びつくからですね。しかし、
それとは正反対こそが正しい、図々しい確信、裏付けのない肯定こ
そよほど情けないと主張するほうが、よほど真実に近いのではない
でしょうか。肯定が今のように持て囃されるのは、それが幸福、安寧
と結びつくからにすぎません。いま必要なのは、肯定と幸福の結び
つきを断ち切ることです。

カールステン・ヘラー、
ハンス＝ウルリヒ・オブリストとのインタヴューに応えて
（パルケット 77号、2006年）

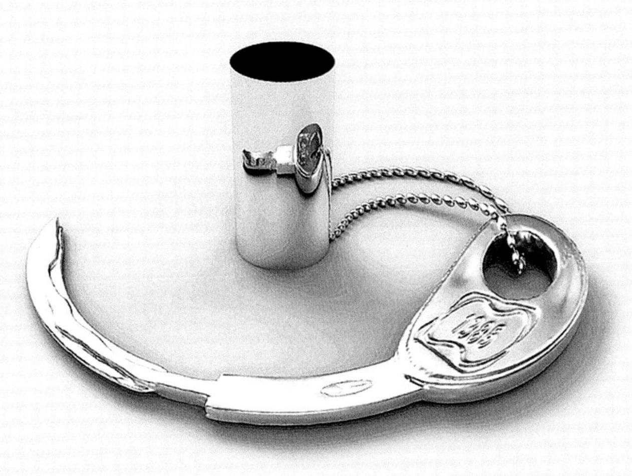

JENNY HOLZER

With You Inside Me Comes the Knowledge of My Death, 1994

Silver snake ring with inscription,
sterling silver, 925/000,
matt, centrifugal cast, hand-finished,
felt-lined wooden case,
1 5/8 x 3 3/8 x 2 1/8" (4,1 x 8,8 x 5,5 cm),
produced by Patrick Muff, Cologne,
Ed. 75/XX, signed and numbered

EDITION FOR PARKETT 40/41

Vicious circle. An ominous poetic text, taken from the artist's current work-in-progress LUSTMORD, insinuates itself on its wearer in the form of a serpentine silver ring.

"The fact that Holzer's 'mock-cliché' truisms sound like the vices, virtues, and prescriptions printed at the turn of the century is at least stylistically no accident, for as she has said about these, her first writings: 'I try to polish them so they sound as if they had been said for a hundred years, but they're mine…'"

Joan Simon
Parkett No. 40/41, 1994

ジェニー・ホルツァー

あなたがわたしの中にいると、自分が死ぬとはどういうことか判ってくる　1994

銀の指輪に銘刻、純銀、925/000、艶消し、
遠心形に鋳造、手仕上げ、
フェルトで裏打ちした木製ケース、
4.1×8.8×5.5cm、
制作：パトリック・ムフ社（ケルン）、
Ed. 75/XX、署名、番号入り

パルケット・エディション 40/41

悪循環。ポエティックだが不吉な文章は、制作中の《LUSTMORD》からの引用。蛇を象った銀の指輪に身をやつし、身につける者にいつのまにか取り入る。

ホルツァーの「決まり文句まがい」の自明の理が悪徳、美徳、世紀末の刷り物によくある人生の指針風に聞こえるのは、文体から見るかぎり偶然ではない。本人がそれについて、初期の文章についてこう語っていることからも、それは明らかだろう。「もう百年も語り継がれてきたような響きをもたせようとして、できるだけ磨きをかけています。ただ考えたのは、わたしです……」

ジョーン・サイモン
（パルケット 40/41号、1994年）

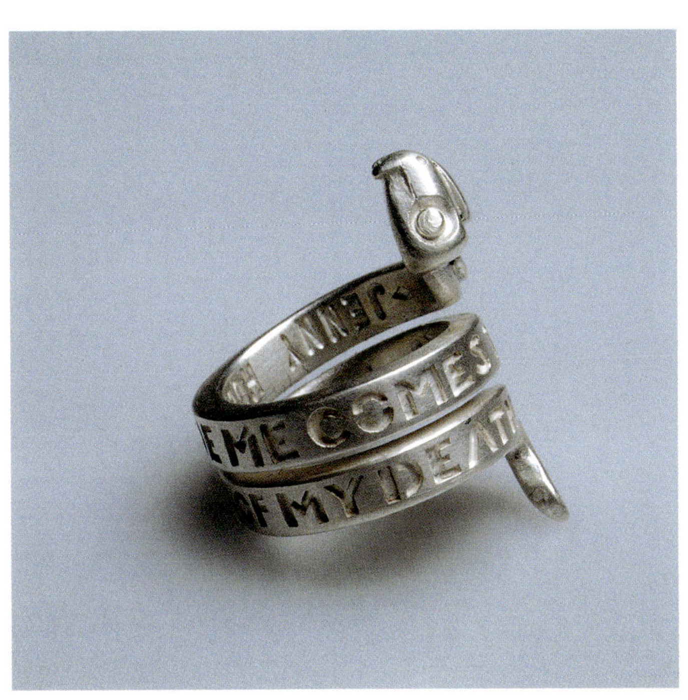

REBECCA HORN

The Double, 1987

Silver-plated brass hammer,
9 $^7/_8$ x 3 $^3/_{16}$ x $^1/_4$" (25,4 x 8 x 0,6 cm),
Ed. 99/XX, placed in a signed and
numbered box

EDITION FOR PARKETT 13

Double trouble. Twin heads facing in opposite
directions, made to accomplish identical if
uncertain tasks, characterize an idiosyncratic
tool from the premier engineer of the fanciful.

"The transitions in Rebecca Horn's world are in a state
of flux between pretense and reality, spirituality and
surface appearance, seeming and being, between
live event and fiction. And everything appears to be
sustained by the calming sense of control exercised
by the rituals in which humans and machines are
caught up."

Bice Curiger
Parkett No. 13, 1987

レベッカ・ホルン

ダブル　1987

真鍮に銀メッキした小さなハンマー、
25.4×8×0.6cm、
Ed. 99/XX、署名、番号入りの箱に収納

パルケット・エディション 13

ダブル・トラブル。ふたつのヘッドが逆向きなのは、
あやふやながら似通った役割を果たすためだろう。いか
にも奇抜なもの作りの第一人者の作らしい、風変わりな
道具。

レベッカ・ホルンの世界に生じる変転は見せかけと現実、精神性とう
わべのみかけ、外観と本質、進行中の出来事と虚構をはさんで流動
状態にある。そしてすべては、人間と機械をともに捲きこむ儀式のコ
ントロール下にある安心感によって支えられているように思われる。

ビーチェ・クリガー
（パルケット 13号、1987年）

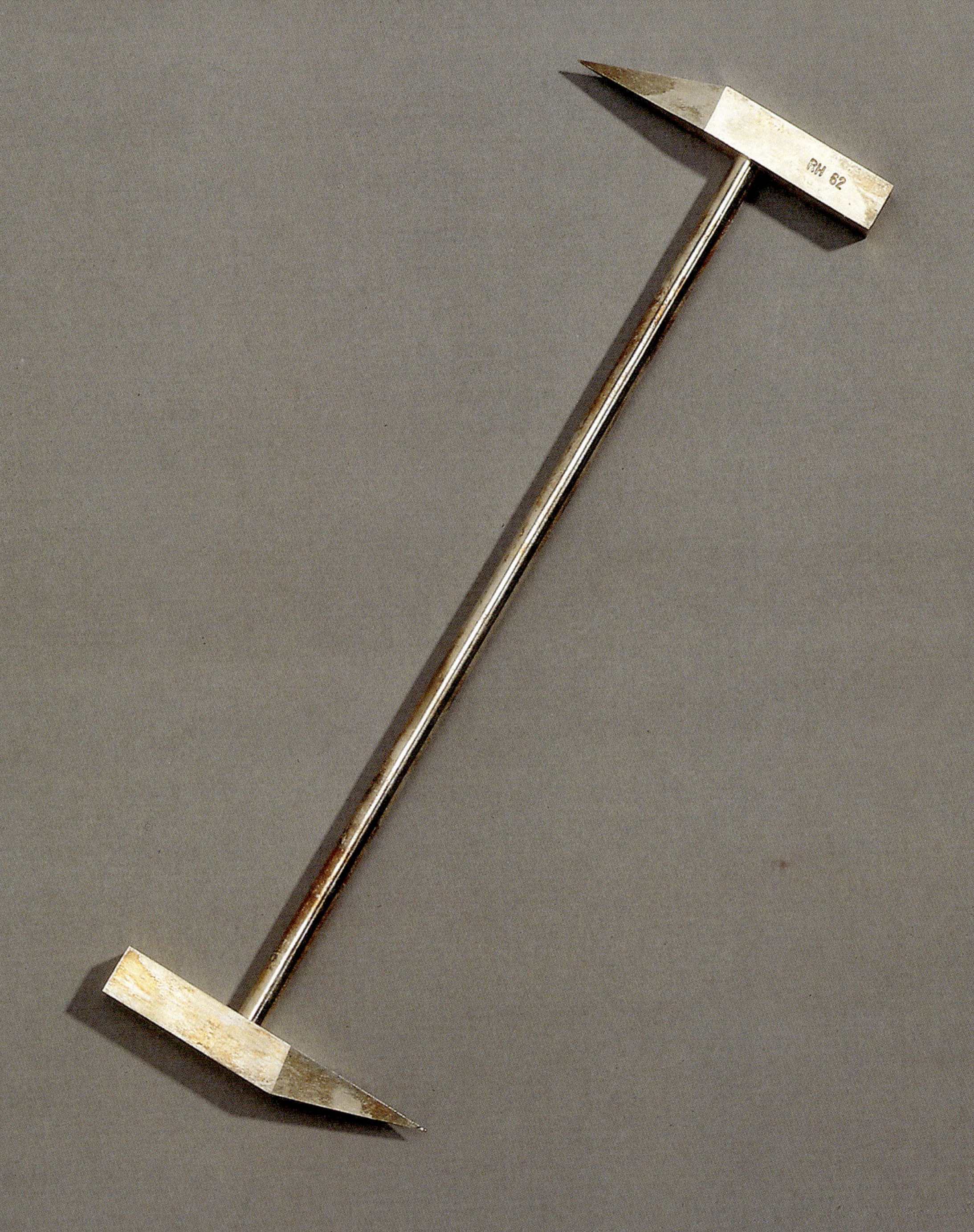

RM 62

REBECCA HORN

Swan Ladder, 1994

Swan's feather in metal-frame box
with glass funnel, ink, glass windows
front and back, mirror, 12 1/4 x 8 1/4 x 3 1/8"
(37,5 x 21 x 8 cm), packed in wooden box
with Styrofoam, 18 3/4 x 13 x 8 7/8"
(47,5 x 33 x 22,5 cm),
Ed. 45/VI, signed and numbered

EDITION FOR PARKETT 40/41

Glass menagerie. Invisible written worlds, visible unwritten worlds reverberate in a cosmos of multiple reflections.

"The works of Rebecca Horn make us think about
the brusque, the sudden, the unexpected, the
instantaneous. They likewise lead us to reflect
upon waverings and alternations."

Gilbert Lascault
Parkett No. 40/41, 1994

レベッカ・ホルン

白鳥の梯子　1994

金属枠の箱に収めた白鳥の羽根、ガラスの漏斗、
インク、前後はガラス窓、鏡、37.5×21×8cm、
木箱に収め発砲スチロールで保護、
47.5×33×22.5cm、
Ed. 45/VI、署名、番号入り

パルケット・エディション 40/41

ガラスの動物園。書かれはしたが見えない世界と書かれていないが見える世界が、複雑に反射する世界のなかに反響する。

レベッカ・ホルンの作品は唐突さ、突発、予期せぬこと、即時性に
ついての思考をうながす。また同様に、動揺、交替についても考
えるようにしむける。

ジルベール・ラスコー
（パルケット 40/41号、1994年）

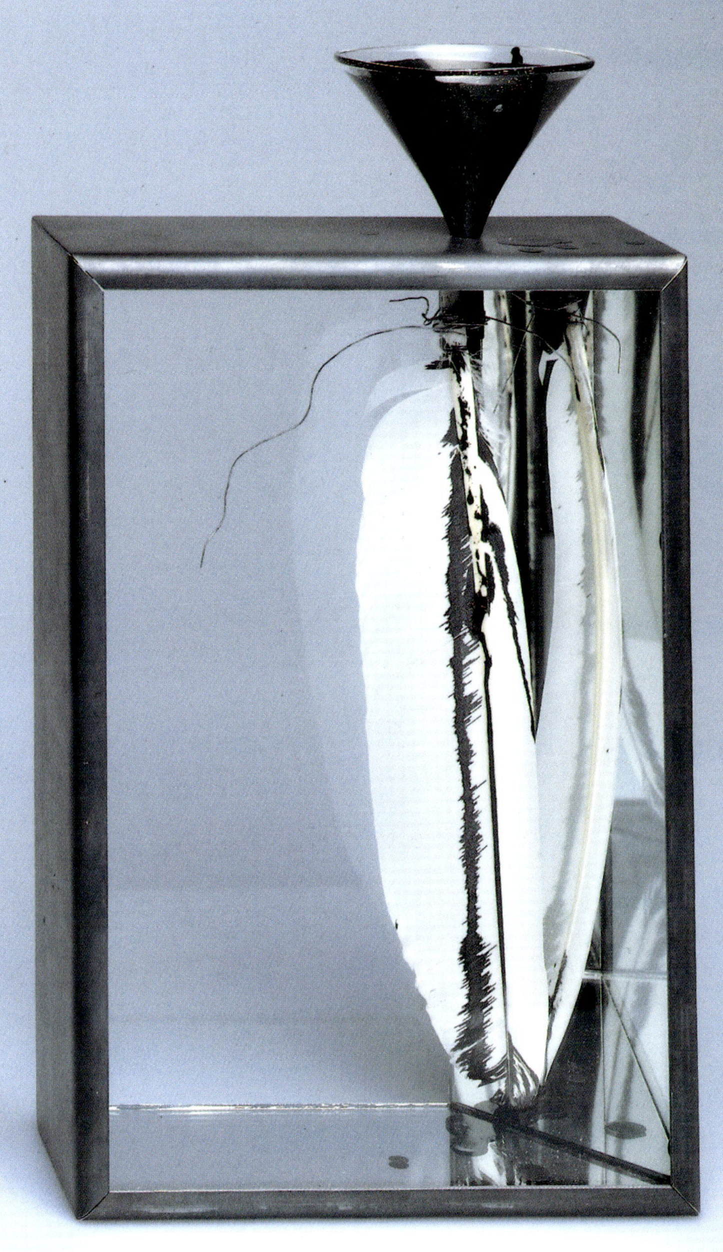

RONI HORN

From: You Are the Weather, 1998

Two-color silkscreen on Arches,
20 x 24" (50,7 x 60,4 cm), in wooden
frame, 20 ³/₄ x 24 ³/₄" (54,4 x 64,5 cm),
printed by Lorenz Boegli, Zurich,
Ed. 60/XX, signed and numbered

EDITION FOR PARKETT 54

Atmospheric traces of mood: changes of climate mapped in a constellation of words.

"Horn is fascinated by Hitchcock's attraction to women and the cinematic consequences of his lack of satisfaction; by Kafka's hatred of fur, teeth, children, flowers, meat, and heavy furniture as a reflection of his introverted sensuality; by Dickinson's reclusiveness and the passion that seemed to be reserved exclusively for the mundane world that surrounded her; by Pasolini's and Polanski's raw sensuality. Horn knows that sexuality crystallizes on the circumference of one's being and that it is symptomatic of the center of human existence. Thus Horn asserts her place in the world by introducing her pathology into the pure geometry of the ideal world."

Jerry Gorovoy
Parkett No. 54, 1998/99

ロニ・ホーン

《あなたは天気》より　1998

アルシュ紙にシルクスクリーンの
2色刷り、50.7×60.4cm、
木製額縁：54.4 ×64.5cm、
刷り：ロレンツ・ボエリ（チューリヒ）、
Ed. 60/XX、署名、番号入り

パルケット・エディション 54

大気に残る雰囲気の痕。気候変動がことばの星座に写像される。

ホーンはヒッチコックの女好きなこと、また満足を得られなかったことが映画にどのような影響をおよぼしたかに強い興味を抱く。またカフカが内向的な好色性を反映して毛皮、歯、子供、花、肉、そして重い家具を憎んだこと、ディキンソンが隠遁生活を営み、周囲をとりまくありきたりな世界にのみ情欲の対象を求めたようにみえること、パゾリーニとポランスキーの剥き出しの色好みにも尽きぬ興味を覚える。ホーンは性愛が本人の存在の周縁で結晶化し、それが人間存在の中心をなすことを示す兆候であることを知っている。そこでホーンは自らの病理を理想的な世界の純粋な幾何学性に導入することによって、世界の中の自らの居場所はそこにあると主張する。

ジェリー・ゴロヴォイ
（パルケット 54号、1998/99年）

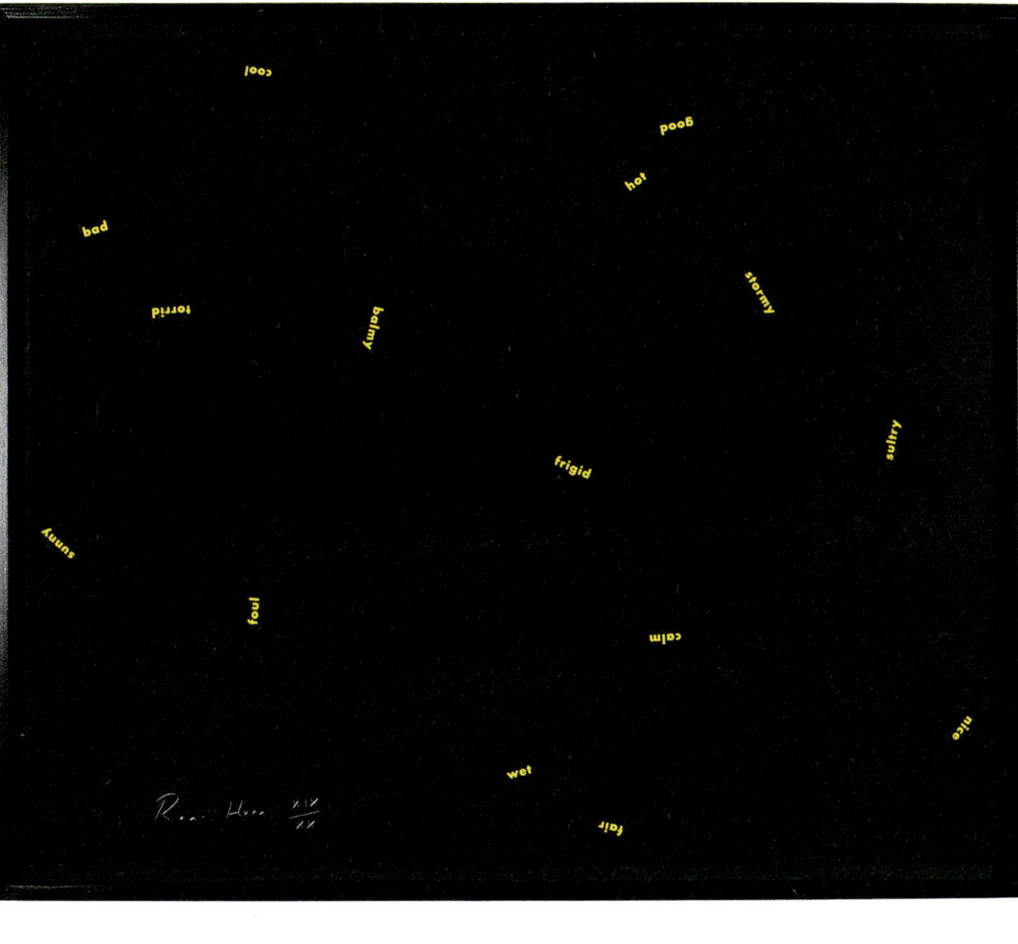

cool
good
hot
bad
stormy
torrid
balmy
sultry
frigid
sunny
foul
calm
nice
wet
fair

GARY HUME

Snowman, 1996

Silkscreen on pink felt,
printed by Print Workshop, London,
12 x 12" (29,9 x 29,9 cm),
Ed. 55/XX, signed and numbered

EDITION FOR PARKETT 48

Impervious to warmth and weather:
a bold and bonny snowman aglow against
a soft, sunset pink.

"In fact, the artist himself has likened his canvases to
flesh, suggesting that the underpainting takes on the
function of skin in relation to the surface paint's role
as makeup. Like skin, these paintings act as interfaces
between the realm of subject and object, viewer and
viewed, drawing us into the orbit of their saccharine
sheen while at the same time maintaining a high-gloss
barrier to any unwelcome entry."

Douglas Fogle
Parkett No. 48, 1996

ゲイリー・ヒューム

雪だるま　1996

ピンクのフェルトにシルクスクリーン、
刷り：プリント・ワークショップ（ロンドン）、
29.9×29.9cm、
Ed. 55/XX、署名、番号入り

パルケット・エディション 48

暖気にも天候にも影響されません。禿げ頭で痩せっぽ
ちの雪だるまは柔らかい、夕陽のようなピンク色を背
に、燃え立つように輝く。

じつはヒューム自身がカンヴァスを肉体になぞらえ、表面の絵具が
化粧とすると、下塗りは肌の機能を果たすと示唆した。皮膚とおなじ
ように、これらの絵画は主体と客体、見る者と見られる物の世界が
触れ合う面として作用し、わたしたちをサッカリンのような光沢の軌
道に引き寄せながら、歓迎されざる侵入に対する艶やかな防壁を維
持しつづける。

ダグラス・フォグル
（パルケット 48号、1996年）

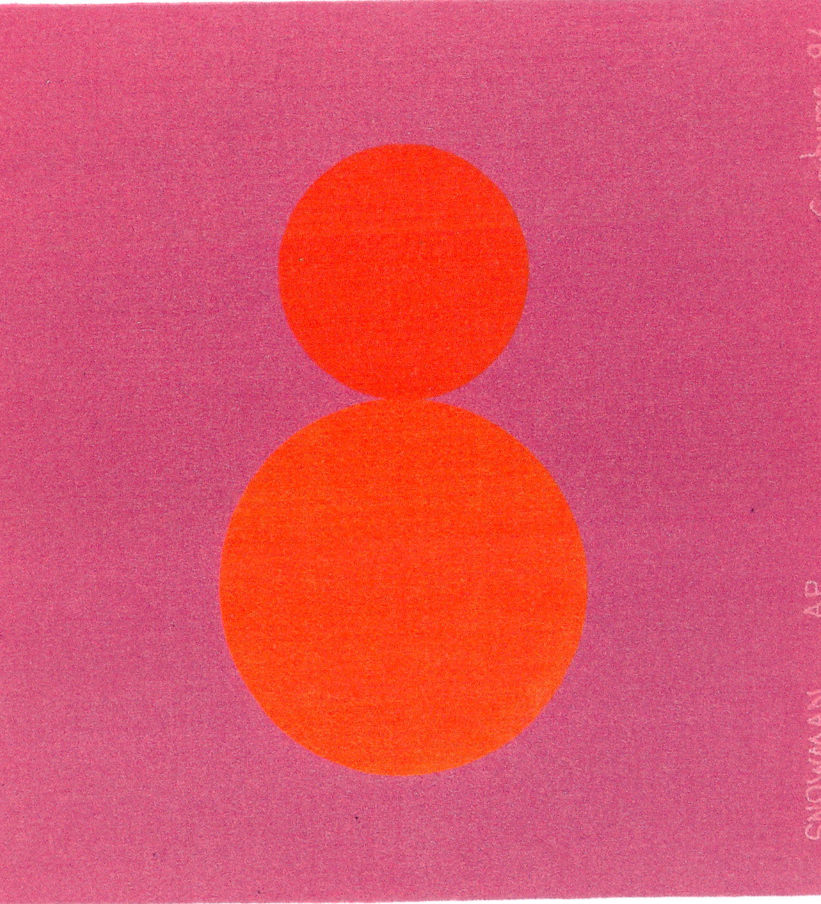

Gary Hume 96
AP
SNOWMAN

PIERRE HUYGHE

All But One, 2002

Windchime for outdoor use,
5 hand-tuned aluminium tubes,
1 3/8" (6,1 cm) diameter each,
top hanging ring 2" (5,2 cm),
black cord, black wood striker,engraved
aluminium wind plate, 4" (10,2 cm)
diameter, overall length: 55 1/8" (140 cm),
overall diameter: 8" (20,5 cm),
manufactured by Jeff Kile, Grace Note
Windchimes, Mariposa, California,
Ed. 70/XXX, signed and numbered
certificate

EDITION FOR PARKETT 66

Speak, memory: the serendipity of capricious winds gives the familiar a new twist.

"There is always a strong sense of performance within
tales, the sense that they exist, somehow, only in
their telling and this is something of which Huyghe
is undoubtedly aware. ... Like Poe, Huyghe is able to
present a certain degree of closure while allowing an
immense and productive openness at its center, like a
traveler into the unknown, prepared and yet desiring
the unexpected."

Jeremy Millar
Parkett No. 66, 2002

ピエール・ユイグ

ひとつを除いて　2002

戸外用ウィンドベル、
手作りで調音したアルミ管：直径6.1cm、
上部の吊り下げ用リング：5.2cm、
黒紐、黒い木製の槌、
彫りこみのあるアルミ製風受けプレート：
直径10.2cm、全長140cm、
全体の直径20.5cm、
制作：ジェフ・ライルネグレイス・ノート・
ウィンドチャイム社（カリフォルニア州マリポーザ）、
Ed. 70/XXX、署名、番号入り証明書

パルケット・エディション 66

記憶よ、語れ。思いがけないものを発見する気まぐ
れな風の能力が、見慣れたものに新しいひとひねりを
あたえる。

物語のなかにはつねにパフォーマンスの強力な感覚があり、それは
語られるところにのみ存在する感覚でもあるが、ユイグはまちがい
なくこれに気づいているとおもう……ポーがそうであったように、ユ
イグも中心に莫大な、そして豊穣な開放感をもたせながら、一定程
度の閉ざされた感覚を提示することができる。未知の世界に歩みい
ろうとする旅行者が、心構えはできていても、予期せぬものとの出
会いを待ち望むように。

ジェレミー・ミラー
（パルケット 66号、2002年）

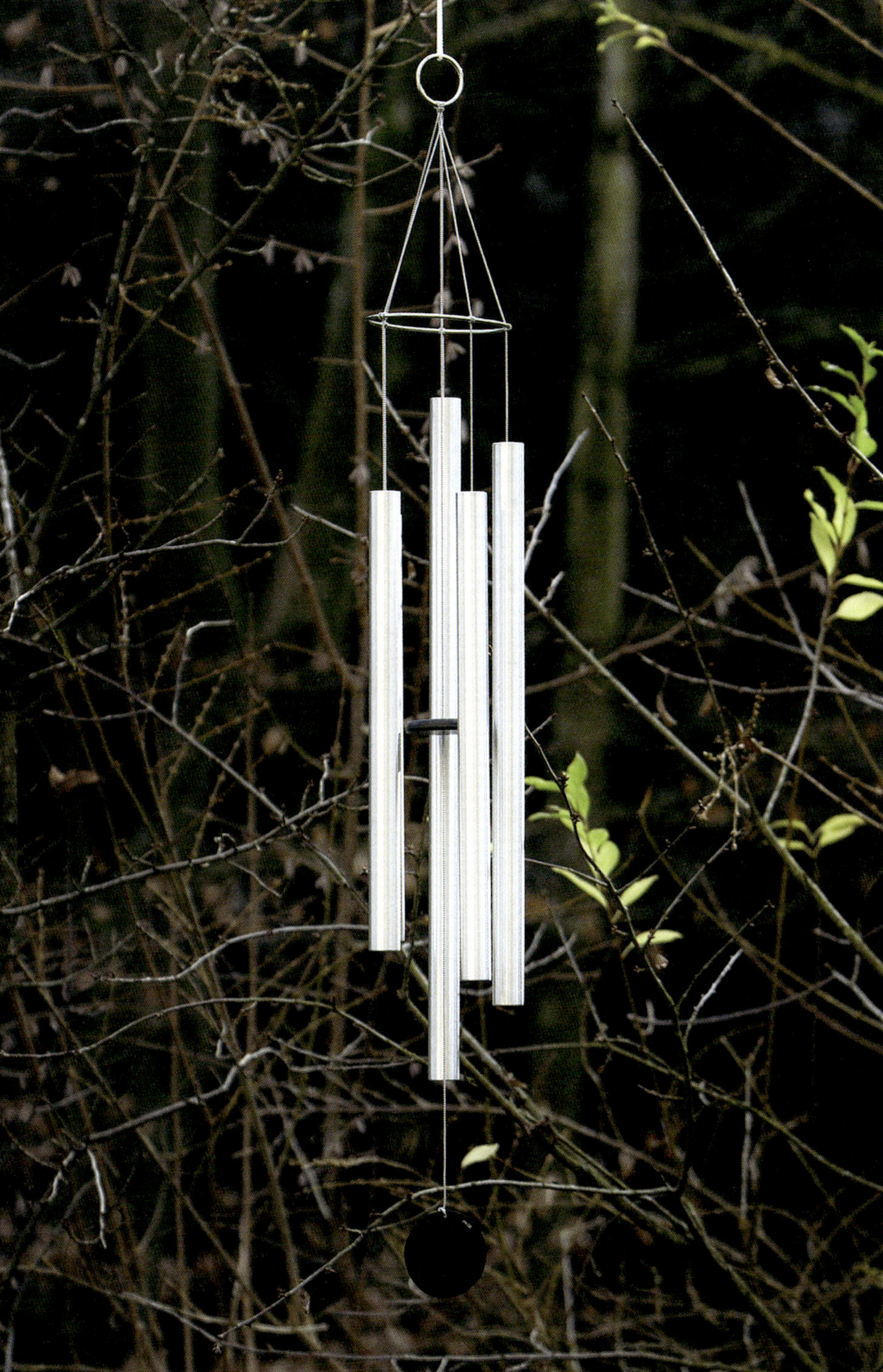

CHRISTIAN JANKOWSKI

Christian Jankowski reads
50 Parkett Artists Collaborations,
2007–2008

50 unique photographs by
50 photographers,
approx. 9 ³/₄ x 7 ³/₄" (25 x 20 cm) each,
Ed. 1/II, each signed and numbered

EDITION FOR PARKETT 81

He is far gone, far gone... What do you read
my lord? Pictures, pictures, pictures.

"Gazing at the pieces (Living Sculptures), it is as
though we see their possible states converging. We see
hard, metal art products that subscribe to highbrow
values of exclusivity and critique become one with an
ephemerally performative form of entertainement,
reflecting the pop-cultural values of accessibility and
empathy; and while collectors appraise the material
used in the production process, children clamber all
over the figures."

Jörg Heiser
Parkett No. 81, 2007

クリスチャン・ヤンコウスキー

クリスチャン・ヤンコウスキーが 50 の
パルケット・アーティストのコラボレーション
を読む　2007-2008

50人の写真家による
それぞれ1点きりの写真 50枚、
25×20cm、
Ed. 1/II、それぞれ署名、番号入り

パルケット・エディション 81

かれは遠くに行ってしまった、行ってしまった……
旦那、なにをお読みですか？　写真、写真、写真。

作品（生きた彫刻）を見つめるのは、可能な状態が収束するのを
見るようなもの。少数のひとのために作られ、批評対象となるハイ
ブローな価値を尊ぶ硬い、金属製の美術品が、娯楽にふさわしい
つかのまのパフォーマンス的な形式と一体化し、とっつきやすさ
と感情移入を優先する大衆文化の価値観を反映するのを目の当た
りにする。コレクターが作品の制作過程で用いられた素材の価値
を鑑定する間に、子供たちは生きた彫刻にところかまわずとりつ
き、よじのぼろうとする。

イェルク・ハイザー
（パルケット 81号、2007年）

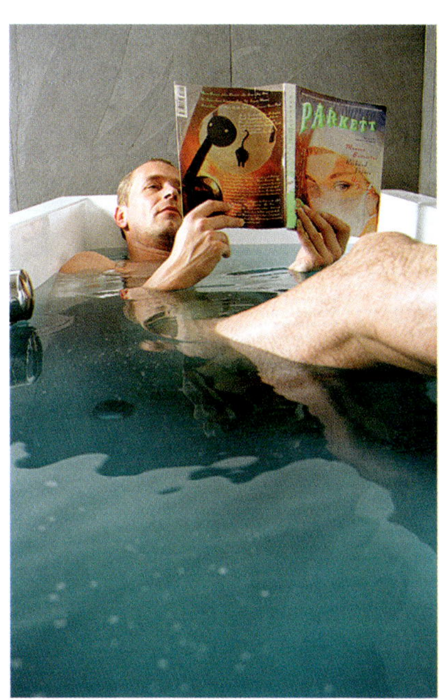

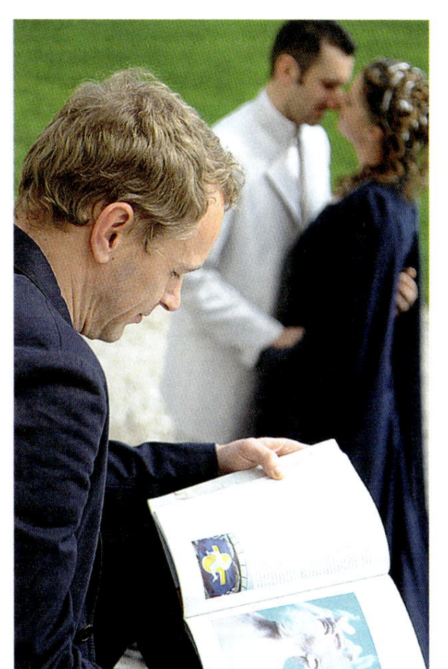

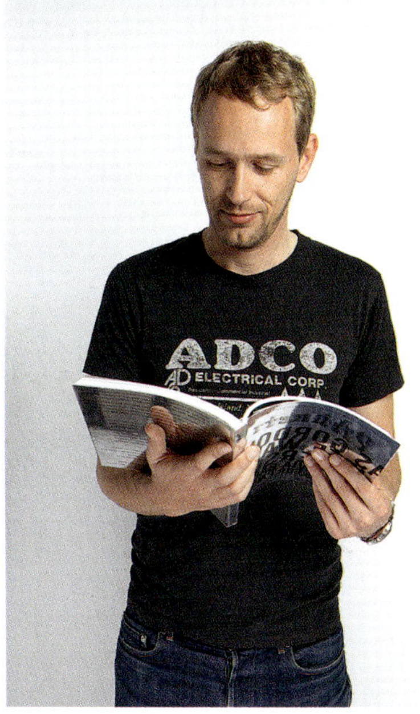

ILYA KABAKOV

Two Friends, 1992 / Citation, 1992

Silkscreened acid-free cardboard box with
two plastic flies and a paper script
(in Russian) attached, English and
German translations provided,
2 x 4$^1/_2$ x 5$^5/_8$" (5,2 x 11,5 x 14,4 cm),
Ed. 50/XX, signed and numbered

Silkscreened picture and plastic fly
mounted on paper and cardboard in
hand-printed passe-partout,
wood frame with acrylic glass,
13$^5/_8$ x 9$^1/_2$ x 1" (34,7 x 24,2 x 2,5 cm),
printed by Lorenz Boegli, Zurich,
Ed. 50/XX, signed and numbered

EDITION FOR PARKETT 34

"To be a fly is not to be a somebody; it means
to be in some condition." Two parables about
existence play on the ready analogies to be
made between the life of humans and the life
of flies.

"No one travels more these days than Ilya Kabakov.
And in no one else's work are the suction of finite
spaces and the vacuum of infinite spaces more
powerfully felt or more deftly shown to be two aspects
of the same uncanny force."

Robert Storr
Parkett No. 34, 1992

イリヤ・カバコフ

ふたりの友だち　1992／引用　1992

シルクスクリーンでプリントした無酸ボール紙の箱、
プラスティックのハエ 2匹、
（ロシア語の）文を記した紙、
英語とドイツ語の翻訳付き、
5.2×11.5×14.4cm、
Ed. 50/XX、署名、番号入り

シルクスクリーンで刷った絵と
プラスティックのハエを紙にマウント、
ボール紙の台紙に手刷り、
木の額縁とアクリル、
34.7×24.2×2.5cm、
刷り：ロレンツ・ボエリ（チューリヒ）、
Ed. 50/XX、　署名、番号入り

パルケット・エディション 34

「ハエであることは、ひとかどの人物であることを意味
しない。ある条件下にあることを意味する」。存在に関
するふたつの比喩は、人間の暮らしとハエの暮らしの
間の手軽な類比と戯れる。

昨今、イリヤ・カバコフ以上に旅をするひとはいない。ほかのだれ
の作品を見ても、有限空間の吸引力と無限空間の真空状態をこれ
以上強力に感じさせるもの、あるいは、それが同一の不可解な力の
ふたつの側面であることをこれ以上巧みに提示するものはない。

ロバート・ストア
（パルケット 34号、1992年）

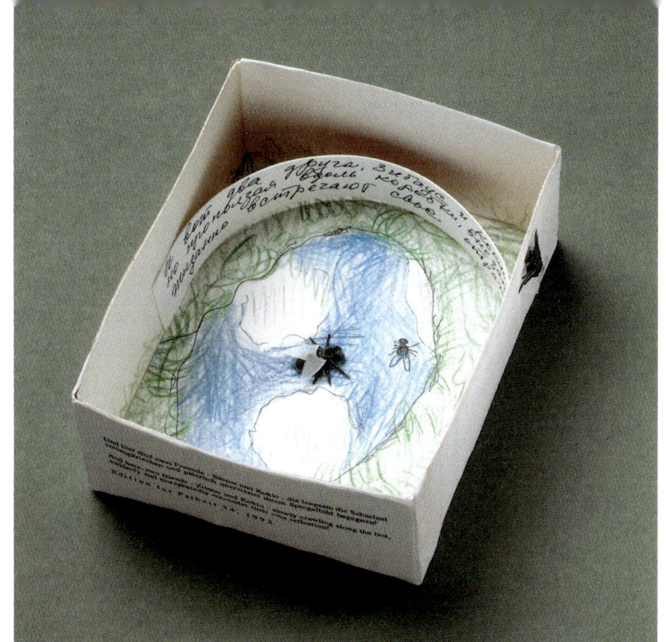

Und hier sind zwei Freunde ... die langsam ihr ... Schneinel
... krochen und plötzlich ihrem Spiegelbild begegnen!
And here are two friends ... Zilma and Kokia, slowly crawling along the ...
... ously meeting their own reflection!
Edition for Parkett 34, 1992

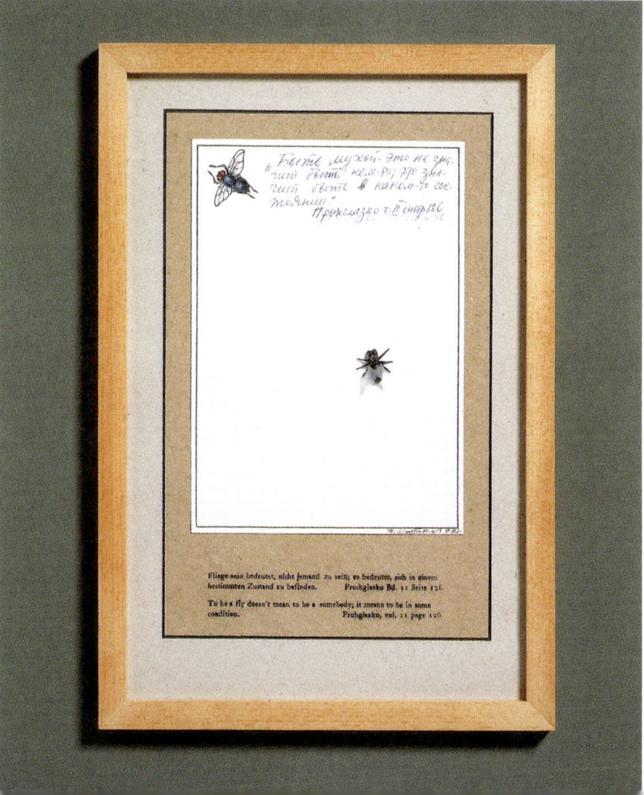

Fliege sein bedeutet, nicht jemand zu sein; es bedeutet, sich in einem
bestimmten Zustand zu befinden.   Prohglaszko Bd. 11 Seite 126

To be a fly doesn't mean to be a somebody; it means to be in some
condition.   Prohglaszko, vol. 11 page 126

ANISH KAPOOR

Untitled, 2003

Perspex, handtinted stocking, paint,
10¼ x 10¼ x 15" (26 x 26 x 38 cm),
Ed. 60/XX, signed and numbered
certificate

EDITION FOR PARKETT 69

Miniature metaphysical maelstrom: stretched in space to the breaking point and beyond.

"'I have always felt drawn,' Kapoor has said, 'towards some notion of fear in a very visual sense, towards sensations of falling, of being pulled inwards, of losing one's sense of self.' Spend time with any work and before long you will feel an unmistakable shift in the coordinates of space and you take for granted. That shift, that sliding of the ground from under your feet, is not always subtle, something you might miss if your mind is less than fully concentrated on the work before you."

Norman Bryson
Parkett No. 69, 2003

アニッシュ・カプーア

無題　2003

アクリル樹脂、手で着色したストッキング、絵具、
26×26×38cm、
Ed. 60/XX、署名、番号入り証明書

パルケット・エディション 69

ミニチュアの形而上学的大渦巻き。破けるまで、さらにその先まで引き伸ばされて。

「きわめて視覚的な意味で、恐怖の観念、落下する感覚、内側に引きこまれたり、自分を意識することができなくなりそうな感覚に前々から惹きつけられてきました」とカプーアは語る。どの作品でもいいから、しばらくつきあってみれば、当然そうあるべきと思う空間のつながりがくずれてゆくのが、まちがいに感じられるだろう。そのずれ、足元の地面が滑ってゆく感覚は、いつでも感じ取れるものとはかぎらず、目の前にある作品に十分に集中していなければ、気づかずにすぎてしまうかもしれない。

ノーマン・ブライソン
（パルケット 69号、2003年）

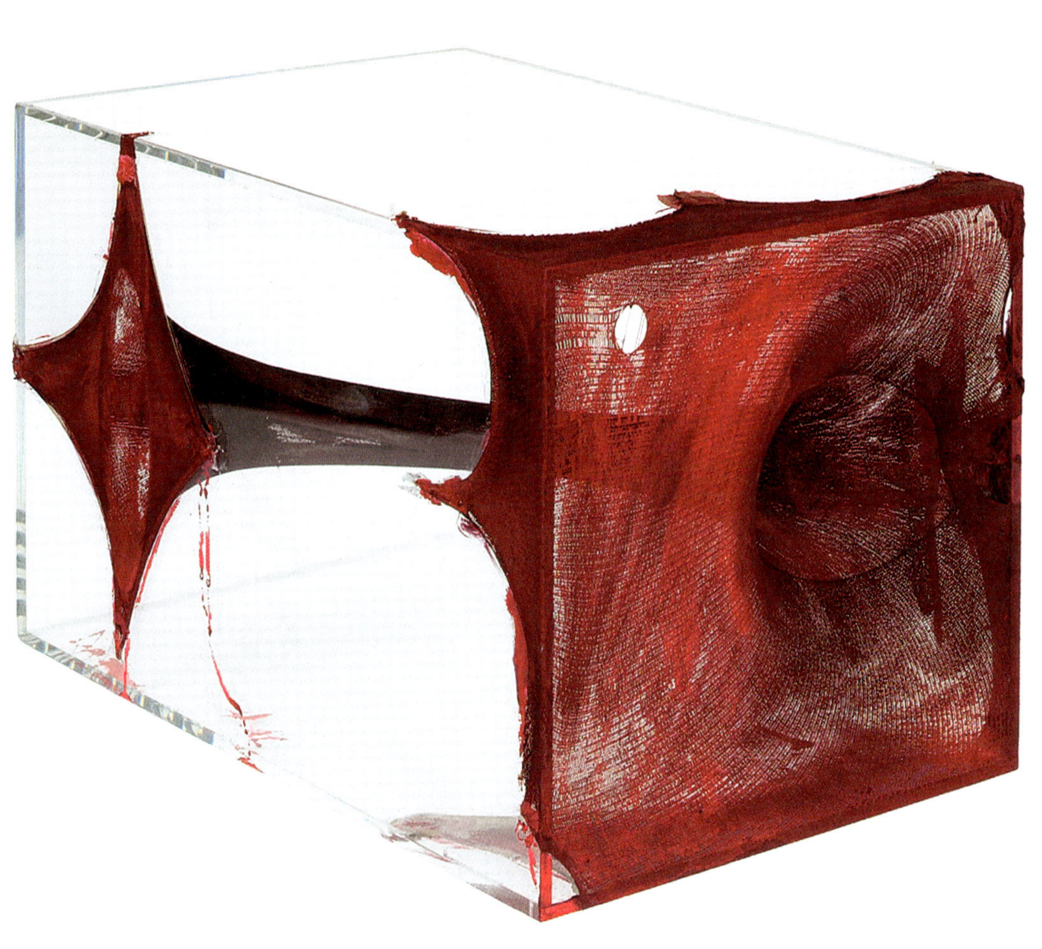

ALEX KATZ

Black Pond, 1989

Woodcut on Goya paper,
11 3/8 x 18 1/8" (65 x 79,6 cm),
printed by John C. Erickson, New York,
Ed. 100/XX, signed and numbered

EDITION FOR PARKETT 21

Artificial nature. A deft exercise in Katz's ongoing exploration of pictorial flatness and poetic symmetry, this stylized woodcut on the most delicate of papers is a quiet moment of reflection from a preternatural world.

"Alex Katz practices a very particular kind of society portraiture. His paintings may resemble billboards, or they may adopt the more intimate scale of the painted sketch, but they are always... portraits in an extended sense—slices of life ennobled by a deadpan iconic American eye."

Brooks Adams
Parkett No. 21, 1989

アレックス・カッツ

黒い池　1989

ゴヤ・ペーパーに木版、65×79.6cm、
刷り：ジョン・C. エリクソン（ニューヨーク）、
Ed. 100/XX、署名、番号入り

パルケット・エディション 21

人工的な自然。カッツが継続する絵画の平面性と詩的対称性をめぐる探究の巧みな試行、繊細きわまる紙をかざる様式化された木版画は、超自然的世界に続く静かな思索のひととき。

アレックス・カッツは上流人士のきわめて特殊な肖像画を描く。カッツの絵は看板広告に似ることもあれば、絵具を使いながらスケッチ風のこじんまりしたサイズにもなるけれども、つねに肖像画の意味合いを拡張したもの、つまりアメリカのシンボルでもある感情のこもらない視線によって、気高さを増した人生のひとひらである。

ブルックス・アダムズ
（パルケット 21号、1989年）

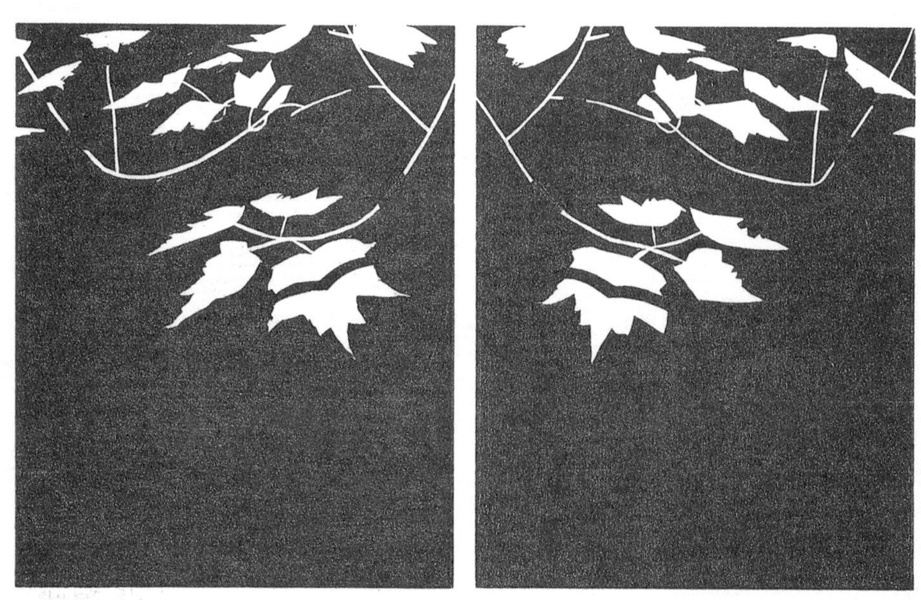

ALEX KATZ

Sunny, 2004

Silkscreen on aluminum,
5 1/8 x 5 7/8 x 2" (13 x 15 x 5 cm),
printed by Atelier für Siebdruck Lorenz
Boegli, Zurich,
Ed. 70/XXX, signed and numbered

EDITION FOR PARKETT 72

I had a dog, his name was Sunny. Was that a dog, was that a dog. That's what people keep asking.

"You get an idea or conception of what you think art should be. It's kind of complicated how you receive it, because you receive a lot from just thinking about it, and other things pop into it. So, I would say, how you arrive at a conceptual basis is as intuitive as anything else, and how you direct that conception to a material object is complicated, because you try, and it fails, and you try, and it's off, and you try this, and you try that, and it works, finally, something works, and you've just stumbled your way into it."

Alex Katz
Parkett No. 72, 2004

アレックス・カッツ

サニー　2004

アルミにシルクスクリーン、
13×15×5cm、
刷り：ロレンツ・ボエリ（チューリヒ）、
Ed. 70/XXX、署名、番号入り

パルケット・エディション 72

以前、犬を飼っていた。名前はサニー。あれは犬だったの？　ねえ、あれは犬だったの？　ひとは今でもわたしにそう訊ねる。

きみも美術とはこうであるべきというアイデアなり、考えをもっているだろう。それをどう受けとめるかは、かなり複雑な話で、そのことを考えるだけでも、かなりいろいろなことを受け取ることになるし、そこにほかのことも思いがけずわりこんでくる。というわけで、思想的な基礎にどのようにたどりつくかは、何につけそうしたものだけれども、直観的なもので、そうした観念をどのようにして物であるオブジェに向けるかも一筋縄ではいかない。なぜなら試してみても失敗し、またやってみても、的外れ、こっちを試し、あっちを試ししているうちに、とうとうどれかがうまくいく、つまり躓いたのが吉とでて、たまたまうまくいくわけだ。

アレックス・カッツ
（パルケット 72号、2004年）

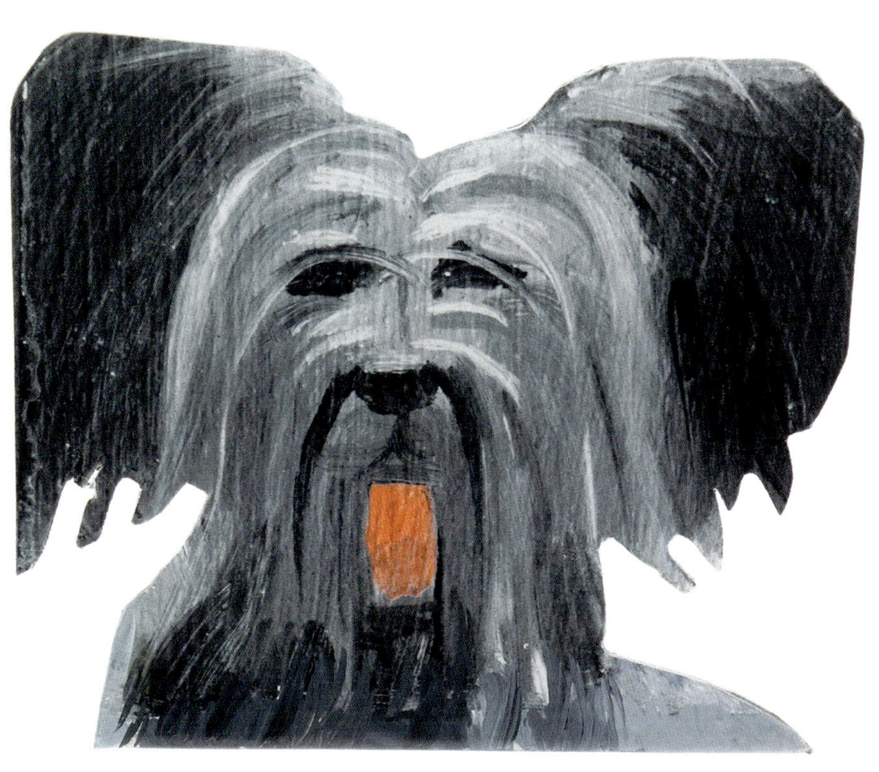

MIKE KELLEY

Goethe Quote, 1992

B/W photograph with silkscreened mat
in black wooden frame with Plexiglas,
25 x 17 ¹/₂" (63,7 x 44,7 cm),
Ed. 60/XX, signed and numbered

EDITION FOR PARKETT 31

A tawdry imagination. Intellectual noblesse
combined with thriftstore fetishism leaves a
Goethe quote wobbling on the brink.

"The man cracking the circus whip, the one
encouraging our higher officials to jump through
hoops is Mr. Kelley; for some time now, Kelley has been
herding toy animals and homemade dolls into his
wall reliefs and sculptural tableaux, training them to
perform intellectual feats, parrot artistic statements,
to act out his fantasies about the world and how it
works."

Lane Relyea
Parkett No. 31, 1992

マイク・ケリー

ゲーテの引用　1992

モノクローム写真、
シルクスクリーンでプリントしたマット、
アクリルをはめた黒い木の額縁、
63.7×44.7cm、
Ed. 60/XX、署名、番号入り

パルケット・エディション 31

安っぽい想像力。気高い知性に古着屋仕込みのフェ
ティシズムがむすびつくと、ゲーテの引用が瀬戸際で
ぐらつくことになる。

男はサーカスの鞭を鳴らす、輪くぐりをするようにお偉方をけしか
けているのは、ケリー氏である。ここしばらく、ケリーは玩具の動物
や手作りの人形を壁掛け用のレリーフや彫刻的なタブローに導いて、
知恵のあるところを見せる芸や芸術に関する所信表明をおうむ返し
に口にしたり、世界に関わり、世界がどのように機能しているかに関
わる自らの幻想を実際に演じている。

レイン・レリイア
（パルケット 31号、1992年）

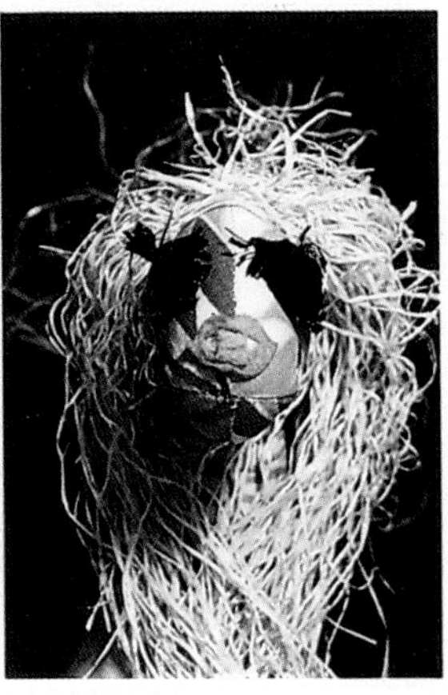

Imagination lies in wait as the most powerful enemy.
Naturally raw, and enamored of absurdity
it breaks out against all civilizing restraints
like a savage who takes delight in grimacing idols.
(Goethe)

ELLSWORTH KELLY

Red Curve, 1999

Single-color lithograph,
10 x 7½" (25,3 x 19,2 cm),
printed by Gemini, Los Angeles,
Ed. 70 and 30 A.P.,
signed and numbered

EDITION FOR PARKETT 56

A curve is a curve is a curve.

"One does not often encounter such quintessential 'art'
as the art of Ellsworth Kelly. It radically sets itself off
against what is not art—thereby actually putting itself
on the same level as the objects in our lives and thus
entering into a dialogue with them."

Simon Maurer
Parkett No. 56, 1999

エルズワース・ケリー

赤い曲線　1999

一色のリトグラフ、25.3×19.2cm、
刷り：ジェミナイ（ロサンゼルス）、
Ed. 70＋30 A.P.、署名、番号入り

パルケット・エディション 56

曲線は曲線である曲線は曲線である。

エルズワース・ケリーの芸術のように、掛け値なしの「芸術」と出会
うことはめったにない。ケリーの作品は、芸術でないものと自らの
対比を根源から際立たせる。そうすることによって、自らをわたした
ちの暮らしのなかで出会う物と同じレベルに置き、対話を始める。

サイモン・マウラー
（パルケット 56号、1999年）

WILLIAM KENTRIDGE

Medusa, 2001

Anamorphic lithograph on chine collé,
printed on 6 different pages from the 1906
French Larousse Encyclopedia,
image diameter: 24⁴/₅" (63 cm),
paper size: 30¹¹/₁₆ x 30¹¹/₁₆" (77 x 77 cm),
printed by The Artists' Press, Johannesburg,
mirror-finish steel cylinder,
diameter 3¹/₂" (9 cm), height 5" (12,7 cm),
weight 2 lbs (750 g),
Ed. 60/XX, signed and numbered

EDITION FOR PARKETT 63

Mystery solved in mirrored captivity: the gorgon's head with serpents entwined and the painstaking efforts of the water bearer.

"No stranger to tragedy in life and on the stage,
[Kentridge] truly has served as a messenger of the
obscene and has taken on the burden of drawing
ethical conclusions from historical events that are
often overwhelmingly evil. His is an art not only of
politics, as it has often been viewed, but also an art
of theodicy that considers with great deliberation
the problems involved in witnessing, telling, and
concluding in the face of unremitting state violence."

Susan Stewart
Parkett No. 63, 2001

ウィリアム・ケントリッジ

メデューサ　2001

chine collé にリトグラフで歪んだ像をプリント、
1906年版ラルース百科事典の6ページを使用、
図柄：直径 63cm、
紙：77×77cm、
刷り：アーティスツ・プレス（ヨハネスブルグ）、
鏡面仕上げのスティール製シリンダー：
直径 9cm、高さ 12.7cm、重量 750g、
Ed. 60/XX、署名、番号入り

パルケット・エディション 63

囚われの姿を鏡に映して謎が解ける。蛇の生えるゴルゴンの頭と水瓶座の労を惜しまない努力。

人生、そして演劇の悲劇に通じたケントリッジは、卑猥さを伝える使者の役割を存分に果たし、圧倒的に邪悪なことの多い歴史的な出来事から、教訓的な結論を引き出す重責を担った。ケントリッジはしばしば言われるように、ただ政治的なアート手がけるばかりではなく、絶えず暴力が用いられる状況に直面して、それを目撃し、語り伝え、結論をひきだすことを考察対象とする神義論に関わるアートにもとりくんでいる。

スーザン・ステュアート
（パルケット 63号、2001年）

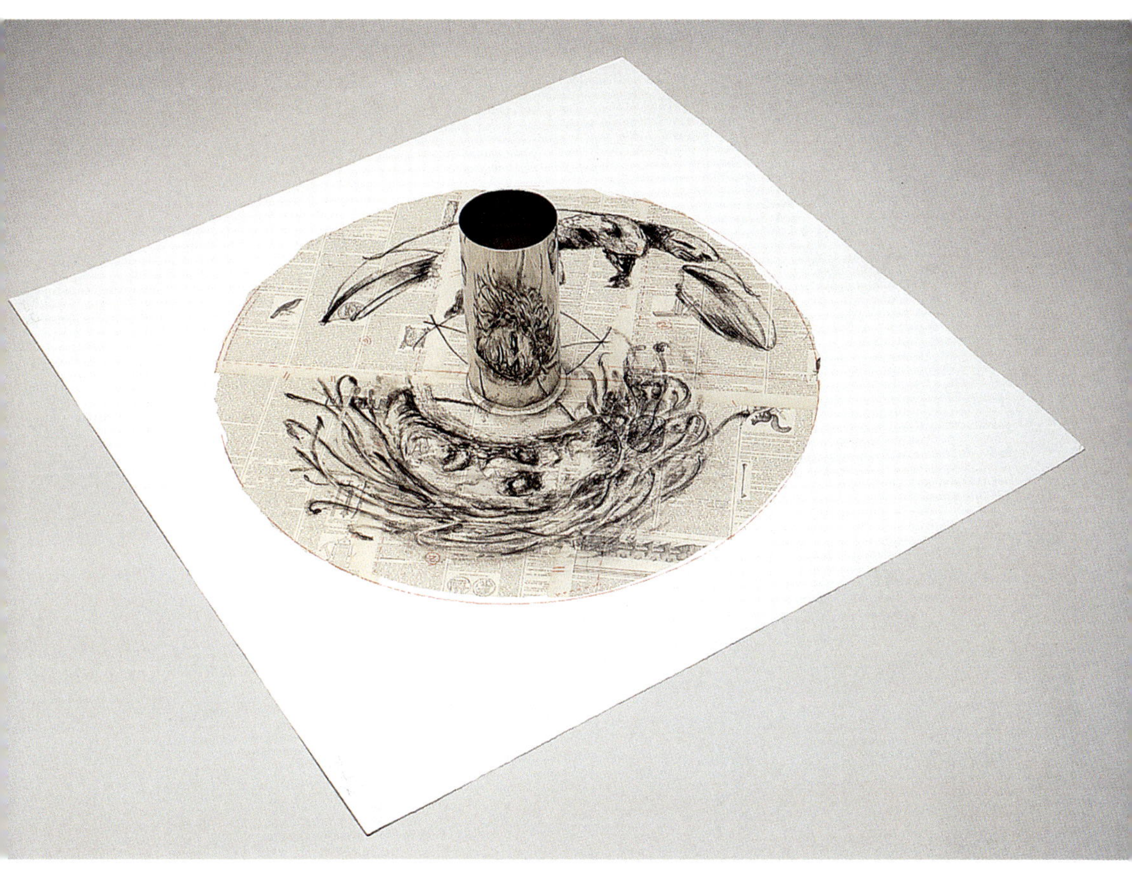

JON KESSLER

Habeas Corpus, 2007

Sculpture, opaque and transparent
non-toxic urethane, instant urethane
pigments, orange polyester satin fabric,
cap, glasses, mask, ear muffs,
sneakers, cable tie, 6 $^3/_4$ x 3 $^1/_2$ x 2 $^3/_4$"
(17 x 9 x 7 cm), production by
Gamla Model Makers, Feasterville, PA,
Ed. 60/XX, signed and numbered
certificate

EDITION FOR PARKETT 79

An image arrested in time, forever etched into
memory, icon of unseen events.

"What unheard-of, hackerly skills will be required for
art in tomorrow's video-broadband Internet: when a
so-called web 'page' is nothing like a 'page.' When video
compositors and web-design software can mix, match,
and munge a chunk of text, annotations, hotlinks,
static images, video snippets, music tracks? And it all
comes gushing straight out of the same pipe, a bub-
bling slumgully of creolized media."

Bruce Sterling
Parkett No. 79, 2007

ジョン・ケスラー

人身保護法　2007

彫刻、有害物質をふくまない半透明、
透明のウレタン、速乾性ウレタン顔料、
オレンジ、サテン風ポリエステル繊維、帽子、
眼鏡、マスク、イア・マフ、スニーカー、ケーブル・タイ、
17×9×7cm、
制作：ガムラ・モデル・メーカーズ社
（ペンシルヴァニア州フィースターヴィル）、
Ed. 60/XX、署名、番号入り証明書

パルケット・エディション 79

時間の流れのなかに固定されたイメージ、永遠に記憶に
刻まれた、人目に触れることのない出来事のシンボル。

ビデオがブロードバンド通信でやとりとりされる明日のインターネッ
ト世界にふさわしいアートには、前代未聞の、ハッカーまがいのいっ
たいどのような技術が求められるのか。いわゆるウェブ「ページ」は、
「ページ」とは似ても似つかない。ビデオ編集とウェブ・デザインのソ
フトが膨大な文章、注釈、ホットリンク、静止画像、ビデオの断片、音
楽のトラックをとりまぜ、とりあわせ、解読の難しいパスワードにも
仕立てられる時代である。しかもそれがすべて同じパイプから、クレ
オール化されたメディアとなり水っぽく泡だちながら、どっと吹き出し
てくる。

ブルース・スターリング
（パルケット 79号、2007年）

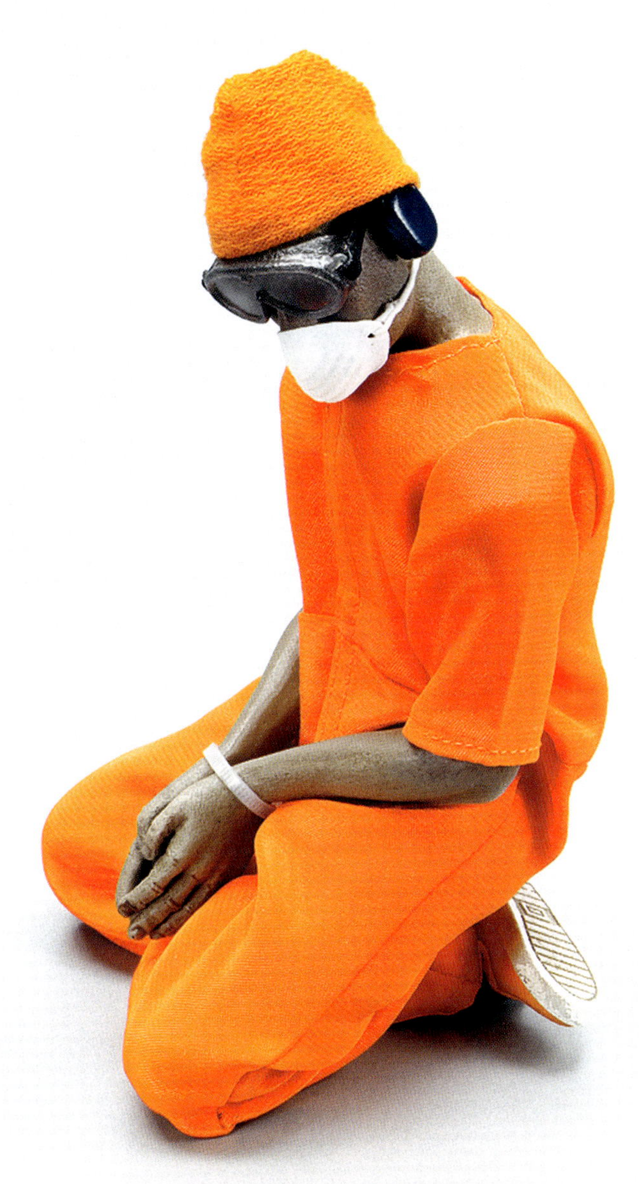

KAREN KILIMNIK

Rapunzel, 1998

Spindle of gold thread (hair) on bed
of moss (thread and moss are separately
packaged to be assembled by the
collector), Plexiglas box,
approx. 4 x 8 x 10" (10,5 x 25,1 x 20,1 cm),
Ed. 45/XX, signed and numbered
certificate with diagram by the artist

EDITION FOR PARKETT 52

Love's Labor's Found.

"Unlike other painters who focus on the well-known,
the beautiful, and the dynamic between the famous
and the secondary... Kilimnik is less absorbed in their
perfection... Kilimnik is a bit of a killer. She loves to
love them but at times they seem to get on even her
nerves. Each character, from fairy tale princesses and
birds, to heiresses, orphans, and models, becomes a
vessel for a broad mixture of self-doubt and conceit."

Collier Schorr
Parkett No. 52, 1998

カレン・キリムニック

髪長姫　1998

苔の床にのせた金色の糸の束（髪）、
糸と苔は別々に包装、コレクターが組み上げる、
アクリル箱、
約10.5×25.1×20.1cm、
Ed. 45/XX、署名、番号入り証明書、
アーティストの描いた組立図

パルケット・エディション 52

恋の骨折り得。

よく知られた者、美しい者、有名人ととりまきの勢力関係に注目
するアーティストたちとは異なり……キリムニックは完璧さにはさ
ほど気をとられない……キリムニックはなかなか油断がならない。
作品であつかう人物が好きなのが気に入ってはいるものの、とき
にはかれらにも苛立つことがある。登場人物のひとりひとりが、お
とぎ話の王女様でも小鳥でも、金持ちの跡取りでもみなしごでも、
モデルであっても、自信喪失と自惚れのいりまじる感情を湛える
器となる。

コリアー・ショール
（パルケット 52号、1998年）

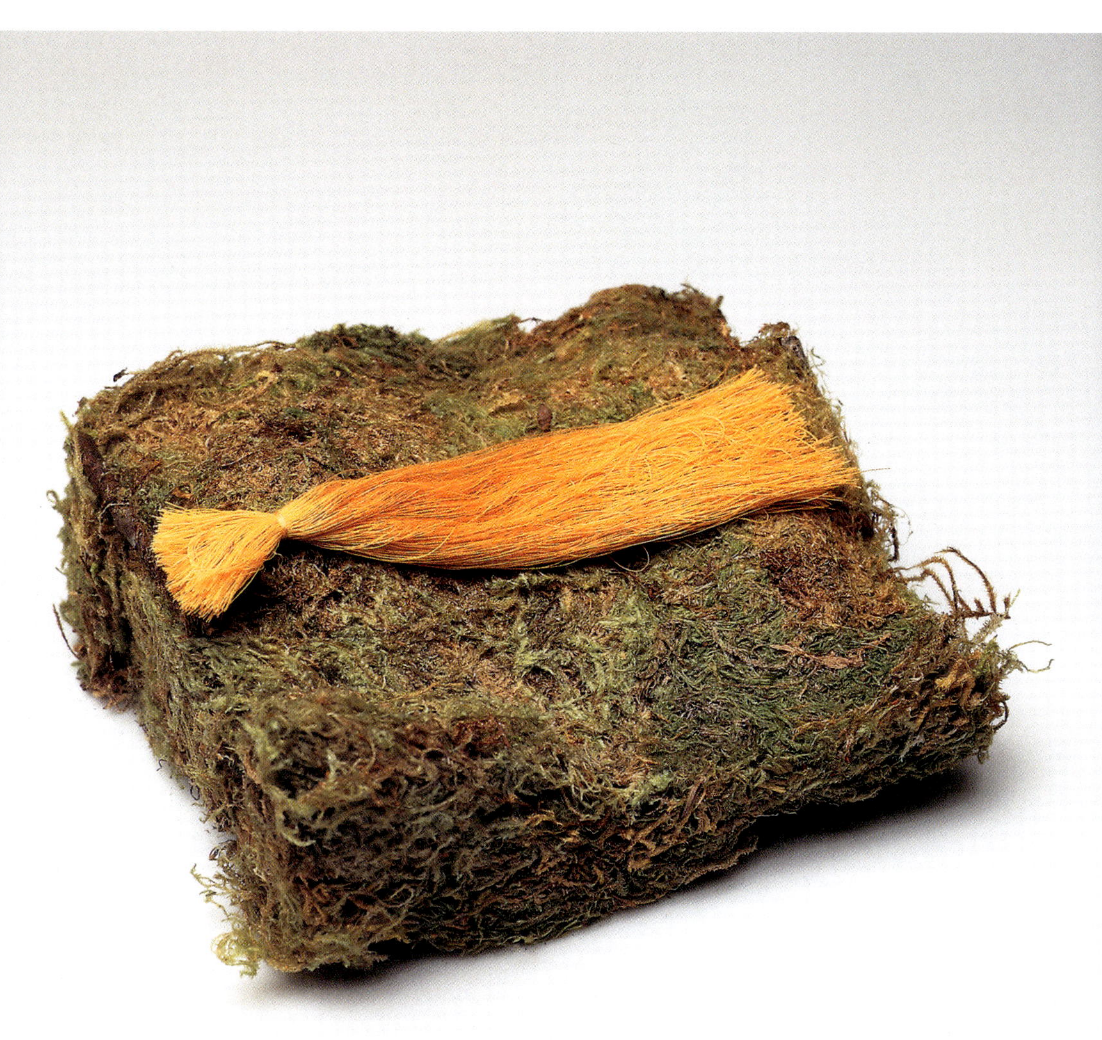

MARTIN KIPPENBERGER

80 Unique Books, 1989

Printed in offset, 6 x 3 ¾" (13,2 x 9,5 cm),
260 pages, inserted in the magazine,
Ed. 80/XX, signed and numbered

EDITION FOR PARKETT 19

Art in the age of mechanical reproduction.
Unique little books, created by turning the
techniques of offset printing inside out,
each containing a single photograph from
the artist's collection of naughty snapshots,
maddeningly reproduced through every page.

"In Kippenberger's work visual subjects follow an order
which is that of the dehierarchized way of reading the
world that distinguishes the masses who have not
been thoroughly cultivated from the masses who have;
such as can be seen, for instance, in the anti-bourgeois
order of values and importance found in tabloid news-
papers and other subcultural or pop-cultural sites,
where sense (and the power that feeds parasitically off
it) plays no part in determining the order of priority of
meaning."

Diedrich Diederichsen
Parkett No. 19, 1989

マルティン・キッペンベルガー

一冊ずつ内容の異なる80冊の本　1989

オフセット印刷、13.2×9.5cm、
260ページ、本誌に綴じこみ、
Ed. 80/XX、署名、番号入り

パルケット・エディション 19

機械を用いた複製万能時代の芸術。オセフット印刷の
技術を逆手にとって創りだされた一冊ずつ内容の異な
る80冊の小さな本には、アーティストがこっそり集め
たスナップショットの中から選ばれた1枚が、始めから
終わりまで延々と印刷されていて、見ていると頭がおか
しくなりそう。

キッペンベルガーの作品では、視覚的主題が教化の充分でない大衆
と充分な大衆を区別する世界を、上下関係抜きに読解させる指示に
したがう。それはたとえばタブロイド版の新聞、サブカルチャーや大
衆文化の現場の反ブルジョア的価値や重要性の判断基準にも見るこ
とができる。そうした場では感覚（そして寄生虫的に養分を吸い上
げる権力）は意味の優先順位を定めるうえで、なんの役割もはたさ
ない。

ディードリヒ・ディーダーリッシェン
（パルケット 19号、1989年）

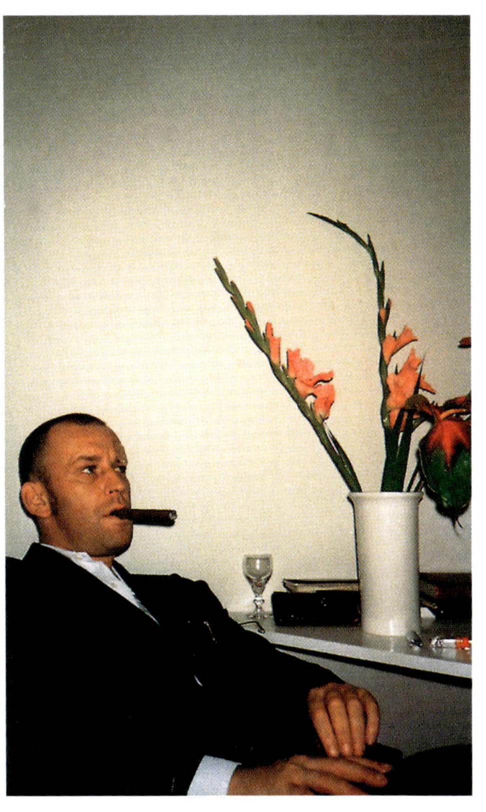

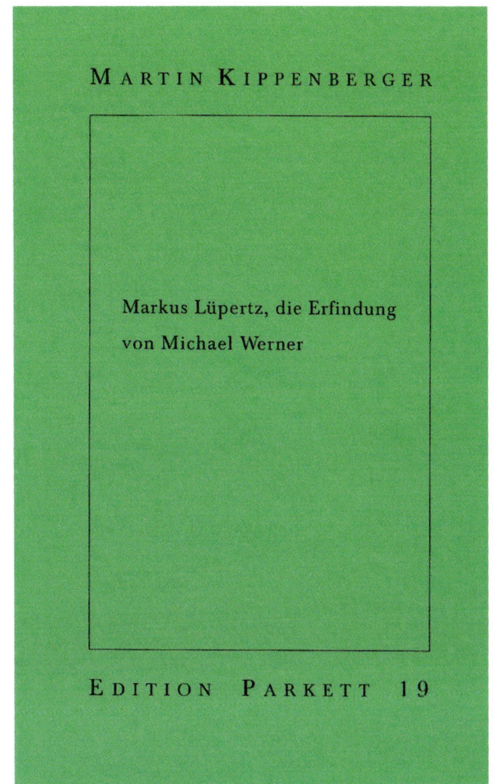

MARTIN KIPPENBERGER
Markus Lüpertz, die Erfindung
von Michael Werner
EDITION PARKETT 19

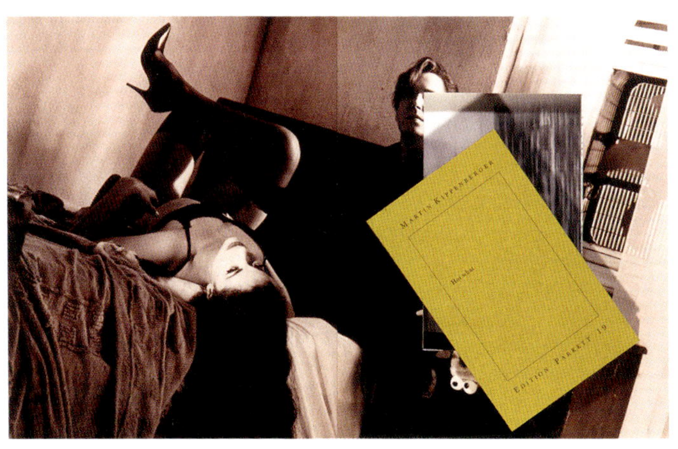

IMI KNOEBEL

Cementi, 1992

Concrete and ferric oxide,
9 1/2 x 4 3/4 x 3" (23,9 x 11,9 x 7,5 cm),
Ed. 100/XX, signed and numbered

EDITION FOR PARKETT 32

Laws of gravity. Concrete laced with pigment yields a surface so delicate that the three-dimensional form to which it belongs appears to float right off the wall.

"Knoebel's work, finally, has to do with progress and regression, construction and destruction, and indeed, most poetically, with childhood, in the light of actual space and place."

Lisa Liebmann
Parkett No. 32, 1992

イミ・クネーベル

セメント　1992

コンクリート、酸化鉄、
23.9×11.9×7.5cm、
Ed. 100/XX、署名、番号入り

パルケット・エディション 32

重力の法則。顔料を塗布されたコンクリートの表面はきわめて優美なため、3次元のフォルムが壁から浮き上がって見える。

クネーベルの作品が実際にある空間、場所に置かれると、やがて進展と後退、構築と破壊、そしてじつはきわめて詩的に、子供時代に関わることが明らかになる。

リサ・リーブマン
（パルケット 32号、1992年）

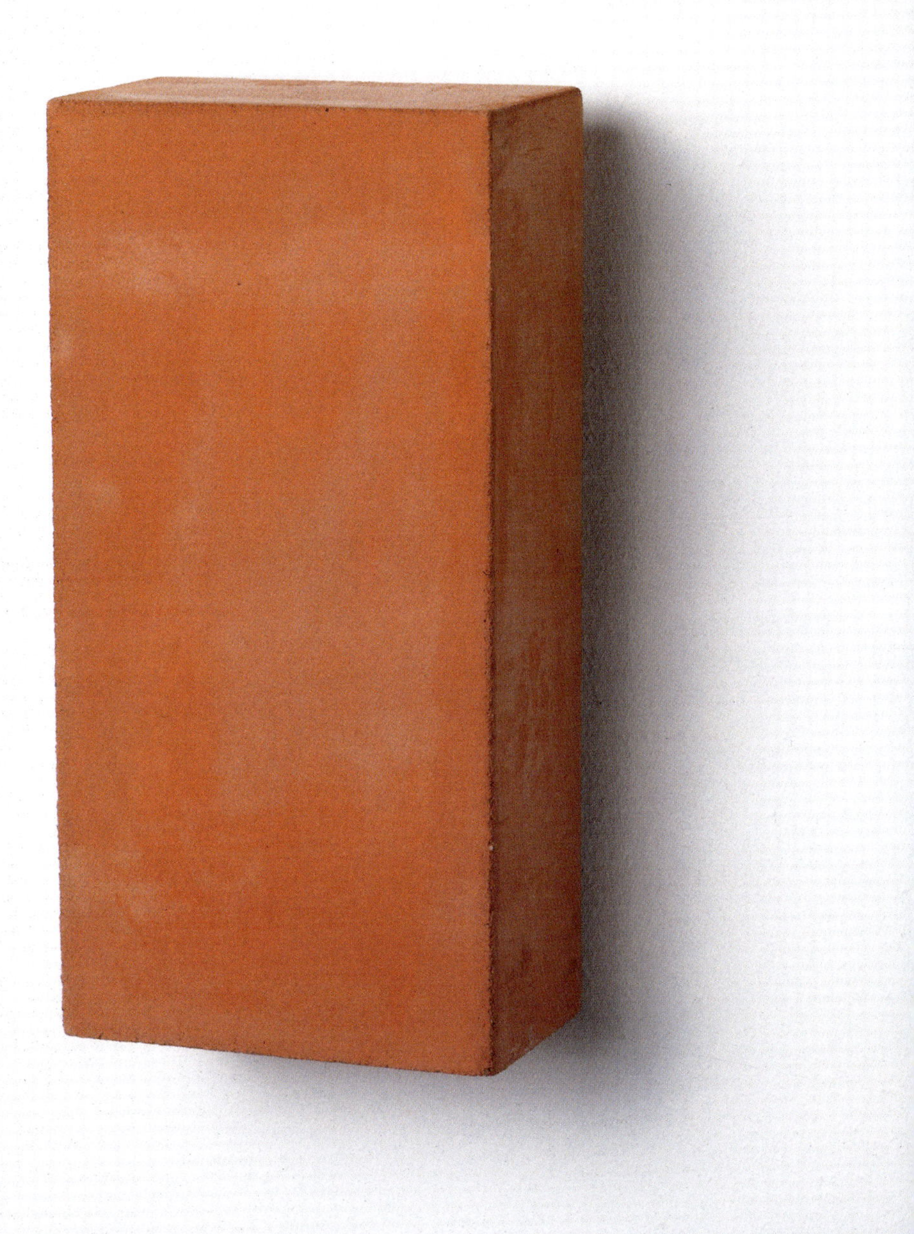

JEFF KOONS

Signature Plate, 1989

Porcelain, with a decal fired at 1652 F, diameter 10¼" (26 cm), made by Porzellanfabrik Langenthal, Switzerland, Ed. 80/L, numbered, signature integrated into the picture

EDITION FOR PARKETT 19

Keepsake kitsch. Neither Elvis, nor the Queen Mother smiles from this quaint china souvenir—their place has been gleefully usurped by Jeff Koons and his pig.

"Jeff Koons's art is most amusing. It is provocative in the most archly targeted way. It makes grown art critics sick."

Glenn O'Brien
Parkett No. 19, 1989

ジェフ・クーンズ

引き出物　1989

絵付けし900℃で焼いた磁器、直径26cm、制作：ランゲンタール磁器製造（スイス）、Ed. 80/L、絵柄の一部に番号と署名を挿入

パルケット・エディション 19

キッチュな記念品。風変わりな土産品の磁器から微笑みかけるのはエルヴィスでもなければ、皇太后でもない—かれらの指定席は嬉しそうに押しかけてきたジェフ・クーンズと愛豚に奪われた。

ジェフ・クーンズの作品はじつに楽しい。悪戯っぽく狙いを定めて、ひとを挑発する。大人の美術評論家は辟易するばかり。

グレン・オブライエン
（パルケット 19号、1989年）

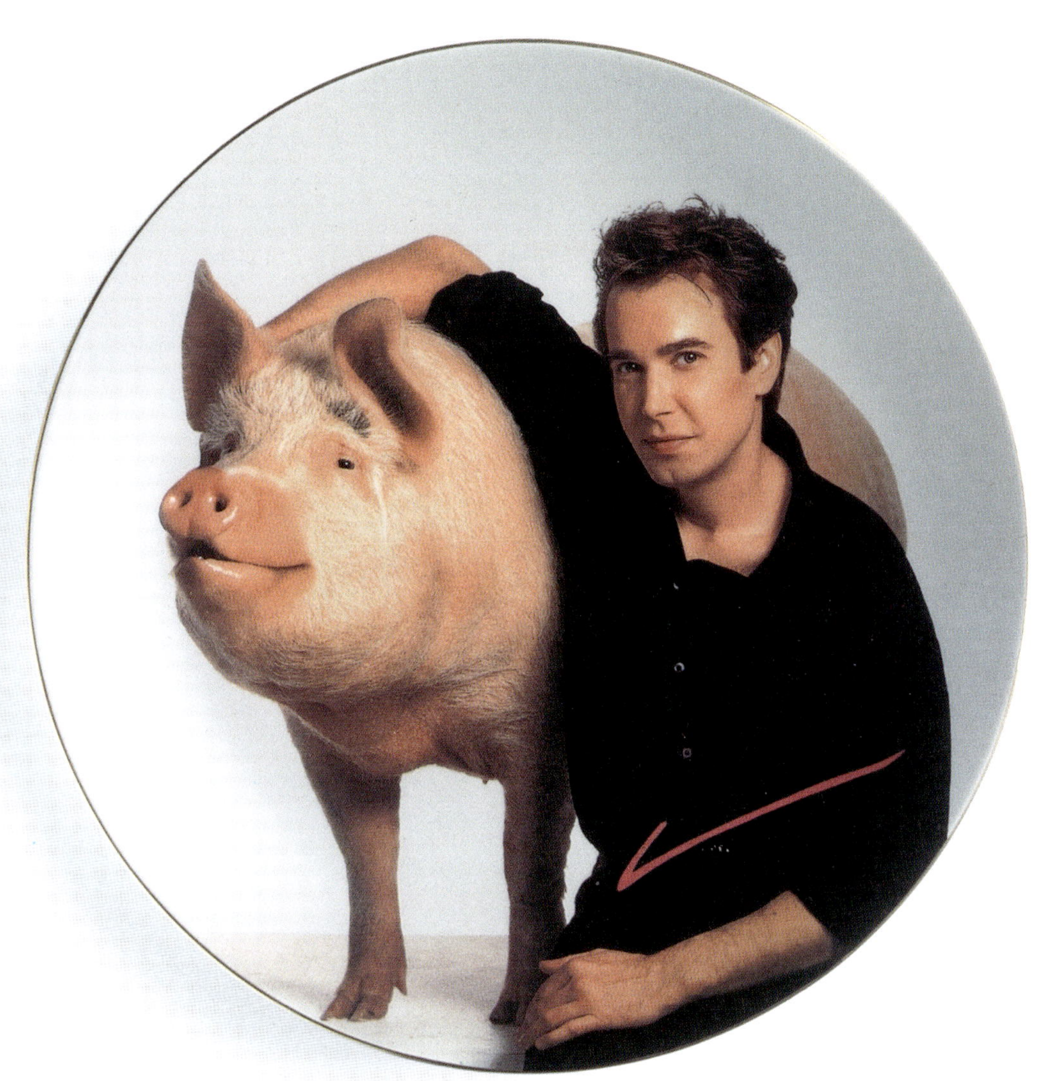

JEFF KOONS

Inflatable Balloon Flower (Yellow),
1997

PVC,
approx. 51 x 59 x 70" (128 x 148 x 180 cm),
manufactured by Schultes, Vienna,
Ed. 100/XL, signed and numbered

EDITION FOR PARKETT 50/51

Miraculum helvum magnum.

"Like a capricious genie, Jeff Koons gives people far
more than they secretly ask for. In the toylike reflective
surfaces of these works, one sees a morally distorted
self, a primal, naked persona shamefully satisfying an
unbridled appetite for sensation, the child one never
grew up to be."

Vik Muniz
Parkett No. 50/51, 1997

ジェフ・クーンズ

風船の花（黄色）　　1997

ポリ塩化ビニール、
約128×148×180cm、
制作：シュルテス社（ウィーン）、
Ed. 100/XL、署名、番号入り

パルケット・エディション 50/51

大型の黄色い奇跡。

気まぐれな天才のように、ジェフ・クーンズはひとびとの密かな願い
を遙かに上回るものをあたえる。光を反射する玩具のようなこれら
の作品の表面に、ひとは倫理的に歪んだ自己、感覚の歓びを求めて
底無しの欲望を恥ずかしげもなく満たそうとする根源的な、赤裸々
なペルソナを見る。成長してそうなることのついになかった子供の
姿をそこに認める。

ヴィク・ムニツ
（パルケット 50/51号、1997年）

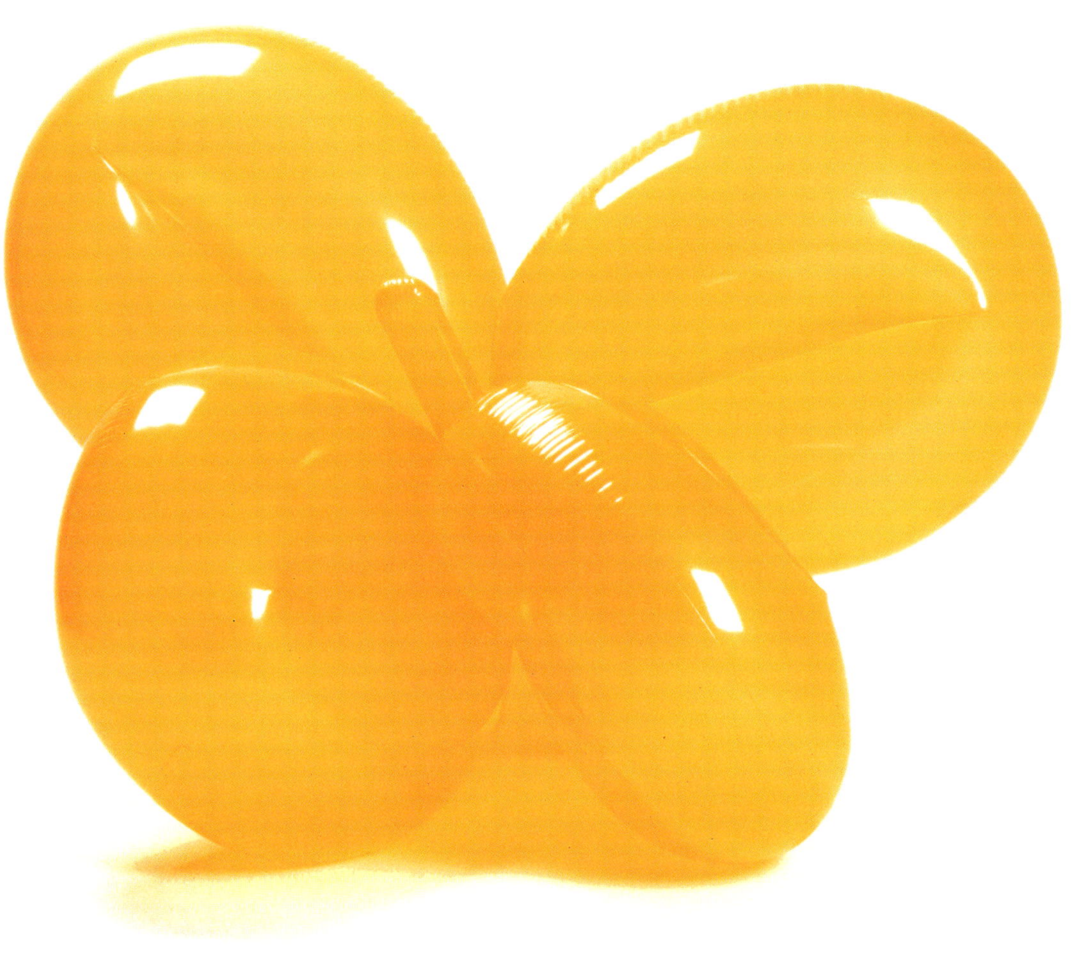

JANNIS KOUNELLIS

Untitled, 1985

Photo-etching, aquatint and scraping
on Zerkall-Vellum, bound in the
magazine, 10 x 8¼" (25,5 x 21 cm),
printed by Peter Kneubühler, Zurich,
Ed. 80/XX, signed and numbered

EDITION FOR PARKETT 6

Private postcard. With fireworks and swans
as punctuation, the brooding sky and rippling
waters of Zurich send a message from the
birthplace of Parkett.

"I am interested in an experience that is not literally
surrealistic but one that leaves room for fantasy, that
opens up possibilities in the sense of an inner life.
Reality is so terribly obsessive. An abstract, geometric
work, like a Mondrian... It's extraordinary but you can
find other means today, freer forms of life than these
rigid, mystical ones."

Jannis Kounellis
in: Ein Magnet im Freien, Berne/Berlin, 1992

ヤニス・クネリス

無題　1985

フォト・エッチング、アクアチント、
スクレイピング、ツェルカル社製ヴェラム紙、
本誌に綴じこみ、25.5×21cm、
刷り：ペーター・クノイビューラー（チューリヒ）、
Ed. 80/XX、署名、番号入り

パルケット・エディション 6

私家版絵はがき。白鳥と花火をアクセントに、チューリ
ヒの重くたれこめる空と湖面のさざ波が、パルケット
誕生の地からメッセージを送り届ける。

シュルレアリスムとは言いきれないまでも、幻想を楽しむ余地が
あり、内面の可能性を広げるような経験に興味がある。現実はあま
りに強迫観念を生みやすい。抽象的で、幾何学的な作品、たとえば
モンドリアンのような……それは素晴らしいけれども、今ではまた
べつのやり方をみつけることができる。ああいった堅苦しくて神が
かりなものではなく、もっと自由な生きかたが可能になった。

ヤニス・クネリス
『Ein Magnet im Freien』ベルン／ベルリン、1992年

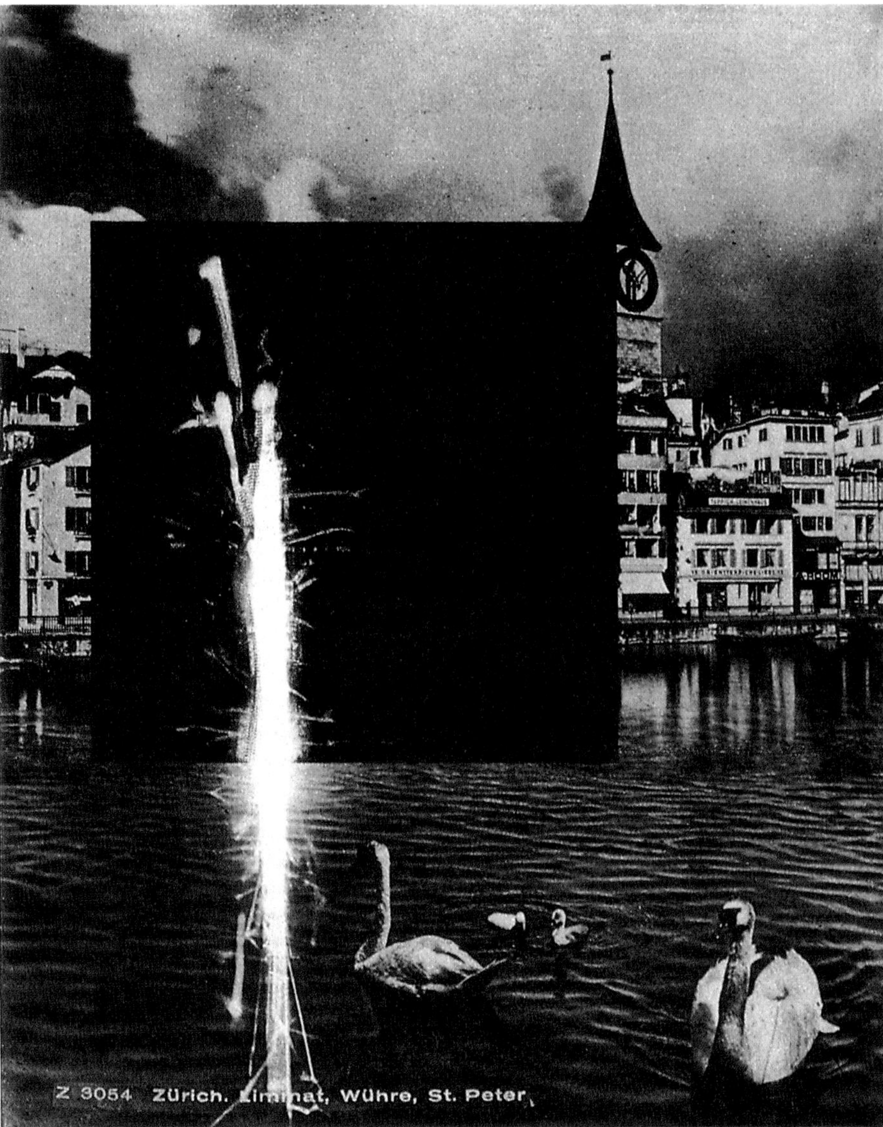

Z 3054 Zürich. Limmat, Wühre, St. Peter

YAYOI KUSAMA

Infinity Nets, 2000

Silkscreen print on mirror,
10 x 8¼" (25,5 x 21 cm),
Ed. 70/XXX, signed and numbered
on the back

EDITION FOR PARKETT 59

Nosce te ipsum. A fragmented whole becomes enmeshed in reflections on infinity.

"She achieves a protean transformation of the 'polka dot' pattern into the accumulation of banal found objects (airmail stickers, working gloves, sofa springs) and stuffed protruding sculptural units and maintains stylistic independence from major artistic schools of her time—Abstract Expressionism, Pop, Minimalism, Nouvelle Tendence—while indicating some overlap with their experimental characteristics."

Midori Matsui
Parkett No. 59, 2000

草間彌生

無限の網　2000

鏡にシルクスクリーンでプリント、
25.2×21cm、
Ed. 70/XXX、裏面に署名、番号入り

パルケット・エディション 59

汝自身を知れ。断片化された全体が無限に反映して網の目にからまる。

草間は「水玉」模様からありふれた品々（航空便用の切手、軍手、ソファのばね）の集積、そして突起物のある詰め物をいくつも連ねる彫刻作品へと多様な変容を遂げ、しかも時代の主流であった抽象表現主義、ポップ、ミニマリズム、新傾向などの運動については、それらの実験性とはいくぶん重なる部分も示しながらも、独立独歩のスタイルを維持した。

松井みどり
（パルケット 59号、2000年）

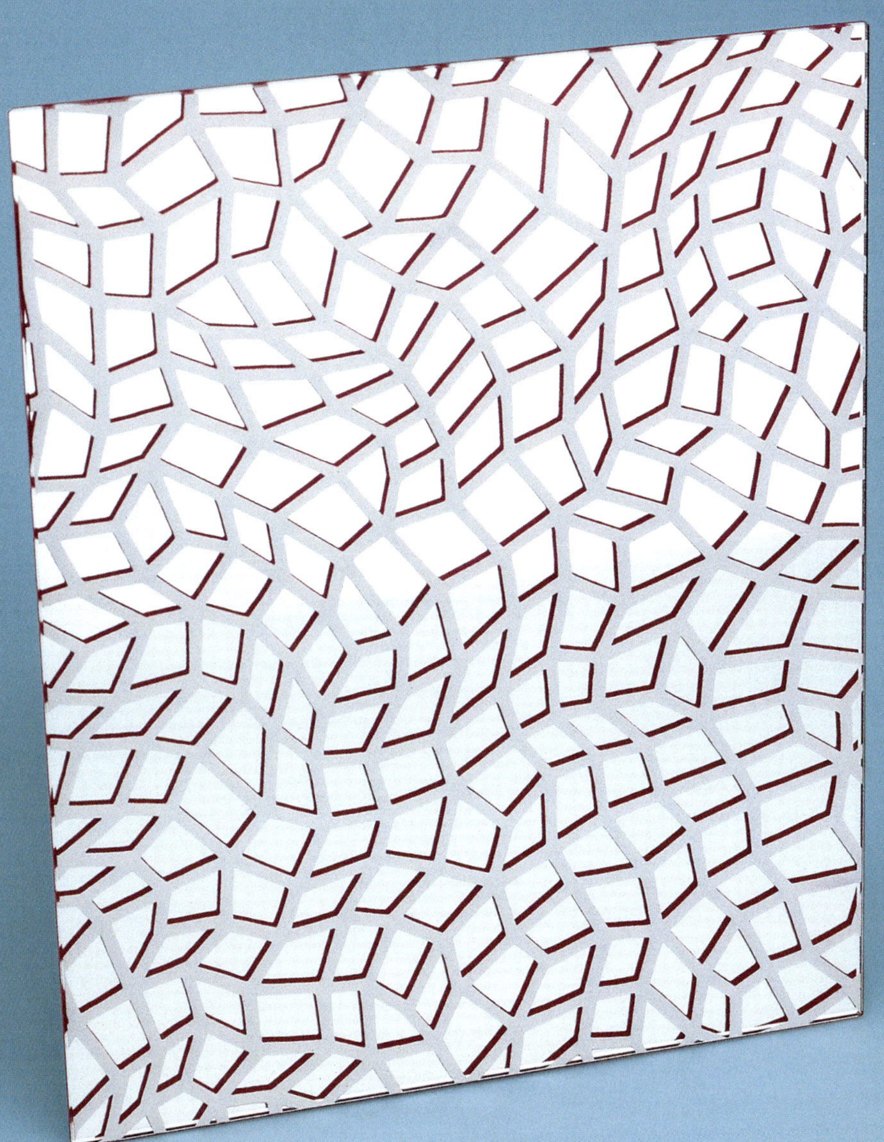

WOLFGANG LAIB

A Wax Room for a Mountain, 1994

Silkscreen, oilstick on Rivoli SK2 240g,
19 1/2 x 16 1/8" (49,2 x 40,9 cm),
printed by Lorenz Boegli, Zurich,
Ed. 75/XL, signed and numbered

EDITION FOR PARKETT 39

Trace elements. A delicate rendering in golden wax of a secluded place in the future, a mountain sanctuary to be built by the artist in the Pyrenees.

"For Wolfgang Laib, the pollen, like the milk, beeswax, rice, and marble, is a material with properties that extend beyond his individual powers of invention; and he accepts this, playing the role of mediator rather than creator, combining organic materials that have invisible energies—perhaps even healing powers."

Clare Farrow
Parkett No. 39, 1994

ヴォルフガング・ライプ

山用のワックスルーム　1994

シルススクリーン、オイルスティック、
リヴォリ SK2、240g、49.2×40.9cm、
刷り：ロレンツ・ボエリ（チューリヒ）、
Ed. 75/XL、署名、番号入り

パルケット・エディション 39

痕跡の要素。ライプが将来ピレネー山中に建築する予定の、人里離れたやすらぎの場所を金の蜜蝋で繊細に描いた。

ヴォルフガング・ライプにとって、花粉はミルクや蜜蝋、米や大理石と同じように、ひとりの人間の有する発明能力をこえた属性をもつ素材なのである。ライプはこの事実を認め、創作者ではなく仲介者の役割に徹し、不可視のエネルギー、おそらくは治癒力さえ備えた有機物を組み合わせる。

クレア・ファロウ
（パルケット 39号、1994年）

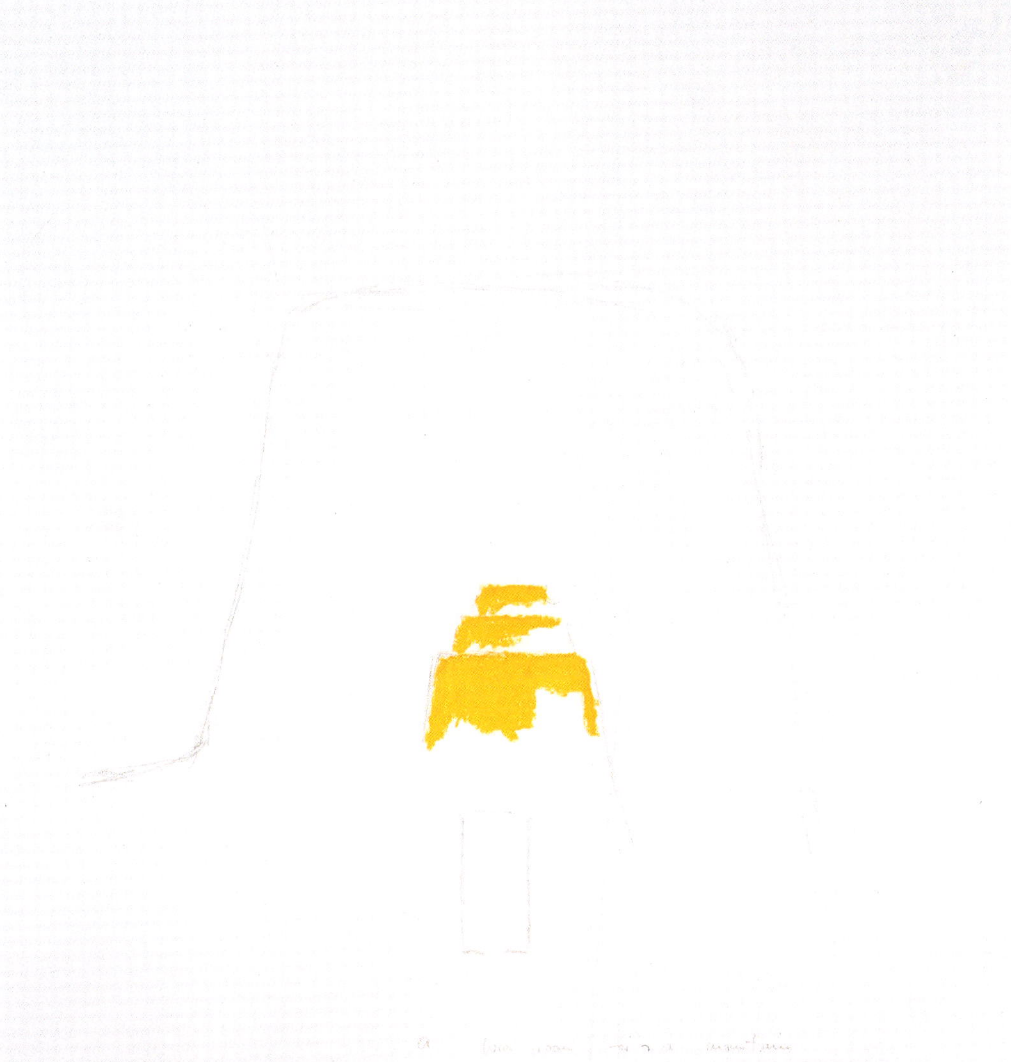

24/75

MARIA LASSNIG

A Pair of Gloves, 2006/2009

6-color silkscreen print on
Arches 88 paper 300 g/m², rein Hadern,
paper size: 28 x 20 3/4" (71 x 52,7 cm),
image size: 24 x 16 7/8" (68,6 x 50,8 cm),
Printed by Atelier für Siebdruck
Lorenz Boegli, Zurich.
Edition of 45/XX, signed and numbered

EDITION FOR PARKETT 85

"My grip on love
slips through my hand,
where will it land?"

"In short, Lassnig has not settled down; she has geared
up. The only tip-off that these were the fantasies of
an old woman comes when she herself is the center of
the action, as she is in several pictures with unsparing
attention to her own nudity. But woe to the spectators
who look down the barrel of the gun she points out
at them in one such picture, thinking that she won't
shoot."

Robert Storr
Parkett No. 85, 2009

マリア・ラスニック

手袋　2006/2009

6色刷りシルクスクリーン、
アルシュ88紙、300g/㎡、
ラグ100%、
図柄：71×52.7cm、
紙：68.6×50.8cm、
刷り：ロレンツ・ボエリ（チューリヒ）、
Ed. 45/XX、署名、番号入り

パルケット・エディション 85

捕まえたと思った愛が
するりと私の手をすり抜けた
行き着く先は何処？

要するに、ラスニックはまだ落ちつくには至らない。老女の夢想を窺
わせるのは、本人が主役となる場合にかぎられ、自らの裸体に容赦
ない眼差しを注ぐいくつかの絵画がそれにあたる。しかし絵の中の
老女がこちらに向ける銃身を見下ろして、撃つもんかとたかをくくる
見物人に災いあれ。

ロバート・ストア
（パルケット 85号、2009年）

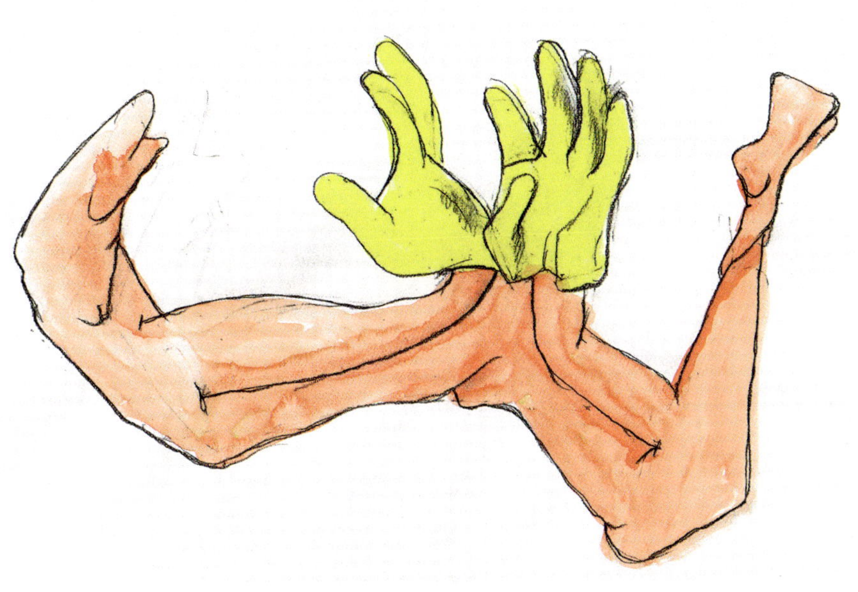

ZOE LEONARD

1 Hour Photo & Video, 2007/2008

C-print, paper size: 18 x 13"
(45,7 x 33 cm), image: 8$^{1}/_{2}$ x 8$^{1}/_{2}$"
(21,6 x 21,6 cm), printed by
My Own Color Lab, New York,
Ed. 40/XXV, signed and numbered

EDITION FOR PARKETT 84

Where the raw urban fabric redefines
visions of human progress.

"It has often been noted that Leonard, in her prints,
keeps the black border that occurs in the printing
process rather then cropping it out, as a way of
integrating the problematics of viewing into the work."

Elisabeth Lebovici,
Parkett No. 84, 2009

ゾーイ・レオナルド

1時間写真＆ビデオ　2007/2008

Cプリント、紙：45.7×33cm、
図柄：21.6×21.6cm、
プリント制作：マイ・オウン・カラー・DPE
（ニューヨーク）、
Ed. 40/XXV、署名、番号入り

パルケット・エディション 84

粗野な都市住民が、人間は進歩するという考え方を
塗り替える。

これまでにもしばしば指摘されてきたように、レオナルドは、プ
リントの過程で生じる黒い縁取りをトリミングせずに残し、それ
によって物を見ることにともなう不確定要素を作品の内部にとり
こむ。

エリザベス・リボヴィッチ
（パルケット 84号、2009年）

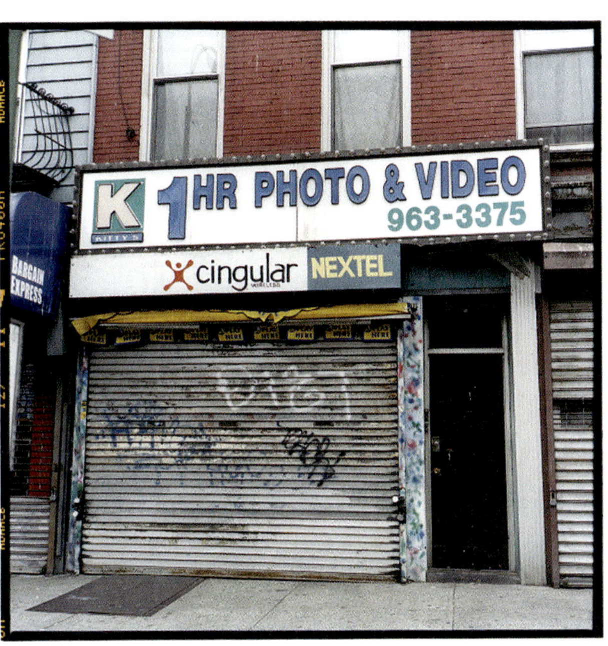

K KITTY'S
1 HR PHOTO & VIDEO
963-3375
cingular WIRELESS
NEXTEL
BARGAIN EXPRESS

SHERRIE LEVINE

Two Shoes, 1992

Pair of children's shoes, brown leather,
each 6$\frac{1}{2}$ x 2$\frac{1}{2}$ x 2$\frac{1}{2}$" (15,8 x 6 x 5,8 cm),
Ed. 99/XXXVI, signed and numbered

EDITION FOR PARKETT 32

A new pair of shoes. Many years ago,
Sherrie Levine found and sold pairs of small
shoes in a gallery in New York. A refined
version, handmade in Italy from softest
leather and suede, retraces the artist's first
steps.

"It is into this story, the story of art history as narrative
of becoming in which each proper name becomes
a historical site, that Sherrie Levine has always
'liberated' her objects. But it is also where she has
always found them."

Howard Singerman
Parkett No. 32, 1992

シェリー・レヴィーン

ふたつの靴　1992

子供靴 1足、茶色の革、各々15.8×6×5.8cm、
Ed. 99/XXXVI、署名、番号入り

パルケット・エディション 32

新品の靴1足。何年も前にシェリー・レヴィーンはニュー
ヨークの画廊で小さな靴を1足みつけて、それを売った
ことがあった。今回はとびきり柔らかな革とスエードを
用いたイタリア製、手縫いの高級版を通して、レヴィー
ン初期の足跡をふりかえる。

シェリー・レヴィーンが常々オブジェを「解き放って」きたのは、物語、
固有名詞が歴史の場となる、生成の説話としての美術史の物語のな
かである。しかしそれはまたレヴィーンがそれらを発見した場所でも
あった。

ハワード・シンガーマン
（パルケット 32号、1992年）

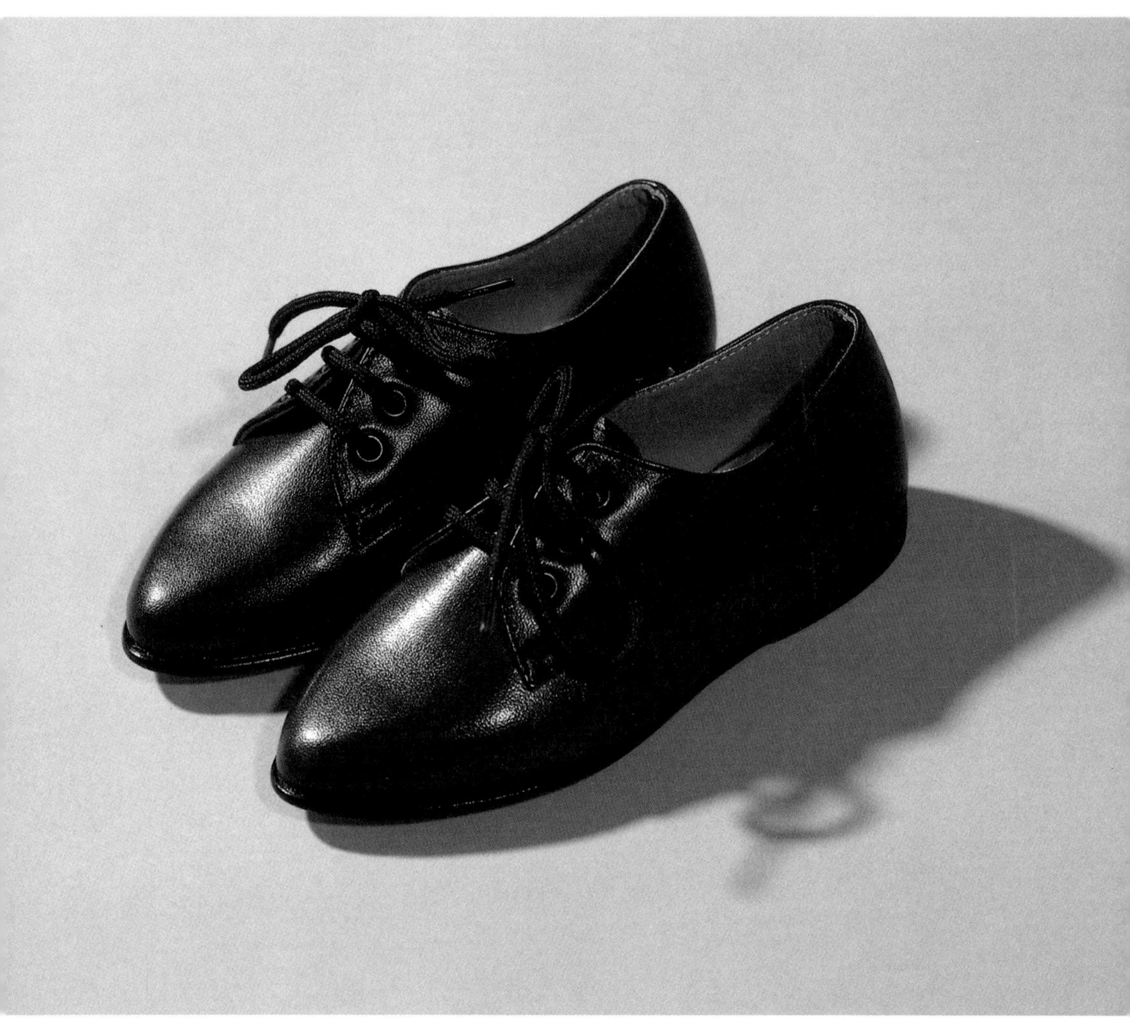

SARAH LUCAS

Lion Heart, 1995

Cast metal, approx. 2 ³/₄ x 2 ³/₄ x 1³/₄"
(7 x 7 x 4,5 cm), 50 pieces of cast lead,
50 pieces of cast brass,
produced at the Jäger Brothers Foundry,
Pfäffikon SZ, Switzerland,
Ed. 100/XXX, signed and numbered

EDITION FOR PARKETT 45

Yang and yang. Brass balls or lead balloons,
a rude trophy, cast as heroic kitsch or mortal
weight.

"Sarah Lucas gives as good as she gets. She's a
code-breaker and a ball-buster, a saboteur and a
spy. Elegantly in-your-face, Lucas is a smutty, salt-
of-the-earth lout whose unequivocal work is raw and
loud and startling. It is also efficient and concise. In
her art, Lucas doesn't mince words and she doesn't
waste them either. She gets quickly to the point—and
the point usually has to do with the ways women are
viewed in society."

Jerry Saltz
Parkett No. 45, 1995

サラ・ルーカス

ライオン・ハート（勇猛な人）　　1995

金属を鋳造、7×7×4.5cm、
鉛の鋳造 50個、真鍮の鋳造 50個、
制作：イェーガー兄弟鋳造所、
（プフェフィコンSZ、スイス）、
Ed. 100/XXX、署名、番号入り

パルケット・エディション 45

陽と陽。真鍮の球か鉛の風船、粗野な戦利品、英雄気
取りのキッチュあるいは致命的な重荷としての鋳造。

サラ・ルーカスはやられたらやり返す。規則は破り男には甘い顔
を見せず、破壊、諜報に精を出す。淑やかに何を言うかとおもえば、
「そうれ、みろ」、下卑た地の塩、手本にしたい図々しさだが、作品
は勘違いする余地もなく露骨で喧しくひとの度肝を抜く。それに効
率が良く、無駄がない。制作を始めれば、上品ぶった遠回しな話し
方は無用、無駄口も叩かない。まっすぐ要点を突く、その要点はた
いがい女が世間でどうみられているかに関わる。

ジェリー・サルツ
（パルケット 45号、1995年）

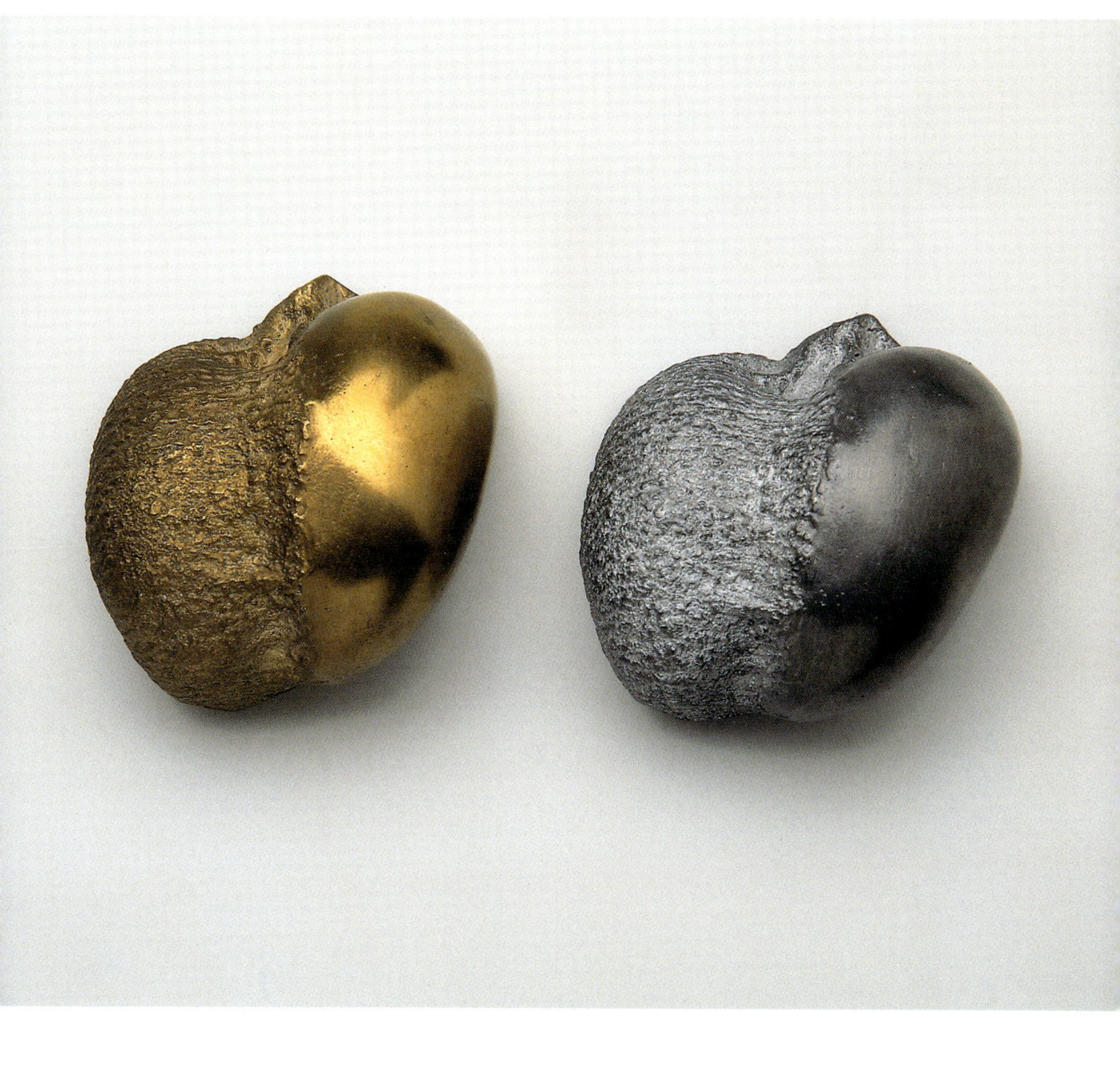

CHRISTIAN MARCLAY

My Bad Ear, 2004

Life-size bronze cast by
Modern Art Foundry, Astoria, NY,
Ed. 60/XX, signed and numbered

EDITION FOR PARKETT 70

Soundseeing—A silent witness to the fugitive, but omnipresent world of music.

"A great deal of Marclay's output, possibly the majority of it, is visual or plastic in nature. And yet even this is as much about sound recording; perhaps more so, because it concerns the ubiquity of sound in culture. Marclay's work is about the socially inscribed 'flip side' of sound; it is about the very fact that I could use the phrase 'flip side' as unthinkingly as I just did, realizing only as I typed it that the term derives from records, and is thus infinitely apropos for use there."

Philip Sherburne
Parkett No. 70, 2004

クリスチャン・マークレイ

ぼくの悪い耳　2004

鋳造した等身大のブロンズ、
制作：モダン・アート鋳造
（ニューヨーク市アストリア）、
Ed. 60/XX、署名、番号入り

パルケット・エディション 70

音を見る—その場限りでも、そこかしこにある音楽の世界の無口な目撃者。

マークレイの作品の多く、おそらく大半は視覚か造型性を特質とする。しかしここでは音声の録音も同じく重視され、文化に音が遍在することを扱っている以上、その比重のほうが高いのかもしれない。マークレイの作品は社会的に刻印された音の「B面」に関わる。肝心なのはわたしが今のように無意識のうちに「B面」ということばを使うという事実、タイプを打ちながらこの言い方はレコードから派生したもので、となればまさにここで使うのにもってこいと気づいたという事実なのである。

フィリップ・シャーバーン
（パルケット 70号、2004年）

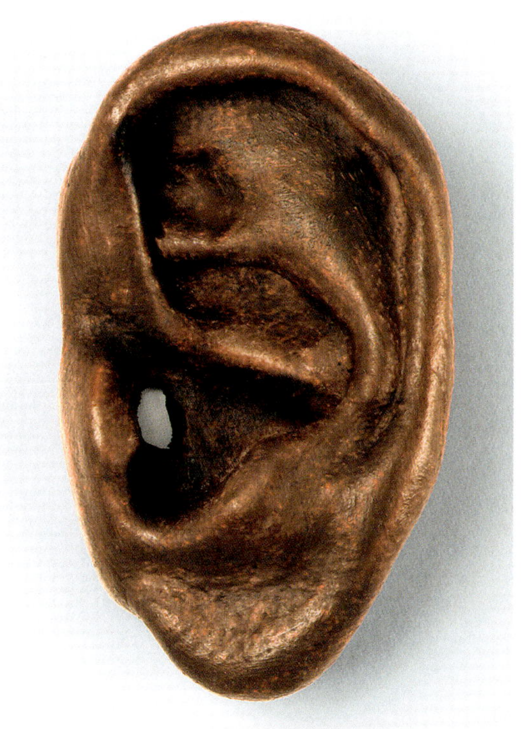

BRICE MARDEN

Etching for Parkett, 1986

Sugar lift and aquatint on Rives BVK,
bound in the magazine,
10 x 8¼" (25,5 x 21 cm),
printed by Jennifer Melby, New York,
Ed. 100/X, signed and numbered

EDITION FOR PARKETT 7

Eye-music. Composed on Parkett layout-sheets, lines, bars and smudges of ink build to a visual crescendo in this six-panel leporello.

"The physical singularity of Marden's paintings may be attributed to the fact that from the very start he pitched his work with resolute intensity to this key of chromatic enigmas—literally with the mystery-tones of gray—and as he advanced, he simply compounded the chords, adding sharps or flats, moving from minor to major scales."

Lisa Liebmann
Parkett No. 7, 1986

ブライス・マーデン

パルケットのためのエッチング　1986

シュガーリフト、アクアチント、
リヴ BVK紙、本誌に綴じこみ、
25.5×21cm、
刷り：ジェニフェー・メルビィ（ニューヨーク）、
Ed. 100/X、署名、番号入り

パルケット・エディション 7

目で聴く音楽。パルケットのレイアウト用紙に作曲。線、小節を区切る縦線、インクの染みが6枚つづりの蛇腹に視覚のクレシェンドを描きだす。

マーデンの絵の物としての特性は、絵を描きはじめた頃から断固として作品を謎の色、文学的にも謎の色とされる灰色の調性に合わせたこと、そして制作をつづけるなかでシャープやフラットを添え、短調から長調に転調して和声を複雑にしていったことに求められる。

リサ・リーブマン
（パルケット 7号、1986年）

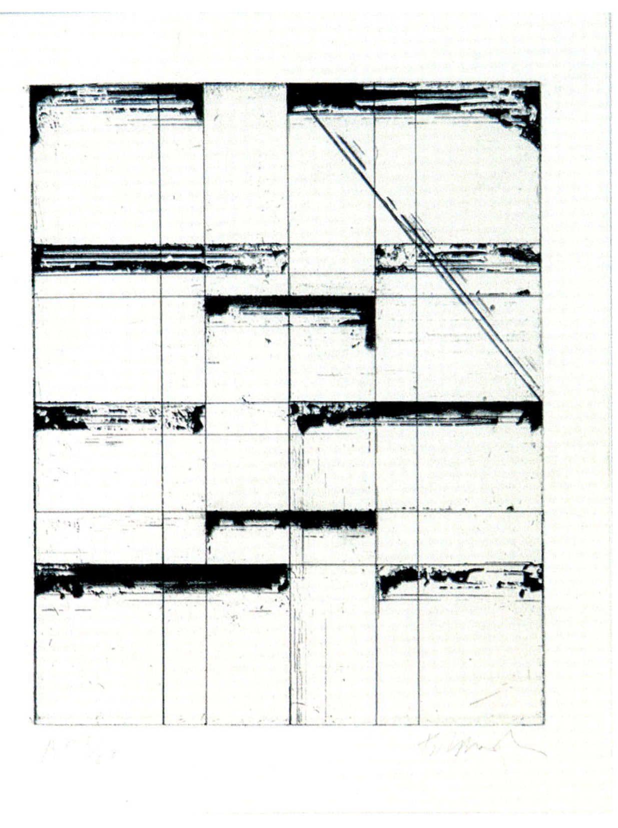

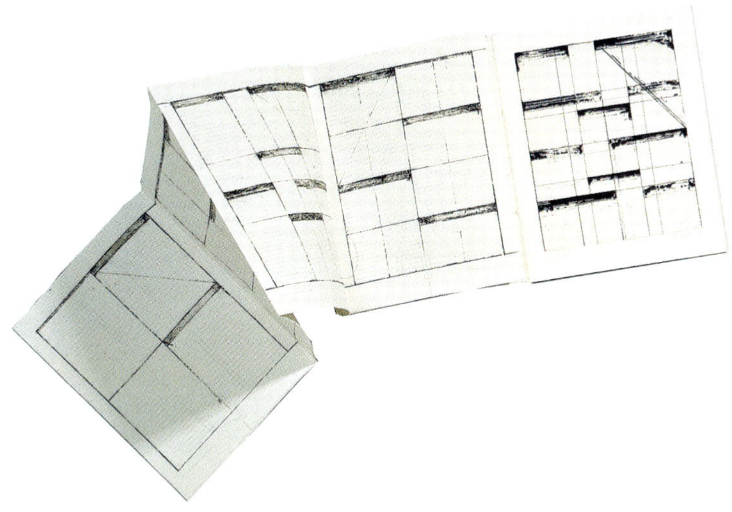

PAUL McCARTHY

Peter Paul Skin Sample, 2005

15 color photographs
(digital laser prints) in cardboard box,
6⁵/₈ x 10" (16,8 x 25,4 cm) each,
Ed. 36/XII, signed and numbered
certificate

Billy Club, 2005

Unique sculptural object, PVC, rubber
foam, gaffers tape, variable dimensions,
approx. 20 x 4 x 4" (55 x 10 x 10 cm),
Ed. 36/XII, signed and numbered
certificate

EDITION FOR PARKETT 73

Skin-deep fragments get under your skin
in this candidly uninhibited and touchingly
intimate memento mori.

Empty threats? Hyperagression kept in
check by the soft core of art.

"I was interested in therapy, and I talked about venting.
I made a hollow box covered in—the type of bent metal
hot rods (Vented Cube Drawing, 1975). Then I wrote this
poem about venting. Venting the subconscious. I want
to vent a situation..."

Paul McCarthy, interview with Jeremy Sigler
Parkett No. 73, 2005

ポール・マッカーシー

ピーター・ポール皮膚見本　2005

15枚組カラー写真（デジタル・レーザー・プリント）、
ボール紙の箱入り、各16.8×25.4cm、
Ed. 36/XII、署名、番号入り証明書

棍棒　2005

1点ずつ形の異なるオブジェ、
ポリ塩化ビニール、フォームラバー、
ガファーテープ、サイズはまちまち、
約55×10×10cm、
Ed. 36/XII、署名、番号入り

パルケット・エディション 73

気取らず率直な、いじらしいほど人懐こいこのメメント・
モリの、皮相さがひとの興味をかきたてる。

ただの脅し？　極端な血の気の多さが芸術の穏やかさに
よって抑えられる。

心理療法に興味があって、感情の発散について話をした。わたしは中
が空の閉じた箱—the type of bent metal hot rods（《通気孔のあ
る立方体ドローイング》1975）を作ってみた。それから感情を発散
することについて、こんな詩を書いた。潜在意識を発散する。状況の
捌け口をつくりたい……

ポール・マッカーシー
ジェレミー・ズィグラーのインタヴューに応えて
（パルケット 73号、2005年）

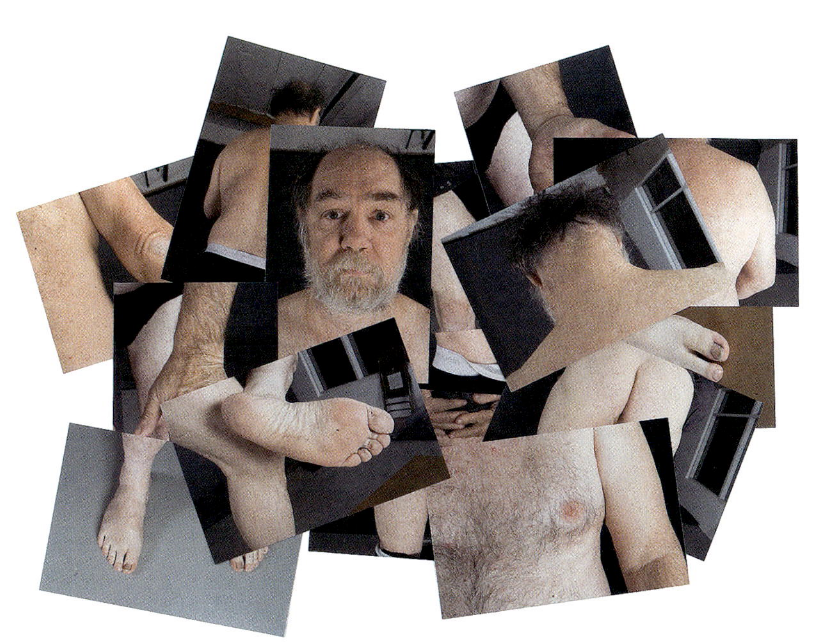

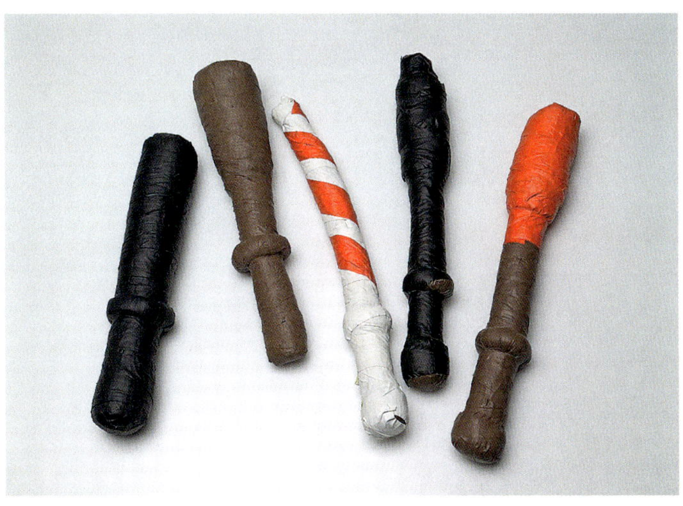

JOSIAH McELHENY

From an Alternative Modernity
(Mirror for Bruno Taut), 2009

Colored glass, laminated between low-iron
glass, and low-iron chrome mirror,
18 1/2 x 14 x 1 1/4 " (47 x 35,5 x 2,5 cm),
approx. 11lb (5kg),
Produced by Schott Architectural Solutions,
Grüneplan, Germany
Ed. 35/XX, signed and numbered
certificate

EDITION FOR PARKETT 86

A reflective object without shadow...

"I'd like to start with a phrase I've heard you use:
'quixotic confluences'—things that come together in
totally unforeseen ways that continue to resonate.
You told me that sometimes you begin a work by
responding to a story or event, and that during the
course of this pursuit, something else tends to come
up which overlays the piece."

Lynne Cooke, interview with Josiah McElheny
Parkett 86, 2009

ジョサイア・マッケルヘニー

もう一つの近代性より
（ブルーノ・タウトのための鏡）　2009

彩色ガラスで構成、低アイロン・ガラスと
クローム鏡の間に挟み、ラミネート、
47×35.5×2.5cm、
約5kg、
制作：ショット建築ソリューションズ
（グリューネプラン、ドイツ）
Ed. 35/XX、署名、番号入り証明書

パルケット・エディション 86

影もなく照り返し光るオブジェ...

あなたが口にした「絵空事のような合流」から話を始めようとおもい
ます。まったく予想外のかたちで一緒になり、残響のように後を引く
もの。ちょっとした物語や出来事をきっかけに制作にとりかかること
があって、そういうときにはえてして途中で何かが現れることが多く、
それが作品に層を成して重なってゆくと言ってましたね。

リン・クック
（パルケット 86号、2009年）

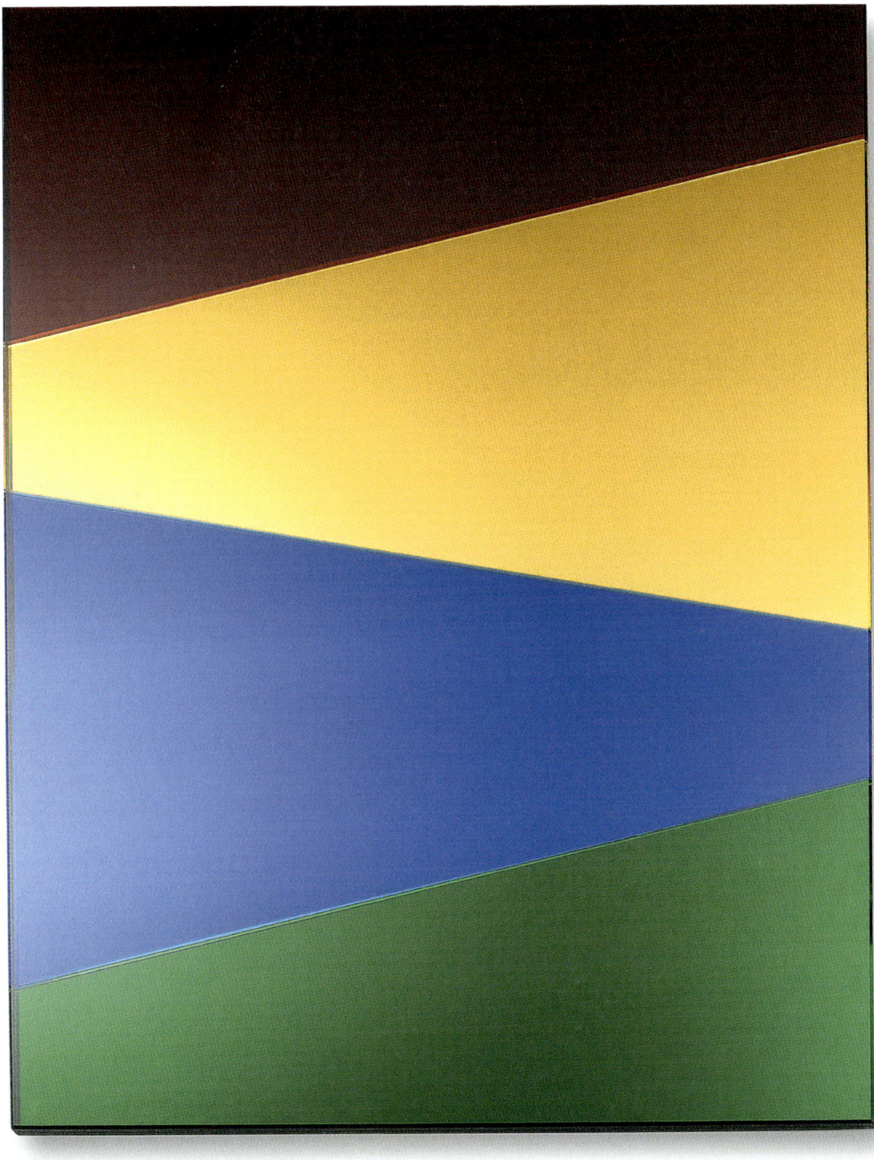

LUCY McKENZIE

Untitled, 2006

5-color silkscreen
on Somerset Satin,
paper size: 29 1/2 x 22" (75 x 55,5 cm),
image: 22 1/2 x 15" (57 x 38 cm),
printed by Bernie Reid,
Edinburgh, Scotland,
Ed. 60/XX, signed and numbered

EDITION FOR PARKETT 76

A shooting star musing on the secret of the unicorn after fierce encounter with a true riot grrl.

"Well, of the top of my head, there's a connection with certain currents in British Painting—artists such as R. B. Kitaj and Stanley Spencer—and with German painters like Otto Dix or the Austrian, Gustav Klimt. On top of this, I'm interested in processes, in the production of pathos—as in the work of Käthe Kollwitz, for instance. One characteristic of my paintings is certainly the use of trompe-l'oeil effects, flat picture grounds, and a form of literalness. I like insidiousness and things that are supposed to manipulate the viewer. But probably the biggest influence on my painting technique is my dilettantism."

Lucy McKenzie, interview with Isabelle Graw
Parkett No. 76, 2006

ルーシー・マッケンジー

無題　2006

5色刷りシルクスクリーン、サマーセット・サテン紙、
紙：75×55.5cm、図柄：57×38cm、
刷り：バーニー・リード
（エディンバラ市、スコットランド）、
Ed. 670/XX、署名、番号入り

パルケット・エディション 76

流れ星は本物の「riot grrl」（フェミニストのロックバンド）との激しい出会いにひきつづき、一角獣の秘密について想いをめぐらす

思いつくことから話すけど、英国絵画のある潮流、たとえばR.B.J.キタイやスタンリー・スペンサーなどの画家と、ドイツのオットー・ディックスやオーストリアのグスタフ・クリムトの間には関連があるでしょう。それだけではなくて、わたしはペーソスの生まれる過程にも関心があった。たとえばケーテ・コルヴィッツの作品。わたしの絵の特徴のひとつに、騙し絵の効果を使うことがある。平らな画面、それからありのままの描き方。狡賢いのも好きで、絵を見る人を思いどおりに操れるとされているものも好き。ただわたしの技法に一番大きな影響をおよぼしたのは、素人っぽさをなくしたくないという気持ちでしょうね。

ルーシー・マッケンジー、
イザベル・グローのインタヴューに応えて
（パルケット 76号、2006年）

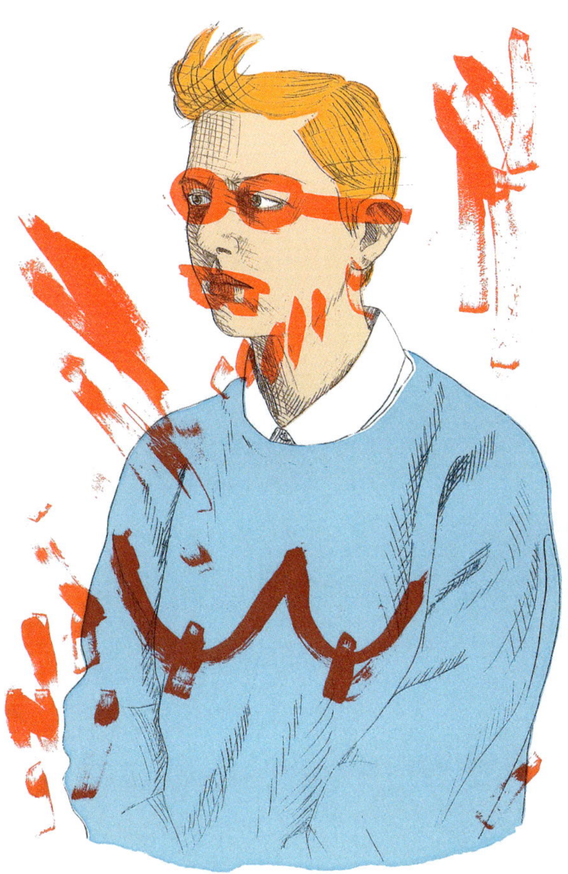

JULIE MEHRETU

Untitled, 2006

5-color etching, engraving and drypoint
on Somerset white textured 300g/m^2,
paper size: 23^1/$_4$ x 28^1/$_4$" (60 x 71,7 cm),
image: 16 x 20" (40,5 x 50 cm),
printed by Greg Burnet,
Burnet Editions, New York,
Ed. 60/XXV, signed and numbered

EDITION FOR PARKETT 76

Here's neither bush nor shrub, to bear off any
weather at all, and another storm brewing.
(Shakespeare, The Tempest act 2, scene II)

"As ever, architectural and urban planning designs
still form the undercurrent and starting point of her
paintings. The artist deploys a wide range of drawings
that she finds in a variety of sources. She constantly
alternates between different types of architectural
drawings—elevations, plans, and perspectival
drawings. The result is a complex aesthetic warp
and weft. The plans she uses are of buildings and
structures that have immense social, political, and
cultural significance as architectural systems and
infrastructures that shape our everyday lives: places
such as airports, urban spaces, sports fields or
churches, where large numbers of people congregate."

Madeleine Schuppli
Parkett No. 76, 2006

ジュリー・メーレトゥ

無題　2006

5色刷りエッチング、エングレーヴィング、
ドライポイント、
サマーセット・ホワイト・テクスチャード紙 300g/㎡、
紙：60×71.7cm、図柄：40.5×50cm、
刷り：グレッグ・バーネット・エディションズ
（ニューヨーク）、
Ed. 60/XXV、署名、番号入り

パルケット・エディション 76

雨風をしのごうにも藪も茂みもない、またひと荒れ来
そうだってのに。（シェイクスピア『テンペスト』第2幕
第2場、松岡和子訳、ちくま文庫）

以前にも増して、建築と都市計画のデザインがメーレトゥの絵画の
伏流、そして出発点をなしている。メーレトゥはさまざまな出典か
ら集めた、多様なドローイングを利用する。立面図、平面図、パース
など、用いる建築図面の種類をたえず変えてゆく。その結果得られ
るものは、複雑に交錯する美学の緯糸と経糸。用いられる図面は
わたしたちの日常生活のあり方を方向づける建築の制度および基
幹施設として、社会、政治、文化的に巨大な意義を有する建築物や
建物のもので、たとえば空港、都市空間、運動施設、教会など、多
くの人々が集まる場所でもある。

マドレーヌ・シュープリ
（パルケット 76号、2006年）

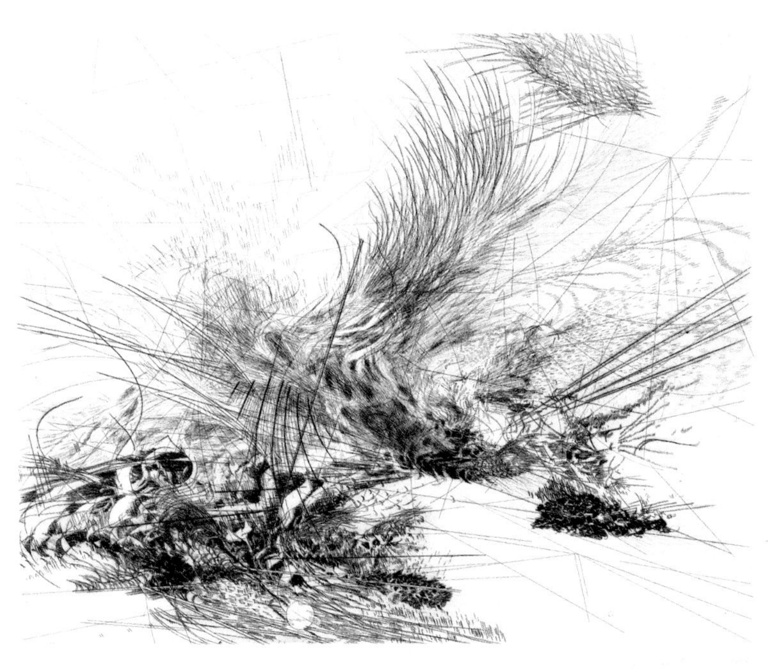

MARIO MERZ

Untitled, 1988

Etching, sugar lift, drypoint, aquatint
on Hahnemühle 300 g/m^2,
bound in the magazine,
image size: 16 x 10" (40,8 x 25,5 cm),
printed by Peter Kneubühler, Zurich,
Ed. 100/XXIX, signed and numbered

EDITION FOR PARKETT 15

Urban Eskimo. Inventor's doodle or
cosmologist's scheme, explorer's map or
architect's sketch—this etching follows as
part of the artist's ongoing obsession with
the forms of nomadic shelter.

"The work of Mario Merz leaves the impression of
a compulsive urge toward transcendence. On the
one hand, he is himself a kind of Second Coming,
considerably less glorious than was anticipated,
bringing confirmation of another postponement in
the offing, a third and fourth and fifth Coming. On the
other hand, he is the last futurist left standing in the
wake of a future that has exhausted itself in an orgy
of big bangs."

Jeanne Silverthorne
Parkett No. 15, 1988

マリオ・メルツ

無題　1988

エッチング、シュガーリフト、
ドライポイント、ハーネミュール紙 300g/㎡、
本誌に綴じこみ、
図柄：40.8×25.5cm、
刷り：ペーター・クノイビューラー（チューリヒ）、
Ed. 100/XXIX、署名、番号入り

パルケット・エディション 15

都会のエスキモー。発明家のいたずら書き、天文学者
の天象図、探検家の地図、建築家のスケッチにも見え
るこのエッチングは、今も遊牧民の住まいの形に寄せる
メルツの強い関心から生まれたもの。

マリオ・メルツの作品は、超越性をめざすやむにやまれぬ衝動を
印象づける。一方で、メルツ自身がキリストの再臨のようなもの、期
待したほど荘厳でもなく、まもなく延期され、3度目、4度目、5度目
の再臨がくるという御告げを伝える。他方では、ビッグバンの大騒
ぎにまぎれて疲弊した未来の航跡に、ただひとり取り残された未来
派でもある。

ジャンヌ・シルヴァーホーン
（パルケット 15号、1988年）

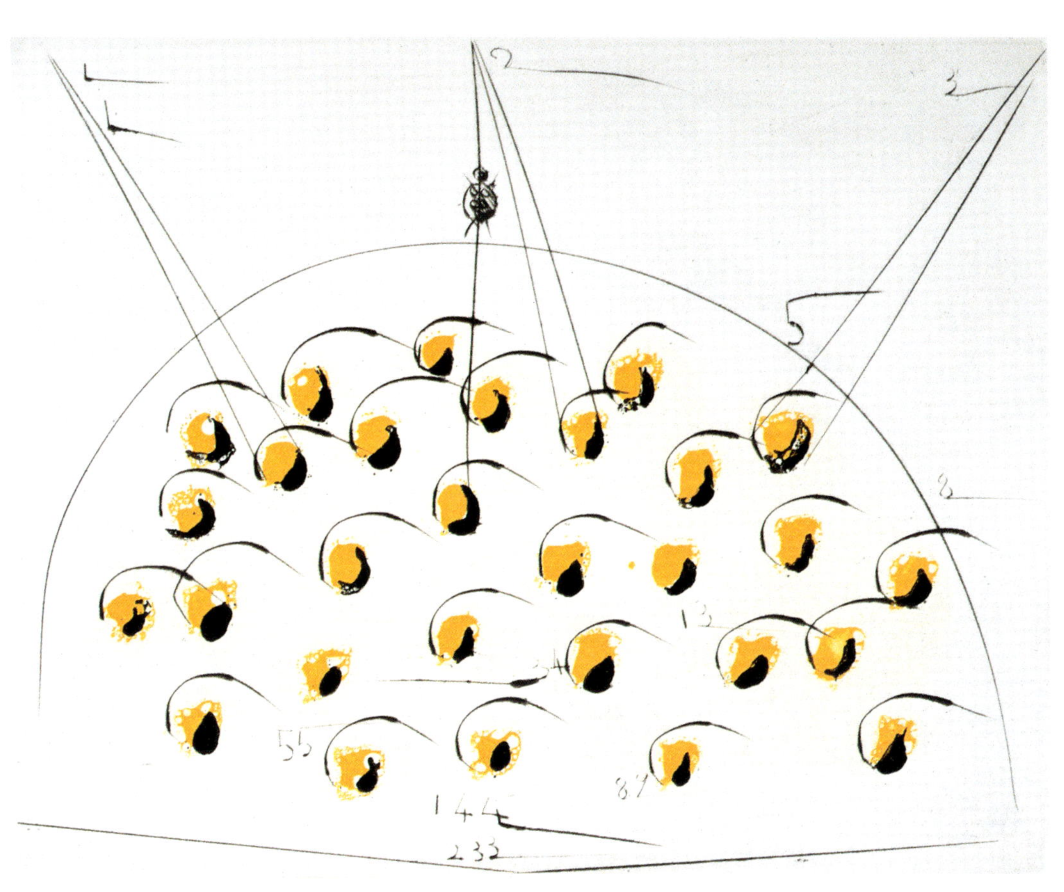

BEATRIZ MILHAZES

Batucada, 2009

18-color silkscreen print with foil
stamping, on Arches 88 paper,
300 g/m², rein Hadern,
13 ³/₈ x 11 ¾" (35 x 30 cm),
printed by Atelier für Siebdruck
Lorenz Boegli, Zurich,
Edition of 45/XX, signed and numbered

EDITION FOR PARKETT 85

The heart of the matter in the limelight, throbbing against a background of ornament.

"'Time' and 'transformation' are explored repeatedly
in Beatriz Milhazes' work in ways that confront and
contradict the idea of painting as a static art form.
One key to this lies in the surfaces of her works.
Frequently her pictorial field is interrupted by various
kinds of disturbances or aberrations. Erosions,
apparent abrasions, paint losses ..., revisions,
reworkings ... complicate and destabilize the integrity
of the work's surface."

Tanya Barson
Parkett No. 85, 2009

ベアトリス・ミリャーゼス

バトゥカダ　2009

18色刷りシルクスクリーン、
ホイルのスタンプ、アルシュ88紙、300g/㎡、
ラグ 100%、34×29.8cm、
刷り：ロレンツ・ボエリ（チューリヒ）、
Ed. 45/XX、署名、番号入り

パルケット・エディション 85

装飾的な背景の前で、肝心要が脚光を浴び、脈動する。

ベアトリス・ミリャーゼスの作品では「時間」と「変容」が、静的な
美術形式としての絵画の概念と対峙し、これに反駁する形でくりか
えし探究される。その鍵のひとつは、作品の表面に見いだせる。ミ
リャーゼスの画面は様々な妨害や逸脱によって頻繁に中断される。
腐食、明らかな剥離、絵具の欠落……修正、補整……が作品の表面
の統一感を損ない、動揺させる。

タニヤ・バーソン
（パルケット 85号、2009年）

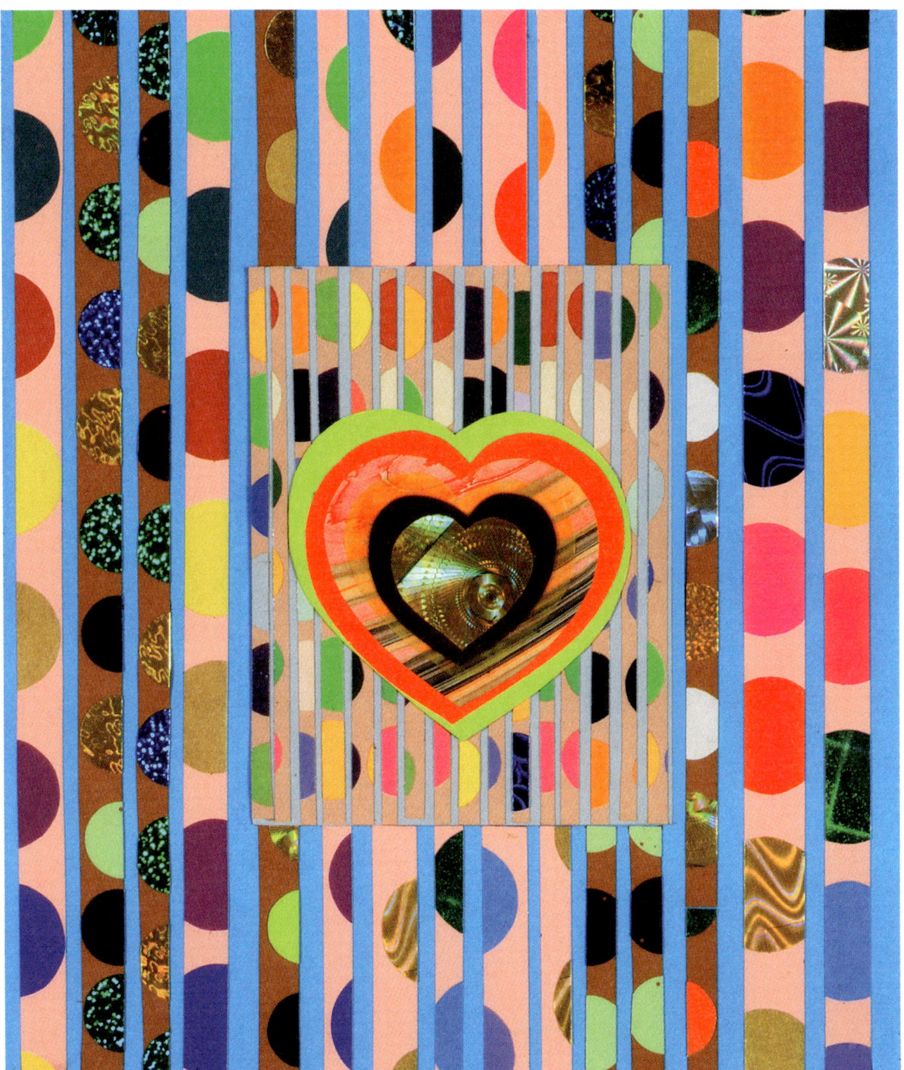

MARILYN MINTER

Pamela Anderson, 2007

C-print,
paper size: 20 1/2 x 16" (52 x 40,5 cm),
image: 19 1/2 x 12 3/4" (49,5 x 32,5 cm),
Ed. 60/XX, signed and numbered

EDITION FOR PARKETT 79

Relentless artistic investigation transforms woman as object into an image of unsettling beauty.

"The work–the effort–peeks out from beneath the surface of these people (and these paintings) in the beads of sweat that so often cover the models. At the very end of her interview with artist Mary Heilmann, Minter affirms both her pleasure in looking at pictures of other bodies, and the constant failure of her own body to conform to a received image: 'armpits with hair growing out of them, sweat running into the eyes, eyelashes that clump together because of too much mascara.' Heilmann replies, 'Completely abstract. Like the materiality of abstract painting, nature surfaces and interrupts the effort to create a flawless image, like weeds pushing their way through the sidewalk.'"

Katy Siegel
Parkett No. 79, 2007

マリリン・ミンター

パメラ・アンダーソン　2007

Cプリント、
紙：52×40.5cm、
図柄：49.5×32.5cm、
Ed. 60/XX、署名、番号入り

パルケット・エディション 79

執拗な芸術的探究がオブジェとしての女を、不穏な美のイメージに変化させる。

これらの人々（そしてこれらの絵画）の表層からは労力あるいは努力が、モデルの身体をしじゅう覆う汗の雫となって滴り落ちる。アーティストのメアリー・ハイルマンとのインタヴューのしめくくりに、ミンターは他人の肉体の写真を見るのが楽しいこと、そして自分の肉体は、世間の認めるイメージによく順応しそこなうと認めている。「脇の下からは毛がはみだし、目には汗が流れこみ、マスカラを塗りすぎて睫毛は上下がくっついてしまう」。それに対してハイルマンはこう応える。「完全な抽象ね。抽象絵画の物質性と同じことで、欠点のないイメージを創りだそうとして努力すると、自然が顔をだし、邪魔をする。舗石のすきまからむりやり顔を出してくる雑草のように」。

ケイティ・シーゲル
（パルケット 79号、2007年）

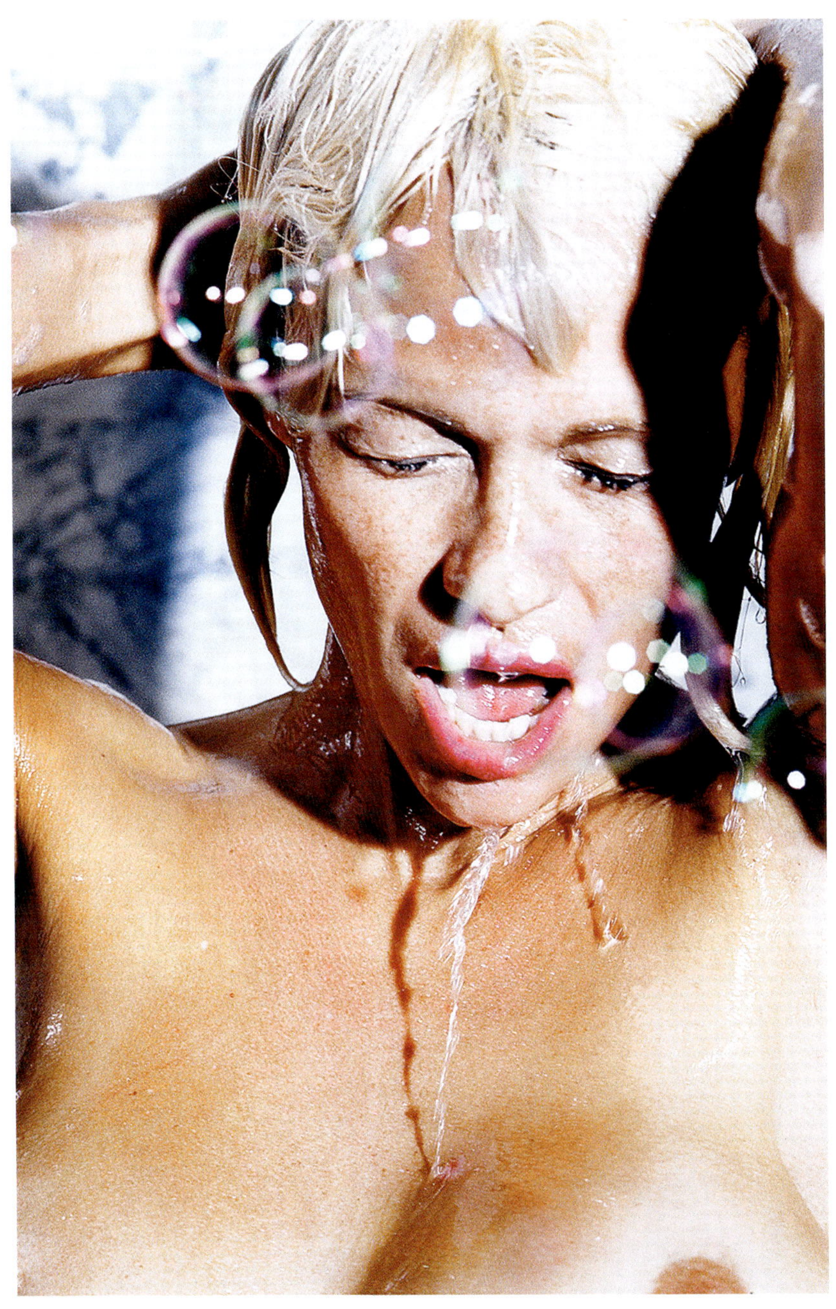

TRACEY MOFFATT

From the "Up in the Sky"
Photo Series, 1997

4-color offset lithograph,
image size: 17 1/8 x 21" (43,3 x 53,5 cm),
on archival book design paper,
20 x 27" (50,8 x 68,4 cm),
printed by Link Printing, Sydney,
Ed. 60/XX, signed and numbered

EDITION FOR PARKETT 53

A blazing void. The distilled force of a
moment wrest out of time and context.

"...her work dramatizes, in many different ways,
the primal violence of socialisation—the invariably
traumatic way in which each individual must be
'inserted' into an ever-widening set of social,
institutional frames: family, school, community, nation.
...And this rite of passage is for her characters as for
each of us never a total success-indeed, it is often a
botched job."

Adrian Martin
Parkett No. 53, 1998

トレイシー・モファット

シリーズ写真「空の上で」より　1997

4色カラーオフセット・リトグラフ、
図柄：43.3×53.5cm、
無酸ブック・デザイン用紙：50.8×68.4cm、
刷り：リンク・プリンティング（シドニー）、
Ed. 60/XX、署名、番号入り

パルケット・エディション 53

燃えさかる空虚。時間と文脈からもぎ取られた瞬間の
凝縮された力。

モファットの作品は、社会化に根ざす根源的な暴力性を、多様な
方法を用いて劇的に表現する。ひとは誰しも家族、学校、コミュニ
ティ、国家など、ますます幅を広げる一方の社会的，制度的枠組み
に、どうしても後にトラウマを残すかたちで「挿入」されなければ
ならない。そしてこの通過儀礼はモファットの作品の登場人物に
とって、わたしたちにとってと同じように、完全な成功裏に終わる
ことは決してない。多くの場合、それはしくじりに終わる。

エイドリアン・マーティン
（パルケット 53号、1998年）

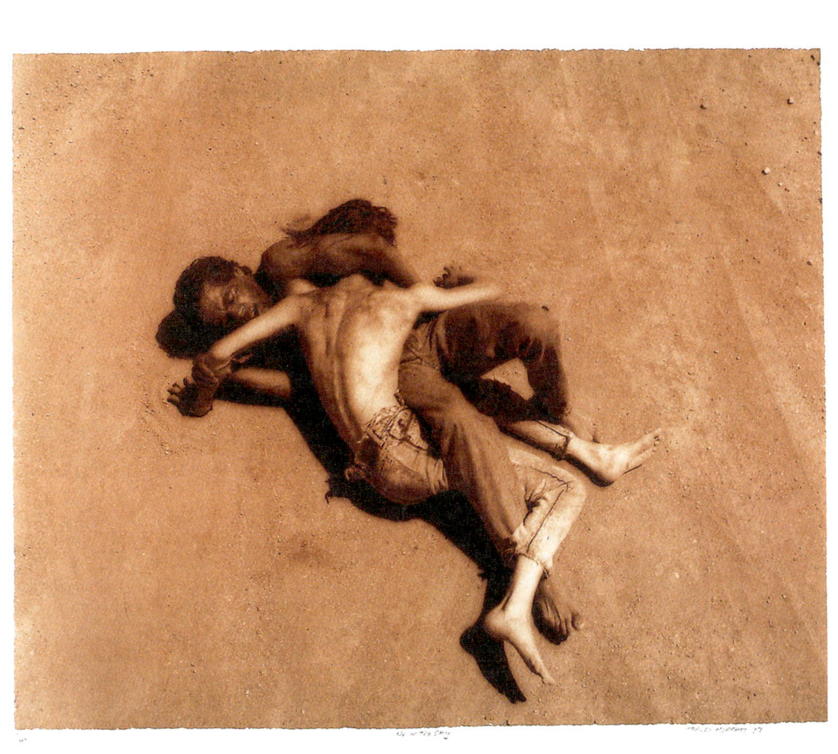
Us in the Sky

MARIKO MORI

Star Doll, 1998

Doll with microphone, earphones,
boots, white stockings, red plaid skirt,
top in blue, black and white, transparent
bracelets, yellow shoulder pads,
brooch and blue hair, 10$\frac{1}{4}$" (26 cm) high,
Ed. 99/XX, signed and numbered

EDITION FOR PARKETT 54

Shooting star: When collective identity
colides with cyber culture, the child of future
is born.

"In Mori's work since 1996 the contours and shaping
pressures of the contemporary image-stream
are explored less by way of the classical-modernist
strategy of distanciation and analysis than by
impersonation: She uses her body as a lens that
captures the light of the contemporary image-stream,
and through certain enhancements and exaggerations
makes it clear what the image-stream really wants
of us."

Norman Bryson
Parkett No. 54, 1998/99

森万里子

スター・ドール　1998

マイクとイヤホンをつけた人形、ブーツ、
白のストッキング、赤いチェックのスカート、
青・黒・白の上着、透明のブレスレット、
黄色の肩パッド、ブローチ、青い髪、
高さ：26cm、
Ed. 99/XX、署名、番号入り

パルケット・エディション 54

流れ星。集団のアイデンティティがコンピューター文化
と衝突するとき、未来の子供が誕生する。

1996年以降、森の作品では現代のイメージの流れの輪郭、形を定
めようとする圧力が、古典的近代主義者の異化効果と分析を通じる
よりも、物真似によって探究されてきた。森は自分の身体を現代の
イメージの流れが放つ光を捉えるレンズ代わりに、ある種の魔法と
誇張を用いて、イメージの流れがわたしたちに何を求めているかを
明らかにした。

ノーマン・ブライソン
（パルケット 54号、1998/99年）

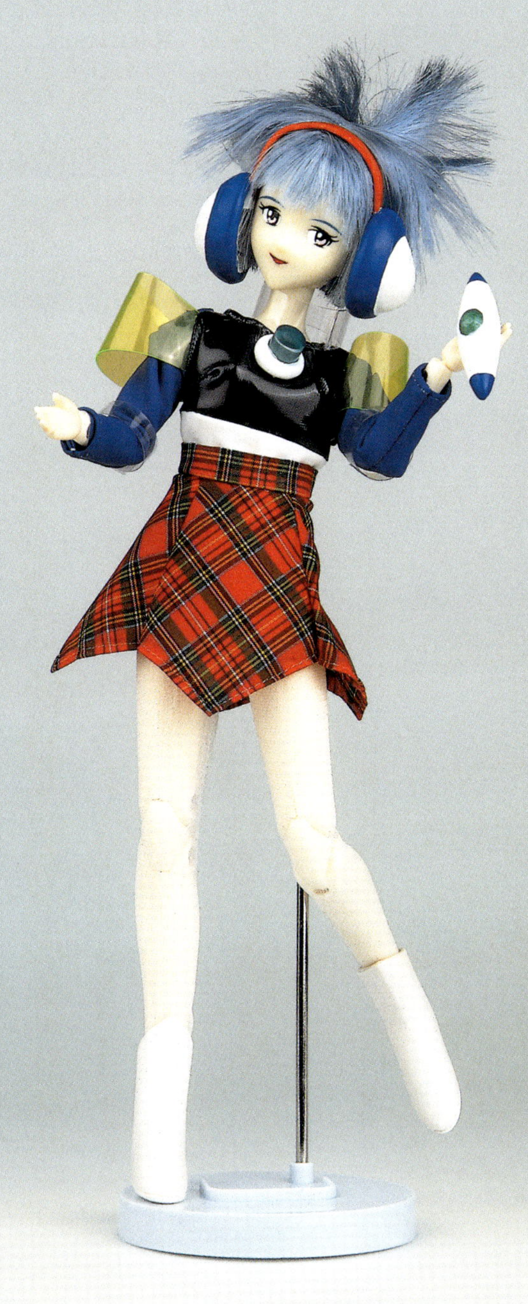

MALCOLM MORLEY

Ancient Chinese Horses, 1998

11-color lithograph,
23 1/4 x 33 7/8" (59 x 86 cm),
on Somerset soft white paper,
28 3/4 x 38" (73 x 96,4 cm),
printed by Maurice Sanchez,
Derrière l'Etoile Studio, New York,
Ed. 60/XX, signed and numbered

EDITION FOR PARKETT 52

A trio of mighty steeds galloping across continents and centuries of color in search of their dream riders.

"Morley's work method—and he is an artist who cultivates the most refined ironies—is obsessive and scrupulous, almost mantra-like. The first paintings that brought him notoriety, his superrealist ocean-liners of the 1960s, derive from photographs that he divided in little squares so that he could copy them with the greatest possible accuracy. Seen from a distance, these works look like photographs, but close up they disclose themselves as jubilant pictorial feasts made up of tiny, dynamic brushstrokes."

Enrique Juncosa
Parkett No. 52, 1998

マルコム・モーリー

古代中国の馬　1998

11色刷りリトグラフ：59×86cm、
サマーセット・ソフト・ホワイト紙：73×96.4cm、
刷り：モーリス・サンチェス、
デリエール・レトワール・スタジオ（ニューヨーク）、
Ed. 60/XX、署名、番号入り

パルケット・エディション 52

力強い軍馬３頭が夢にみた騎手を求めて、色彩の世紀と大陸を早駆けしてゆく。

モーリーの仕事ぶり―モーリーは極上のアイロニーを育てたアーティストである―はなりふりかまわず、几帳面で、呪文を唱えているようにさえ見える。モーリーの名を初めて世間に広めたのは、1960年代に豪華客船をスーパーリアリスト風に描いた作品だったが、この時はできるかぎり正確な模写をめざして、写真を小さな正方形に分割した。離れてみると、まるで写真のような絵が、近づくと、躍動感溢れる細かな筆遣いからなる、描く喜びに満ちた絵であることがわかる。

エンリケ・フンコーサ
（パルケット 52号、1998年）

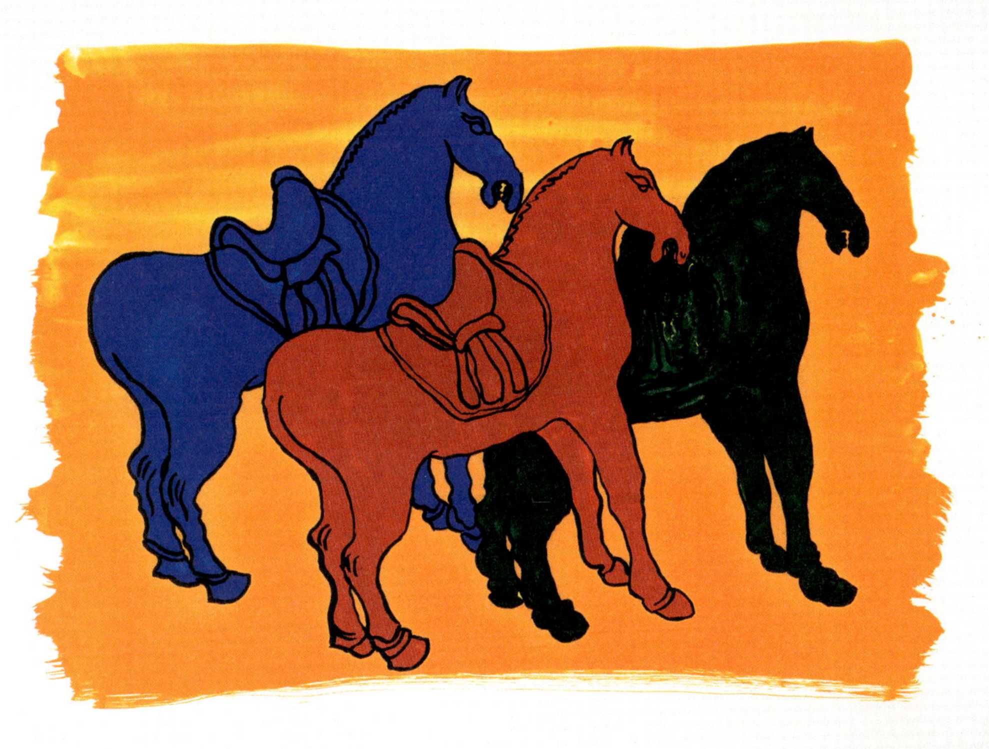

SARAH MORRIS

Capital (A Film by Sarah Morris),
2001

8-color silkscreen
on 300g/m² Somerset Satin,
60 x 40" (151,4 x 101,4 cm),
designed by Sarah Morris/Peter Saville,
printed by Coriander Studio Ltd., London,
Ed. 70/XX, signed and numbered

EDITION FOR PARKETT 61

In and out of line: look up, look through, look
into the deceptive transparence of structure.

"Sarah Morris's work languishes in the perceptual
fields of late-twentieth and early-twenty-first century
capitalism. This world is made of flat grids which
mimic perspective while denying the phenomenal
experience of the referent (of which there is none
except codes and signals drawn from the language of
geometric abstraction; modernist urban architecture;
Op Art; the poetics of everyday life stripped of the
experience of everyday life)."

Thyrza Nichols Goodeve
Parkett No. 61, 2001

サラ・モリス

首都（サラ・モリス映画作品）　2001

8色刷りシルクスクリーン、
サマーセット・サテン紙 300g/㎡、
151.4×101.4cm、
デザイン：サラ・モリス、ピーター・サヴィル、
刷り：コリアンダー・スタジオ（ロンドン）、
Ed. 70/XX、署名、番号入り

パルケット・エディション 61

線の中に入ったり、外に出たり。上を見て、透かして
見て、透明のように目を欺く建物の中を覗きこんで。

サラ・モリスの作品は20世紀後半、21世紀初期資本主義の知覚
領域で物憂げに滞る。この世は遠近法を模しながら、指示対象の
現象的体験を拒む平板な格子から成り立つ。（指示対象にも、幾何
学的抽象の言語から抽出された符号と記号以外になにもない。近
代主義的な都市建築、オプアート、日常生活の体験を剥奪された
日常生活の詩学）

ティルザ・ニコルズ・グッドイーヴ
（パルケット 61号、2001年）

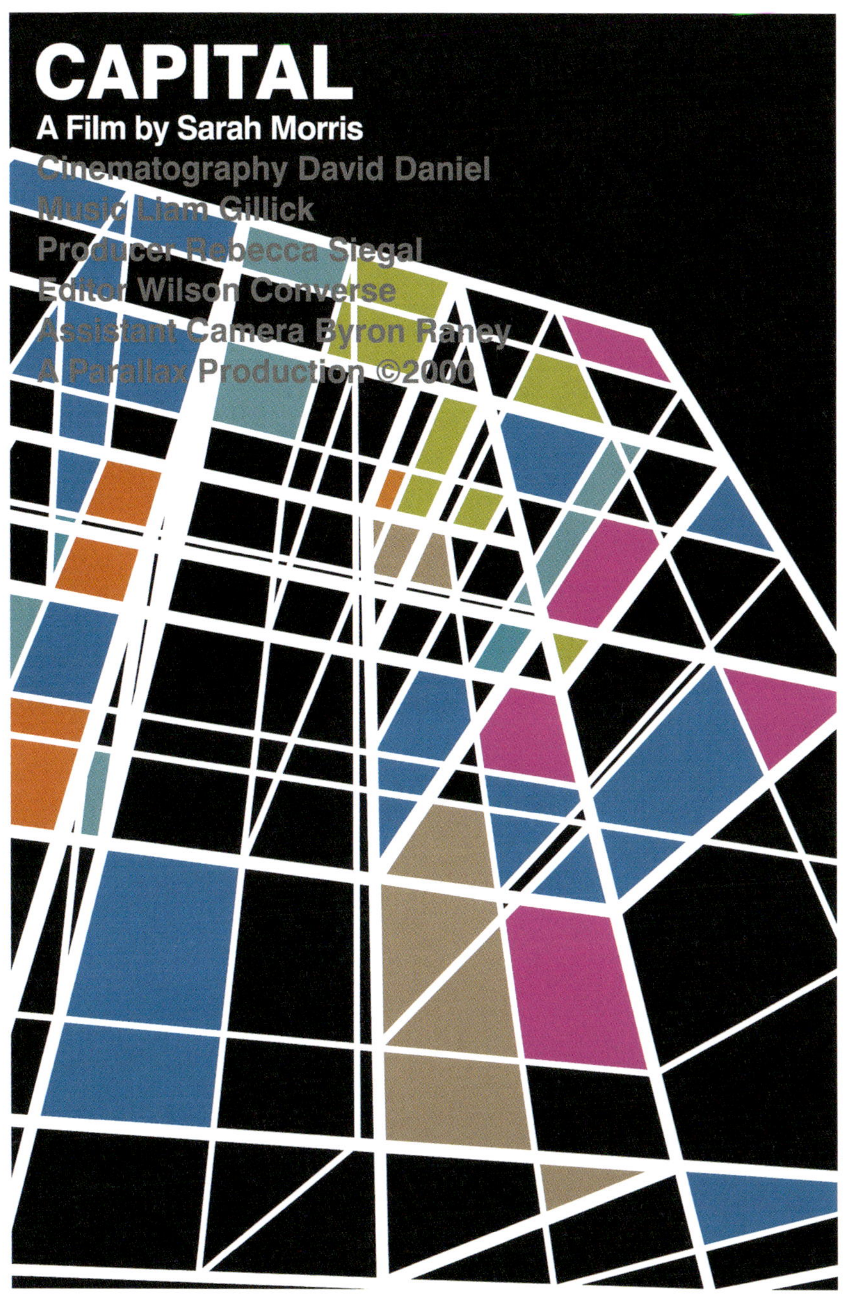

CAPITAL
A Film by Sarah Morris
Cinematography David Daniel
Music Liam Gillick
Producer Rebecca Siegal
Editor Wilson Converse
Assistant Camera Byron Raney
A Parallax Production ©2000

JUAN MUÑOZ

Augenblick (Glimpse), 1995

Hand-etched glass, the image
becomes momentarily visible by
breathing on the glass,
4 3/4 x 3 1/2 x 1/8" (12 x 9 x 0,3 cm),
Ed. 70/XXV, signed and numbered

EDITION FOR PARKETT 43

Vanishing point. An image as tenuous and
fugitive as breath on a pane of glass.

"Muñoz's sculptures are inviable, incomplete,
restricted bodies that no longer define a human,
integral, and self-determined posture, but rather a
semi-, pseudo-, or post-human condition in which
the place of the body is less the result of the positive
affirmation of a will, an individuality, or a desire than
the result of a system of external spatial relations
and determinations."

Alexandre Melo
Parkett No. 43, 1995

フアン・ムニョス

Augenblick（瞥見）　1995

手で刻印したガラス、ガラスに息を吹き
かけると瞬間的にイメージが目に見える、
12×9×0.3cm、
Ed. 70/XXV、署名、番号入り

パルケット・エディション 43

消点。ガラスに吹きかけた息ほどにうつろいやすく、
影の薄いイメージ。

ムニョスの彫刻は目に見えず、未完成で、すでに人間らしい、完
結した、自らが選んだ姿態をとることのない制約を受けた身体
であり、身体の場が積極的な意志、個性、欲望の肯定する結果で
あるよりも、外部空間との関係、限定の体系の産物であるような、
半人間的、擬似人間的、人間であることをやめた後の状況である。

アレクザンドル・メロ
（パルケット 43号、1995年）

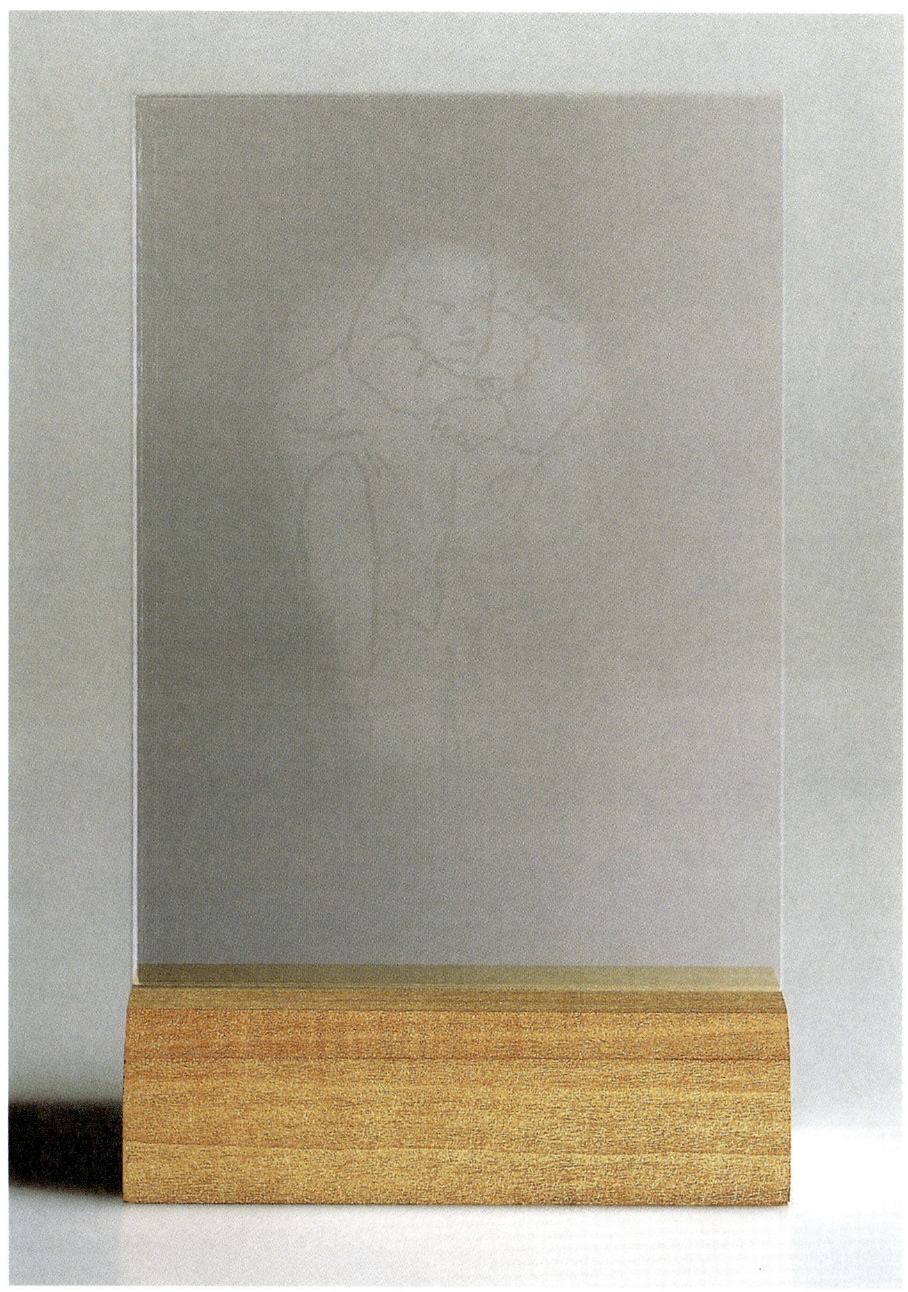

JEAN-LUC MYLAYNE

No. 37 – 38, Août 1982

Two color photographs,
9 1/2 x 9 1/2" (24 x 24 cm) each,
mounted back to back on aluminum
under Plexiglas, encased in a massive,
free-standing wooden frame,
14 3/8 x 14 3/8 x 2 3/4" (36,5 x 36,5 x 7,3 cm),
Ed. 48/XII, with signed and numbered
certificate

EDITION FOR PARKETT 50/51

Implacable time. Two moments irreconcileably united and eternally severed.

"…Each of his unique photographs represents not
merely the one-thousandth of a second it takes for the
camera to click its shutter but also the days, weeks,
and months of devotion and patience it takes to build
a bond of trust with a subject. The crux of his work is
the moment at which the bird returns the gaze of the
photographer. It is a glance not of hostility or mistrust
but of recognition. The individual bird accomplishes a
task still difficult for most of humanity: to recognize
itself as one of many species."

Mark Dion
Parkett No. 50/51, 1997

ジャン＝リュック・ミレーヌ
No.37-38　1982年 8月

カラー写真2枚 (24×24cm) を
背中合わせにアルミ板にマウント、
アクリル・カバー付きのどっしりとした
木製の額 (36.5×36.5×7.3cm) に収める、
Ed. 48/XII、署名、番号入り証明書

パルケット・エディション 50/51

無情の時。和解不能に結ばれ、永遠に仲を裂かれたふたつの時機。

ミレーヌの風変わりな写真はどれひとつとっても、カメラのシャッターが降りるのに必要な1000分の1秒のみならず、被写体と信頼の絆を築くのに必要な何日、何週間、何か月かの献身と忍耐を表現する。作品の要点は、小鳥が写真家に視線を投げ返す瞬間である。その眼差しは敵意や不信感ではなく、相手の存在を認めたことを示している。一羽の小鳥が、人間の大半にはいまだに手に余る作業をなしとげる。鳥は自らを多くの種のなかのひとつと悟っている。

マーク・ディオン
（パルケット 50/51号、1997年）

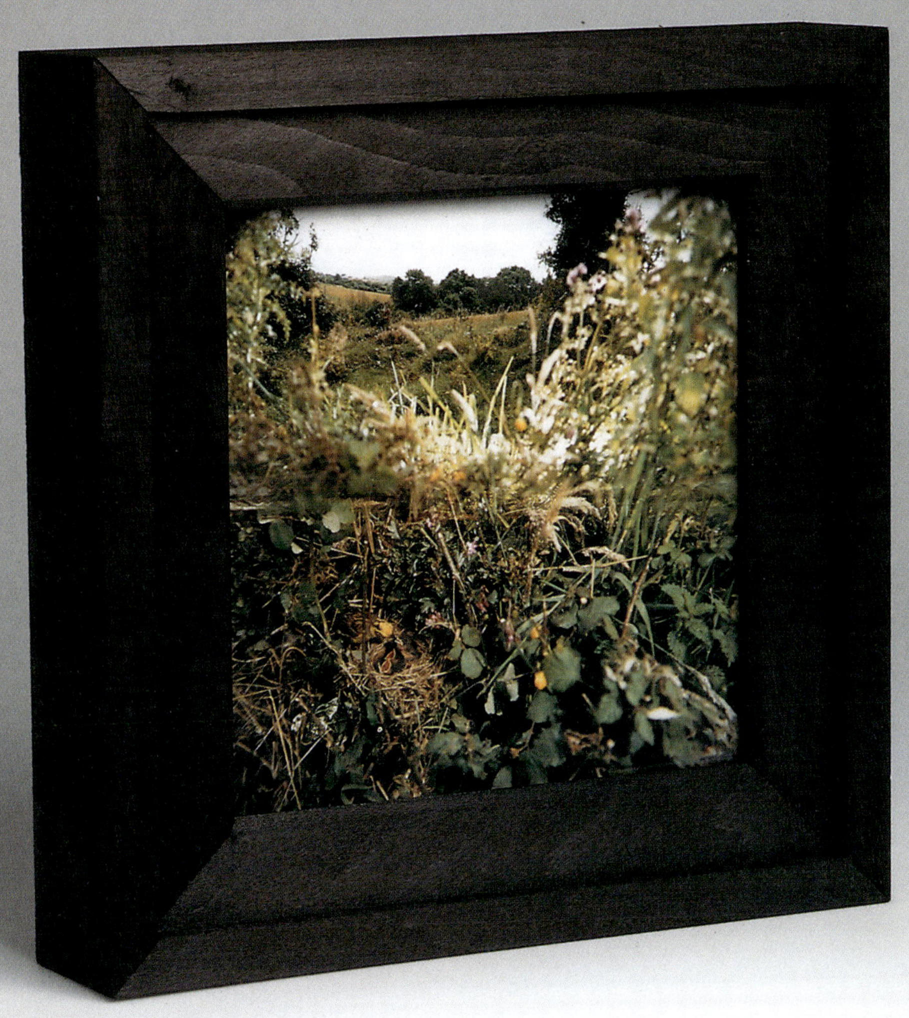

JEAN-LUC MYLAYNE

No. PO-65, Face to Face,
April/May 2001

C-print, transparency,
image size: 9 1/2 x 9 1/2" (24 x 24cm),
Mounted between Altuglass,
15 x 15 x 2 3/4" (38 x 38 x 7cm),
weight 16,5 lb. (7,5 kg),
2 C-prints, 9 1/2 x 9 1/2" (24 x 24 cm),
Artist designed certificate including
a close-up photograph of the bird
facing the apple, 5 1/2 x 5 1/2" (14 x 14cm),
Edition of 38/XXII, signed and numbered
certificate

EDITION FOR PARKETT 85

Nature communes with itself,
sublimely indifferent to human
intervention.

"… he is not looking for the iconic, historical moment
or event, but rather for the coincidental encounter
experienced in his case only by the photographer and
the bird. Time, patience, and an unwavering mental
focus based on a profound passion for his subject
informs Mylayne's work as an artist."

Josef Helfenstein
Parkett No. 85, 2009

ジャン＝リュック・ミレーヌ

NO.PO-65、向かい合わせ、
4月／5月　2001年

Cプリント、トランスペアレンシー、
図柄：24×24cm、
アルテュグラス2枚でサンドイッチ状にマウント、
38×38×7cm、

重さ：7.5kg、
Cプリント2点、各24x24cm
リンゴと向き合う小鳥のクローズアップ写真を
ふくむ証明書をミレーヌ自身がデザイン、
14×14cm、
Ed. 38/XXII、署名、番号入り証明書

パルケット・エディション 85

自然は人間の干渉など少しも意に介すことなく、自ら
と親しく交わる。

象徴的、あるいは歴史的な瞬間や出来事ではなく、作者は写真家
と小鳥が経験する偶然の出会いを探し求める。時間、忍耐、そして
被写体に寄せる限りない愛着に根ざす揺るぎない集中力が、アー
ティストとしてのミレーヌの作品の特徴をなす。

ヨーゼフ・ヘルフェンシュタイン
（パルケット 85号、2009年）

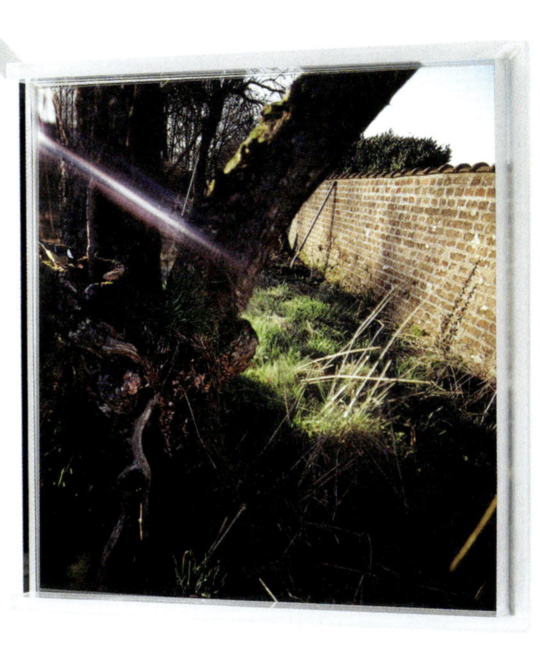

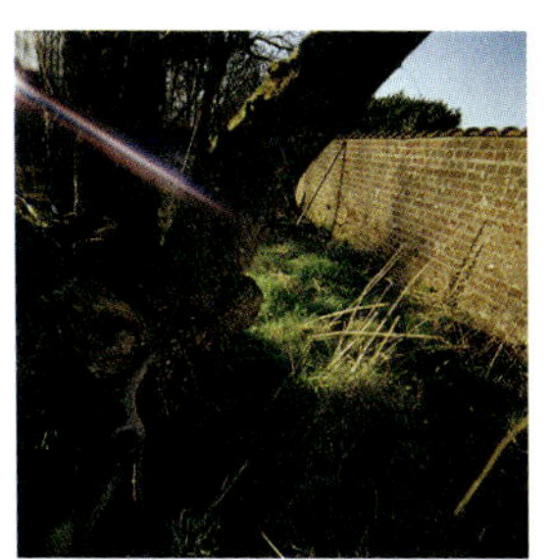

Front / 表

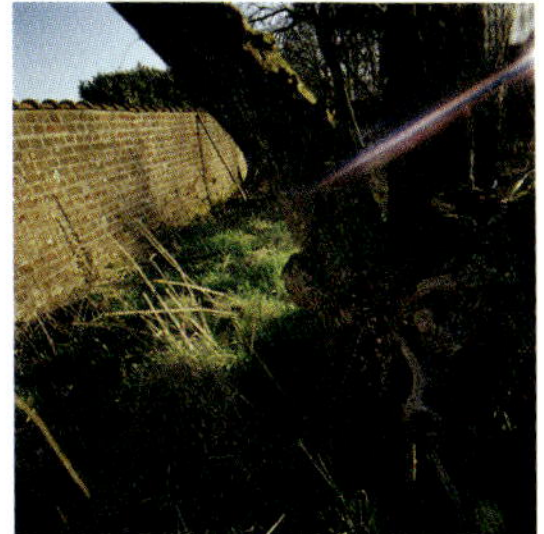

Back / 裏

EDITION FOR PARKETT
N° 85

JEAN-LUC MYLAYNE

N° PO-65, FACE TO FACE, Avril mai 2004
38 cm x 38 cm x 7 cm   (24 cm x 24 cm)

CERTIFICATE OF AUTHENTICITY
with detail (14 cm x 14 cm)

Le 7 Mai 2009   38/38

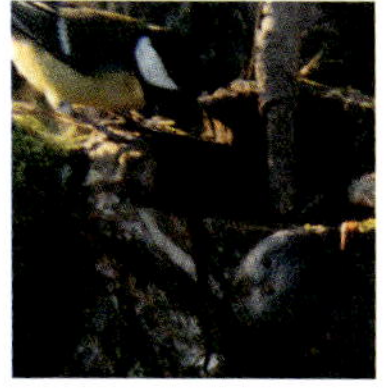

BRUCE NAUMAN

Violent Incident—Man-Woman,
Segment, 1986

Videotape, 30 min., time of one sequence:
28 sec., color, sound,
Ed. 200/XX, signed and numbered

EDITION FOR PARKETT 10

Eye for eye. In a pas-de-deux of violent
pratfalls and angry jokes, a romantic
tête-à-tête between man and woman
degenerates into murderous symmetry.

"One suspects that Nauman would agree with
Wittgenstein that language has meaning only in use,
and its users are bodies. In the recent work,
he seems to want to metaphorically slow language
down (perhaps now recognizing that it cannot be
really stopped to show that, although language may
live on, bodies do not)."

Jeanne Silverthorne
Parkett No. 10, 1986

ブルース・ナウマン
暴力沙汰―男-女、部分　　1986

ビデオテープ、30分、
1シーンの長さ：28秒、
カラー、有声、
Ed. 200/XX、署名、番号入り

パルケット・エディション　10

目には目を。男女ふたりがくりひろげる荒っぽい尻餅と
怒りにまかせた冗談、ロマンティックな差し向かいの
パ・ドゥ・ドゥがいよいよ行き詰まり、殺意のシンメト
リーに転落する。

言語は使用されて初めて意味をもち、使用者は身体であるという
ヴィトゲンシュタインの説に、ナウマンも同意するのではないだろ
うか。最近の作品では、言語の速度を隠喩的に緩めようとしている
ように見受けられる（そのことを示すために、本当に言語を停止さ
せることはできないと気づいたのかもしれない。言語は生き延びて
も、身体はそうはいかない）。

ジャンヌ・シルヴァソーン
（パルケット　10号、1986年）

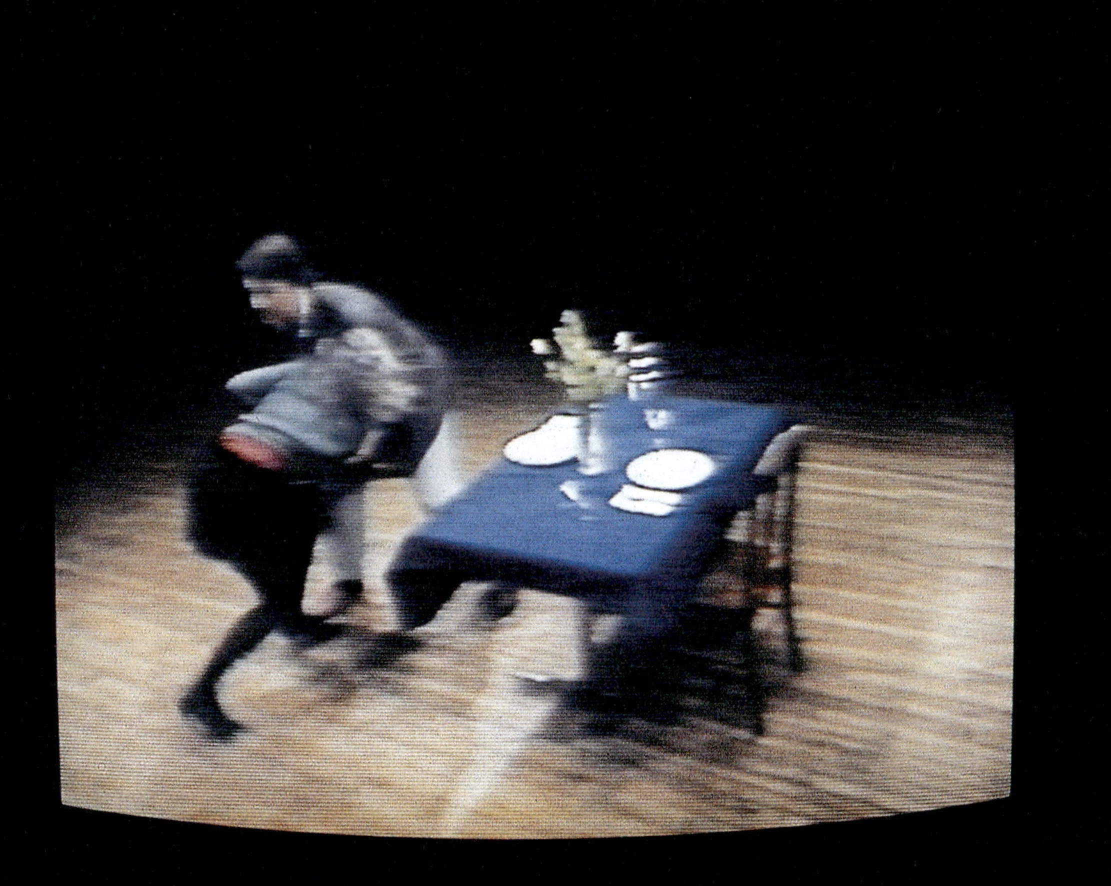

ERNESTO NETO

Phytuziann, 2006

Green lycra tulle and polypropylene
pellets, 17 ¾ x 10 ¾ x 2"
(45 x 27 x 5cm); weight: 4 lb. (900 g),
Ed. 60/XX, signed and numbered

EDITION FOR PARKETT 78

Do touch: the metamorphosis of perception is in the hands of the beholder.

"Ernesto Neto views himself as an illegal street vendor from Rio de Janeiro—a typical product of the underground economy exacerbated by the social marginalization attendant on inflated capitalist globalization. To evade state repression, street vendors display their merchandise on blankets that they pack up and swiftly take away the minute they spot trouble. Similarly, Neto works with the portability of large dimensions; his project, so he says, is carried around 'inside small eggs, like culture in the time space of the social body.'"

Paulo Herkenhoff
Parkett No. 78, 2006

エルネスト・ネト

フィトゥジアン　2006

緑のリクラ製チュール、ポリプロピレンの粒、
45×27×5cm、重さ：900g、
Ed. 60/XX、署名、番号入り

パルケット・エディション 78

お触りください。知覚の変容は見る者次第。

エルネスト・ネトはリオ・デ・ジャネイロ出身のもぐりの露天商を自認する。これは資本主義の野放図なグローバル化に伴い社会からの落ちこぼれが増加し、そのため膨脹した地下経済の典型的な産物にほかならない。国家の規制を逃れるため、露天商は商品を毛布に乗せて披露し、面倒が起こりそうな気配を察知すれば、さっさと片づけてよそに立ち去る。これと同じく、ネトは持ち運びできる大きな作品を作る。作品は、本人の言葉によると、「社会的身体の時空間の中にある文化のように、小さな卵に入れて持ち運べる」。

パウロ・ハーケンホフ
（パルケット 78号、2006年）

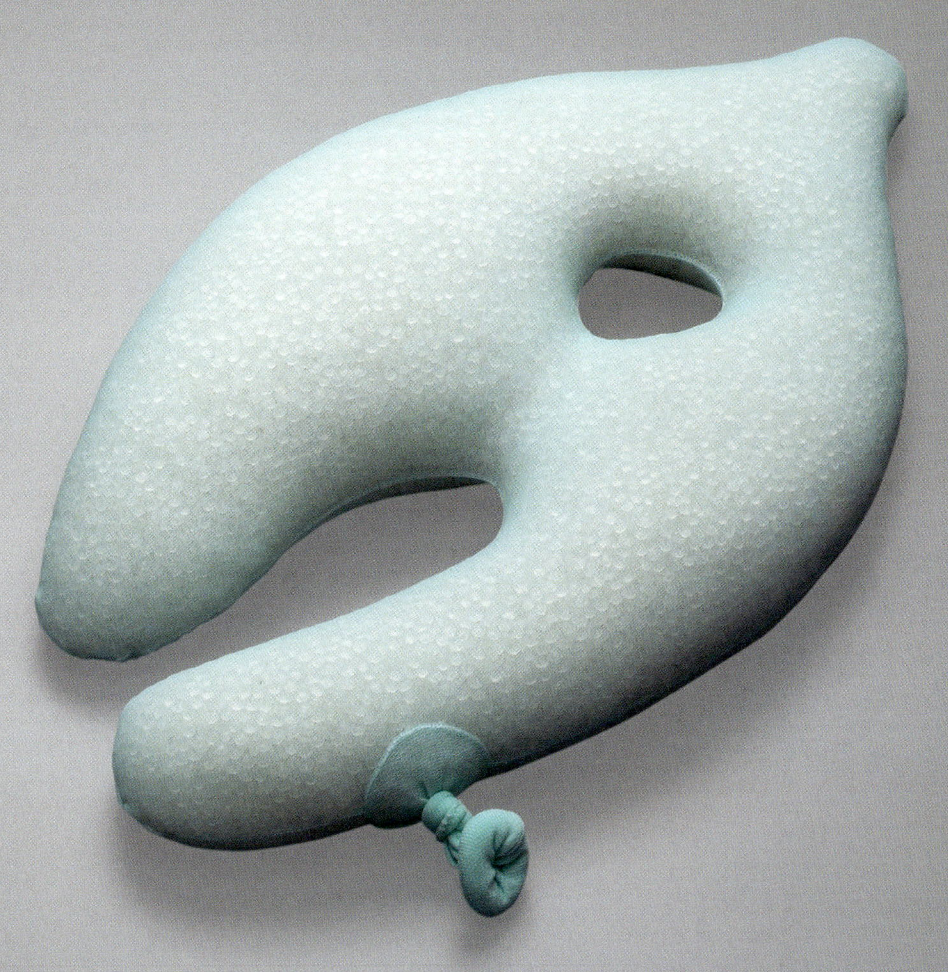

OLAF NICOLAI

Georg's Pillow, 2007
(Replica of a pillow from George
Lukács' sofa in his study at Belgrad
Kai, Budapest)

Handwoven pillowcase, hand-dyed
sheep's wool and red silk, 18 $\frac{1}{2}$ x 20"
(47 x 51cm), made by the Department
of Textiles, Institute of Applied Arts,
Schneeberg, Germany,
Ed. 35/XX, signed and numbered
certificate

EDITION FOR PARKETT 78

A mimetically charged pillow which offers an
invitation to reflect on Georg Lukács' favorite
theme, realism.

"Nicolai uses the license that his status as an artist
gives him to be free of academia—free to abuse
sources and reconfigure images and objects of entirely
different statuses. Thus, while remaining securely
within the identity of an artist, Nicolai performs a
role as a researcher and combiner—a turner-upside-
down-of-things to see what they look like from another
angle, and ultimately create new modes of visibility.
His strategy, it would seem, is a fine one at this
point in our cultural development, given the current
moment's political exhaustion and the universalizing
of 'creativity' for bland economic ends."

Chales Esche
Parkett No. 78, 2006

オラフ・ニコライ

ジェルジの枕　2007
（ブダペストのベオグラード・カイにあった
ジェルジ・ルカーチの書斎のソファに置かれていた
クッションのレプリカ）

手織りのクッション・カバー、
手染めの毛糸、赤い絹、47×51cm、
制作：装飾美術学校染織学科
（シュネーベルク市、ドイツ）、
Ed. 35/XX、署名、番号入り証明書

パルケット・エディション 78

擬態をおもわせるクッションはジェルジ・ルカーチの
好んだテーマ、リアリズムについての思索をうながす。

ニコライはアーティストの身分がもたらす学究的世界に煩わされず
にすむ自由、つまり出典を誤用し、まったく状況の異なるイメージや
オブジェを再構成する自由を利用する。こうしてアーティストのアイ
デンティティの内部に確実にとどまりながら、研究者、まとめ役の役
割をはたす。物事を逆転させて別の角度から見るとどうなるか試し、
最終的には視覚の新様式を創出する。ニコライの戦略はどうやら文
化発展のこの段階では、政治が疲弊し、甘ったるい経済的利益追求
のために「創造性」が無国籍化していることも考えると、優れたもの
のように見える。

シャレス・エッシュ
（パルケット 78号、2006年）

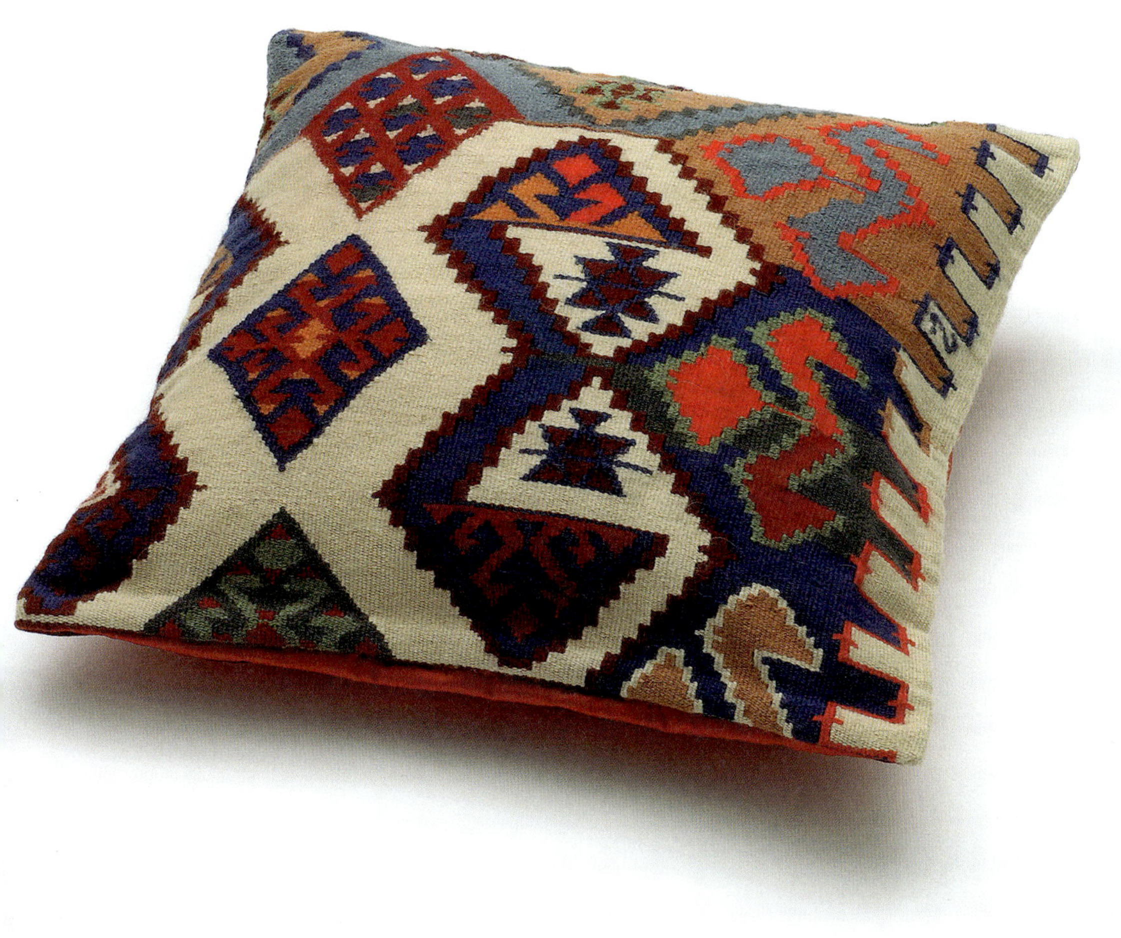

CADY NOLAND

(Not Yet Titled), 1996

Cardboard, lacquer-based sanding
sealer and aluminum enamel spray paint,
(please note: surface inflections differ
from one piece to another),
56 x 54" (142 x 137 cm),
Ed. 50/XV, signed and numbered

EDITION FOR PARKETT 46

Sparkling, silvered stocks—hinting perhaps at the crumbling elegance of pilloried lives?

"Imagine, then, each of Cady Noland's installations
as an entry into an ever-collecting, mortally transient,
tactile encyclopedia of visceral Americana, where
each entry is constructed of principled materials
(for instance, aluminum), storied objects (handcuffs,
rubber tires, Budweiser beer cans, bug sprayers,
American flags, wire mesh baskets and fences), and
embodied ephemera (Patty Hearst, Charles Manson,
Wilbur Mills, Vince Foster): Art as encyclopedia,
history as vaudeville."

Thyrza Nichols Goodeve
Parkett No. 46, 1996

ケディ・ノーランド

（今のところまだ題はついていない）
1996

ボール紙、ラッカー系サンディングシーラー、
アルミ・エナメル・スプレー塗料
　（表面の光の反射具合は1点ずつ異なる）、
142×137cm、
Ed. 50/XV、署名、番号入り

パルケット・エディション 46

銀色の光を放つ足枷台—晒者にされた人生の、脆くも崩れゆく高雅さを仄めかしているのだろうか。

さてケディ・ノーランドのインスタレーションひとつひとつを、素顔
のアメリカに関する百科事典、たえず収録数を増やしつづけ、あく
まで一過性だが生々しい百科事典の見出しと考えてみよう。見出
しはそれぞれ原則的な素材（たとえばアルミ）、物語を秘めたオブ
ジェ（手錠、ゴムタイヤ、バドワイザー・缶ビール、殺虫剤のスプレー
缶、星条旗、金網の籠や柵）、肉体を得た短い命（パティ・ハースト、
チャールズ・マンソン、ウィルバー・ミルズ、ヴィンス・フォスター）で
構成される。百科事典としての美術作品、ヴォードヴィル仕立ての
歴史。

シルザ・ニコルズ・グッドイーヴ
（パルケット 46号、1996年）

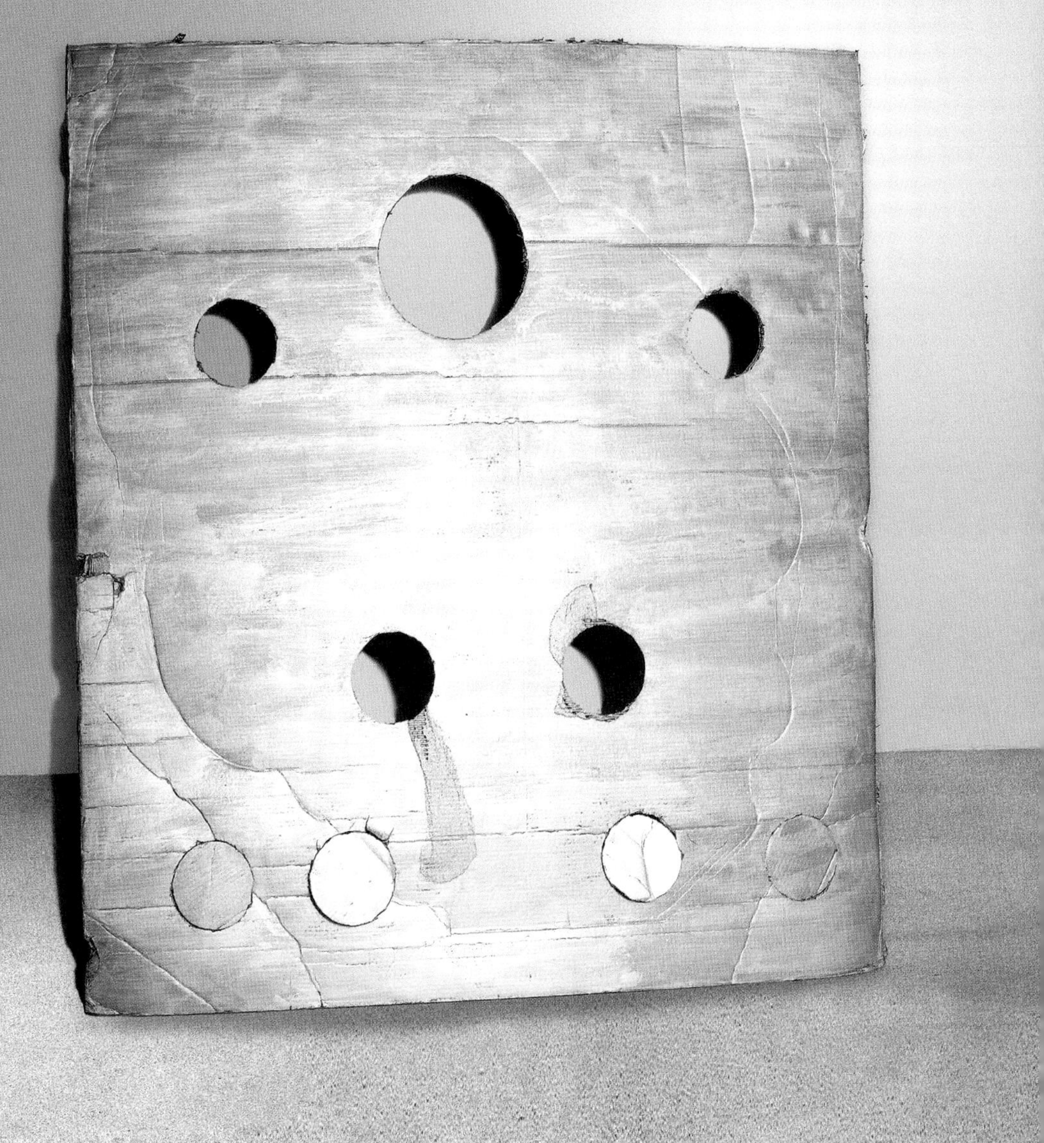

ALBERT OEHLEN

L. P. A., 2007

Etching and Charbonnel black ink
on Hahnemühle Dürer Etching White
300 g/m², paper size: 20 3/4 x 26 1/2"
(53 x 66,5 cm), image: 13 3/4 x 20 1/4"
(35 x 51,5 cm), printed by Greg Burnet,
Burnet Editions, New York,
Ed. 60/XX, signed and numbered

EDITION FOR PARKETT 79

Mental décollage—not the archeology of
eroded snipes and billboards but the beat
interference of digital collisions.
(Glenn O'Brien)

"There is method in his madness, madness in his
method. Oehlen employs error as method, but if it is
deliberate, is it error? Logic is more inescapable than
it looks. It's not enough putting one foot in front of
another; maybe you need to put one foot in front of
somebody else's or put the foot in the mouth where
it belongs."

Glenn O'Brien
Parkett No. 79, 2007

アルバート・オーレン

L. P. A.　2007

エッチング、シャルボネル社の黒インク、
ハーネミュール・デューラー・エッチング・ホワイト紙
300g/㎡、
紙：53×66.5cm、図柄：35×51.5cm、
刷り：グレッグ・バーネット、
バーネット・エディションズ（ニューヨーク）、
Ed. 60/XX、署名、番号入り

パルケット・エディション 79

知性の離陸—崩れかけた吸いさしや大看板の考古学
ではなく、デジタル化された衝突へのビート的介入。
（グレン・オブライエン）

オーレンの狂気には方法論があり、方法論に狂気がある。オーレ
ンはしくじりを方法として用いるが、意図的になされたとすると、
それをしくじりと呼べるだろうか。論理はみかけよりしつこくつい
てまわる。片方の足をもう一方の前に出すのでは充分でない。片足
を、だれかよその人の片足の前に出す必要があるのではないか。そ
れとも片足を口につっこむとか。もともとそれが本来の場所なの
だし。

グレン・オブライエン
（パルケット 79号、2007年）

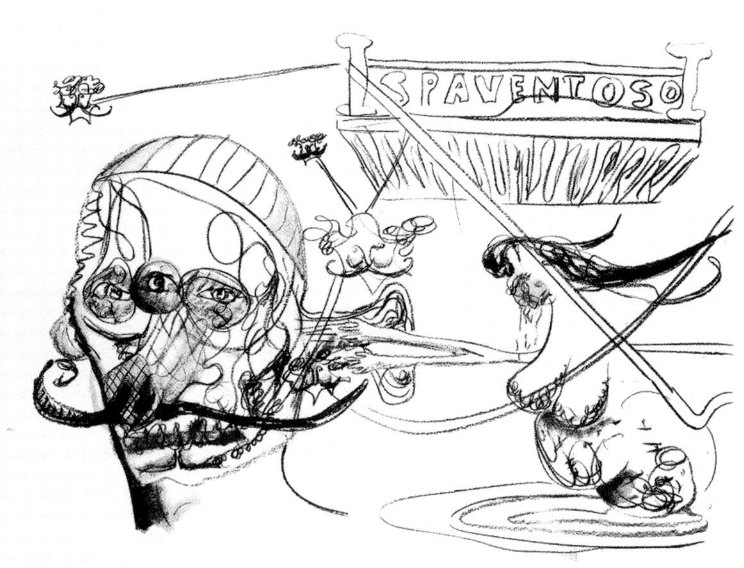

SPAVENTOSO

MERET OPPENHEIM

Glove, 1985

Goat suede with silk-screen and
handstitched, included in Parkett issue,
5 5/8 x 3 2/4" (21,3 x 9,3 cm),
Ed. 150/XII, signed and numbered

EDITION FOR PARKETT 4

Hand in glove. Realizing an original design
from 1936—the year of the creation of the
famous "Furlined Teacup"—the demurely
savage chic of these gloves turns the hands
of the wearer inside out.

"Meret Oppenheim's abstruse, multi-leveled work
sometimes stubbornly eludes facile interpretation;
her virtuoso performance on many instruments at
once has long left viewers at something of a loss. On
a picture done early in 1933 she wrote the laconic
statement: 'Well, then we'll live a little later.' Only
gradually, after the critic's stodgy demand for clear
development and stylistic consistency had paled,
yielding to a growing fascination for the unfettered
approach of recent art, Meret Oppenheim has finally
come into her own."

Jacqueline Burckhardt
Parkett No. 4, 1985

メレット・オッペンハイム

手袋　1985

山羊スエード皮にシルクスクリーン、
手で縫いとり、パルケット本誌に挿入、
21.3×9.3cm、
Ed. 150/XII、署名、番号入り

パルケット・エディション 4

手袋をはめた手。1936年（世に名高い《毛皮で覆わ
れたティーカップ》が制作された年）にさかのぼるデ
ザインをエディション化。とりすました手袋の洗練さ
れた野性が、使い手の皮膚を裏返す。

難解で重層的なメレット・オッペンハイムの作品は、安易な解釈
をときに頑に撥ねつける。多様な楽器を操る名人芸で、オッペン
ハイムは鑑賞者を長年にわたり煙に巻いてきた。活動を始めて間
もない1933年に描いた絵に、オッペンハイムはずばり一言、こ
う記した。「それなら、しばらくしてから生きることにしましょ
う」。発展の明確な方向性や様式の一貫性をくどくど求める評論
家の声がしだいに遠のき、枷を逃れた近年のアートの自由な行き
方を称賛する声の高まりに取って代わられた今になって、メレッ
ト・オッペンハイムはようやく正当な名声を手に入れた。

ジャクリーヌ・ブルクハルト
（パルケット 4号、1985年）

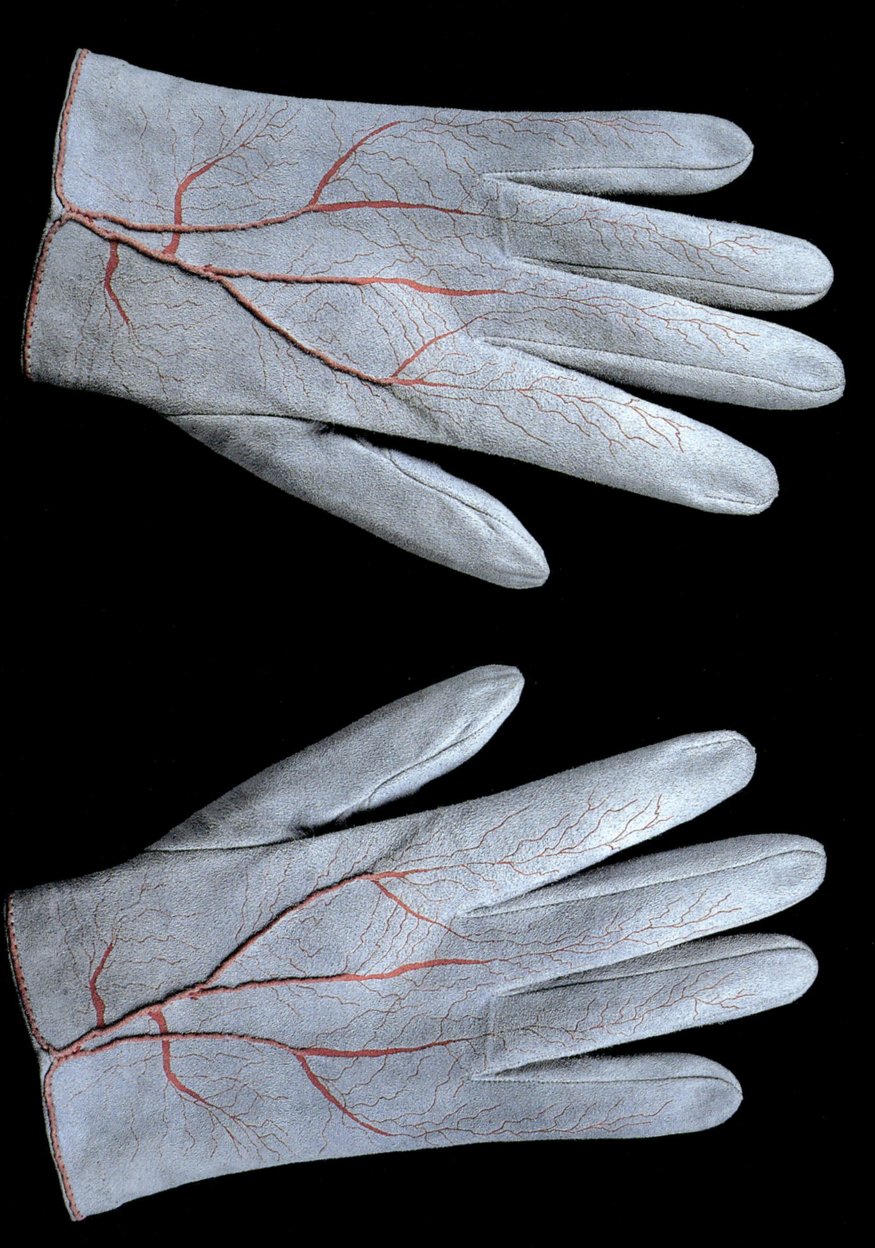

GABRIEL OROZCO

Light through Leaves, 1996

Iris computer print, archival water-based
ink on paper (500g/m² Somerset Satin
100% cotton rag), produced by
Cone Laumont Editions, New York,
image size: 20 x 30 1/8" (50,9 x 76,5 cm),
paper size: 22 x 32 1/8" (55,9 x 81,5 cm),
Ed. 60/XX, signed and numbered

EDITION FOR PARKETT 48

Oneness and plurality. Particles of light
fluttering in a tangle of leaves and twigs,
electronically filtered and reinvented.

"We are looking at an artist who analyzes the alphabet
created by sculpture in art history, and then mixes it
with the alphabet created by things in reality. Inside
Orozco's work, a series of threads are woven, but along
those threads the communication flow is interrupted
by knots of meaning. These knots are, simply, those
things—transformed into sculpture—which break the
circuit of artistic language. The logical and historical
consequences of the artwork are subverted or, at least,
diverted."

Francesco Bonami
Parkett No. 48, 1996

ガブリエル・オロスコ

木漏れ日　1996

アイリス・コンピューター・プリント、
高耐久性水性インク、
サマーセット・サテン・100％コットン・ラグペーパー
500g/㎡、
刷り：コーン・ローモント・エディションズ
（ニューヨーク）、
図柄：50.9×76.5cm、紙：55.9×81.5cm、
Ed. 60/XX、署名、番号入り

パルケット・エディション 48

単一性と複数性。光の粒子が錯綜する木の葉と枝の狭間
ではためき、電子フィルターを透して新たな姿に生まれ
変わる。

わたしたちは今、美術史上の彫刻が創りだしたアルファベットを分析
し、それを現実に存在する物が創りだしたアルファベットと混ぜ合わ
せるアーティストを目の当たりにしている。オロスコの作品の内部で
は一連の糸が織り上げられているが、その糸の傍らで情報伝達の流れ
は意味の結び目によって中断される。これらの結び目は、彫刻に作り
替えられ、芸術言語の循環を妨げるものである。美術作品の論理的、
歴史的帰結は覆されるか、少なくとも本来の道筋から逸らされる。

フランチェスコ・ボナミ
（パルケット 48号、1996年）

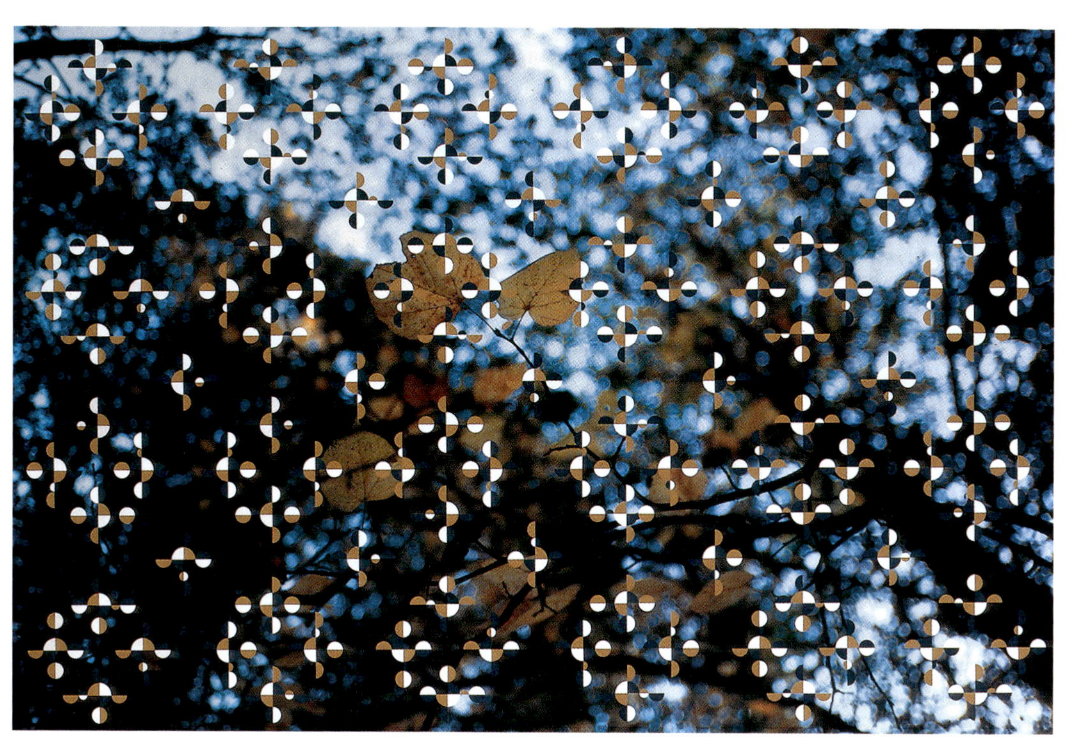

TONY OURSLER

Talking Light, 1996

Compact disk with artist's voice
(running time approx. 15 min.), light bulb,
sound organ kit, the light bulb reacts to
the frequency of the voice on the CD,
installation manual,
Ed. 50/XX, signed and numbered

EDITION FOR PARKETT 47

Force of dramatic character is transformed
into pure energy. The light source, correlated
to a sound organ, waxes and wanes according
to the fluctuating intensity of the performed
text.

"I've always been interested in things which are on
the verge of falling apart but which still maintain their
original quality. It's a constant battle because I have a
pretty low boredom threshold. At the beginning when
I started looking at Structuralist films, I just couldn't
stand all that repetition. Our culture is obsessed with
the whole horror-sex-violence thing. It's a weird form
of refinement, like bonsai. We love to watch it, and I'm
obsessed by the fact that we love to watch it."

Tony Oursler, interview with Louise Neri and Tracy Leipold
Parkett No. 47, 1996

トニー・アウスラー

おしゃべり電球　1996

アウスラーの声を録音したCD（収録時間約15分）、
電球、音声を光に変換する装置、
電球はCDから流れる声の周波数に反応する、
設置マニュアル、
Ed. 50/XX、署名、番号入り

パルケット・エディション 47

劇的な性格をもつ力が、純粋なエネルギーに変換され
る。光源は発声器官と相関し、読み上げられるテキスト
の強度の変動にともない明るさを増減させる。

崩壊寸前にあっても、本来の性質を保っているものにずっと関心が
あった。ぼくはひどく飽きっぽいほうなので、戦いに明け暮れたよ。
構造主義の映画を見はじめたころは、あのくりかえしがどうにも
我慢がならなかった。ぼくらの文化は、ホラーとセックスと暴力に
夢中なんだ。特殊な方角に高度化したもので、たとえてみれば盆
栽のようなものかな。ぼくらはそうしたものを見るのが大好きだし、
ぼくにはそのことが気になってしょうがない。

トニー・アウスラー、
ルイーズ・ネリ＆トレイシー・レイポルトのインタヴューに応えて
（パルケット 47号、1996年）

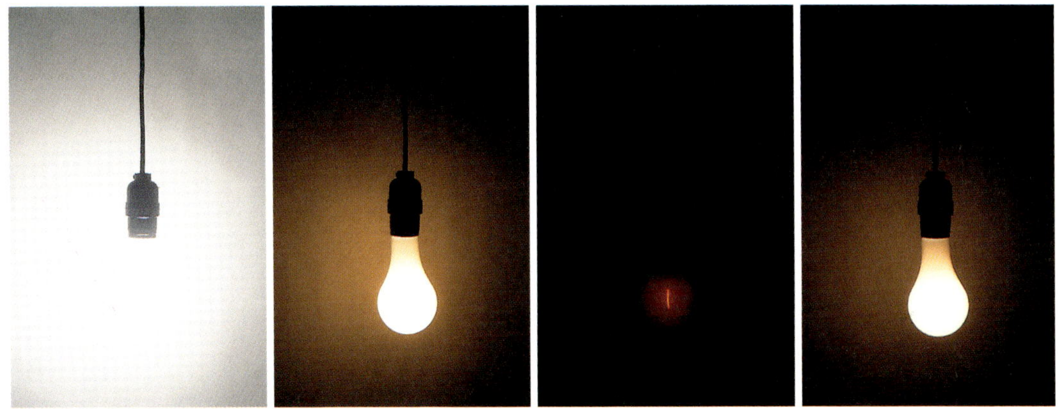

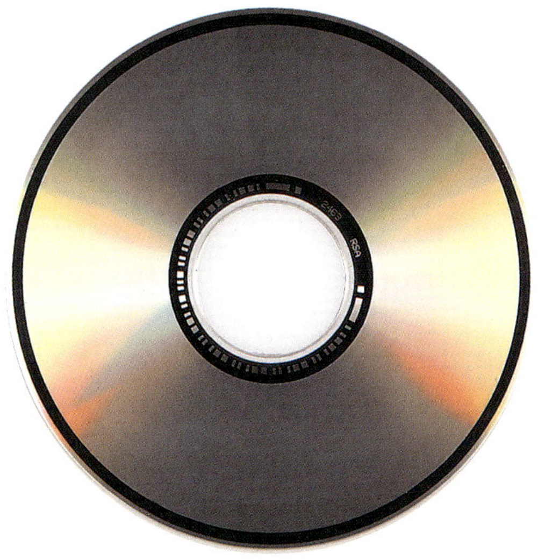

LAURA OWENS

Untitled, 2002

Handprinted 10-color lithograph on tan
BFK Rives with three collage elements:
one handpainted with watercolor on
blue Magnani Pescia, two on white BFK
Rives, the color of the moon will vary
with each print, 18 x 12" (46 x 30,6 cm),
printed by Ed Hamilton, Hamilton Press,
Venice, California,
Ed. 70/XXIV, signed and numbered
on the back

EDITION FOR PARKETT 65

Blue Moon... And then suddenly appeared
before me, the only one my arms could ever
hold.

"The work has a double life, the parts of which are
separate, yet deeply connected. On one level, it's a
picture of a better world: a peaceable kingdom where
all of nature co-exists in idyllic harmony. On another,
simultaneous, level, it's a painting: an elaborately
composed arrangement of paint on canvas that is
inevitably part of a complex dialogue with the whole
history of the medium. There is a constant back and
forth between the creation of a pictorial world and the
act of painting itself. For the work to be successful,
a certain harmony needs to be achieved that will
encompass both elements."

Russell Ferguson
Parkett No. 65, 2002

ローラ・オーエンズ

無題　2002

手刷り10色リトグラフ、
タン BFK リヴ紙に3種のコラージュ
　（水彩でマニャーニ・ペシアに手描きしたものが1種、
白のBFK リヴ紙に描いたものが2種）、
月の色はプリント毎にまちまち、46×30.6cm、
刷り：エド・ハミルトン、ハミルトン・プレス社
　（カリフォルニア州ヴェニス）、
Ed. 70/XXIV、裏面に署名、番号入り

パルケット・エディション 65

ブルー・ムーン……すると突然わたしの前に現れたの
は、腕に抱けるただひとつのもの。

美術作品にはふたつの側面があり、それぞれ分かれていながら、深
く結びついてもいる。あるレベルでは、それはよりよい世界の姿、自
然界のすべてが牧歌的な調和を保って共存する泰平な王国である。
もう一方の、並行するレベルでは、それは絵画である。カンヴァスの
上に絵具を高度に構成して配置したもので、こちらはメディアの総
体的な歴史との複雑な対話の一部にならざるをえない。絵画的世
界の創造と、絵を描く行為そのものとの間には、つねに往来がある。
作品が成功するためには、両方の要素をともにふくむある種の調和
が達成されなければならない。

ラッセル・ファーガソン
（パルケット 65号、2002年）

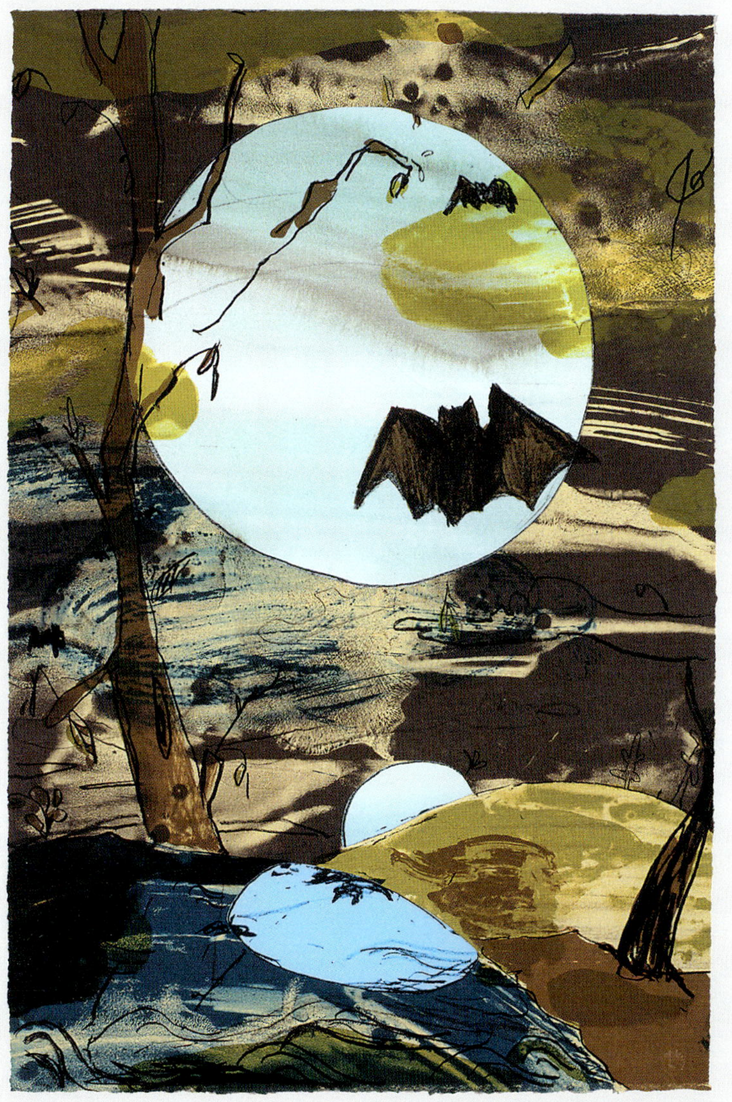

JORGE PARDO

Untitled, 1999

Unique sculpture, archival paper
mounted on cardboard, colored pencil,
approx. 9 $\frac{7}{8}$ x 4 x 4" (25 x 10 x 10 cm),
Ed. 55/XX, signed and numbered
certificate

EDITION FOR PARKETT 56

The weightlessness of the third dimension.

"We all know that no holds are barred when Jorge
Pardo is at work. Neither floor covering nor pictures,
books nor beds, lamps, houses nor boots escape
his attention. He addresses such diverse fields as
interior design, arts and crafts, graphic design, and
architecture. Common to these uncommon works
is one thing only: They all deal in curious cycles of
contradictory settings... Pardo speaks of tonality that
motivates his delight in speculative experimentation."

Christina Végh
Parkett No. 56, 1999

ホルヘ・パルド

無題　1999

1点ずつ形の異なる彫刻、
中性紙をボール紙にマウント、色鉛筆、
約25×10×10cm、
Ed. 55/XX、署名、番号入り証明書

パルケット・エディション 56

3次元の無重力感覚。

ホルヘ・パルドが仕事にかかれば、したい放題なのは周知の通り。
床の絨毯も絵も、本もベッドも、ランプも、家もブーツもパルドの
視線を免れることはできない。パルドは室内装飾、応用美術、グラ
フィック・デザイン、建築など多様な分野を手がける。共通性のな
いこれらの仕事に共通するのはただひとつ、すべてが矛盾をふくむ
奇妙な循環をあつかうこと……パルドは投機的な実験の楽しさの
もとにある調性について語る。

クリスティーナ・ヴェーグ
（パルケット 56号、1999年）

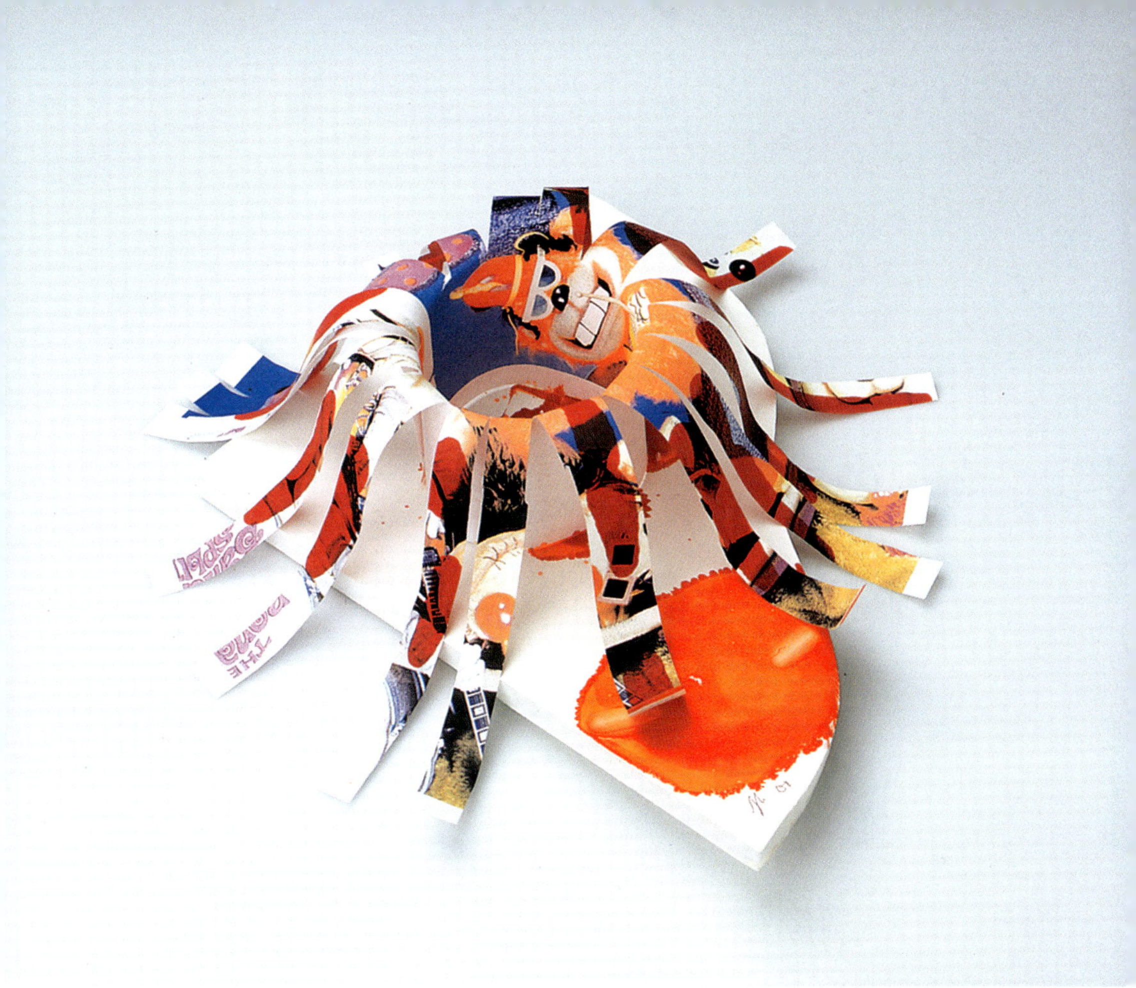

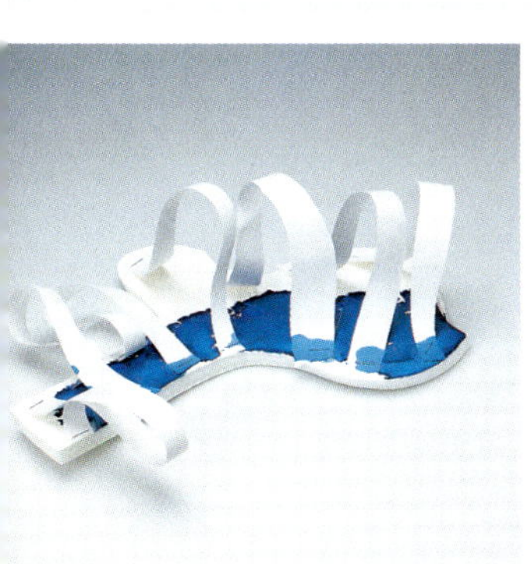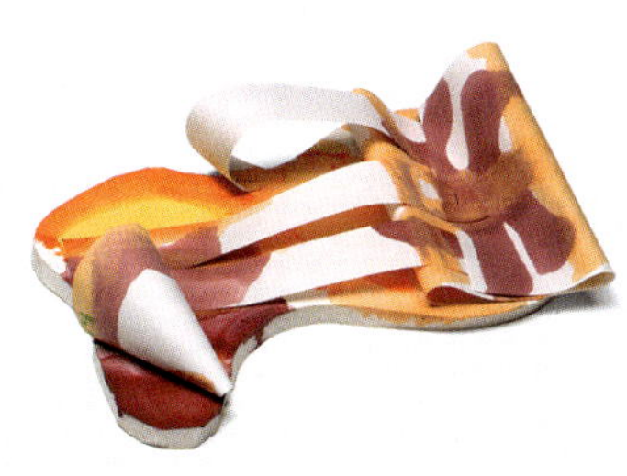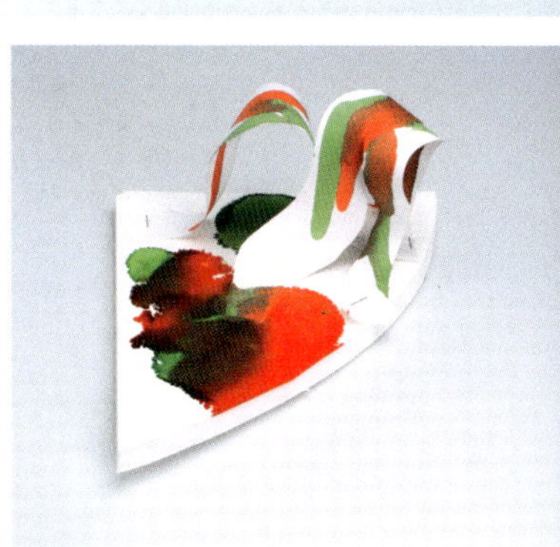

MAI-THU PERRET

A Portable Apocalypse Ballet
(Red Ring), 2008

Sculpture, opaque non-toxic polyurethane
resin, color cast with instant polyurethane
pigments, clothing designed by Ligia Dias,
beige viscose fabric with white accents
and metal buttons, black leather belt,
modacrylic light brown wig, solid cast
polyurethane resin base, painted, neon
ring powered by 12 V CE and UL approved
universal wall adapter, 14 ¾ x 7 x 7"
(37,5 x 17,8 x 17,8 cm) production by Gamla
Model Makers, Feasterville, PA, USA,
Ed. 45/XX, signed and numbered certificate

EDITION FOR PARKETT 84

The purity of the circle, unassailable with eyes closed in order to see.

"…Perret explores the ambivalence between object and
action, the gap between a transitive instrument (either
revolutionary or ritualistic) and the object reified by a
sociocultural, institutional, or market-based system.
Her work, as she conceives of it, is a dispassionate as-
sessment of forms and the hypothetical permanence
of their messages."

Julien Fronsacq,
Parkett No. 84, 2008

マイ＝チュー・ペレ

ポータブル黙示録バレエ（赤いリング）
2008

彫刻、不透明なポリウレタン樹脂、
速乾性ポリウレタン系顔料により着色成形、
衣裳デザイン：リジア・ディアス、
ベージュ色のビスコース繊維に白の縁取り、
金属製ボタン、黒皮ベルト、
モドアクリル繊維ライト・ブラウン色ウィッグ、
硬質ポリウレタン樹脂の土台、塗装、
ネオン・リング：直流12Vアダプターで電流供給、
37.5×17.8×17.8cm、
制作：ガムラ・モデル・メーカー社
（ペンシルヴァニア州フィースターヴィル市）、
Ed. 45/XX、署名、番号入り証明書

パルケット・エディション 84

リングの純潔。見るために目を閉じては攻め手なし。

ペレは物と行為の間の曖昧さ、（革命的であっても儀式的であって
も）移行に資する手段と社会文化的、制度的、あるいは市場機軸型
システムによって具象化されるオブジェの間の隔たりを追求する。
ペレの作品は、構想された段階では、フォルムとそれが伝えるメッ
セージの仮定に基づく永続性を冷静に査定しようとする。

ジュリアン・フロンサック
（パルケット 84号、2008）

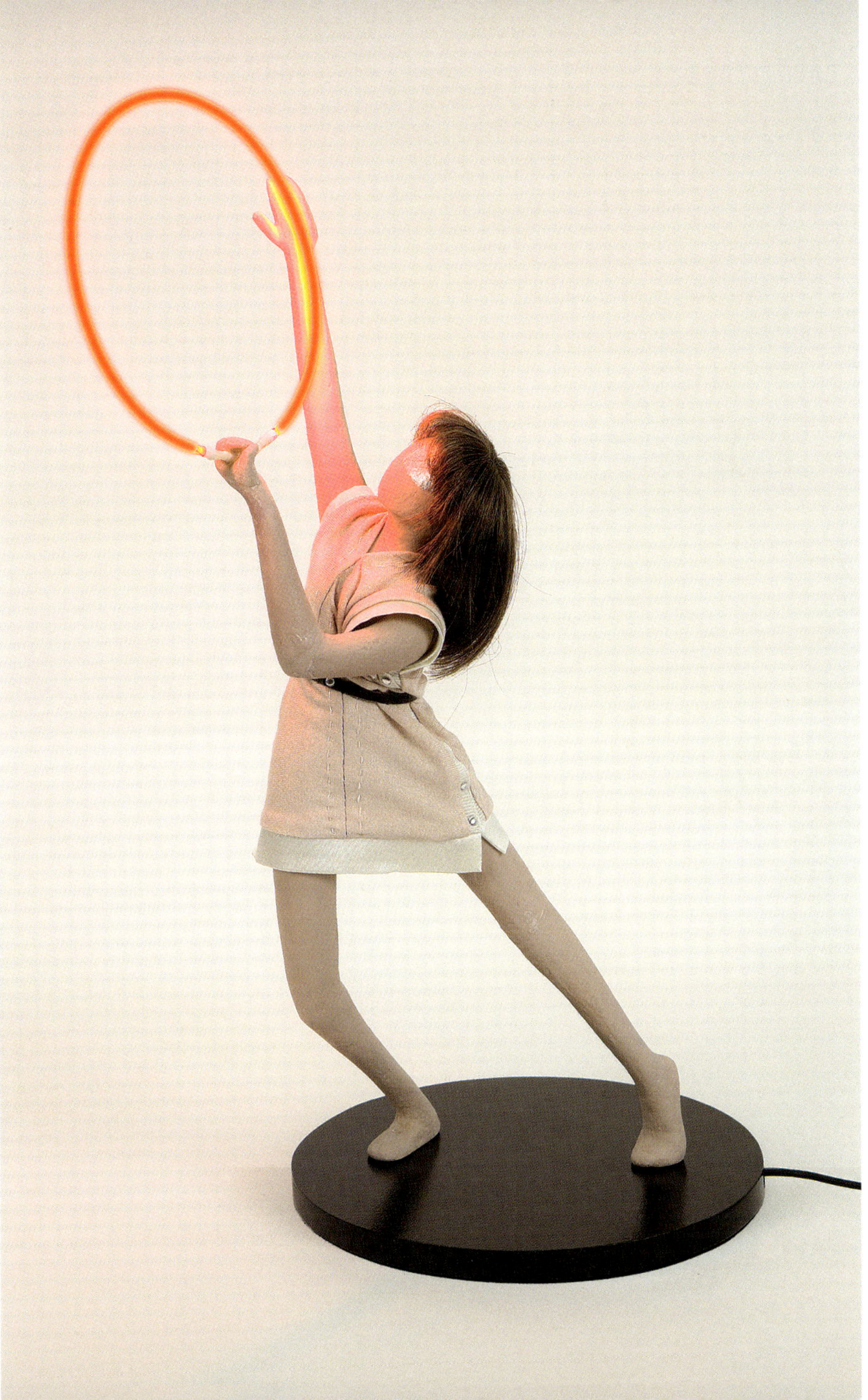

RAYMOND PETTIBON

Untitled (Justly Felt and Brilliantly Said), 1996

Silkscreen, handwritten texts by the artist
which vary in each edition, pressed flower,
printed by Lorenz Boegli, Zurich,
on Arches 120g/m^2,
approx. 9 $^5/_8$ x 7 $^5/_8$" (24,4 x 19,4 cm),
a 10-part foldout,
full length 9 $^5/_8$ x 76 $^3/_4$" (24,4 x 194 cm),
Ed. 60/XX, signed and numbered

EDITION FOR PARKETT 47

Riding the waves. A swell of words and images. Whooping with joy, seeking to maintain a precarious balance, persevering in focused silence.

"By placing texts in unique, single drawings, Pettibon has found a means of surmounting his intrinsic difficulty and revealing the aesthetic potential of 'bad' commercial mass literature within the framework of his art. Pettibon is not the only artist over the past few decades to pursue such ends in incorporating texts in his work; others have also grasped this opportunity—both literally and figuratively. (...) His pictures serve the interests of poetry, which—given the hegemony of the mechanically-printed word in current culture—cannot afford the appropriations and recontextualizations which have already become standard practice in art."

Boris Groys
Parkett No. 47, 1996

レイモンド・ペティボン

無題（正当に感知され、見事に語られた）
1996

シルクスクリーン、
アーティストによる手書きのテキスト
（1点毎に内容は異なる）、押し花、
刷り：ロレンツ・ボエリ（チューリヒ）、
アルシュ紙 120g/㎡、約24.4×19.4cm、
折り畳み10枚綴り、
24.4×194cm、
Ed. 60/XX、署名、番号入り

パルケット・エディション 47

波に乗る。もりあがる言葉と映像。嬉しさのあまり歓声をあげ、意識を集中し、沈黙に耐えながら、あやうくバランスをとる。

一枚の一点かぎりの素描にテキストを添えることによって、ペティボンは内因性の困難を克服し、作品の枠組みのなかで大量生産される売らんかなの「低俗な」小説にも美術品として機能する潜在力があることを明らかにする。過去数十年の間、作品にテキストを採り入れそうした目標を追求したアーティストはペティボンひとりにかぎらない。ほかにもこのチャンスを直接的に、そしてまた比喩的に掴んだアーティストはいる。ペティボンの絵は詩の役に立つ。機械によって印刷された文字がヘゲモニーを握る文化の現況を考えると、美術界で当たり前のように通用する借用や再文脈化であっても、詩にはまだ敷居が高いのだろう。

ボリス・グロイス
（パルケット 47号、1996年）

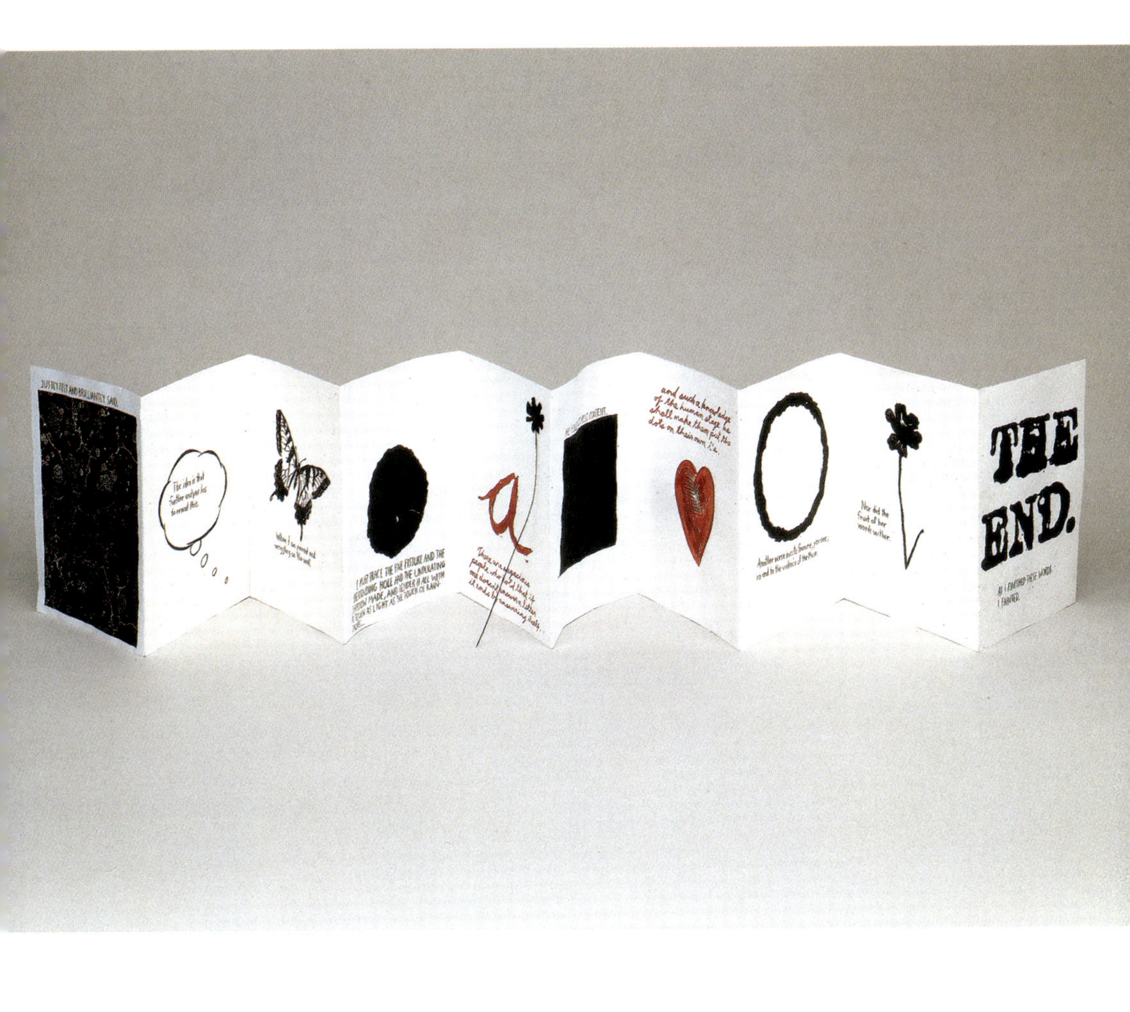

JUST BE FELT AND BRILLIANTLY SAID.
The idea is that further analysis has to reveal this.
THE END.
AS I FINISHED THESE WORDS, I FAINTED.

ELIZABETH PEYTON

Oscar and Bosie, 1998

Two-color lithograph on hand-tinted
Somerset Satin, lightly finished with
pearlescent dust, ca. 22 $^3/_8$ x 24 $^3/_4$"
(58,4 x 62,1 cm), printed by Maurice
Sanchez and James Miller,
Derrière l'Etoile Studio, New York,
Ed. 60/XX, signed and numbered

EDITION FOR PARKETT 53

...druggy, lush and androgynous, yet somehow removed from human touch.

"These are all people who I have made part of my
daily life. I read about them or listen to their music
for pleasure. I look for books about them, but I'm not
even thinking about work at this point. Then I see a
particular image of them and I really want to make
pictures of them. And then I do it. It's very seamless.
Life and work are not so separated. You know that
excitement when you're walking down the street and
you see someone who attracts you? Suddenly, just for
a second, all possibilities are open."

Elizabeth Peyton, interview with Linda Pilgrim
Parkett No. 53, 1998

エリザベス・ペイトン

オスカーとボウジー　1998

2色刷りリトグラフ、
手彩色したサマーセット・サテン紙、
真珠の光沢のある粉末を軽く塗布、
約58.4×62.1cm、
刷り：モーリス・サンチェス、ジェイムズ・ミラー、
デリエール・レトワール・スタジオ（ニューヨーク）、
Ed. 60/XX、署名、番号入り

パルケット・エディション 53

麻薬が効いているのか、艶かしく、中性的ながら、どこか人間らしさを欠いている。

このひとたちは、わたしの日常生活の一部になりました。話を聞い
て、かれらの音楽を聴いて楽しみました。このひとたちに関する本
を探したけれど、今のところ仕事のことは考えていません。それか
ら、ある時、かれらの映像を見て、どうしても絵を描きたくなりま
した。そして、実際に描いたのです。そこまではスラスラ運びまし
た。人生と仕事はそれほど遠く離れたものでもないのですね。道
を歩いていて、素敵だなと思えるひとを見かけた時の心のときめ
きを、あなたも知っていますね。突然、ほんの一瞬、あらゆる可能
性が目の前に開けるのです。

エリザベス・ペイトン、
リンダ・ピルグリムのインタヴューに応えて
（パルケット 53号、1998年）

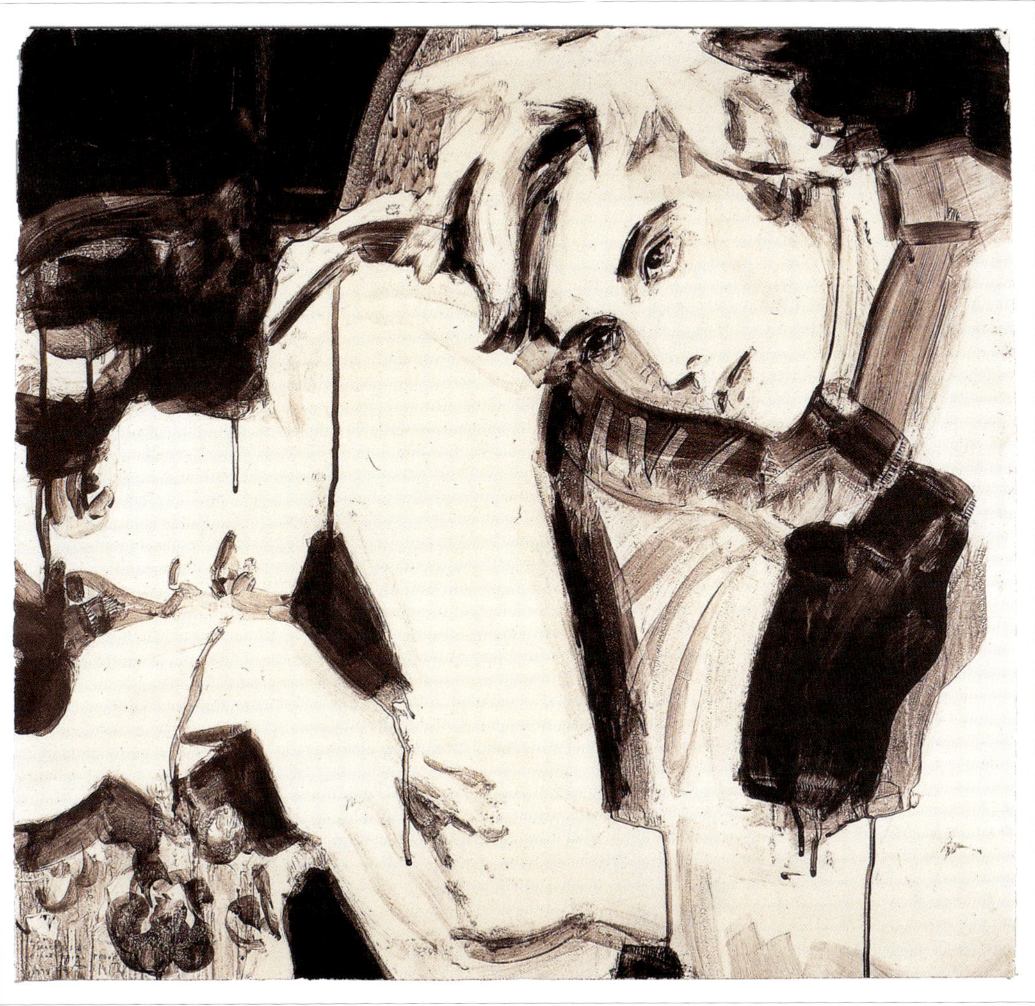

RICHARD PHILLIPS

Miss Parkett, 2004

5-color lithograph on
Somerset white paper,
paper size: 26 x 20 $^3/_{16}$" (66 x 51,3 cm),
image size: 21 $^1/_4$ x 16 $^1/_{16}$" (54 x 40,8 cm),
printed by Maurice Sanchez, Derrière
l'Etoile Studio, New York,
Ed. 70/XXVI, signed and numbered

EDITION FOR PARKETT 71

There once was a lady of fashion who posed
for an artist so dashing, that they both took
the leap and jumped into the deep of a
journal we all know is splashing.

"Whatever the case, it is better NOT to see these
pictures in reproduction, but to see the originals, live
and physical, no matter how much they pretend to be
infinitely reproductible. It is best to see them the way
they claim they do not want to be seen: face-to-face.
Because only then can one sense the special nature of
the change and the prolonged sessions during which
the artist appropriates this painting."

Jutta Koether
Parkett No. 71, 2004

リチャード・フィリップス

ミス・パルケット　2004

5色刷りリトグラフ、
サマーセット・ホワイト紙：66×51.3cm、
図柄：54×40.8cm、
刷り：モーリス・サンチェス、
デリエール・レトワール・スタジオ（ニューヨーク）、
Ed. 70/XXVI、署名、番号入り

パルケット・エディション 71

昔々上流婦人がおりまして、ある絵描きのモデルになっ
たところ、このひとがあまりに颯爽としているものです
から、ふたりは思いきって出奔、だれもが大成功をして
いると知っている雑誌の中に飛びこんだのでありまし
た。

とにかく、これらの絵は複製を見ずに、オリジナルを見るべきだ。ど
れほど複製しやすく見えるにしても、絵の息吹き、物としての手触り
が感じられるオリジナルを見るのがよい。そういうふうには見られ
たくないという見方、つまり正面から向かい合う形で見るのがよい。
なぜならそうして始めて、変化と、画家がこの絵を描こうとして写生
に費やした長い時間の特殊な性格を感じ取ることができるからであ
る。

ユッタ・ケザー
（パルケット 71号、2004年）

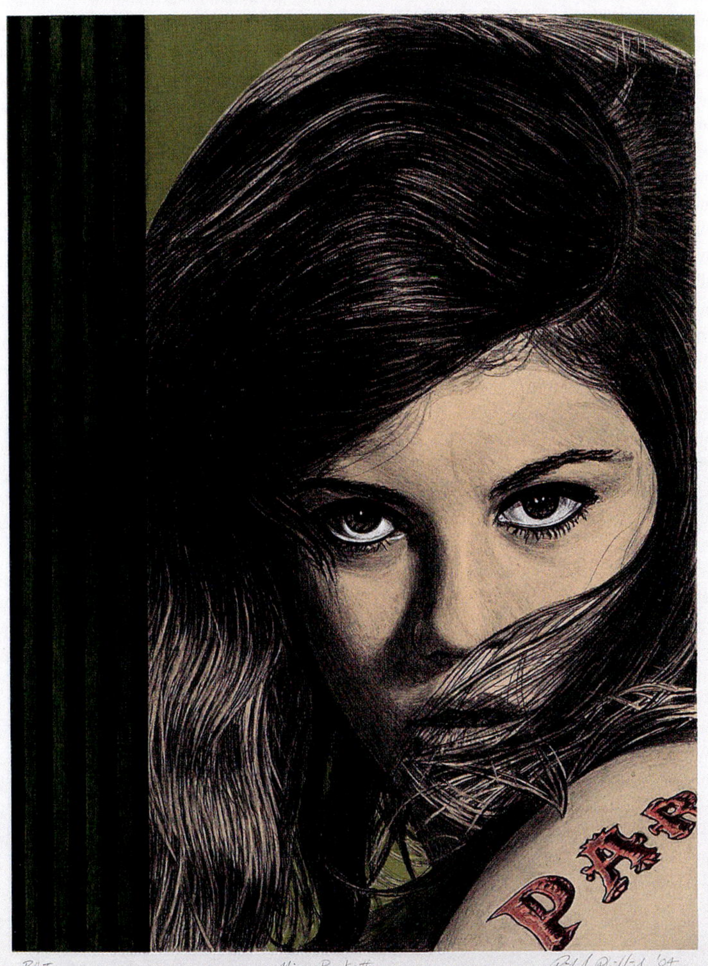

BAT
Miss Parkett
Robert Phillips '04

SIGMAR POLKE

Desasters und andere bare Wunder,
1982/84

60/5 E. A. unique photographs,
11 3/16 x 15 1/2" (30 x 40 cm),
signed and numbered

EDITION FOR PARKETT 2

Alchemist's signature. Sixty unique photographs enlarged from a strip of film that has been developed with the aid of raspberry brandy, coffee, Prill detergent, and other chemical secrets.

"Sigmar Polke with his consistently effortless use of old and new, rich and poor materials, applies a gentle insight and an unswerving determination to everything he does, endowing his imagery with an irrefutable validity."

Bice Curiger
Parkett No. 2, 1984

ジグマー・ポルケ

惨事並びに露な驚異　1982/84

60/5 E.A. 1点ずつ異なる写真、
30×40cm、
署名、番号入り

パルケット・エディション 2

錬金術師の署名。ラズベリー・ブランデー、コーヒー、プリル洗剤などの化学的秘薬の数々を用いて現像したフィルムを引き伸ばした1枚ずつ映像の異なる写真。

ジグマー・ポルケは古いもの、新しいもの、高級なもの、低級なもの、あらゆる素材をいつもながら苦もなく使いこなし、手がける作品のすべてに物静かな洞察と揺るぎない決意を注ぎ、作りだす映像にだれにも否定のできない妥当性を賦与する。

ビーチェ・クリガー
（パルケット 2号、1984年）

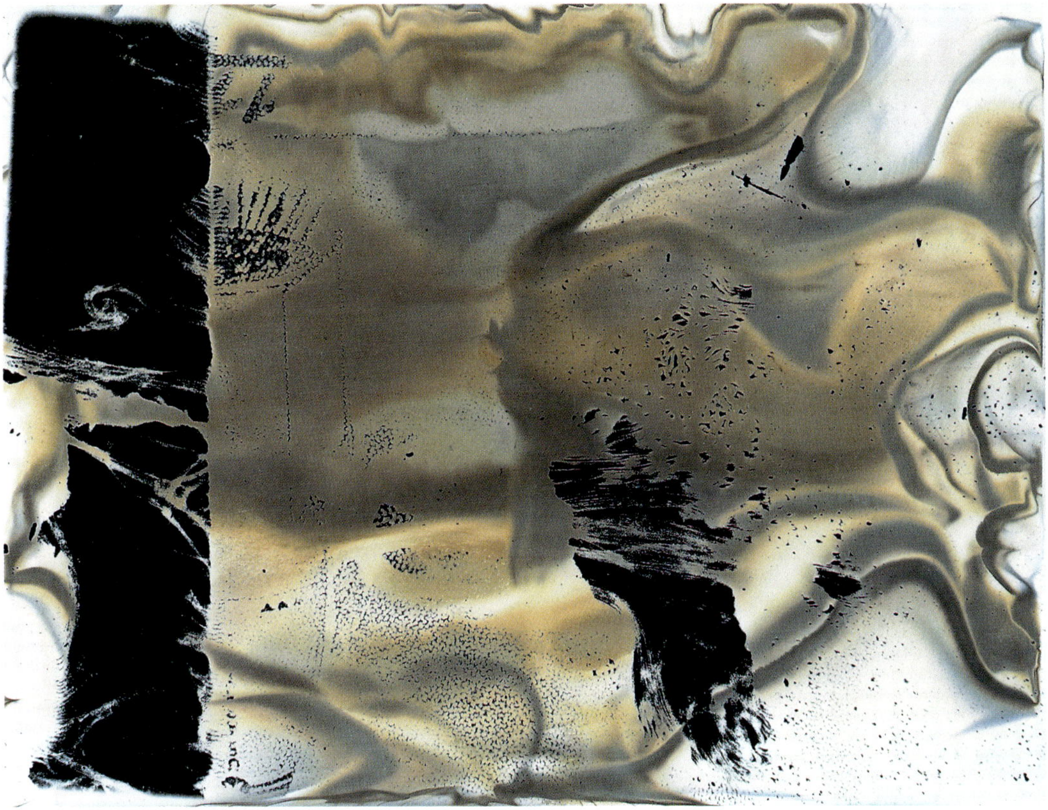

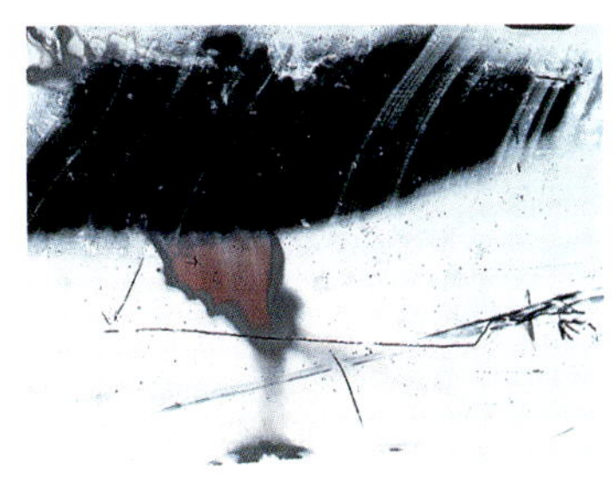

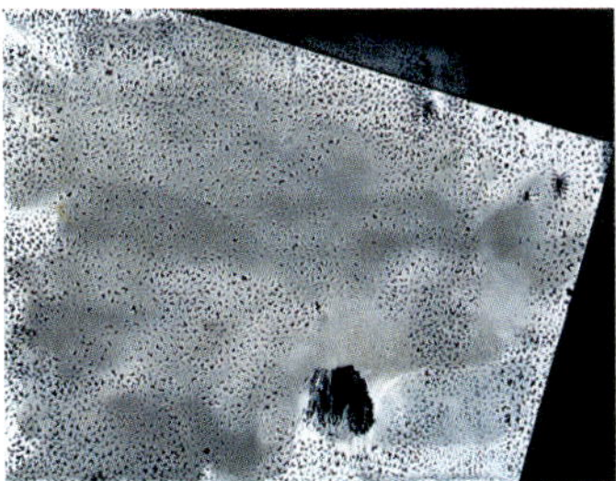

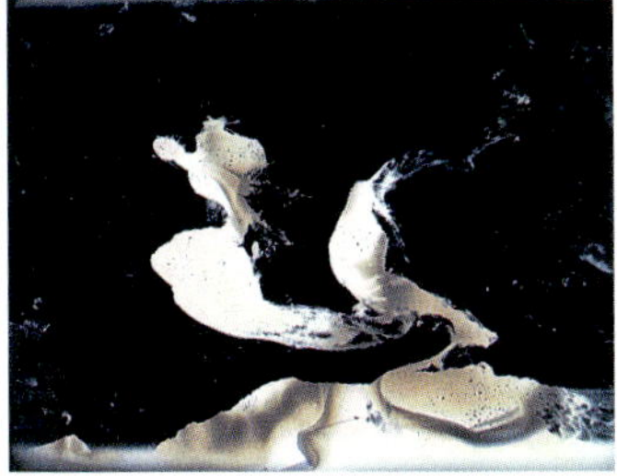

SIGMAR POLKE

Dr Pabscht het z'Schpiez
s'Schpäckbschteck z'schpät
bschteut, 1980/91
(tongue twister in Swiss-German:
The pope ordered the bacon cutlery
in Spiez too late)

Computer reproduction
mounted on stretcher, in vinyl,
19 $^5/_8$ x 15 $^3/_4$" (50,2 x 40,3 cm),
Ed. 100/XX, signed and numbered

EDITION FOR PARKETT 30

Fantastic voyage. Reversing his signature
process of imitating mechanical reproductive
techniques by hand, Polke employs high-tech
computer graphics to send an image of a
silverware case, pirated via Max Ernst from a
19th century mail order catalogue, on a flight
through time, space, and media.

"Somehow, for all the visual excitement of their
collective presence, each picture of Polke's as it
flickers before us, seems simultaneously drawn
backward into the time and place of its creation and
sucked upward into some wheeling constellation of
enduring cultural concerns."

Dave Hickey
Parkett No. 30, 1991

ジグマー・ポルケ

法皇はシュピーツでベーコン用のナイフを
注文したが、時すでに遅し　1980/81
（スイスで話されているドイツ語の早口言葉）

コンピューター・グラフィックによりビニールに描画、
ストレッチャーにマウント、
50.2×40.3cm、
Ed. 100/XX、署名、番号入り

パルケット・エディション 30

素敵な旅。機械を用いた複製技術を手作業で模す
トレードマーク的な手法を逆転させ、ポルケはハイテク
なコンピューター・グラフィックスを用いて、マックス・
エルンストを介して拝借した19世紀の通信販売カタロ
グから銀食器のケースのイメージを、時間、空間、メディ
アを越えて送りとどける。

なぜか、いくつもまとまってあるときには視覚を大いに刺激するに
もかかわらず、ポルケの絵の一枚一枚が目の前でまたたくとき、それ
は同時に描かれた時と場に引き戻され、いつまでも色あせない文化
的関心事の旋回する星座に向かい、上空に吸い上げられてゆくよう
な気がする。

デイヴ・ヒッキー
（パルケット 30号、1991年）

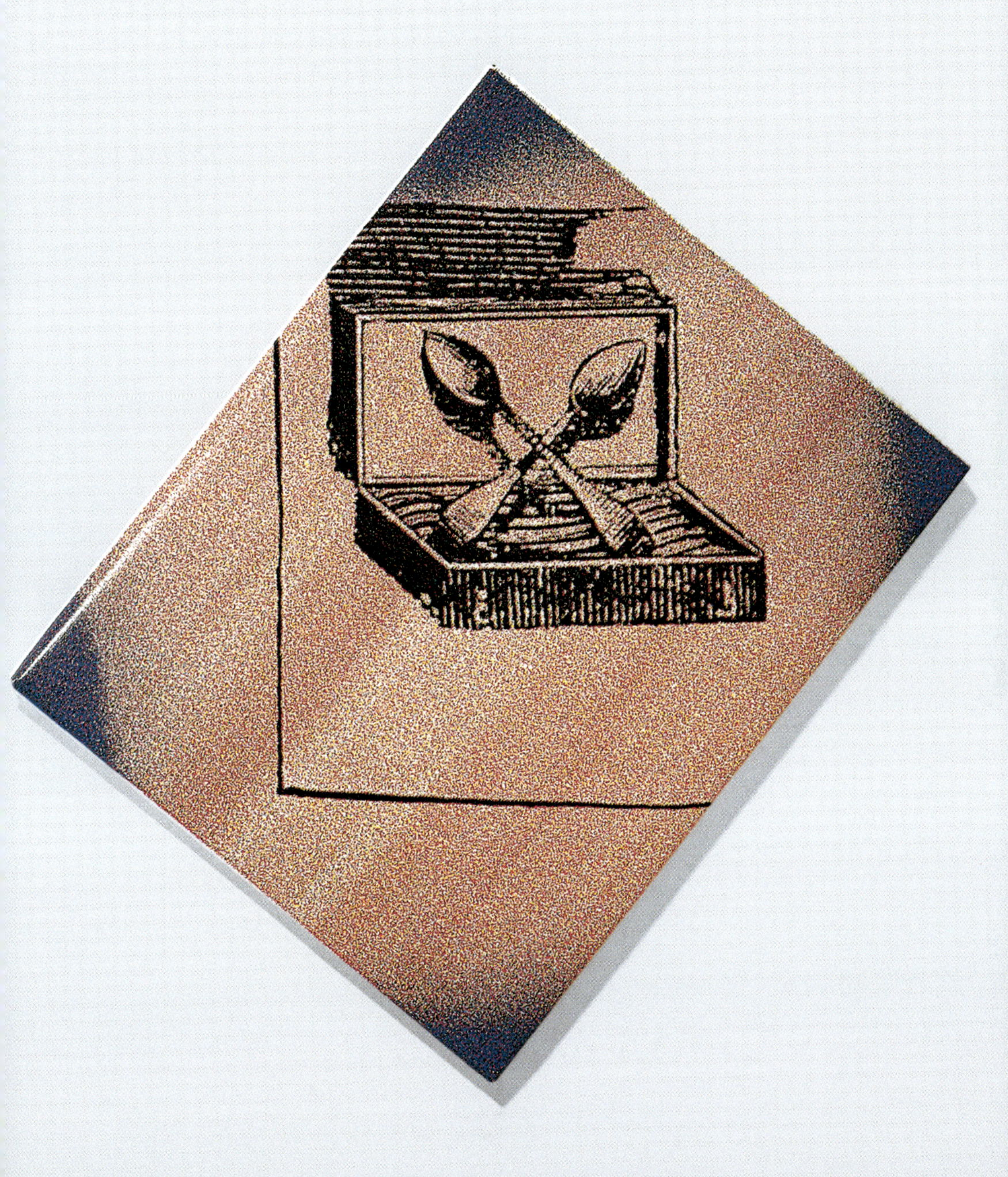

SIGMAR POLKE

Untitled, 1994

Volume of Parkett made of overprint
paper, individual sheets bound at
random, 10 x 8¼" (25,5 x 21 cm),
Ed. 25/X, signed and numbered,
and Ed. 25/X with an original contribution
(gouache), signed and numbered

EDITION FOR PARKETT 40/41

Master marksman. Chance hits the mark on overprint paper in a fireworks of acrobatic multi-meaning.

"By discovering a vital metaphorical means of equating
the higher domain of art with all efforts to attain
'knowledge of higher worlds' (Rudolf Steiner), Sigmar
Polke has staked out a vast playing field for himself.
With the frivolity dictated by gravity, he has let evil
snakes loose in spaces cluttered up with metaphysical
ladders. Starting with the painterly fabric of dots
from blown-up newspaper photographs, he annexed
the mental substance attendant upon them as a
provocative snake pit."

Bice Curiger
Parkett No. 40/41, 1994

ジグマー・ポルケ

無題　1994

重ね刷りした紙で制作したパルケット、
紙のシートは無作為に製本、25.5×21cm、
Ed. 25/X、署名、番号入り、
Ed. 25/X、オリジナル（グワッシュ）付き、
署名、番号入り

パルケット・エディション 40/41

射撃の名人。アクロバットまがいの多義性の花火のなかで、重ね刷りした紙の的を偶然が射抜く。

美術の高踏領域を、「高度な世界の知識」（ルドルフ・シュタイナー）
をめざすすべての努力と同等のものにする生き生きとした隠喩的な
方法を見いだすことにより、ジグマー・ポルケは自分自身のために広
大な遊び場を確保した。重力に起因する気まぐれを発揮し、隠喩的な
梯子でごたついた空に邪悪な蛇を放してやった。新聞写真を引き伸ば
したドットの絵画的な構造を手がかりに、それに伴う知的要素を挑発
的な蛇の穴として採り入れた。

ビーチェ・クリガー
（パルケット 40/41号、1994年）

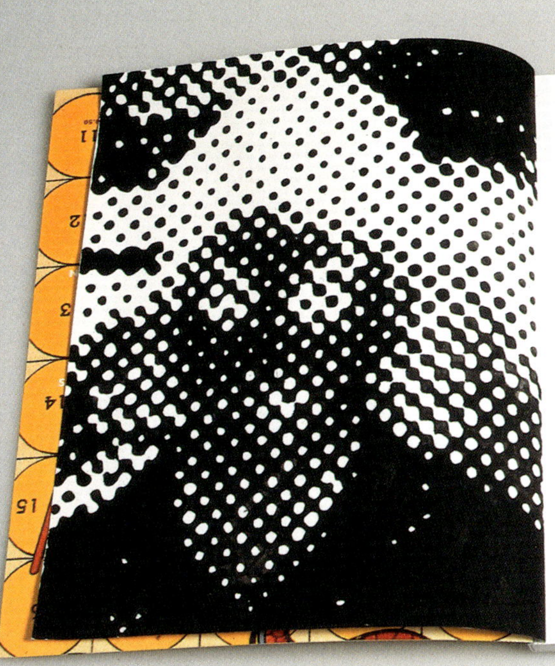
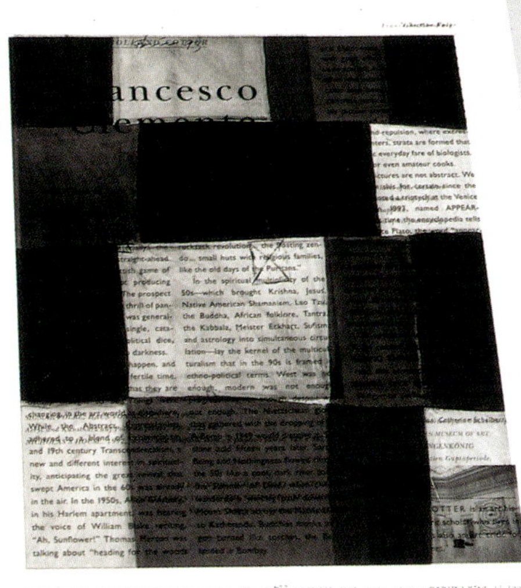
ancesco
Clemente

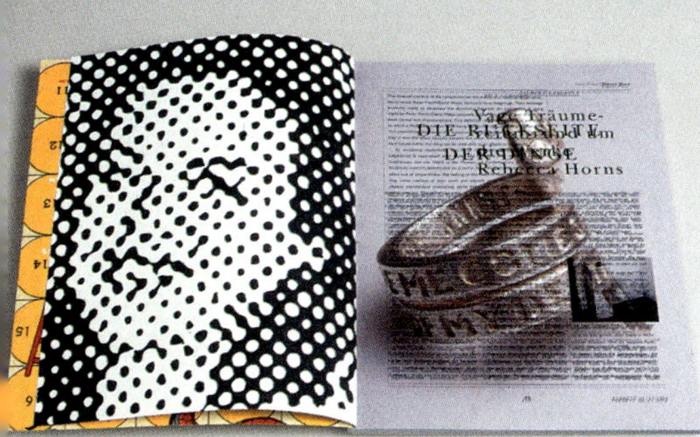
Vage Träume—
DIE RÜCKSEITE
DER DINGE
Rebecca Horns

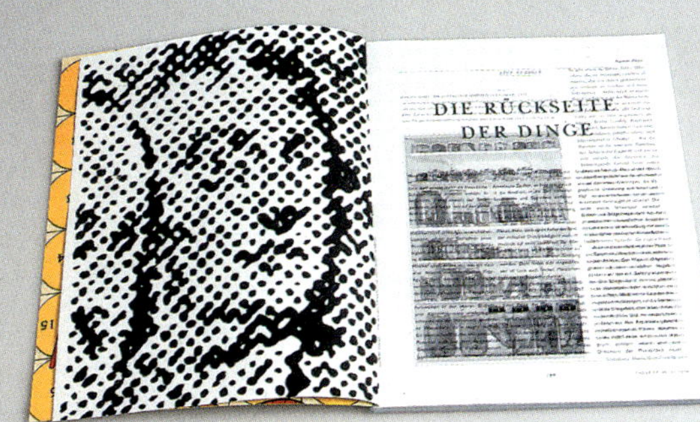
DIE RÜCKSEITE
DER DINGE

RICHARD PRINCE

Good Revolution, 1992

Presentation gold record with engraved
plaque mounted on C-print, framed,
includes a playable vinyl record by the
artist, recorded both sides, "Good
Revolution" (1:46) and "Don't Belong" (1:46),
arranged and performed by Richard Prince,
recorded and mixed at Harmonic Ranch
by Mark Degliantoni, September 1992,
$20^1/_2$ x $16^1/_2$" (52 x 41,9 cm),
Ed. 80/XX, signed and numbered

EDITION FOR PARKETT 34

Greatest hits. A weaver of fictions awards
himself the industry's highest accolade—a
gold record—complete with winning cover
design and haunting "lyrics."

"Prince's style of appropriation is not about the
transgressive aspect of the process, that is, stealing
from popular culture to turn it inside out and reveal its
manipulative aspect; rather, he mines it to unearth the
myths that crystallize American culture."

Daniela Salvioni
Parkett No. 34, 1992

リチャード・プリンス

良い革命　1992

ゴールド・レコード表彰額、
Cプリントに銘板をマウント、額装、
プリンスの演奏を録音した再生可能なレコード、
両面録音、「良い革命」（1 分46秒）、
「属さず」（1 分46秒）、
編曲・演奏：リチャード・プリンス、
録音・ミックス：ハーモニックス・ランチ、
技師：マーク・デリアントーニ、
1992年9月、
52×41.9cm、
Ed. 80/XX、署名、番号入り

パルケット・エディション 34

グレイテスト・ヒッツ。絵空事を紡ぐのが得意なアー
ティストが、業界最高峰の「ゴールド・レコード」賞を見
栄えよくデザイン、一度見たら忘れられない「歌詞」も
添えて、自分自身に贈る。

プリンスのアプロプリエーションのスタイルは違反性、つまり大衆文
化からの盗用を裏返し、操作されたものである側面を暴露するので
はなく、大衆文化を採掘し、アメリカ文化の結晶した神話を掘り起こ
す。

ダニエラ・サルヴィオーニ
（パルケット 34号、1992年）

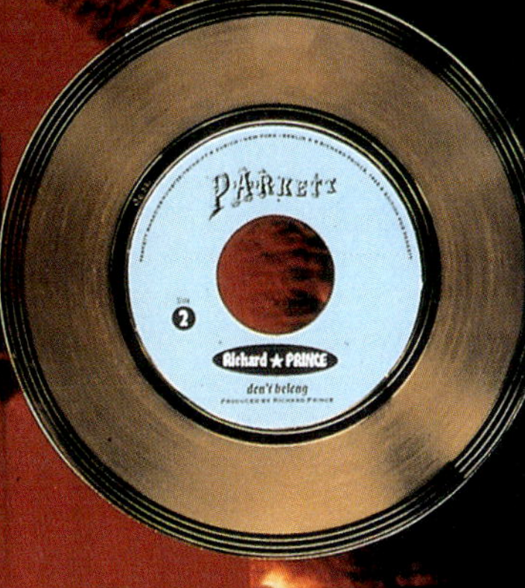
Richard Prince
good revolution
PARkett
Richard ★ PRINCE
don't belong
PRODUCED BY RICHARD PRINCE
RICHARD PRINCE
GOOD REVOLUTION
1992
1/80

RICHARD PRINCE

It's a Free Concert from Now on,
2004

Ektacolor print,
paper size: 30 x 40" (76,2 x 101,6 cm),
image size: 30 x 33 1/2" (76,2 x 85,1 cm),
Ed. 66/XXVI, signed and numbered

EDITION FOR PARKETT 72

Woodstock revisited, where memory resides
in the backlit darkness of invented mythology.

"He owns concretely. He owns the stuff of his (and
our culture's) dreams—houses, rare books, and
cars—and he turns that stuff into art by hijacking
their images. He acquired all that he has by taking
aesthetic possession. His work, by employing a canny
approach to the mediated image, takes abstract
ownership of a type of imagery that deals with desire
and consumption."

Dike Blair
Parkett No. 72, 2004

リチャード・プリンス

これからはフリー・コンサート　2004

エクタクローム・プリント、
紙：76.2×101.6cm、
図柄：76.2×85.1cm、
Ed. 66/XXVI、署名、番号入り

パルケット・エディション 72

ウッドストック再訪。記憶は背後から光に照らされる
作り物の神話のなかにある。

プリンスは具体的にとりこむ。自分（そして我々の文化）が夢見
たもの、家、稀覯本、車をとりこみ、イメージをハイジャックし、そ
れらを美術作品にしたてあげる。手持ちの物はすべて、美しさを
我が物とすることによって入手した。プリンスの作品は媒介された
イメージに抜け目ない接近法を採用することより、欲望と消費に関
わる類のイメージの抽象的な所有権を確立する。

ダイク・ブレア
（パルケット 72号、2004年）

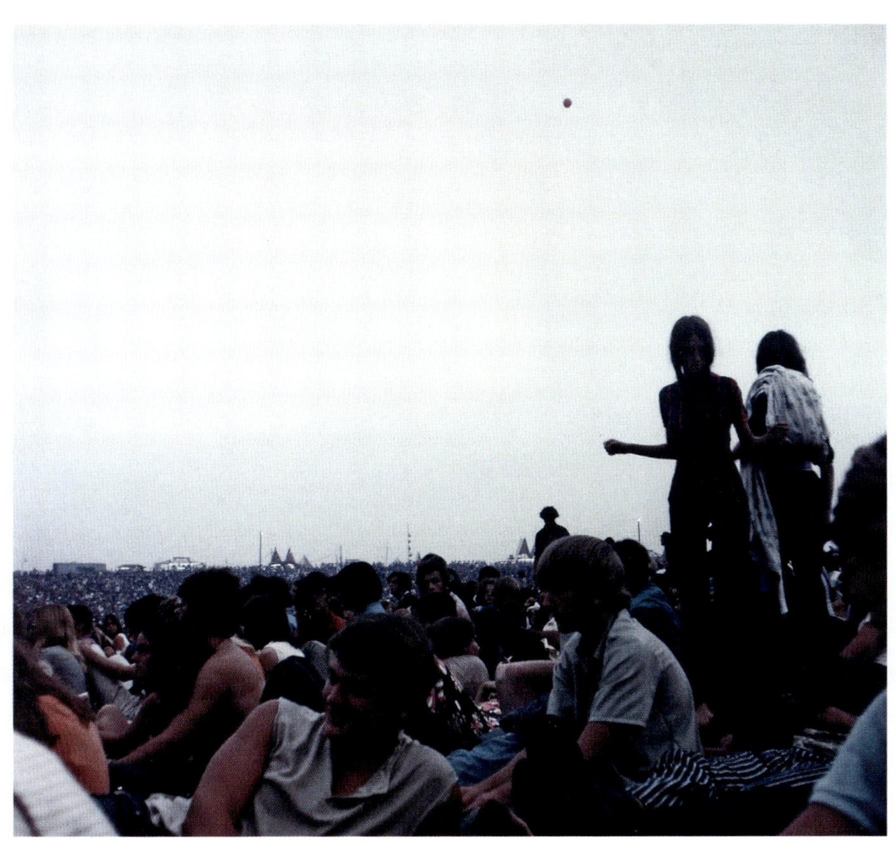

Woodstock 1969. I took this picture Friday evening around seven thirty. I had just turned nineteen. It was the only picture I took that weekend. I had gone to Woodstock with only one exposure in my camera. I thought I could buy film in the nearest town. Not knowing what I was getting into, I thought I could get out of it. You know, "come and go." "Coming" was hard enough (it took six hours to travel the last twenty miles), and "leaving" was impossible. Anyway, realizing I was there to stay, I decided not to save my only exposure but rather get rid of it as fast as I could. So I just stood up, whirled around and (click) took it.   – Richard Prince

MICHAEL RAEDECKER

The Other Side, 2002

13-color silkscreen print on pure silk
satin scarf with handrolled border,
33 1/2 x 33 1/2" (81,2 x 81,2 cm),
detail from the back of the painting
INCOMPLETE (2002), produced by
Fabric Frontline, Zurich,
Ed. 99/LI, signed and numbered
certificate

EDITION FOR PARKETT 65

Twice incomplete yields complete perfection: a humble shack threaded in reverse visibility and reproduced on exquisite silk.

"It has rightly been said that Michael Raedecker's paintings are 'unsettling': we do not readily comprehend what is actually happening in them nor do they offer us an ideal viewing distance from which we might feel that the image coalesces into an accessible whole. The paint, the various kinds of threads, and the other materials sometimes pasted and painted over, work at cross purposes. (...) On closer examination, loose hairs and threads stuck into the paint, along with protruding lumps of paint, evoke miniature landscapes, which then again approximate the complete image first seen in the painting, and so on."

Bart Verschaffel
Parkett No. 65, 2002

マイケル・レデッカー

反対側　2002

13色刷りシルクスクリーン・プリント、
純絹サテン・スカーフ、縁は手縫いでまつり絎け、
81.2×81.2cm、絵画作品《未完成》裏面の部分図、
制作：ファブリック・フロントライン（チューリヒ）、
Ed. 99/LI、署名、番号入り証明書

パルケット・エディション 65

2度の未完成が完璧な完成にいたる。糸で縫われ見えないはずが見えるようになったみすぼらしい小屋が、素晴らしいシルクに再現される。

マイケル・レデッカーのペインティングは見るものを動揺させるという主張は正しい。そこで何か起こっているのかすぐにはわからないし、イメージがとっつきやすい全体像に溶けこむと思えるような、絵を見るのに最適な距離もあたえてくれない。絵具、様々な種類の糸、それからなにやかやが糊付けされ、そのうえから絵具を塗られたものも、さっぱりまとまりがない。近寄って詳しく調べれば、ほつれた髪と糸が絵具にくっつき、突き出した絵具のかたまりと重なって、ミニチュアの風景をおもわせるが、それがまた絵を見たときに最初に目についた全体像に近いものになるという具合である。

バート・フェルシャフェル
（パルケット 65号、2002年）

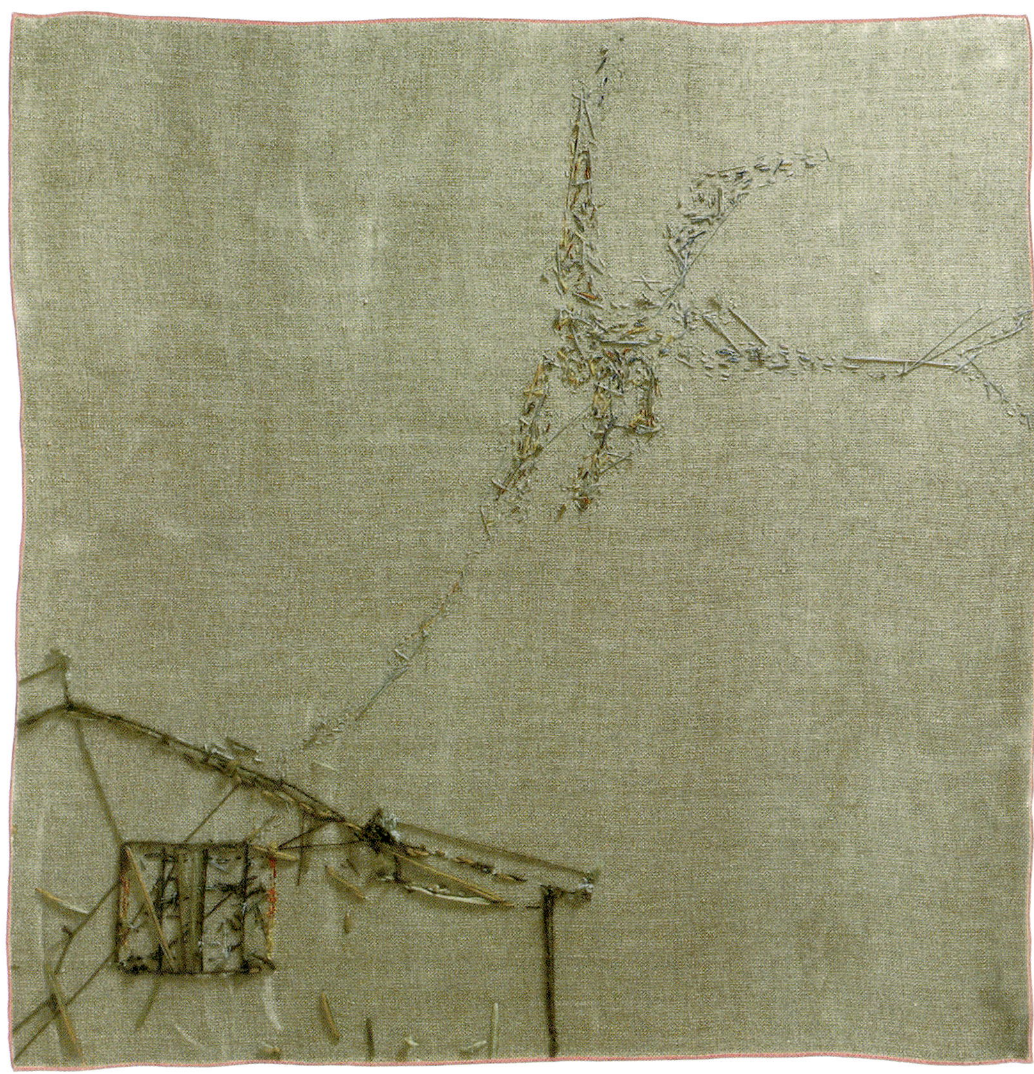

MARKUS RAETZ

Untitled, 1986

Aquatint and sugar lift on
Zerkall-Vellum, bound in the magazine,
10 x 16¹/₂" (25,4 x 42 cm),
printed by Peter Kneubühler, Zurich,
Ed. 100/XV, signed and numbered

EDITION FOR PARKETT 8

Tunnel vision. As perception reaches out into the world, so the perceptible world reaches in. A visual conundrum captured in an image as whimsical and mysterious as Zen koan.

"Since the 1960s, Markus Raetz has been playing with a perspective that is not mathematical but at once pragmatic and intuitive. It leads him to explore distortions obtained by certain—extravagances of perspective, sometimes pushed to the point of anamorphisis. Such works present a problematic of the function of sight, replacing the conventional hierarchy of the eye over the world."

Claude Ritschard
Parkett No. 42, 1994

マークス・レーツ

無題　1986

アクアチント、シュガーリフト、
ツェルカル社製ヴェラム紙、
本誌に綴じこみ、25.4×42cm、
刷り：ペーター・クノイビューラー（チューリヒ）、
Ed. 100/XV、署名、番号入り

パルケット・エディション 8

棒視（視野狭窄の一種）。知覚が世界に手をさしのべれば、知覚しうる世界が向こうから近寄ってくる。禅の公案のように、気まぐれで神秘的なイメージに捉えられた視覚の語呂合わせ。

1960年代以降、マークス・レーツは遠近法と戯れてきたが、それは数学的というより実際的、直観的なものだった。そこからレーツはある種の遠近法の行き過ぎ、時には歪像作用を起こすまでに追いこまれた遠近法のもたらす歪みを検証しはじめた。そうした作品は視覚の機能にまつわる不確定要素を明らかにし、目が世界に対して優位に立つ旧来の上下関係を放逐する。

クロード・リチャード
（パルケット 42号、1994年）

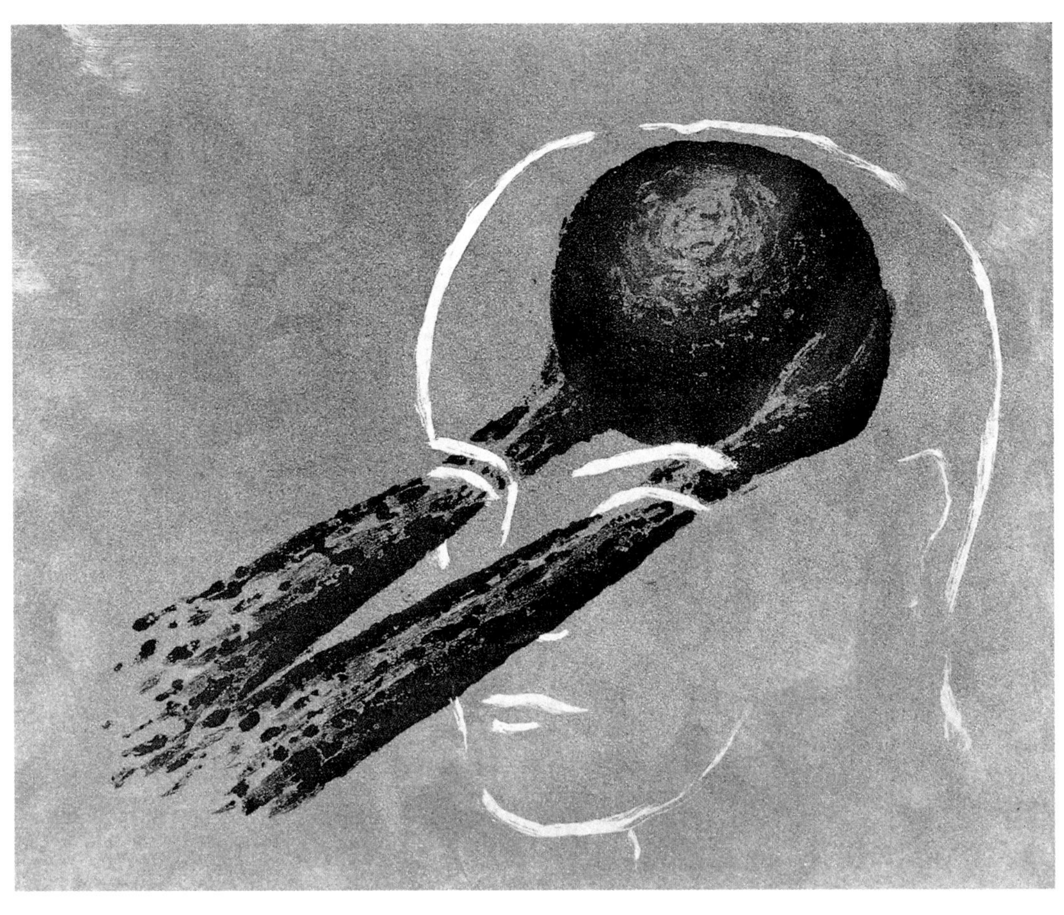

CHARLES RAY

The Most Beautiful Woman in
the World, 1993

Photo edition, each comprising a set
of nine unique color snapshots of
Tatjana Patitz, 4 x 6" (14,8 x 10,2 cm),
Ed. 60/XXIII, signed and numbered

EDITION FOR PARKETT 37

Between real and ideal. A relentless informal
photo session with supermodel Tatjana
Patitz yielded disarmingly familiar keepsake
snapshots of an extraordinary girl next door.

"Generic, infinitely reproducible, Ray himself became
the consumerized ideal, an American standard, at
once the victim and the victimizer of technological
replication."

Klaus Kertess
Parkett No. 37, 1993

チャールズ・レイ

世界で一番美しい女性　1993

写真のエディション、
それぞれタチアナ・パティッツの9枚の
カラー・スナップ写真のセットからなる、
14.8×10.2cm、
Ed. 60/XXIII、署名、番号入り

パルケット・エディション 37

現実と理想の間。スーパーモデルのタチアナ・パティッ
ツの普段着の姿を執拗に撮影した結果、ご近所の素敵
なお嬢さんの、見ているとつい頬が綻びそうなスナッ
プ写真ができあがった。

ありきたりで、いくらでも複製できるレイ自身が、消費生活の理想
像、アメリカ的基準となり、先進技術を用いたレプリカ作りの犠牲
者、加害者両方の役回りを一手に引き受けた。

クラウス・ケルテス
（パルケット 37号、1993年）

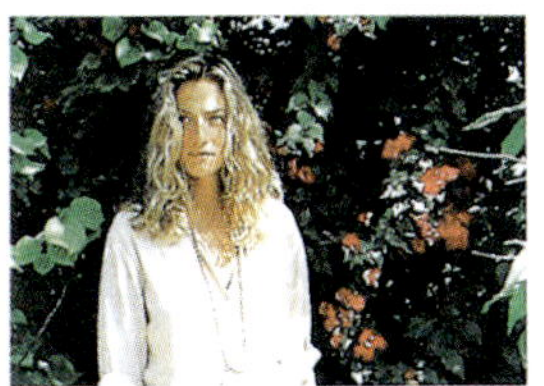
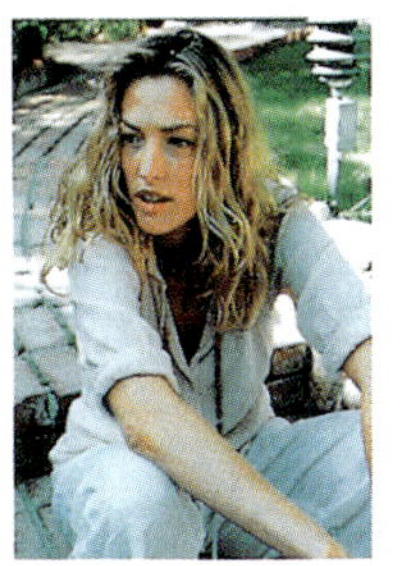
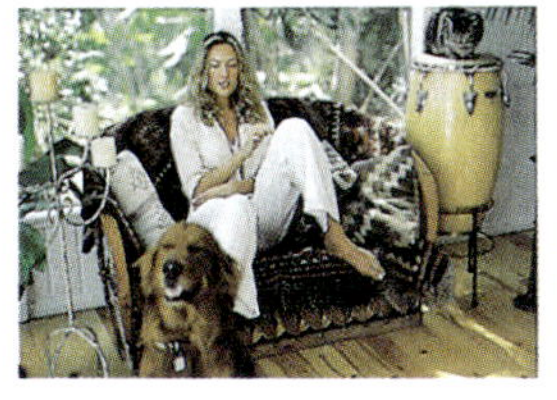
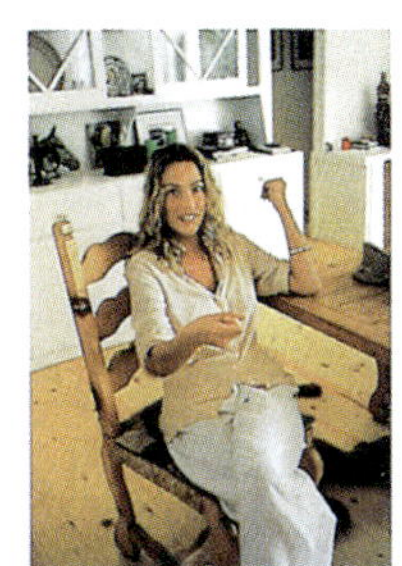
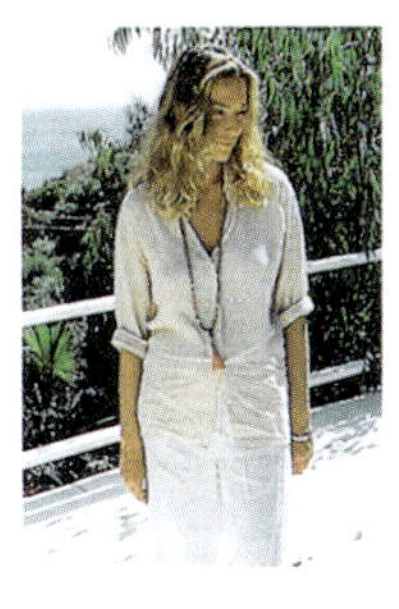
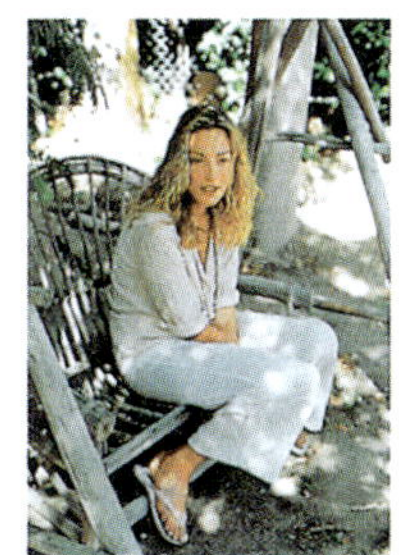
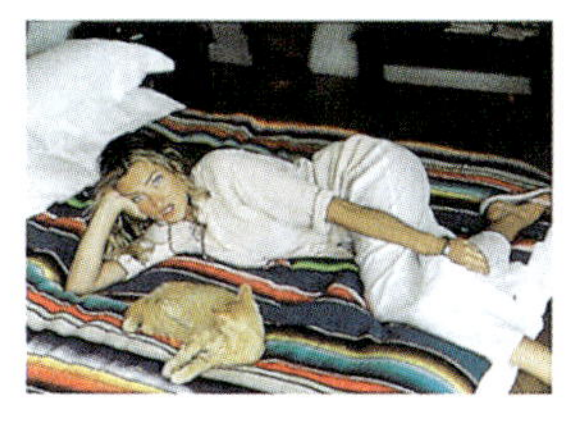
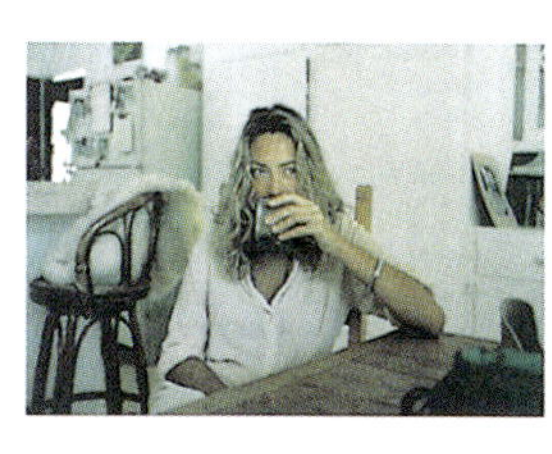
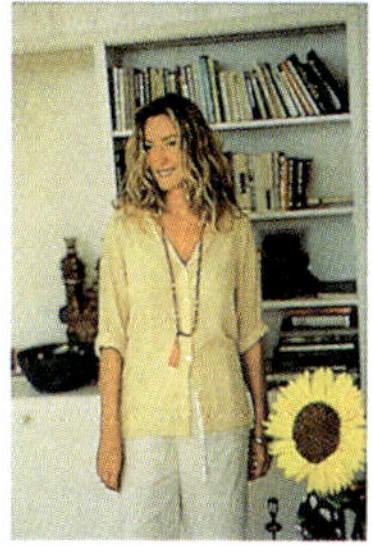
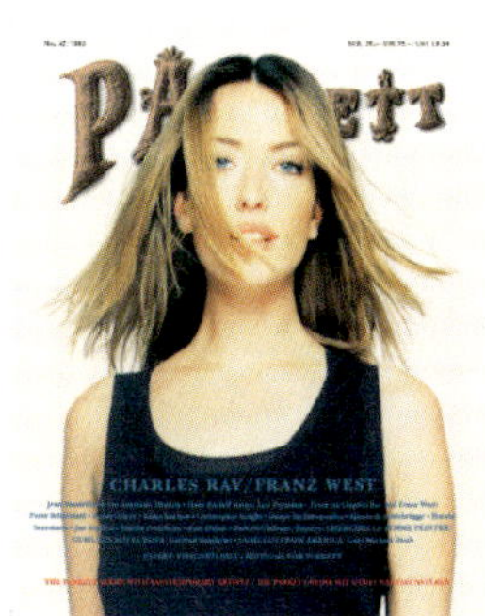

Parkett Cover 37

JASON RHOADES

Bottle Pumpkin from Perfect World,
2000

Hand-painted gourd with seeds
that last 2000 years, backpack
(each different), 11 snapshots,
round cardboard container/pedestal,
Ed. 70/XX, signed and numbered
certificate

EDITION FOR PARKETT 58

Ready for traveling. Jason Rhoades has
distilled the eclectic world of his rampant
installations into a single gourd.

"'...When I build something, I build it for literally two
or three people, for the interaction at that point.'
Despite the often gigantic scale on which he works,
the essence of his practice remains surprisingly
intimate. The larger-than-life stereotypes that fill
Rhoades's work fade into their real role. They are
merely vehicles that get the artist and his audience
to somewhere else. In the end the smoke and mirrors
of explanation with which Rhoades both illuminates
and obfuscates his work act like the mile of string that
Duchamp wound around the space of the 'First Papers
of Surrealism' exhibition in 1942, a simultaneously
translucent yet impenetrable medium within which
floats the real content of the work."

Russell Ferguson
Parkett No. 58, 2000

ジェイソン・ローズ

パーフェクト・ワールドからやってきた
瓶型カボチャ　2000

手で着色したひょうたん、
2000年生命を保つ種入り、
バックパック（個々に異なる）、
11枚のスナップ写真、
ボール紙製円形収納箱（台座）、
Ed. 70/XX、署名、番号入り証明書

パルケット・エディション 58

いざ旅立とう。ジェイソン・ローズは奔放なインスタ
レーション作品のなんでもありの世界を蒸留して、たっ
たひとつのひょうたんに中身を収めた。

「なにか作るとき、ぼくはほんとうに2、3人のひとのために、その
ときの付き合いを深めるために作っているんです」。作品の規模は
しばしば巨大であっても、作家活動の本質はいつでも驚くほどの親
密さを保った。ローズの作品にみちあふれる桁外れのステレオタイ
プは、しずしずと本来の役割に収まる。ローズが説明と称する煙幕
と鏡の類は、作品をときあかすと同時にいっそうわけがわからなく
させて、つまるところデュシャンが1942年に企画した「第1回ペー
パー・オブ・シュルレアリズム展」の会場に張りめぐらせた全長1マイ
ルの紐と同じように、透き通っていながら通過はできないメディアと
して作用し、作品の真の内容はそのなかに浮遊する。

ラッセル・ファーガソン
（パルケット 58号、2000年）

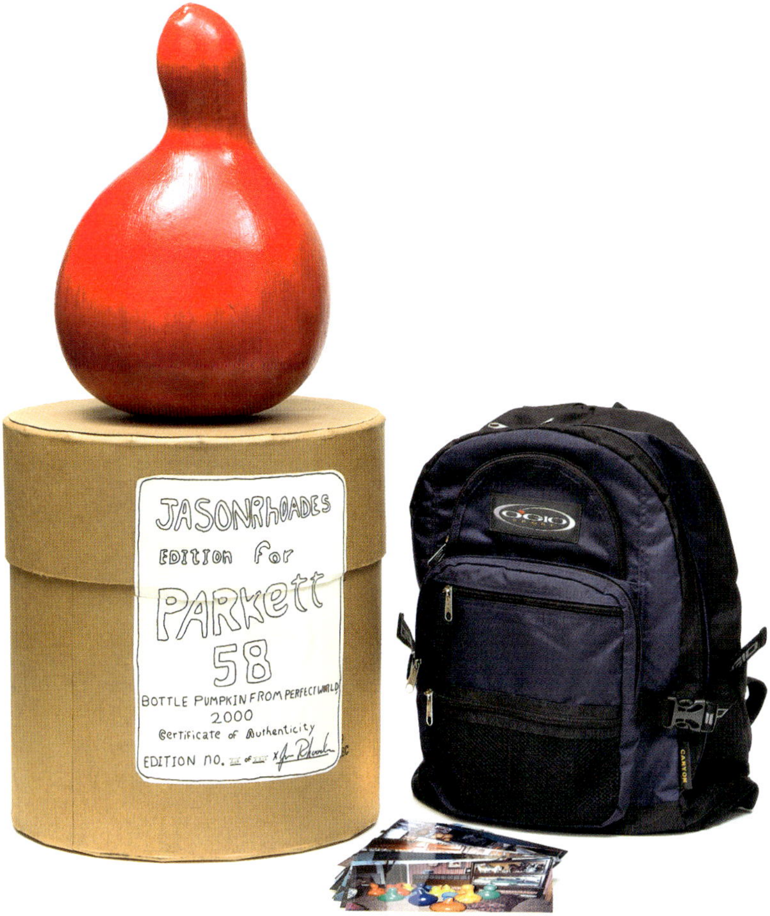

JASONRHOADES
EDITION for
PARKETT
58
BOTTLE PUMPKIN FROM PERFECT WORLD
2000
Certificate of Authenticity
EDITION NO. XX of XXV

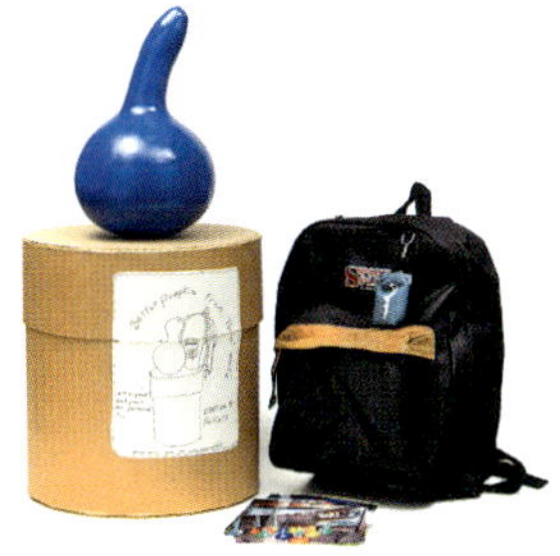

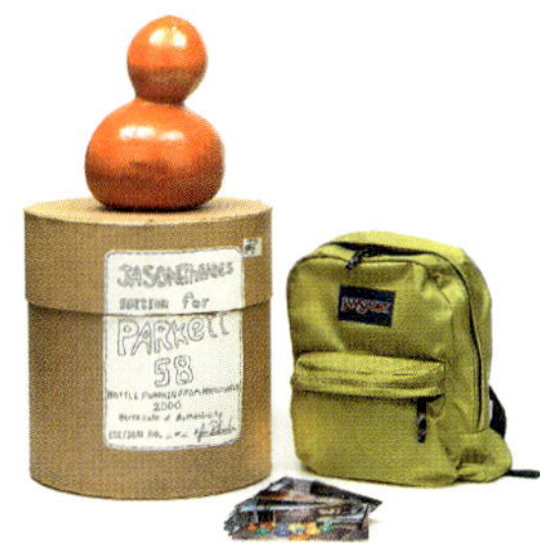

GERHARD RICHTER

Green-Blue-Red, 1993

Oil on canvas,
11 $^4/_5$ x 15 $^3/_4$" (30 x 40 cm) each,
Ed. of 115 originals, signed and
numbered (789–1 to 789–115) on verso

EDITION FOR PARKETT 35

Theme and variation. A sequence of original
paintings chart the chromatic flux of a flow of
iridescent hues.

"Gerhard Richter's work investigates and explores
malaise—that void, that gap, that speck of death,
that violence we carry inside us—reality as a screen
compared to the unbearable real. Painting inscribes
the tragic dimension—tragedy concerning that area
where death encroaches on life."

Birgit Pelzer
Parkett No. 35, 1993

ゲルハルト・リヒター

緑 - 青 - 赤　1993

カンヴァスに油彩、30×40cm、
オリジナル作品 115点、
裏面に署名と番号 (789-1 から 789-115 まで) 入り

パルケット・エディション 35

主題と変奏。油彩によるオリジナル作品の連なりが、
光沢のある色相の流れのたえまない変化を図示する。

ゲルハルト・リヒターの作品は不安を探り、究めようとする。わたし
たちの心についてまわるあの虚しさ、もどかしさ、死の予感、そして
暴力、つまり堪えがたい現実と対比される映写幕としての真実性。
絵画は悲劇的色彩を銘記する。悲劇は死が生を蚕食する領域に
およぶ。

ブリギット・ペルツァー
（パルケット 35号、1993年）

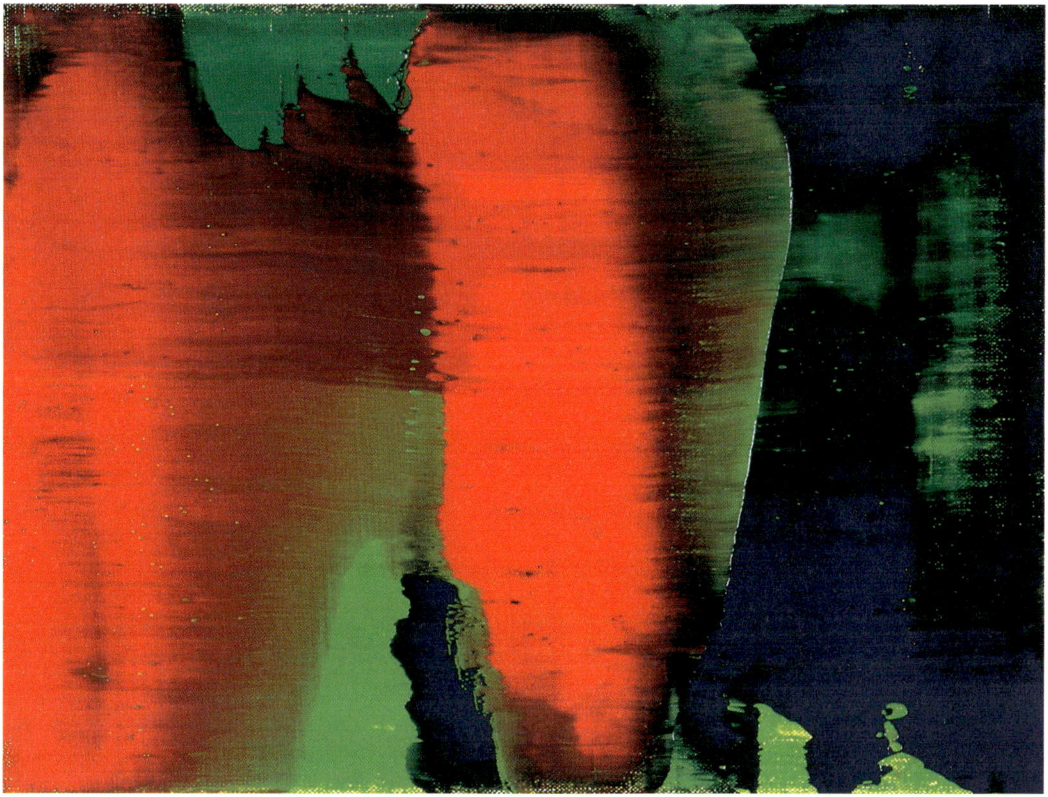

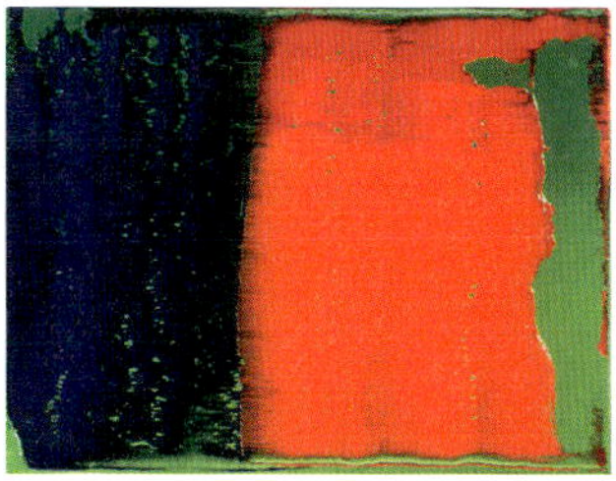

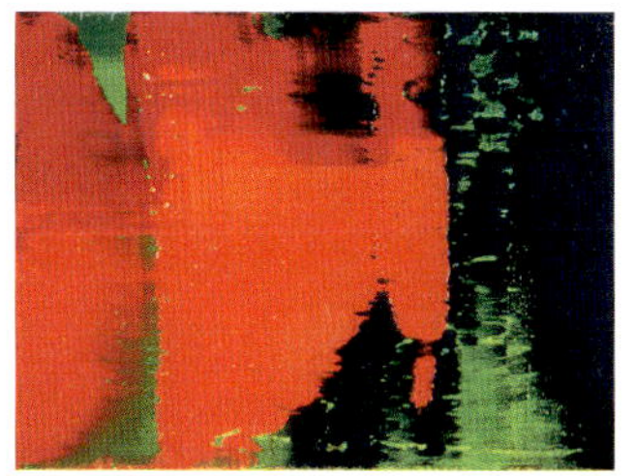

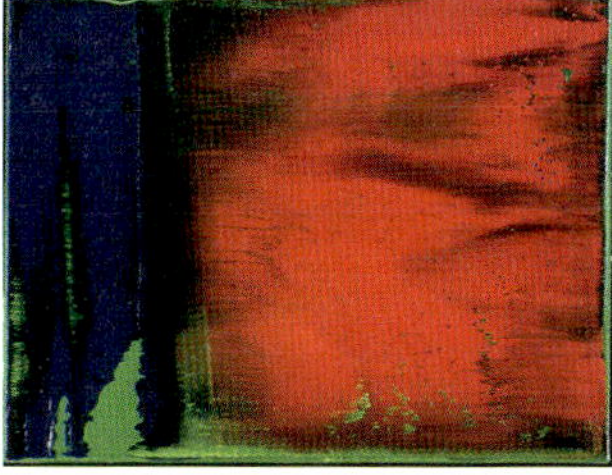

BRIDGET RILEY

Going Across, 2001

Silkscreen print on Somerset satin,
paper size: 24 1/4 x 36" (61,6 x 91,4 cm),
image size: 16 1/2 x 28 7/8" (42 x 73 cm),
printed by Sally Gimson for
Artizan Editions, Hove, England,
Ed. 90/X, signed and numbered

EDITION FOR PARKETT 61

Elusive illusion: no foreground, no background, no depth, no surface, and all of them at once.

"By seducing and conflating the relationship between shape and pattern, Riley's paintings invariably compromise both the spatial arrangements that relate pattern to syntax and the autonomous boundaries that relate shapes to external referents. This persistent, subversive instability is the single constant in Riley's practice—the attribute that keeps her paintings from devolving into dead formalism or dissolving into absent signification."

Dave Hickey
Parkett No. 61, 2001

ブリジット・ライリー

よこぎってゆく　2001

サマーセット・サテン紙に
シルクスクリーン・プリント、
紙：61.6×91.4cm、図柄：42×73cm、
刷り：サリー・ギムソン、
アーティザン・エディションズ（ホーヴ市、イギリス）、
Ed. 90/X、署名、番号入り

パルケット・エディション 61

つかまえにくい幻覚。前景もなく、背景もなく、奥行きもなく、表面もなく、そして同時にそのすべてであるような。

形と図案の関係を誘惑、融合させることによって、ライリーの絵画は図案を文法にむすびつける空間の配置と、形を外部の指示対象に結びつける自律的な境界の双方をつねに危うくする。この執拗な、周囲の安寧を破綻させかねない不安定性こそ、ライリーの創作活動に一貫する唯一の要因だろう。これがあるために、ライリーの絵画は血の気の失せたフォルマリズムに転落することも、意味の不在に解消することも免れる。

デイヴ・ヒッキー
（パルケット 61号、2001年）

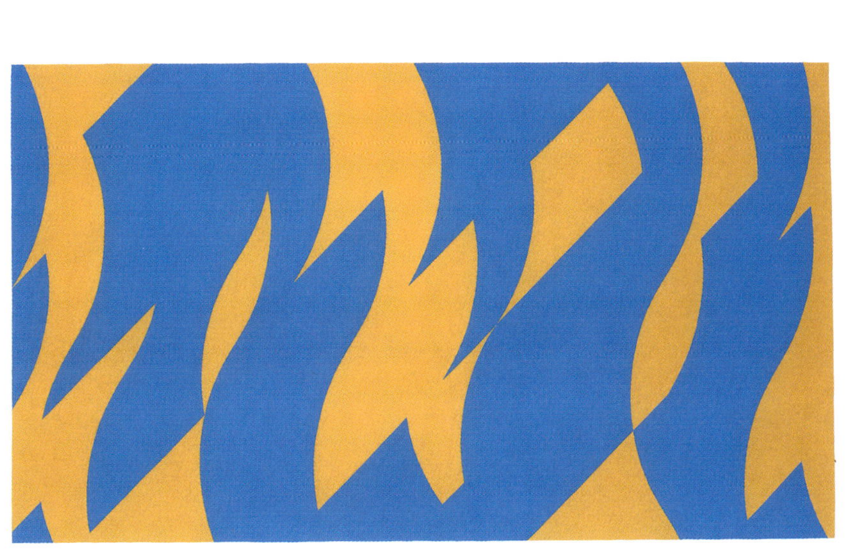

PIPILOTTI RIST

I've Only Got Eyes for You—
(Pin Down Jump Up Girl), 1996

3-D image, color photograph under
lenticulated film, mounted on flexible
plastic with four suction cups, to be
attached to TV screen when not in use,
photograph by Rita Palanikumar,
8¼ x 11" (20,8 x 27,8 cm),
Ed. 80/XX, signed and numbered

EDITION FOR PARKETT 48

Peeping tomboy. Are you lonesome tonight?

"Pipilotti Rist… exploits the general acceptance of the
video medium as a kind of substitute for the easel
painting—and, above all, its role as a component of
spatial installations. The specific appeal of video, as
employed by Rist, also incorporates such shadow
disciplines as the pop video, the television commercial,
and the trailer. Here, Rist's idiom, schooled in
Expanded Cinema, receives a highly contemporary
infusion of entertainment value. The rheme of art has
become her theme; hence the self-dramatization that
encompasses not only the means of production but
also her existential self-definition as a subject within
society, as a woman, and as an artist."

Marius Babias
Parkett No. 48, 1996

ピピロッティ・リスト

あなたしか見えない
（ピン・ダウン・ジャンプ・アップ・ガール）
1996

3-D 映像、カラー写真に
微小凸レンズフィルムを被せ
4個の吸引カップをとりつけた柔軟の
あるプラスティックにマウント、
不使用時はテレビの画面にとりつける、
写真：リタ・パラニクマール、20.8×27.8cm、
Ed. 80/XX、署名、番号入り

パルケット・エディション 48

覗き見の好きなお転婆さん、今夜はひとりかい？

ピピロッティ・リストはメディアとしてのビデオがイーゼル絵画の
一種の代替物として、とりわけ一定の空間を占めるインスタレーショ
ンの構成要素としての役割を一般に認められている事実を活用する。
リストのビデオ作品の魅力は、ポップ・ビデオやテレビのコマーシャ
ル、予告編など日陰の分野を採り入れたこととも無縁ではない。こう
して、リストの作風は「Expanded Cinema」に学び、きわめて現代
的な娯楽としての価値を注入される。芸術のテーマがリストのテー
マとなり、制作手段ばかりか社会のなかに生きるひとりの人間、女性、
そしてアーティストとしての実存的な自己の実体認識までも視野に
収めた自己の演劇化が発生する。

マリウス・バビアス
（パルケット 48号、1996年）

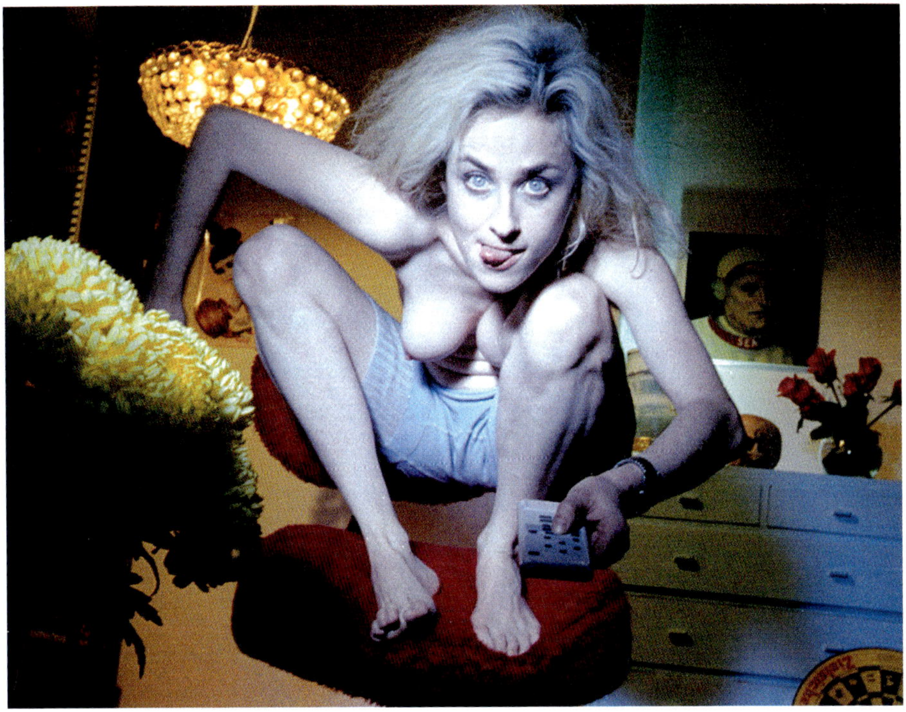

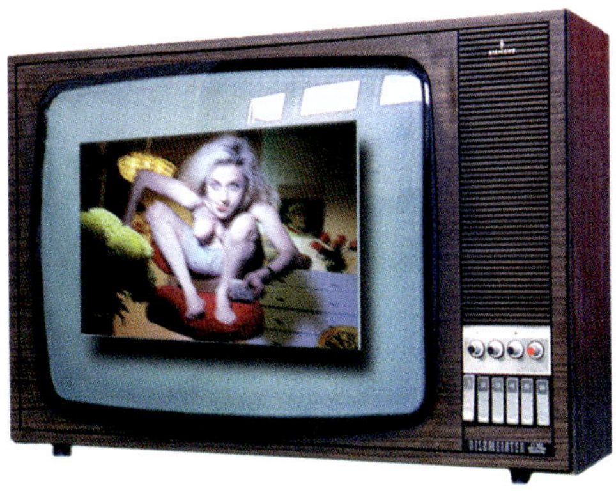

PIPILOTTI RIST

The Help, 2004

Cut-out, 4-color print on fabric,
ca. 70 $^7/_8$ x 43 $^5/_{16}$" (178 x 110 cm),
with 7 straight pins (plus 7 spare pins)
to fasten it to a wall, a chair, or a table,
support, Thomas Ryner, Photo by
Martin Stollenwerk, printed by
Plotfactory, Weisslingen, Switzerland,
Ed. 70/XX, signed and numbered

EDITION FOR PARKETT 71

Delusions of grandeur: When the help takes
a rest and joins us at table.

"I keep working at my material until it resembles my
own synaptic activities and mental states. Aren't all
cultural practitioners motivated and driven by the
need to materialize their inner images as a means of
escapting their isolation?"

Piplotti Rist, interview with Elisabeth Roth
Parkett No. 71, 2004

ピピロッティ・リスト

ヘルプ　2004

切り抜き、布地に4色刷り、178×110cm、
壁・椅子・テーブルなどにとりつけるための
まっすぐなピン7本（スペア7本）、
サポート：トマス・ライナー、
写真：マーティン・ストーレンヴェルク、
刷り：フロットファクトリー
　（ヴァイスリンゲン市、スイス）、
Ed. 70/XX、署名、番号入り

パルケット・エディション 71

誇大妄想。助けが休みをとり、ともにテーブルを囲む
とき。

素材がわたし自身の染色体の活動や心理状態に似てくるまで、作
業をつづけます。文化に関わるひとは誰でも、孤独から逃れるため
に、心の中にあるイメージを形あるものにする必要に迫られ、そう
するように駆り立てられているのではないでしょうか。

ピピロッティ・リスト、
エリザベス・ロスのインタヴューに応えて
　（パルケット 71号、2004年）

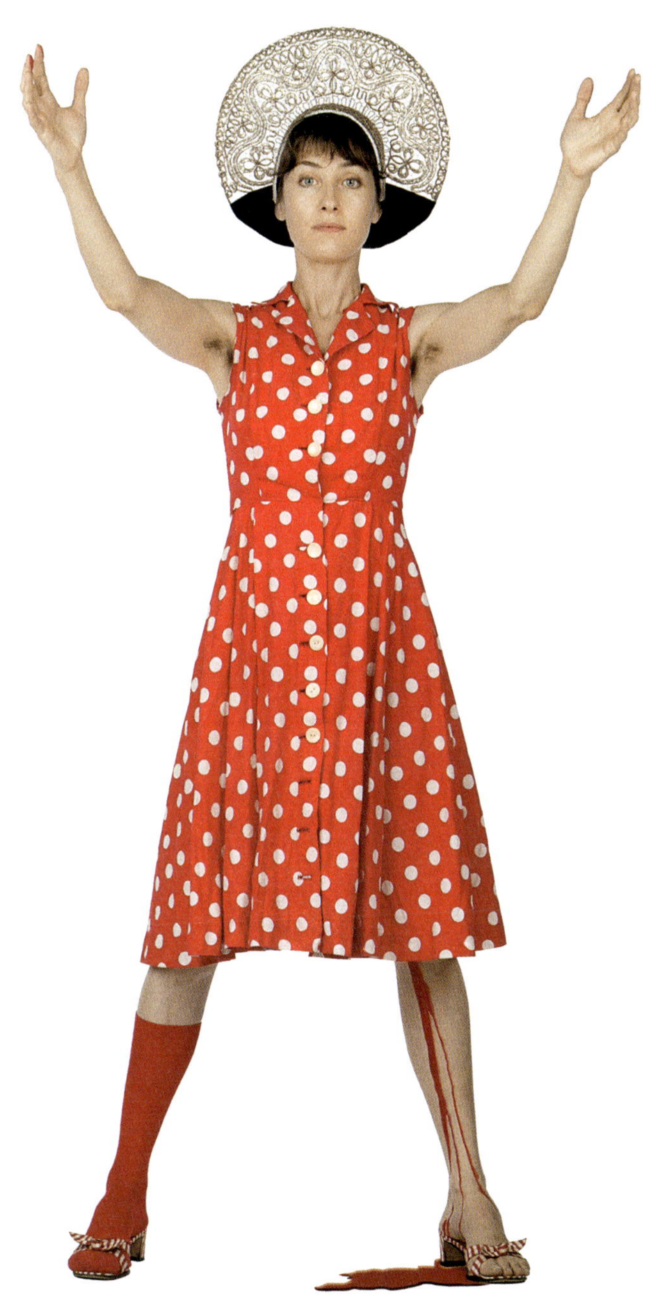

MATTHEW RITCHIE

The Bad Need, 2001

Wall work, cut-out of adhesive-
backed vinyl, approx. 36 $\frac{1}{4}$ x 40 $\frac{1}{4}$"
(95,2 x 106,6 cm), to be installed at a
height of 41 $\frac{1}{2}$" (105,5 cm) o.c. on a wall
surface (with a minimum size of
96 x 72" / 243,7 x 183 cm) painted
with the eggshell acrylic paint supplied
as part of the edition, accompanied
by an annotated artist's book,
Ed. 70/XXVIII, signed and numbered

EDITION FOR PARKETT 61

The writing on the wall as universal pattern.

"Matthew Ritchie is interested in the trace, the mark,
the diagrammatic and inscriptural aspects of science.
Powerful abstractions of the world, these graphemes
are made to intersect in his work with other
abstractions drawn from popular culture: computer
avatars, Japanese anime, film noir. Looking at his
paintings is like being in one of Dorothy's cyclones—
one minute a one-celled organism wheels by, the next
minute a sequence of skulls streams along from a
school chart on evolution. All are bound together in
a furiously active matrix of colors applied in umixed
adjacent tones... the flat juxtapositions make it seem
map-like... although there is enough play with values
to destabilize that reading and create some sense
of depth in the whirling forms."

Peter Galison & Caroline Jones
Parkett No. 61, 2001

マシュー・リッチー

悪い必要　2001

壁にとりつける作品、
裏面が粘着性のビニールの切り抜き、
95.2×106.6cm、
壁面の高さ105.5cmの位置に掛ける、
壁はエディション付属の低光沢アクリル塗料で塗装、
アーティストによる解説冊子付き、
Ed. 70/XXVIII、署名、番号入り

パルケット・エディション 61

壁に書いた宇宙の雛型。

マシュー・リッチーは痕跡、形跡、刻印を残す科学の側面に興味
をもつ。世界に源を発する強力な抽出物であるこれらの書記素は、
リッチーの作品の中で、コンピューターのアバター、日本のアニメ、
フィルム・ノワールなど、大衆文化から集めた他の抽出物と交錯
する。リッチーの絵を見るのは、「オズの魔法使い」の主人公ドロ
シーをまきこんだ竜巻の中にいるようなもので、単細胞の有機物
が目の前を横切ったとおもうそばから、動物の進化の様子を描い
た学校のポスターから抜け出したような、頭蓋骨のパレードが現れ
るといった案配。そのすべてが、隣り合う色調の入り混じらない鮮
烈な色彩のマトリックスによって、ひとつに結びつく……そうした
読解をあやふやにし、渦巻くフォルムに奥行き感をあたえる価値観
との戯れは十分に行われているにしても、平面上に対置されている
ため、地図のような印象をともなう。

ピーター・ギャリソン、キャロライナ・ジョーンズ
（パルケット 61号、2001年）

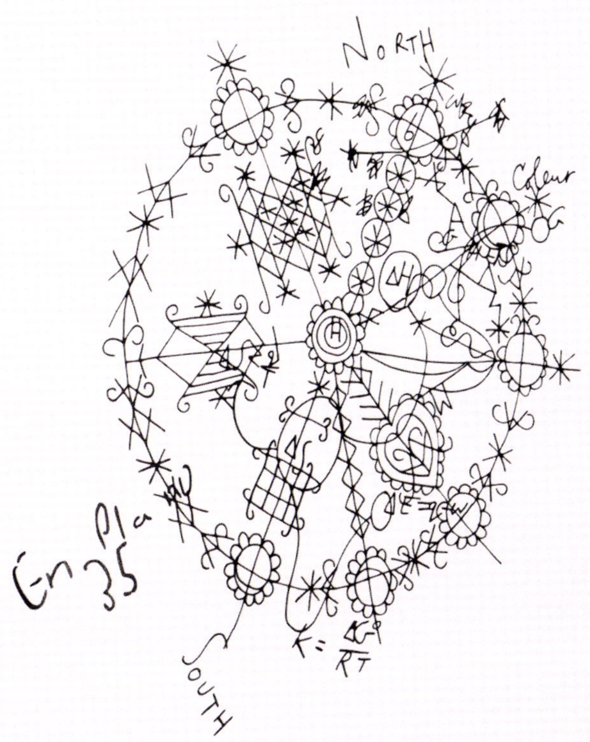

NORTH
Couleur
En Pl a 35
SOUTH

TIM ROLLINS + K.O.S.

Winterreise – Wasserfluth, 1989

Acryl, mica and offset print on
Saunders rag, mounted on rag board,
11 $^7/_8$ x 8 $^{15}/_{16}$" (30,2 x 22,7 cm),
Ed. 80/XX A. P., originals, signed and
numbered

EDITION FOR PARKETT 20

Visual music. In a school in the Bronx, Tim
Rollins + K.O.S. immerse themselves in
Schubert's "Winterreise." The result: a page
of the score as pale as snow—a sign of
conciliation and a gathering of new strength.

"Tim Rollins: I love what we do with our projects. We
drive people crazy because they can't figure out what
it is. Is it social work? Is it a school? Is it an art project?
Is it a fraud? Is it socialism? Is it rehabilitation for
juvenile delinquents? Richard Cruz: All and none of
the above!"

Tim Rollins + K.O.S, dialogue
Parkett No. 20, 1989

ティム・ロリンズ ＋ K.O.S.

『冬の旅』／「溢れる涙」　1989

アクリル、雲母、
ソンダーズ・ラグ紙オフセット・プリント、
ラグボードにマウント、
30.2×22.7cm、
Ed. 80/XX A.P. すべてオリジナル、署名、番号入り

パルケット・エディション 20

目で見る音楽。ブロンクス区の学校で、ティム・ロリンズ
＋ K.O.S.はシューベルトの『冬の旅』に没頭する。その
結果生まれたものは、雪のように白い楽譜の1ページ。
それは宥和の徴、新たな力の結集。

ティム・ロリンズ「ぼくらのプロジェクトが気に入っていますよ。いっ
たい何がなんだか見当がつかなくて、みな頭を抱えているようだけ
ど。社会奉仕活動なのだろうか。これでも学校か。美術の作品作り
か。いんちきか。社会主義か。不良少年の更生活動かってね」
リチャード・クルス「その全部で、どれでもない！」

ティム・ロリンズ ＋ K.O.S.の対話
（パルケット 20号、1989年）

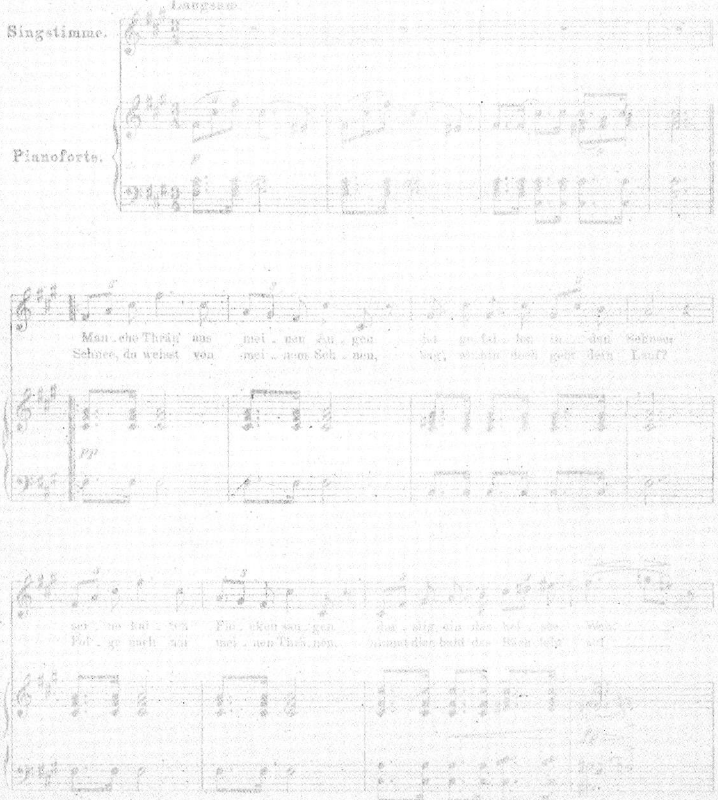

VI.
Wasserfluth
Langsam.
Singstimme.
Pianoforte.
Man . che Thrän' aus mei . nen Au . gen ist ge . fal . len in . . den Schnee,
Schnee, du weisst von mei . nem Seh . nen, sag', wohin doch geht dein Lauf?
ih . re kal . ten Flo . cken sau . gen dur . stig ein das hei . sse Weh.
Fol . ge nach nur mei . nen Thrä . nen, nimmt dich bald das Bäch . lein auf.
F. S. 493.

UGO RONDINONE

All Moments Stop Here and Together We Become Every Memory That Has Ever Been, 1998

Stone from the Valle Maggia, Ticino,
Switzerland, approx. 12 x 8 x 4"
(21,5 x 28 x 14 cm), approx. weight:
14 to 20 lbs. (7–10 kg), Polaroid photo
of the stone by the artist,
Ed. 50/XX, signed and numbered

EDITION FOR PARKETT 52

This too, too solid stone: all the world locked into the timeless embrace of the ages.

"The Pop dandy is aware of the aesthetic surfaces to which he owes his subjectivity and enjoys taking both serious and ironic stabs at it and himself. His melancholy is articulated in camp; he celebrates his longings in a lusty mix of excessive empathy and affectionate self-irony. He acts out his life in a self-devised aesthetic universe, an isolated space that is filled with the media of his longing, with the pictures and the music that he loves. There he plays a game of sentimental identification and contemplative self-detachment that allows him to enjoy his melancholy split ego."

Jan Verwoert
Parkett No. 52, 1998

ウーゴ・ロンディノーネ

すべての瞬間はここで停止し、我々はともに かつて存在したあらゆる記憶となる　1998

スイスのティッチーニ州マッジア峡谷で採取した石、
約21.5×28×14cm、約7-10kg、
石を作家が撮影したポラロイド写真、
Ed. 50/XX、署名、番号入り

パルケット・エディション 52

これもまた、じつに固い石。世界のすべてが時間を越えた時代の抱擁のなかに閉じこめられる。

ポップな伊達男は主観性の支えを美的表層と見抜いたうえで、そちらと自分自身に真面目でもあれば皮肉っぽくもある茶々を入れてご満悦。当人は気鬱を不似合いに表現する。願望は、度を越した感情移入と自身に向ける愛しげなアイロニーの旺盛な混淆により、祝福される。自ら編み出した美的世界、自らの願望のメディアで満ちた隔離された空間で、大好きな絵と音楽にあわせて自らの人生を演じきる。そこでロンディノーネが演じるのは、分裂した自我の憂鬱を楽しめる感傷的な自己確認、そして観照的な自己客観化のゲームである。

ヤン・フェルウォールト
（パルケット 52号、1998年）

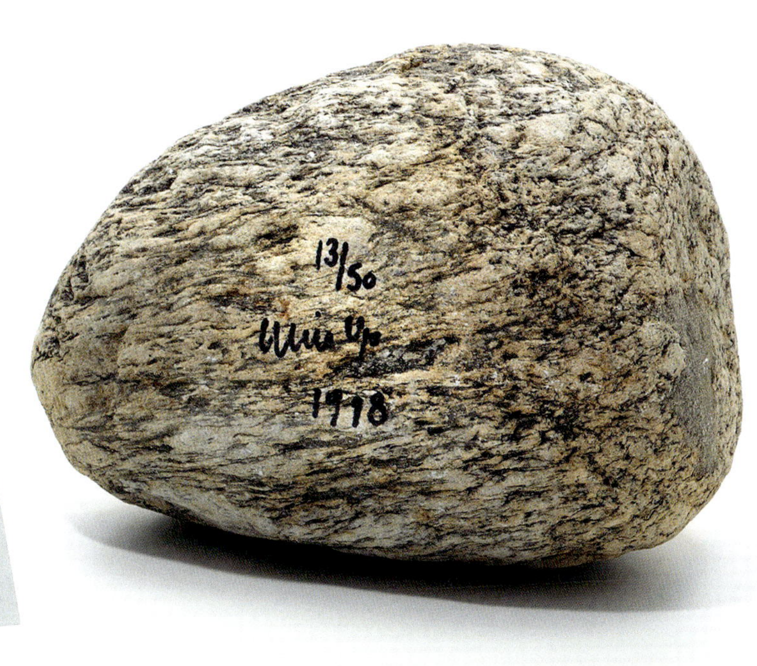

13/50
1978

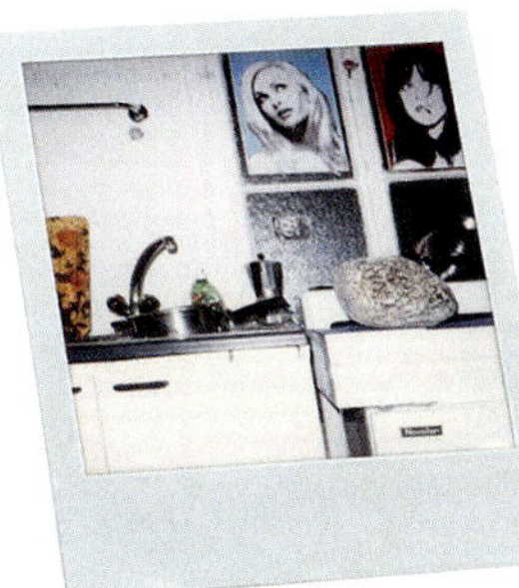

JAMES ROSENQUIST

Drifter: Speed of Light, 2000

9-color lithograph on Somerset soft white paper, 17 1/4 x 14 5/8" (44 x 37,1 cm), printed by Maurice Sanchez, Derrière L'Etoile Studio, New York, Ed. 60/XX, signed and numbered

EDITION FOR PARKETT 58

Macroscopic is not necessarily big. For once the artist renders his macro-universe on a single sheet of paper.

"James Rosenquist undoubtedly deserves to be called a 'monumentalist' among American Pop artists and his tactics clearly pay off when the relationship between 'subject matter' and 'size' is right. Twenty-five feet of painting at one stretch is not only a rarity in Pop art. The only exceptions, perhaps, are Claes Oldenburg's objects and a few of Andy Warhol's late works."

Zdenek Felix
Parkett No. 58, 2000

ジェームズ・ローゼンクィスト

漂流物。光速　2000

9色刷りリトグラフ、
サマーセット・ソフト・ホワイト紙：44×37.1cm、
刷り：モーリス・サンチェス、
デリエール・レトワール・スタジオ（ニューヨーク）、
Ed. 60/XX、署名、番号入り

パルケット・エディション 58

巨視的なものはかならずしも大きくなくてもよい。この時にかぎり、ローゼンクィストは自らの巨大な宇宙を1枚の紙に描ききった。

ジェームズ・ローゼンクィストがアメリカのポップ・アーティストの中で「超大作の描き手」と呼ばれる資格のあるのはたしかで、「主題」と「サイズ」が合致したときに、その戦略はじつに大きな成果をあげる。7.5メートルが一続きの絵には、ポップ・アートに限らず、滅多にお目に掛からない。わずかな例外としてクレス・オルデンバーグのオブジェと、アンディ・ウォーホルの晩年の作のいくつかがあるくらいだろう。

ズデニク・フェリックス
（パルケット 58号、2000年）

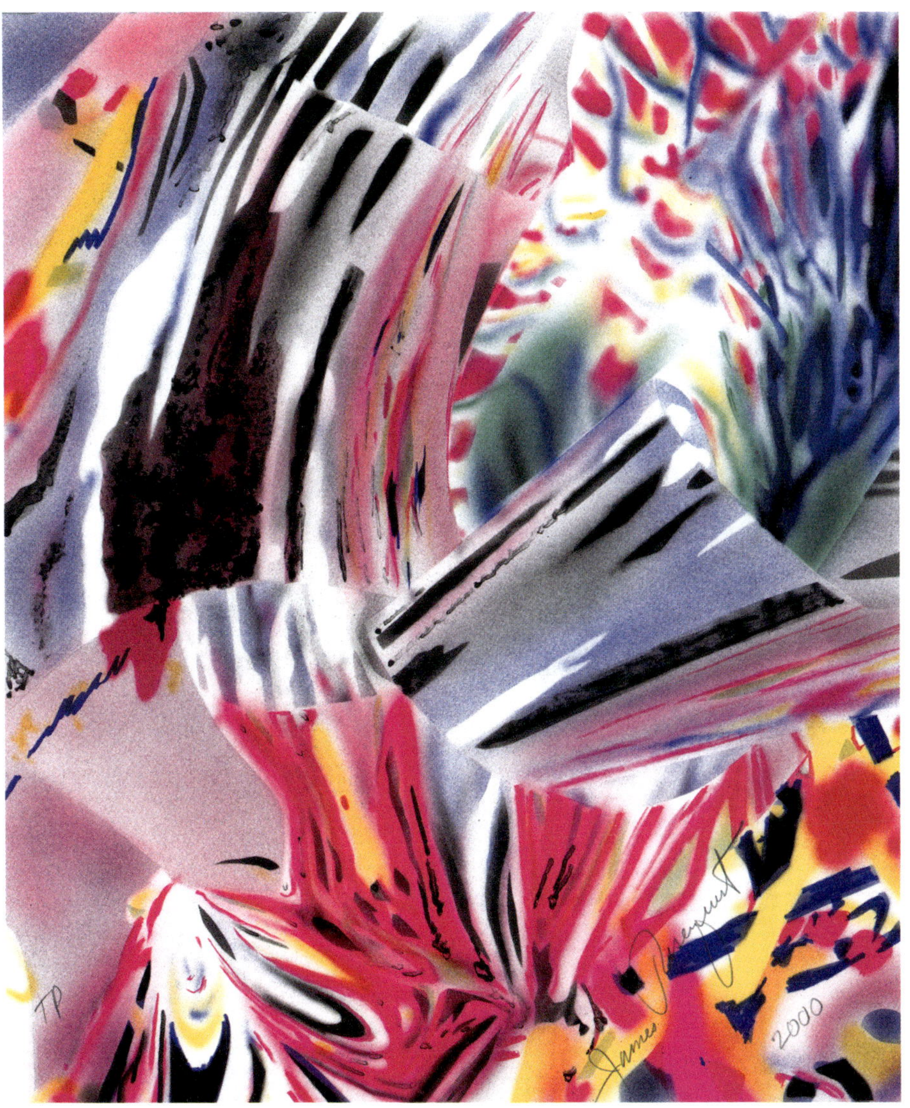
TP
James Rosenquist
2000

SUSAN ROTHENBERG

Bear Skin Rug, 1995

Synthetic latex,
12¼ x 12½ x 2" (31 x 32 x 5 cm),
cast by Art Foundry, Santa Fé,
Ed. 70/XX, signed and numbered

EDITION FOR PARKETT 43

Ursa Minor. A miniature pelt as talisman rather than trophy.

"Susan Rothenberg always outlines, structures, isolates emotion. She has transformed the sounding-board of painting into a sound shape. ... Breathing is metaphorically taken out of the painting and transferred to the subject matter. The painting is condensation, condensed in the subject matter, but the subject matter is not the prime mover of the painting. It joins the painting at the juncture of idea, immense feeling, and the necessity of painting."

Jean-Christophe Ammann
Parkett No. 43, 1995

スーザン・ローゼンバーグ

熊皮のラグ　1995

合成ゴム、31×32×5cm、
制作：美術鋳造社（サンタ・フェ）、
Ed. 70/XX、署名、番号入り

パルケット・エディション 43

小熊座。トロフィよりお守りにふさわしいミニチュア裸皮

スーザン・ローゼンバーグはいつでも感情の輪郭を示し、構成し、分離させる。絵の共鳴板を音の形に変化させる……呼吸は隠喩的に絵画から抜き取られ、主題に移し替えられた。絵画とは凝縮することであり、主題に凝縮されるけれども、主題は絵画の主な原動力ではない。主題は絵画を思想、巨大な感情、そして絵画の必要性の接点に結びつける。

ジャン＝クリストフ・アマン
（パルケット 43号、1995年）

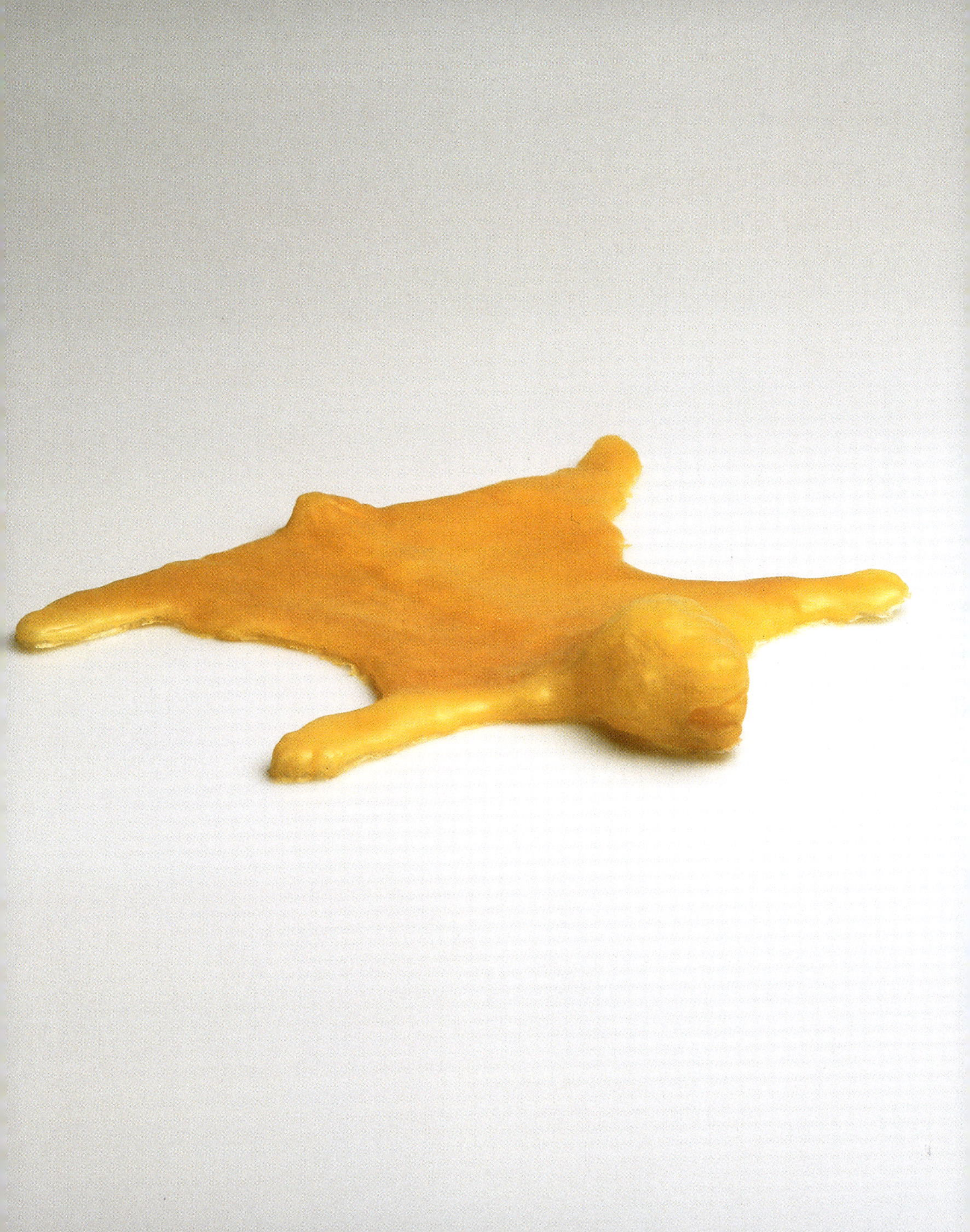

THOMAS RUFF

C-Prints, 1991

Two C-prints (photos: ESO),
each 19 1/2 x 19 1/2" (50 x 50 cm),
with astronomic data silkscreened on
front and back of transparent wrappers,
Ed. 50/X each, signed and numbered

EDITION FOR PARKETT 28

Milky ways. Phantasmagoric photographs of
the night sky and its galaxies are reversed
into peppered white fields upon which
a single lode-star is pinpointed by its
astronomical data.

"Common uses of the medium [photography], its
division into genres, its social function, and the ease
with which it can be misused, are themes which
pervade all of Ruff's work."

Marc Freidus
Parkett No. 28, 1991

トーマス・ルフ

Cプリント　1991

Cプリント2枚 (photos: ESO) 、各50×50cm、
透明カバーの表裏に天体のデータを
シルクスクリーン・プリント、
各Ed. 50/X、署名、番号入り

パルケット・エディション 28

天の川。夜空に輝く銀河を撮影した走馬灯をおもわ
せる写真は反転され、胡椒をまぶした白い広がりとな
り、そこに天体のデータにもとづき道標となる唯一の
星が正確に記される。

メディア (写真) の一般的な用法、ジャンルへの分類、社会的機能、
そして誤用の容易さがルフの作品のすべてに行き渡っている。

マーク・フレイダス
 (パルケット 28号、1991年)

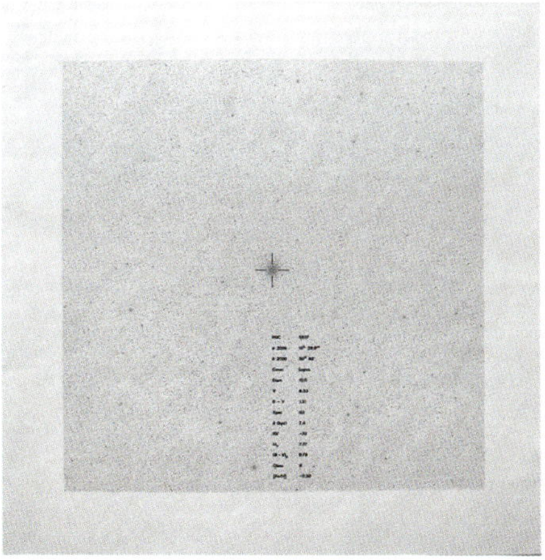

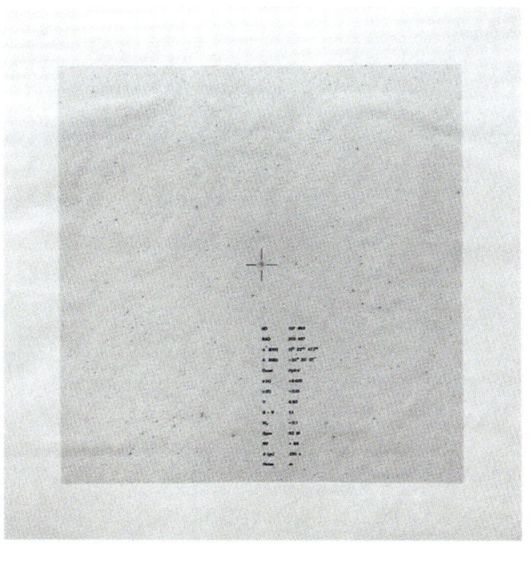

EDWARD RUSCHA

Hell ½ Way Heaven, 1988

Lithograph on Rives,
10 x 24" (25,5 x 61 cm),
bound in the magazine,
printed by Ed Hamilton, Los Angeles,
Ed. 80/18 A. P., signed and numbered

EDITION FOR PARKETT 18

Where in the world. Is Heaven up and Hell down, or vice-versa? In typically cryptic fashion, Ruscha leaves us in blue limbo, somewhere in-between.

"Ruscha's art is a vivid, and sometimes sweetly poignant, silhouette of the displaced psyche that fitfully inhabits mass culture."

Christopher Knight
Parkett No. 18, 1988

エドワード・ルシェ

Hell ½ Way Heaven
（地獄・中途・天国）　　1988

リトグラフ、リヴ紙：25.5×61cm、
本紙に綴じこみ、
刷り：エド・ハミルトン（ロサンゼルス）、
Ed. 80/18 A.P.、署名、番号入り

パルケット・エディション 18

世界のどこで。天国は上、地獄は下、それとも逆？持ち前の謎かけめいた方法で、ルシェはわたしたちをブルー・リンボ（蒼ざめた地獄の辺土）に、狭間のどこかに置き去りにする。

ルシェの作品は鮮烈で、ときに甘やかに胸をうつ、発作的に大衆文化に居場所を見いだす、行き場をなくした精神のシルエット。

クリストファー・ナイト
（パルケット 18号、1988年）

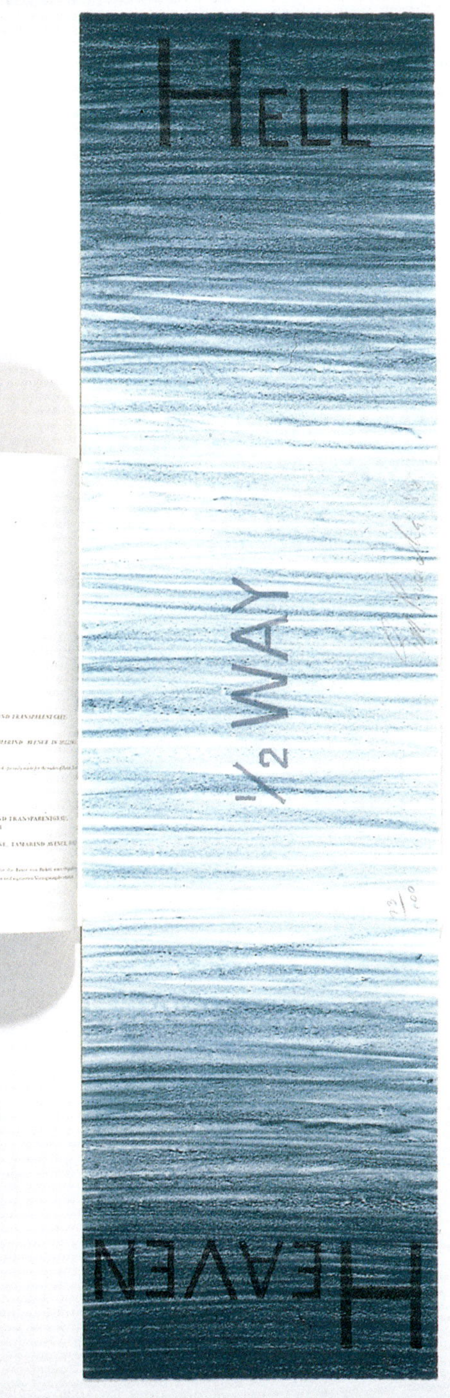

EDITION FOR PARKETT

EDWARD RUSCHA, HELL ½ WAY HEAVEN

LITHOGRAPHY IN THREE COLORS (BLUE GREEN, OPAQUE GREY AND TRANSPARENT GREY),
DRAWN ON ALUMINUM PLATES, PRINTED ON RIVES.
EDITION 100 IMPRESSIONS, SIGNED AND NUMBERED.
PRINTED BY ED HAMILTON AT JUNE WAYNE'S STUDIO ON TAMARIND AVENUE IN INGLEWOOD,
CALIFORNIA, JULY 1988.

Each issue of the magazine is created in collaboration with an artist, who contributes an original work, specially made for the readers of Parkett. Besides appearing in the regular edition, this is also available in a signed and Limited Deluxe Edition.

EDWARD RUSCHA, HÖLLE ½ WEG HIMMEL

LITHOGRAPHIE IN DREI FARBEN (BLAU GRÜN, OPAKGRAU UND TRANSPARENTGRAU),
GEZEICHNET AUF ALUMINIUMPLATTE, AUF RIVES GEDRUCKT.
AUFLAGE 100 EXEMPLARE, SIGNIERT UND NUMERIERT.
GEDRUCKT VON ED HAMILTON IM STUDIO VON JUNE WAYNE, TAMARIND AVENUE, INGLEWOOD, CALIFORNIA, JULI 1988.

Jede Nummer der Zeitschrift entsteht in Collaboration mit einem Künstler, der eigens für die Leser von Parkett eine Originalarbeit gestaltet. Dieses Werk ist in der gesamten Auflage abgebildet und zusätzlich in einer limitierten und signierten Vorzugsausgabe erhältlich.

PARKETT 18 1988

EDWARD RUSCHA

Vine / Melrose, 1999

Two-color Lithograph on Rives,
22 1/4 x 30 1/8" (56,8 x 76,3 cm),
printed by Hamilton Press, Venice,
California,
Ed. of 60/XX, signed and numbered

EDITION FOR PARKETT 55

Los Angeles: an intersection where angels
do not fear to tread.

"Ruscha throws out connections and images that
initially look controlled, even cold, and then you
realize—none of it makes any sense, in the accepted
sense of the word. They're about finding new meanings
in things, about seeing something fresh in the dullest
or most contained of spaces. You won't ever get it, if
getting it is what you want."

Jennifer Higgie
Parkett No. 55, 1999

エドワード・ルシェ

ヴァイン／メルローズ　1999

2色刷りリトグラフ、
リヴ紙：56.8×76.3cm、
刷り：ハルミトン・プレス（カリフォルニア州ヴェニス）、
Ed. 60/XX、署名、番号入り

パルケット・エディション 55

ロサンゼルス。天使たちが渡るのを恐れない交差点。

ルシェは当初はコントロールされているように見え、冷やかとさえ
思えた関連性とイメージを放り出す、するとことばの通常の意味で
は、それがなにも意味しないことに気づく。物事に新しい意味を見
いだすこと、これ以上ないほどうっとうしく、不自由な空間で、なに
か新鮮なものを見ることが、作品の目指すもの。それはしかし決して
手に入らない、たとえ手に入れることがあなたの望みであっても。

ジェニファー・ヒギー
（パルケット 55号、1999年）

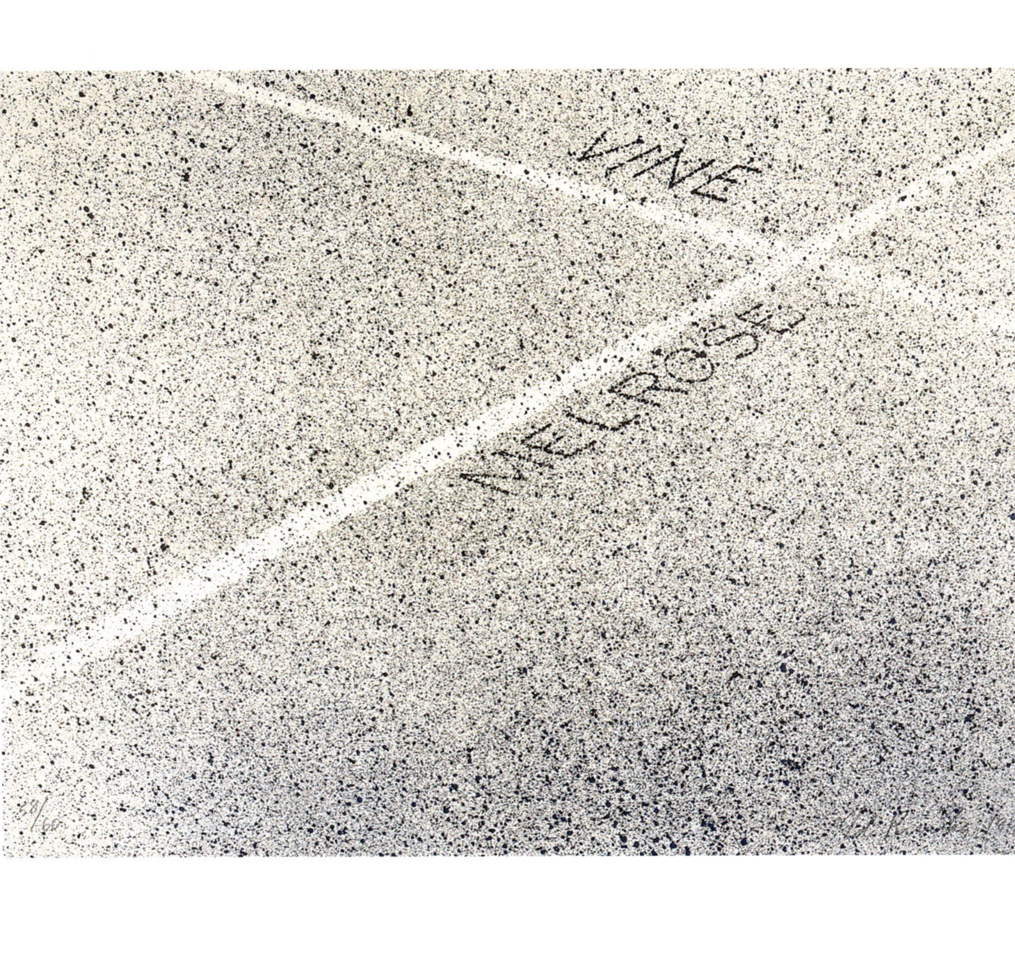

WINE
MELROSE

ANRI SALA

Airport, 2005

C-print,
paper size: 20 1/2 x 27 9/16" (52 x 70 cm),
image size: 16 1/2 x 23 5/8" (42 x 60 cm),
Ed. 60/XX, signed and numbered
certificate

EDITION FOR PARKETT 73

A barren place among places: the facelessness of technology vies with the eloquence of distant hills in a divided universe.

"The documentary form of Sala's videos succeeds in extracting from experiance the sensation of the timeless continuation of lives, cities, or instincts in the midst of the aggregate of history. The films seem almost buoyed by the sense that life goes on, even in times of spacial upheaval and historical crisis. Sala's work offers insight into the life that emerges at the very moment when hermeneutic categories are suspended."

Jan Verwoert
Parkett No. 73, 2005

アンリ・サラ

空港　2005

Cプリント、
紙：52×70cm、
図柄：42×60cm、
Ed. 60/XX、署名、番号入り証明書

パルケット・エディション 73

荒野の中の荒野。分裂した世界の中で、科学技術の匿名性が遠い丘陵の雄弁さと張り合う。

サラのビデオ作品のドキュメンタリー風の形式は、歴史の集積のただなかにあって、経験から人生、都会、あるいは本能が時間を越えて持続する感覚を見事に抽出する。フィルムは歴史的な危機、地理的な激変のさなかにも人生はつづくという感覚によって、鼓舞されているようにみえる。サラの作品は解釈学の範疇が停止したまさにその時に浮上する、人生の洞察を提供する。

ヤン・フェルウォールト
（パルケット 73号、2005年）

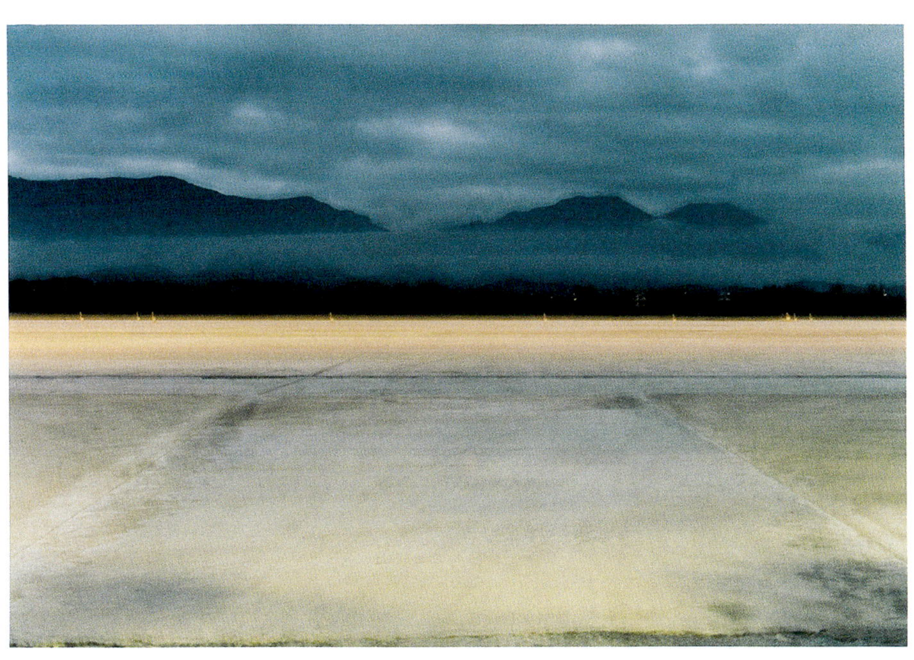

WILHELM SASNAL

Concorde Is Dead, 2004

Color contact print from engraved
negative on Kodak paper,
12 ⁵/₈ x 18 ⁷/₈" (31 x 47 cm),
Ed. 60/XX, signed and numbered

EDITION FOR PARKETT 70

The end of an era: another flight of fancy
consumed by the inexorable march of
civilization.

"Wilhelm Sasnal's economy lies in the fact that
he consistently allows his viewers to share in this
unresolved ambivalence and the tragic, naive longing
to grasp the uungraspable. An ambivalence that might
be described as the basis of Sasnal's visual stock-
taking of identity or, to repeat, as a kind of defect of
the faculty of perception. Despite their easy 'legibility',
his pictures resist interpretation while still being of
great significance in terms of historical mentality,
subculture and opposition."

Gregor Jansen
Parkett No. 70, 2004

ヴィルヘルム・サスナル

コンコルドはもう飛ばない　2004

文字を彫りつけたネガのコンタクト・プリント、
コダック社の印画紙、31×47cm、
Ed. 60/XX、署名、番号入り

パルケット・エディション 70

一時代の終わり。文明の無情な行進によって消費され
たまたひとつの空想の飛翔。

ヴィルヘルム・サスナルの理法は、未解決の躊躇と把握不能なもの
を把握したがる世間知らずの悲劇的な願望を、鑑賞者とつねに分か
ち合うことにある。この躊躇は、サスナルによるアイデンティティの
視覚的棚卸しの基礎、あるいは、くりかえしになるが、知覚能力の欠
損として説明されうるだろう。サスナルの写真は「読み取りやすい」
にもかかわらず、解釈を拒みながら、歴史的な心理、サブカルチャー、
抵抗に関しては大きな意味をもちつづける。

グレゴール・ヤンセン
（パルケット 70号、2004年）

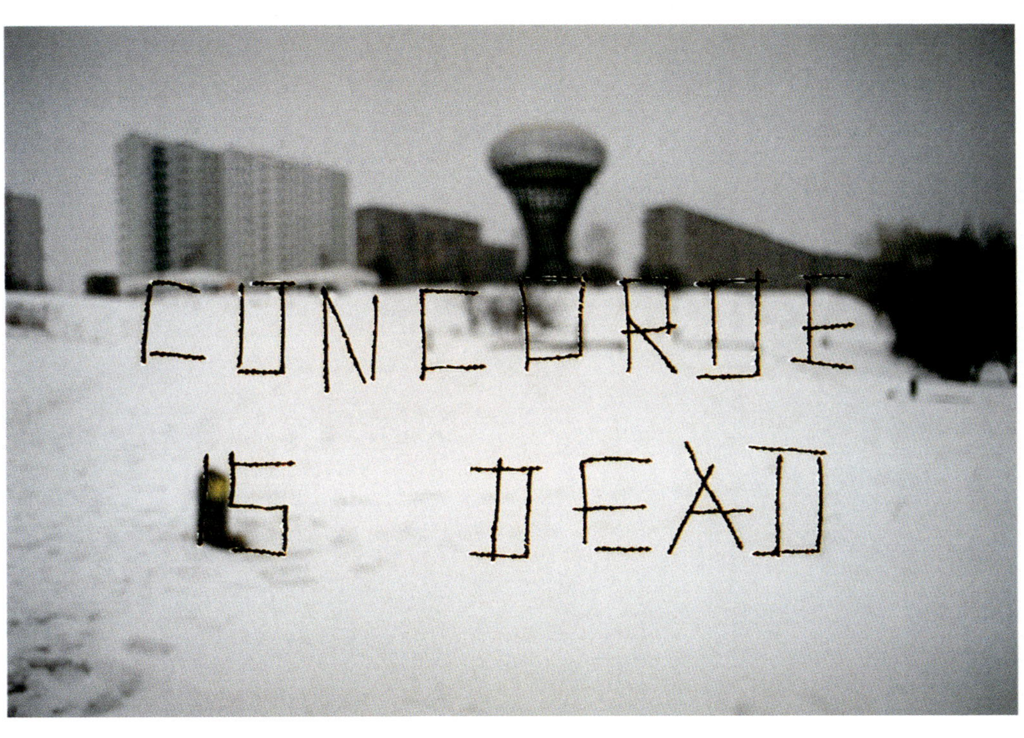

CONCORDE
IS DEAD

GREGOR SCHNEIDER

The German Contribution,
Bower, Venice, 2001

Two color photographs in
handpainted frames with passe-
partouts made by the artist,
image size: 9$^{1}/_{2}$ x 6$^{4}/_{5}$" (23,1 x 17,1 cm);
frames: 16$^{1}/_{2}$ x 12$^{1}/_{2}$" (41,7 x 31,8 cm),
Ed. 60/XX, signed and numbered

EDITION FOR PARKETT 63

The Archaeology of the everyday. There may
be more not only under the floor or between
the walls but overhead as well.

"With his own hands [Gregor Schneider] reproduces
existing rooms in the same place and subsequently,
for exhibition purposes, reconstructs these in another
place. Thus, he takes over and affirms an existing
building, constantly seeking to make a connection
with what it is not, with an uncanny undertow that
fundamentally questions the existential possibility of
living, of finding refuge in a house. He contextualizes
the house with itself in order to locate the other side
of its meaning."

Ulrich Loock
Parkett No. 63, 2001

グレゴール・シュナイダー

ドイツの貢献、バウアー、ヴェニス　2001

カラー写真 2枚、手で塗装した額、
アーティスト自身が制作したマット、
図柄：23.1×17.1cm、
額：41.7×31.8cm、
Ed. 60/XX、署名、番号入り

パルケット・エディション 63

日常の考古学。床の下や壁の間だけでなく、頭上にも、
もっとあるかもしれない。

グレゴール・シュナイダーは自らの手で実際に存在する部屋を同じ
場所に再現し、その後、展覧会を行うために、それらを別の場所に
建て直す。こうしてシュナイダーは既存の建物を引き継ぎ、肯定し、
自分とはちがうものと関連づけ、また生きること、家に逃げ場を見
いだす実存的な可能性を根源的に問う神秘的な引き波にもたえず
関連づけようと試みる。シュナイダーは家をそれ自体と併せて文脈
に収め、その意味合いの別の側面を見定めようとする。

ウルリヒ・ロック
（パルケット 63号、2001年）

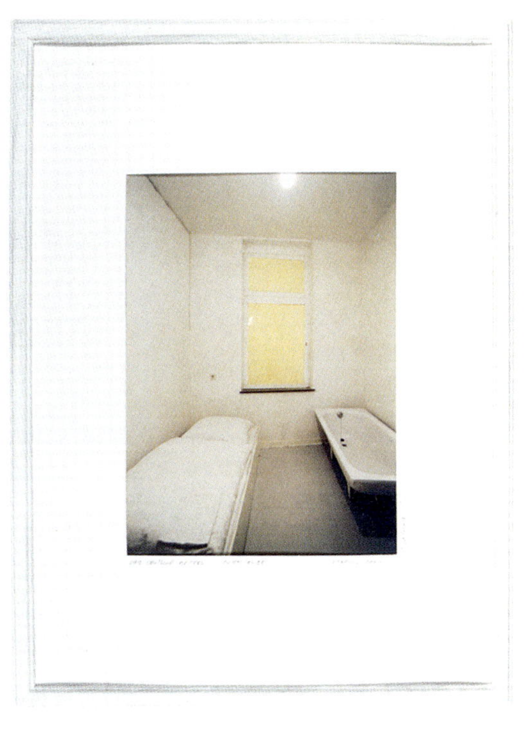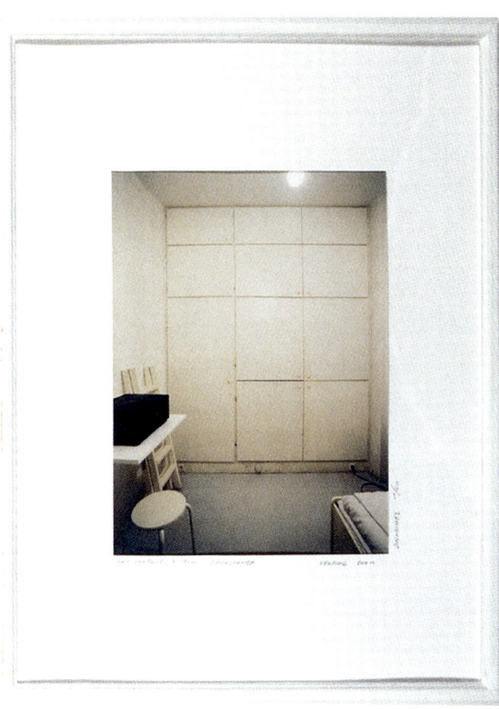

THOMAS SCHÜTTE

Olga's Wallpaper, 1996 (1977)

Lithograph, stone-pulled, 5 colors,
printed by Felix Bauer, Cologne,
on handmade Indian Vellum, 250g/m^2,
40$^1/_8$ x 27" (101,5 x 68,4 cm),
Ed. 60/XX, signed and numbered

EDITION FOR PARKETT 47

Rainbow bright. Lighthearted wallpaper, about to float away like a magic carpet, inspires flights of fancy on tapestries, spaces, and the people who live with them.

"Thomas Schütte's oeuvre possesses a rare quality: It is contemporary without being modernist. It possesses subjectivity, but a subjectivity devoid of egoism. It possesses versatility of expression along with the rigor of a program it sometimes hides and sometimes reveals. Schütte's concern is the representation of the human condition as it is right now. But what fascinates me is the fact that he is not interested in either a utopian or a catastrophic future, or why he doesn't drift into golden ages located in some imaginary past. Schütte is a realist: He represents what he sees using materials directly linked to that vision, materials anchored in the literalness of the image."

Bartomeu Mari
Parkett No. 47, 1996

トーマス・シュッテ

オルガの壁紙　1996（1977）

リトグラフ、石版使用、5色、
刷り：フェリックス・バウアー（ケルン）、
手漉きインディアン・ヴェラム紙250ｇ/㎡、
101.5×68.4cm、
Ed. 60/XX、署名、番号入り

パルケット・エディション 47

虹のような明るさ。屈託のない壁紙、魔法の絨毯のように今にもどこかへ飛んでゆきそう、絨毯、空間、そこに暮らす人々に向かって想像力は羽ばたく。

トーマス・シュッテの作品には比類ない特質がある。近代主義的でなく、現代的なのである。主観性を有するが、その主観性に自己中心的なところは少しもない。融通の利く表現力と並行して、ときに隠し、ときに露呈させる計画の厳密さももちあわせる。シュッテの関心は、人間の置かれた状況を、今のこのままの状態で表現することにある。わたしがとくに興味を惹かれるのは、かれがユートピア的な未来にも、破滅的な未来にも興味をおぼえないこと、そして空想の過去のどこかに存在する黄金時代に彷徨いこまないことである。シュッテはリアリストである。シュッテは自分の目で見たものとじかに結びつく素材、そしてイメージの散文性につなぎとめられた素材を用いて、目で見たものを表現する。

バールトミュー・マリ
（パルケット 47号、1996年）

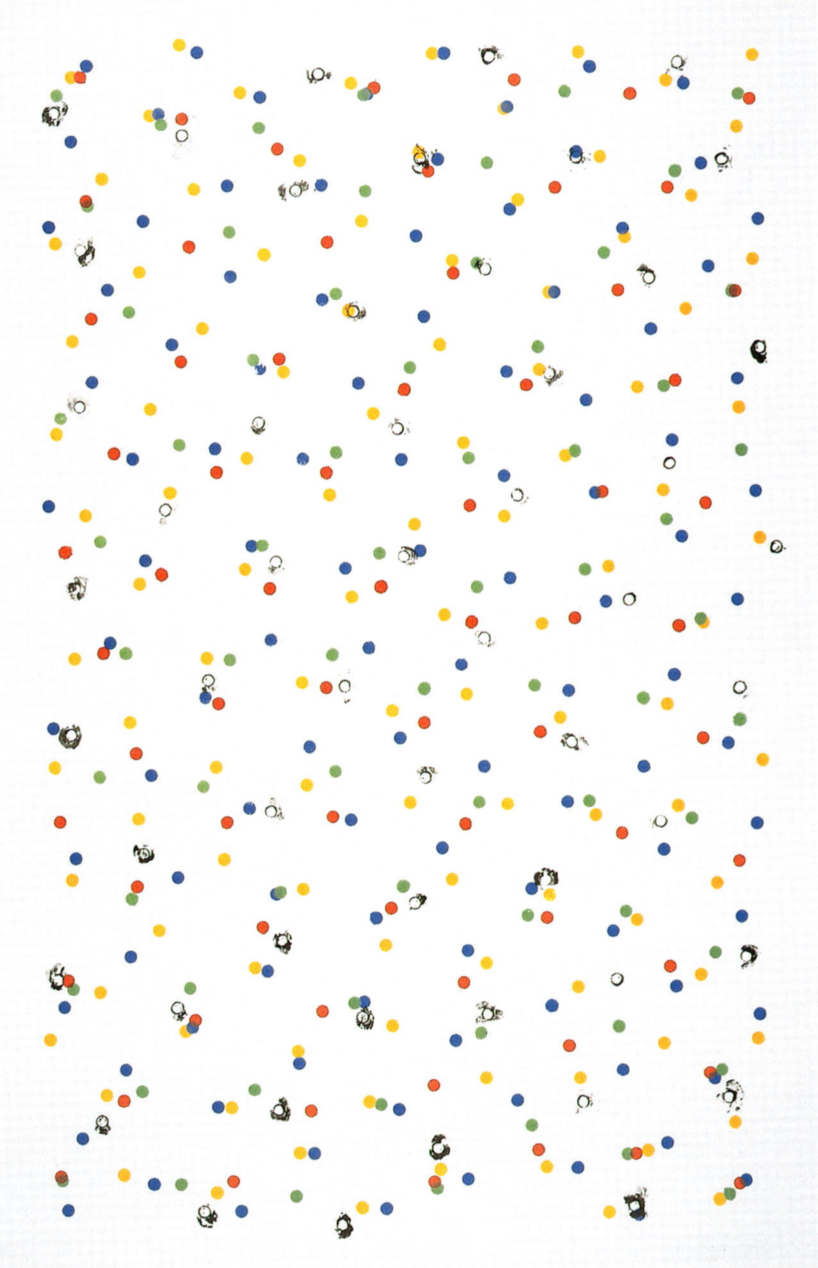

DANA SCHUTZ

Untitled (Head of Timothy Leary), 2005

11-color lithograph with wood printing
elements on Rives cover white 350g/m^2,
paper size: 28^1/$_8$ x 26^1/$_8$" (71,5 x 66,5 cm),
image: 24 x 22^1/$_2$" (61 x 57 cm),
printed by Maurice Sanchez,
Derrière L'Etoile Studio, New York,
Ed. 55/XXV, signed and numbered

EDITION FOR PARKETT 75

Leary in the sky with diamonds.

"The artist's absurd, dreamy images stir deeply
hidden anxieties: dogs lose their heads, teeth mutate
into wooden stakes, gravity becomes an obsession.
Everything is in the grips of being transformed or
dissolved; things emerge only to fall apart again.
The world is out of joint. The bizarre figures all
seem somehow related; they are disturbing and of a
grotesque exaggeration and ironic twist that radiates
an unfathomable lightness."

Katrin Wittneven
Parkett No. 75, 2005

デイナ・シュッツ

無題（ティモシー・リアリーの頭）　2005

11色刷りリトグラフ、木版刷り、
リヴ・カヴァー・ホワイト紙350g/㎡、
紙：71.5×66.5cm、図柄：61×57cm、
刷り：モーリス・サンチェス、
デリエール・レトワール・スタジオ（ニューヨーク）、
Ed. 55/XXV、署名、番号入り

パルケット・エディション 75

リアリー・イン・ザ・スカイ・ウィズ・ダイアモンズ。

不条理で、夢見るようなシュッツのイメージは、心の奥底に隠され
た不安を揺さぶる。頭をなくす犬、木の杭に姿を変える歯、重力は
妄想となる。すべては変化か解消の途上にあって、そこから逃れる
ことはできない。浮上してもかならず再び崩れ落ちる。世界は調子
が狂っている。奇妙な人物はみななにかしら関連があるらしい。か
れらは気にさわり、グロテスクな誇張とアイロニックなひねりが、
底知れぬ軽やかさを放射する。

カトリン・ウィットネヴン
（パルケット 75号、2005年）

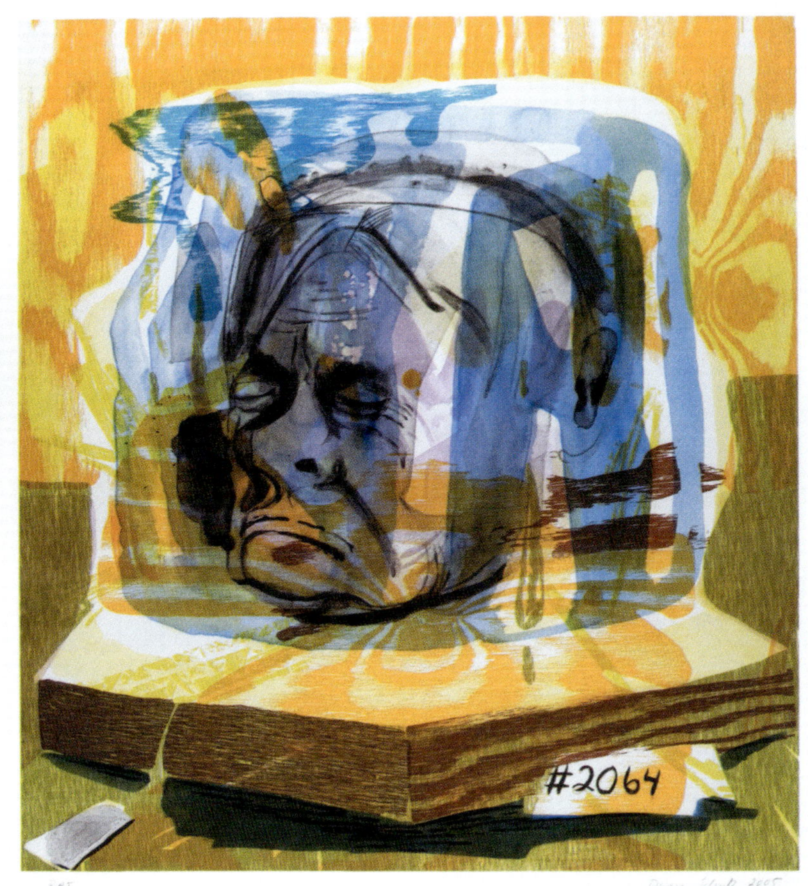

#2064

RICHARD SERRA

Bilbao 1, 2005

Etching,
paper size: 22 ¾ x 27 ½" (58 x 70 cm),
image size: 17 ¾ x 23 ½" (45 x 60 cm),
printed by Gemini G.E.L., Los Angeles, CA,
Ed. 35, signed and numbered

EDITION FOR PARKETT 74

Wave upon wave, a spectrum leaves the
confines of the paper, and escapes into an
infinity of weightlessness.

"'The Matter of Time' immerses its viewers in
circumstances that make the embodiment of the eye
undeniable. It forces upon its viewers the question
'who sees?' And in the astonishing ambiguities and
fugitive impressions it generates, this ensemble of
works extends that question beyond curiosity about
one's own nature as an observer, to the social curiosity
of 'who sees what I see, and how do we know?' In
other words, Serra's art, which we see fulfilled in
'The Matter of Time,' offers itself as a set of devices
for reconstructing our view of the world, starting not
with the question 'what can be known?' but with the
question 'what can be shared?'"

Kenneth Baker
Parkett No. 74, 2005

リチャード・セラ

ビルバオ1　2005

エッチング、紙：58×70cm、
図柄：45×60cm、
刷り：ジェミナイ G.E.L
（カリフォルニア州ロサンゼルス）、
Ed. 35、署名、番号入り

パルケット・エディション 74

波から波へ、スペクトルは紙の制約を離れ、重さのな
い無限の広がりへ逃げてゆく。

「時間の問題」は目の形象化を否定できない状況に、鑑賞者を
とっぷり漬ける。鑑賞者に「だれが見るのか？」と問い詰める。そ
して自ら呼び起こすおどろくほど曖昧で捉えどころのない印象の
なかで、これらの作品の集成はその問いを、観察者としての自らの
性質に向かう好奇心を越えて、「わたしが見ているものをほかにだ
れが見ているか、そしてわたしたちにはどうしてそれがわかるか」
という社会的な好奇心にまで広げてゆく。言い換えるなら、わたし
たちはセラの作品が「時間の問題」として成就されるのを目の当た
りにしたが、それは「何を知ることができるか」ではなく「何を分か
ち合えるか」を問うことから始めて、わたしたちの世界観を再構築
する道具一式となるのである。

ケネス・ベーカー
（パルケット 74号、1991年）

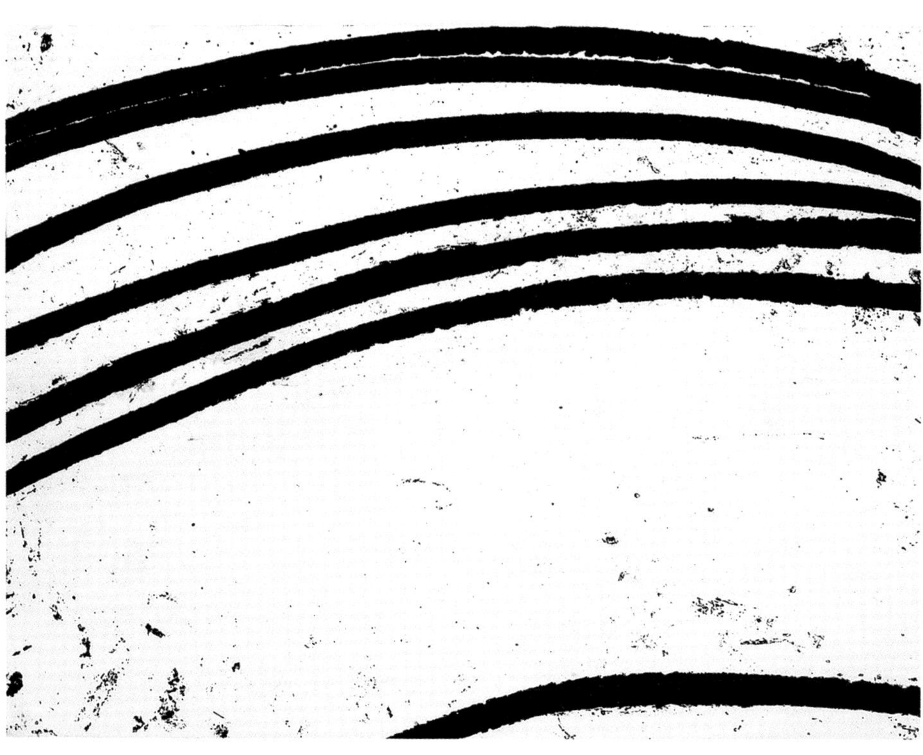

CINDY SHERMAN

Untitled, 1991

Printed silk, padded, in gilded wooden
frame, 8 ³/₈ x 6 ⁷/₈" (21,3 x 17,4 cm)
with frame,
Ed. 100/XX, signed and numbered

EDITION FOR PARKETT 29

The little house of horrors. A silken
greasepaint grotesque rendered in startling
3-D threatens to burst from its keepsake
frame.

"They say that with her approach to photography
the line between painting and photography starts
oscillating. Success is immediate, uncomplicated,
undisputed, as if it were (still) child's play."

Ursula Pia Jauch
Parkett No. 29, 1991

シンディ・シャーマン

無題　1991

シルクにプリント、パッド入り、
金色に塗った木の額、
額装時21.3×17.4cm、
Ed. 100/XX、署名、番号入り

パルケット・エディション 29

ザ・リトル・ハウス・オブ・ホラー。絹のようになめらか
なドーランが目ざましい3-Dで描かれ、飾りの額から
飛び出そうとする。

シャーマンの写真へのアプローチによって、絵画と写真を隔てる境
界線が震動しはじめたとひとは言う。成功は（いまでも）児戯のよ
うに、素早く、面倒なく、議論の余地もない。

ウルスラ・ピア・ジャウシュ
（パルケット 29号、1991年）

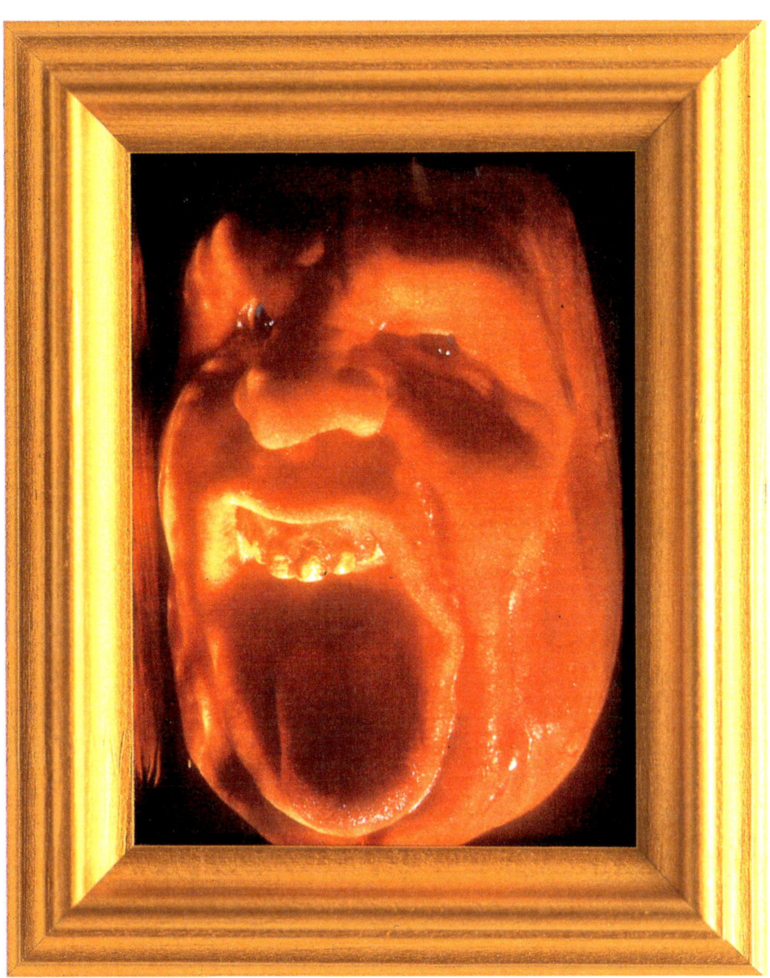

ROMAN SIGNER

Fireman's Glove with Photograph,
1995

Heat-resistant glove, length 13 ³/₄"
(35 cm), still from a video by Aleksandra
Signer, approx. 5 ¹/₈ x 7 ¹/₈" (13 x 18,2 cm),
Ed. 80/XV, signed and numbered

EDITION FOR PARKETT 45

Red alert. A fireman's protective glove plays
an active role as a mock traffic signal.

"Action and sculpture, dynamics and stasis in Roman
Signer's oeuvre do not oppose each other but are
rather different states of the same structure. It is
a structure that displays the potential of future,
energetic change; it is transformation as transient
shape; it is detritus as traces of past events. The
sculptural form in Signer's oeuvre, the static object in
space is expanded—liquefied, as it were—to include
the dimension of time."

Konrad Bitterli
Parkett No. 45, 1995

ローマン・シグナー

消防士用の手袋と写真　1995

耐熱手袋、長さ：35cm、
アレグザンドラ・シグナー作ビデオのスティル写真、
約13×18.2cm、
Ed. 80/XV、署名、番号入り

パルケット・エディション 45

非常態勢。消防士を保護する手袋が交通信号の代役
を務める。

ローマン・シグナーの作品では行為と彫刻、動と静が対立するより
も、同一構造の異なる状態として存在する。構造は未来の潜在力、
エネルギッシュな変化を表現する。それはつかのまの姿をとった
変身であり、過去の出来事の痕跡としての有機堆積物である。シグ
ナーの作品に見られる彫刻的なフォルム、空間の中に静止するオブ
ジェは拡張され、いわば液化され、時間の次元を内包する。

コンラッド・ビッテルリ
（パルケット 45号、1995年）

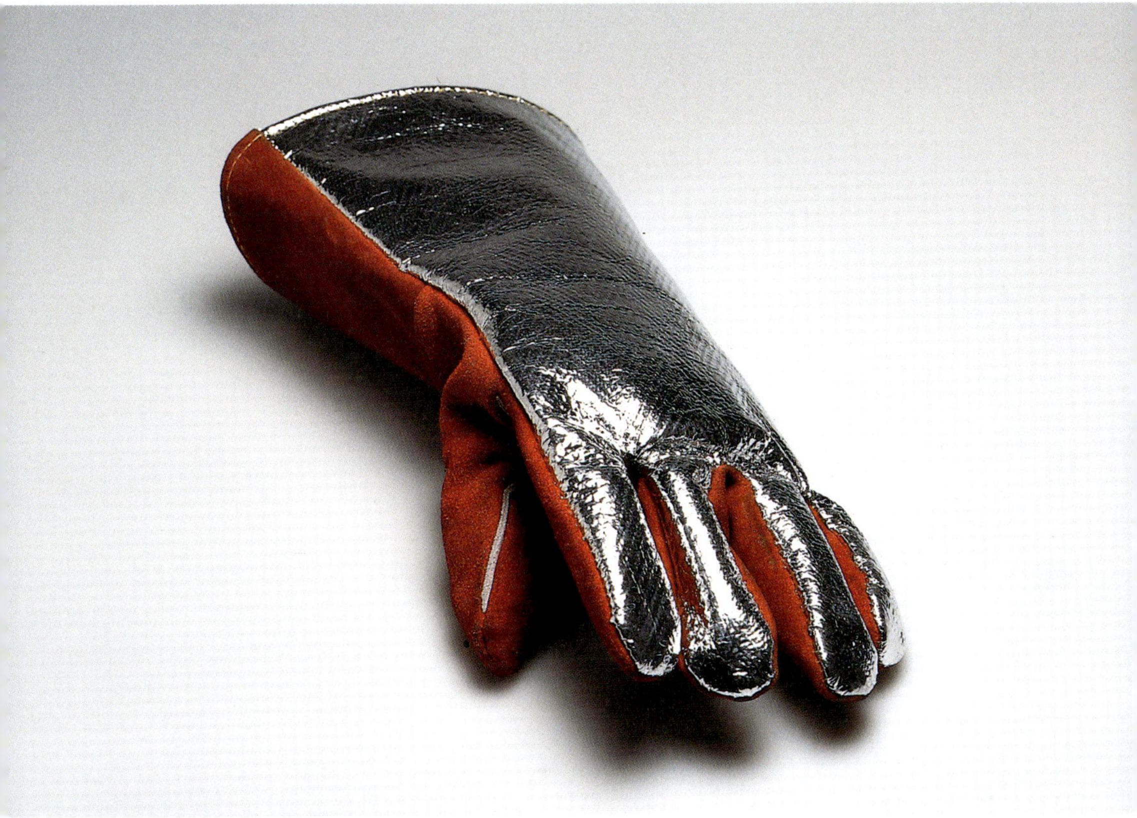

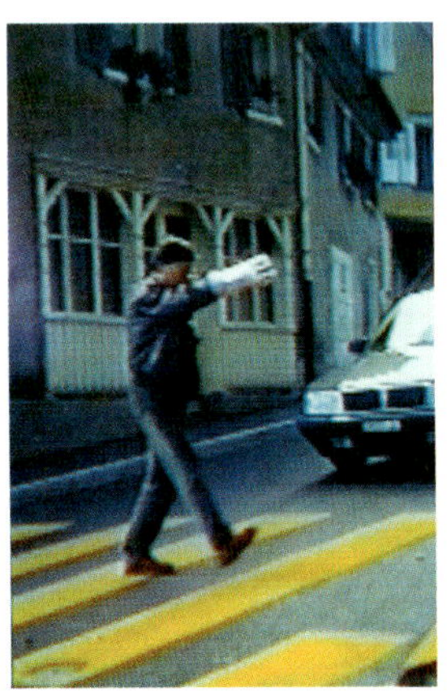

ANDREAS SLOMINSKI

Folding Rule, 1999

The rule will be delivered extended,
length: 78 $^{11}/_{16}$" (200 cm),
Ed. 55/XX, signed and numbered certificate

EDITION FOR PARKETT 55

Measure for Measure—every inch a hyper-reality that begs authenticity and gauges only imponderables.

"And so we gaze at the Slominski traps, at some point we suddenly see that they are indeed peculiar, very strange objects—strange, that is to say, from an artistic point of view. The really strange, peculiar thing about them is their ever taut, ever perilously enticing beauty which does not really seem to be geared towards our synaesthetic sensibilities but towards the sensory capacities of rats, grouse, or orange slugs (and how to outwit these)."

Patrick Frey
Parkett No. 55, 1999

アンドレアス・スロミンスキー

おりたたみ定規　1999

定規は伸ばした状態で配送される、
長さ：200cm、
Ed. 55/XX、署名、番号入り証明書

パルケット・エディション 55

目には目を。どの1インチをとっても本物を求め、測り知れない物のみを計測するハイパー・リアリティ。

わたしたちはソロミンスキーのしかけた罠を見つめ、あるところまでくるといきなりそれがたしかに風変わりな、奇妙なオブジェだと気づく。奇妙というのは、美術の視点から見てということである。ほんとうに奇妙で、風変わりなのは、このうえなく厳格で、危険なほど魅惑的な美しさが、共感する力のあるわたしたちの感受性ではなく、ネズミやライチョウ、あるいはナメクジ、（どのようにしてそれらの裏をかくか）に向けられていることだろう。

パトリック・フライ
（パルケット 55号、1999年）

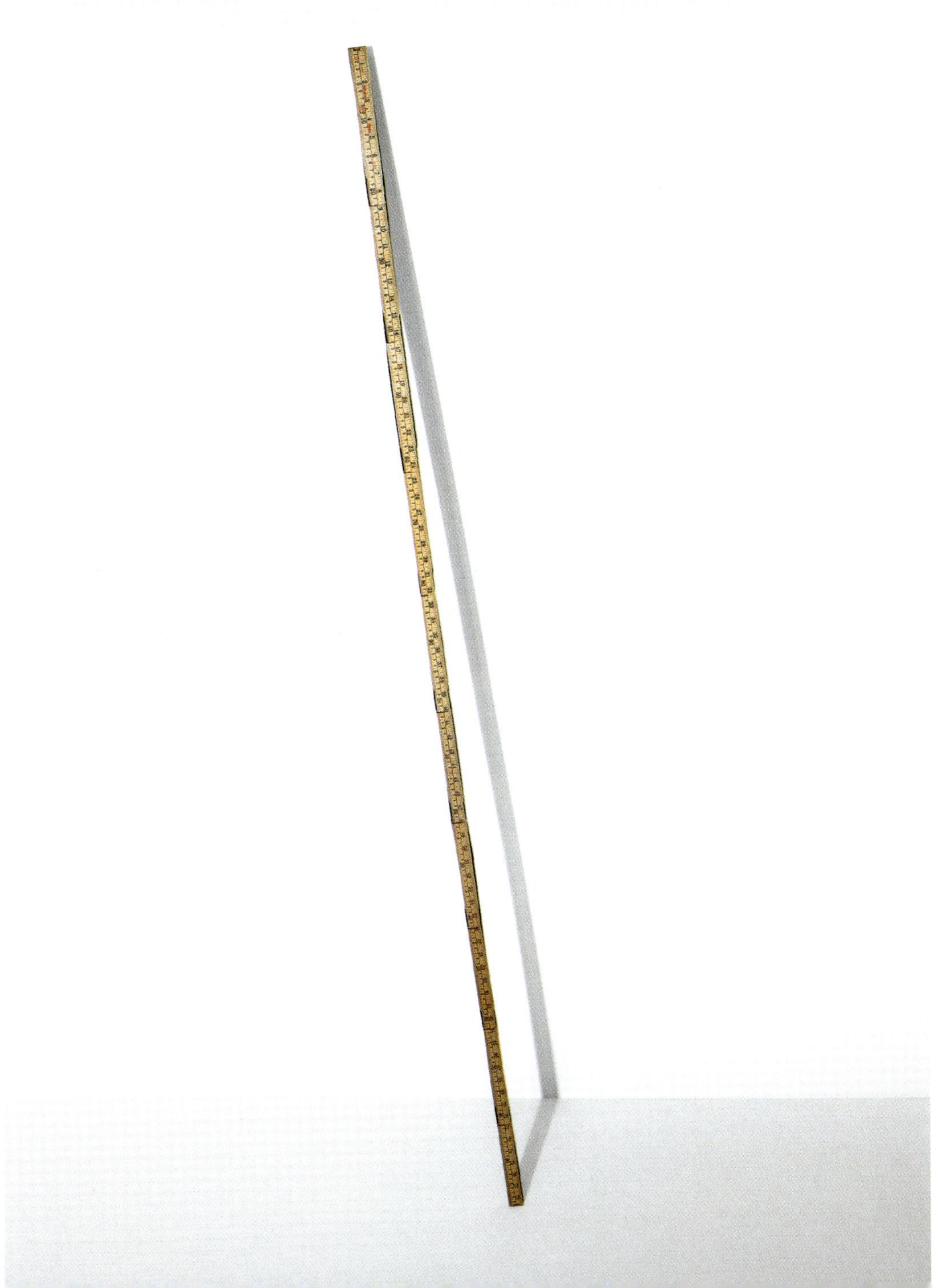

JOSH SMITH

Parkett Book Collage, 2009

Mixed media, ink and collage
on wood (front and back),
Each work unique, 24 x 18 x ¾"
(61 x 45,7 x 1,9 cm)
Ed. 38/XV, signed and numbered

EDITION FOR PARKETT 85

It can always be done again—same, same but different—when artistic passion prevails.

"He 'thinks in paint,' as evidenced by the sheer quantity of works he produces—a phenomenon deliberately displayed in his installations. The picture is not conceived as a closed site, nor as something completed, but merely as one stage in a continuous process of creation."

Anne Pontégnie
Parkett No. 85, 2009

ジョシュ・スミス

パルケット・ブック・コラージュ　2009

ミクスト・メディア、インク、コラージュ、
板（表、裏）、1点ずつ異なる、
61×45.7×1.9cm、
Ed. 38/XV、署名、番号入り

パルケット・エディション 85

いつでもやり直すことはできる—前と同じに、同じでも違うふうに—芸術家の情熱が奏功するかぎり

スミスが「絵具で思考する」ことは、手がける作品の驚くべき数からも見てとれる。作者はこの現象をあえて意図してインスタレーションに表現する。絵画は閉じられた場とも、完結したものとも見なされず、持続する創造過程のたんなる一段階であるに過ぎない。

アン・ポンテニー
（パルケット 85号、2009年）

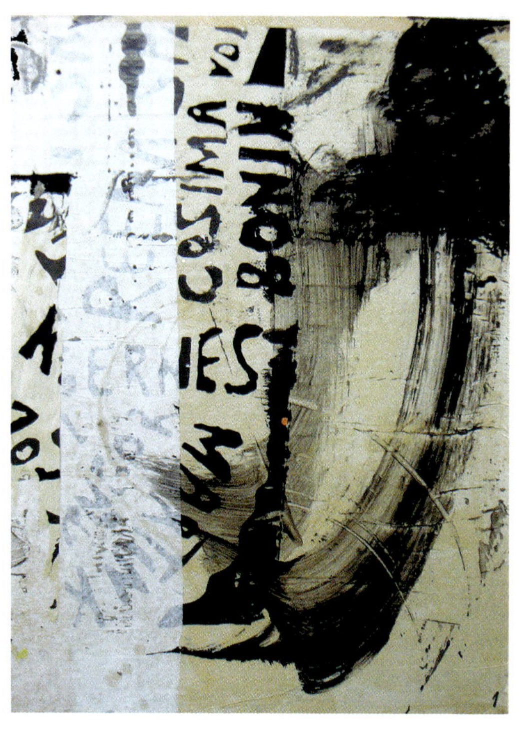

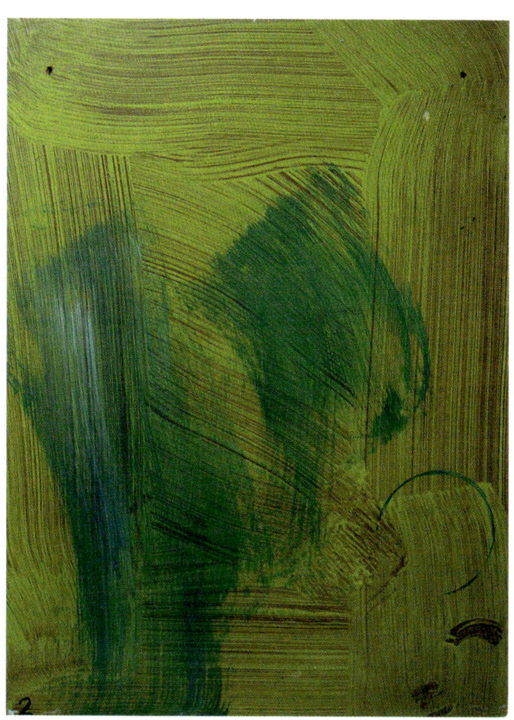

Front / 表

Back / 裏

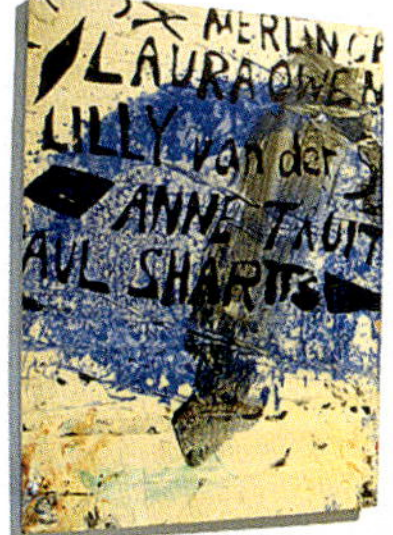

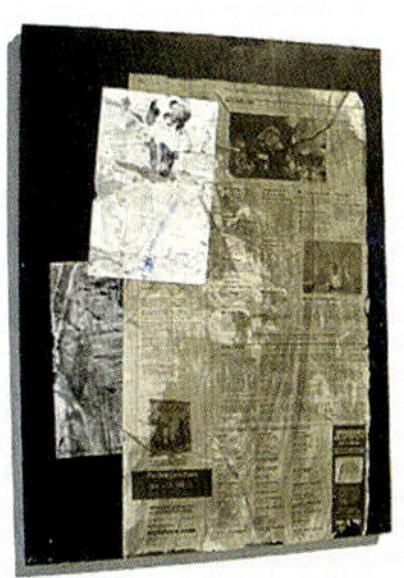

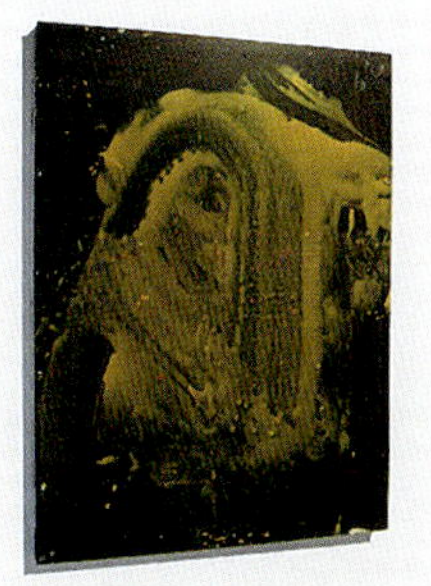

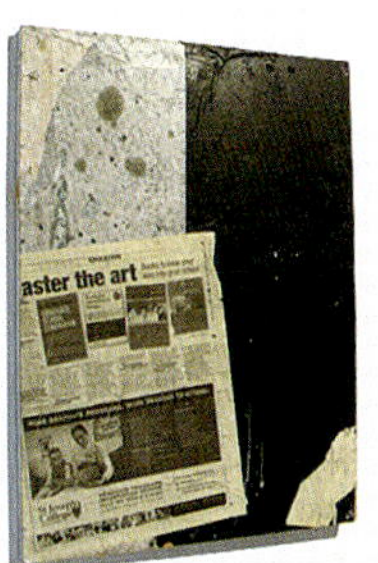

RUDOLF STINGEL

RS, 2006

Signet ring, 18 carat gold,
approx. 1 x $^{3}/_{4}$ x $^{1}/_{2}$" (2,5 x 2 x 1,5 cm),
jewelery box, production by
Markus Frühauf, jeweler, Meran, Italy,
Ed. 22/XVI, initials engraved and
numbered

EDITION FOR PARKETT 77

Wear it right side down, to seal a friendship,
as kings once did.

"In most cases, however, Stingel's works are both
medium and membrane in one. They are skin. They
record traces of use-of being walked on, of tearing,
of flaking. As permeable membranes, they mark and
'regulate' the locus of border and transition in spatio-
physical terms (between wall and picture, floor and
covering, painting and sculpture, architectural and
institutional space), and in temporal-economical
terms (between that which produces and that which
consumes)."

Jörg Heiser
Parkett No. 77, 2006

ルドルフ・スティンゲル

RS　2006

認印付きの指輪、金18K、
約2.5×2×1.5cm、
宝石箱、
制作：マルクス・フリュハウフ宝石細工
　（メラノ市、イタリア）、
Ed. 22/XVI、イニシャルを刻印、番号入り

パルケット・エディション 77

正しい方を下にして指にはめ、王たちがかつて行った
ように、友誼を固めたまえ。

ほとんど場合、しかし、スティンゲルの作品はメディアと膜がひとつ
になったものである。つまり皮膚。使用の痕、上から踏まれ、ちぎ
られ、薄く剥がれた痕を記録する。透過性の膜として、空間−物理
的な意味（壁と絵、床と絨毯、絵と彫刻、建築的空間と制度的空間
の間）と時間−経済的な意味（生産するものと消費するものの間）
で、境界と転移の場を示し、また「調整」する。

イェルク・ハイザー
（パルケット 77号、2006年）

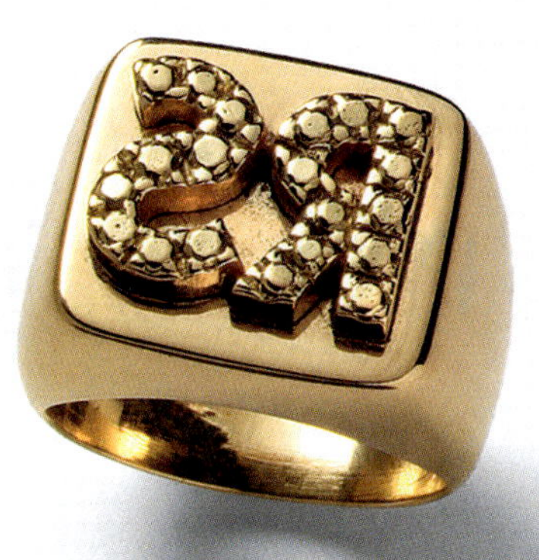

BEAT STREULI

Oxford Street, 1998

Laserchrome print on Agfa high-gloss paper, poster with 32 colored and b/w photographs, enlarged by Grieger GmbH, Dusseldorf, 53 1/8 x 39 3/8" (132 x 50,6 cm), Ed. 60/XX, signed and numbered

EDITION FOR PARKETT 54

Singular and isolate: Immersed in the human river of our cities, we see in the light of morning occasional flashes of the individual beeings that we are.

"Surprised in heavily trafficked spaces or in moments of rest, the impromptu actors he chooses for his photos seem neither very old nor very young. They compose a mosaic of unknown characters who become recognizable when we identify the everyday in their gestures. Streuli lends dignity to the infinite encounters that secretly take place day after day in the center of the city: Students? Young professionals? White-collar workers? Unwittingly they pose for a meticulous and patient observer who is capable of distilling the quintessential human element that manifests itself when someone pauses in the clamor of daily routine."

José Lebrero Stals
Parkett No. 54, 1998/99

ベアト・ストロイリ

オックスフォード・ストリート　1998

レーザークローム・プリント、アグファ光沢紙、
32点のカラー／モノクロ写真を集めたポスター、
引伸し：グリーガー社（デュッセルドルフ）、
132×50.6cm、
Ed. 60/XX、署名、番号入り

パルケット・エディション 54

奇異と孤立。都会を行く大河のような人の流れにとっぷり漬かり、わたしたちは朝の光が照らしだす、ほかのだれともちがうひとりひとり（それはつまりわたしたち）の姿が、ときおり閃くのを見る。

ストロイリが被写体に選ぶにわかづくりの役者たちは、交通量の激しさに驚き、あるいは一時くつろいだとしても、とりわけ年寄りにも、若くも見えない。かれらは見覚えのない人物のモザイクを構成するが、その身振りもだれもがふだんからするものとわかれば、親しみも感じさせる。ストロイリは都会の中心で日々密かに、数限りなく起こる出会いを尊厳のあるものにする。学生？　専門職に就いた若者？　ホワイトカラーの勤め人？　忙しい日常に訪れる息抜きの折にかいま見える真の人間らしさを抽出する能力に長けた、辛抱強く、注意深い観察者の前で、かられはそれと気づかずに、ポーズをとる。

ホセ・レブレロ・スタルス
（パルケット 54号、1998/99年）

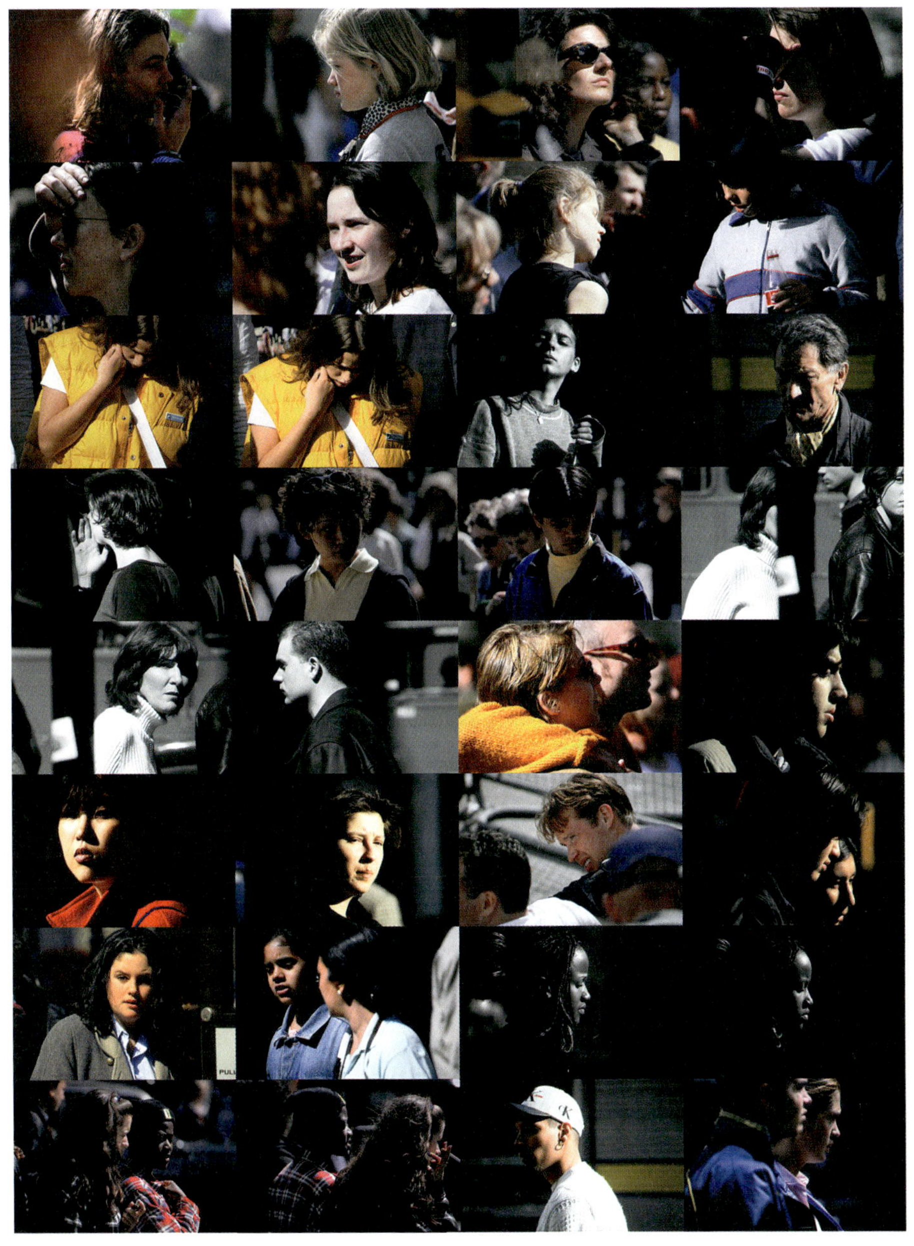

THOMAS STRUTH

Jiangxi Zhong Lu, Shanghai 1996

Color photograph, C-print, 1997,
sheet: 16 $^1/_{16}$ x 20 $^1/_{16}$" (40,6 x 50,6 cm);
image: 14 $^3/_{16}$ x 18 $^1/_8$" (36,7 x 46 cm),
Ed. 60/XX, signed and numbered

EDITION FOR PARKETT 50/51

A moment in Shanghai. Remote and yet oddly familiar.

"Like many photographers, Struth watches and waits. But he's not interested in catching something, or in catching someone out. Responding to an increasing interest in photographing people, some he knows and others he does not, Struth has taken extreme care to resist the temptations of voyeurism."

James Lingwood
Parkett No. 50/51, 1997

トーマス・シュトゥルート

江西中路、上海　1996

カラー写真、Cプリント、1997、
紙：40.6×50.6cm、
図柄：36.7×46cm、
Ed. 60/XX、署名、番号入り

パルケット・エディション 50/51

上海のひととき、遠い土地だが、不思議なほど親しみを覚える。

写真家の多くと同じように、シュトゥルートも目を凝らし、待ち構える。ところがシュトゥルートはなにかを捉えたい、だれかを見つけ出したいと思っているわけではない。人物写真に対する関心の高まりに応え、相手が知っているひとであっても、知らないひとであっても、シュトゥルートは覗き見趣味の誘惑に負けないように、細心の注意を払う。

ジェイムズ・リングウッド
（パルケット 50/51号、1997年）

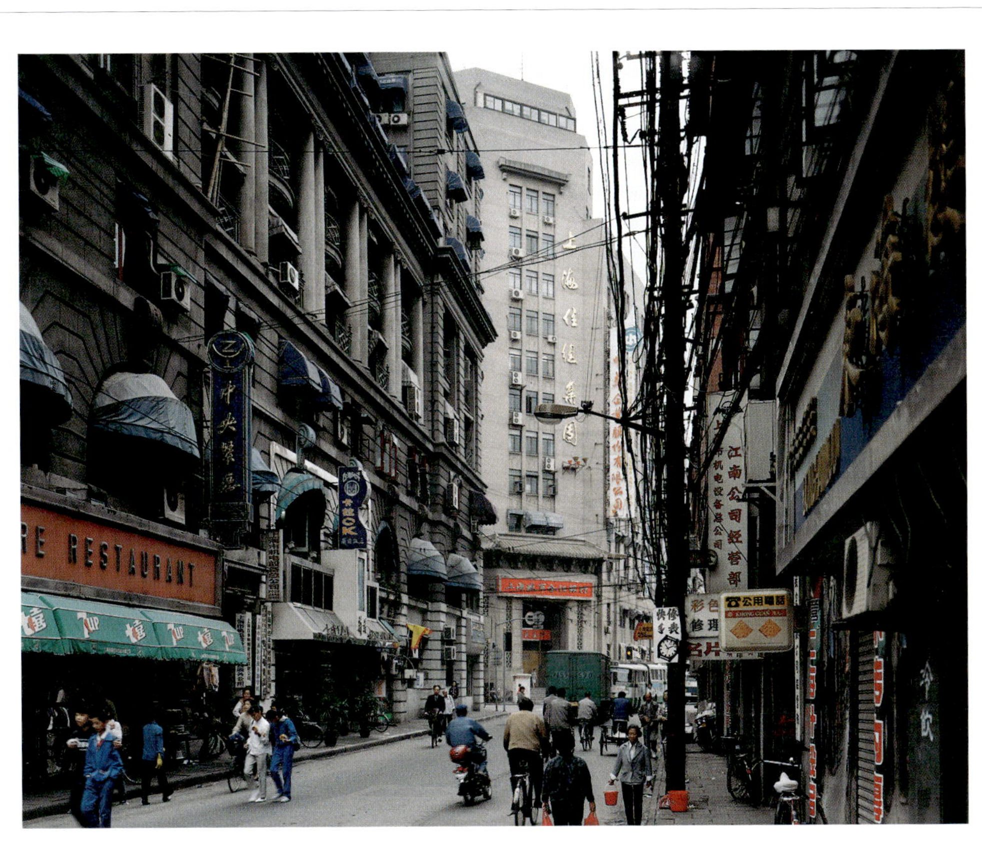

HIROSHI SUGIMOTO

Night Seascape, Ionian Sea, Santa
Cesarea, 1990 /
Day Seascape, English Channel,
Weston Cliff, 1994

Miniature photograph, paulownia box,
rice paper-lined inner felt lid,
silver-plated knob (hand made in Japan),
image: approx. 2 x 1 $^5/_8$" (4,2 x 5,3 cm),
box: approx. 6 $^1/_4$ x 5 x 1 $^3/_4$"
(4,6 x 15,7 x 12,8 cm).
Ed. of 35/X day and 35/X night,
signed and numbered

EDITION FOR PARKETT 46

Quintessential photography—the vast
horizons of night and day bedded in a
beautiful little box.

"'Maybe I am already half dead.'—Hiroshi
Sugimoto. I am almost inclined to take Hiroshi
Sugimoto at his word. Since 1976 he has been
elaborating on three basic themes—dioramas,
movie theatres, and seascapes—and almost every
picture shares the same quiet morbidity, as if all
his prints had been developed in embalming fluid."

Ralph Rugoff
Parkett No. 46, 1996

杉本博司

夜の海景、イオニア海、サンタ・チェザレア
　　1990
昼の海景、イギリス海峡、ウェストン・クリフ
　　1994

ミニチュア写真、桐箱、
ライスペーパーで裏打ちしたフェルトの蓋、
銀メッキしたノブ（日本で手作り）、
図柄：4.2×5.3cm、箱：4.6×15.7×12.8cm、
Ed. 35/X（昼）、Ed. 35/X（夜）、署名、番号入り

パルケット・エディション 46

写真の真髄—夜と昼の広大な水平線が美しい小箱
に収められた。

「わたしはもう半ば死んでいるのかもしれない」（杉本博司）。
このことばを信じても良いような気もする。1976年以降、杉本
は3つの基本的なテーマ（ジオラマ、映画館、海景）と取り組ん
できたが、その写真のほとんどすべてが、まるで防腐処理液で
現像されたかのように、穏やかな罹患状態にある。

ラルフ・ルゴフ
（パルケット 46号、1996年）

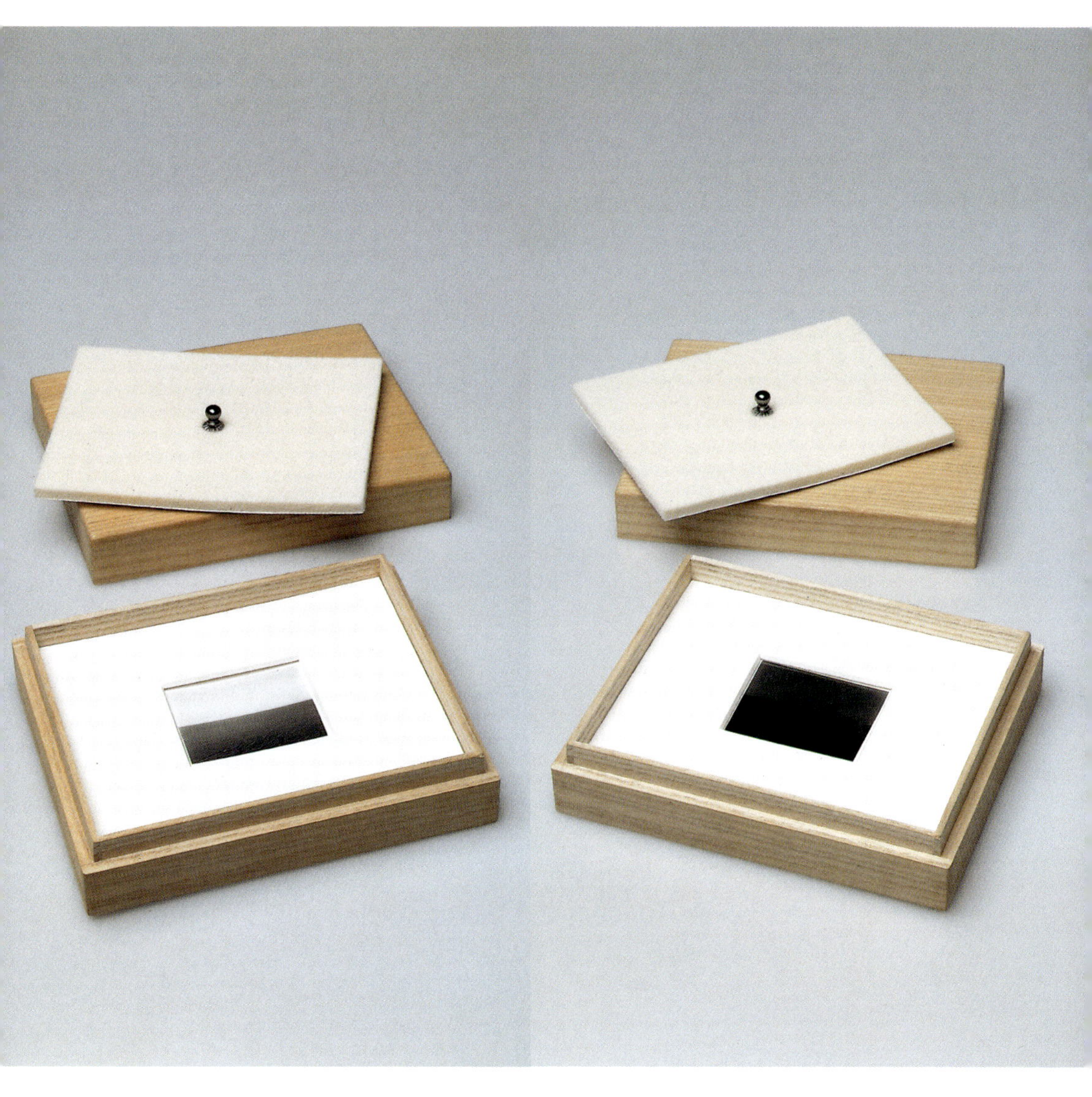

PHILIP TAAFFE

Lineament Monotypes, 1990

Lithographic ink on Japanese paper,
made in Naples 1990,
19 1/2 x 15 3/4" (49,5 x 40 cm),
Ed. of 55 individually printed monotypes

EDITION FOR PARKETT 26

Mining abstraction. A series of sixty
ornamental abstract monotypes reveals the
exponential permutations and combinations
of color and form contained in the obdurate
arabesque of the lineament.

"Taaffe's paintings are suffused with abandoned
architecture, perambulations left open, fraught
with possibilities—not closed, limited, bounded,
imprisoned, like the grid. Tying ribbons around the bars
of Western abstraction, he undermines stability with
pinwheels, rotation, movement, access."

Jeff Perrone
Parkett No. 26, 1990

フィリップ・ターフ

線形模様のモノタイプ　1990

1990年ナポリ製手漉き紙にリトグラフ用インク、
49.5×40cm、
Ed. 55、1枚ずつ刷られたモノタイプ

パルケット・エディション 26

抽象の採掘。60点の装飾的な抽象模様のモノタイプ
は、線形模様の頑固なアラベスクの含む色彩とフォル
ムの順列組合せが、指数関数的な数に上ることを明ら
かにする。

ターフの絵画には廃墟や中断されたそぞろ歩きをおもわせる跡がひ
しめき、多くの可能性を秘めている。それも格子とは異なり、閉ざさ
れ、制限され、囲われ、拘束されてはいない。西洋の抽象の鉄格子
にリボンを結わき、ターフは風車、回転、運動、出入りを使って均衡
を揺るがす。

ジェフ・ペローネ
（パルケット 26号、1990年）

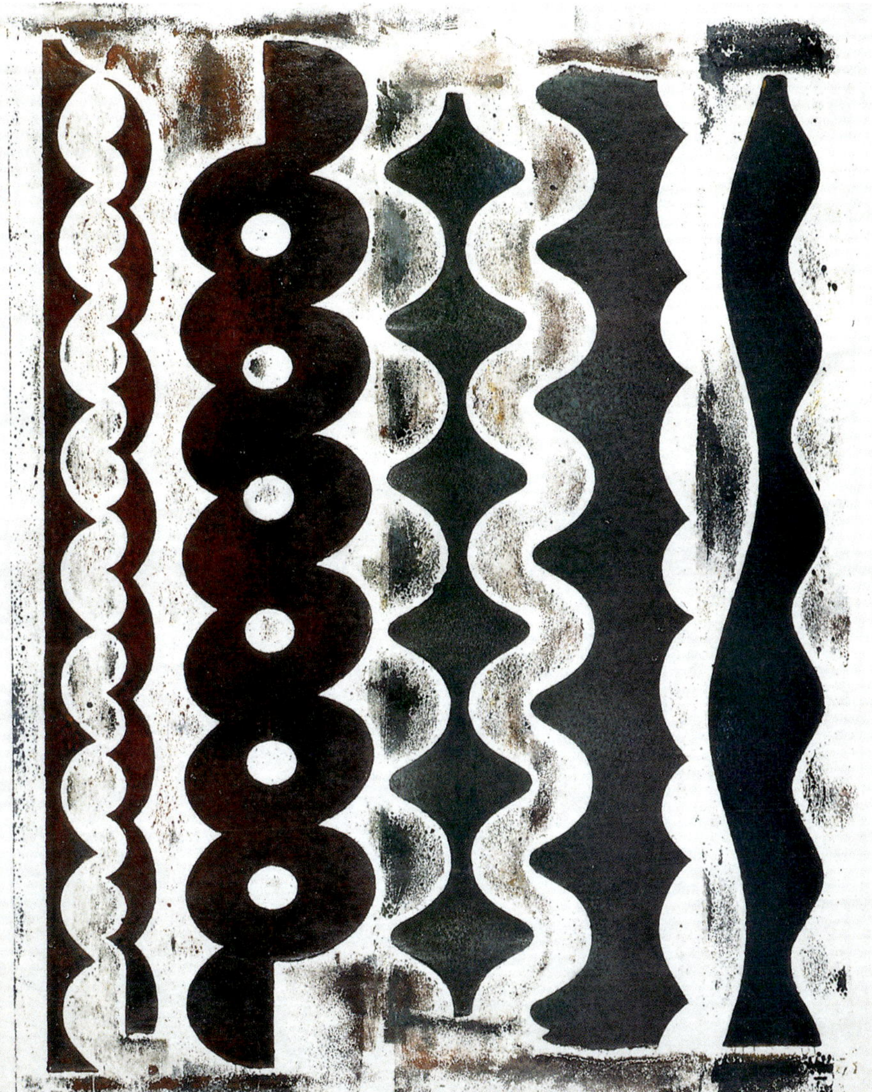

SAM TAYLOR-WOOD

Five Revolutionary Seconds XIV
(Sketch), 1999

C-print, 360-degree panorama shot,
2 3/4 x 16 1/2" (6,9 x 49,1 cm),
Ed. 50/XX, signed and numbered

EDITION FOR PARKETT 55

A loop in space and time: The revolution has
been arrested, each figure suspended in the
moment of "taking a giant step."

"Not only does Sam Taylor-Wood construct a seamless
yet heterogeneous space, in which people are both in
close proximity, yet also infinitely distant, because,
though in a mutually shared space, they inhabit
another site: the scene of their private theater. Her
photographic presentation is such that, even as it
elicits our desire for narrative, it frustrates our hope
for narrative coherence and closure."

Elisabeth Bronfen
Parkett No. 55, 1999

サム・テイラー＝ウッド

革命的な5秒間　XIV（スケッチ）
1999

Cプリント、360度パノラマ撮影、
6.9×49.1cm、
Ed. 50/XX、署名、番号入り

パルケット・エディション 55

空間と時間のループ。革命は抑止され、登場人物は各々
「大きな一歩」を踏み出そうとする瞬間、動きを停め
る。

サム・テイラー＝ウッドは継ぎ目なく、しかし異なる成分からなる空間
を組み立てるばかりでない。またその空間で人々がごく身近にいなが
ら、限りなく遠くにいるのは、同じ空間を共有しながら、かれらの居
場所はまた別にあるからである。それはかれらの私的な演劇の一場面。
そのためテイラー＝ウッドの写真は、物語を欲するわたしたちの気持
ちを顕在化させても、物語のまとまりと結末を求める期待には応えて
くれない。

エリザベス・ブロンフェン
（パルケット 55号、1999年）

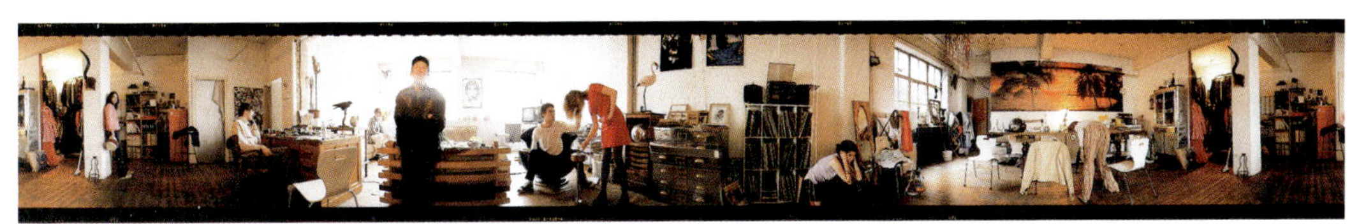

DIANA THATER

Untitled, 2000

DVD (Digital Video Disc)
with endless loop, no sound,
Ed. 150/XXX, signed and numbered

EDITION FOR PARKETT 60

Bees in hexagons, rooms filmed, brightness
of shadows, and quantum physics.

"Diana Thater considers the perception of animals
in parallel with a human perception which may
be described as either conditioned by technology
(the camera-assisted human) or as a product of it
(the human wholly dependent on the idea of the
photographic, i.e., as a post-human realization of
itself). What is to be compared here is not the animal
and the human but the animal and the apparatus, and
while the work's content may be projected on the wall,
its subject is the viewer in the gallery."

Jeremy Gilbert-Rolfe
Parkett No. 60, 2000

ダイアナ・セイター

無題　2000

DVDエンドレス・ループ、無声、
Ed. 150/XXX、署名、番号入り

パルケット・エディション 60

六角形のなかのハチ、撮影された部屋、影の明るさ、
そして量子力学。

ダイアナ・セイターは動物の知覚を、科学技術に慣らされた（カメラ
の助けを借りる人間）、あるいはその産物（写真的なものの概念、す
なわち人間以後に起こるそれ自身の実現に完全に依拠する人間）で
ある人間の知覚と同列のものとみなす。ここで比較すべきは動物と
人間ではなく、動物と装置であり、作品の内容は壁に映写されるが、
作品の主題は画廊を訪れる鑑賞者である。

ジェレミー・ギルバート＝ロルフ
（パルケット 60号、2000年）

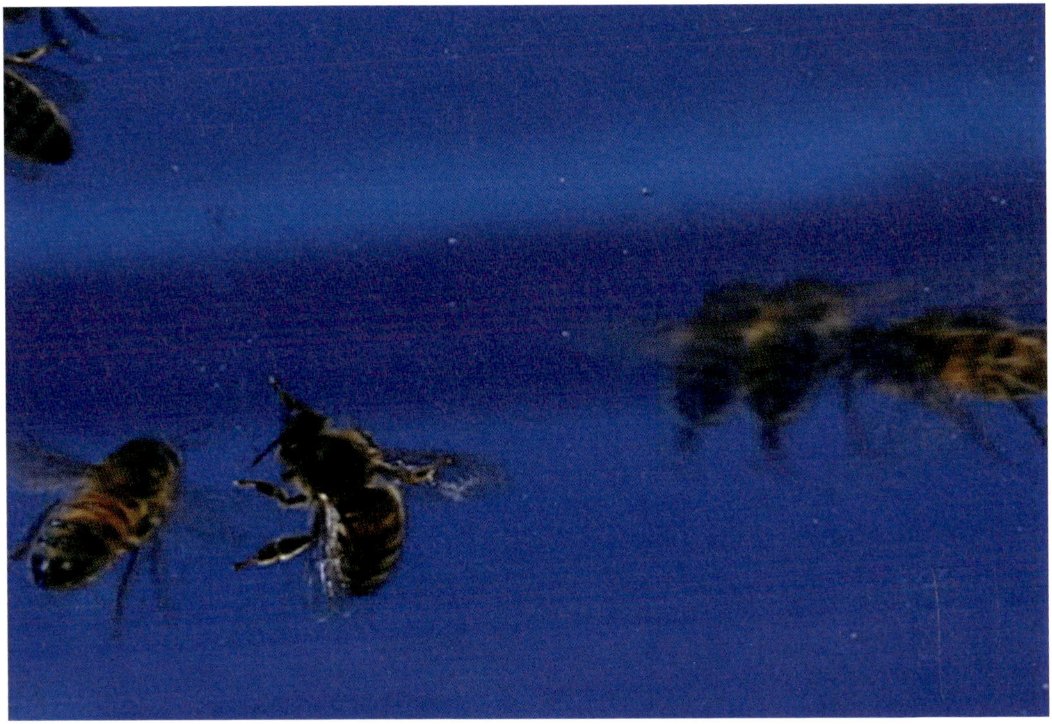

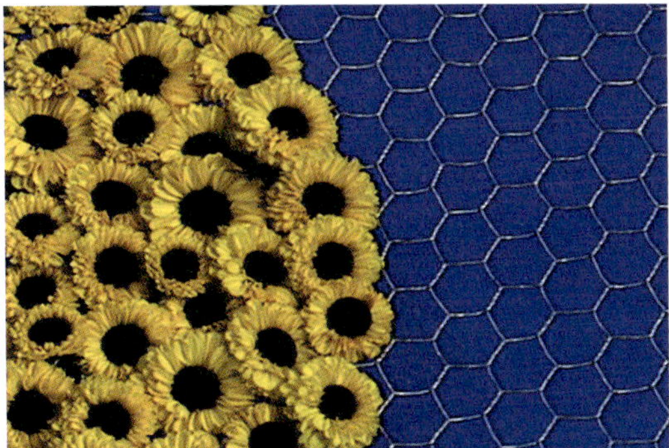

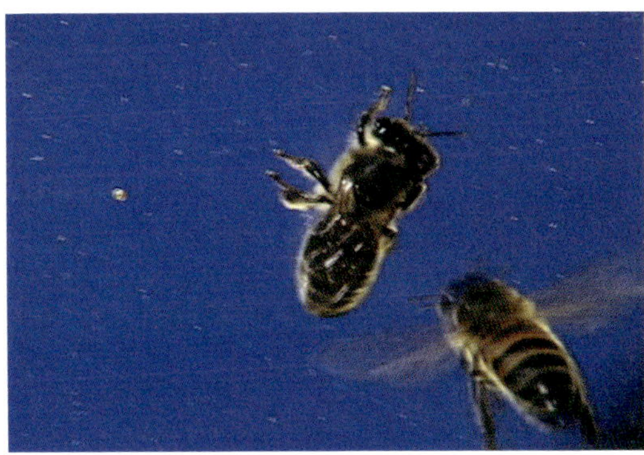

WOLFGANG TILLMANS

Parkett Edition, 1992–98

60/X unique works on color-negative
photographic paper,
ca. 16 x 12" (40,5 x 30,5 cm),
signed and numbered

EDITION FOR PARKETT 53

De-subjectivized signals: From classical
contemplation of an object to universal
structures.

"Tillmans's photos project a special aura due to their
innate temporal element. His photos evoke in you the
sense of having visited some place similar, or spent the
same sort of intimate time with friends. That is owing
to the fact that, through the manipulation of distance,
his shots always indicate his presence, participating
in the scene not as a voyeur but as someone with a
strong empathy for those being photographed."

Midori Matsui
Parkett No. 53, 1998

ヴォルフガング・ティルマンス

パルケット・エディション　1992-98

それぞれにイメージの異なる60/X種の作品、
カラー反転写真印画紙：約40.5×30.5cm、
署名、番号入り

パルケット・エディション 53

主観的を妨げる信号。オブジェの古典的な熟視から
普遍的な構造へ。

ティルマンスの写真は時間的な要素を内包して、特別なオーラを放
つ。写真を見ると、どこか似たようなところを訪ねたり、同じように
友だちと親しい時間を過ごしたことがあるような気がする。それは
距離の操作によって、ティルマンスの写真がつねに撮影者の存在を
暗に示し、それも覗き見するよそ者ではなく、撮影された人々と心の
通い合う人物として、その情景の中にいることを知らせるからである。

松井みどり
（パルケット 53号、1998年）

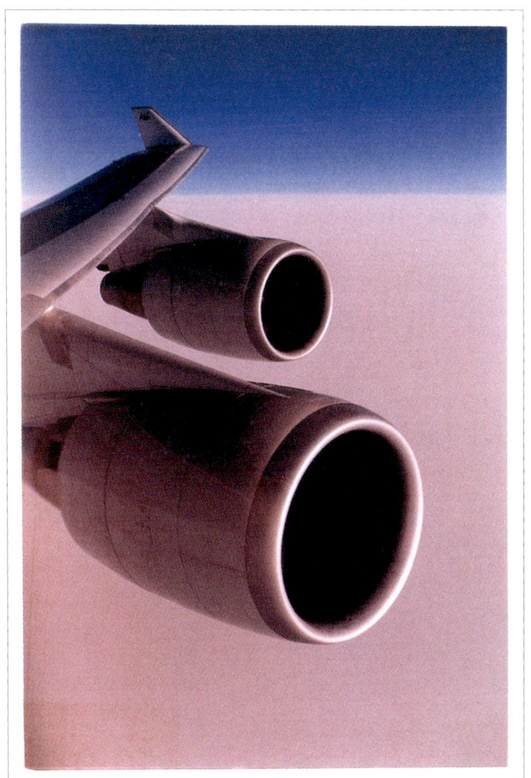

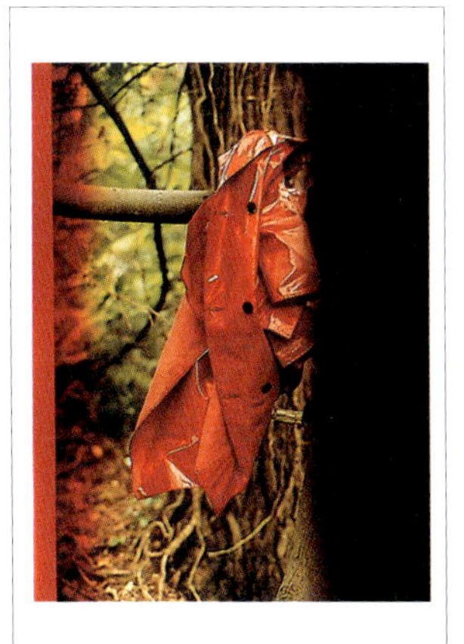

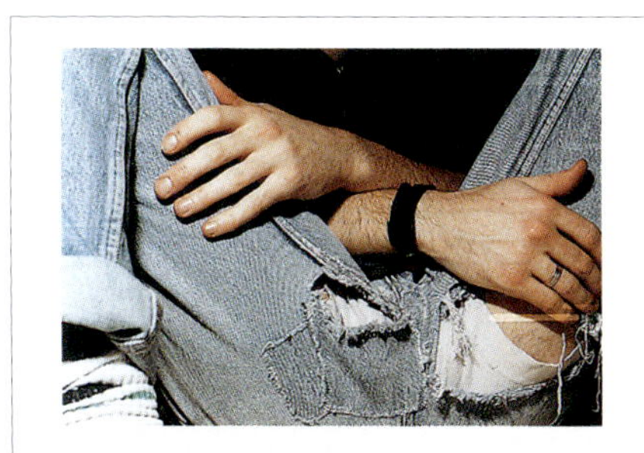

RIRKRIT TIRAVANIJA

Untitled, 1995, (450/375)

Gold-rimmed Ray Ban glasses
with engraving on the lenses:
LONG RIVER
A SINGLE LINE
ORANGE SAFFRON
AT TWILIGHT,
5 $^3/_8$ x 1 $^3/_4$" (2,5 x 16 x 6,7 cm),
Ed. 80/XXV, numbered,
with certificate and artist's seal

EDITION FOR PARKETT 44

Instrument of heightened perception.
A self-portrait perhaps or a picture of the
part played by the artist as he brings into
focus the daily chores blurred by habit.

"Art has many different levels and you have to make
your own level. You have to decide where you want to
be, and then just go for that. It doesn't have to do with
anything else in the world. Just yourself. You get there,
and maybe nobody sees it, but you get there. It is, at
least as I think of it, a spiritual thing."

Rirkrit Tiravanija
Parkett No. 44, 1995

リクリット・ティラヴァニャ

無題 1995 （450/375）

レイバンの金縁眼鏡、レンズに銘刻：
長い川
一本の線
オレンジ色のサフラン
黄昏時に
2.5×16×6.6cm、
Ed. 80/XXV、番号入り、証明書、アーティストの印章

パルケット・エディション 44

高度な知覚を得るための道具。おそらく自画像、ある
いは習慣化して印象のぼやけた日常の雑用に焦点を絞
り、ティラヴァニャが演じるアーティストの役柄の絵。

アートにはさまざまなレベルがあり、きみも自分のレベルを作る
必要がある。どこにいたいか決め、あとはそれを目指して突進する。
世界のなにかほかのものと関わる必要はない。きみだけがいれば
よい。きみはそこにたどりつく。ひょっとするとだれも見ないかも
しれない。しかしきみはそこにたどりついた。その行為は、少なく
ともわたしの考えるかぎり、信仰にかかわる。

リクリット・ティラヴァニャ
（パルケット 44号、1995年）

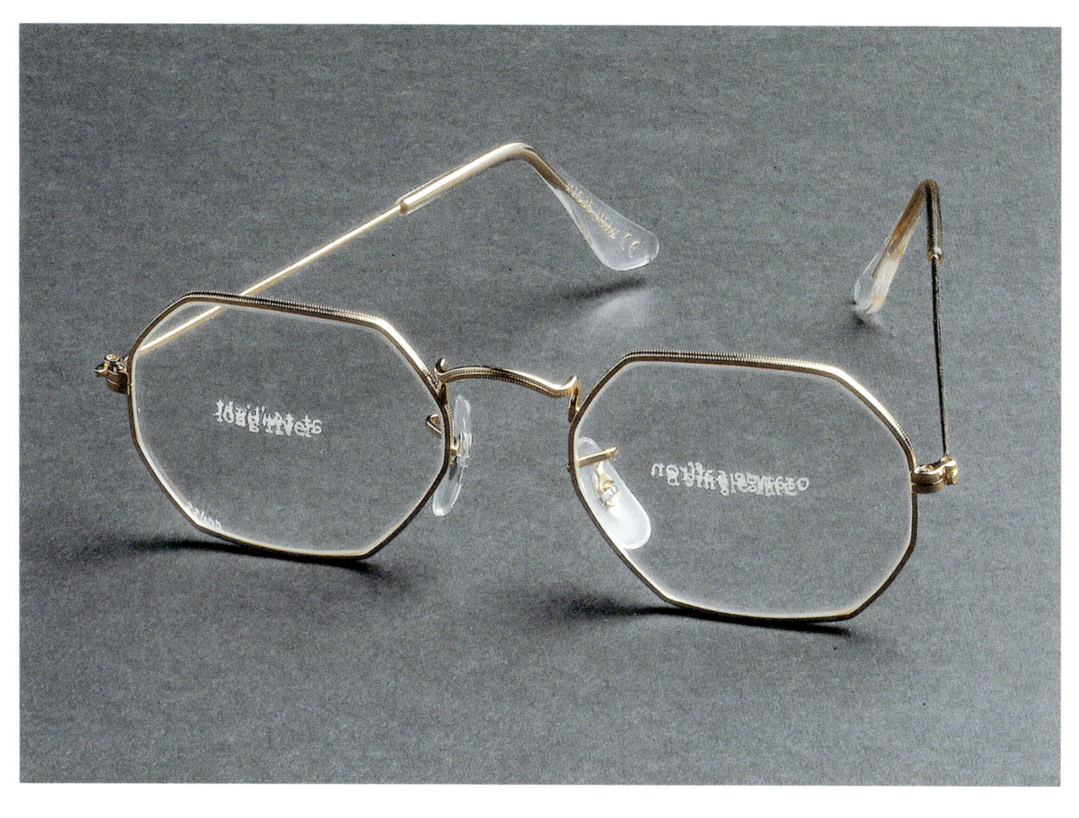

FRED TOMASELLI

Cyclopticon, 2003

Surface-mounted pigment print on
Plexiglas, 12 x 12" (30,1 x 30,1 cm),
printed by David Adamson,
Adamson Editions, Washington, D.C.,
Ed. 60/XXX, signed and numbered

EDITION FOR PARKETT 67

The anatomy of a mind spewing a tidy universe of chaotic invention.

"His signature pieces are compelling, hybrid objects: ersatz, or maybe surrogate paintings, or tapestries, or quilts, or mosaics. Their various components—both over-the-counter and controlled pharmaceuticals, street drugs, natural psychotropic substances and other organic matter, collaged elements from printed sources, and hand-painted ornament—are all suspended in gleaming layers of clear, polished, hard resin. Forms implode, explode, oscillate, buzz, loop, swirl, and spiral.—The combined effect, neither determinably real nor fully illusionistic, is at once electrifying and de-stabilizing."

James Rondeau,
Parkett No. 67, 2003

フレッド・トマセーリ

キクロプティコン　2003

アクリルの表面に顔料でプリント、
30.1×30.1cm、
刷り：デイヴィッド・アダムソン、
アダムソン・エディションズ（ワシントンDC）、
Ed. 60/XXX、書名、番号入り

パルケット・エディション 67

混沌とした発明の整然とした宇宙を吐く知力の解剖図。

トマセーリの特徴がよく現れた作品は吸引力の強い、混合物である。絵画の模造、あるいは代用物、タペストリー、キルト、モザイクなど。多様な構成物—市販薬、処方薬、街中で売買される薬、向精神作用のある天然素材などの有機物、印刷物のコラージュ、手描きの装飾—はすべて透明な、磨き上げられた、固い樹脂の光る層のなかに宙づりにされる。フォルムは内へ外へと破裂し、震動し、ブンブン音をたて、宙返りし、渦を巻き、らせん状に回転する。それらが組み合わさって生ずる効果は、はっきり実在もしなければ完全な幻覚でもないが、見るものを感電したように痺れさせ、心を揺さぶる。

ジェイムズ・ロンドー
（パルケット 67号、2003年）

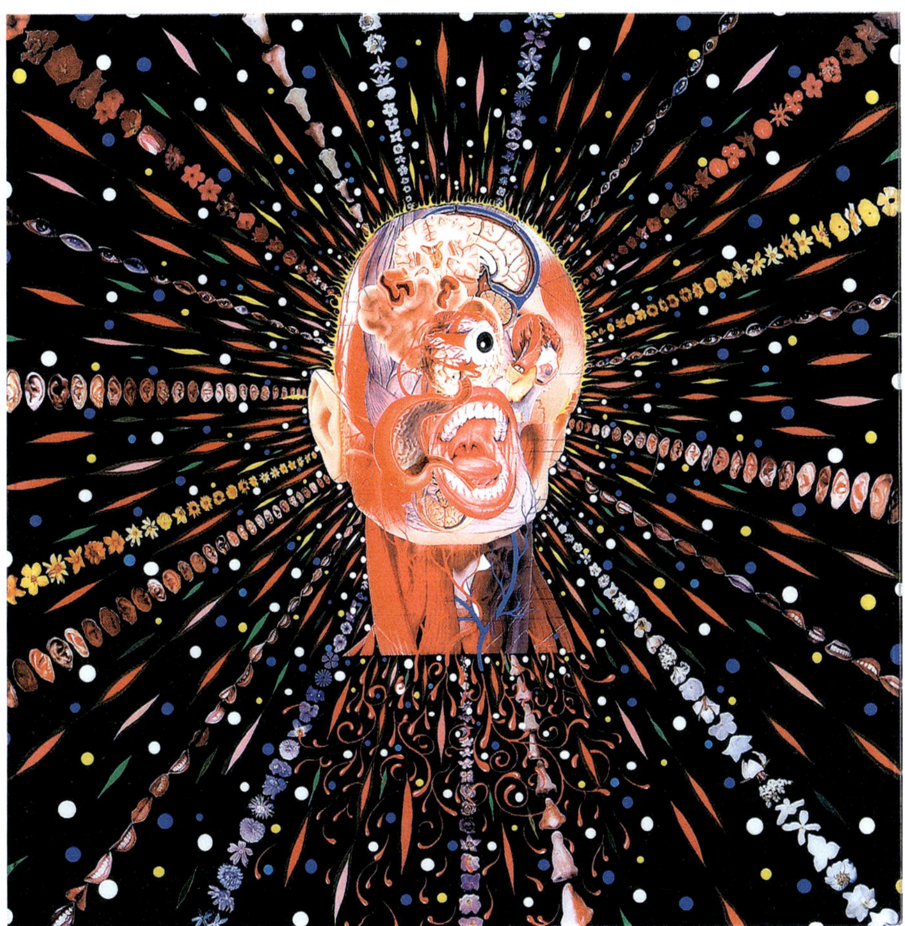

ROSEMARIE TROCKEL

Studio Visit, 1992

Photo-etching and acid-free
transparent foil in embossed strawboard
matte, mounted on wood with hanger,
image: 8¼ x 8¼" (21 x 21 cm);
frame: 15 x 13 x ⅜" (38 x 33 x 0,8 cm),
printed by Peter Kneubühler, Zurich,
Ed. 80/XX, signed and numbered

EDITION FOR PARKETT 33

Mind's eye view. An intimate perspective of the studio that places the viewer inside the secret cave of the artist's left eye.

"What language cannot do easily, and what Trockel achieves in her composite objects, is the simultaneous: she makes us spectators, at one and the same moment, of high art objects—and their tending, after hours, by the cleaner."

Anne M. Wagner
Parkett No. 33, 1992

ローズマリー・トロッケル

アトリエ訪問　1992

フォト・エッチング、無酸透明ホイル、
エンボス加工を施した黄ボール紙マット、
板にマウント、吊り金具付き、
図柄：21×21cm、額：38×33×0.8cm、
刷り：ペーター・クノイビューラー（チューリヒ）、
Ed. 80/XX、署名、番号入り

パルケット・エディション 33

知力の目が見るもの。鑑賞者をアーティストの左目の秘密の洞の内部に置いて見る、身近なアトリエの景色。

ことばでは容易になし遂げられないものの、様々な物をとりあわせたトロッケルのオブジェが達成するのは、同時性である。トロッケルはわたしたちをまったく同じ瞬間に高級な美術品の鑑賞者にし、定刻を過ぎれば掃除機を渡して世話係にする。

アン・M. ワグナー
（パルケット 33号、1992年）

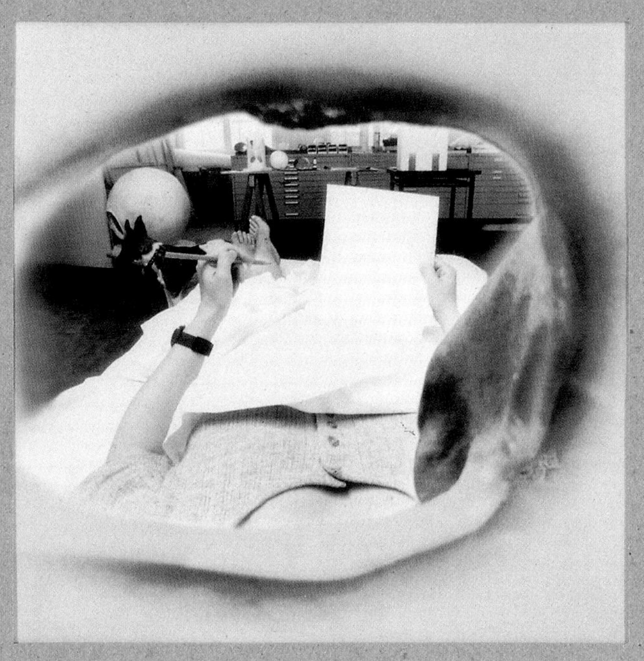

JAMES TURRELL

Squat, Juke, Carn, Alta, 1990

Four aquatint editions on Zerkall 250g/m^2,
each 10 x 8 $^{11}/_{24}$" (25,5 x 21 cm),
one of them bound in the magazine,
printed by Peter Kneubühler, Zurich,
Ed. 40/X each, signed and numbered

EDITION FOR PARKETT 25

Speed of light. These experimental forays into
the medium of etching yield light as material,
not illusion, in the contours of the printed
image.

"Turrell treats light as substance. Instead of stone,
wood, clay or bronze, he 'molds' light—artificial or
natural—whose density displays a barely visible but
fluctuating, palpable presence: palpable through
perception. The visitor who exposes himself to this
perception is inevitably and bluntly confronted with
himself.

Jean-Christophe Ammann
Parkett No. 25, 1990

ジェームズ・タレル

スクウォット、ジューク、カーン、オルタ
1990

アクアチント 4点、ツェルカル紙 250g/m^2、
各25.5×21cm、1点を本紙に綴じこみ、
刷り：ペーター・クノイビューラー（チューリヒ）、
各Ed. 40/X、署名、番号入り

パルケット・エディション 25

光速。エッチングを用いた実験では、光は錯視ではな
く物質として、プリントされたイメージの輪郭に痕を残
す。

タレルは光を物質としてあつかう。石、木、土、あるいはブロンズの
代わりに、（人工、自然を問わず）光を「成形する」。光の密度はかろ
うじて目に映るが変動し、触知のできる存在であることを示す。触
知は知覚を通してなされる。この知覚に自らをさらす訪問者は避け
がたく、容赦なく、自らに直面する。

ジャン＝クリストフ・アマン
（パルケット 25号、1990年）

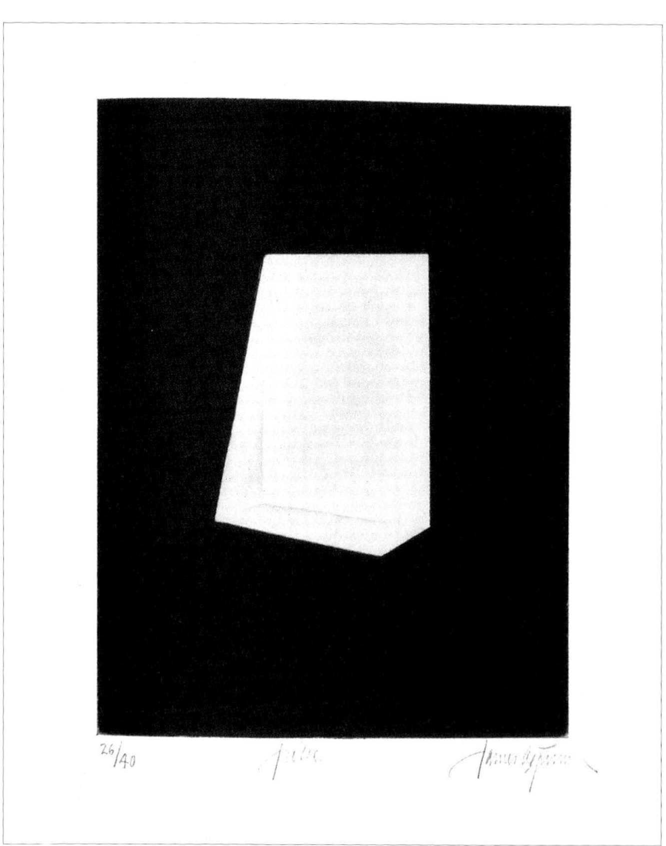

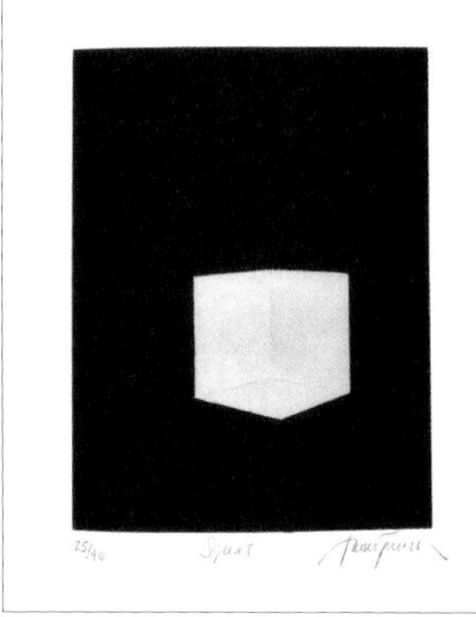

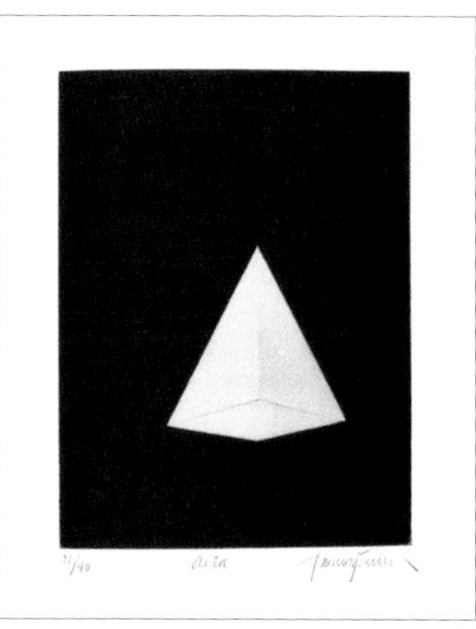

LUC TUYMANS

Silence, 1990–2000

Men's cotton shirt with reproduction of
the artist's painting SILENCE, 1991,
shirt design by Walter van Beirendonck,
3 sizes (S, M, L)

Hand-stiched version
made by Trois-Quarte, Antwerp,
Ed. 20/XXV, signed and numbered
certificate

Silkscreen version
printed by Lorenz Boegli, Zurich,
Ed. 99/XXX, signed and numbered
certificate

EDITION FOR PARKETT 60

Born to wear: give this child a voice.

"Painting, like any memory, always comes too late
and too soon. It mediates between the uncatchable
moment of the past and a thought that springs
from it. Luc Tuymans's pictures show this mediating
relationship by including elements of the medial
source after which they were painted: the fleetingness
and the light of photographic paper, film or video stills."

Hans Rudolf Reust
Parkett No. 60, 2000

リュック・タイマンス

沈黙　1990-2000

男物の綿のシャツに
タイマンスの絵画《沈黙》の複製をプリント、
シャツのデザイン：ヴァルター・ファン・ベイレンドンク、
3サイズ（S. M. L.）

手縫い版
制作：トロワ・カルト（アントワープ）
Ed. 25/XXV、署名、番号入り証明書

シルクスクリーン版
刷り：ロレンツ・ボエリ（チューリヒ）、
Ed. 99/XXX、署名、番号入り証明書

パルケット・エディション 60

着るために生まれた。この子に声をあげて。

絵画は、あらゆる記憶と同じように、いつも来るのが遅すぎるか、さ
もなければ早すぎる。過去の捉えられない瞬間と、そこから湧き
でる思考の間を仲介する。リュック・タイマンスの絵は、絵を描くも
とになったメディアの要素（印画紙、映画、ビデオ・スティル）のうつ
ろいやすさ、そして光をとりこんで、こうした仲介の関わりを表現す
る。

ハンス・ルドルフ・ロイスト
（パルケット 60号、2000年）

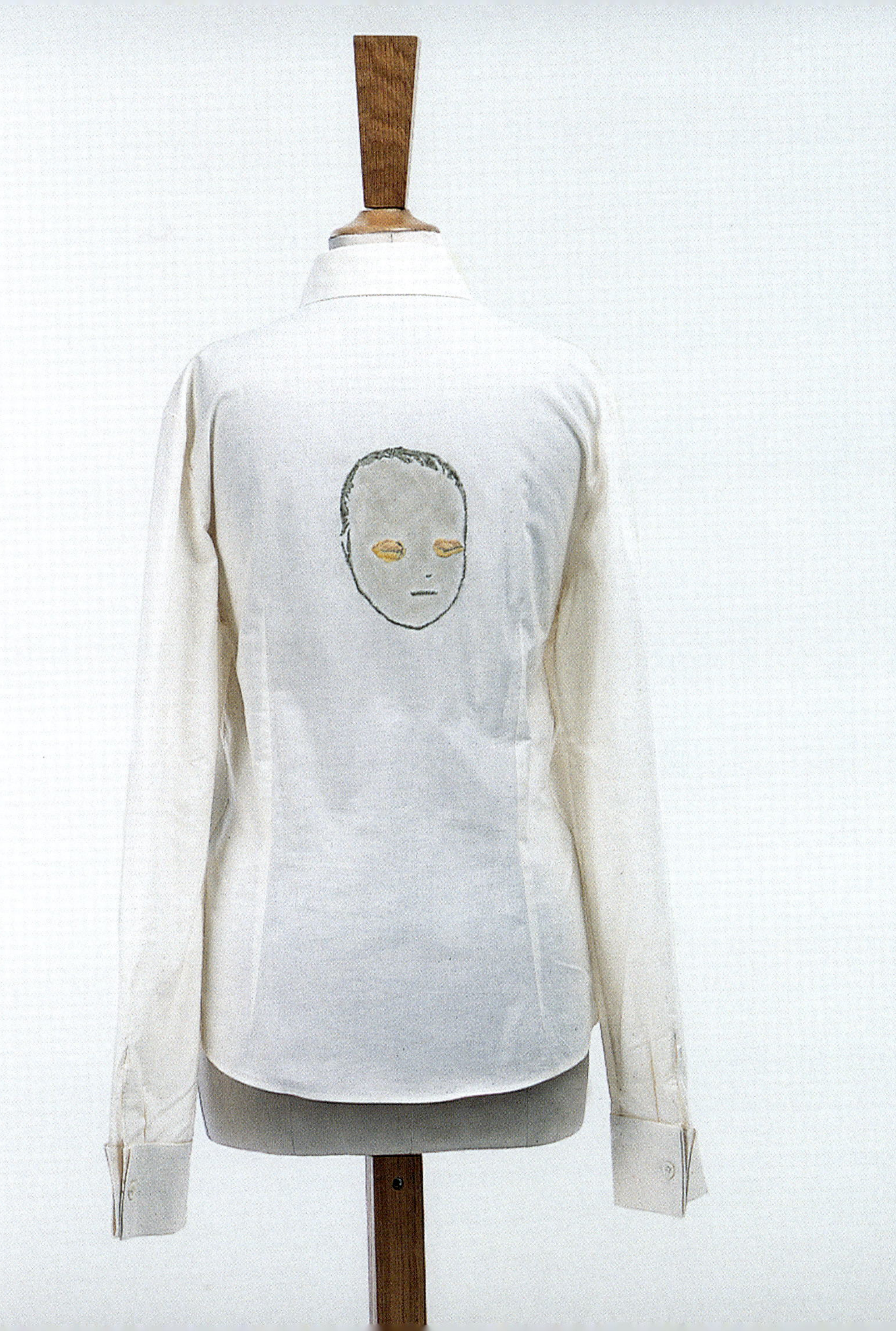

KEITH TYSON

Parkett Paperweight, 2004

Pebble on copper plate, partially painted
in enamel, mounted on rubber base,
3 ^{15}/$_{16}$ x 3 ^{15}/$_{16}$" (10 x 10 cm), ca. 1 ^{9}/$_{16}$"
(4 cm) high, each piece is unique in its
combination of plate, pattern, pebble,
paint, and position, and each comes
with a signed pattern sheet showing
its specific design within the
100 different possibilities,
Ed. 75/XXV, signed and numbered

EDITION FOR PARKETT 71

The complexity of chaos: Deceptively harnessed in ten times ten geometries.

"Faced with the contradiction inherent in the
notion that the infinitude of all possibilities should
be grasped by the structures of our minds and,
consequently, that the expanding universe is purely an
extrapolation of a finite universe, Keith Tyson devises
strategies to invent rules. He neither comes up with
static 'world pictures' nor with linear sequences of
pictures. Instead he seeks completely new rules by
which a major player could generate his own worlds."

Hans Rudolf Reust
Parkett No. 71, 2004

キース・タイソン

パルケットのための文鎮　2004

銅板の上に石、エナメルで部分的に塗装、
ゴムの土台にマウント、
10×10cm、高さ約4cm、
銅板、模様、石、塗装、位置は1点ずつ異なる、
100種の可能性のなかから
唯一選んだデザインを示すパターン・シートに署名し、
それぞれに添付、
Ed. 75/XXV、署名、番号入り

パルケット・エディション 71

混沌の複雑さ。10×10の幾何学に鞁具をつけて
繋ぎ、ひとを惑わす。

可能性はすべて無限であることはわたしたちの知力の構造によっ
て把握されなければならず、したがって膨脹する宇宙はたんに
限りある宇宙の敷衍にすぎないとの観念に内在する矛盾に直面
し、キース・タイソンは規則を発明する戦術を考案する。タイソン
は静的な「世界の絵」も、絵画の線的な連鎖ももちださない。そ
の代わりに主役たちがそれぞれ独自の世界を生みだせるような、
まったく新しい規則を追求する。

ハンス・ルドルフ・ロイスト
（パルケット 71号、2004年）

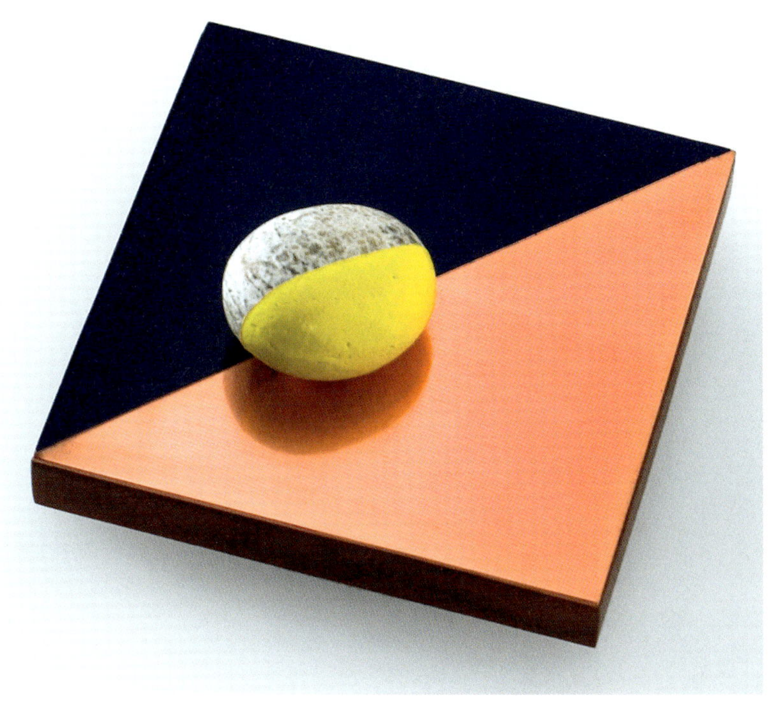

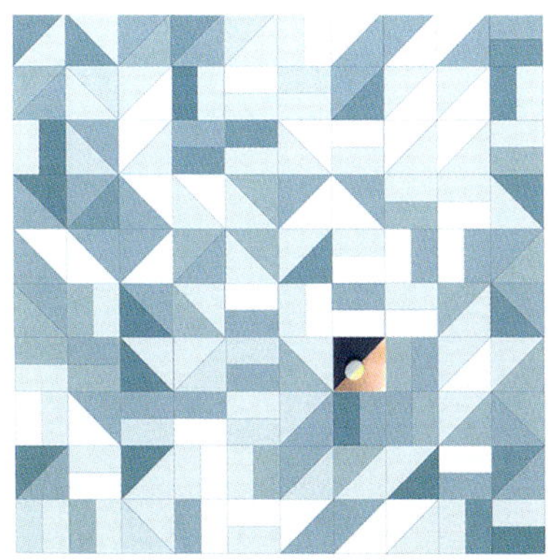

COSIMA VON BONIN

Colour Wheel, 2007

Stainless steel, polypropylen
handles, enameled in 7 colors,
$18^{1}/_{2}$ x $2^{1}/_{4}$" (47 x 6 cm),
production by Saygel & Schreiber, Berlin,
Ed. 45/XX, signed and numbered
certificate

EDITION FOR PARKETT 81

Take the pastry of concept, roll it out with the colors of the rainbow, and serve it up with a dollop of debate.

"That the word 'monster' resonates in monstrare,
the Latin word for 'to show', is probably more than
a coincidence, and the world von Bonin serves up
is indeed monstrous with its outsized mushrooms,
rockets, and octopuses that look as if they had just
escaped from an old-fashioned Jules Vernes film
adaptation, not to mention the gigantic, floppy stuffed
animals and her soft pictures or 'rags,' as she calls
them."

Dirk von Lowtzow
Parkett No. 81, 2007

コズィマ・フォン・ボニン

色の輪　2007

ステンレス・スティール、ポリプロピレンの把手、
7色のエナメルで塗装、47×6cm、
制作：セイゲル＆シュライバー（ベルリン）、
Ed. 45/XX、署名、番号入り証明書

パルケット・エディション 81

観念の練り粉を用意し、虹色の麺棒で伸したら、ちょっぴり論争を添えて食卓へお運びください。

ラテン語で「見せる」を意味する「monstrare」に「モンスター」の
響きが感じられるのは、おそらく偶然ではないのだろう。フォン・ボ
ニンが食卓に運ぶ世界は、まるでジュール・ヴェルヌ原作の古い映画
のセットから逃げ出してきたような特大のキノコやロケット、蛸、は
たまた巨大でへなへなしたぬいぐるみの動物、本人が「ラグ」とよぶ
柔らかな絵までちりばめて、まさにモンスターと呼ぶにふさわしい。

ディルク・フォン・ロウツォウ
（パルケット 81号、2007年）

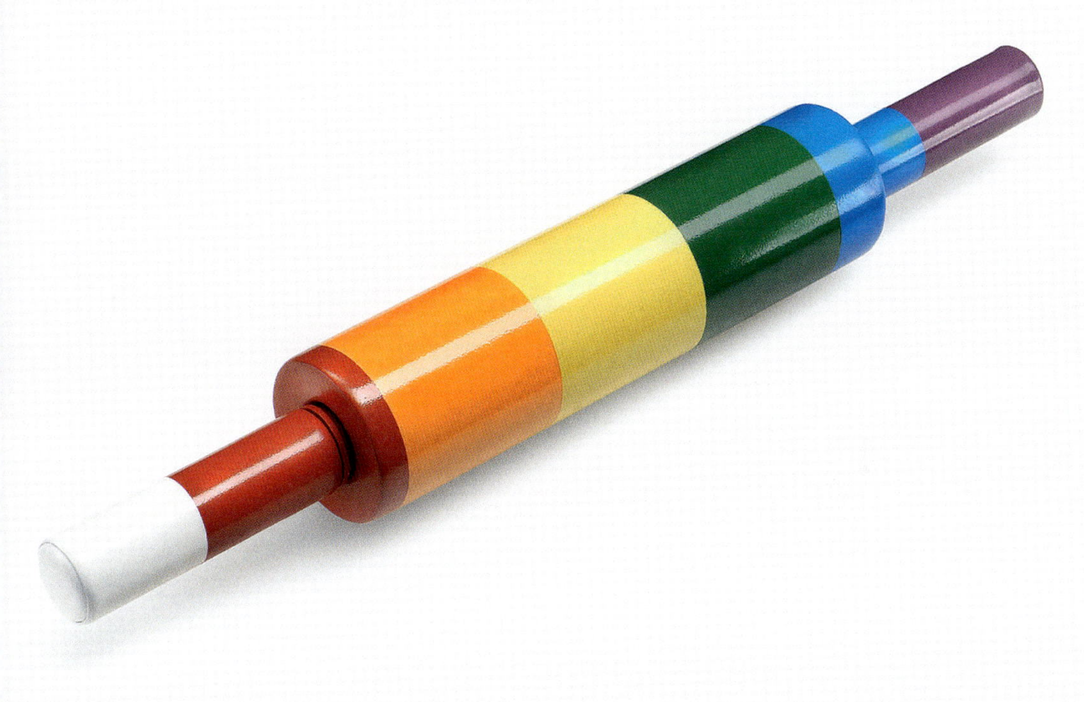

KARA WALKER

Boo-hoo, 2000

Linocut on Arches Cover White,
40 x 20 ¹/₂" (100,8 x 52,4 cm),
printed by Maurice Sanchez,
Derrière L'Etoile Studio, New York,
Ed. 70/XXX, signed and numbered

EDITION FOR PARKETT 59

Paradise revisited: Eve shows the evidence.

"Walker's unwieldy imagination is fixated with race in the starkest and most American of terms, black and white, as they were forged in the ante-bellum South, a time not so long ago in a galaxy called here."

Hamza Walker
Parkett No. 59, 2000

キャラ・ウォーカー

ブー・フー　2000

アルシュ・カバー・ホワイトにリノカット、
100.8x52.4cm、
刷り：モーリス・サンチェス、
デリエール・レトワール・スタジオ（ニューヨーク）、
Ed. 70/XXX，署名、番号入り

パルケット・エディション 59

楽園再訪。イーヴが証拠をお見せします。

ウォーカーの無骨な想像力は人種問題に病的に執着して離れない。その人種問題とは南北戦争以前の南部で、大昔でもない時期に、此処と呼ばれる銀河で形成された、露骨きわまりない、優れてアメリカ的な黒人と白人の対立である。

ハムザ・ウォーカー
（パルケット 59号、2000年）

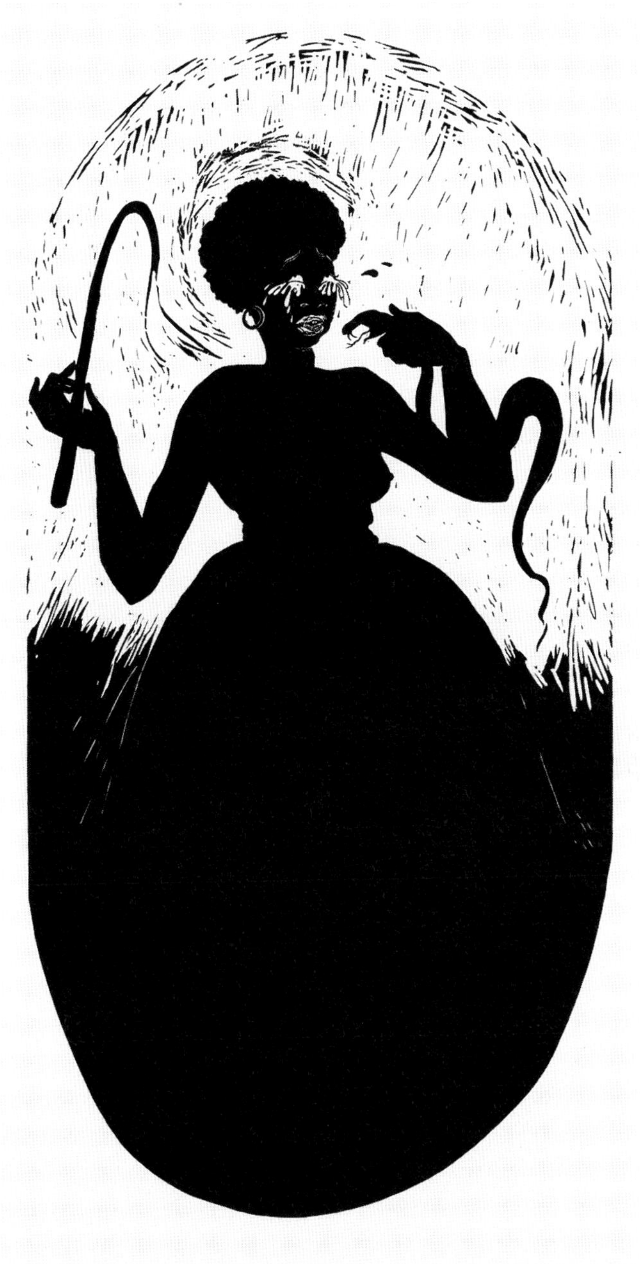

JEFF WALL

Boy on TV, 1989
(from "Eviction Struggle")

Cibachrome print,
13 ³/₄ x 14 ¹/₂" (35 x 37 cm),
photograph by Mancia/Bodmer, Zurich,
Ed. 80/XX, signed and numbered

EDITION FOR PARKETT 22

Freeze frame. A child's anxiety and disbelief
are digitally registered and trapped on a TV
screen, a "micro-gesture" extracted from
the general state of social tension and crisis
depicted in Wall's epic Eviction Struggle.

"Wall's images reflect a reality which surrounds us,
but which we do not necessarily want to face: racism,
solitude, exploitation, poverty, the difficulty of relations
between the sexes. Though anonymous, his characters
are a part of each one of us."

Béatrice Parent
Parkett No. 22, 1988

ジェフ・ウォール

テレビに映る少年　1989
（《立ち退き反対闘争》より）

チバクローム・プリント、35×37cm、
写真：マンシア・ボドマー（チューリヒ）、
Ed. 80/XX、署名、番号入り

パルケット・エディション 22

ストップモーション。少年の不安と驚愕がデジタル技
術を用いてテレビの画面上に捉えられ、保存される。
ウォールの大作《立ち退き反対闘争》は、社会的な緊
張、危機の普遍性から抽出された「微細な身振り」を描
きだす。

ウォールの映像は身近にあるにもかかわらず、わたしたちが必ずし
も直視しようとしたがらない現実（人種差別、孤独、搾取、貧困、男
女関係の難しさ）を映しだす。どこのだれかわからなくとも、登場人
物はわたしたちひとりひとりの一部でもある。

ベアトリス・ペアレント
（パルケット 22号、1988年）

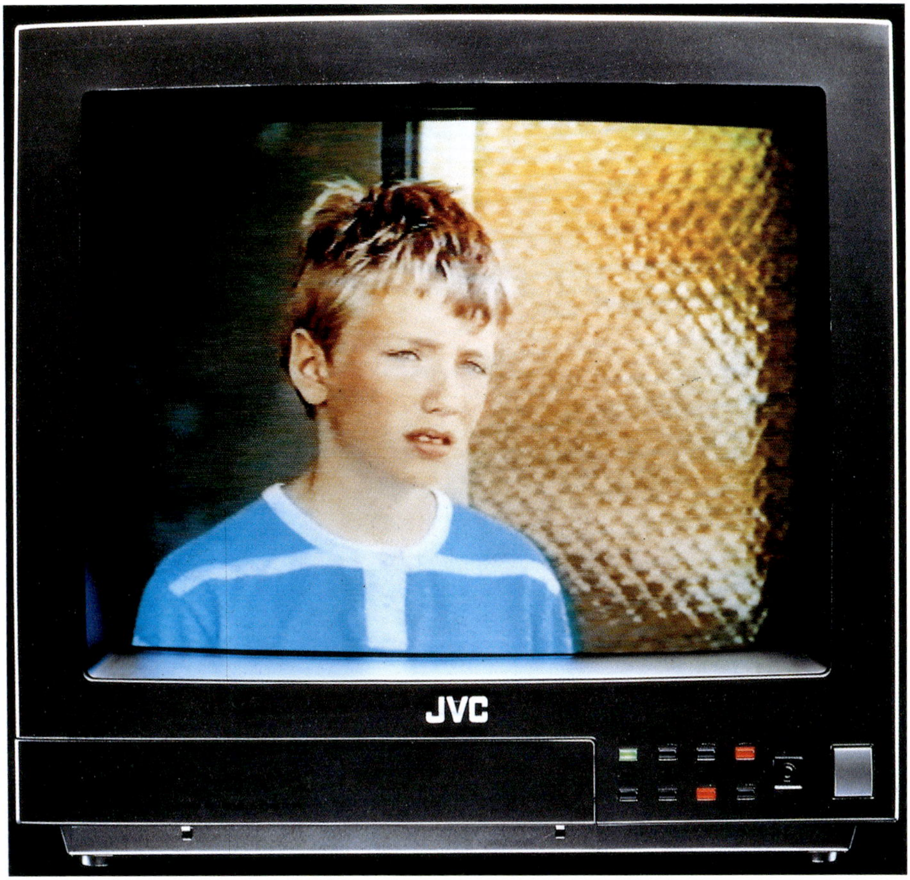

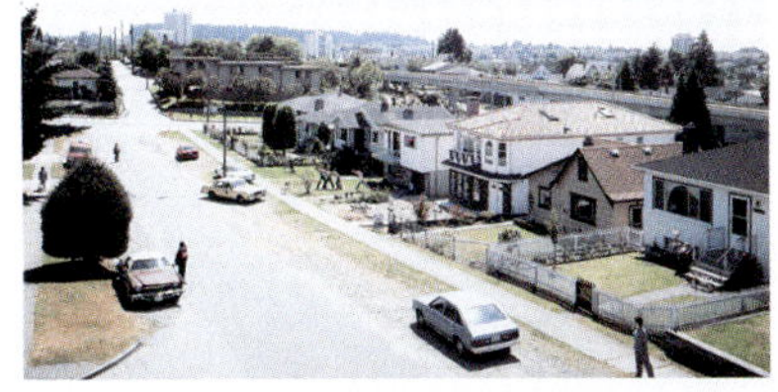

JEFF WALL

Untitled (Edition for Parkett), 1997

Silver gelatin contact print,
image approx. 7 1/2 x 9 5/8" (24,4 x 19,3 cm),
printed on archival paper,
approx. 15 3/4 x 17" (40 x 43,2 cm),
Ed. 50/XXV, signed and numbered

EDITION FOR PARKETT 49

Stepping across boundaries:
The solitude of a single sole bears witness.

"What we see in each picture are two images, one
which Wall builds and the second which we invent in
an instant, depending on what we saw on television
that day, what article we read, what argument we
participated in. As viewers, we find ourselves in a
fragile place, a conflicted moment when stereotype
and predisposition rush to finish sentences that never
had beginnings."

Collier Schorr
Parkett No. 49, 1997

ジェフ・ウォール

**無題（パルケットのためのエディション）
1997**

シルヴァー・ゼラチン・コンタクト・プリント、
図柄：約24.4×19.3cm、
無酸紙：約40×43.2cm、
Ed. 50/XXV、署名、番号入り

パルケット・エディション 49

境界を踏み越す。片方の靴裏の寂しさが証言する。

それぞれの写真にわたしたちはふたつのイメージをみる。ひとつは
ウォールが組み立てたもの、もうひとつは、その日テレビで何を見
たか、どんな記事を読んだか、どのような議論を交わしたかによっ
て左右される瞬間に、わたしたちが創作するもの。鑑賞者としてわ
たしたちは脆い場に身を置いている。ステレオタイプと素因が始ま
りのない文を慌てふためいて終わらせようとする脆い場所、紛糾し
た瞬間にわたしたちはいる。

コリエ・ショール
（パルケット 49号、1997年）

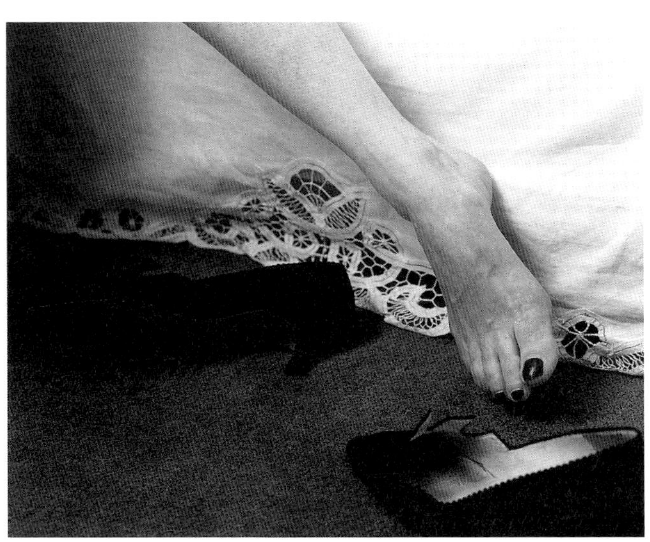

ANDY WARHOL

Photo Edition for Parkett, 1987

Machine-sewn and inserted in a
parchment cover in the special edition
of Parkett, 9 3/4 x 7 3/4" (24,8 x 19,9 cm),
Ed. 120, signed and numbered

EDITION FOR PARKETT 12

Social X-ray. Skeletons proliferate like guests
at a macabre cocktail party in this quartet of
repeated images sutured into a patchwork
memento mori.

"Andy was what sports fans call a most valuable player.
His work is more valuable now, but not because of
some laws of marketing, but because he's not around
himself. Those works are souvenirs and relics. They're
pieces of Andy."

Glenn O'Brien
Parkett No. 12, 1987

アンディ・ウォーホル

パルケットのためのフォト・エディション
1987

機械で綴りパルケット特別号の羊皮紙の表紙に挿入、
24.8×19.9cm、
Ed. 120、署名、番号入り

パルケット・エディション 12

社交のレントゲン写真。縫合され、死を表徴するパッチ
ワークとなった映像のくりかえす四重奏には、薄気味悪
いカクテルパーティーのゲストのように、骸骨が増殖す
る。

アンディはスポーツのファンに言わせれば、最高殊勲選手のような
もの。アンディの作品の価値は前より上がっているけれど、それは
マーケットのなにかしらの法則のせいではなく、アンディ自身がもう
いなくなってしまったから。作品は形見、遺品。アンディの一部でも
ある。

グレン・オブライエン
（パルケット 12号、1987年）

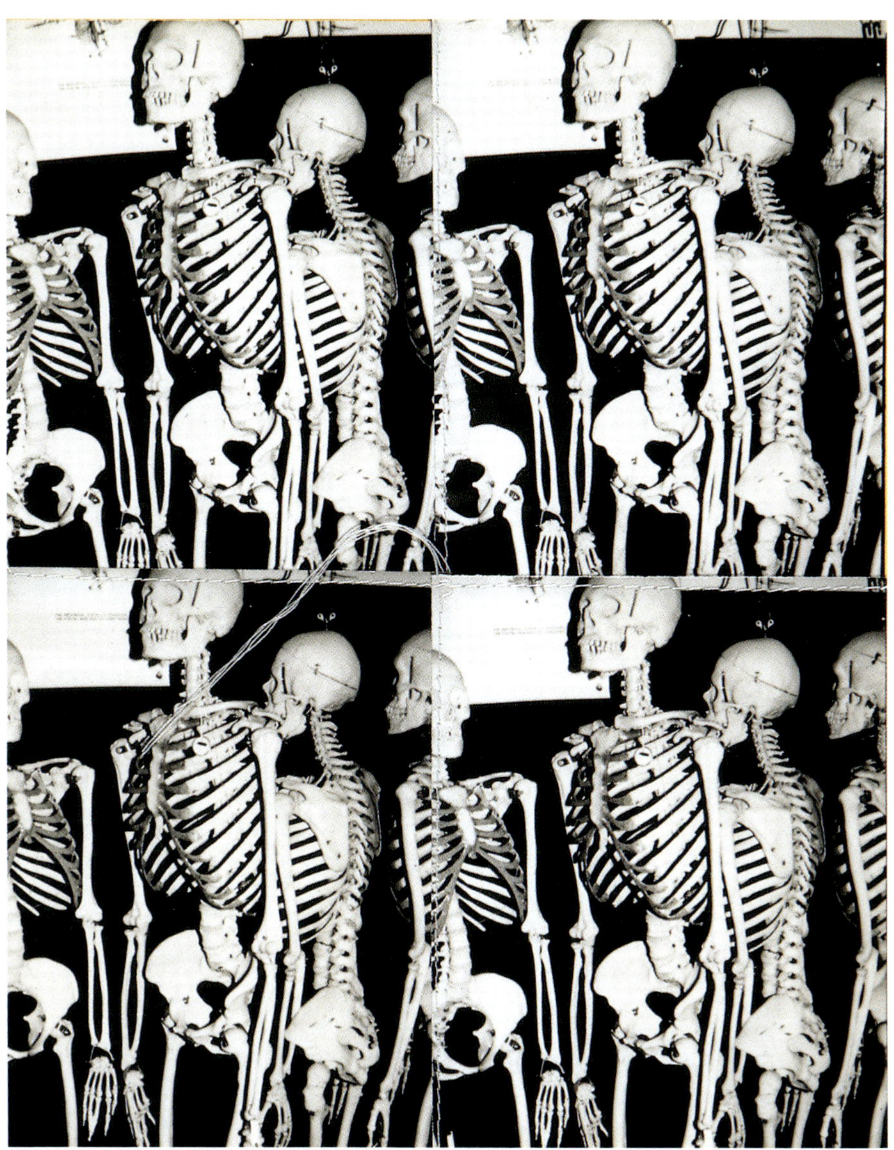

REBECCA WARREN

Poincaré, 2006

Pompom and shoe, hand painted,
mixed media,
2 ³/₄ x 2 ¹/₂ x 2 ³/₈" (7 x 7 x 6cm),
Ed. 35/XX, signed and numbered
certificate

EDITION FOR PARKETT 78

The slipper overlooked in foam as aphrodite emerges.

"In Warren's art… what you can hold onto in iconographical terms counts for less than what you can't, and what matters most are the implications and effects of her refusals. When she got back the ruined cast of BOBO, for example, she began working back into it, piling more febrile, finger-worked masses of clay onto its already-exploited armature—generally speaking this is not done, but Warren never saw a restriction she didn't immediately want to transgress—and the result, given a title intentionally difficult to pronounce, was DOU DOU CHÉ (2006)."

Martin Herbert
Parkett No. 78, 2007

レベッカ・ウォーレン

ポアンカレ　2006

ポンポンと靴、手彩色、
ミクスト・メディア、
7×7×6cm、
Ed. 35/XX、署名、番号入りの証明書

パルケット・エディション 78

アフロディーテの誕生時には泡にまぎれて見過ごされた靴。

ウォーレンの作品において、図像のもつ意味として手がかりになるものは、手がかりにならないものより重要でなく、もっとも大切なのはウォーレンの拒否に伴う含意とその効果である。たとえばBOBOの壊れた像が手元に戻ったときには、またそれに手を加えはじめた。以前にもまして熱心に、すでにたっぷり手をかけた骨組みに、粘土の塊を指で捏ねてつけ足した。普通に考えれば、そんなことはしないものだが、ウォーレンときたら、規制があれば、とりあえずそれを破ってみたくなる質なので、その結果は、わざわざ発音しにくいタイトルまでつけた《DOU DOU CHÉ》（2006）である。

マーティン・ハーバート
（パルケット 78号、2007年）

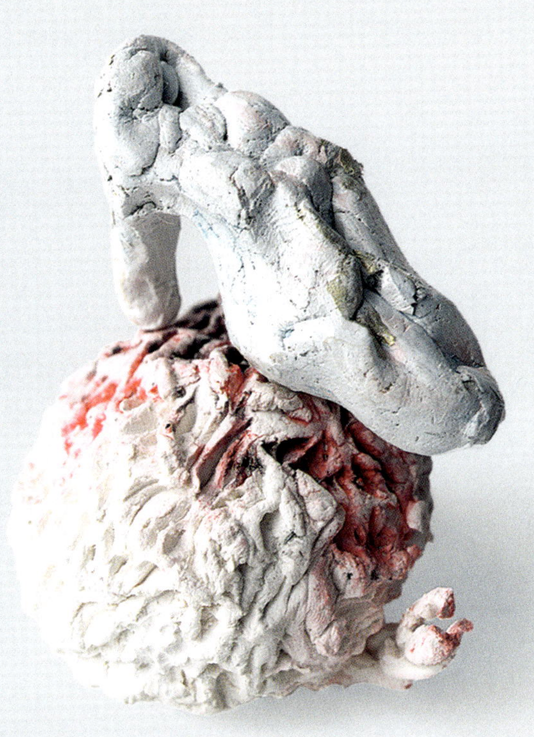

GILLIAN WEARING

Sleeping Mask, 2004

Wax (reinforced by polymer resin),
paint, 8 ¼ x 5 ⁵⁄₁₆" (20,5 x 13,8 x 8 cm),
produced by Making Objects Ltd.,
London,
Ed. 60/XX, signed and numbered

EDITION FOR PARKETT 70

Inverting the cothurnus, from foot to face,
from sound to silence, from the swagger of
conceit to the truthfulness of disguise.

"It was strange that when I was younger I thought of
my mother as older in the picture and when I retur-
ned to it, I realized that hers was the face of a young
woman that I didn't recognize and hadn't seen before!
It took my own aging to make me really appreciate and
understand my mother as her younger self. I could see
in the photograph my mother, myself, and someone I
could never have known at that age."

Gillian Wearing, interview with Cay-Sophie Rabinowitz
Parkett No. 70, 2004

ジリアン・ウェアリング

寝顔のマスク　2004

ワックス（ポリマー樹脂で強化）、絵具、
20.5×13.8×8cm、
制作：メイキング・オブジェクツ社（ロンドン）、
Ed. 60/XX、署名、番号入り

パルケット・エディション 70

足から顔へ、音から静寂へ、自惚れて闊歩するより人目
に立たずに真心を尽くすように、コトルヌス（上げ底靴）
を裏返す。

今より若かった頃には、写真の中の母は年上に見えたけれど、しばら
く経ってから見直してみたら、それが前に一度も見たことのない、見
知らぬ若い女性の顔だったの。自分が年をとって初めて、若い女性
だったころの母のことがよくわかるようになりました。その写真に
映っている母、わたし自身、それから若いころには知ることのできな
かったひとの姿を見ることができます。

ジリアン・ウェアリング、
カイ＝ソフィ・ラビノヴィッツのインタヴューに応えて
（パルケット 70号、2004年）

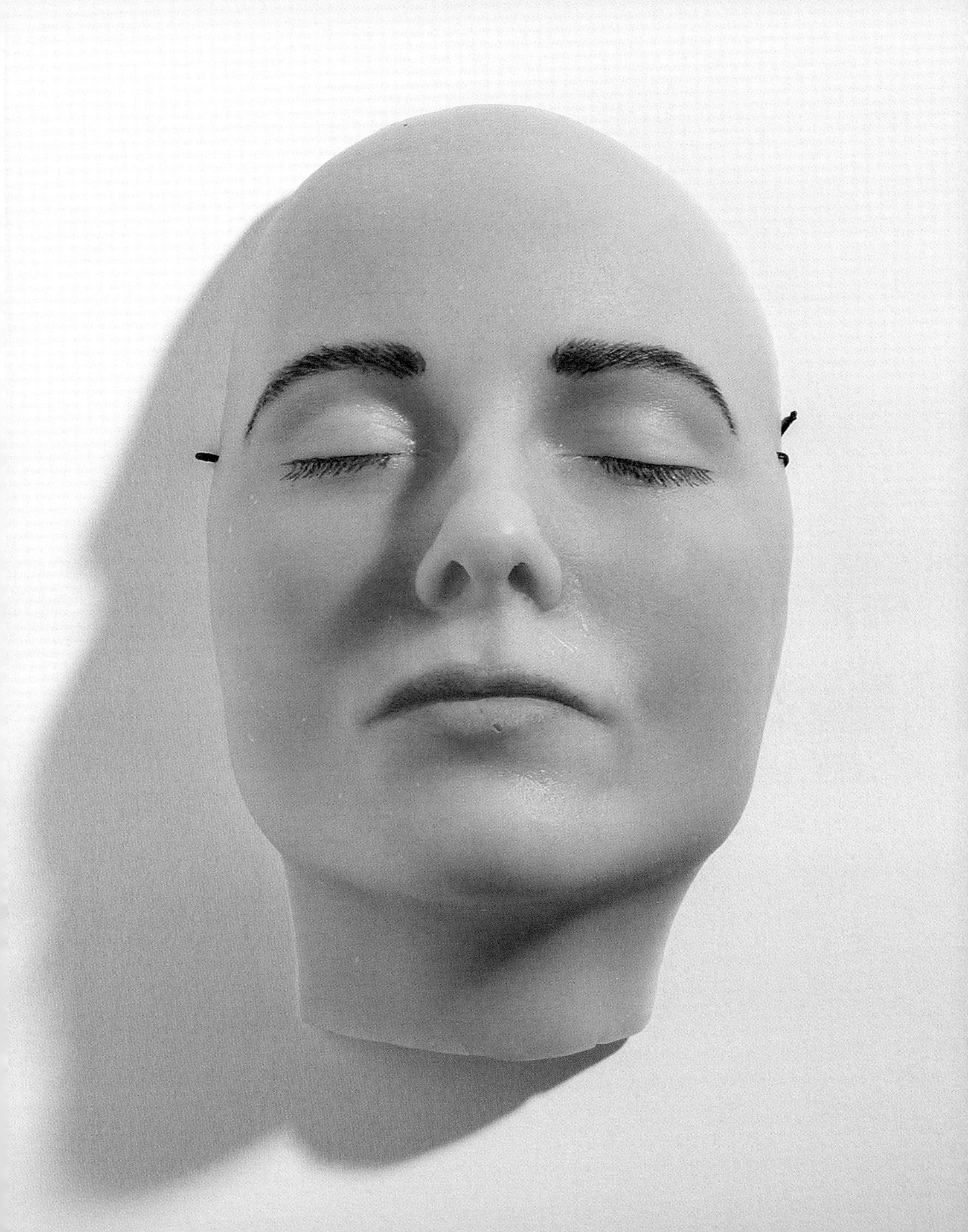

LAWRENCE WEINER

Unter den Linden—Under Lime
Trees, 1994

Rubber stamp,
approx. 7 1/2 x 3 3/4 x 3 1/2"
(19 x 10 x 8,8 cm), with red ink pad
in silkscreened card-board box
printed by Lorenz Boegli, Zurich,
Ed. 80/XXV, signed and numbered

EDITION FOR PARKETT 42

The meaning that comes away
from the work of art.
Berlin's historic street transforms—
through the act of translation—
into a metaphor of poetry and nature.

"The dialectical beauty of Weiner's work is its extreme
freedom of meaning coupled with fundamentally being
about what it says it's about."

Daniela Salvioni
Parkett No. 42, 1994

ローレンス・ウェイナー

ウンター・デン・リンデン―菩提樹の下で
1994

ゴム印、約19×10×8.8cm、
赤インクのスタンプ台、
シルクスクリーンでプリントしたボール紙の箱、
刷り：ロレンツ・ボエリ（チューリヒ）、
Ed. 80/XXV、署名、番号入り

パルケット・エディション 42

美術作品から離れてゆく意味。古い歴史のあるベルリ
ンの大通りが、翻訳という行為に仲介されて、詩と自然
の隠喩に変容をとげる。

ウェイナーの作品の弁証法的な美しさは、意味の自由を究めつつ、
それが関わると語るものに根源的に関わるところに在る。

ダニエラ・サルヴィオーニ
（パルケット 42号、1994年）

UNDER LIME TREES
UNTER DEN LINDEN

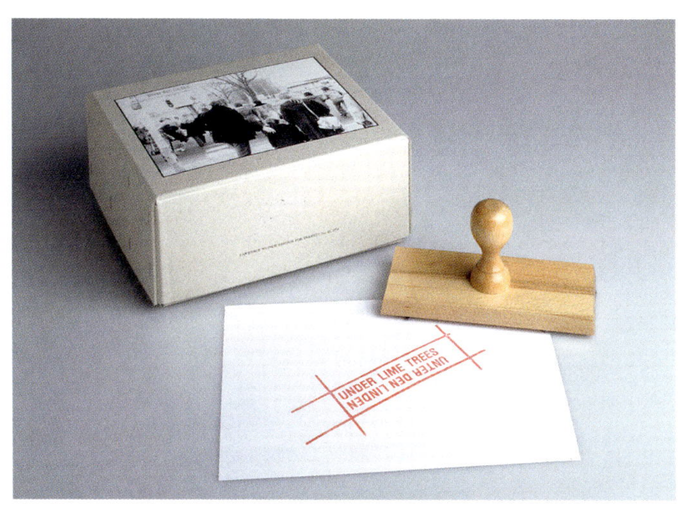

JOHN WESLEY

Boyfriends, 2001

6-color silkscreen
on Coventry 290 g/m^2,
image size: 28 x 35" (71,2 x 88,9 cm),
paper size: 31 x 38" (81 x 96,5 cm),
printed by Bob Blanton,
Brand X Editions, New York,
Ed. 70/XXX, signed and numbered

EDITION FOR PARKETT 62

Hairline, coastline: a mental and physical topography.

"Wesley's painting looks like nothing else out there. …the most conspicuous characteristics of his work from the seventies on—its insistent flatness, powdered pastel palette, cartoon/cinematographic narratives, embrace of the sexually charged encounter, sophisticated anthropomorphism, and mannered drawing—have enormous appeal amid a digital revolution that has provoked yet another rethinking of the medium."

Linda Norden
Parkett No. 62, 2001

ジョン・ウェスリー

男友だち　2001

6色刷りシルクスクリーン、
コヴェントリー紙 290g/㎡、
図柄：71.2×88.9cm、紙：81×96.5cm、
刷り：ボブ・ブラントン、
ブランド X エディションズ（ニューヨーク）、
Ed. 70/XXX、署名、番号入り

パルケット・エディション 62

生え際、水際。心理、物理の形態学。

ウェスリーの絵画はほかのどれにも似ていない……70年代以降の作品のもっとも目立つ特徴は—執拗な平面性、粉っぽいパステル風の色調、漫画／映画的な物語性、性的予感を湛えた出会いに向ける関心、高度に洗練された擬人化、様式化された素描—絵画というメディアの新たな見直しを促すデジタル革命のさなかに、大きな魅力を発揮した。

リンダ・ノーデン
（パルケット 62号、2001年）

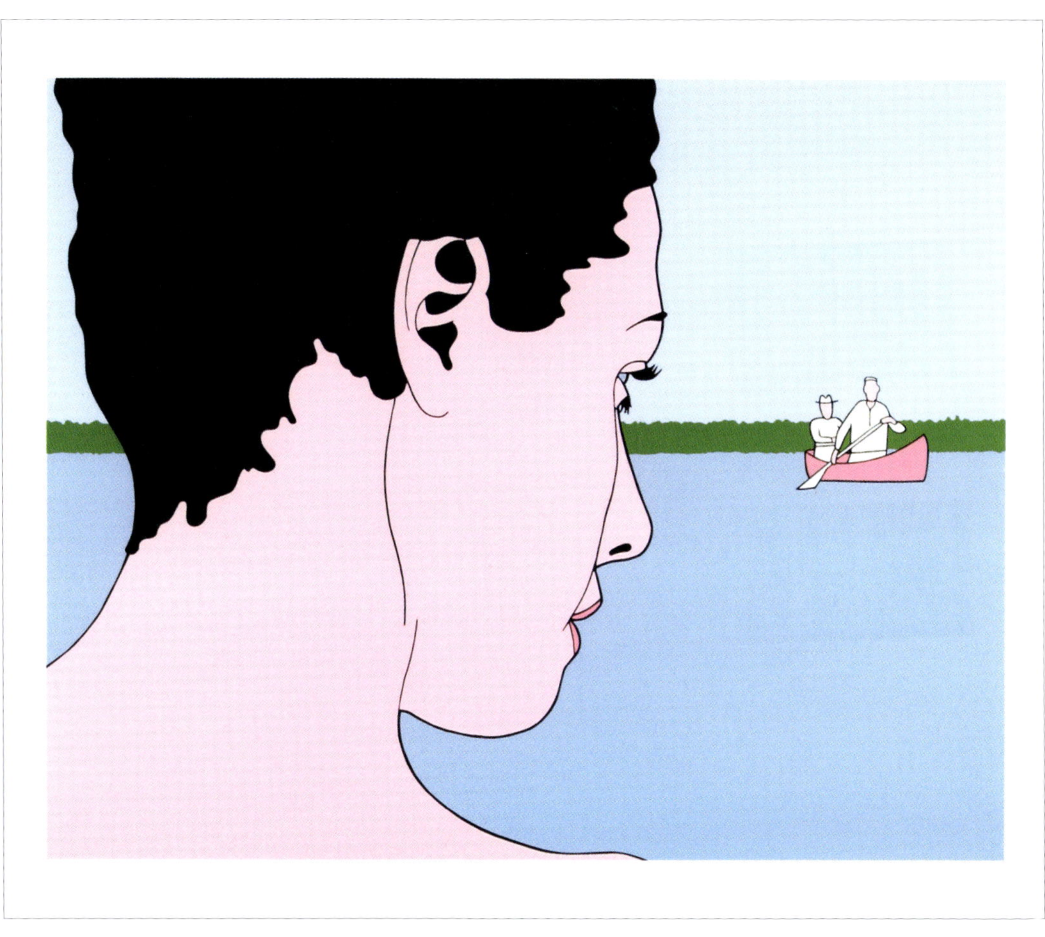

FRANZ WEST

Pouch for Parkett, 1993

Printed African fabric, chain,
10 $^5/_8$ x 9 $^5/_8$" (26,2 x 24,5 cm),
Ed. 180/XX, signed and numbered

EDITION FOR PARKETT 37

Totem tote. A Parkett-sized pouch fashioned
from hand-printed African fabric is a useful
article for a specific purpose.

"Despite their sedate qualities as couches and chairs,
and pedestal-mounted or hand-held sculptures, Franz
West's works seem always to belie another mission,
as though publicly their masquerade was quietly
aesthetic, but privately their purpose was fetishist
and host to some orgiastic activity."

Jan Avgikos
Parkett No. 37, 1993

フランツ・ヴェスト

パルケット用ポーチ　1993

プリント柄のアフリカの布地、チェーン、
26.2×24.5cm、
Ed. 180/XX、署名、番号入り

パルケット・エディション 37

トーテム・トート。手刷りでプリントしたアフリカ産の布
地でこしらえたパルケット・サイズのポーチは、用途を
限定した便利な一品。

ソファや椅子、台座に載せたり手でもつ彫刻のように落ちついた風
情でありながら、フランツ・ヴェストの作品はいつでもそれとは別の
使命をもつらしく、表向きは淑やかに美しさを装いながら、人目に
立たないところではフェティシュを意識して、乱痴気騒ぎを主催する。

ヤン・アヴギコス
（パルケット 37号、1993年）

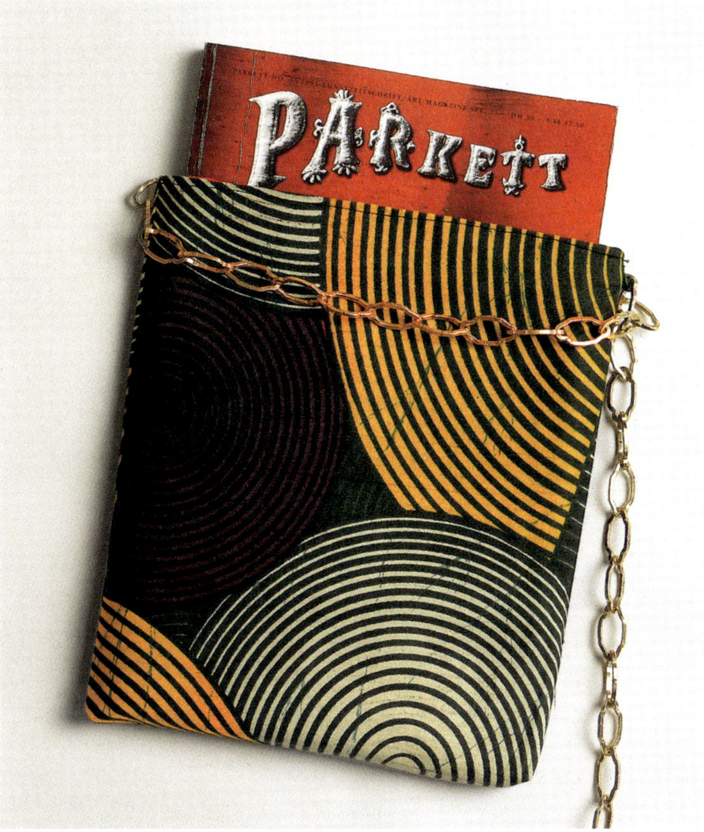

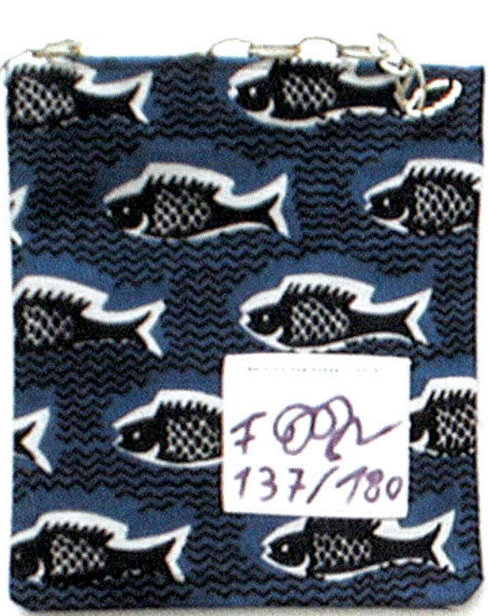
137/180

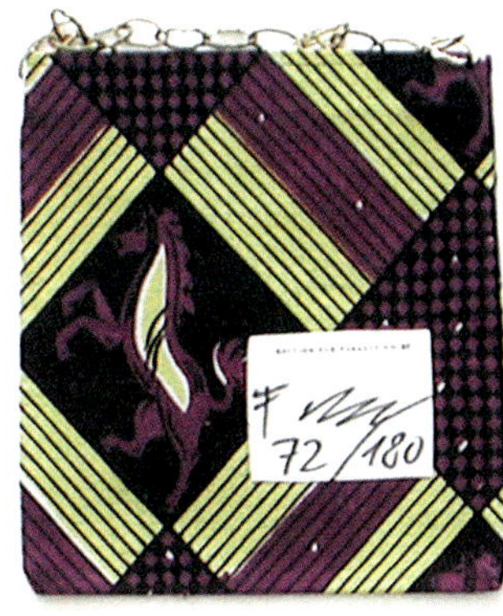
72/180

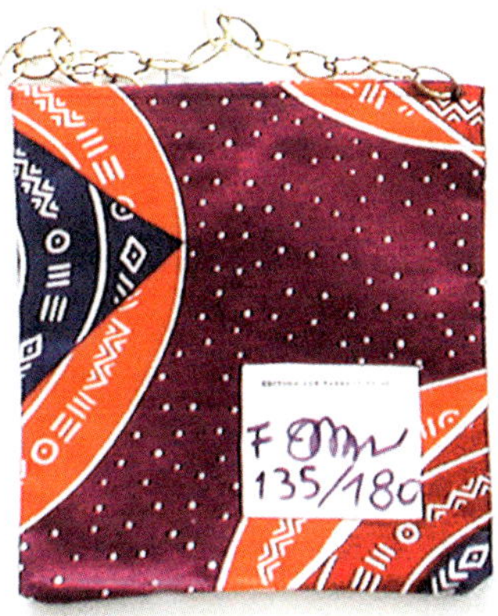
135/180

FRANZ WEST

2 x 20 Years of Parkett, 2004

Bookshelf, reinforcing steel,
plexiglas, four wheels,
47 1/4 x 23 5/8 x 11 13/16" (120 x 60 x 30 cm),
Ed. 99/XX, signed and numbered
certificate

EDITION FOR PARKETT 70

This wheeled companion to the globetrotter's
"Pouch for Parkett" (1993) will house all the
volumes of Parkett through 2024.

"You can't catch up with things that are evident-
beautiful, right, definitely compelling (as their defining
opposites). It's a matter of being ahead of calculation
or design or definition by exactly that distance that
establishes their usefulness."

Franz West, interview with Bice Curiger
Parkett No. 70, 2004

フランツ・ヴェスト

パルケットの2x20年　2004

本棚、強化スティール、アクリル、
キャスター 4個、
120×60×30cm、
Ed. 90/XX、署名、番号入り証明書

パルケット・エディション 70

世界を股にかけて飛びまわる人の《パルケット用ポーチ》（1993）と対をなすキャスター付きのこの品には、2004年までに刊行されたパルケットの全巻を収納できる。

見た目そのままの物、（判定基準となる対極として）美しく、正しく、紛いようもなく魅力的なものとはつきあいようがない。有用性を確定するその間隔の分だけきちんと打算、たくらみ、定義に先んじることが肝心だ。

フランツ・ヴェスト、
ビーチェ・クリガーのインタヴューに応えて
（パルケット 70号、2004年）

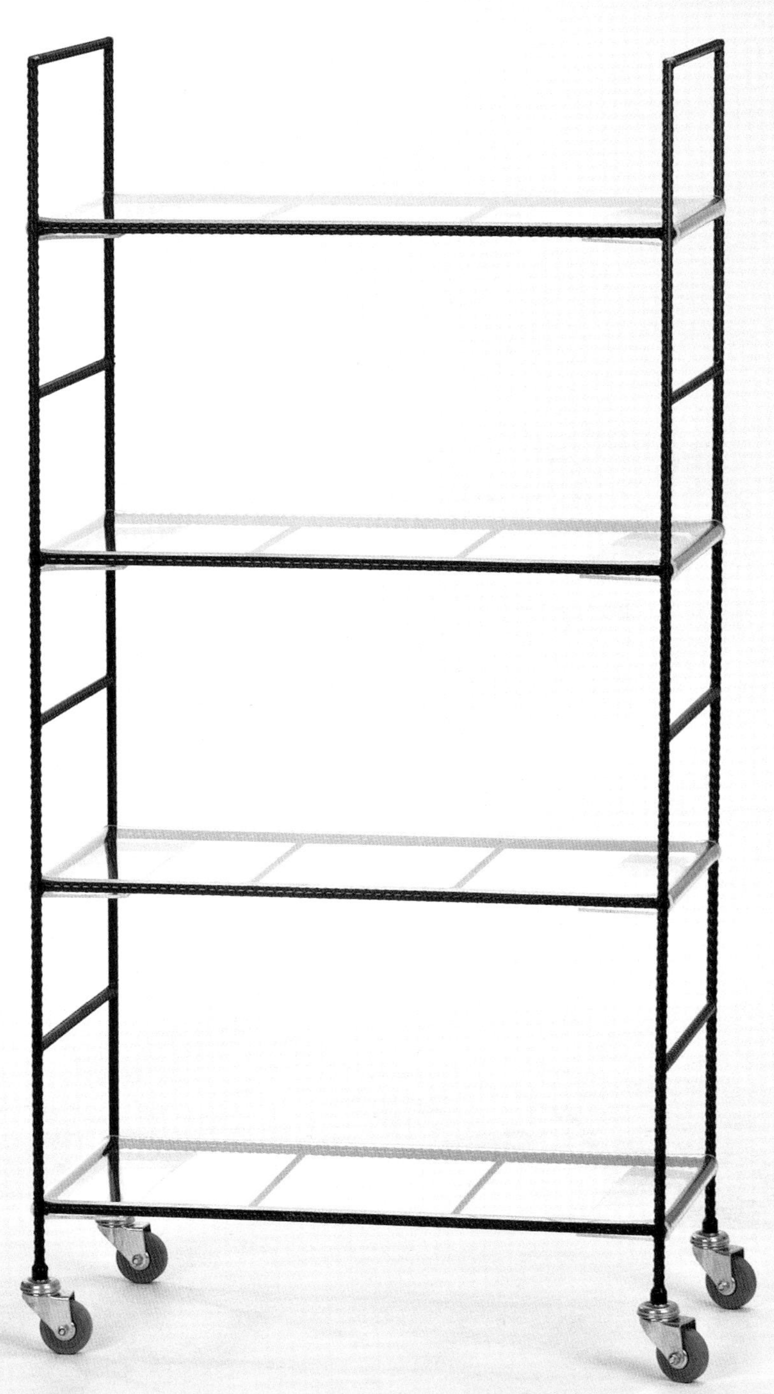

RACHEL WHITEREAD

Switch, 1994

Object, plaster (prestia ortho) and brass,
3¹/₂ x 3¹/₂ x 1¹/₈" (2,8 x 8,9 x 8,9 cm),
Ed. 60/XXV, signed and numbered

EDITION FOR PARKETT 42

Negative charge. A domestic light switch box,
cast inversely in delicate plaster, becomes an
impenetrable source of embalmed energy.

"'I use furniture as a metaphor for human beings,'
says Whiteread. But as well as metaphor it is
extension. Whiteread's casts of sinks, baths, and
mattresses make poetic play of the introversions and
extroversions of the body they propose."

Neville Wakefield
Parkett No. 42, 1994

レイチェル・ホワイトリード

スイッチ　1994

オブジェ、石膏 (prestia ortho) 、真鍮、
2.8×8.9×8.9cm、
Ed. 60/XXV、署名、番号入り

パルケット・エディション 42

負電荷。家庭用照明のスイッチ・ボックスを、肌理の細
かな石膏で裏返しに成形すると、防腐処理済エネル
ギーの神秘的な供給源となる。

「わたしは家具を人間の隠喩に用います」とホワイトリードは語る。
しかしそれは隠喩でもあれば、延長でもある。ホワイトリードが象る
流し、風呂、マットレスは、指名する身体の内翻、外翻と詩的に戯れ
る。

ネヴィル・ウェイクフィールド
（パルケット 42号、1994年）

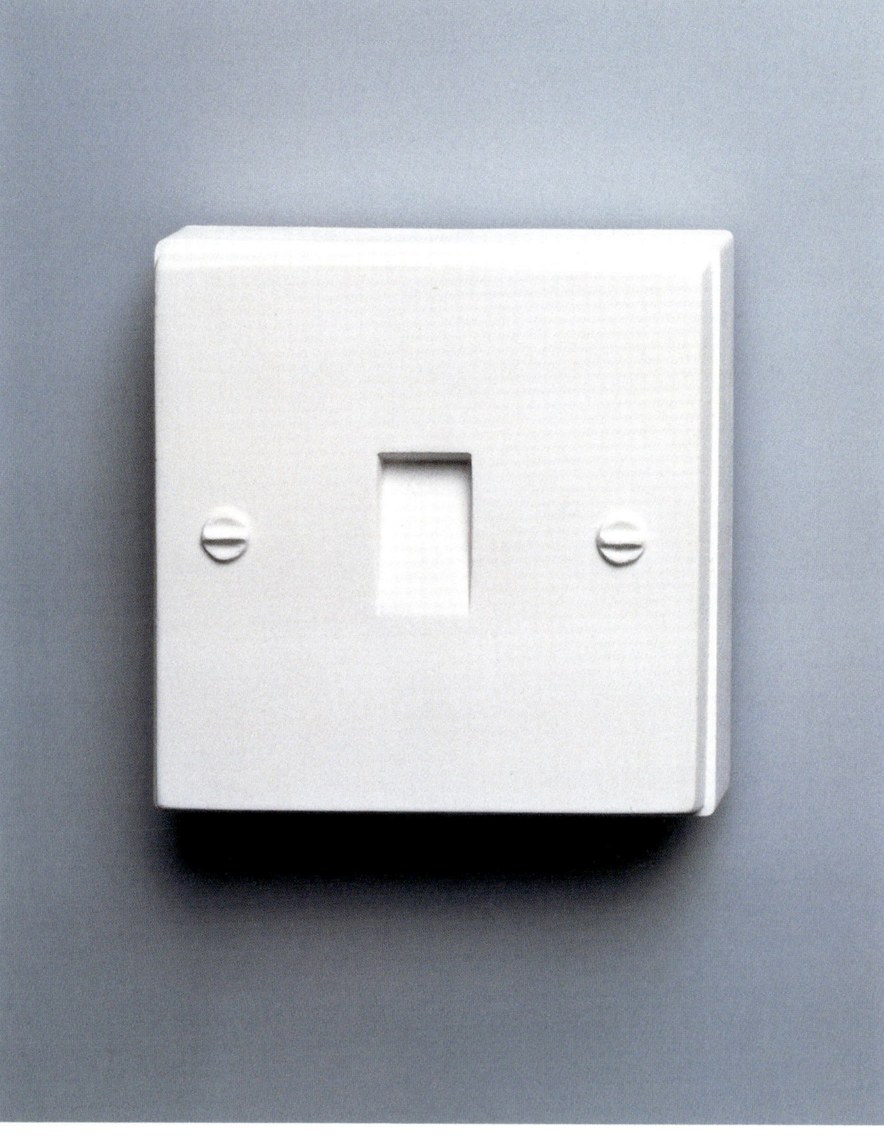

SUE WILLIAMS

Untitled (Edition for Parkett), 1997

Three-layer lithograph on transparent
archival Mylar, each image-layer printed
in a different color on a separate loose
sheet, 10 x 16¹/₂" (25,5 x 42 cm),
printed by Maurice Sanchez and James
Miller, Derrière L'Etoile Studio, New York,
Ed. 60/XXV, signed and numbered

EDITION FOR PARKETT 50/51

Transparent trinity. A layered set piece in three colors.

"Filled with the frenetic, automatic energy of sex,
Williams' elaborate webs seem like vast abstract
tissues of unconscious material being woven
in someone's head. To make private traumas public
can sometimes seem to be a strangely depriving
experience for what remains of a sense of self.
Williams says that when she's alone with herself
she sometimes gives herself 'the willies,' but
by transforming these neuroses into high-spirited
aesthetic practice she has found a way of giving them
to us instead."

Leslie Camhi
Parkett No. 50/51, 1997

スー・ウィリアムズ

無題 (パルケットのためのエディション) 1997

透明のマイラー (ポリエステルフィルム) に
リトグラフの3層プリント、
各層はシート1枚ずつに色を違えてプリント、
25.5×42cm、
刷り：モーリス・サンチェス、ジェイムズ・ミラー、
デリエール・レトワール・スタジオ (ニューヨーク)、
Ed. 60/XXV、署名、番号入り

パルケット・エディション 50/51

透明な3位1体。3色3層のセット作品。

熱っぽく、とめどないセックスのエネルギーがみなぎるウィリムズ
の緻密な網は、だれかが頭のなかで織る意識のない素材が描く広
大な抽象模様のように見える。私的なトラウマを公表すると、後に
残る自己の意識に、ときに奇妙な喪失感を背負わせることにもな
りかねない。ウィリアムズはひとりきりでいると、ときに「ぞっとす
る」ことがあると言うが、そうしたノイローゼ症状を気持ちの昂る
作品制作に転換することによって、わたしたちに肩代わりさせる方
法を見いだした。

レスリー・カムイ
(パルケット 50/51号、1997年)

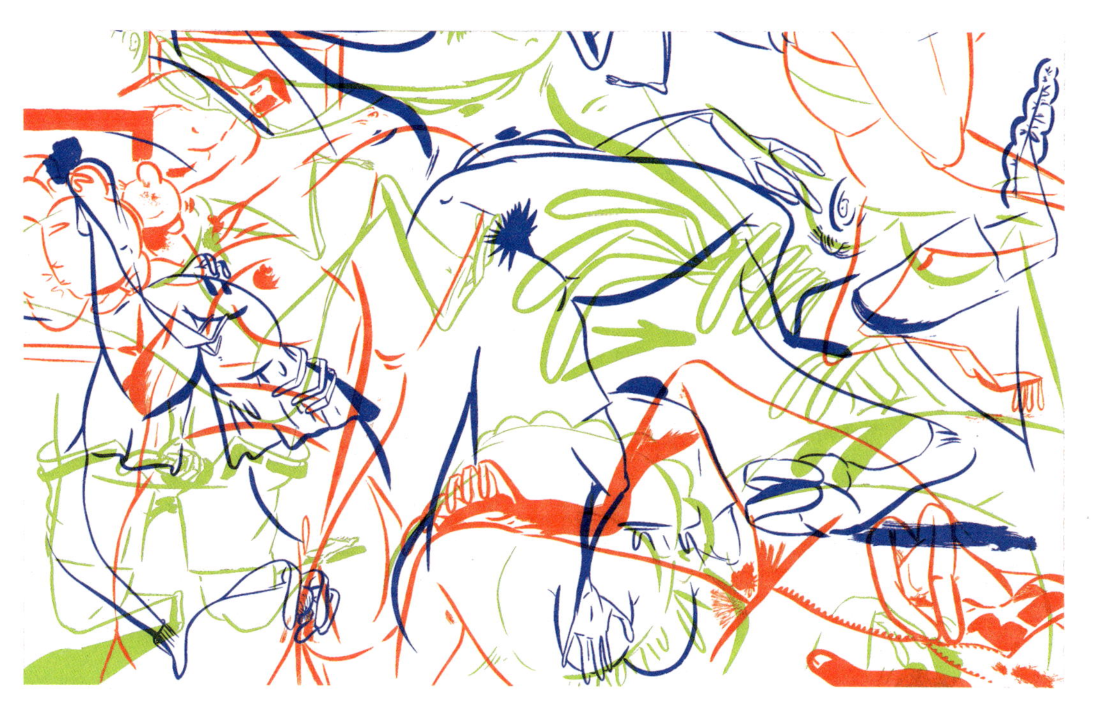

ROBERT WILSON

A Letter for Queen Victoria, 1988

Lithograph on Rives,
10 x 24" (25,3 x 61 cm),
bound in the magazine,
printed by Champfleury, Paris,
Ed. 80/XV, signed and numbered

EDITION FOR PARKETT 16

The director's notebook. This animated three-part lithograph is a reminder that every one of Wilson's dramatic theater works has its genesis in a powerful, light-filled drawing.

"…by choosing theater as his medium, Wilson gained extraordinary power over the very properties which visual artists have labored hardest to represent, although it cost him the visual artist's ordinary power to make things permanent."

Ellen Levy
Parkett No. 16, 1988

ロバート・ウィルソン

ヴィクトリア女王への手紙　1998

リヴ紙にリトグラフ、
25.3×61cm、
本誌に綴じこみ、
刷り：シャンフルーリ（パリ）、
Ed. 80/XV、署名、番号入り

パルケット・エディション　16

演出家のノート。3枚綴りの躍動感のあるリトグラフは、ウィルソンの手がける演劇はどれもその起源を力強く、光に満ちた素描に遡ることを思い出させてくれる。

……演劇を自らのメディアとしたウィルソンは、視覚芸術に携わる者が表現にもっとも手を焼く特質をあやつる素晴らしい力を獲得したが、そのために視覚芸術家にとってはごくあたりまえの、作品を持続的な形あるものにする能力を失うことになった。

エレン・レヴィ
（パルケット　16号、1988年）

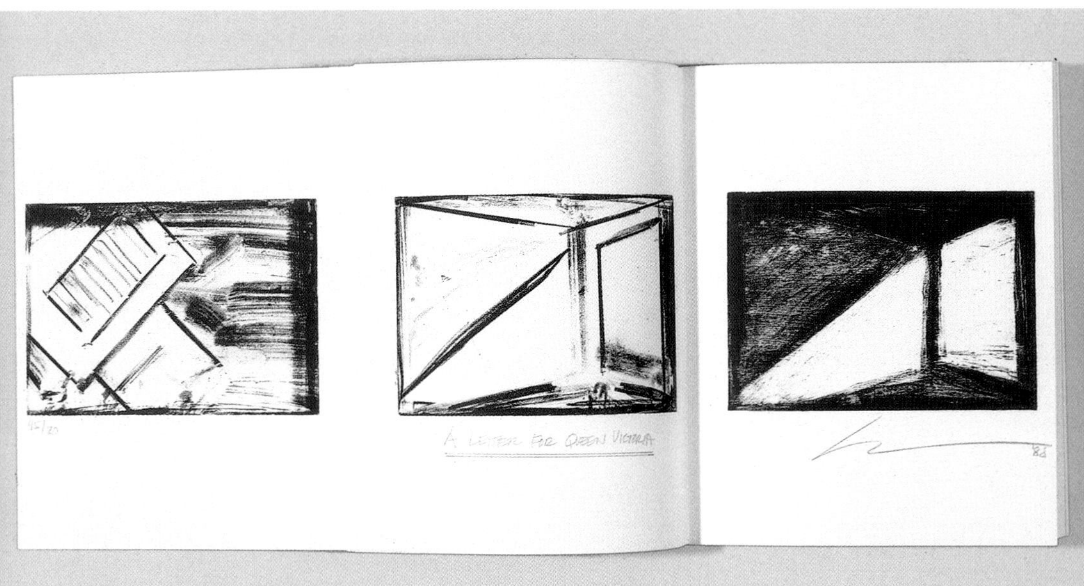
A LETTER FOR QEEN VICTRA

CHRISTOPHER WOOL

Untitled, 1992

Black-and-white photograph,
10 x 8" (25,4 x 20,3 cm),
Ed. 70/XX, signed and numbered

EDITION FOR PARKETT 33

Word into image. RUN DOG RUN beat a
tattoo in an earlier cycle of paintings; here it
becomes a fleeting presence captured in a
painterly snapshot.

"Wool looks you in the face; he says what you're used
to hearing; he disrupts the communicative power of
words; he affirms the communicative power of letters.
Someone is shouting, but you can't tell if that person
is trying to make you understand or insisting that you
don't have a clue."

Greil Marcus
Parkett No. 33, 1992

クリストファー・ウール

無題　1992

モノクロ写真、25.4×20.3cm、
Ed. 70/XX、署名、番号入り

パルケット・エディション 33

イメージにおりこまれたことば。初期の絵画には RUN
DOG RUNと刺青をほどこした。ここではそれが、絵
をおもわせるスナップ写真に捉えられた束の間の姿と
なった。

ウールはきみの顔をじっと見つめる。きみには聞き慣れたことを言
う。ことばの伝達力を混乱させる。文字の伝達力を肯定する。だれ
かが叫んでいる、しかしきみにはそのひとがきみにわからせようと
しているのか、それともきみには見当もつかないと言い張っている
のか、わからない。

グレイル・マルクス（33号、1992年）

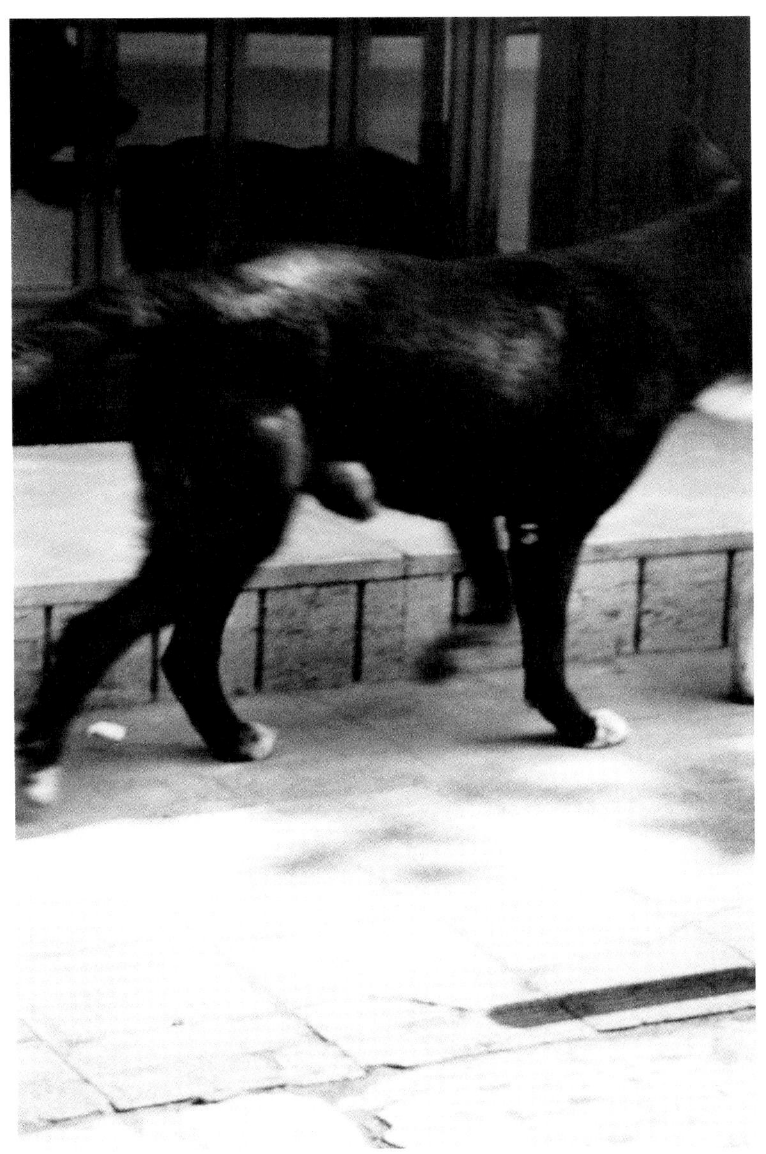

CHRISTOPHER WOOL

Wool 2008, 2008

2-color silkscreen on
Dur-O-Tone Newsprint,
paper size: 38 x 25" (96.5 x 61cm),
image size: 32 x 24" (81,3 x 61 cm),
printed by Brand X Editions, New York,
Ed. 45/XX, signed and numbered

EDITION FOR PARKETT 83

Clean-cut time, neat, tidy and manageable;
the woolly foreground tells a different story.

"As Wool has gradually pulled away from language, he
has moved ever closer to paintings that slip further
and further into the void. There is a real menace that
comes with the fog and the rot and the glimpses of
graffiti hanging in the air like satanic versions of the
Northern Lights."

Richard Flood
Parkett No. 83, 2008

クリストファー・ウール

ウール 2008　2008

シルクスクリーン2色刷り、
デュロトーン・ニューズプリント紙：96.5×61cm、
図柄：81.3×61cm、
刷り：ブランド X エディションズ（ニューヨーク）、
Ed. 45/XX、署名、番号入り

パルケット・エディション 33

すっきりとした時間、さっぱりしてこぎれい、そしてあ
つかいやすい。ぼんやりした前景は、また別の事情を
物語る。

ウールは言語から徐々に身を退くにしたがい、虚空にただ滑り落
ちてゆくばかりの絵に接近していった。そこには霧と腐食、ちらり
と見えるオーロラの悪魔版に似た、宙づりの落書きにともなう本
当の脅威がある。

リチャード・フラッド
（パルケット 83号、2008年）

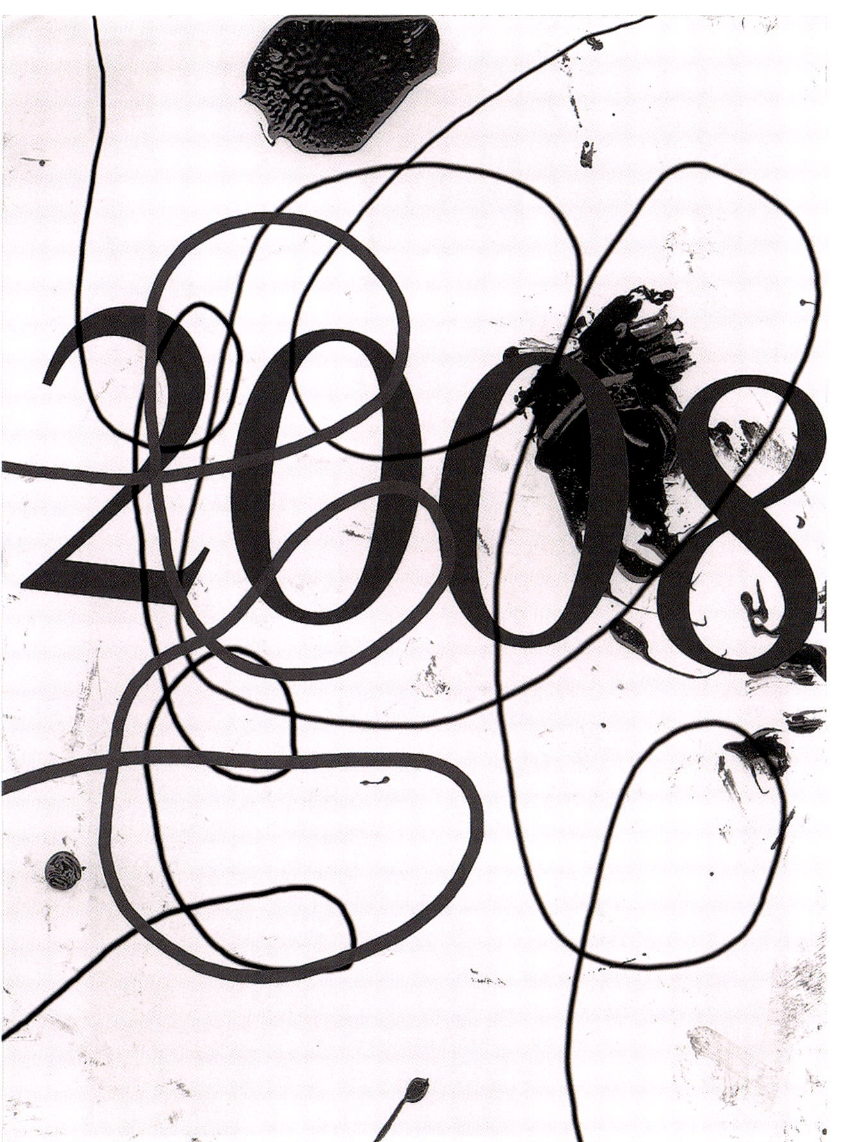

YANG FUDONG

Ms. Huang at M. Last Night, 2006

Black-and-white photograph,
Lambda print on Kodak Endura paper,
paper size: 19 1/2 x 29 1/2" (50 x 75 cm),
image: 18 7/8 x 28 3/4" (48 x 73 cm),
Ed. 60/XX, signed and numbered
certificate

EDITION FOR PARKETT 76

Ms. Huang on a ride, Shanghai at night.

"Perhaps Yang Fudong's works hark back to a experience common to members of my generation. We had the privilege of being part of two markedly different social and cultural systems, for we experienced the rapid transition from the intense political sentiments of the Cultural Revolution to a capitalist and consumerist society. We are the experimental products in the social laboratory of first modern and then contemporary China."

Zhang Wei
Parkett No. 76, 2006

ヤン・フードン（楊福東）

ホワンさん、昨夜Mにて　2006

白黒写真、
コダック社製エンデュラにランバ・プリント、
紙：50×75cm、図柄：48×73cm、
Ed. 60/XX、署名、番号入り証明書

パルケット・エディション 76

夜の上海、ドライブするホワンさん。

ヤン・フードンの作品は、わたしの世代に属するものが共有する体験に回帰するものなのだろう。わたしたちはふたつのまったく異なる社会、文化体制に属する機会にめぐまれた。文化大革命の強烈な政治意識から、資本主義的な、消費万能主義社会への急激な移り変わりを経験した。わたしたちはまずは近代的、つづいて現代的な中国の社会的な実験の産物にほかならない。

チャン・ウェイ
（パルケット 76号、2006年）

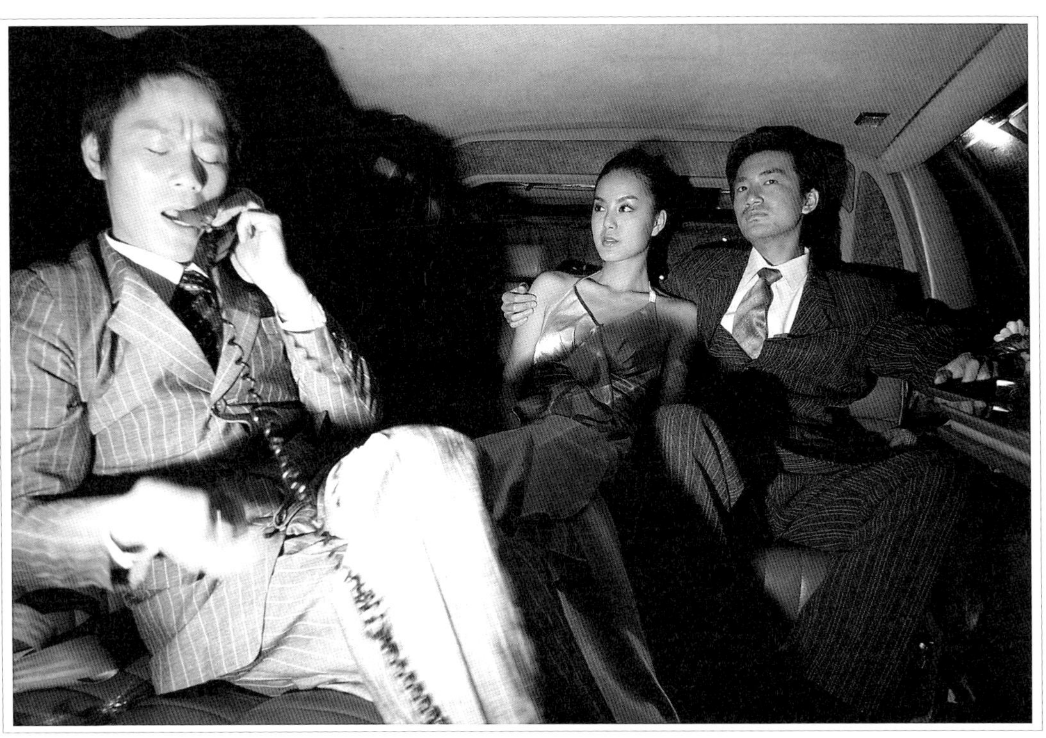

Artists' Sketches and Letters
アーティストのスケッチと手紙

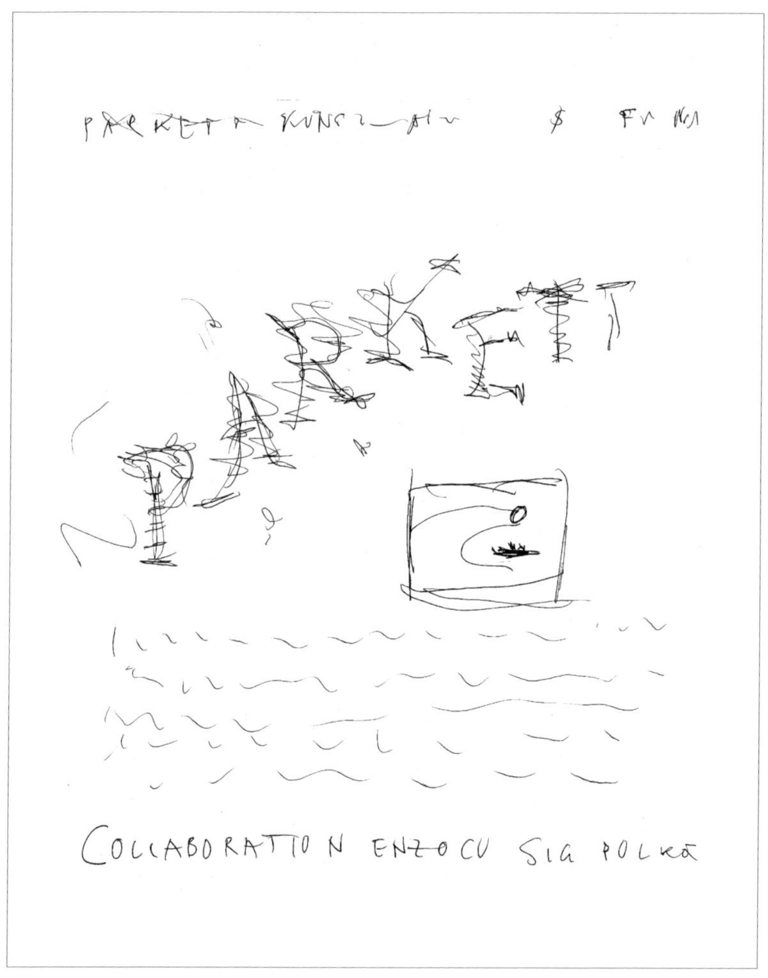

Parkett no. 1, first sketch for logo
パルケット1号、ロゴの最初のスケッチ

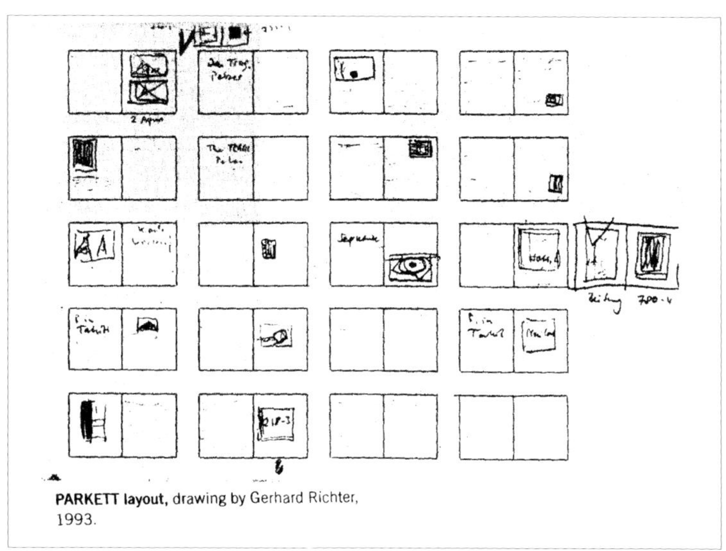

PARKETT layout, drawing by Gerhard Richter, 1993.

Gerhard Richter, layout sketch for Parkett 35
ゲルハルト・リヒター、パルケット35号のレイアウト・スケッチ

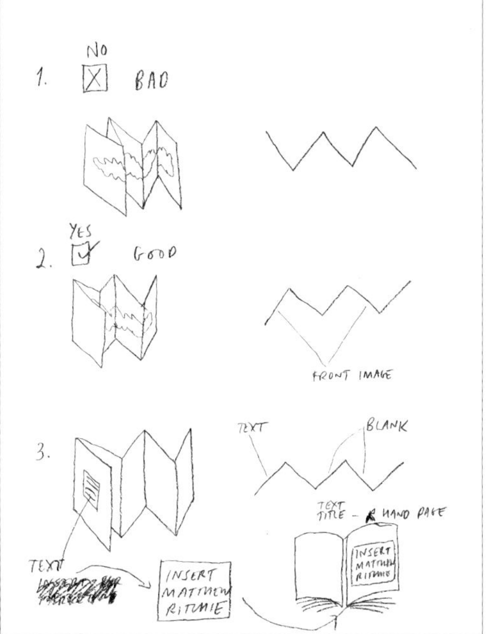

Matthew Ritchie, layout sketch Insert, Parkett 54
マシュー・リッチー、パルケット54号の綴じ込み付録のレイアウト・スケッチ

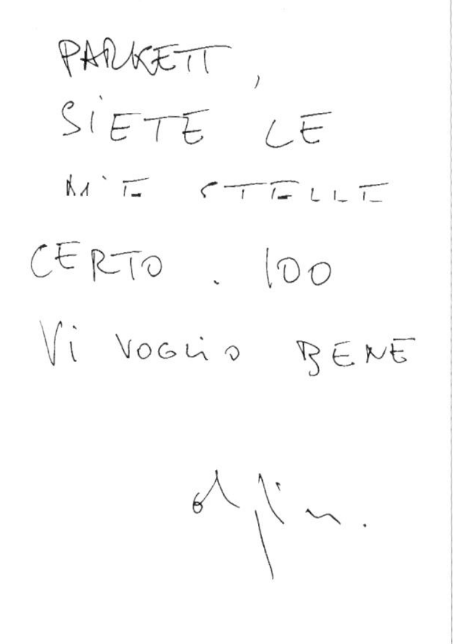

Alighiero Boetti, fax, edition for Parkett 24
アリギエロ・ボエッティ、ファクシミリ、パルケット24号のためのエディション

LOUISE BOURGEOIS

October 4/88

Dear Bice,

Jerry just brought me
Parkett and I am
delighted with the
Insert. I really mean it!!!!
Thank you for everything.

P.S. Could I, please have a
couple of copies.

Meilleures amitiés and love
Louise

Louise Bourgeois, letter, Insert Parkett 17
ルイーズ・ブルジョワ、手紙、パルケット17号のインサート（ページ・アート）

Pipilotti Rist, sketch, edition for Parkett 47
ピピロッティ・リスト、スケッチ、パルケット47号のためのエディション

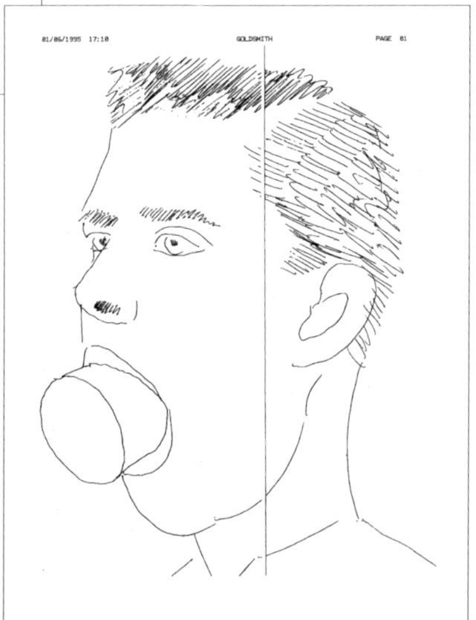

Maurizio Cattelan, sketch, edition for Parkett 59
マウリツィオ・カテラン、スケッチ、パルケット59号
のためのエディション

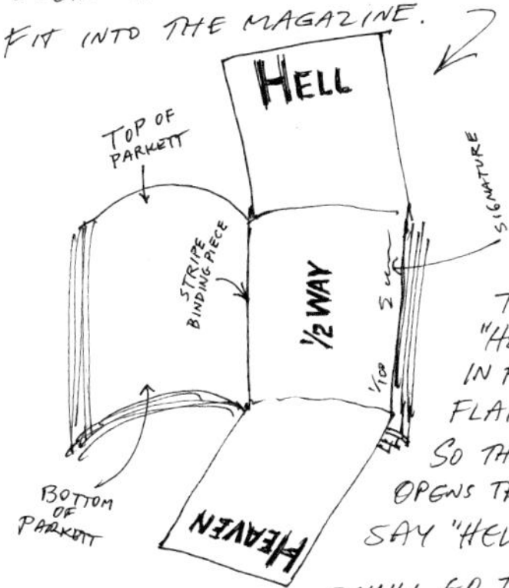

EDWARD RUSCHA

AUG. 10, '88

DEAR DIETER —
AS YOU MAY KNOW, THE PRINTING FOR THE PARKETT EDITION IS COMPLETED AND I SIGNED ALL THE PRINTS YESTERDAY. I WANTED TO MENTION ONE THING: I WANTED TO MAKE IT CLEAR HOW I HAVE IN MIND FOR THE PRINT TO FIT INTO THE MAGAZINE.

THE FLAP SAYING "HEAVEN" SHOULD FOLD IN FIRST, THEN THE FLAP THAT SAYS "HELL" SO THAT WHEN A PERSON OPENS THE PRINT IT WILL SAY "HELL" FIRST.

I UNDERSTAND SOMEONE WILL GO TO ED HAMILTON AND TAKE THE PRINTS BY HAND TO ZURICH. THAT IS WHAT WE CALL "TENDER LOVING CARE"! IT WAS GOOD MEETING YOU AND WALTER. KEEP ME INFORMED ON THE PROJECT. BEST WISHES Ed R—

Ed Ruscha, letter, edition for Parkett 18
エドワード・ルシェ、手紙、パルケット18号のためのエディション

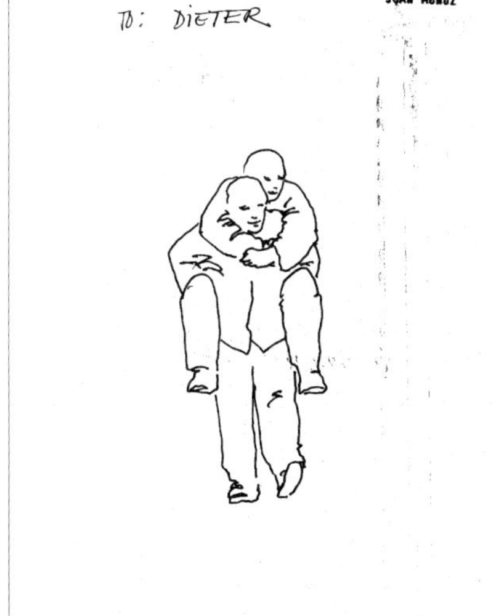

Juan Munoz, fax, edition for Parkett 43
フアン・ムニョス、ファクシミリ、パルケット43号のためのエディション

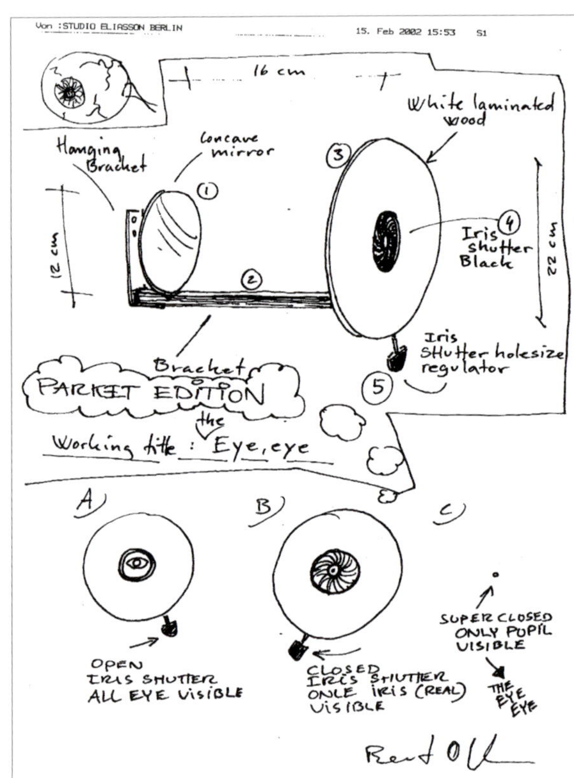

Olafur Eliasson, sketch, edition for Parkett 64
オラファー・エリアソン、スケッチ、パルケット64号のためのエデション

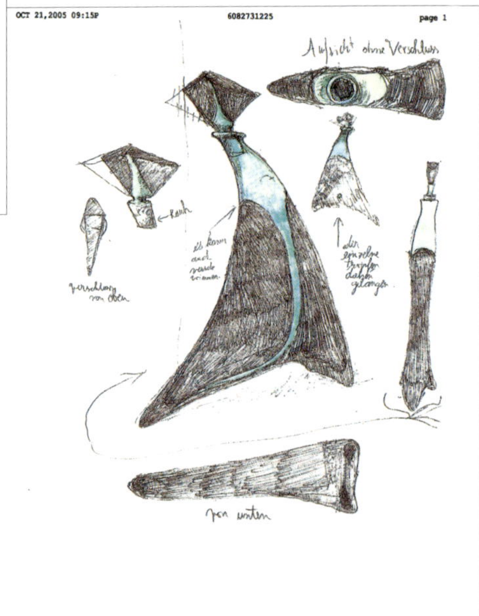

Kai Althoff, sketch, edition for Parkett 75
カイ・アルトフ、スケッチ、パルケット75号のためのエデション

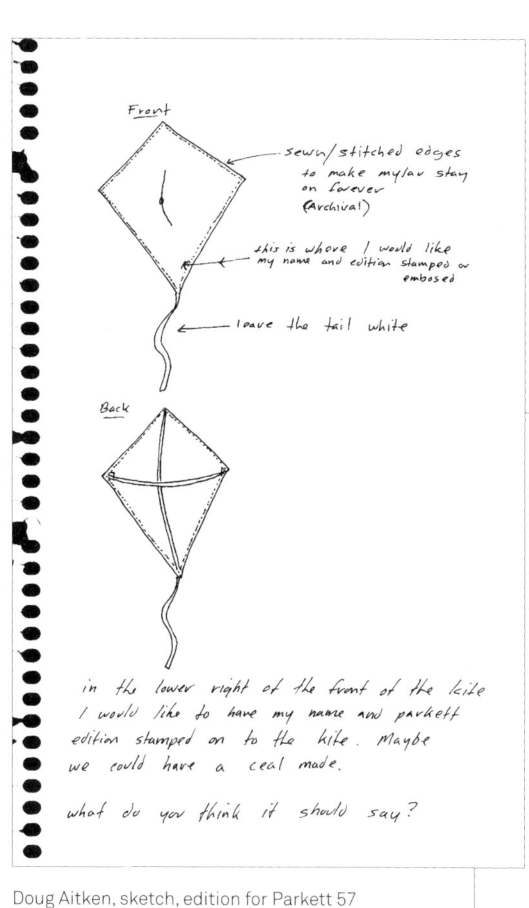

Doug Aitken, sketch, edition for Parkett 57
ダグ・エイケン、スケッチ、パルケット57号のためのエディション

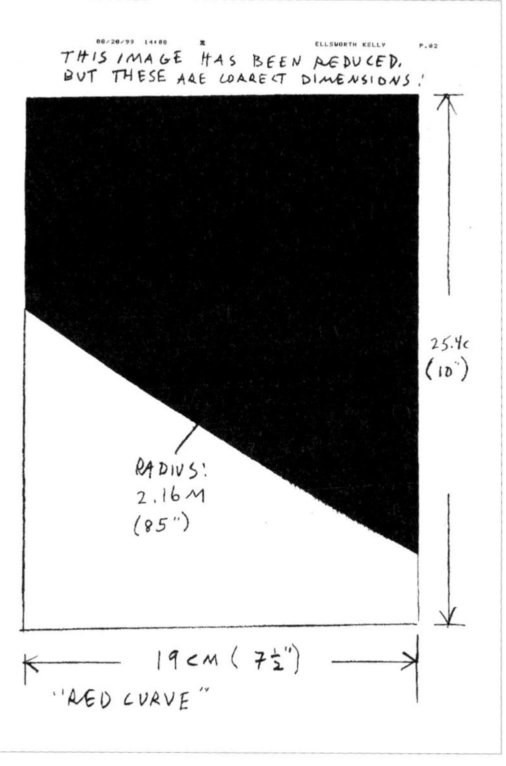

Ellsworth Kelly, sketch, edition for Parkett 56
エルズワース・ケリー、スケッチ、パルケット56号のためのエディション

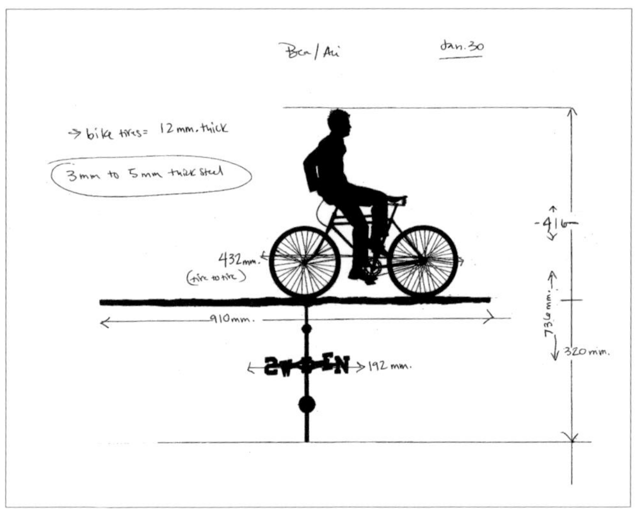

Rodney Graham, sketch, edition for Parkett 64
ロドニー・グレアム、スケッチ、パルケット64号のためのエディション

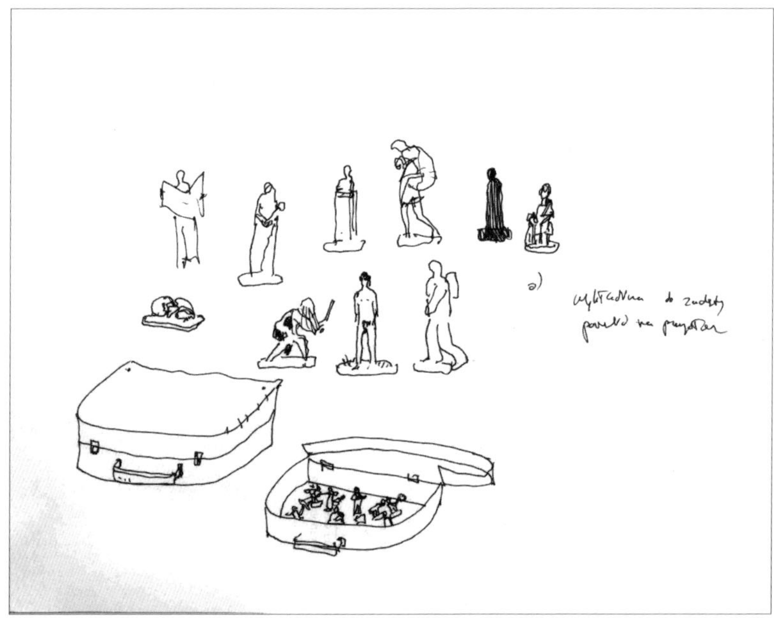

Paweł Althamer, sketch, edition for Parkett 82
パヴェウ・アルトハメル、スケッチ、パルケット82号のためのエディション

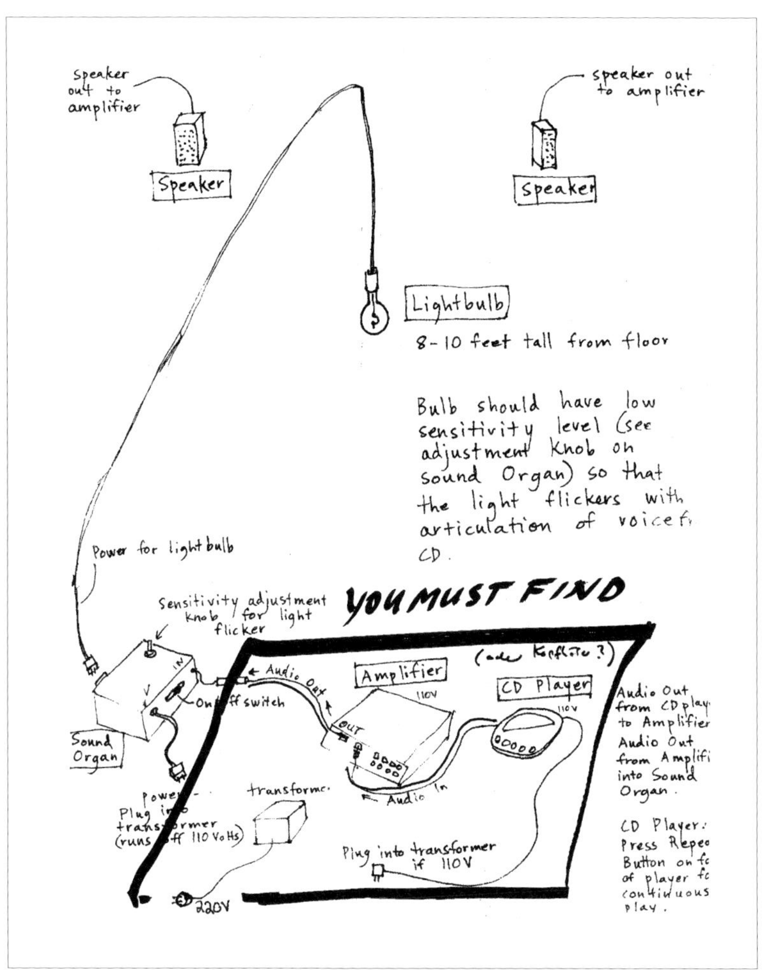

Tony Oursler, sketch, edition for Parkett 47
トニー・アウスラー、スケッチ、パルケット47号のためのエディション

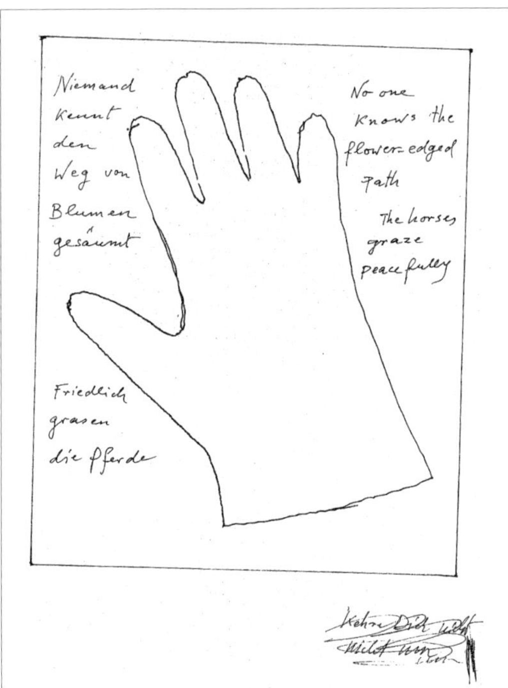

Meret Oppenheim, sketch, edition for Parkett 4
メレット・オッペンハイム、スケッチ、パルケット4号のためのエディション

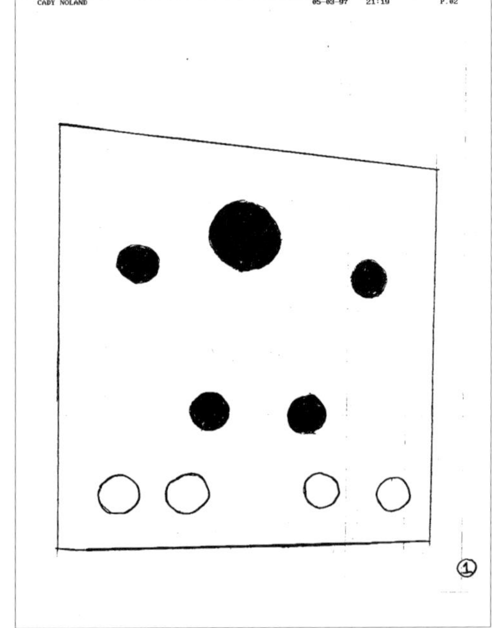

Cady Noland, fax, edition for Parkett 46
ケディ・ノーランド、ファクシミリ、パルケット46号のためのエディション

09/10/00 WED 09:16 FAX 212 271 0704   TEL NO.   →→→ PARKETT ZURICH   ☑001
                                                                      2000. 5.10 16:44   P. 1

Dieter & Ben/Ali

YAYOI KUSAMA

May 9.2000
Ali Subotnick

Dear Ali Subotnick,

I received your fax of May 3.
I am quite enthusiastic to your project and wondering what kind of work I should
produce.
Right now I am polishing my ideas.
I will let you know as soon as I get my ideas in shape.

Yours Sincerely,

Yayoi Kusama

Yayoi Kusama, letter, edition for Parkett 59
草間彌生、手紙、パルケット59号のためのエディション

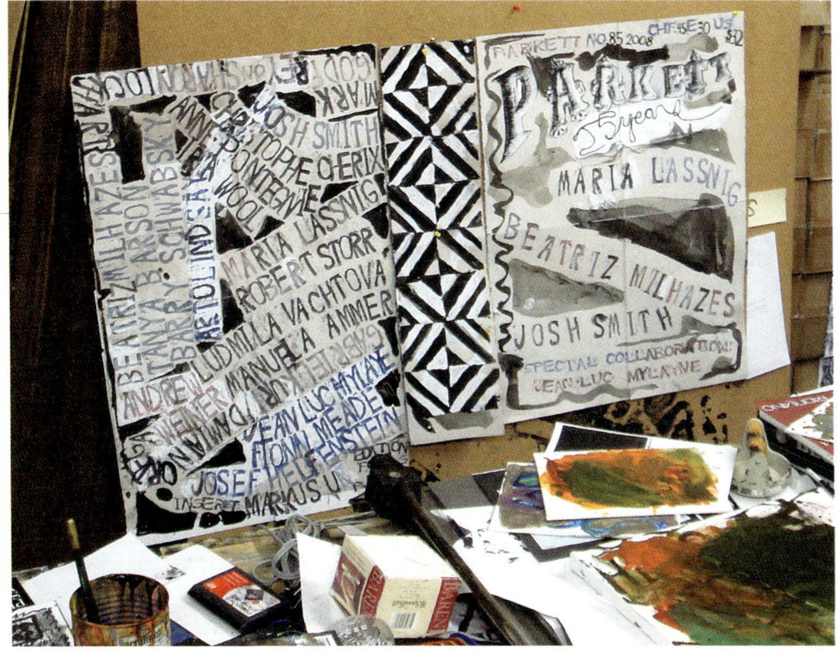

Josh Smith, studio, cover design, Parkett 85
ジョシュ・スミス、アトリエ、パルケット85号の表紙デザイン

Exhibitions in Public Institutions
美術館での展覧会歴

Kanazawa, 21st Century Museum of Contemporary Art (September 2009)
"200 Art Works – 25 Years"
The most complete museum exhibition to date presents all 200 works
made by artists for Parkett since 1984, with catalog.

Zurich, Kunsthaus (November, 2004–February, 2005)
"Parkett – 20 Years of Artists' Collaborations",
curated by Miriam Varadinis, with catalog.

Venice, Palazzo Remer (June–October, 2003)
At the occasion of the Biennale this exhibition presented
all Parkett editions in Venice.

Dublin, Irish Museum of Modern Art (June–October, 2002)
"Beautiful Productions"

London, Whitechapel Art Gallery (July–August, 2001)
In its Centenary the Whitechapel Gallery presented a Parkett exhibition entitled
"Beautiful Productions: Art to Play, Art to Wear, Art to Own",
curated by Iwona Blazwick.

New York, Museum of Modern Art (April–June, 2001)
"Collaborations with Parkett: 1984 to Now",
curated by Deborah Wye, with catalog.

Geneva, Centre d'Art Contemporain (November, 1999)

Siena, Palazzo delle Papesse (June–October, 1999)

Cologne, Museum Ludwig (November 1998–January, 1999),
curated by Reinhold Misselbeck, with catalog.

Humlebaek, Denmark, Louisiana Museum (September–October, 1996)
Curated by Lars Grambye

Los Angeles, MAK-Center at the Schindler House (March–June, 1995)
Catalog "Silent & Violent" edited by Peter Noever.

Geneva, Centre de Gravure Contemporaîne (April–May, 1992)

Marseille, Centre de la Vieille Chariteé, Museés de Marseille (February–March, 1991)

Zurich, Helmhaus (January–February, 1989)

Frankfurt, Portikus (September–October, 1988)

Paris, Centre Georges Pompidou (April–June, 1987)

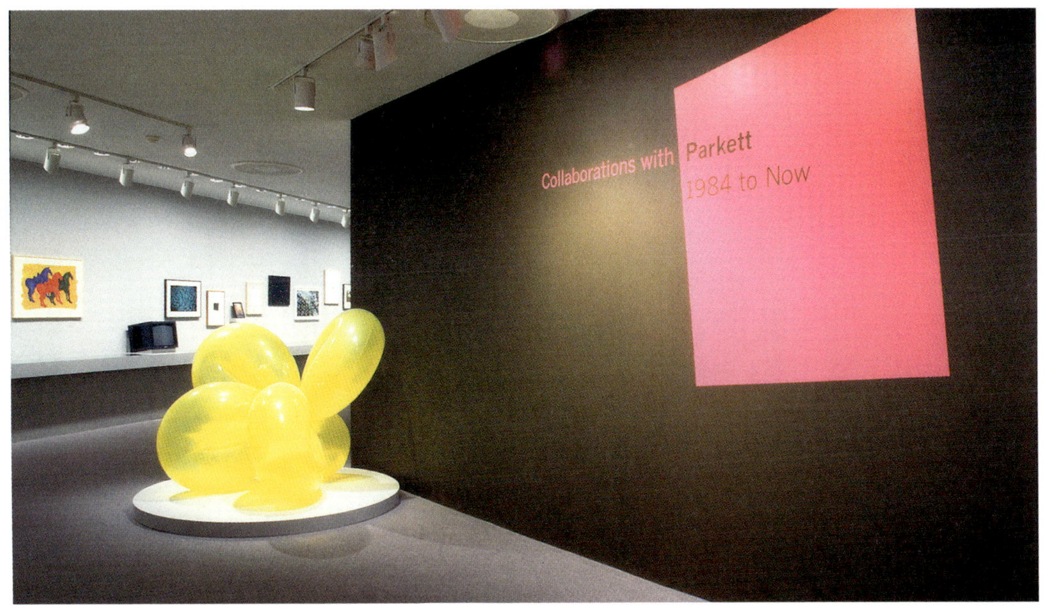

Parkett Exhibltion at the Museum of Modern Art, New York, 2001

Inserts
インサート（ページ・アート）

Faithful to its core principle of working closely with artists, PARKETT has invited 75 artists to work directly with the format of the magazine and the offset printing process. The artists have each produced a series of original artists' pages, an on-going study in the freedom within a book and in the rhythm and flow of the pages. A special CD ROM features all 75 inserts on one disc.

アーティストと密接な協力のもとで誌面作りを行なうという基本方針に基づいて、パルケットは雑誌の形態とオフセット印刷技法の範囲で作品を制作するよう、75人のアーティストに呼びかけた。アーティストはそれぞれ独自のページ・アートを複数のページにわたって制作し、このシリーズは誌面に自由奔放性を取り込み、リズムや流れをもたらす新たな試みとなった。全75点の「インサート」を一枚のディスクに収録した、特製CD-ROMが制作されている。

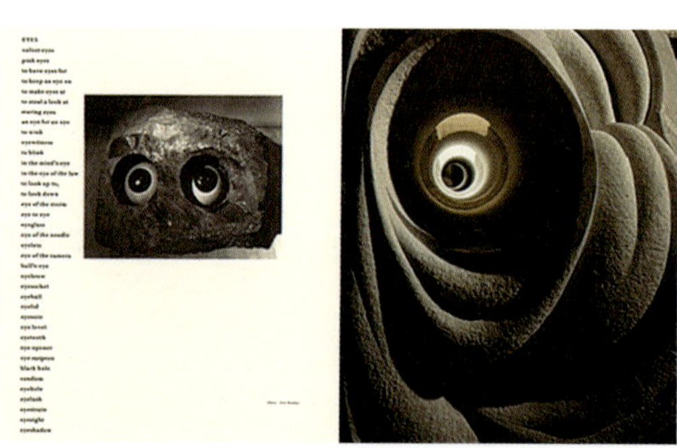

Louise Bourgeois, from Insert in Parkett 17

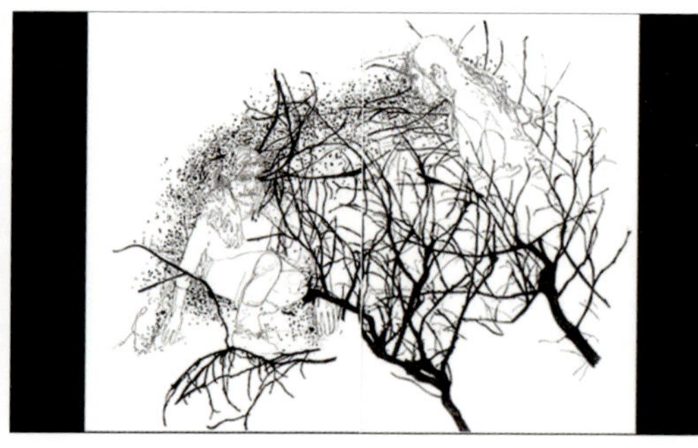

Loredana Sperini, from Insert in Parkett 72

Doug Aitken no. 57 / 1999
John Armleder no. 46 / 1996
Silvia Bächli no. 49 / 1997
John Baldessari no. 7 / 1985
Lothar Baumgarten no. 6 / 1985
Thomas Bayrle no. 52 / 1998
Sadie Benning no. 82 / 2008
Jeremy Blake no. 63 / 2002
Barbara Bloom no. 35 / 1993
Henry Bond no. 58 / 2000
Louise Bourgeois no. 17 / 1988
Matthew Brannon no. 73 / 2005
Kerstin Brätsch no. 83 / 2008
Rudi Burckhardt no. 48 / 1996
Daniel Buren no. 66 / 2003
Balthasar Burkhard no. 75 / 2005
Richmond Burton no. 36 / 1993
David Byrne no. 23 / 1990

Ernst Caramelle no. 27 / 1991
Beth Coleman &
Howard Goldkrand no. 77 / 2006
Anne Collier no. 78 / 2006
Robert Crumb no. 69 / 2004
Hans Danuser no. 44 / 1995
Tacita Dean no. 50/51 / 1997
Marcel Dzama no. 67 / 2003
Günther Förg no. 12 / 1987
Ryan Gander no. 80 / 2007
General Idea no. 15 / 1988
Nan Goldin no. 42 / 1994
Peter Greenaway no. 26 / 1990
Andreas Gursky no. 20 / 1989
Nic Hess no. 70 / 2004
Damien Hirst no. 32 / 1992
Candida Höfer no. 31 / 1992
Roni Horn no. 39 / 1994

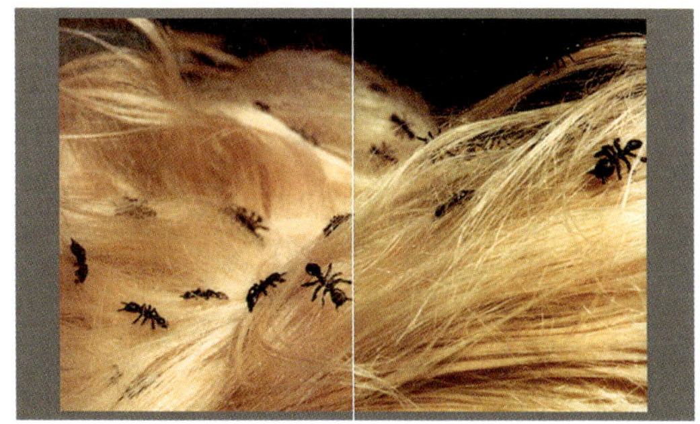

Cindy Sherman, from Insert in Parkett 24

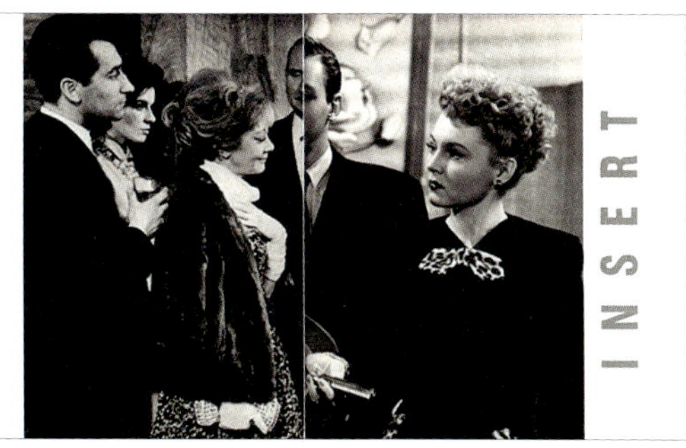

John Baldessari, from Insert in Parkett 7

Jonathan Monk no. 68 / 2003
Toba Khedoori no. 50/51 / 1997
Barbara Kruger no. 11 / 1986
Liz Larner no. 28 / 1991
Zoe Leonard & Cheryl Dunye no. 47 / 1996
Sherrie Levine no. 16 / 1988
Glenn Ligon no. 30 / 1991
Nate Lowman no. 79 / 2007
Robert Mapplethorpe no. 8 / 1986
Tatsuo Miyajima no. 34 / 1992
Rudi Molacek no. 38 / 1993
A.R. Penck no. 10 / 1986
Dan Perjovschi no. 71 / 2004
Sigmar Polke no. 13 / 1987
Elliott Puckette no. 45 / 1995
Lou Reed no. 65 / 2002
Pipilotti Rist no. 37 / 1993
Matthew Ritchie no. 54 / 1998
Edward Ruscha no. 9 / 1986
Adrian Schiess no. 33 / 1992
Shirana Shahbazi no. 60 / 2000

Steven Shearer no. 76 / 2006
Cindy Sherman no. 24 / 1990
David Shrigley no. 53 / 1998
Amy Sillman no. 64 / 2002
Robert Smithson no. 43 / 1995
Loredana Sperini no. 72 / 2004
Anselm Stalder no. 19 / 1989
Frances Stark no. 86 / 2009
Gerda Steiner / Jörg Lenzlinger no. 62 / 2001
John Stezaker no. 84 / 2008
Beat Streuli no. 25 / 1990
Niele Toroni no. 29 / 1991
Rosemarie Trockel no. 14 / 1987
Markus Uhr no. 85 / 2009
Kara Walker no. 55 / 1999
Boyd Webb no. 18 / 1988
William Wegman no. 21 / 1989
Christopher Wool no. 22 / 1989
Heimo Zobernig no. 81 / 2007
Andreas Züst no. 59 / 2000

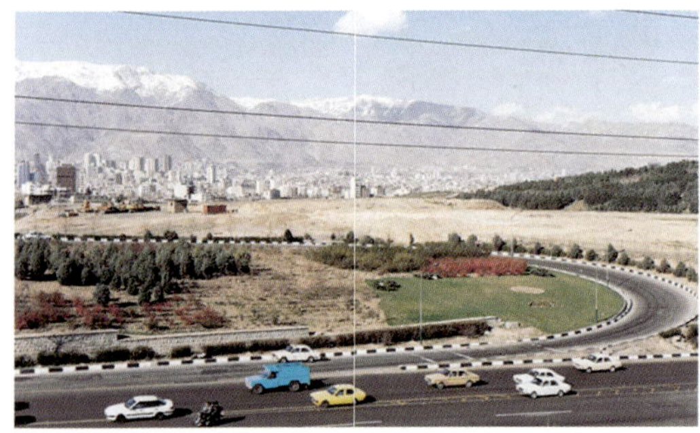

Shirana Shahbazi, from Insert in Parkett 60

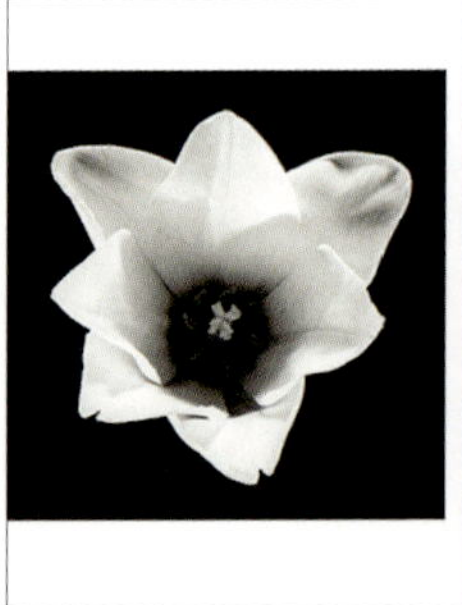
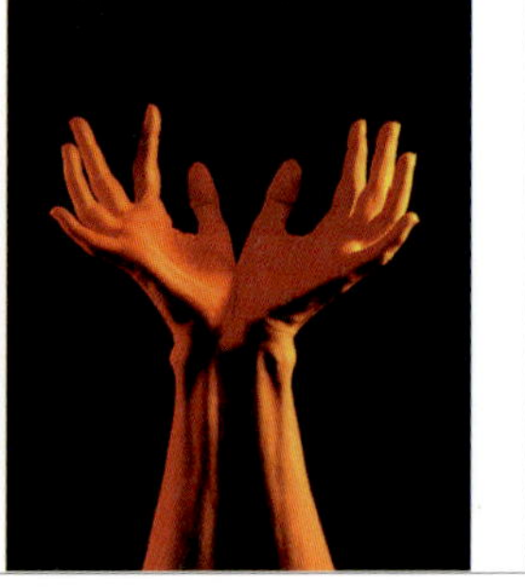

Robert Mapplethorpe, from Insert in Parkett 8

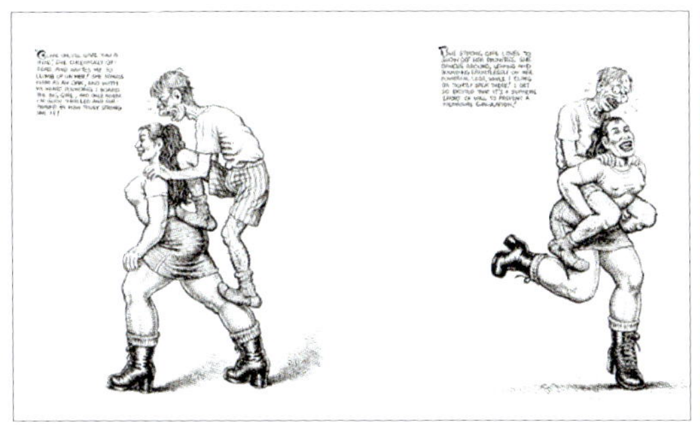

Robert Crumb, from Insert in Parkett 69

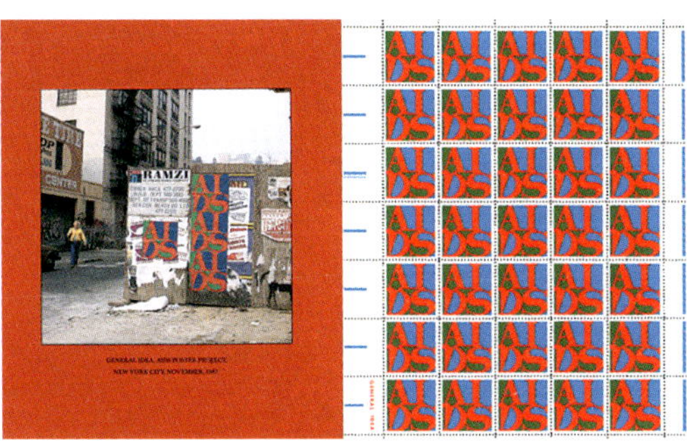

General Idea, from Insert in Parkett 15

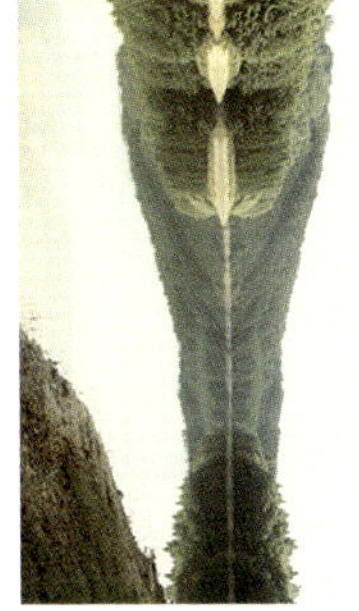

Sigmar Polke, from Insert in Parkett 13

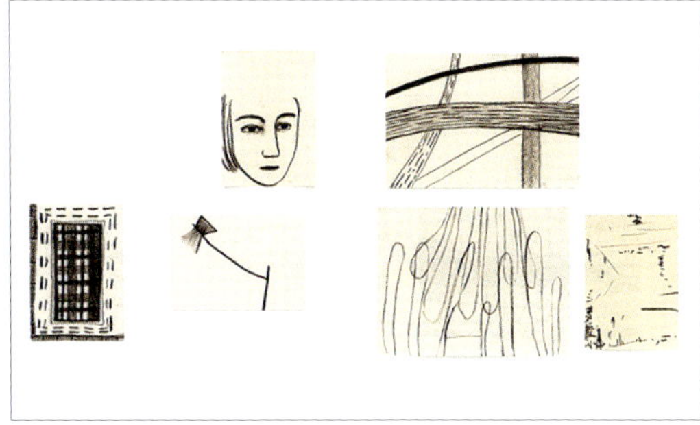

Silvia Bächli, from Insert in Parkett 49

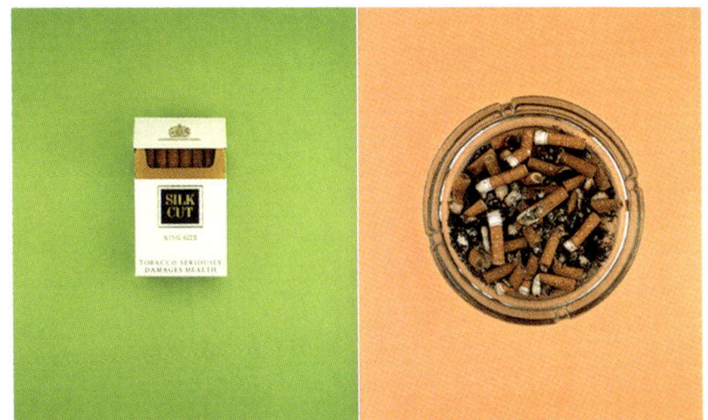

Damian Hirst, from Insert in Parkett 32

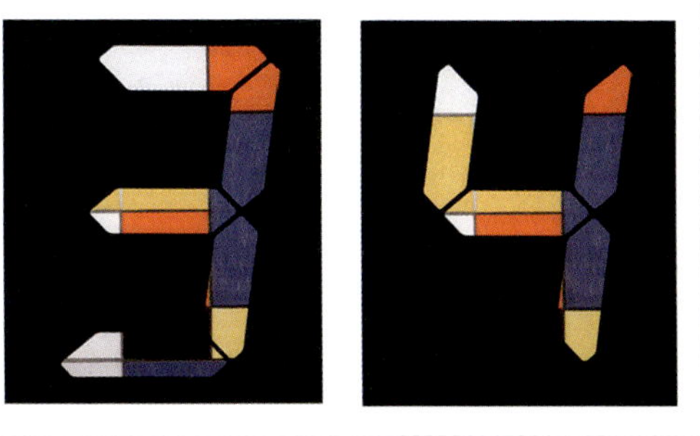

Tatsuo Miyajima, from Insert in Parkett 34

Spines
背表紙

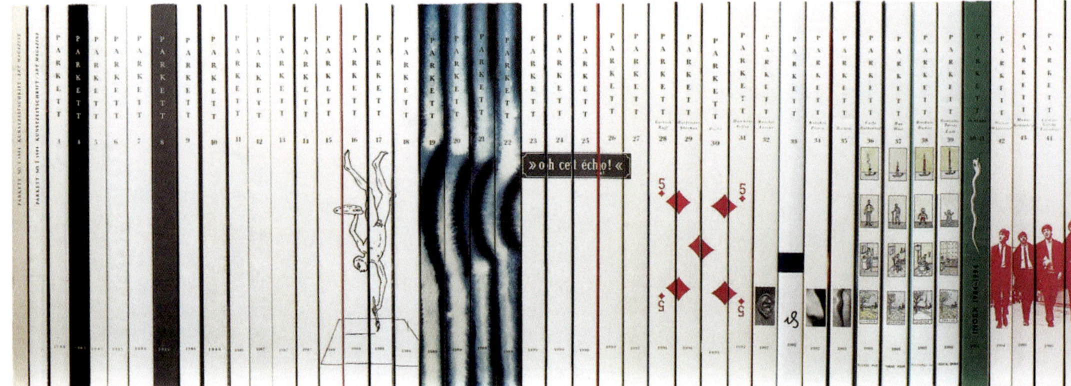

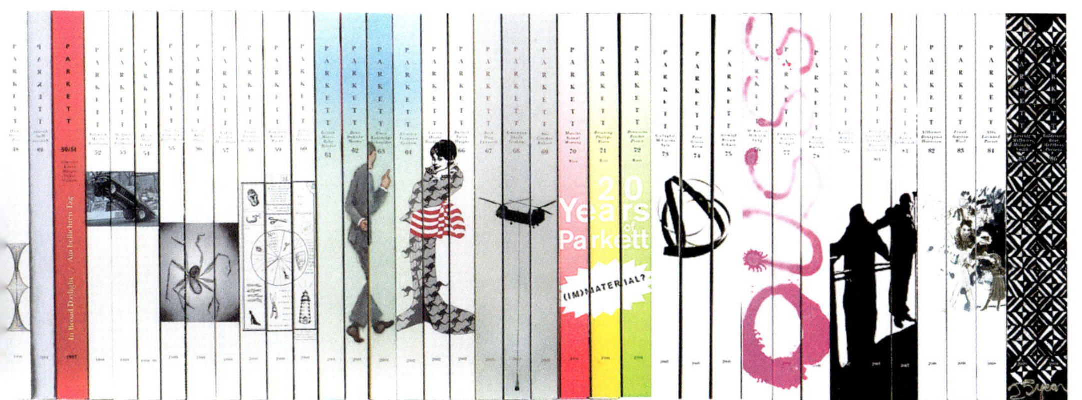

Publications: 86 Volumes – 1400 Texts
バックナンバー（86巻、1400記事）

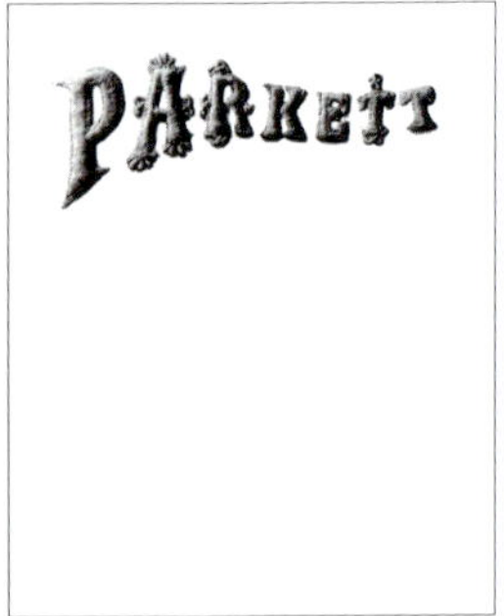

No. 86: Philippe Parreno
Carol Bove, Josiah McElheny
John Baldessari
Insert: Frances Stark

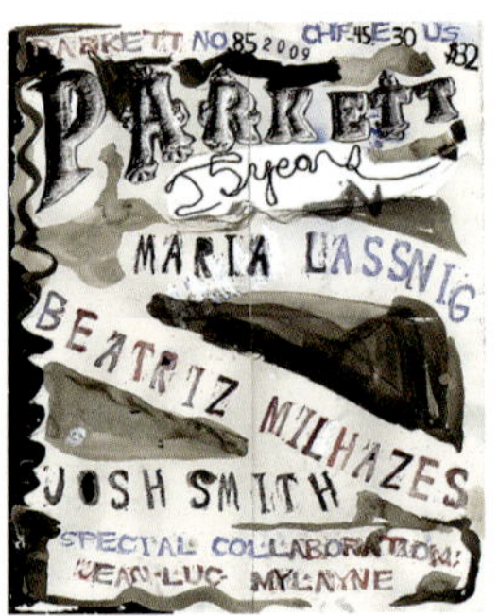

No. 85: Jean-Luc Mylayne
Maria Lassnig, Josh Smith
Beatriz Milhazes
Insert: Markus Uhr

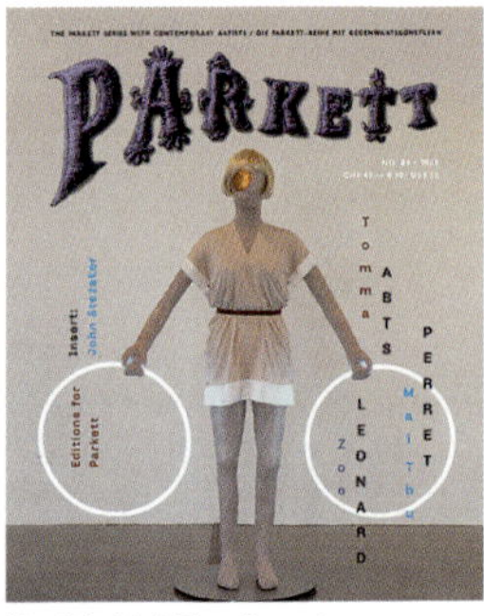

No. 84: Mai-Thu Perret
Zoe Leonard
Tomma Abts
Insert: John Stezaker

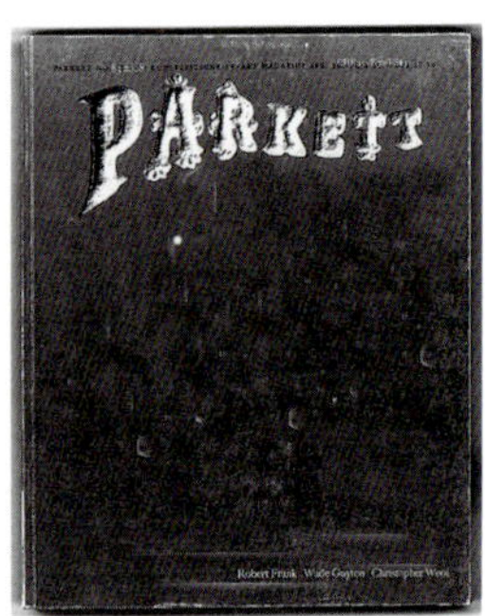

No. 83: Christopher Wool
Wade Guyton
Robert Frank
Insert: Kerstin Brätsch

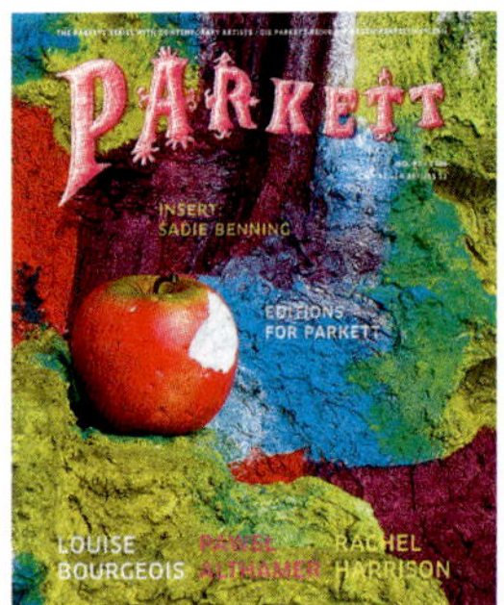

No. 82: Paweł Althamer
Louise Bourgeois
Rachel Harrison
Insert: Sadie Benning

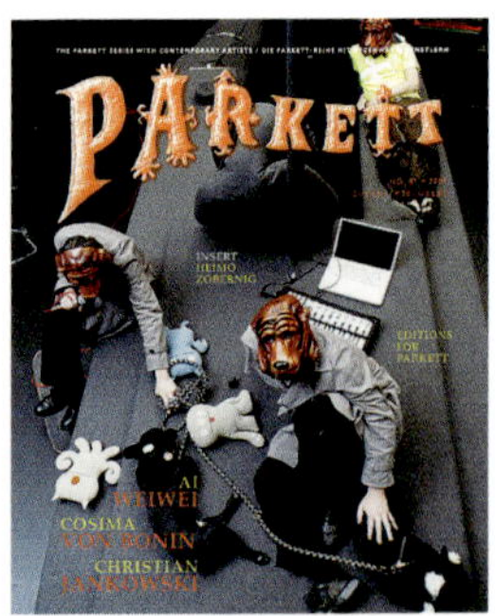

No. 81: Cosima von Bonin
Ai Weiwei
Christian Jankowski
Insert: Heimo Zobernig

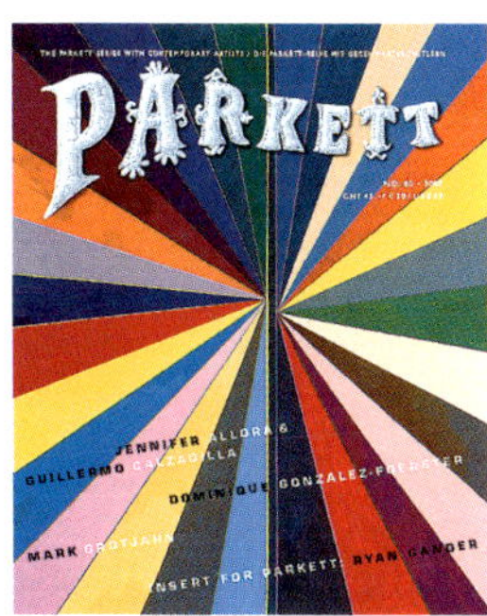

No. 80: Mark Grotjahn
Dominique Gonzalez-Foerster
Jennifer Allora & Guillermo Calzadilla
Insert: Ryan Gander

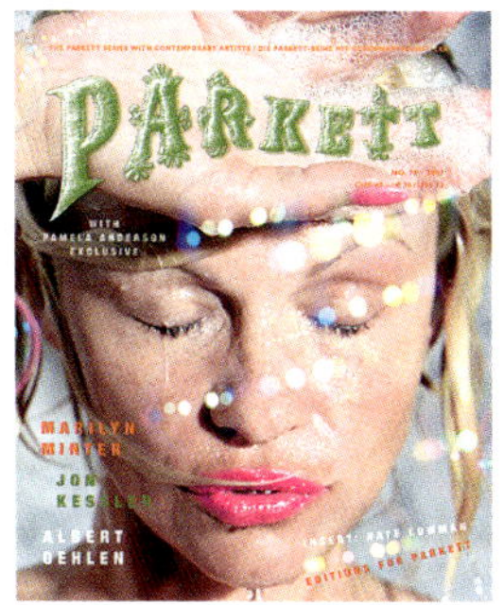

No. 79: Marilyn Minter
Jon Kessler
Albert Oehlen
Insert: Nate Lowman

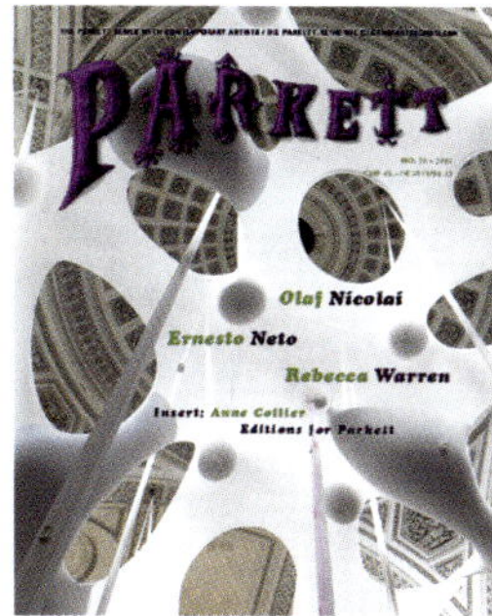

No. 78: Ernesto Neto
Rebecca Warren
Olaf Nicolai
Insert: Anne Collier

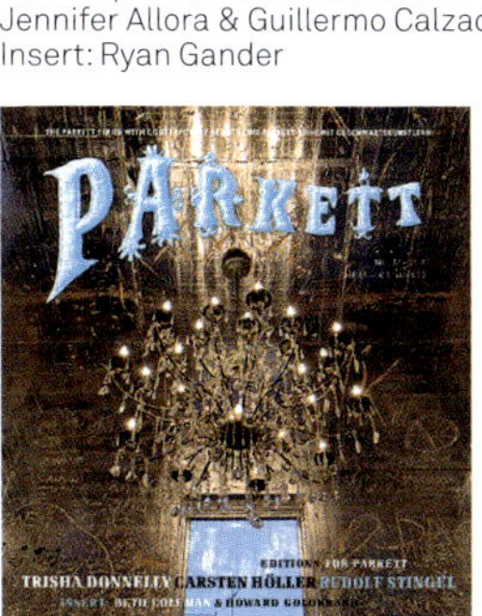

No. 77: Carsten Höller
Rudolf Stingel, Trisha Donnelly
Insert: Beth Coleman,
Howard Goldkrand

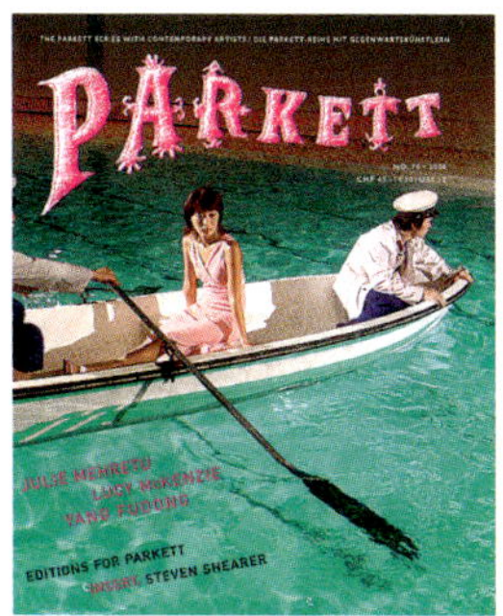

No. 76: Lucy McKenzie
Yang Fudong
Julie Mehretu
Insert: Steven Shearer

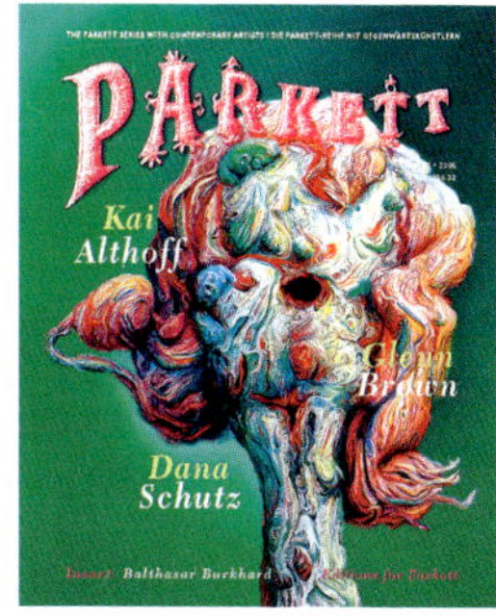

No. 75: Glenn Brown
Kai Althoff
Dana Schutz
Insert: Balthasar Burkhard

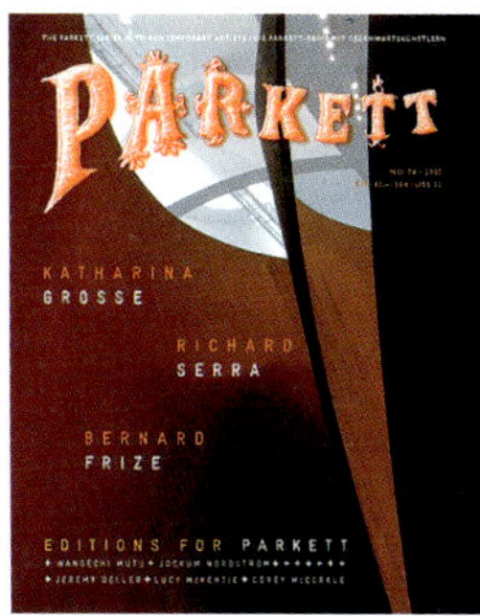

No. 74: Bernard Frize
Richard Serra
Katharina Grosse

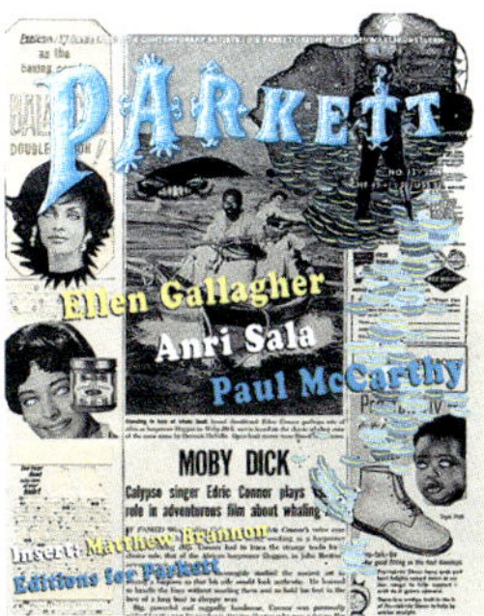

No. 73: Anri Sala
Ellen Gallagher
Paul McCarthy
Insert: Matthew Brannon

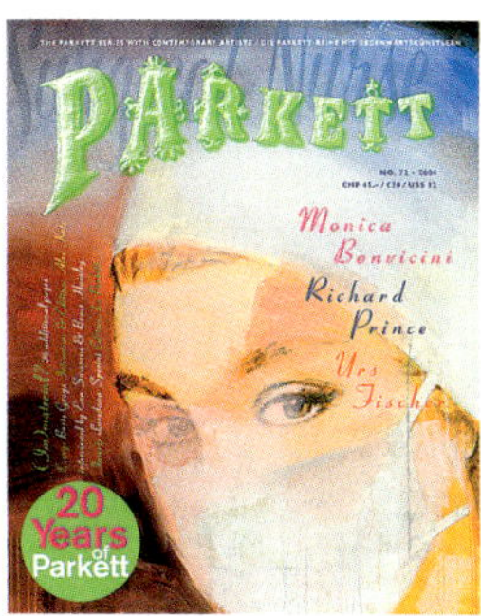

No. 72: Monica Bonvicini
Alex Katz, Richard Prince
Urs Fischer
Insert: Loredana Sperini

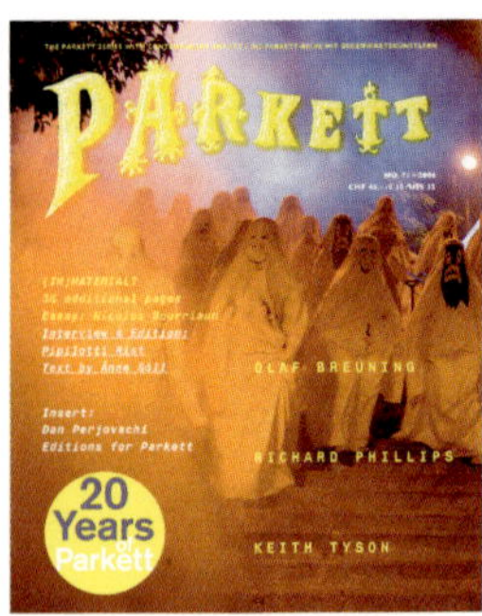

No. 71: Olaf Breuning
Pipilotti Rist, Keith Tyson
Richard Phillips
Insert: Dan Perjovschi

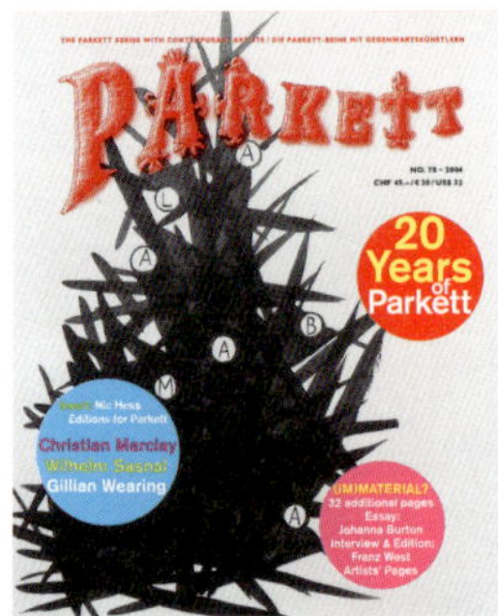

No. 70: Christian Marclay
Franz West, Gillian Wearing
Wilhelm Sasnal
Insert: Nic Hess

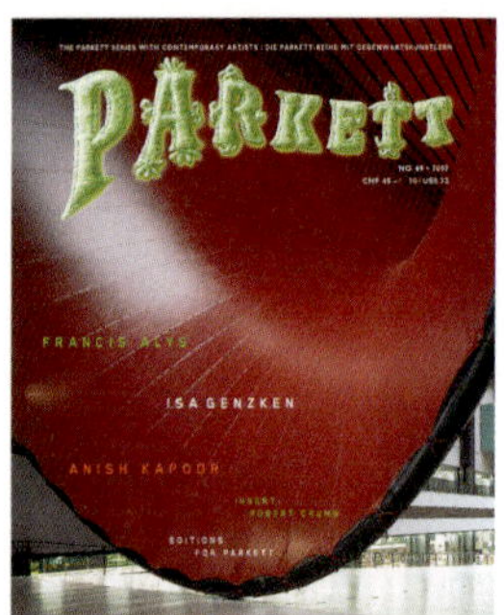

No. 69: Francis Alys
Anish Kapoor
Isa Genzken
Insert: Robert Crumb

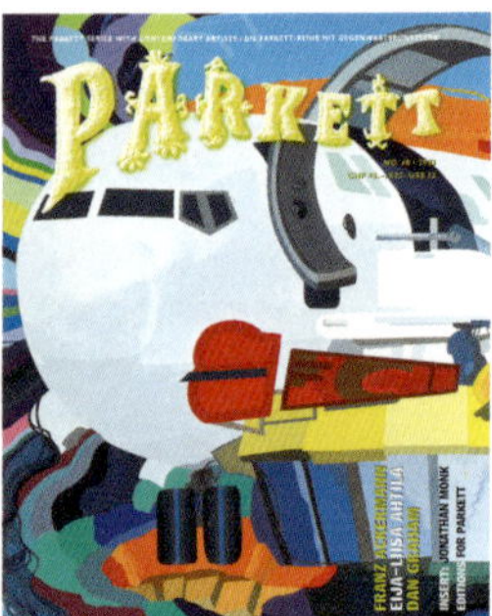

No. 68: Dan Graham
Eija-Liisa Ahtila
Franz Ackermann
Insert: Jonathan Monk

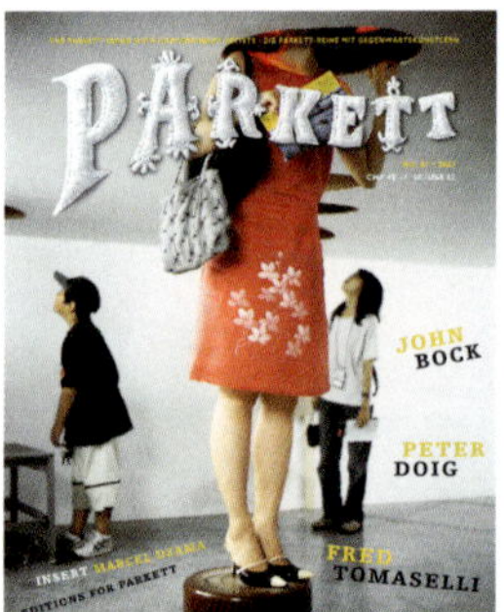

No. 67: Fred Tomaselli
Peter Doig
John Bock
Insert: Marcel Dzama

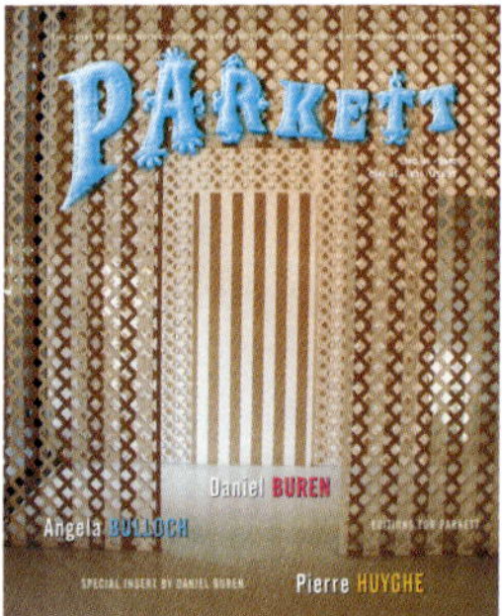

No. 66: Daniel Buren
Angela Bulloch
Pierre Huyghe
Insert: Daniel Buren

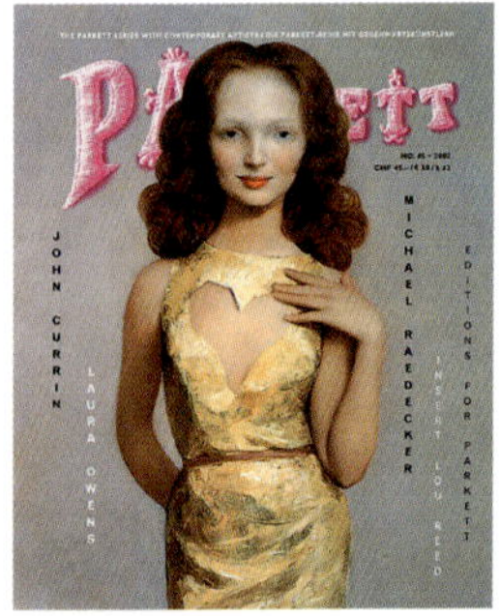

No. 65: John Currin
Michael Raedecker
Laura Owens
Insert: Lou Reed

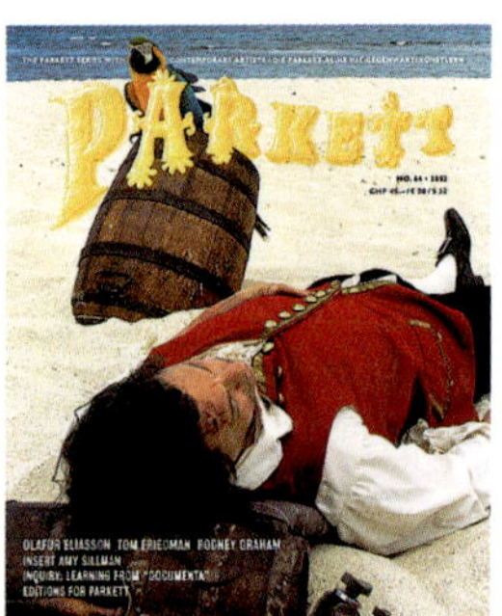

No. 64: Rodney Graham
Tom Friedman
Olafur Eliasson
Insert: Matthew Brannon

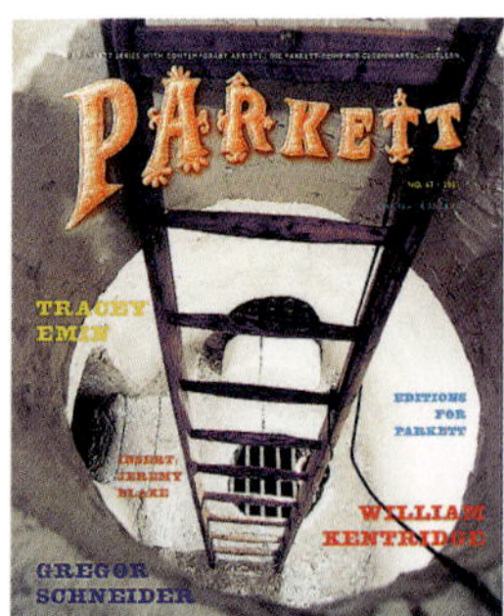

No. 63: Gregor Schneider
William Kentridge
Tracey Emin
Insert: Jeremy Blake

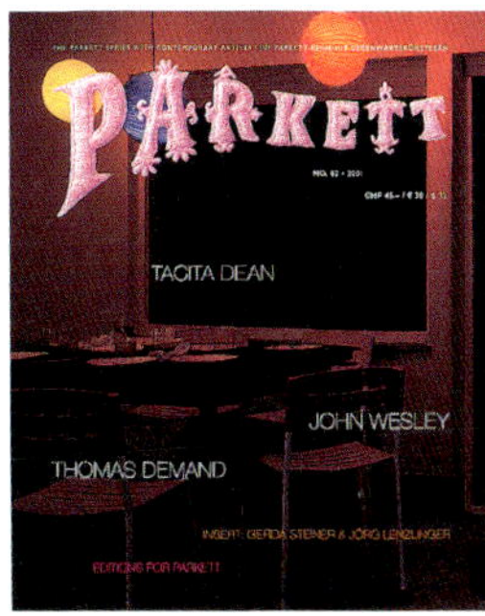

No. 62: John Wesley
Tacita Dean, Thomas Demand
Insert: Gerda Steiner,
Jörg Lenzlinger

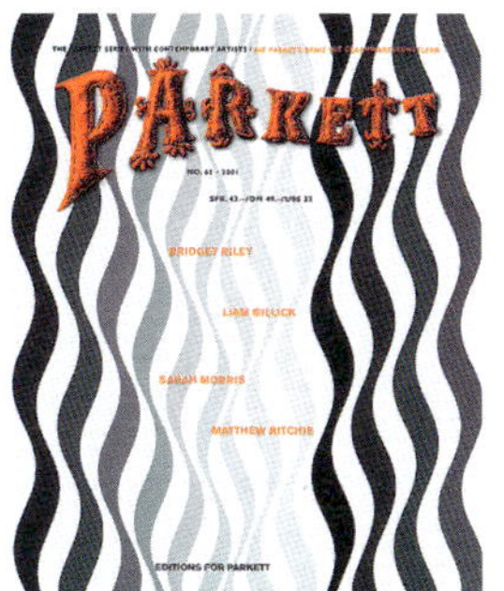

No. 61: Liam Gillick
Sarah Morris, Bridget Riley
Matthew Ritchie
Insert: Nate Lowman

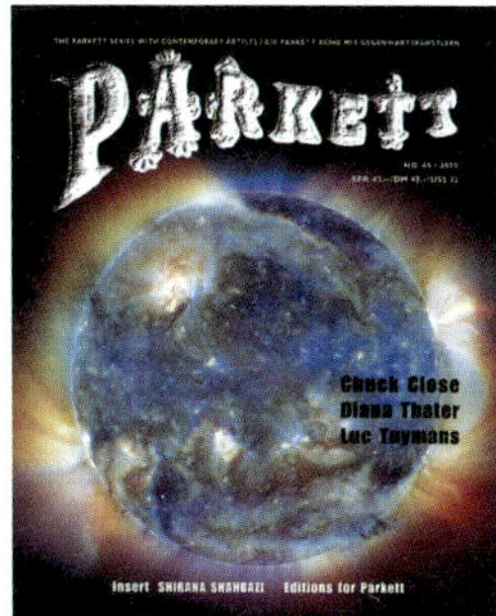

No. 60: Chuck Close
Diana Thater
Luc Tuymans
Insert: Shirana Shahbazi

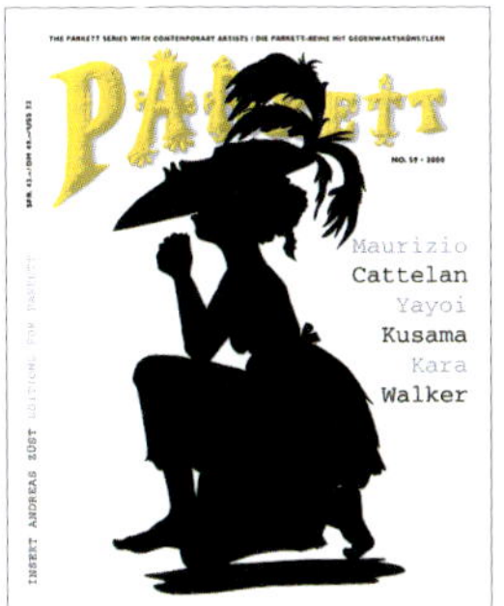

No. 59: Maurizio Cattelan
Yayoi Kusama
Kara Walker
Insert: Andreas Züst

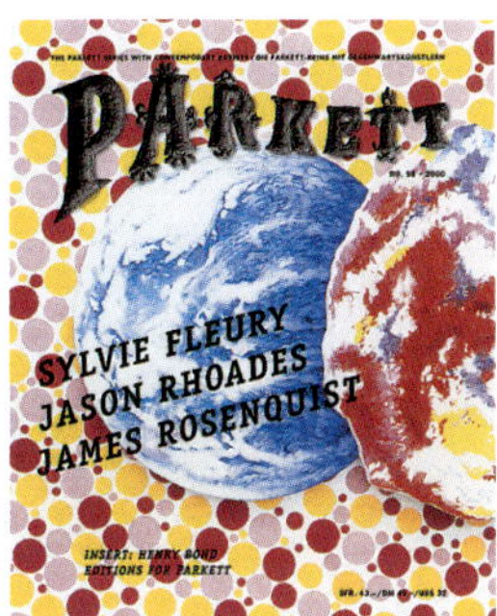

No. 58: James Rosenquist
Sylvie Fleury
Jason Rhoades
Insert: Henry Bond

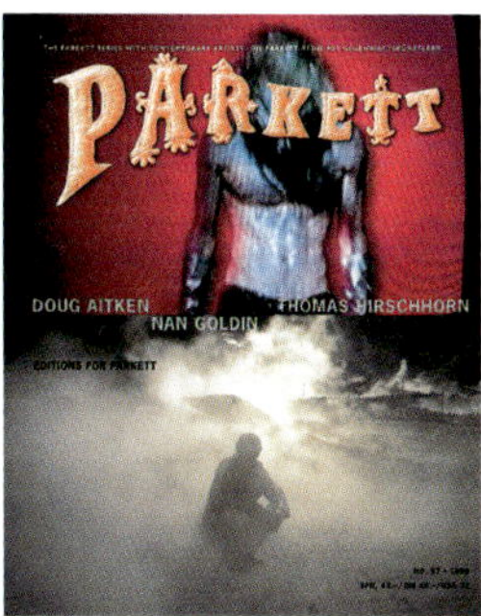

No. 57: Doug Aitken
Nan Goldin
Thomas Hirschhorn
Insert: Doug Aitken

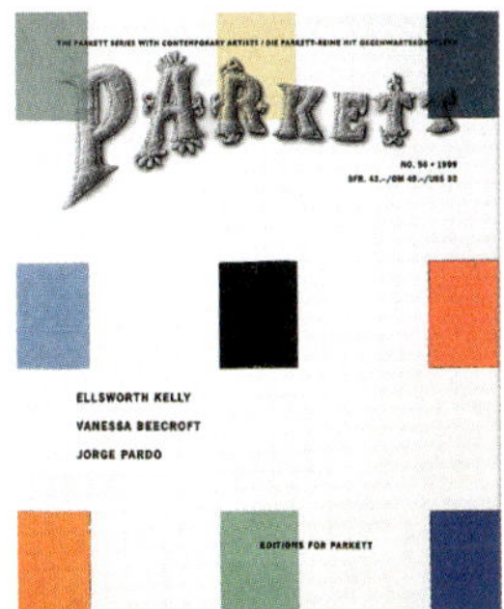

No. 56: Ellsworth Kelly
Vanessa Beecroft
Jorge Pardo

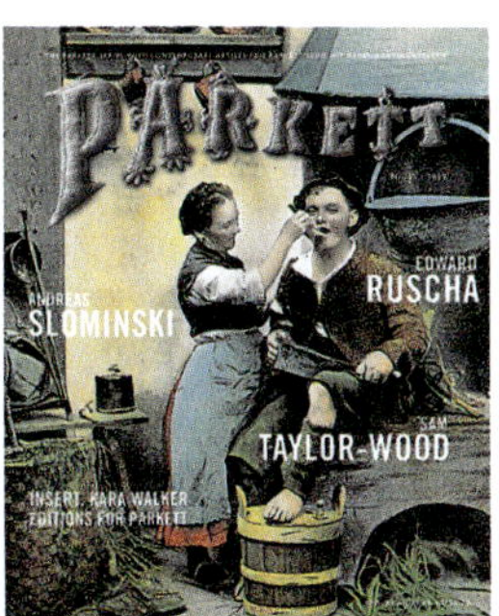

No. 55: Edward Ruscha
Andreas Slominski
Sam Taylor-Wood
Insert: Kara Walker

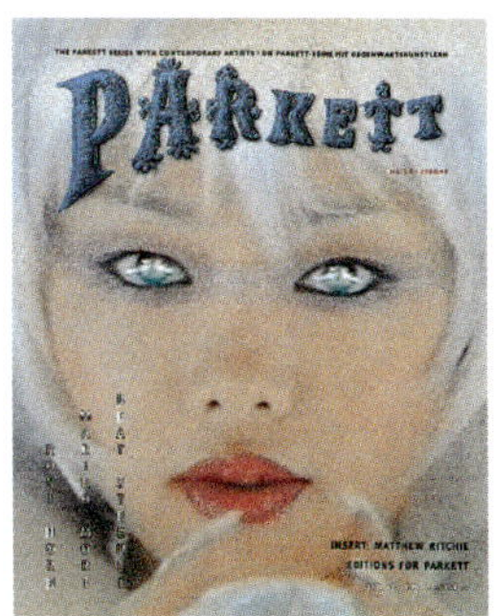

No. 54: Roni Horn
Mariko Mori
Beat Streuli
Insert: Matthew Ritchie

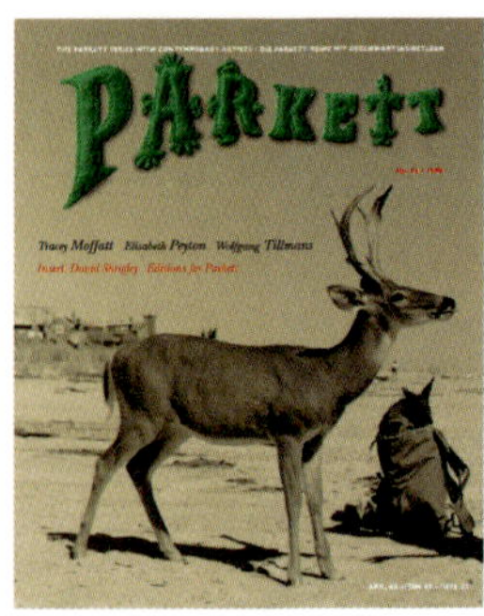

No. 53: Tracey Moffatt
Elizabeth Peyton
Wolfgang Tillmans
Insert: David Shrigley

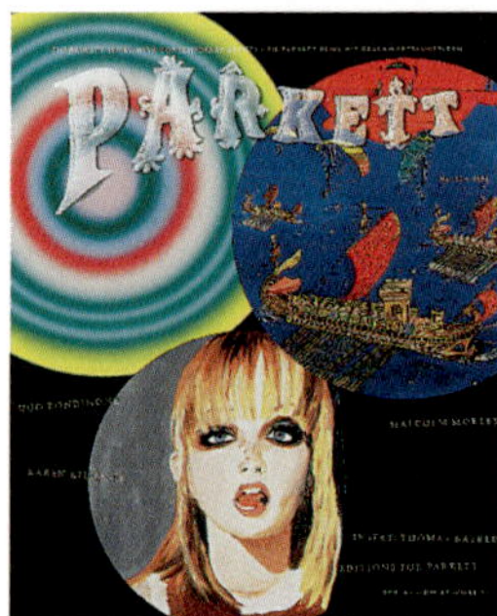

No. 52: Karen Kilimnik
Malcolm Morley
Ugo Rondinone
Insert: Thomas Bayrle

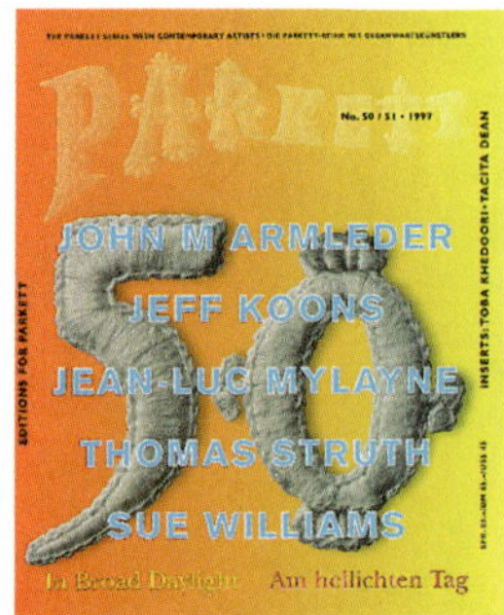

No. 50/51: John M Armleder
Jeff Koons, Jean-Luc Mylayne
Thomas Struth, Sue Williams
Insert: Toba Khedoori, Tacita Dean

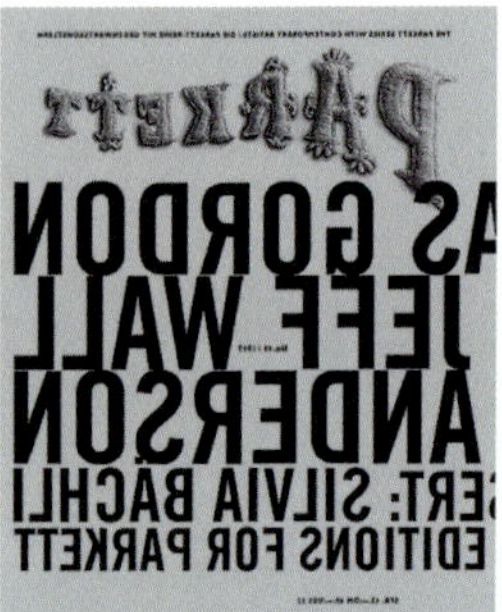

No. 49: Laurie Anderson
Douglas Gordon
Jeff Wall
Insert: Silvia Bächli

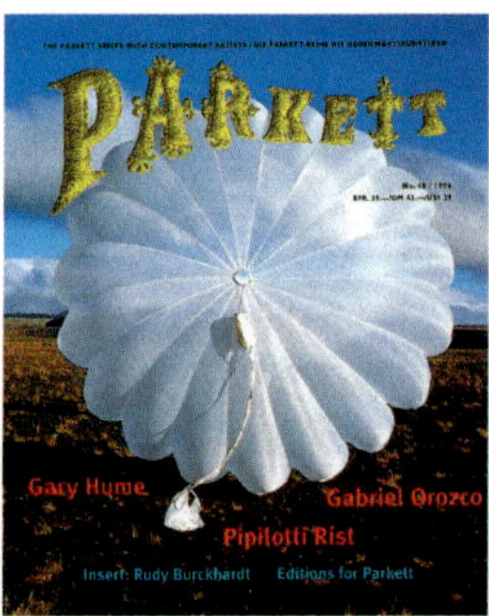

No. 48: Gary Hume
Gabriel Orozco
Pipilotti Rist
Insert: Rudy Burckhardt

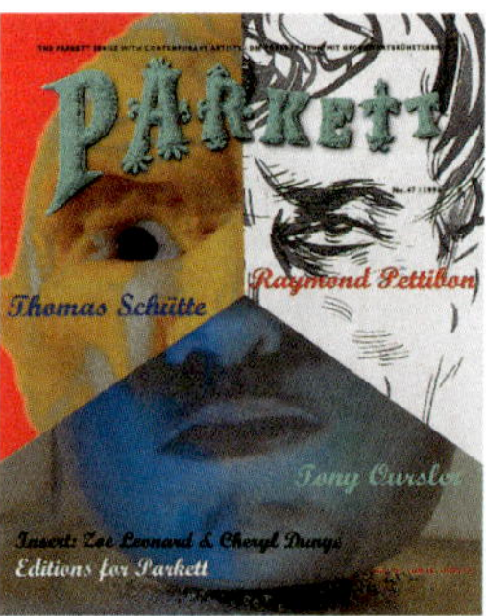

No. 47: Tony Oursler
Raymond Pettibon
Thomas Schütte
Insert: Zoe Leonard & Cheryl Dunye

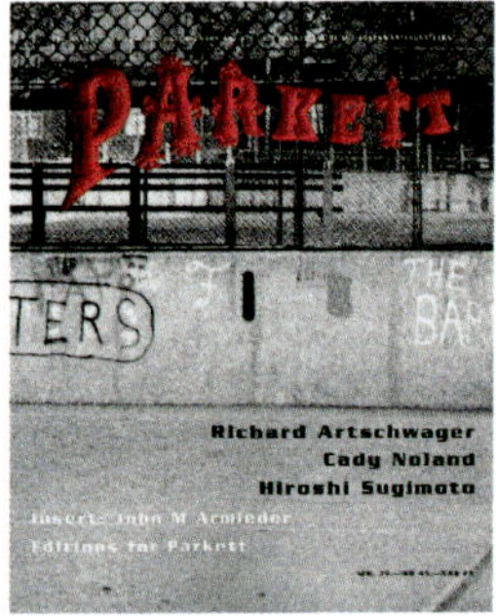

No. 46: Richard Artschwager
Cady Noland
Hiroshi Sugimoto
Insert: John M. Armleder

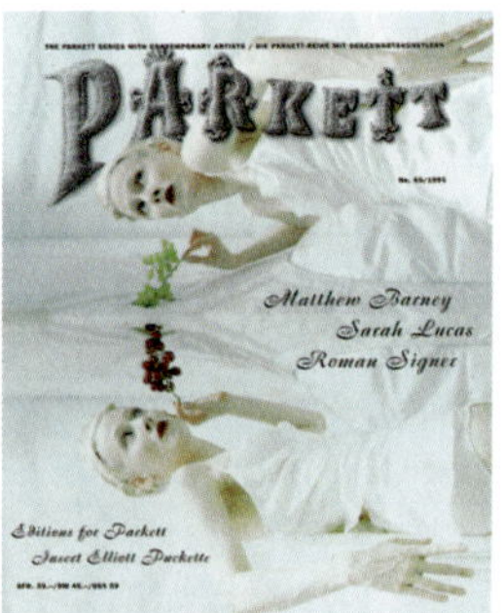

No. 45: Matthew Barney
Sarah Lucas
Roman Signer
Insert: Elliott Puckette

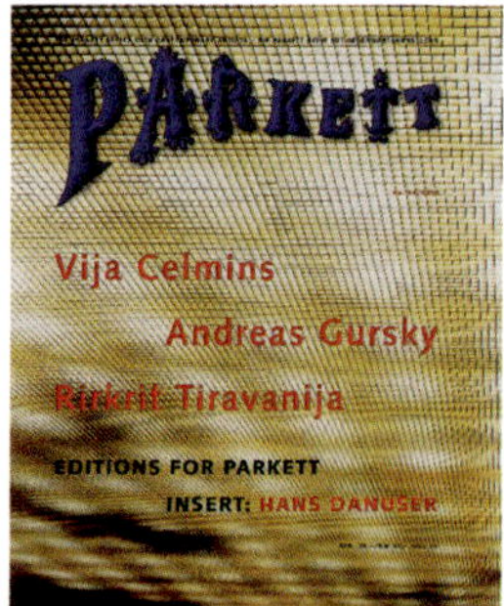

No. 44: Vija Celmins
Andreas Gursky
Rirkrit Tiravanija
Insert: Hans Danuser

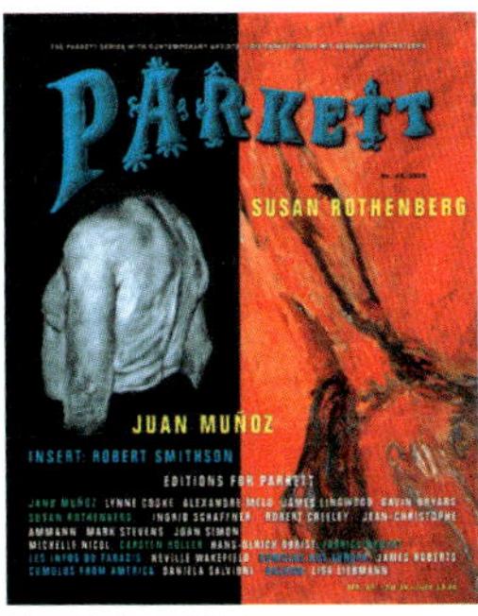

No. 43: Juan Muñoz
Susan Rothenberg
Insert: Robert Smithson

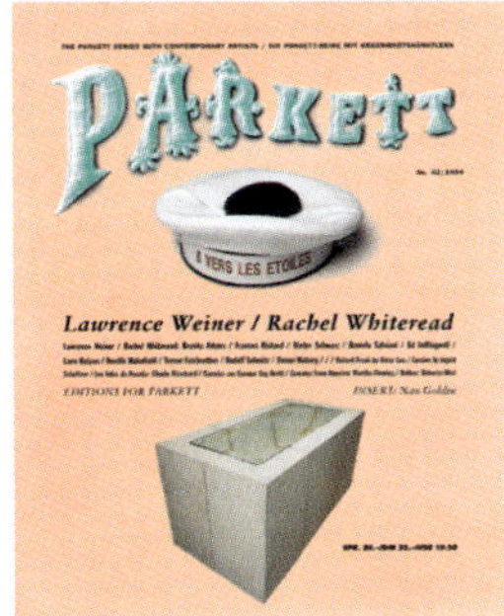

No. 42: Lawrence Weiner
Rachel Whiteread
Insert: Nan Goldin

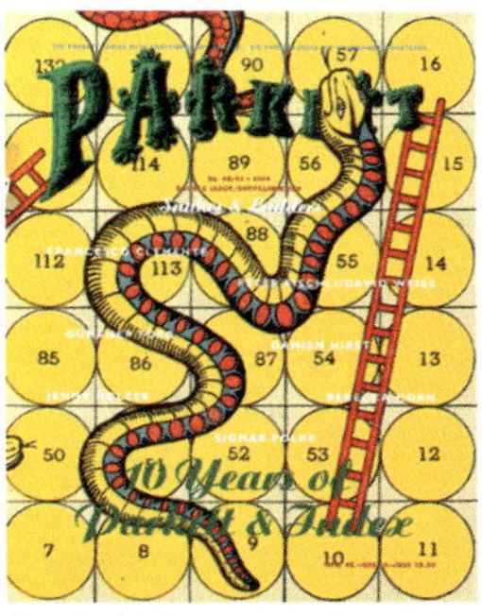

No. 40/41: Francesco Clemente,
Günther Förg, Peter Fischli/David Weiss
Damien Hirst, Jenny Holzer
Rebecca Horn, Sigmar Polke

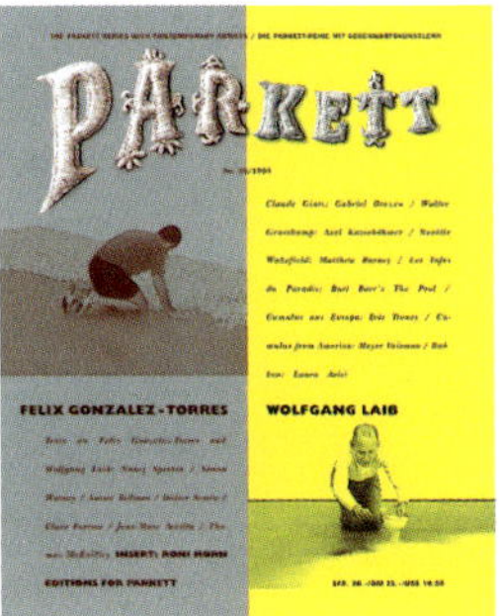

No. 39: Felix Gonzalez-Torres
Wolfgang Laib
Insert: Roni Horn

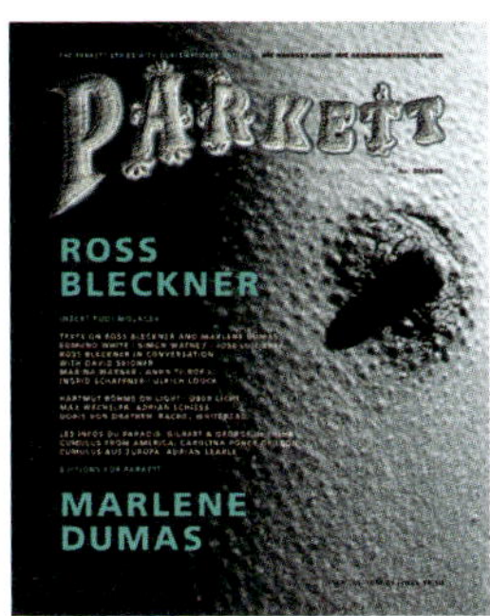

No. 38: Ross Bleckner
Marlene Dumas
Insert: Rudi Molacek

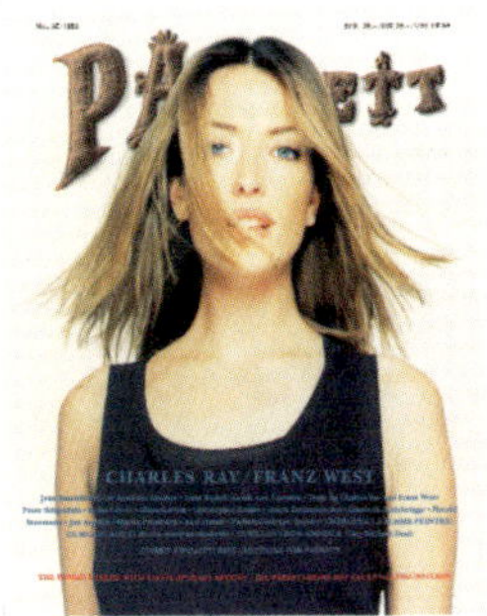

No. 37: Charles Ray
Franz West
Insert: Pipilotti Rist

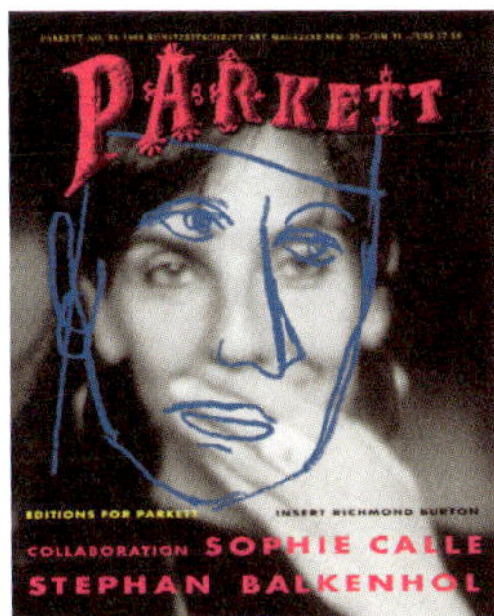

No. 36: Stephan Balkenhol
Sophie Calle
Insert: Richmond Burton

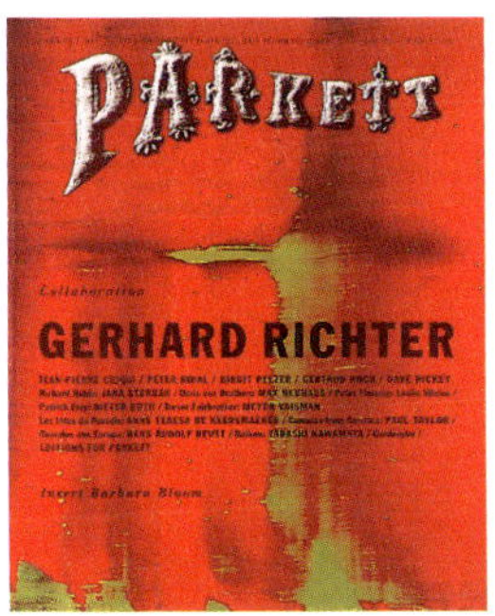

No. 35: Gerhard Richter
Insert: Barbara Bloom

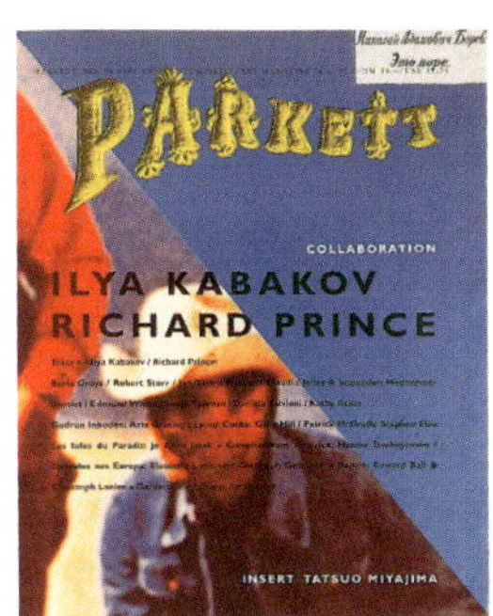

No. 34: Ilya Kabakov
Richard Prince
Insert: Tatsuo Miyajima

No. 33: Rosemarie Trockel
Christopher Wool
Insert: Adrian Schiess

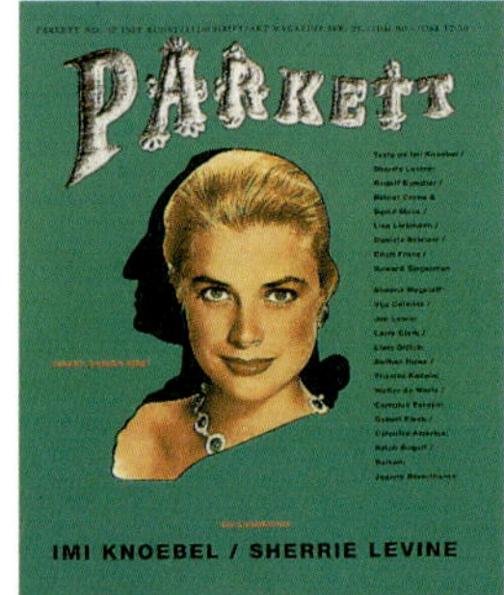

No. 32: Imi Knoebel
Sherrie Levine
Insert: Damien Hirst

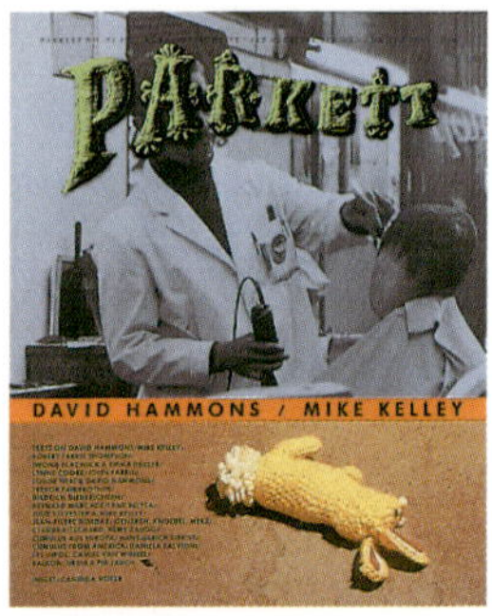

No. 31: David Hammons
Mike Kelley
Insert: Candida Höfer

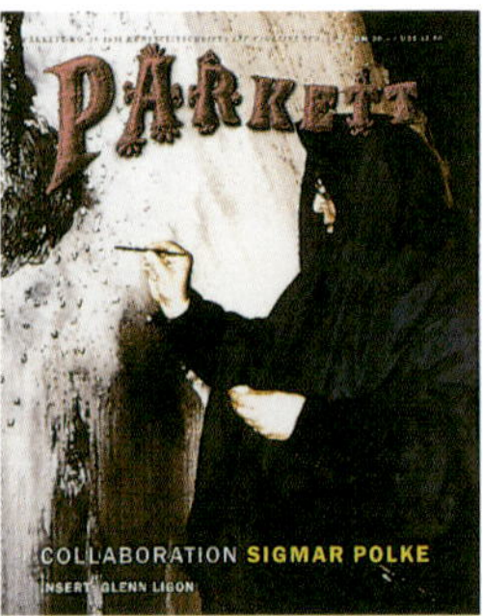

No. 30: Sigmar Polke
Insert: Glenn Ligon

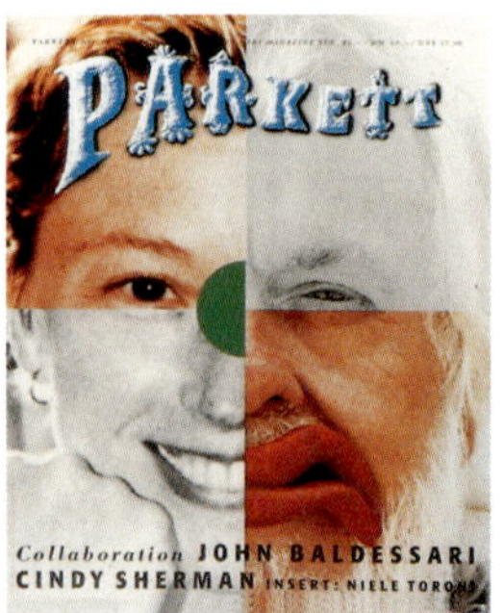

No. 29: John Baldessari
Cindy Sherman
Insert: Niele Toroni

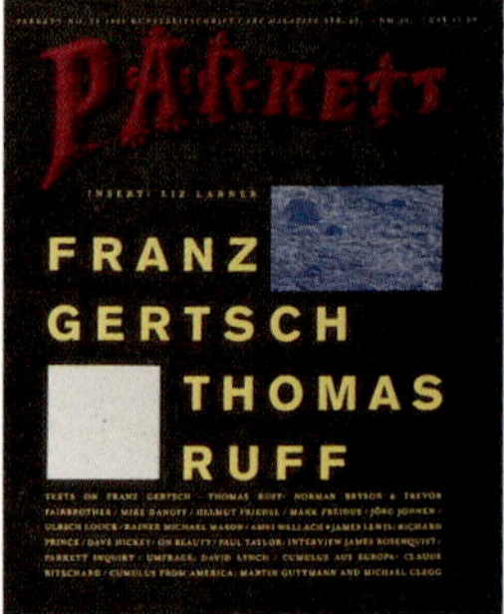

No. 28: Franz Gertsch
Thomas Ruff
Insert: Liz Larner

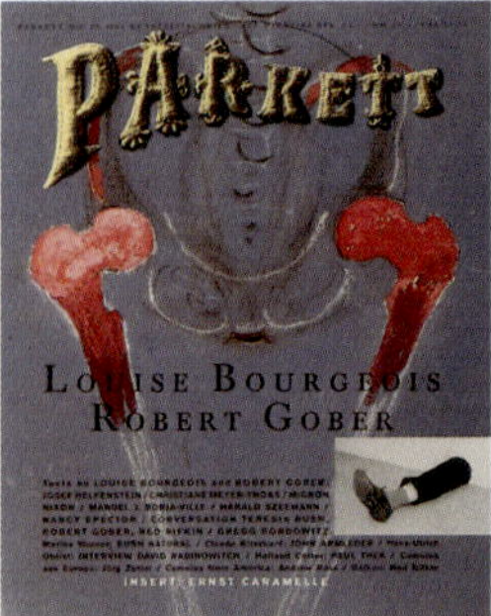

No. 27: Louise Bourgeois
Robert Gober
Insert: Ernst Caramelle

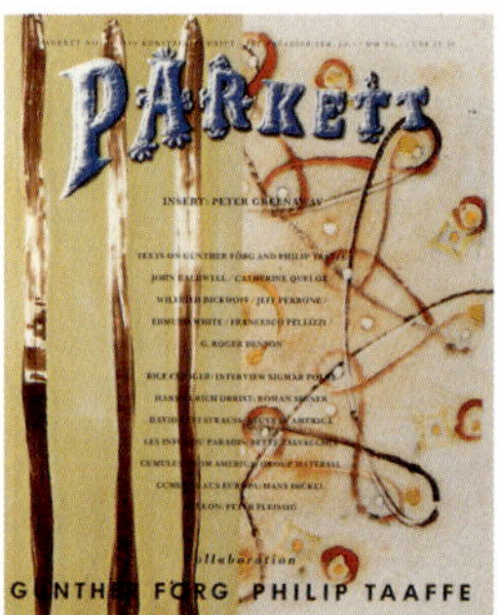

No. 26: Günther Förg
Philip Taaffe
Insert: Peter Greenaway

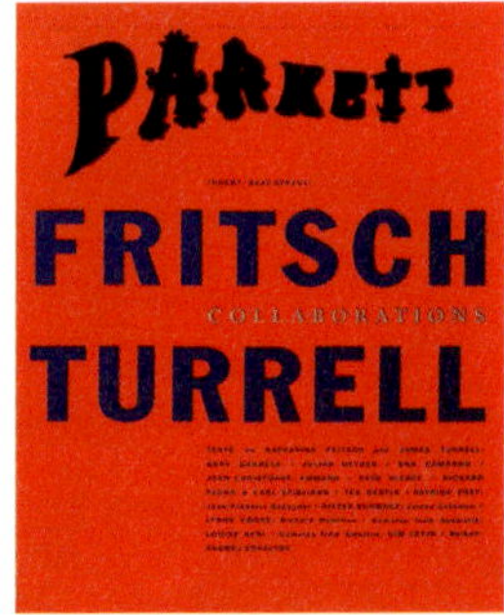

No. 25: Katharina Fritsch
James Turrell
Insert: Beat Streuli

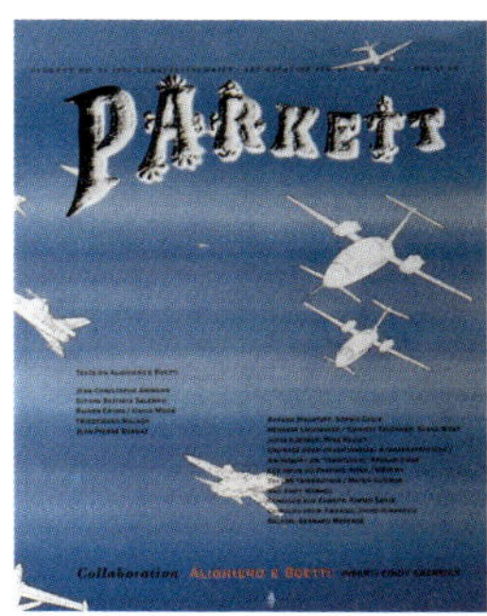

No. 24: Alighiero e Boetti
Insert: Cindy Sherman

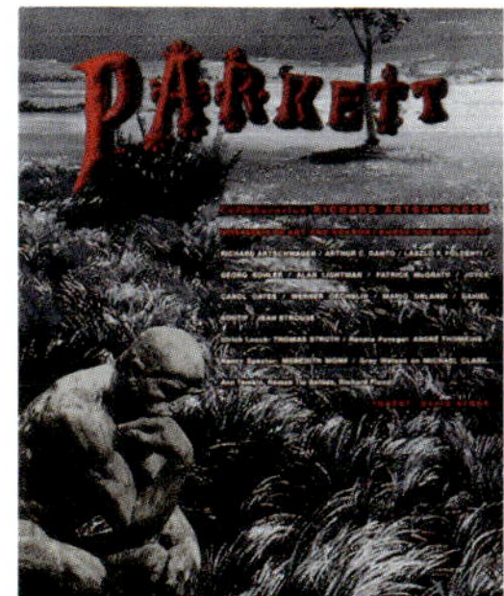

No. 23: Richard Artschwager
Insert: David Byrne

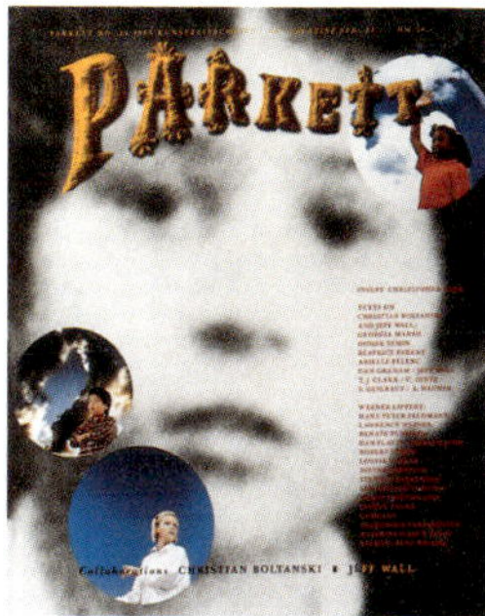

No. 22: Christian Boltanski
Jeff Wall
Insert: Christopher Wool

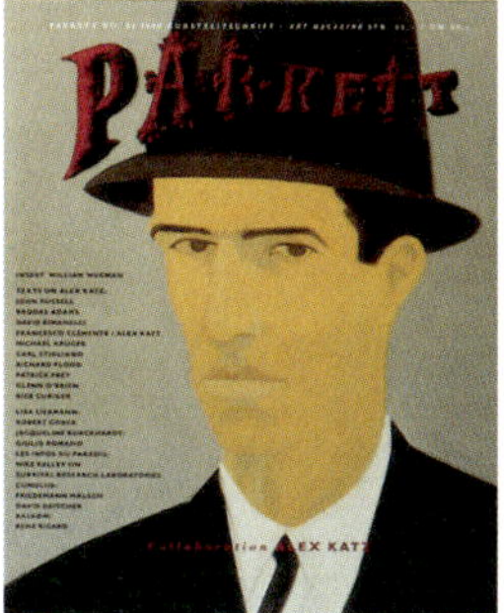

No. 21: Alex Katz
Insert: William Wegman

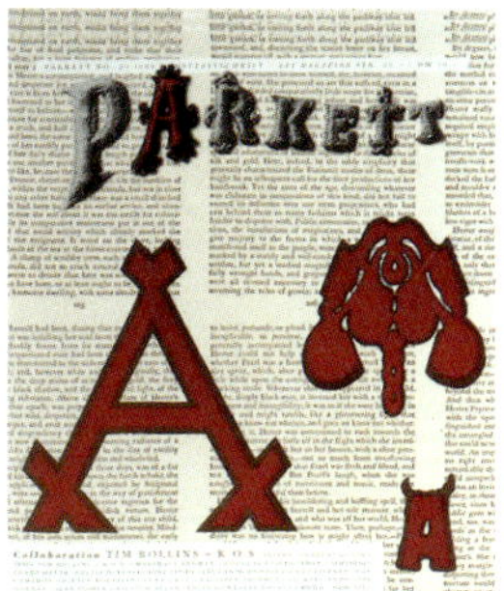

No. 20: Tim Rollins + K.O.S.
Insert: Andreas Gursky

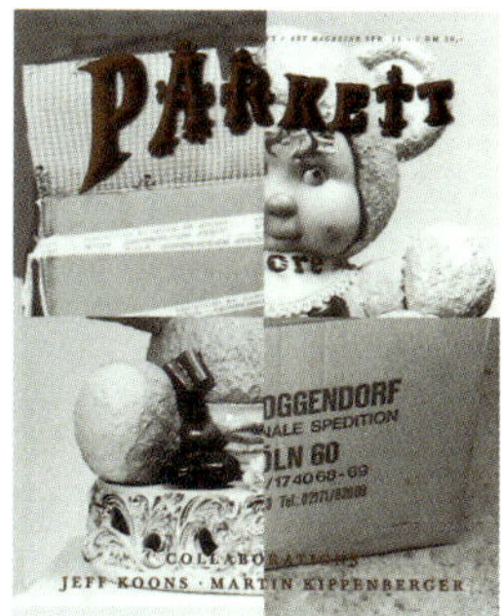

No. 19: Jeff Koons
Martin Kippenberger
Insert: Anselm Stalder

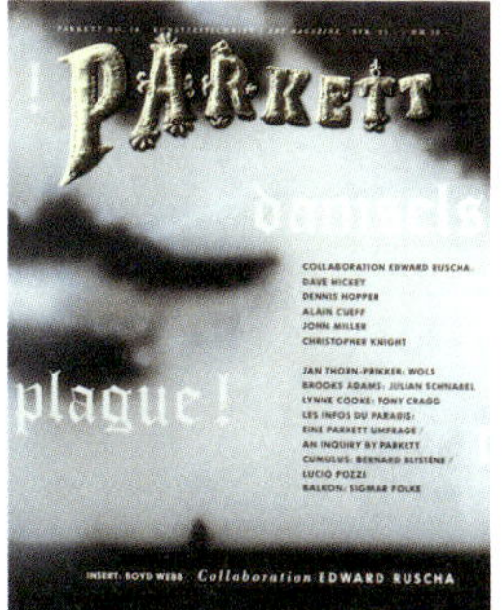

No. 18: Edward Ruscha
Insert: Boyd Webb

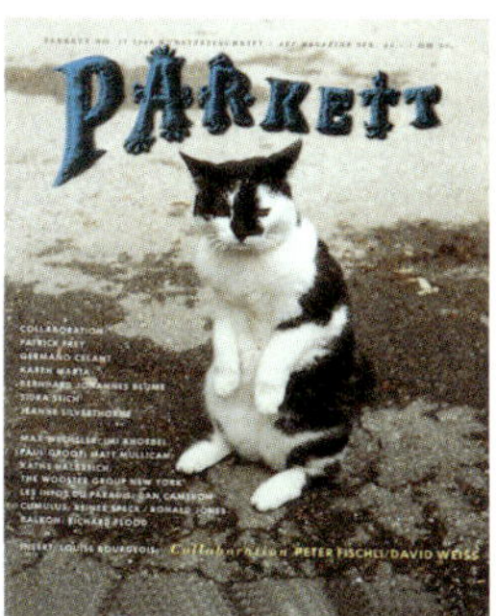

No. 17: Peter Fischli/David Weiss
Insert: Louise Bourgeois

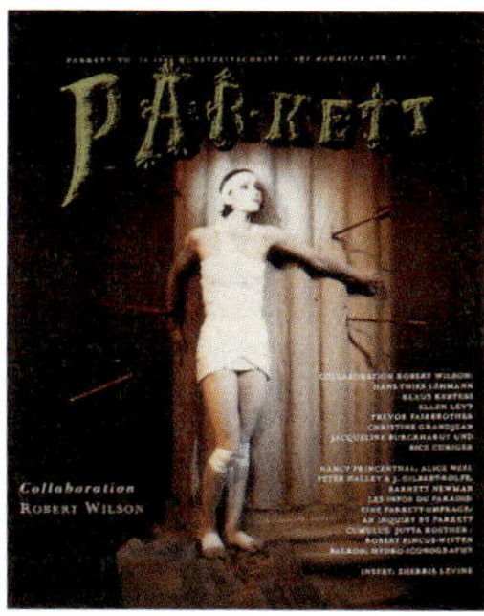

No. 16: Robert Wilson
Insert: Sherrie Levine

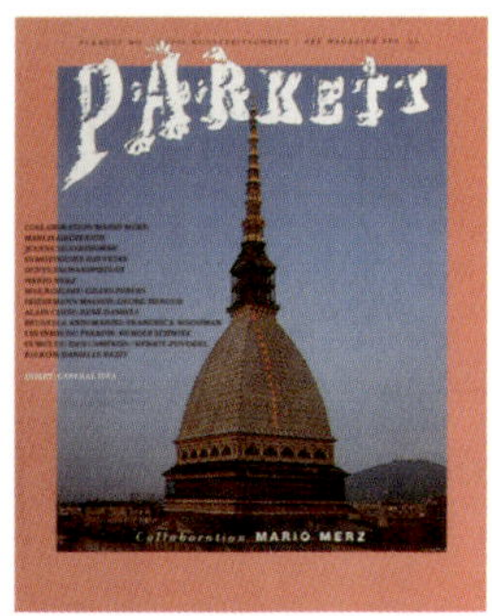

No. 15: Mario Merz
Insert: General Idea

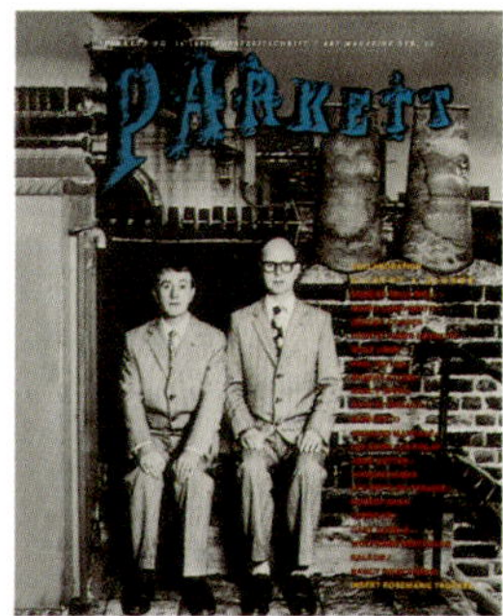

No. 14: Gilbert & George
Insert: Rosemarie Trockel

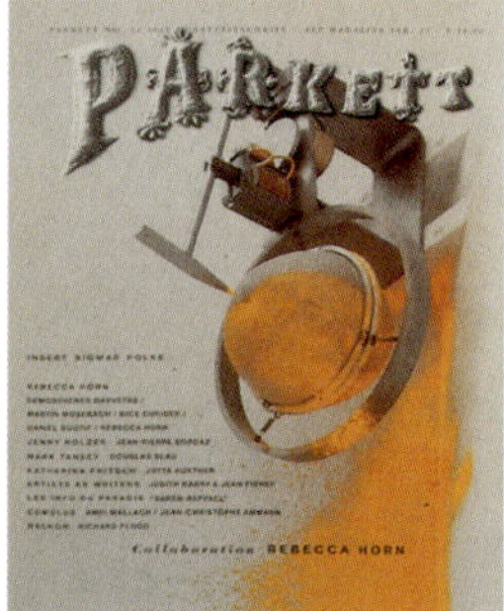

No. 13: Rebecca Horn
Insert: Sigmar Polke

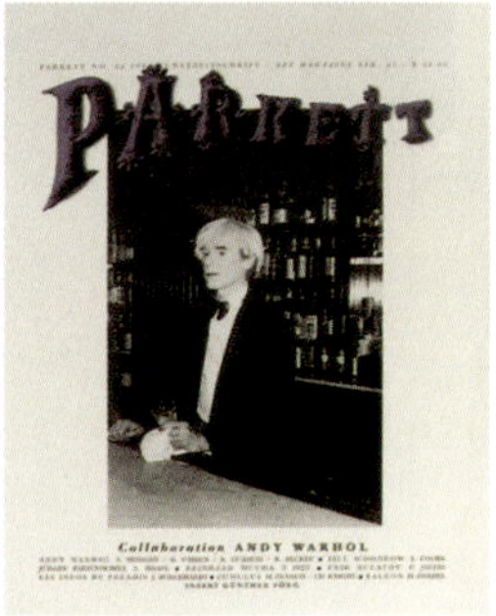

No. 12: Andy Warhol
Insert: Günther Förg

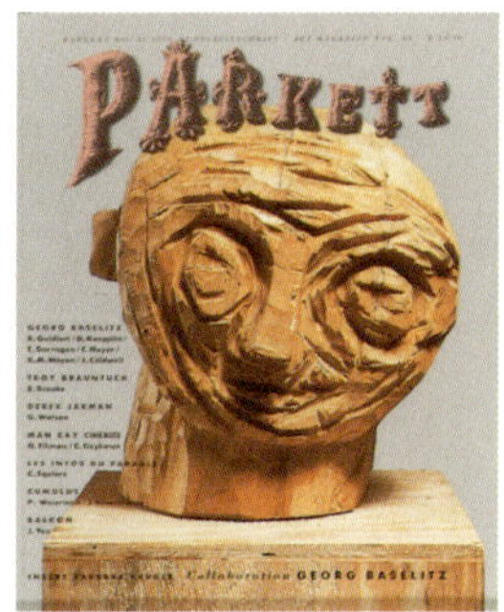

No. 11: Georg Baselitz
Insert: Barbara Kruger

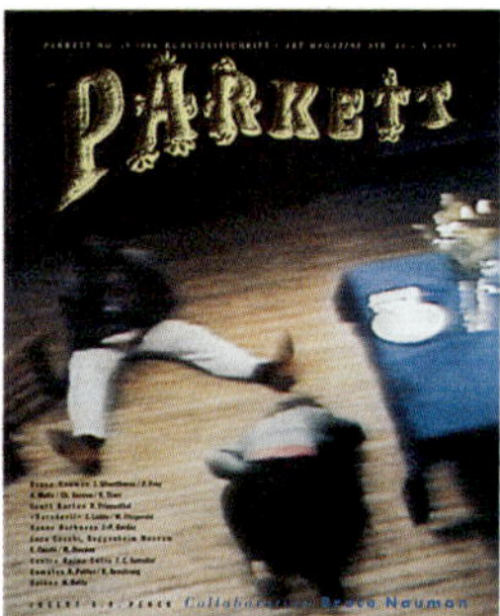

No. 10: Bruce Nauman
Insert: A.R.Penck

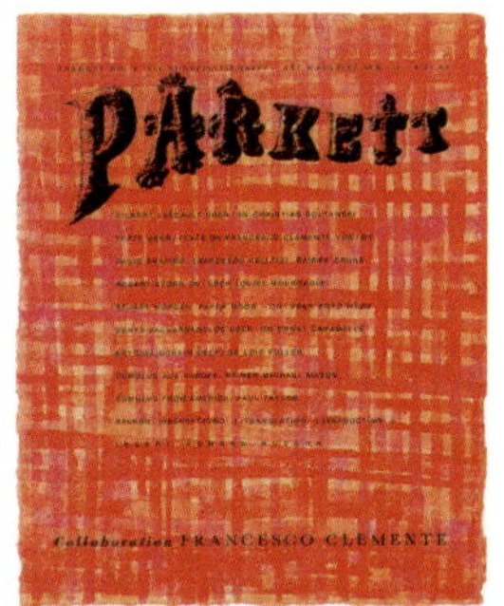

No. 9: Francesco Clemente
Insert: Edward Ruscha

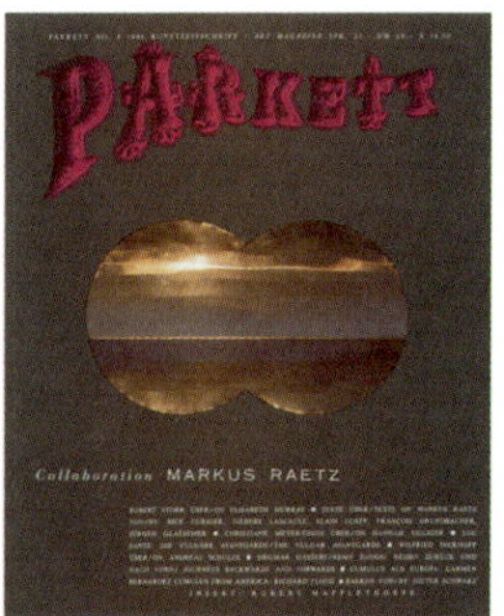

No. 8: Markus Raetz
Insert: Robert Mapplethorpe

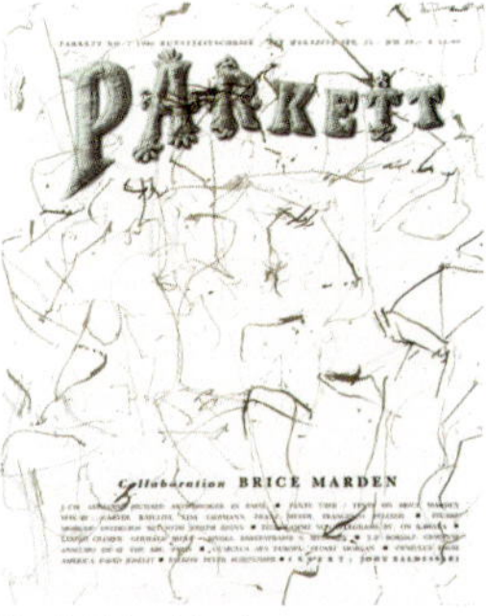

No. 7: Brice Marden
Insert: John Baldessari

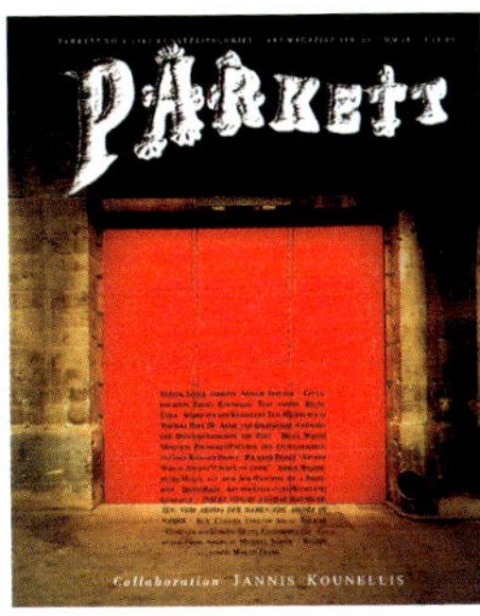

No. 6: Jannis Kounellis
Insert: Lothar Baumgarten

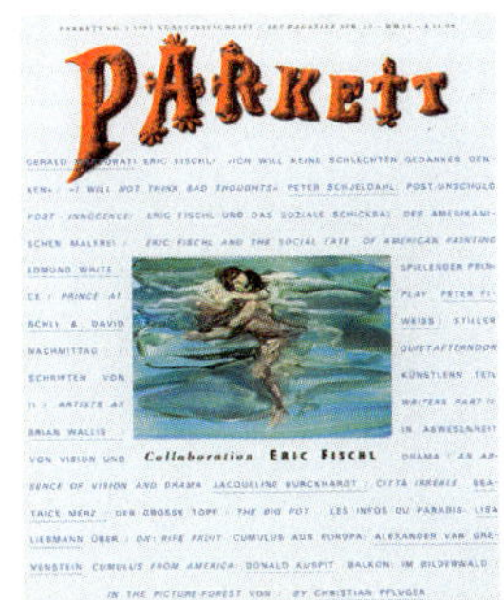

No. 5: Eric Fischl

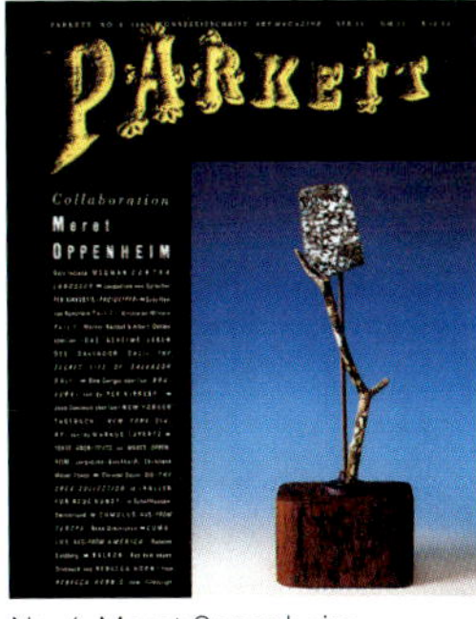

No. 4: Meret Oppenheim

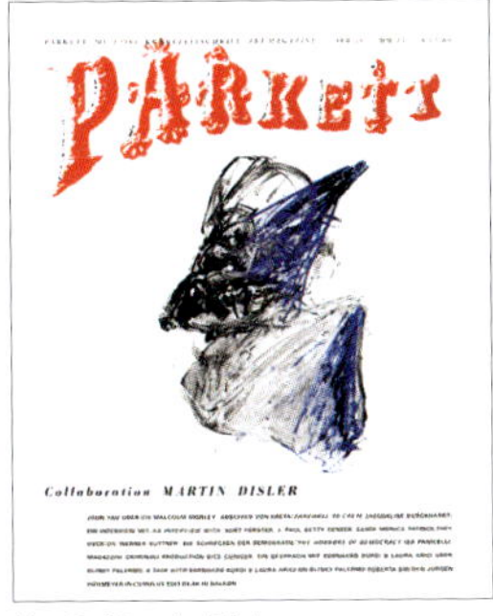

No. 3: Martin Disler

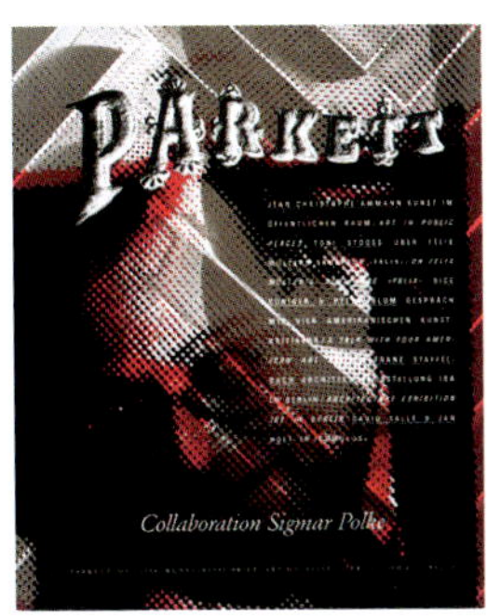

No. 2: Sigmar Polke

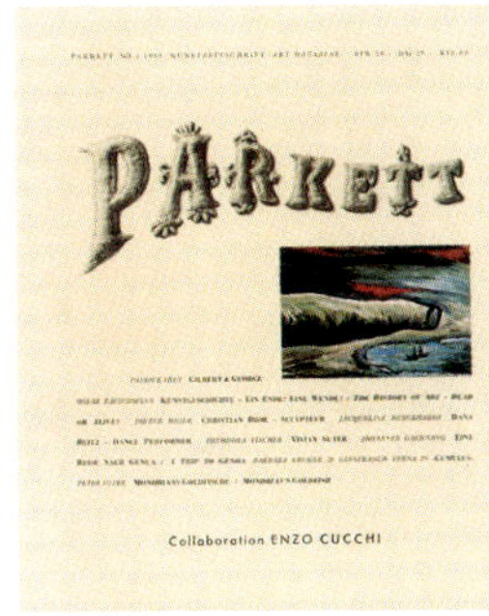

No. 1: Enzo Cucchi

Authors' Index alphabetically
執筆者一覧（アルファベット順）

This index lists all 800 authors and their 1400 texts published in Parkett 1–86. Each text is referenced by the respective issue number and the title of the text. If the text focuses on specific artists, their names are also listed. Texts, interviews and discussions by more than one author are listed separately under each author's name. Further information on all Parkett authors and texts is available from the search engine at www.parkettart.com/search.

この執筆者一覧は、パルケット1号から86号までの、800人の執筆者名と掲載記事1400本を網羅したものである。それぞれの記事について、掲載された号数と記事のタイトルも記載してある。記事が特定のアーティストについて執筆されたものであれば、該当アーティスト名も併記した。記事、インタビュー、論評などで、複数の執筆者が関与しているものは、それぞれの執筆者名別にも掲載してある。パルケットの執筆者や記事についての詳しい情報は、インターネットで検索できる。www.parkettart.com/search

Masthead Parkett
パルケット誌奥付

PARKETT Zürich New York

Bice Curiger Chefredaktorin/Editor-in-Chief; **Jacqueline Burckhardt** Redaktorin/Senior Editor; **Bettina Funcke** Redaktorin USA/Senior Editor US; **Jeremy Sigler** Redaktionsassistenz USA/Associate Editor US; **Mark Welzel** Textredaktion und Produktion/Editing and Production; **Hanna Williamson-Koller · Simone Eggstein** Graphik/Design, **Trix Wetter** Graphisches Konzept/Founding Designer (–2001); **Catherine Schelbert** Englisches Lektorat / Editorial Assistant for English; **Claudia Meneghini Nevzadi & Richard Hall** Korrektorat/Proofreading

Beatrice Fässler Vorzugsausgaben, Inserate/Special Editions, Advertising; **Nicole Stotzer** Buchvertrieb, Administration/Distribution, Administration; **Mathias Arnold** Abonnemente/Subscriptions; **Andrea Urban** Vorzugsausgaben, Inserate und Abonnemente USA/Special Editions, Advertising, and Subscriptions US

Jacqueline Burckhardt – Bice Curiger – Dieter von Graffenried Herausgeber/Parkett Board; **Jacqueline Burckhardt – Bice Curiger – Dieter von Graffenried – Walter Keller – Peter Blum** Gründer/Founders

Dieter von Graffenried Verleger/Publisher

www.parkettart.com

PARKETT-VERLAG AG, QUELLENSTRASSE 27, CH-8031 ZÜRICH
TEL. 41-44-271 81 40, FAX 41-44-272 43 01

PARKETT, NEW YORK, 145 AV. OF THE AMERICAS, N.Y. 10013
PHONE (212) 673-2660, FAX (212) 271-0704

The texts of this book are typeset in Akkurat (light, regular, bold),
and 0-ATF-ShinGo (light, regular, medium)

Printed on Condat Périgord hochweiss, matt 135 g/m^2,
Cover 350 g/m^2

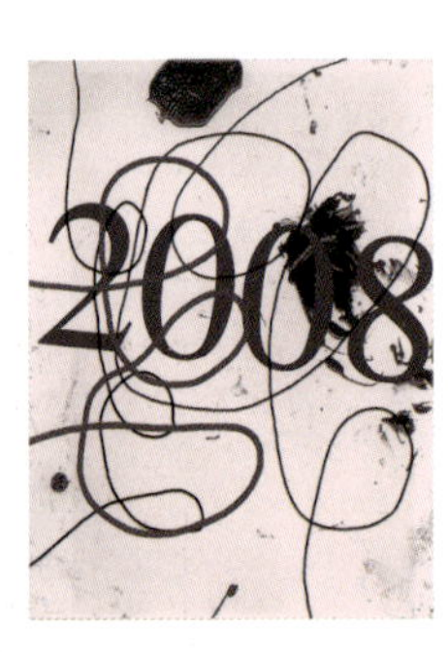
2008

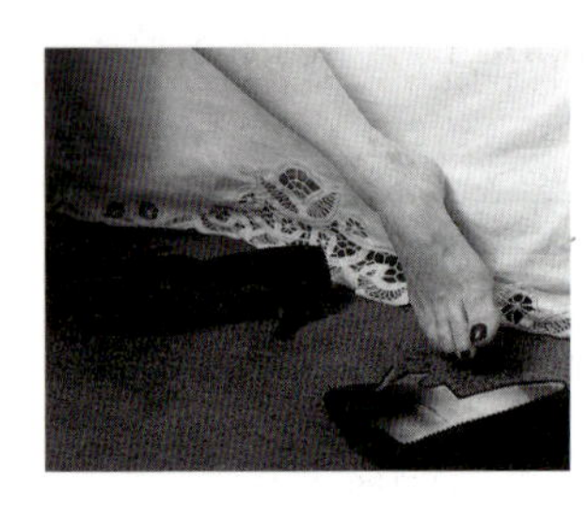

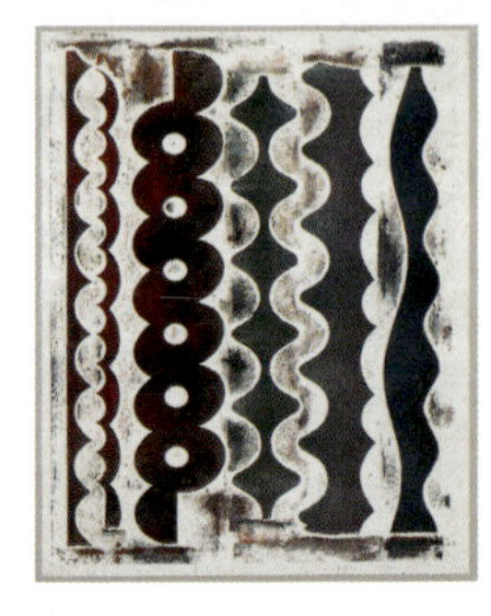

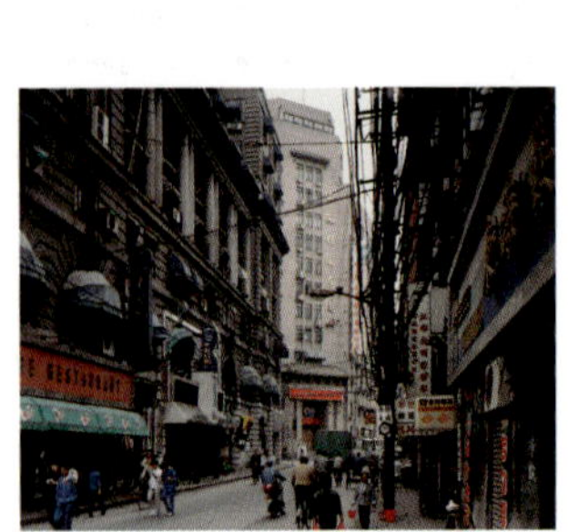

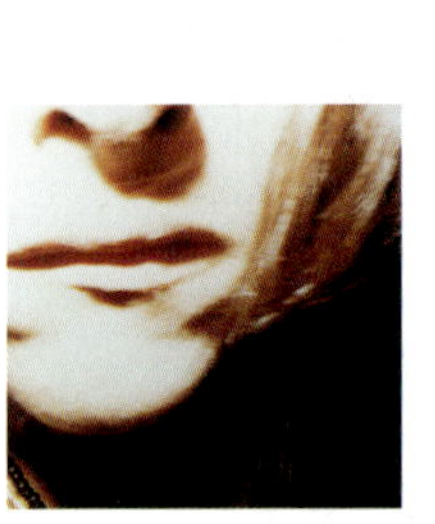

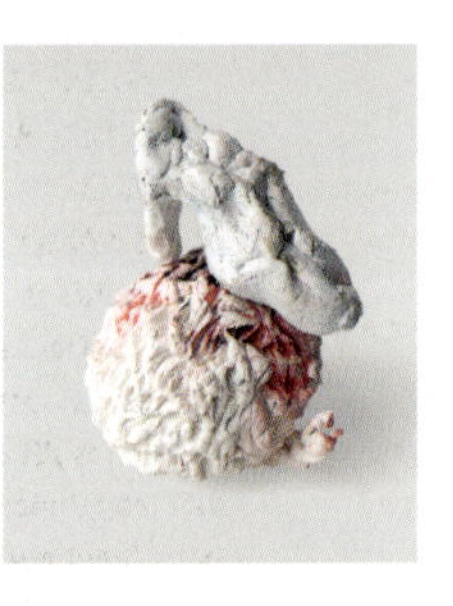

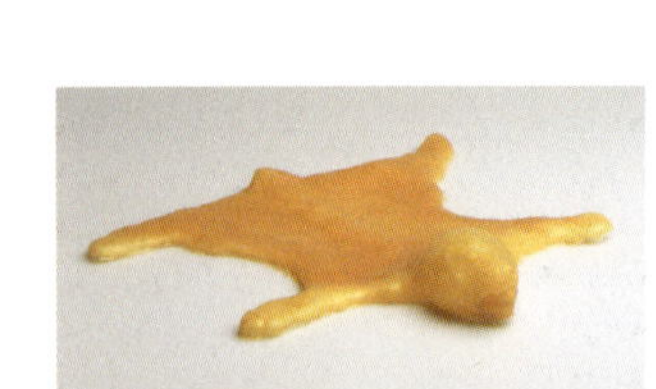

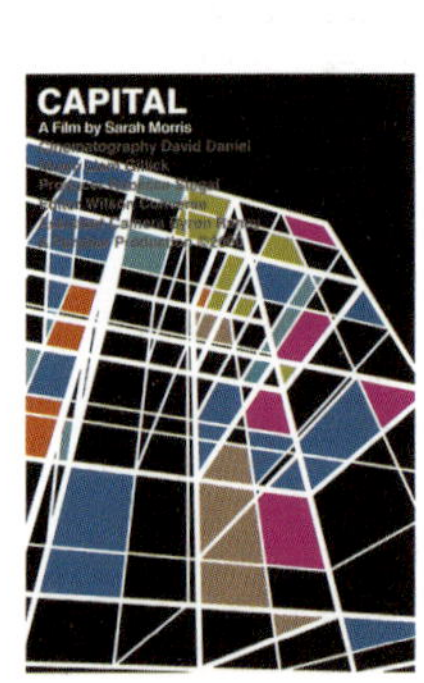
CAPITAL
A Film by Sarah Morris

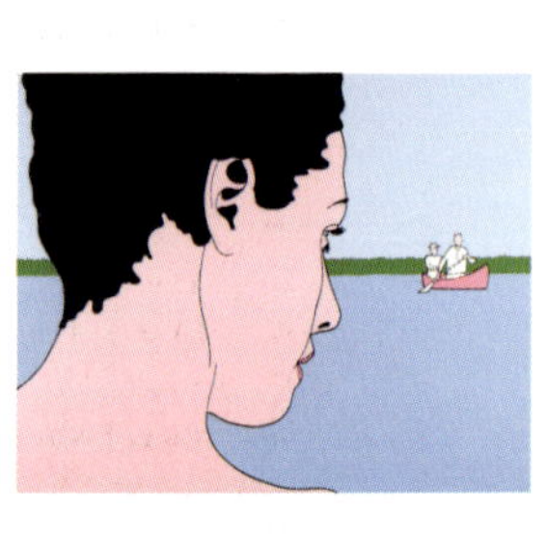

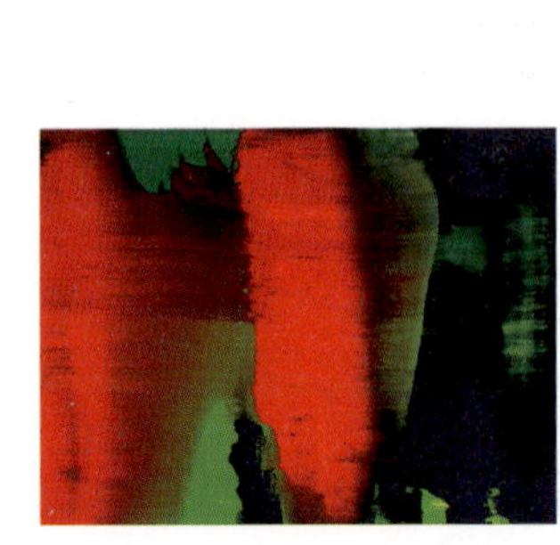

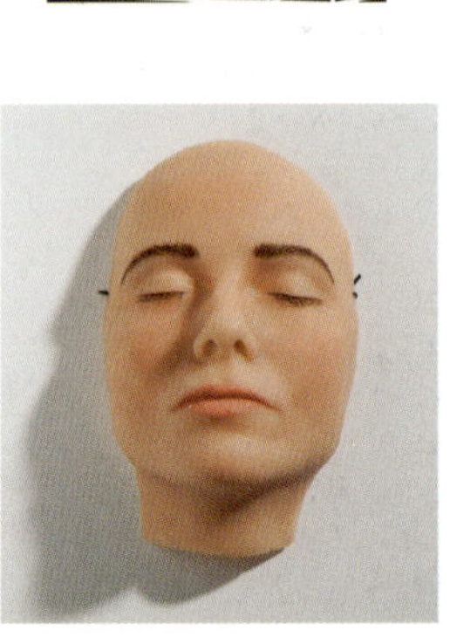

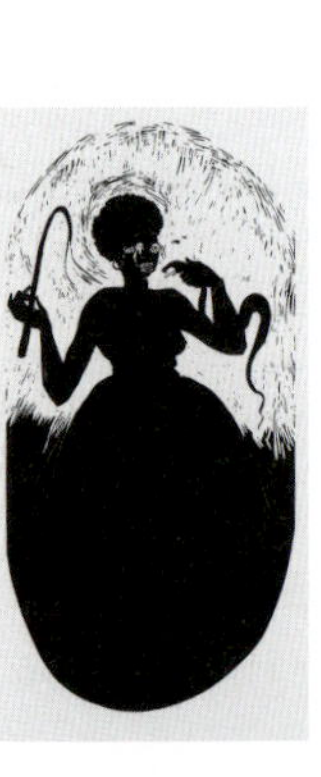